NAPOLEON

ALSO BY MICHAEL BROERS

NAPOLEON

---⚜---

THE DECLINE AND FALL
OF AN EMPIRE:
1811–1821

MICHAEL BROERS

PEGASUS BOOKS
NEW YORK LONDON

NAPOLEON

Pegasus Books, Ltd.
148 West 37th Street, 13th Floor
New York, NY 10018

Copyright © 2022 by Michael Broers

First Pegasus Books cloth edition August 2022

Interior design by Maria Fernandez

Maps designed by Michael Siegel, Department of Geography, Rutgers University

Library of Congress Cataloging-in-Publication Data is available.

ISBN: 978-1-63936-177-9

10 9 8 7 6 5 4 3 2 1

Printed in the United States of America
Distributed by Simon & Schuster
www.pegasusbooks.com

For Sue, for all she does
(and Woody, of course!)

And for John Merriman,
a great scholar, and an even greater friend.

CONTENTS

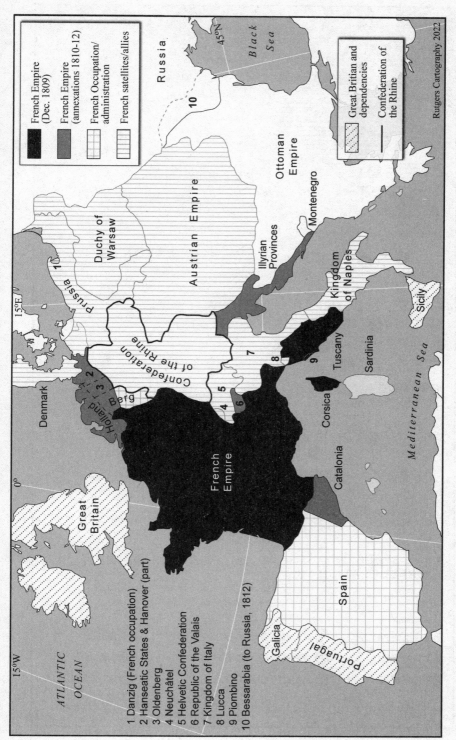

Europe in 1812.

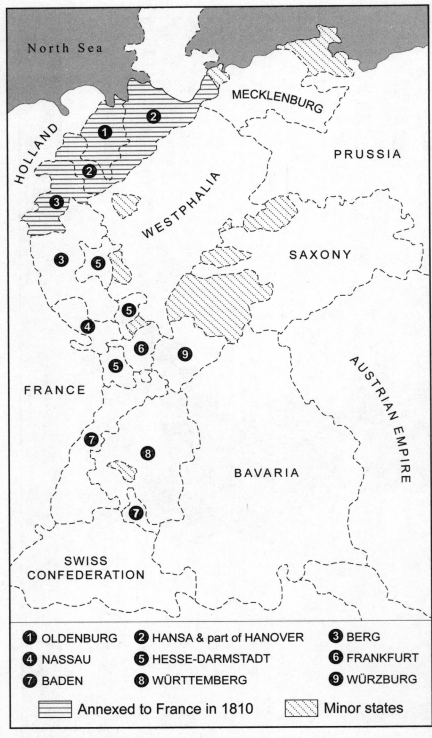

North Sea

HOLLAND

MECKLENBURG

PRUSSIA

WESTPHALIA

SAXONY

FRANCE

AUSTRIAN EMPIRE

BAVARIA

WÜRTTEMBERG

SWISS
CONFEDERATION

❶ OLDENBURG	❷ HANSA & part of HANOVER	❸ BERG
❹ NASSAU	❺ HESSE-DARMSTADT	❻ FRANKFURT
❼ BADEN	❽ WÜRTTEMBERG	❾ WÜRZBURG

Annexed to France in 1810   Minor states

The Confederation of the Rhine.

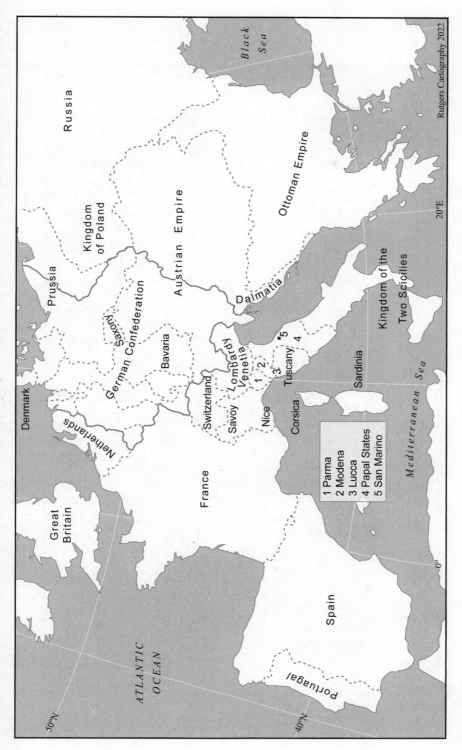

Europe in 1815.

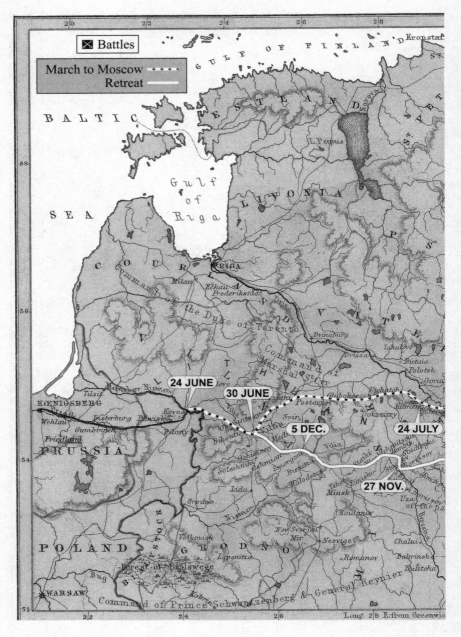

Russian campaign of 1812. *Courtesy of the David Rumsey Map Collection, David Rumsey Map Center, Stanford Libraries.*

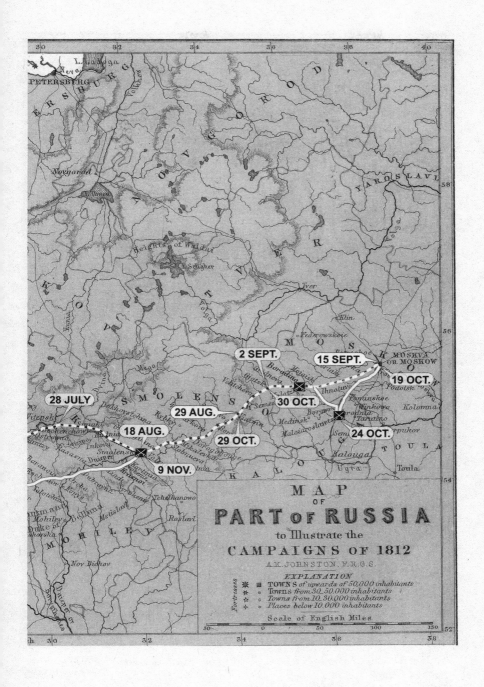

MAP
OF
PART OF RUSSIA
to Illustrate the
CAMPAIGNS OF 1812
A.K. JOHNSTON, F.R.G.S.

EXPLANATION
TOWNS of upwards of 50,000 inhabitants
Towns from 30-50,000 inhabitants
Towns from 10-30,000 inhabitants
Places below 10,000 inhabitants

Fortresses

Scale of English Miles

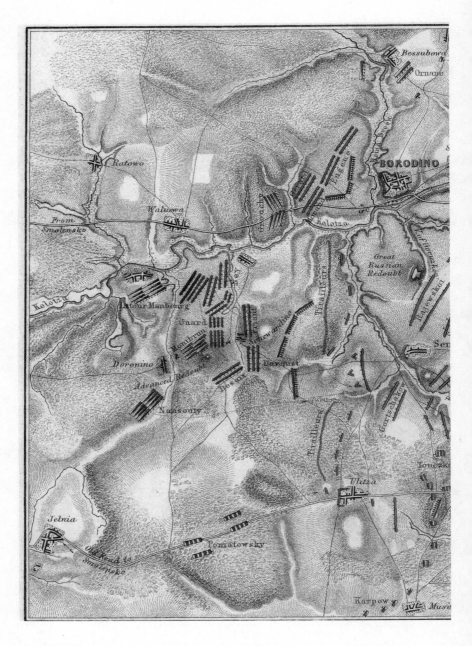

Battle of Borodino. *Courtesy of the David Rumsey Map Collection, David Rumsey Map Center, Stanford Libraries.*

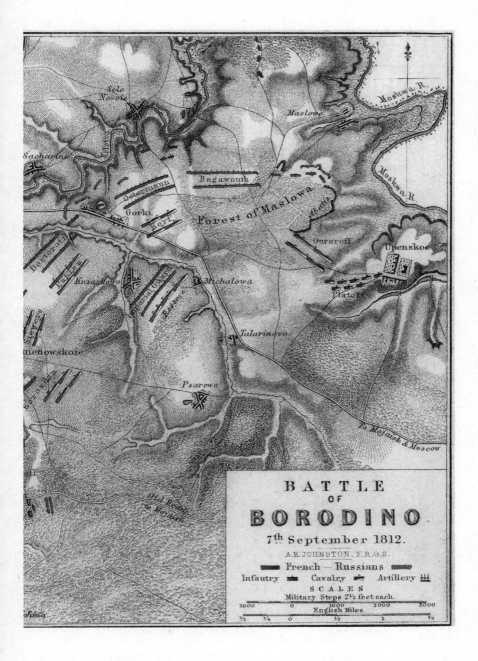

BATTLE
OF
BORODINO
7th September 1812.

A.K.JOHNSTON, F.R.G.S.

French — Russians

Infantry — Cavalry — Artillery

SCALES
Military Steps 2½ feet each.

1000   0   1000   2000   3000

English Miles.

½   ¼   0   ½   1   ½

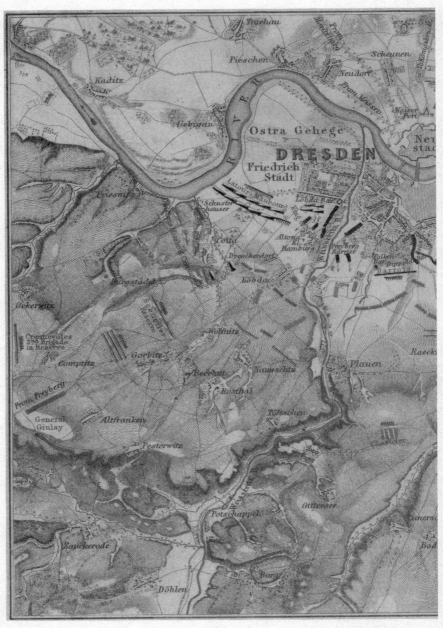

Battle of Dresden. *Courtesy of the David Rumsey Map Collection, David Rumsey Map Center, Stanford Libraries.*

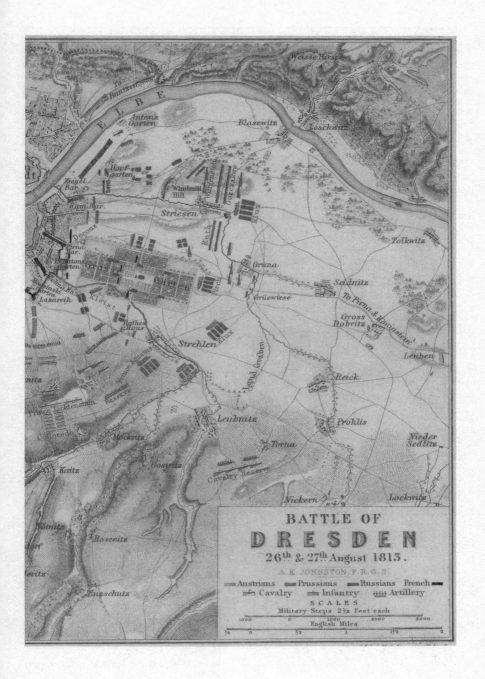

BATTLE OF
DRESDEN
26th & 27th August 1813.

A.K. JOHNSTON, F.R.G.S

Austrians   Prussians   Russians   French

Cavalry   Infantry   Artillery

SCALES
Military Steps 2½ Feet each

| 1000 | 0 | 1000 | 2000 | 3000 |

English Miles

| ¼ | 0 | ½ | 1 | 1½ | 2 |

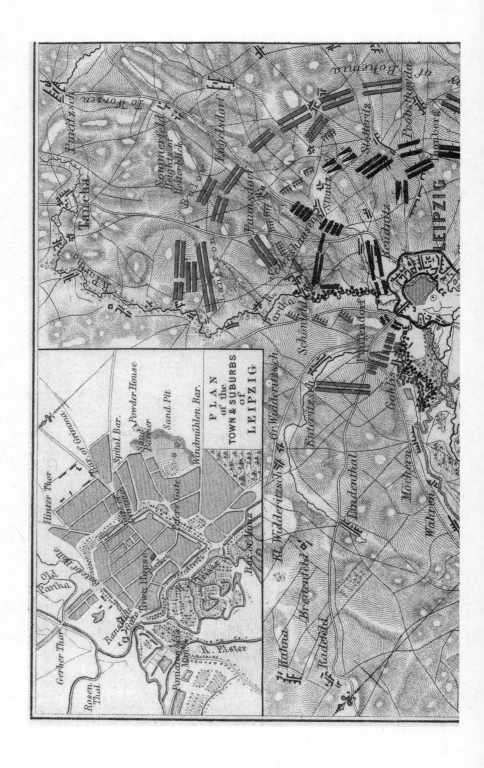

PLAN
of the
TOWN & SUBURBS
of
LEIPZIG

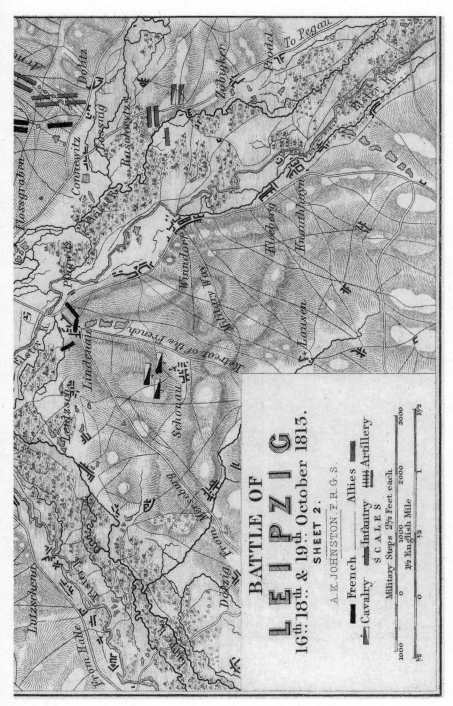

Battle of Leipzig. *Courtesy of the David Rumsey Map Collection, David Rumsey Map Center, Stanford Libraries.*

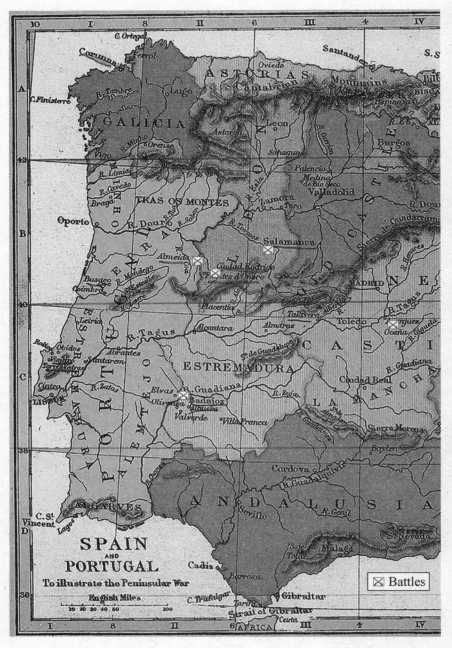

Spain, 1811–1813. *Courtesy of "The Public Schools Historical Atlas" by Charles Colbeck. Longmans, Green; New York; London; Bombay. 1905.*

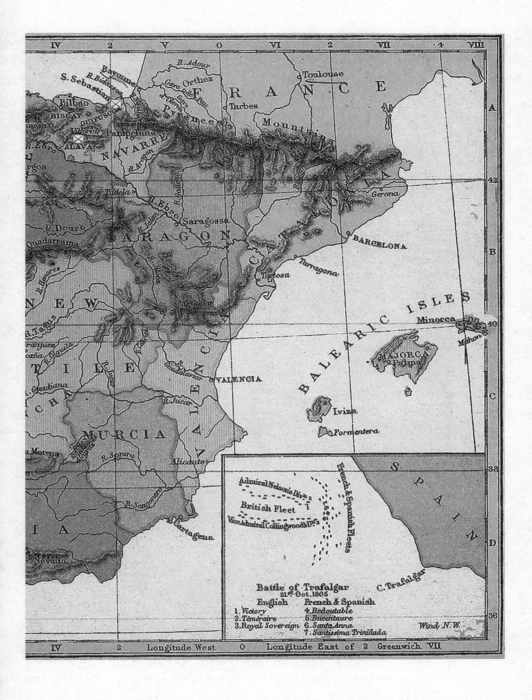

Battle of Trafalgar
21ˢᵗ Oct. 1805
English   French & Spanish
1. Victory   4. Redoutable
2. Téméraire   5. Bucentaure
3. Royal Sovereign 6. Santa Anna
                   7. Santissima Trinidada

Wind N.W.

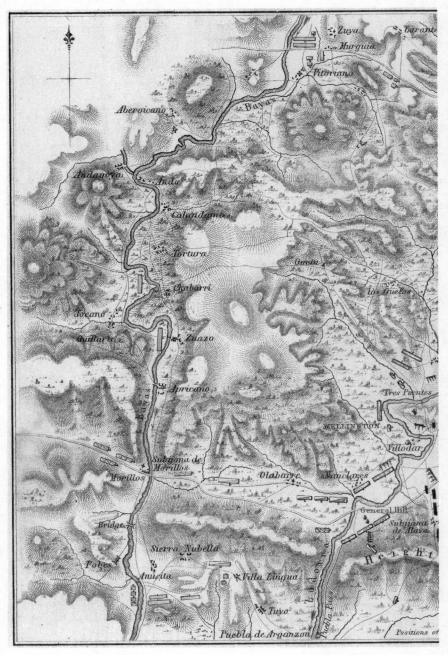

Inset: Battle of Vitoria. *Courtesy of the David Rumsey Map Collection, David Rumsey Map Center, Stanford Libraries.*

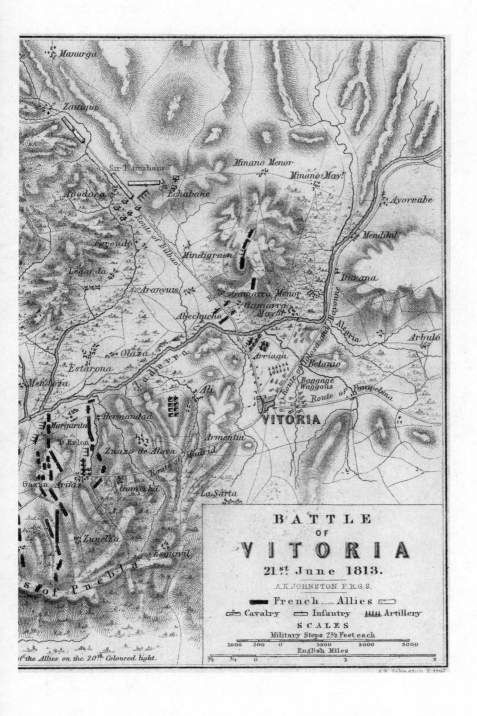

BATTLE
OF
VITORIA
21st June 1813.

A.K.JOHNSTON. F.R.G.S.

French ▬▬ Allies ▭

Cavalry ⬭ Infantry ⬭ Artillery

SCALES
Military Steps 2½ Feet each

1000   500   0   1000   2000   3000
English Miles

½   ¾   0   1   2

of the Allies on the 20th. Coloured light.

J.B. Johnston. Edinᵗ

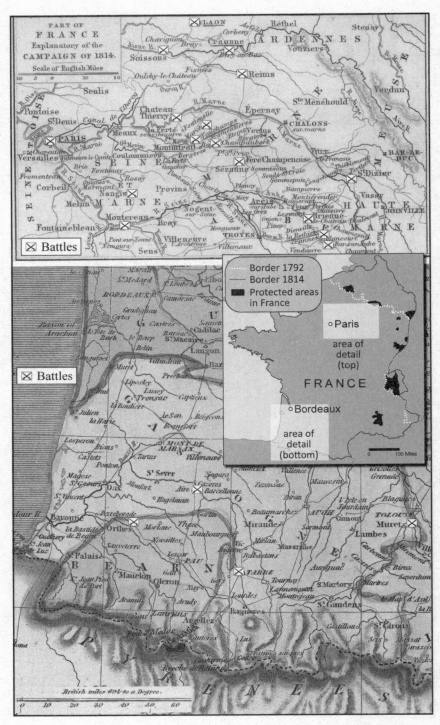

1814 Campaign of France. *Courtesy of "The Public Schools Historical Atlas" by Charles Colbeck. Longmans, Green; New York; London; Bombay. 1905.*

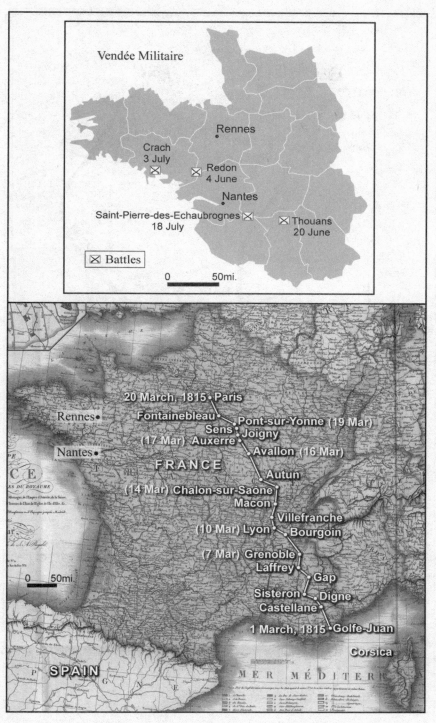

France 1815 'Flight of the Eagle.' *Courtesy of "The Public Schools Historical Atlas" by Charles Colbeck. Longmans, Green; New York; London; Bombay. 1905.*

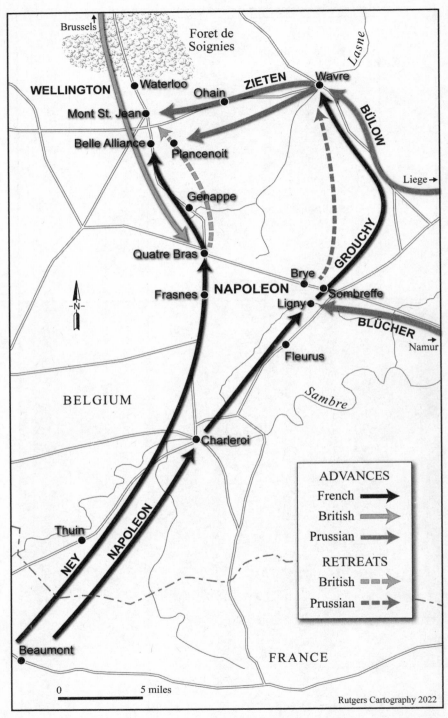

Start of Campaign, Battle of Waterloo. *Courtesy of "The Public Schools Historical Atlas" by Charles Colbeck. Longmans, Green; New York; London; Bombay. 1905.*

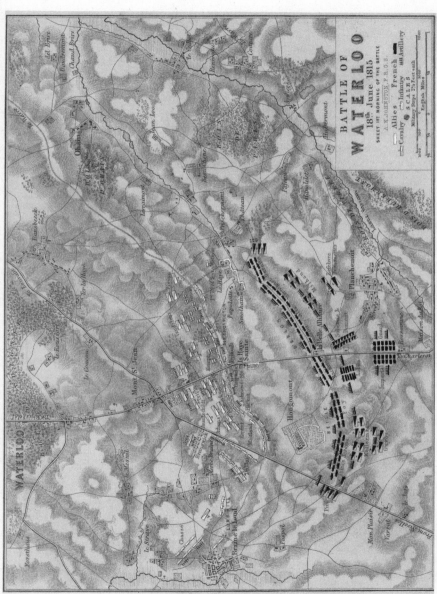

Battle of Waterloo. Courtesy of "The Public Schools Historical Atlas" by Charles Colbeck. Longmans, Green; New York; London; Bombay. 1905.

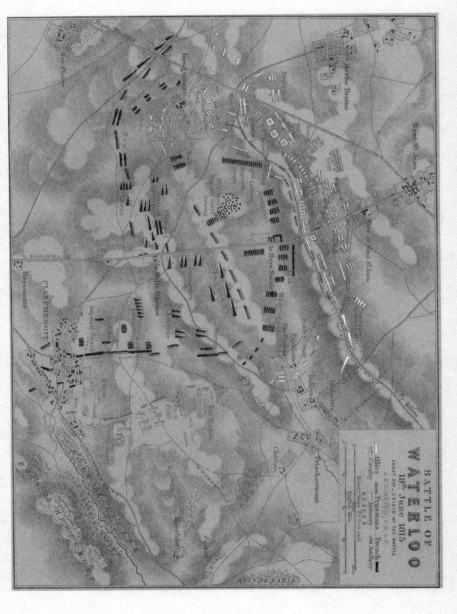

Battle of Waterloo. *Courtesy of "The Public Schools Historical Atlas" by Charles Colbeck, Longmans, Green; New York; London; Bombay, 1905.*

PRELUDE

INTO THE FLAMES

*J*ournée is one of the most evocative words in the French language. It can mean simply a day's work, the time between rising and going to bed. It also stands for "an historic day," a day of destiny. July 1, 1810, was one such for Napoleon.

That morning he wrote one of the most infamous, important letters of his eventful life: ". . . [Y]our services are no long[er] agreeable to me. It would be appropriate if you left (Paris) within twenty-four hours . . . This letter contains no further points."[1] In this terse fashion, Napoleon achieved the long-cherished ambition of ridding himself of Joseph Fouché, his minister of police, indispensable and a viper in his bosom in almost equal measure from the outset. Now, for the first time, Napoleon felt secure enough to expel a man who had plotted against him two years before, survived in office, and become still more influential. This letter was followed immediately by one to Fouché's successor, General Jean-Marie Réné Savary, ". . . I want him to retire to Nice . . . behaving as if he were in exile . . . he must exercise no influence there, nor receive any honors. . . ."[2] At last, Napoleon was free. In the course of the morning, he dispatched two detailed letters to Admiral Decrès, his minister of the navy, which projected the rebuilding of the French fleets, the first concerted effort to do so since the catastrophe of Trafalgar in 1805.[3] The invasion of England, another long-cherished hope, was now rekindled.[4] It was a day to deal with all-consuming, age-old obsessions.

Nor did the *journée* end there. That evening, Prince Karl of Schwarzenberg, the Austrian ambassador to Paris, held a sumptuous ball for Napoleon and Marie-Louise in his embassy at the beautiful Hôtel de Montesson, in western Paris.[5] Even the Montesson was too small for the fifteen hundred people who replied to the two thousand invitations issued, so a wooden pavilion was erected in the garden, linked to the house by a gallery, also of wood. Partitions were created within it by pleated tapestries of muslin. Rain was forecast, and to prevent water leaking in, and to dry the muslin and wood quickly, the pavilion had been coated in ethane, an odorless, colorless gas that absorbs water. The main hall was lit by a gigantic chandelier; there were seventy-three smaller ones, each with forty candles, distributed around the pavilion. Napoleon and Marie-Louise arrived about 11:00 P.M., to trumpet fanfares. When the dancers of the Paris Opera, recently reinvigorated by Napoleon's efforts, had finished performing, the dancing began. Marie-Louise left her throne and began to chat and banter with her entourage, while Napoleon "worked the room" with his usual bonhomie. At about 11:30 P.M., there was a gust of wind. The wooden struts of the ceiling burst into flames, raining cinders and sparks onto the crowd. Those in the main hall were not immediately aware of the danger until the fire consumed the muslin partitions. Then the gallery caught fire, blocking any escape to the Hôtel. The pavilion had become a death trap. Napoleon kept calm, turned to Marie-Louise, and said simply, "Let's go, there's a fire," hustling her out by the exit reserved for dignitaries. He put her in a coach to get her back to Saint-Cloud, where the imperial couple were residing, but he left her at the edge of Paris, and returned to take charge.

In the meantime, chaos reigned. The flames from the roof set peoples' hair alight, consuming their light summer dresses and gold-gilt gowns. The chandeliers crashed down on the wooden floor, setting it ablaze and blocking the few remaining exits. A stampede began; those knocked to the ground were trampled underfoot. Death by asphyxia ensued. There was now only one way out, a stair into the garden, but it could not cope with one thousand or more people, as more wind whipped the flames. Caroline, Napoleon's sister and the Queen of Naples, was normally the steeliest of the Bonapartes, her imperial brother included, but her nerves were shattered, an emphatic sign of how terrifying the inferno had become. Trying to punch and kick her way out, while screaming in terror, she fell, but was picked up and carried out by Jérôme Bonaparte and Klemens von Metternich, an act they may later have had cause to regret—within four years, she would betray them both. Eugène kept his pregnant wife, Augusta-Amélie of Bavaria, close to him. Apparently doomed in the throng, fate took a hand: a quick-witted man, Napoleon's trusted lieutenant spotted a small hole in the canvas and slipped them both to safety. Among the dead was Pauline of Schwarzenberg, the young, vivacious sister-in-law of the ambassador, a mother of eight, who shortly before had opened the dancing with Eugène. She had been crushed under the falling ceiling. Those who escaped stumbled around, half-naked, often scarred by appalling burns. Many simply collapsed, exhausted. Servants scurried among them, doing what they could. Real help only came from one of Napoleon's reliable technocrats, Regnault de Saint-Jean d'Angély, who quickly converted his nearby residence into a makeshift hospital.

A mere forty-eight hours before the ball, Schwarzenberg and the Parisian authorities had thought to post six firemen at the ball, but they were completely overwhelmed by the scale of the fire, despite their heroic efforts to contain it and save lives. Napoleon rushed back to the scene about midnight, now wrapped in his military gray greatcoat, with Marshal Bessières at his side, and they gave Schwarzenberg what help they could. A torrential rain began to fall, putting out the fire by about 3:00 A.M. and turning what was left of the pavilion to mush. The police turned up about 4:00 P.M. and began their investigation, and the search for bodies. Only then did Napoleon go back to Saint-Cloud.

Napoleon's valet, Constant, recorded in his memoirs that Napoleon was more upset than he had almost ever seen him, choked with an emotion he never expressed in his own misfortunes.[6] Constant's are among the most dubious of the many untrustworthy memoirs of the period, however.[7] Even so, Napoleon indisputably reacted in ways very much in character. Initially, he believed reports that the firemen present had been drunk, and ordered them sacked, along with several more in the service.[8] However, when the results of the report of July 2 reached him, and made him aware of their heroism, he revoked his own order and commended them. It did not go as well for those in charge, however. Ten days after the fire, he ordered the complete reorganization and expansion of the Paris fire service. This entailed mass dismissals from its higher and middle echelons, and a more effective public service resulted, setting it on the footing it still has today. As in so many other spheres of the French state, Napoleon's quick reaction established lasting, effective change. Throughout the investigations, Napoleon loyally protected Schwarzenberg, determined that no blame be attached to his new Austrian allies. Realpolitik was never far away. However, the report lambasted the architect of the pavilion, Pierre Bénard, who was jailed briefly, and saw his reputation ruined. The prefect of Paris, Louis Dubois, remained in his post, but was severely reprimanded by Napoleon for having gone to the country during the event. Many at the time felt he should have been sacked for not preventing the looting that followed the fire, when an unknown mass of jewelry discarded or lost by those fleeing the fire was left scattered around the scene.

Public disquiet among Parisians extended beyond the actual events. There had been another "Austrian marriage," when the rulers of France had reversed what many saw as the "natural order of things," by allying with the traditional enemy. On May 16–17, 1770, the ill-starred union of the future Louis XVI and Marie Antoinette, the aunt of Marie-Louise, took place at Versailles. At a fireworks display held as part of the marriage festivities on the present-day Place de la Concorde, a fire broke out killing 132 people. Dread parallels, inevitably, were quickly drawn. In a fashion typical of him, Napoleon drew a veil over the tragedy, as far as the public was concerned. The death of a person of such renown as Pauline of Schwarzenberg was impossible to hide, but the official press registered her as the sole fatality. The actual number was probably closer to ninety, according to the police reports. It was not the first time Napoleon had lied shamelessly about casualties. Nor would it be the last.

1

A NEW ORDER OF THINGS

❧ ———————————————————————————— ❧

On December 10, 1810, Napoleon declared to the Senate, "A new order of things directs the universe."[1] This was bombastic, but it was not hubris. Now, for the first time since 1805, he could devote himself to the governance of his "universe" because he had humbled all comers. This "new order of things" was decreed when his new wife, Marie-Louise, was heavily pregnant with his son, and that the new order was to be Napoleon's legacy to his much-cherished heir, but that legacy had to be forged in strife.

The same day he annexed Rome to France, February 17, 1810—and even before his remarriage—Napoleon issued an edict declaring that his first male heir would carry the title "King of Rome." The timing was obviously meant as a blunt instrument with which to beat the pope, but the title carried far deeper significance. It dated from 1110, when the title "King of the Romans" was added to the imperial title to assert imperial authority over the Papacy. In 1508, Maximilian I adopted it as the title assigned to the chosen successor of an emperor during his lifetime.[2] The implications for Pope Pius VII were gratuitously obvious—he was no longer a secular ruler. It was also salt in the wounds of Emperor Francis of Austria, a reminder that he was no longer the Holy Roman Emperor. In early 1810, it also carried potent, if hardly historically accurate, Carolingian implications: Napoleon's heir would, until his succession, be another Bonaparte monarch in the new crypto-feudal imperial construct. He would be the first familial vassal among Napoleon's brothers and sisters. However, by the time Napoléon François Joseph Charles was born on March 20, 1811, all this had become redundant. The future "Napoleon II" would rule over a highly centralized hegemony, more akin to a Roman than a feudal model.

Ineffectual at best, a hotbed of betrayal at worst, Napoleon's vision of a Europe both federal and feudal had all but disintegrated by the spring of 1810. Napoleonic policy, everywhere, embraced abolishing feudalism among the peasant masses, but it was to be reintroduced for his siblings, to bind them into a hierarchy of kings with Napoleon as emperor at the apex of the system, ruling them at one remove. As so often with Napoleon, the essence of a grand strategy emerges in the details. In the midst of lambasting Jérôme, a barely surviving vassal, for allowing himself to become "the laughingstock of Europe," to the point that no marshal of the empire could respect him, Napoleon asserted his vision: "A kingdom is not an empire"; the grand dignitaries of the empire were its kings along with the viceroy of Italy, Eugène. He humbled his brother witheringly: "Do not look for comparisons in Paris (of how to run his Court), you would look like a frog who wants to be as big as a bull."[3]

"The children of the century"

The failure of his Carolingian vision led him back to the "Roman" model of a centralized, uniform empire. The trope of Roman imperialism had reasserted itself in the wake of the crisis of 1809–10, when Napoleon's hegemony had been shaken as never before. The "extraordinary political laboratory" that was Napoleonic Europe, according to the Italian scholar Luigi Mascilli Migliorini, had entered a new phase in 1810.[4] An aristocratic courtier, Louis-Philippe de Ségur, admitted in his memoirs to fretting that this rapid, huge expansion might "lose France in Europe, for when France was Europe, there might be no more France."[5] He need not have worried. "The Great Empire," as it was soon called, was run by the French, in the manner of France, and for the French, from the Baltic to the Strait of Messina.

This process was already well underway. In practice, it meant the system imposed on Napoleon's vast empire was rigid, and to keep it so, it was run in the main by Frenchmen, often with the active participation of their wives. The French officials came from the old core of the empire—which embraced Belgium, the Rhineland, and northern Italy as well as France—and were sent to rule its new peripheries; they were drawn from two different pools of talent. On the one hand, Napoleon turned to tried and trusted collaborators for the most senior posts both in France and beyond. On the other, he was finally able to reach over the revolutionary generation, conferring the middle level of government to his *enfants du siècle*—"the children of the (new) century"—who were drawn from every shade of the political landscape and none, and had been schooled in the system he had created. France had the human wherewithal to supply the higher and middle ranks of its imperial bureaucracy. The civil administration of the newly annexed "Illyrian Provinces" was staffed, at departmental level, wholly with the young auditors of the Council of State, as were the proto-departments of Catalonia, which were earmarked for eventual annexation to France. In March 1811, Napoleon wrote to Louis-Nicolas Davout following the transfer of some of Jérôme's Westphalian territory to direct rule from Paris:

> It is very important that these territories are promptly organized into sub-prefectures (the major subdivision of departments). I envisage German speaking sub-prefects, but (drawn from) old France . . .[6]

He got them.[7]

The "rallying" of large sections of the French elites to the Napoleonic educational system and the careers in an ever-expanding imperial public sphere flooded Europe with *les enfants*. They began in Paris, the capital Napoleon had done so much to make both imposing and alluring. From the corridors of power in the Council of State, where the best among them began as auditors, they were sent forth to be tested on the furthest-flung marches of the empire, but always with the prospect of returning to its heart, if they served well. *Les enfants* were among the best schooled public servants of the age. They were professional bureaucrats.

There was far more to it than professionalism, however. The auditors were imbued with a clear mission to extend the "unbreakable model" to wherever the emperor sent them, for embodied in the Civil Code, its system of judicial administration, and the whole edifice of civil government, was their own vision of enlightened progress. In their eyes, they held the perfect template with which to reform Europe, and Europe would not be reformed until its peoples fitted that template. It took a remarkable degree of confidence and clarity of purpose to rule half a continent by such lights. Madame de Rémusat—possessed of one of the most poisonous pens of the age—saw them as a disaster in the making:

> Only the briefest acquaintance is needed with the attitude and despotic ideas these young men exercised in their own country, to understand what a danger these attitudes had been when the administration of some conquered French province had been given to them.[8]

They were not the children of the Revolution, still less the battered survivors of the Terror and counter-Terror, but the generation that grew into adulthood under the blazing sun of Austerlitz. There was nothing pleasant about these young men, and they made the regime a host of enemies as they went about their routine duties, to say nothing of their ruthless enforcement of conscription. They were determined and effective, nonetheless. However overbearing, arrogant, or even tremulous, "the children of the century" had the "bible" of the French civilizing mission, crystallized in the Civil Code, to guide them: Wherever they went, the walls of the Ghettos crumbled, feudalism was fought tooth and nail in the courts, and civic improvements driven through. They rose to these tasks with as much determination as they showed in enforcing conscription, levying taxes, and crushing armed revolt.

Napoleonic women had their part to play in the new imperial order, and theirs was a far from passive role. When French women came into direct contact with their Italian, Spanish, and even German "sisters," they knew themselves to be the most liberated in Europe, certainly in the social world of the salon and also through their control of the domestic sphere: The Tournon, the aristocratic couple to whom the second city of the empire was entrusted, defiantly flouted the sexist conventions of Roman society in the private sphere by holding mixed dinner parties, and in the public, when Madame Tournon, herself the daughter of a prominent legal family from Nîmes, took charge of the prefectoral office in her husband's absence. Madame Tournon's position in Rome was far from unique. Prefects toured their departments four times a year under Napoleon, to carry out conscription, and in their absence, their wives usually ran the departmental offices. The rougher the frontier, the more unabashed the behavior. The wife of Marshal Suchet did not so much shock as "floor" Catalan and Valencian society by riding in breeches to review the troops, kiss them on both cheeks, and hand out medals, to say nothing of her own very bourgeois, highly intellectual salons in Barcelona and Valencia.[9] The school established by Madame Campan to educate the female orphans of members of the Legion of Honor was created to turn out exactly such women. If the education she, under Napoleon's supervision, prescribed for them fell short of that of later ages, it was certainly liberated—and liberating—by the standards of the time, as witnessed by Campan's justified fears for its survival under the Restoration. Louis XVIII closed the school almost immediately in 1814. He did not want the wives of his prefects, officers, or magistrates educated in modern languages, mathematics, or basic science, still less given only one hour of religious instruction per week, or boarding without a confessor "on site," as had been Campan's system.[10]

Napoleon's "new order of things" had two watchwords from which all else stemmed: centralization and uniformity. He meant for this vision to be stamped emphatically on the next generation of rulers: Napoleon set about refurbishing the châteaux of Meudon, to the west of Paris, in the winter of 1810–11, even before his heir was born. It was to become "the Institute of Meudon," a centralized college where the children of the Imperial family—called officially "the Children of France" regardless of the territories ruled by their parents—were to be educated together. They were to be joined by the children of the leading families of the satellite states in a setting of buildings arranged around the central pavilion in which Napoleon's son would reside. It all came to nothing, but the intent was clear: This was now a French imperium, to be ruled by a "French" ruling class, regardless of where they were born.[11]

Amid all the swirling changes of his "new order of things," there were things that nothing, not even remarriage or the prospect of fatherhood, could alter in Napoleon. In the summer of 1810, while taking the waters at Aix, Josephine had gone boating and fallen in a lake. "For someone born beside the ocean, to die in a lake! Now that would be a fatality, wouldn't it!"[12] he teased her, as always.

The Empire of the Laws

The bedrock of the imperial edifice, like its Roman template, was the law. Its core was the Civil Code of 1804, but these years of relative peace saw another surge of legal reform, both in terms of statute law and in the workings of the administration of justice. This time, however, Napoleonic legal reform had most of continental Europe in its remit. By 1810–11, the changed times turned the regime's attention to the criminal law.

The Civil Code was complete, mature, and ready for export, of a piece, to the rest of Napoleonic Europe, and the young auditors and their judicial equivalents saw that it was, although not without myriad challenges. The same was not true of the criminal law. The early French revolutionaries had drawn up a prototype for a penal code as early as 1791, and it exercised a great influence by the later work of the Napoleonic regimes, but it had yet to be completed by 1810. Napoleon returned from the 1809 campaign determined to hasten its completion: He resumed the chairmanship from Cambacérès, the work sped up, and it was put before the *Corps législatif* in February 1810—after only a month under his chairmanship—and voted into law in March. It came into effect in January 1811.[13]

The major historian of the Penal Code, Pierre Lascoumes, describes it as "in the end, only a reform of that of 1791,"[14] but "a much more precise and systematic professional instrument" in keeping with the process of rationalization and professionalism begun under the Consulate.[15] The real ruptures with the Revolution came in its justifications for punishments and a greater emphasis on the protection of society as a whole, rather than the revolutionaries' insistence on the individualism of both victim and criminal: The 1810 Penal Code argued from the particular and the pragmatic, and simply ignored the emphatic insistence of the code of 1791 on the capacity of the law to perfect humanity. The Napoleonic code explicitly accepted the permanent existence of a debased criminal class that posed a constant threat to public order, thus reflecting the alarmist currents within "the masses of granite" at the rising tide of disorder around them, at a time of economic crisis. The kind of crime that so enraged the masses of granite took place in the rich vineyards around Bordeaux in 1811, when the little town of Moulinet sustained an attack of great violence by a band of deserters who had plagued its environs for some time. They had a vendetta against the mayor, who had informed on them.[16] Personal safety and property all seemed at risk, even in the wealthiest rural areas.

This pessimistic view of the human condition has branded the Penal Code of 1810 as fundamentally repressive.[17] However, the 1810 code actually reduced the proportion of cases subject to the death penalty from 18.3 to 6.4 percent, and reduced those punishable by forced labor from 31.4 to 10.2 percent, using imprisonment and fines for less serious offenses.[18] Nevertheless, Italian jurists, both in the imperial departments and the kingdom of Italy, opposed the ethos of the French codes vociferously, if in vain, when Napoleon imposed a code on them that was virtually a clone of the French project of legal reform.[19] As conscription intensified with the approach of war with Russia, criminality rose in tandem. For Napoleon, this was a way of reassuring the masses of granite that the regime was on their side: "(Public) opinion wanted severe sanctions."[20]

This found its expression less in the text of the Criminal Code than in the manner of its application. Over vast tracts of the empire, there had never been juries for serious criminal trials, and new legislation in 1810 made this state of affairs permanent for the imperial departments in Italy and for most of those in the west and south of France. The "Special Criminal Courts" composed partly of soldiers—usually senior gendarmes—and civilian magistrates were made permanent. Elsewhere, the role of juries was greatly reduced. Napoleon had sought the complete abolition of juries in criminal cases, fearing their amateur nature, but he was firmly overruled by a majority in the Council of State and accepted its opinion.[21] He still valued expert opinion, despite his increasingly embattled attitude to the world around him.

The subtle hand of Jean-Jacques-Régis Cambacérès temporized many of Napoleon's harsher instincts and those of the masses of granite whose views he reflected. The differences between the two men had become more acute since Cambacérès's clear reticence about the divorce of Napoleon and Josephine and even more over the advisability of the Austrian marriage. He feared that many of Napoleon's new policies were bringing the regime far too close to the revival of a society of orders. Napoleon always respected his views, and Cambacérès provided a genuine break on Napoleon during these years. His oblique influence came from drawing many of the regime's power brokers—Napoleon included—closer to Freemasonry.[22] His greatest intervention came over the administration of justice. Cambacérès did not mince words in his memoirs:

> More than once I put it to Napoleon that the laws he was giving to his
> people would prove inadequate if he did not confide them to the hands
> of magistrates (who were) invested with high esteem and placed in
> a position of independence which would make them immune from
> any fear other than that of failing to do their duty . . .[23]

The major restructuring of the court system developed by Cambacérès and realized in 1810 helped achieve this. It was a mixture of centralized, hierarchical professionalization Napoleon could not argue with, and a calibrated policy of assuring an increased independence for the magistrates who ran it. There were obvious parallels with the ancien régime *parlements*: the Courts of Appeal were enlarged and renamed "Imperial Courts," and the local criminal and civil courts were integrated into them, as had been the case before 1789. The senior magistrates were renamed "councillors," as in the *parlements*. The real purpose of Cambacérès's reforms was to bring the local judiciary into closer, more integrated contact with better educated senior magistrates, and to make it easier for the Imperial Courts to oversee the workings of justice at lower levels. Civil and criminal justice were now under the supervision of the same senior court, and this provided an important break on the newly powerful public prosecutors. Cambacérès did not win easily: He successfully opposed Napoleon's idea to fix the number of judges arbitrarily for each Imperial Court, and Treilhard's project to retain two separate chambers (civil and criminal).[24]

According to the Belgian scholar Xavier Rousseau, "After twenty years of hesitation, the new (system) of justice was firmly bound to the state."[25] Cambacérès felt strongly that the law needed to retain its standing to curb the power of that same state. To bolster the status of the magistracy, Cambacérès made court sessions and confirmation of judges more solemn occasions, and restored their ancien régime regalia. Outwardly, these changes appear almost retrograde, and they doubtless drew on Cambacérès's own vanity. Nonetheless, their serious purpose was to erect a brake on the state. One reform he failed to get past Napoleon was to resurrect the corporate status of lawyers. Although Napoleon consented to revive the Bar in the spirit of fostering professionalism, Cambacérès inadvertently reawakened the Jacobin in him:

> His Majesty said that he did not see why the profession of advocate should be more honored than any other . . . Perhaps in seeing one of their number rise to the post of Arch-Chancellor because of the Revolution, they have persuaded themselves that one day they

might become him? That would be like the whole artillery corps giving itself over to ambitious hopes because one of them got to the Throne![26]

Whatever their differences, the two men retained their trust, goodwill, and mutual sense of humor.

The creation of the new structures in 1810 allowed Claude-Ambroise Régnier, the minister of justice, to ask the new heads of the Imperial Courts for their advice on those "who left something to be desired." When the time came to replace them, "the occult hand" of Cambacérès proved the most influential.[27] The object of the exercise was renewal, and as the new system came into being in early March, the empire also acquired another source of new life.

The King of Rome

The "new order of things" now rested on the little boy who came into the world on March 20, 1811, at the Tuileries, the youngest but most exalted *enfant du siècle*. That birth was anything but easy. When the time came, the delivery proved dangerous. Napoleon had summoned Jean-Nicolas Corvisart—one of the most distinguished medical men of the era—but he had yet to arrive as Marie-Louise began an agonizing labor. The only doctor present was Antoine Dubois, an army surgeon all too familiar with the horrors of battle, but with no experience delivering babies.[28] Cambacérès gave an unembellished account of the scene: The atmosphere was one of impending catastrophe, everyone's faces were haggard. Napoleon had just arrived and asked Cambacérès if he had seen Dubois, adding, "I'm afraid he might lose his head. I hope Corvisart gets here soon." Dubois came out of the birthing room, pale and nervous, and told Napoleon that Marie-Louise was in real danger, and that he could do nothing without Corvisart. No crisis could be more personal, but it brought the absolute best out of Napoleon. He diffused the pressure on Dubois, reassuring him:

Conduct yourself as if you were seeing to the son of a cobbler . . . I'm telling you this in the presence of the Arch-Chancellor (the highest legal officer of the Empire). Carry on in complete security. You have my full confidence. No blame will attach to anything you do. But remember that the mother's health must prevail over all other considerations.[29]

Nevertheless, Napoleon almost cheered when Corvisart arrived. Dubois stood aside, and Napoleon went with his old friend to his wife's bedside.

These conversations took place as the agonized screams of a girl barely out of her teens rang out down the long corridors and reverberated across the high ceilings of the Tuileries. Marie-Louise was terrified by her ordeal, and with good reason. Nothing her feminine entourage told her could possibly have prepared her for the horrors of her labor, which were so serious that Corvisart resorted to a breach birth. Napoleon trusted Corvisart implicitly, as he had been his surgeon in the field over many campaigns and helped him through many of his own bouts of illness. Corvisart kept a cool head throughout when others panicked—Napoleon included, by his own later admission, though he took Corvisart's orders when helping to hold down Marie-Louise during the birth. In the midst of it, Marie-Louise cried out to Napoleon, "Will you sacrifice me because I am the Empress?" Witnesses verified his reply to Corvisart that Napoleon recounted in his memoirs, when it looked like the baby might suffocate: "I can have another child with the mother."[30] The life of his wife came first, a sign of genuine humanity, mingled as always with realpolitik, but hardly in keeping with the tenets of the Church. Before Marie-Louise went into labor, Napoleon had been very anxious for any sign of the child's sex; when her danger became apparent, he forgot all about it. When his son was at last safely delivered, Napoleon readily admitted:

The danger had been so great that all etiquette . . . which had been so carefully researched for this occasion, was cast aside, and the infant was taken aside and put on a plank while everyone busied themselves only with his mother.[31]

The King of Rome slept so quietly through it all that, in the general state of anxiety, the assembled company feared he was dead. It was only when Corvisart picked him up that he began to cry, to unanimous hilarity.

The personal crisis over, the regime became a parody of itself. The first into the room was Cambacérès, who dictated the legal corroboration of the birth to a secretary for the registers of the *État Civil*. The Republican formalities dealt with, the imperial pageant began. The boy's appointed governess, the impeccably aristocratic Madame de Montesquiou, took Napoleon-Francis in her arms, swathed him in ermine, and marched into the throne room, declaring to all and sundry, "The King of Rome!" Even before he was presented to the gathered dignitaries, Napoleon led Madame de Montesquiou, her new charge in her arms, to the balcony and together they presented him to the Imperial Guard, assembled outside—they were Napoleon's real family, and they came first. One witness, the Marquise de la Tour du Pin, recalled:

> We relished the incomparable spectacle of these *grognards* of the
> Old Guard, ranged in order, one on each step, every chest decorated
> with the cross (of the Legion of Honor). Any movement was for-
> bidden them, but real emotion broke through those very masculine
> faces, and I saw tears of joy welling up in their eyes.[32]

Orders or no, a huge cheer broke out. It was soon followed by the roar of one hundred cannon salvos (it would have been a mere twenty for a girl) sounding in the background as the King of Rome was placed in his cradle—at last—for the assembled company to pass by. The *grognards* soon "baptized" Napoleon-Francis themselves: he was "the Eaglette."

Napoleon showered generosity on all who had helped. Dubois was made a Baron of the Legion of Honor and given a *dotation* worth 100,000 francs. Madame de Montesquiou and all the other ladies-in-waiting received very generous gifts. It was hard to reward Corvisart, given the honors and wealth Napoleon had already accorded him, so he bestowed upon him the greatest accolade in his gift: From that moment, Corvisart never left the side of the empress and Napoleon-Francis. Napoleon did not risk him in any future campaigns, so crucial did he believe his old friend to be for their well-being. A decree of March 22 bestowed a sum of 250,000 francs from Napoleon's private savings for needy mothers. Marie-Louise got a pearl necklace.[33] Private frugality coexisted with official largesse.

Public holidays, illuminations, and commemorative songs and poems of nauseating mediocrity followed. However, the police noted that the public celebrations petered out after a day or two.[34] In the background, the pastoral letters of several bishops inviting the people to pray for the safe delivery of the empress and her child had to be redrafted under police pressure for not being "happy enough."[35] Shadows of clerical hostility and growing poverty mirrored the hard coming into the world of the regime's great hope.

With an heir came the need to reorder the hegemony that was now held in trust for the son by the father. The baptism of Napoleon-Francis was the moment when the "new order of things" was laid bare for the Bonapartes. It was less about family or Court intrigue, than geopolitics. There was one caveat, however. Napoleon-Francis should have been baptized by Maury, the Cardinal Archbishop of Paris, in whose jurisdiction he was born. Instead, Joseph Fesch, Napoleon's cousin, the Cardinal Archbishop of Lyon, performed the rite, not because Fesch was his relation, but that "Napoleon did not want to take the risk of having his son baptized by a Cardinal-Archbishop who had not been invested by the Pope."[36] If so, it was his last sign of fear of, or deference to, the Holy See.

The Birth of a New Empire

Napoleon used the baptism of his son, on June 9, 1811, to mark the symbolic end of the "Carolingian system" of a federation of satellite states. The only Bonaparte brothers left—barely—in the fold, Jérôme and Joseph, made the journey to Paris for the ceremony in Notre-Dame, Napoleon breaking his long silence with his elder brother. Both were ordered to dress as French princes, not kings; Joseph's Spanish retinue was snubbed, even though he was one of the two godfathers, the other being the absent Emperor Francis.[37] Caroline feared her brother Napoleon's wrath because of her husband Joachim Murat's ill-judged attempts to defy him. She had no need, for Caroline was among the increasingly narrow circle of people Napoleon still trusted. She had always been his favorite sibling, the one he felt most resembled him, and her efforts to follow his orders in Naples, even in defiance of her husband, marked a sharp contrast to his brothers in Napoleon's mind, her singular loyalty only strengthened for him by her kindness to Marie-Louise, when set beside the spite shown her by his other sisters at their wedding. He tried to make this clear to Caroline, when inviting her to the baptism:

> My sister, I hope to associate you with all my happy events, and I hope you will be godmother to my son, whose birth has given me so much joy . . . It would be so agreeable to me to create these new links between my son and my sister.[38]

Caroline still feared coming to Paris, and her sister Pauline stood as the second godmother in Caroline's "political" absence; her antipathy for Marie-Louise notwithstanding, she was harmless. Caroline did not let the chance to advance herself slip, however. She sent the King of Rome a toy coach and two Merino sheep to pull it, in which both father and son delighted.[39]

The baptism of the King of Rome was but an event. The new order of things was meant to find more lasting symbolic expression in a new series of palaces, not only in France but across the empire. As the family courts of the satellite states lost their influence, Napoleon's own European palaces were to usurp them. Rome, "the second city of the Empire," preoccupied Napoleon in a particularly pointed manner. While he lavished money on saving the Vatican and many classical monuments from collapse,[40] he seized Pius's residence and the scene of his arrest, the Quirinal, and transformed it into a temple of militarism: It contained a Hall of the Marshals; Jean-Auguste-Dominique Ingres executed a huge painting of "Romulus carrying to the Temple of Jupiter the weapons of his enemy Acrionius"; another depicted Alexander the Great entering Babylon. The intentional cultural insult to baroque Rome, and to Pius who had enraged Napoleon with his passive resistance, was gross. The Quirinal was to lodge Napoleon for his projected state visit in 1813 and his coronation in a refurbished Vatican. Conversely, the palace of the new King of Rome was not to be in "his" city, but in Paris, where the Trocadéro now stands.[41] It was never completed. In Florence, Napoleon's sister Élisa was now virtually usurped as ruler with the complete annexation of Tuscany to the empire; she retired to Lucca, and Napoleon immediately set about restoring the Pitti Palace for himself. In 1811, he acquired palaces in Antwerp, Turin, and Amsterdam, but Paris remained the real center of power. Its palaces were now peopled by courtiers drawn from all over his hegemony, not just the empire proper: There were now five Poles among Napoleon's chamberlains, alongside Tuscans, Romans, and Belgians. The style of the "Great Empire" is epitomized by the surviving apartments of the Empress Marie-Louise at Compiègne: The furniture is far heavier than that of the ancien régime and the walls and ceilings are covered in Napoleonic symbols: Ns; the golden bees of Clovis, the first Christian king of France and golden eagles. As at Fontainebleau, the colors are bold and brave: gold, red, and white. In Philip Mansel's words, "the effect is one of startling splendor and luxury."[42] "Startling" was the point. This was an exercise in "shock and awe." As Mansel observes:

> The hostility of a large part of the population of the Empire had been one reason for the creation of the court. The court and, indeed, the whole capital city, had a dark side. The Court and the capital were there to intimidate, as well as inspire. It was all intended to be a symbol of the power, magnificence, and stability of the regime.[43]

That symbolism was wholly French. The great empire was now, visibly, an extension of "the great nation," as the French Republic had long dubbed itself.

The Idyll of Saint-Cloud

On the advice of Dubois and Corvisart, the new, nuclear imperial family withdrew from the hubbub of Paris to Saint-Cloud on April 20 to give Marie-Louise the rest and tranquility her health so badly needed. It was punctuated only briefly by the baptism in June, and short trips to Normandy and nearby Rambouillet. Otherwise, something close to a routine of family life took shape.

Napoleon had long made use of Saint-Cloud. Like most Parisians of means, he usually escaped the heat and possible pestilence of Paris in the summer at Saint-Cloud, as it was larger than Malmaison (now the principal home of Josephine, in any case) and more convenient for Paris than Fontainebleau or Compiègne. Normally, Napoleon would have returned to the Tuileries in late summer, but this time he lingered at Saint-Cloud as long as he could, until December. Marie Antoinette liked Saint-Cloud and had done considerable work on it in the 1780s, but it was a private residence. Napoleon did little to change the exterior, but carried out extensive changes to its interior, creating a throne room and other public spaces needed for the court, but he liked it above all as a quiet place where he could work. After 1814, Saint-Cloud certainly struck some English tourists as lacking the overbearing, self-conscious grandeur typical of Napoleon's ever-expanding network of palaces. Whereas Fontainebleau was as voluptuous a palace "as any sultan of Baghdad or monarch of India," Saint-Cloud presented "a scene of astonishing elegance and splendor . . . the Graces themselves might not scorn to repose upon the sofas."[44] Saint-Cloud was as close to normal a setting for the closest to a normal life Napoleon ever came since childhood.

Napoleon had a study on the ground floor, which gave on to Madame de Montesquiou's garden, where he could watch his son play and often joined him. His study was "off limits" even to Hugues Bernard Maret, his civilian chief of staff, but the door was now usually open to Marie-Louise and their son, as he grew. There are numerous anecdotes of the two Napoleons playing with pieces of painted wood and building an eagle together. Such tales are usually based on dubious memoirs,[45] but Napoleon certainly spent as much time with his son and wife as his schedule allowed, and if they did, indeed, play soldiers, it was on a carpet decorated with the insignia of the Legion of Honor.[46]

The private letters of Marie-Louise to her family and friends give the most reliable account of these singular months, and they paint a consistently happy picture. In May, she wrote to Madame Crenneville about her son: "I hope . . . he will be like his father one day, bringing happiness to all around him and who know him . . . My son is astonishing for his age . . . he laughs out loud, already. He is very like the Emperor." He did not know her at first, on her return from a brief trip to Normandy, "but after a few days, I soon renewed my acquaintance with him!" However, he always knew his father, who teased him at the daily meals he always had with his wife and son, much to the annoyance of his aristocratic governess and the astonishment of Marie-Louise.[47] Whether the anecdotes of memoirists are true or not—such as Napoleon teaching his son to drink from a glass or teasing him to eat off his nose[48]—Napoleon and Marie-Louise soon realized they had been brought up in very different cultures that were not only the result of a gulf in their social classes. The historian of gender, Julie Hardwick, describes the emergence of "compassionate marriage" in the 18th century, epitomized by the model set out by Jean-Jacques Rousseau, in his widely read *Émile*.[49] Few marriages were more "pragmatic" in their origins than that of Napoleon and Marie-Louise, but perhaps when he at last got the chance, Napoleon began putting Rousseau, an author he devoured in his youth, into practice. More tangible evidence of Napoleon's belief in the Enlightenment was his insistence in April that Napoleon-Francis be vaccinated when he heard of a virus going about.[50] He certainly had no intention of giving his son the cold upbringing he had witnessed among his aristocratic schoolmates. Even when away on a short inspection in Belgium, Napoleon kept in regular touch with Madame de Montesquiou, writing from Antwerp that ". . . I take real pleasure in your different letters about the good health of the king (of Rome) . . . I want . . . the king to have a good routine from the outset, to give him a good constitution."[51]

Marie-Louise wrote to her father with a mixture of love and bewilderment: "He takes a great deal of interest in his son. He carries him in his arms, and

tries to make him eat, but without success."[52] It may have been quietly grati-
fying for a Habsburg to witness a Napoleonic defeat, but such behavior was
alien to her own upbringing. Marie-Louise was hesitant about these levels of
intimacy, and was afraid to cradle her son in case she hurt him.[53] As she told
Madame Crenneville, the deep emotions she had for her son were "felt, but
not expressed."[54] Napoleon had been brought up differently. It is clear enough
that he treasured time with his family in these months, picnicking with them
on the grounds, taking an evening drive with Marie-Louise, showing patience
when teaching her to ride.

Napoleon's emotional happiness was not matched by his physical health in
these months, though. His legs were often badly swollen and he suffered from
severe sleep deprivation. He remained abstemious of food and alcohol, yet saw his
weight increase with abnormal speed, despite doing everything he could to take
regular exercise through hunting and pursuing his duties as normal. When
the writer Charles Paul de Kock caught a glimpse of him during this time at the
Tuileries, he saw a man "yellow, obese and puffy . . . only a fat man."[55] He was
only forty-two. Napoleon was very open about this on Saint Helena, admitting
that Corvisart had come out to Saint-Cloud several times to try to get him to
try medicines for his stomach problems, and that he tired easily. His sense of
humor reasserted itself at times, nonetheless: On Saint Helena he recounted
how he once asked a secretary to read him a fairy tale to help him get to sleep
and when his aide reached for one, they all burst out laughing.[56]

Napoleon's poor health was no laughing matter for those around him,
however. The months at Saint-Cloud saw drastic contrasts between Napoleon's public behavior and his new family life. A weight of evidence, however
anecdotal, attests to the "intimacy and the gentleness of his marriage" in the
words of one aide-de-camp, the Dutch general Thierry van Hogendorp.[57]
However, there were also many accounts of smashed vases, thrown crockery,
and most convincingly, verbal violence, both oral and committed to paper,
attesting to Napoleon's increasingly hair-trigger temper and lack of his almost
habitual self control: His rages were nothing new, but now they often seemed
spontaneous, rather than stage-managed. It is unlikely that his ill health did

not influence the long streams of vitriol and poor judgment that marked this period, although all the perennial sources of his frustrated aggression—the Church, the English, his siblings—did enough to incense even a healthy Napoleon. Yet, he never took any of this out on his wife or son.

It is impossible to know the exact source of his illness. A plausible and widely accepted explanation is that Napoleon suffered from a severe bladder infection, dysuria.[58] Symptoms strongly resembling stomach cancer had also killed many in his close family, his father included, and all his sisters eventually died showing similar symptoms.[59] None of this was helped by his openly admitted loathing of medical treatments and doctors in general—suspicions that did not extend to surgeons, apothecaries, or midwives—and at one point, Napoleon admitted in his memoirs that Corvisart had even pulled a human stomach out of a handkerchief at Saint-Cloud, shoved it in his face, and made him realize that this was what was inside him.[60] Even so, his resistance to treatment was never really broken down.[61] Napoleon did follow the advice of Corvisart and Dubois over something important, however. They strongly advised Napoleon that Marie-Louise had to avoid another pregnancy at all costs, or her life would be at risk. Napoleon found it hard to believe this of a young, otherwise healthy woman, but he followed professional opinion, as was his wont. They slept apart throughout the "idyll" of Saint-Cloud. It took her some time to be able to take her riding lessons, but once she had learned and felt able, she enthusiastically followed the hunt with Napoleon. In a hint of the capable ruler she went on to be as Duchess of Parma-Piacenza, after the demise of her husband, Marie-Louise held official audiences almost immediately, doing so reclining on a chaise longue until she could sit up.[62]

Napoleon remarked to the great German poet, Johann Wolfgang von Goethe, during one of their meetings that the Revolution had made all life political, that the private world no longer existed. He tried hard at Saint-Cloud to prove himself wrong, but the real world spun on, and the imperial family was its fulcrum. Napoleon had ensured that his cherished, embattled policies of *ralliement* and *amalgame* stood at the heart of the nuclear, imperial family. When Napoleon appointed the Countess Louise-Charlotte-Françoise de Montesquiou-Fézensac as his son's governess, he acknowledged that a certain element of the old order had a vital part to play in shaping the new. Madame de Montesquiou rocked the most important cradle in Europe, and she was a thoroughgoing product of the French nobility, as was her husband, who had replaced Talleyrand as grand chamberlain; he came from an old military family and rallied to Napoleon under the Consulate. His wife was described by General Durand:

> This lady of standing had received an excellent education. She blended a sense of worldliness with a genuine, enlightened piety. Her conduct had always been so measured that no one ever dared attempt to attack her. She was reproached as a little haughty, but it was tempered by politeness and an obliging nature.[63]

The Governess "of the Children of France" (her official title) was a direct descendant of Louvois, the great minister of Louis XIV, one of the major figures in that period of French history. Napoleon—following Voltaire—regarded it as "the great century," when the arts and French military power reached their apex under the aegis of a powerful, dynamic monarchy. In many ways, the key is "enlightened piety," however, for Madame de Montesquiou was not drawn from an obscurantist, reactionary noble milieu. As his conflict with the Church swelled, he chose his Catholics carefully. This choice betokened more than his desire to infuse the court—present and future—with ancien régime decorum. It was a vote of confidence in those nobles who had rallied to him from the outset. The Grand Chamberlain had always taken a great interest in persuading émigré nobles to rally to the regime, and in persuading Napoleon to trust them. He set an example by sending his sons to serve in the Grande Armée, where they fought with distinction; one became an aide-de-camp to Napoleon and followed him into exile on Elba.[64] Napoleon told Madame de Montesquiou in May 1811, even as he detected forces of royalist resistance all around him, "I am without worry in the full confidence I hold you in."[65] It was a political as well as a personal statement.

He looked to a different kind of ralliement when he appointed Louise-Antoi-nette Lannes, Duchess of Montebello—the widow of his old comrade killed at Aspern-Essling in 1809—as lady-of-honor to the new empress. Napoleon felt a deep obligation to her and Lannes's family, and held "La Maréchale" in the highest regard. Indeed, she had become a heroine to those devoted to the regime, an integral part of the Napoleonic myth. Madame Lannes represented a different kind of loyalist, although not as divergent from the milieu of Madame de Montesquiou as is often depicted. Louise-Antoinette is often tarred with the same brush as her rough-hewn husband, the son of Gascon peasants and an apprentice dyer before he joined the revolutionary armies as a private soldier in 1792. Part of these misconceptions about her arose from those surrounding Marie-Louise—that she was dim and had a bawdy sense of humor, as befitting her slow wits.[66] Her future career as Duchesse of Parma-Piacenza belies this, as does any examination of the background of her lady-of-honor. Louise-Antoinette was born into the bourgeoisie of the royal Court; her father, François Guéhéneuc, had been an equerry and valet de chambre to Louis XVI; her mother, a Dame of the Court. They did not emigrate during the Revolution, but came back into public life only under the Consulate, her father rising through the forestry service to become a senator. Louise-Antoinette was generally reckoned "incomparably beautiful."[67] After what amounted to a marriage arranged by Napoleon and brokered by Jean-Baptiste Bessières in 1800,[68] part of her remit was to civilize her new husband, one of the few challenges in life in which she did not wholly succeed. Louise-Antoinette's background gave her standing, while her own adult life reflected something very close to the ideal female leaders Napoleon strove to mould in Madame Campan's colleges. Louise-Antoinette had proved a valuable diplomatic wife during Lannes's time as Napoleon's ambassador to Lisbon in 1801, organizing balls and winning over influential nobles so successfully that when her son was born in Lisbon, the Prince Regent of Portugal himself stood as his godfather. She habitually eclipsed the dowdy wife of the British ambas-sador at the opera.[69] Above all, she showed her hosts that her husband had a *finesse d'esprit* under his brusque manners.[70] Louise-Antoinette was the ideal Napoleonic woman, in every respect.

That ideal nearly rebounded against Napoleon. In 1811, he took a great chance in bringing La Maréchale so deeply into the court, not for her aristocratic background, but because she now harbored a real hatred of Napoleon, blaming him for her husband's agonizing death. She came to the front after the battle of Aspern-Essling, on May 31, 1809, to nurse her Lannes, and stayed for two weeks, returning home believing he would survive. When Lannes's body was sent home, she came to Strasbourg to collect it. Napoleon gave strict orders that she should not be allowed to see it until it had been prepared, but the prefect gave in to her. The sight drove Louise-Antoinette almost mad. The prefect was severely reprimanded, but the damage was done.[71] In his agony, Lannes often reviled Napoleon for "deserting him," and his wife took this in. Napoleon had bestowed a very generous *majorat* on Lannes, the Polish Principality of Siewierz, worth two and a half million francs, although Lannes did not actually apply for the revenues, and had never used the title that went with them. Louise-Antoinette took her hatred of Napoleon out by demanding the title—which she was readily accorded, although Napoleon felt there was no need to flaunt it—but also sought direct control of the revenues, which was not normal practice, as this was administered by the government on a Napoleonic noble's behalf. She pressed her claims with great haste after Lannes's death. This showed great independence of mind and a combative spirit Napoleon admired, even if it was directed against him. Napoleon always looked after La Maréchale and her five sons, but Louise-Antoinette still lent her house in Paris to Arthur Wellesley, Duke of Wellington, in 1814.[72] Nevertheless, she served Marie-Louise loyally and, for his part, Napoleon admired her all the more for it.[73] La Maréchale stood for the newly empowered women of the empire, but also for those tens of millions without voices who hated Napoleon for widowing them, and there would be many more of them in the years to come.

A New Church. An Ancient Quarrel.

If the imperial household became a delicate exercise in *amalgame* and *ralliement*, Napoleon showed few qualms about risking his cherished policy goals in his dealings with the Catholic Church in the first months of 1811. His thirst for confrontation grew apace, even as the state's working relationship with the Church reached crisis point. The fundamental problem was Napoleon's harsh treatment of Pope Pius VII, but its most serious symptom was Pius's refusal to legitimize Napoleon's appointments to an ever-increasing number of vacant sees. Napoleon knew he could not ignore this, for in many places the Church risked being unable to function properly, but he still chose to deal with it aggressively. The potential collapse of public religion risked making the breach between the emperor and the pope all too obvious to the faithful.

By 1811, ten of the sixty episcopal sees in France were vacant, together with two more in the imperial departments in Italy. Some of them were in major cities, Paris among them, and it was here that the first salvos were fired in a new round of the conflict between Pius and Napoleon. When Cardinal Fesch refused to accept Napoleon's nomination to the see of Paris in September 1810, Napoleon turned to Cardinal Maury, who took up the post in November, but without papal investiture. Maury expressed his loyalty to the pope to his cathedral chapter, most of whom accepted him, but his powerful Vicar-Capitular, Paul-Thérèse-David d'Astros, resisted Maury's attempts actually to administer the diocese, blocking him at every step and issuing warnings that Maury's instructions were not legitimate.[74] Pius agreed, and issued a papal "brief" in December, declaring that Maury was acting illegally.[75] Through a remarkable "underground" network, the brief reached d'Astros. D'Astros was a relative of the late Jean-Étienne-Marie Portalis, Napoleon's minister of religion until his death in 1807. He showed the brief to his cousin, Joseph-Marie, Portalis's son and the director of the official print works and government publications, who advised him to keep it to himself. Undeterred, d'Astros read it to several canons of Notre-Dame. A troubled Portalis reported this to the police, but said nothing to anyone else. Napoleon chose his moment to strike perfectly: On New Year's Day 1811, Maury led his chapter—d'Astros included—to the Tuileries to wish Napoleon a happy New Year. The formalities over, Napoleon had them lined up as he would his guard and passed down their ranks. He stopped in front of d'Astros, put one hand on his shoulder and the other on the hilt of his sword: "There are those among you who seek to sow trouble in people's consciences and raise them against authority. I'm talking to you, d'Astros." Maury took d'Astros aside, seemingly to calm him, but instead led him into a room where Savary, the minister of police, was waiting. D'Astros was questioned aggressively about the brief, with Maury present. He admitted he had seen it, and Savary demanded his resignation. When d'Astros refused, Savary told him it was resignation or prison: "Well then, I'm your prisoner" came the reply. He was led home, his papers and office ransacked, and the brief was found hidden in a hatbox. D'Astros was carted off to the military fortress of Vincennes, on the edge of Paris.[76] The chapter of Notre-Dame soon fell into line.

Napoleon was far from finished. Three days later, at a meeting of the Council of State, he turned on Portalis with real fury. In his memoirs, Étienne Denis Pasquier, the chief of police in Paris, recalled his words: "How dare you show yourself in this place after the treason you have committed?"[77] It got worse. Napoleon reminded him that he had sworn he had never seen the brief at the Council of State, in the Hall of the Marshals, no less:

> Did I take you by the scruff of the neck and make you my councillor of state? No. It was an honor you sought. You are the youngest here and probably the only one without personal merit. I have seen in you only the service given by your father. You swore an oath to me. How have you scrambled your principles to suit this manifest violation of that oath? You're among your family here (a reference to Portalis's defense that d'Astros was his cousin). Your colleagues will judge you![78]

Most of those colleagues felt Napoleon had treated Portalis very harshly, but none dared say so at the time. He fled the room as Napoleon ordered him out of Paris by the following night, telling Savary not to let him stop until he was at least forty leagues from the city.[79] His rage did not end there, and his comments to the assembled company revealed the deeper sources of his rage:

I hope I never see anything like this again. It hurt me too much. I have surrounded myself with (men of) every party. I have kept close to my own person émigrés . . . even people who may have wanted to assassinate me . . . They have been loyal to me. Behold! The first person close to me since I have been in government who has betrayed me!

"You write that down" he told the scribe—"'betrayed,' understand?"[80] The cause is less important than the reaction. (Louis, Talleyrand, and Fouché seem to have been forgotten in the heat of the moment.) The sense of ingratitude, of isolation, was palpable. On Saint Helena, Napoleon admitted he had acted wrongly—"Rulers are always wrong when they speak in anger"[81]—but he could not contain himself at the time. The contrast between his reactions to Portalis and d'Astros opens a window on an embattled mind: D'Astros was the old foe in a young frame; Napoleon was ready for him and struck with calculated ruthlessness, laced with confident sarcasm. His treatment of Portalis smacked of the demolition of his brother, Louis. It was personal, shocked, almost unnerved in its rage. Napoleon felt increasingly alone.

Pius, in captivity in Savona since August 17, 1809, soon felt the backlash. On January 2, 1811, Napoleon ordered the governor-general of the region:

. . . [T]he Pope whispers disorder and sedition everywhere . . . I intend to erase the outward signs of consideration I have accorded him, by taking the carriages I gave him back to Turin, and reducing his household allowance from 15 to 12,000 francs per year [in his anger, Napoleon made a rare accounting error—he meant monthly] . . . Keep the Pope away from suspect people who help him correspond . . . It may even be necessary to replace some of his domestic servants . . . Basically, it is essential he is not allowed any communication; if he writes letters, have them sent to the Minister of Religion. The Prefect alone has a right to see them.[82]

The pettiness says as much as the fear of the security breach. Napoleon was already preparing to bring Pius to Paris.[83]

This whole affair had poisoned the air even before Napoleon set about confronting the crisis in the Church, but set about it he did. Napoleon had created a small commission of trusted senior clerics in November 1809, soon after his excommunication from the Church by Pius, chaired by Fesch. In the wake of the "d'Astros affair" and its revelations about Pius's brief, he needed it to spring into action. On January 5—even as Portalis fled Paris—he ordered Félix-Julien-Jean Bigot, his minister of religion, to put three questions to the commission: Did the pope have the right to excommunicate rulers for temporal reasons? Given that Pius has violated the Concordat by not confirming Napoleon's appointments to vacant sees, what methods exist in canon law to give bishops canonical investiture? Napoleon gave these bishops the authority to administer their diocese as Vicars-Capitular; does the pope have the right to prevent them from so doing? Napoleon concluded by evoking the tradition of the Gallican liberties of the French Church, now assailed by "the Pope's spirit of usurpation and arbitrariness."[84] This did not bode well. Underpinning it was Napoleon's own increasing despair with the Concordat, for he now saw that it had left Pius considerable scope to play havoc with episcopal appointments: "If Pius does not agree (to his nominations) the whole of Europe will be notified that the Concordat itself will be abolished, and recourse will be made to a different means of conferring canonical institution."[85]

The commission mendaciously evaded the first question, saying that the bull of excommunication was, indeed, void, as it was triggered by the occupation of Rome, when the text—even if it did not name Napoleon specifically—made the religious nature of the act clear. Even so, Napoleon refused to countenance their conclusions. The commission had avoided the real problem: "Is there a canonical means by which the Pope can be punished for preaching revolt and civil war?" he asked it on March 16. Napoleon had redefined the issue on grounds of national security. However far-fetched, that was now his line. He concluded that the only way forward was to convoke a "Council of the West."[86] Cowed, fearing this would provoke a schism, the commission then fell back on its earlier recommendation of January 27, 1810, that, indeed, only a national council of all the bishops—agreed to by the pope—could resolve the investiture crisis.[87] Napoleon then created a new commission to arrange this. He drew up a circular to the bishops of the empire, convoking them to the council. He then ordered Bigot to bring the new commission together and read it to them before it was published, telling him, "you will inform me, unknown to all of them, what effect it has on the committee, and what you then think needs to be changed." Simultaneously, he ordered Bigot to send three trusted bishops—those of Tours, Nantes, and Trier, all Napoleonic loyalists and respected theologians[88]—to Savona.[89] They put it to Pius that if he agreed to legitimate all Napoleon's appointments to the vacant sees within the six-month period stipulated by the Concordat, he could go back to Rome, but only as its bishop, not as a temporal ruler. Pius spun it out with his unflappable poise.[90]

Even as he held out this excuse for an olive branch, Napoleon bared his Jacobinal fangs on internal clerical dissent. In the following weeks, he arrested the mother superior of Sisters of Charity in Amiens, one of the few remaining convents in the empire (which owed its survival to the terms of the Concordat) simply for knowing of the pope's brief, and threatened to close it. He ordered the arrest of all the clergy of the department of Charente-Inférieure as "enemies of the state."[91] Over March and April, hundreds of priests from the territory of the ex–Papal States, already under arrest in cities in northern and central Italy, were exiled to Corsica for their persistent refusal to swear allegiance to the regime and, even more, for the considerable moral influence they exerted on the communities around them by their defiance.[92]

This was the climate in which the "National Council" met on June 17, 1811. Out of the 149 bishops and archbishops within the empire, the kingdom of Italy, and the Duchy of Berg, 104 attended. Thirteen of those absent were the "black cardinals" who had defied Napoleon at his marriage to Marie-Louise the year before. Others claimed illness, feigned or otherwise, or the infirmity of old age, of whom five were formally excused, while many sees in the two departments of the ex–Papal States were not present because their sees had been abolished after their bishops had refused to take the oath of loyalty to Napoleon.[93] The thirteen bishops Napoleon had appointed without papal investiture were treated with disdain by the majority of the council. Even Fesch, who organized the council, studiously ignored them.[94] The bishop of Troyes openly called their presence "a scandal."[95] The intensity of the breach between the emperor and the pope now became very public, and many bishops made a point of touring their dioceses, calling for calm, before they went to Paris. Police reports spoke of parish clergy in Paris itself intent on stirring up the council against Napoleon.[96]

Proceedings were opened in the splendor of Notre-Dame. Fesch took it upon himself to say the High Mass that inaugurated it, as its president. Fesch's sermon, followed by an address by the bishop of Troyes, both stressed the loyalty and obedience of the French Church to the Papacy. This was in keeping with tradition, but Napoleon reacted with fury. On June 19, he hauled Fesch and the bishops of Trier, Tours, Venice, and Nantes—his trusted "team"—to Saint-Cloud and lambasted them for being so subservient to Pius. He also took umbrage at Fesch referring to himself as "the Primate of the Gauls"—that is, as the head of all the French bishops, the traditional title of the Archbishop of Lyon—without his authorization: ". . . (Y)ou are related to my mother . . . and so that makes you think I will make you head of the Church . . . Europe will now think that I will make you the future Pope!" Fesch calmly stood up to the tirade; Nantes tried to temporize, while the others stood in cowed silence. Napoleon later told the bishop of Nantes that Fesch's independent actions were counterproductive to his policy of trying to overawe the council.[97] To this end, Napoleon issued his own declaration to the council. It was aggressive, referring openly to "the Pope's sinister projects" and ended: "Religion is the right of all peoples, of all nations . . . no one man . . . can have the right to obscure that, to turn it to his profit by confounding the simplest ideas of the spiritual and the temporal, or to confuse consciences." Napoleon added that if the pope prevailed, "Everything the English . . . have ever said about the incompatibility of the Catholic religion to the independence of governments could now be justly applied."[98] It had been drawn up by Pierre Daunou, once an outspoken opponent of Napoleon, for which he had been expelled from the Tribunate before its abolition in 1807.[99] For all that, he now joined Napoleon's attack on the Church with relish, a mark of how unifying the old battles could still be. Daunou "moved sideways" from politics to become the first director of the new Imperial (now National) Archives that Napoleon created in Paris, and this inveterate republican "who harbored a great hatred for the power of the Church"[100] may have felt an added incentive, for it was also at this time Napoleon was planning the transfer of the unparalleled riches of the Vatican archives to Paris.[101] Together, they threw down a gauntlet to the Church, and it was taken up.

A hard core of opposition to Napoleon quickly emerged, centered on Charles-Francois du Bois de Sanzay d'Aviau, the aged and respected archbishop of Bordeaux, who said they had no business discussing anything until Pius was at liberty.[102] He was ably supported by the bishop of the Belgian diocese of Ghent, Maurice-Jean de Broglie. De Broglie's outspoken attacks on the legitimacy of the council were nothing short of a personal repudiation of *amalagme*: This son of a marshal of France was sent to Belgium as a symbol of imperial unity, and was highly prized as a living symbol of *ralliement*. He was named one of the emperor's almoners in 1805.[103] However, in 1810, he refused his promotion to the Legion of Honor in protest at the annexation of Rome to the empire. Now, he found his voice.[104] In their report of July 10, the bishops of Troyes and Tournai admitted that the general view was that the council's decrees would be invalid without the pope's agreement.[105] They were part of a commission of twelve created by the council to oversee its work, theoretically equally divided between pro- and anti-regime prelates. Eight of them, led by the bishops of Ghent and Tournai, replied bluntly to Napoleon that they supported Pius's stand over the investitures for the vacant sees.[106] Napoleon hit back with a chilling response. He dissolved the council, but he did not stop there: He had the bishops of Ghent, Tournai, and Troyes arrested and thrown into Vincennes along with d'Astros. De Broglie (Ghent) and Hirn (Tournai) were more than rebels; they were two more names on the growing list of those whose ingratitude Napoleon did not appreciate, certainly when coming from his own almoners.[107] That day, he told Fesch:

> The extreme displeasure the bad conduct of the bishops of Ghent and Tournai has given me has obliged me to hand them to the police under special supervision . . . (M)ake known to them that they have been taken off the table of officers of my Household. You should no longer consider them as my Almoners.[108]

Napoleon did not dare touch the Archbishop of Bordeaux, whose age might make arrest fatal to him, and inflame a port city badly hit by the blockade. Although tightly monitored by the police, d'Aviau remained able to direct opposition.[109] Jacques-Olivier Boudon, the leading historian of the Napoleonic Church, sees it as significant that Napoleon chose to allow the head of the Church such a forum at a time when he had systematically killed off public debate.[110] He soon repented of it.

Napoleon recalled the council a few weeks later, when he saw that his vicious actions had frightened more of its members than they enraged. However, he unveiled a still more ruthless plan. The investiture crisis was now to be solved entirely by laymen and state methods. All the while, Napoleon had a commission from the Council of State, chaired by his minister of justice, Claude-Ambroise Régnier—a Lutheran—exploring ways by which the civil power could fill the vacant sees. Régnier concluded that Napoleon could resort to the Gallican traditions of the old regime, and allow the metropolitan of a province (the senior bishop in an ecclesiastical province of several dioceses) to fill vacant sees should the pope refuse.[111] He went further: Should the Metropolitan refuse, it would become a matter for the courts, and the *Cours Impériales* could intervene. Régnier then "went for the throat." Discarding the discretion of the magistrate, he accused Pius of orchestrating the crisis "probably driven by pernicious advice." Napoleon had a duty to sort this out, for it was now a question of law and order, and if the Metropolitan or any cleric made trouble over this, it should be a matter for the public prosecutors under the Penal Code.[112] When Napoleon put this to Cambacérès, his only qualm was that the courts might prove reticent when treating the clergy as common criminals.[113] Napoleon now ordered Fesch to "adhere . . . and tell the other bishops with whom you have influence that they must make their declarations . . . This adhesion is important to me and I'm counting on you."[114] This was too much for Fesch. With some courage, he replied:

> I cannot lie to my conscience. I believe that . . . the arrests, the threats of the Minister of Justice, are illegal . . . My conscience would reproach me were I to authorize such methods to decide on such grave issues for the Church . . . The Church alone can submit to them.[115]

In the months to come, Fesch continued to press in vain for the release of the bishops of Ghent and Tournai.[116] Bigot took over "managing" the bishops.

Napoleon now switched tactics, and began mooting that he was prepared to reconvene the council if it would look at these proposals, stressing that his real aim was to get agreement from Pius to fill the vacant sees, thus rendering Régnier's proposals redundant. However, this process had two faces. Throughout mid-July, in a frenzy of activity, Bigot met personally with as many of the bishops as possible, presenting them with a draft decree that would allow Metropolitans to fill sees if the pope delayed more than six months. In exchange, the council would be allowed to send a delegation of its own choosing to Pius to secure his agreement. Parallel to this came Régnier's draconian proposals to the bishops, and with them, the threat of arrest if they did not approve the decree. By July 25, eighty bishops had approved it, Fesch among them, with thirteen holding out against. When the council reconvened in early August, it ratified this.[117] On September 30, Napoleon ordered all the bishops of the council back to their dioceses.[118] "And don't allow any of them to stay in Paris,"[119] he told Bigot a week later, thus confirming in a brusque order the thoughts of Pasquier, the head of the Paris police: "I don't think that

Napoleon ever in his life, under any circumstances, met men whose character and opinions he so miscalculated as over this business."[120]

A delegation from the council went off to Savona on August 22, "comprised (of) the usual storm troopers of Gallicanism."[121] A month later, a draft of a papal brief reached Paris that seemed to accept the decrees of the council. It was cleverly phrased but the original text made no reference to the government and seemed to imply that Pius had summoned the council on his own authority.[122] It caught up with Napoleon in Antwerp, and he noted that "it is nothing to do with me" and that Pius had not given the Metropolitans the right to invest bishops; if this was not forthcoming, he would tear up the Concordat.[123] A month later, from Rotterdam, he told Bigot that only when Pius ratified his appointments to the vacant sees would he give the brief official sanction. He went further:

> The fact is, the Church is in crisis . . . The Pope cannot obtain any
> accommodation . . . nor exercise any spiritual jurisdiction unless
> he approves the decrees of the council, and his position will only
> worsen until he invests all the bishops; only then will he see his
> decrees published and made into law . . .[124]

Napoleon had no intention of waiting for Pius's agreement. On October 6, he declared that if Pius did not simply ratify the decree and confirm his appointments, he would issue his own decree in the Council of State without reference to the Papacy, and order the metropolitans to carry out the investitures. If they refused to do so within six months—or tried to refer it to the Papacy—they would be sent before the courts "for rebellion against the laws . . . in wanting to foment disorder in society . . . (and be) condemned to lose their Episcopal functions, their rights as citizens, and to imprisonment for life." This would be their fate if they entangled themselves with any new brief Pius might issue.[125] A concrete example of what might befall them came in November, when Napoleon told Savary to order the three jailed bishops to resign: "They no longer have my confidence" he remarked with rare understatement.[126] They duly did so, but only one, Tournai, declared he remained loyal to Napoleon. Napoleon appointed a new vicar-general to run the diocese of Ghent until de Broglie was replaced, but the vicar-general promptly refused to do so until a bishop approved by Pius was installed.[127] When Napoleon finally released the three bishops—Ghent, Tournai, and Troyes in December, they were dealt with in the same manner as the "black cardinals." Savary was told to smuggle them out in dead of night, to avoid Paris, and to send the bishop of Troyes to Falaise, Tournai to Orleans, and Ghent to Dijon, all secure areas: "Make them give their word of honor to remain peacefully (there), to have no contact with their (own) dioceses, and to have nothing to do with ecclesiastical affairs."[128]

Ambrogio Caiani's study of the council leaves no doubt that Napoleon's victory had been won by physical, as well as psychological, coercion.[129] It was part of a wider campaign. The same day the delegation set off, the official journal *Le Moniteur* announced that the public auction of confiscated Church properties in the city of Rome had begun.[130] In early October, Napoleon told Bigot in obvious exasperation, "I don't want any *Sulpiciens* in the seminaries of Paris. I have told you a hundred times, and I will repeat it one last one; take steps to abolish this congregation."[131] The *Sulpiciens* were an elite clerical teaching order, specializing in training young priests. Soon, Napoleon extended this policy to the provinces, striking at the dioceses of those bishops who had fallen foul of him. When requests reached him for exemption from conscription from 239 theological students across the empire, he refused to exempt those from the dioceses of the bishops who had "crossed" him at the council, as well as refusing government grants to candidates for the priesthood in those same dioceses.[132] Napoleon's unease about clerical influence was aroused by the rise in requests for the creation of domestic chapels and oratories, usually the preserve of the nobility. This seeming resurgence of piety practiced in private was "worthy of attention" he told Bigot. Although prepared to accord them for country houses, this was only on condition that those possessed of them attended the parish church regularly. "There are too many of these chapels in Paris. Get me a report on this."[133] Catholic royalist nobles now saw themselves as Elizabethan Catholics; if Napoleon did not react like Robert Cecil, he thought like him.

Even as the talks in Savona began, Napoleon told Bigot, "I am too old and too used to Italian trickery to let myself by duped (by Pius)."[134] For the moment, he was content to play the talks along, but Napoleon was framing more ruthless plans for Pius. As winter drew in, however, he had more pressing problems than empty sees.

"Old France" in the New Order

Napoleonic officials often referred quite casually to "old France" as the empire grew, meaning France within the prerevolutionary borders, "the heartland." It was a notion that contradicted Napoleon's imperial vision, but it stuck, and found clearest official expression in Napoleon's economic policies, for the tariff walls of his hegemony did not correspond to the political boundaries he and the revolutionaries before him had so cavalierly redrawn across Europe. By 1810–11, those tariffs barriers increasingly defined his empire. The economic malaise demanded that "France first" drove all before it. Several "treaties" that culminated in the "Trianon" tariff of October 18, 1811 (named for the building at Versailles where it was issued) saw Napoleon draw a new border within this empire: While imperial and allied ports outside the borders of "old France" (including the Belgian departments) remained firmly closed to American and colonial merchants, those within the "Trianon line" were now opened to them. This freedom to trade also allowed the importation of hitherto prohibited goods, in an effort to supply French industry with raw materials and consumers with essential commodities, even if it did so at exorbitant tariff rates. This cut off the new Dutch and Hansa departments from equal, easy trade with what was now their own country, often to the frustration of the French themselves: The Strasbourg Chamber of Commerce saw its requests for easier trade conditions with these departments blocked in 1811.[135]

All was not well behind the Trianon redoubt. In late 1810, a request reached the emperor from a manufacturing business for a loan of no less than 1,500,000 francs to save it from closure. Soon, hundreds more arrived from all over France between January and March 1811. Napoleon insisted on dealing with all of them personally. In his memoirs, François-Nicolas Mollien, Napoleon's minister of the treasury, portrayed a stark landscape of abandoned factories and expensive machinery left to rot because even when the bankrupt properties were seized from their owners, the slump was often so severe that no buyers could be found.[136] Cotton production in Rouen fell by 50 percent in the first months of 1811, because raw material was too expensive and demand for finished goods diminished drastically. Bankruptcies in this one city numbered 110.[137] Delegations arrived from across northeastern France—from Rouen, Amiens, Saint-Quentin—and from Ghent, in Belgium, begging, literally, to be saved from liquidation. This risked throwing between twelve to fifteen thousand men out of work in Amiens alone.[138] Mollien felt Napoleon was spurred into action by Savary, whose reports warned of incipient disorder in this very stable part of the empire.[139] His response was energetic and wholehearted. Napoleon and Mollien devised a gargantuan bailout plan, injecting eighteen million francs into faltering enterprises under carefully calculated, equitable terms of repayment (about half of which still remained unpaid at the fall of the regime, in 1814).[140] Napoleon went further, extending two million francs to Hottinguer, a banker Mollien trusted, to buy up unsold stocks of calico in Rouen, Ghent, and Saint-Quentin.[141] Napoleon was very clear to Mollien: "Carry out these operations secretly."[142] It was an act of largesse he uncharacteristically covered up because he sensed the irregularity of his actions. Although the worst of the crisis was over by mid-July, and none of the well-established manufacturers went under,[143] Mollien felt that the program failed to reach many of those most in need of stimulus, because it simply depended on taking the initiative to petition Napoleon personally, almost on a "first-come-first-serve" basis, rather than through an organized system. Mollien described this as "arbitrary liberality," and felt it probably left as many people embittered as it did grateful. Nor did Napoleon try to lighten their tax burdens by exempting them from his high tariffs. The program was successful as far as it went, but Mollien was unable to fathom how Napoleon could not grasp the basic contradiction in his own behavior: pursing a ruinous blockade, which he knew he had to soften within France.[144]

Mollien observed the economic crisis from within the eye of the storm, and blamed it all on the blockade, but the work of Geoffrey Ellis, the doyen of modern blockade studies, showed that the slump was not "wholly, or even directly" engendered by it, at least within the Trianon line. The root cause was speculative overstocking of a wide range of commodities by French entrepreneurs and manufacturers, and when their foreign outlets defaulted, these stocks could not be sold. In Ellis's words, ". . . the crisis was paradoxically one of glut, of over- rather than under-production, and . . . faltering markets. The problem lay in demand. . . ."[145]

When such problems affected Paris, Napoleon resurrected the policy of the Terror, setting the former sans culottes to war work. In May 1811, he told his minister of war administration, Jean-Gérard Lacuée, in no uncertain terms:

> There are many hatters, hosiers, rope makers, tailors (and) saddlers without work in Paris. I want you to take measures to produce 500 pairs of shoes (for the army) per day, on condition you employ rope makers, and not shoemakers, who will make 15,000 pairs per month . . . You will also (make) 250 shakos (helmets for lancers) per day, thirty saddles per day, and other articles of clothing, making sure that new workers are always employed. As there are other workers who are still unemployed, you will . . . have 100 caissons built.[146]

This was far from an isolated intervention. A few days later, Napoleon ordered still more caissons and cartridges and, revealing his lingering memories of revolutionary unrest, singled out the unemployed of the faubourgs of Saint-Antoine and Saint-Marceau—Robespierre's "heartland"—to build them, along with beds for the Imperial Guard.[147] That same day, the shadow of the Terror and the lingering menace of its rank and file were evident when he told

Duroc, the grand marshal of the palace, to mobilize these skilled artisans in the service of the Imperial Court:

> Faubourg Saint-Antoine lacks work: I want to give it some, particularly in the month before the holidays. Go to Paris and get . . . my architect Fontaine, and order for this month and June 2,000 workers from faubourg Saint-Antoine who make chairs, tables, commodes and armchairs, who are out of work, to get to it at once. Order things needed in the Louvre: chairs, windows, etc. which will be needed for the new gallery (largely to house looted art from Rome) and for Versailles and other palaces . . . Liaise with Fontaine to set up a workshop in the Louvre as of tomorrow and employ as many workers as possible in the demolitions, to give as much work as possible to those without it . . . The works at Versailles should occupy about 2 to 3,000 workers. It seems to me that there is enough work in the parks . . . to occupy plenty of people.[148]

The irony is heavy: The greatest enemies of the old monarchy were being bought off in the cause of bolstering the glory of the new.

While Napoleon attacked the Church almost with relish, an instinctive revolutionary reaction to the slightest defiance in its ranks, he treated the heirs of popular revolution very differently, quite possibly in part because he felt his largesse was appreciated. Napoleon had always taken an interest in the well-being of the sans culottes, giving Paris artificially light conscription quotas and ensuring it was always well provisioned with food—he sacked a prefect early in his rule for failing to do so—but the interventions of 1811 were different. Only one other French government after Napoleon's offered its unemployed workers this kind of support to get them through hard times: The short-lived Second Republic of 1848–49 created the National Workshops during the slump of 1848 at public expense and triggered the civil war between the Parisian artisans and enraged rural taxpayers, which led to the republic's collapse.[149] Napoleon's dictatorial powers and iron grip on France prevented such a backlash.

Textiles were badly hit everywhere, but particularly in the Lyon silk industry. It was saved by the blatant exercise of economic colonialism, and so this long-feared powder keg of unrest was contained. Since 1807, Italian raw silk had been supplied to France at prices and through tariffs advantageous to the French, and Lyon was the major silk manufacturing center of the empire. However, Italian producers had also been able to export their silk through Germany, at better prices. The crisis in the French textile market in 1810 corresponded with a poor silk harvest in Italy, and Napoleon clamped down quickly on the Italians' right to export to Germany. In August, he ordered all Italian raw silk to be sent to Lyon at an even more onerous tariff. Eugène reacted immediately: "I must observe to Your Majesty that the execution . . . of this decree will occasion a great loss and general discontent in the Kingdom of Italy."[150] Napoleon replied with a ruthless clarity on August 23:

> The silks from the Kingdom of Italy all go to England, as they do not make silk in Germany. It makes clear sense that I should want to redirect them to my factories in France, because without them, my silk works, which are the principal source of commerce in France, would suffer considerable losses . . . Italy is independent only because of France; that independence is paid for in its blood, and its victories, and Italy must not abuse this . . . Take for your watchword: France above all . . . I find it singular that there might be some repugnance at the idea of coming to the aid of French industry, and in a way that would hurt the English.[151]

"France above all" is the best known, oft cited phrase in this letter, but it sits cheek-by-jowl with the all-pervasive hatred of Britain and a fierce resentment at the ingratitude of those unconscious of the sacrifices of his troops, both ever more powerful currents in Napoleon's mind.

Napoleon retained a special affection for his original political stronghold, but it had its limits. In October, he backed down somewhat, allowing Italian silks to come to Lyon tariff-free; they could pass through Austrian and German territory to France, but at high rates and the ban on sales outside France remained.[152] During the bad harvests of these years, which affected Italy as much as France, he restricted cereal exports from Italy to France, and showed Milan much the same favor as he did Paris.[153] He exploited his German possessions instead. Massive imports of grain were rushed into the northeastern departments of France, where serious disorder was tempered mainly by the fact that this region was heavily garrisoned.[154] These state interventions aggravated the inflation of grain prices in the Rhineland, itself hit by bad harvests. As a result, even a good harvest in 1813 did not ease the pressure on prices for consumers.[155] The impoverished Dutch departments were stripped of grain to feed northern France. Lyon was saved by imports from Baden and Württemberg.[156] "France first."

Napoleon's luck with a run of good harvests, dating from his accession to power, ended in 1810. Famine now stalked the countryside, as well as the towns and cities, and the crisis took on more terrifying proportions. Famine struck everywhere, but those parts of his empire Napoleon counted on as the most secure were the hardest hit, and soon the most convulsed. Fortunately, the traditionally unruly departments of southern France seemed less touched by disorder of this kind, if hardly immune from misery.[157] The atavistic threat of the "beggars' armies" reemerged for the first time since the coup of Brumaire. In the winter of 1811–12, the prefects of Picardy and coastal Normandy reported enormous bands of "sturdy" beggars roaming the countryside, terrorizing farmers with threats of violence and arson if they were not fed. The prefect of the Cher, in the central Loire valley, painted this portrait for his superiors in the spring of 1812:

> Here is how begging works. In the course of several days, the beg-
> gars (whose numbers exceed all belief) walk about singly, from door
> to door, asking for a piece of bread, and those who dare to refuse

are threatened with arson, with a night break-in, and in numbers of twenty or even thirty, they turn up at isolated farm houses . . . and beg no more, eating, sleeping and even staying for lunch . . . There is not the power to stop them, the prisons cannot hold them.[158]

As a rule, the regime did not respond with repression, preferring to lure the rural vagrants into the towns, where they could benefit from the exceptional decrees providing relief, or to persuade them to go back to their own villages, where they could be kept under watch.[159] These were the circumstances that lent support for the new criminal and penal codes from the masses of granite, as besieged as any French army in Spain.

The year 1812 saw a better harvest, and the worst manifestations of disorder receded accordingly. The exceptional measures of public charity were withdrawn, the slump in textiles eased. Nor was the raging misery of these years universal. Nantes saw a strong upturn in the years 1810–12, the tonnage of ships using its port briefly surpassing prewar levels, probably protected from British pressure by the continental system.[160] Philip Dwyer has explored Napoleon's increasing identification of himself as the "father of people" in these years in his propaganda.[161] His actions give some substance to this, as he flouted the laissez-faire maxims of 1789 and nodded to the populism of the Terror years in the face of widespread hardship. Even if the authorities never openly referred to it, the Jacobin "maximum" on food prices was constantly evoked in practice.[162]

It is very hard to know if that cultivated image hit its mark with his subjects, however. Napoleon had fostered an excellent administrative and policing system, which provided him with reliable information at the most localized levels. This was tested during the crisis of 1810–12. Yet, so effective and pervasive had his censorship become, so tight was his control of any form of expression, that it was impossible for Napoleon to judge whether his largesse had won him popularity or not. He lashed out when opinions he hated reared their heads, and had the repressive machinery to support him. In April 1810, he wrote to his director general of publications

(*La Librairie*): "A work has appeared . . . with the title 'A critical historical essay of the French Revolution' by P. Paganel. This work is full of bad principles . . . Forbid its circulation and ban it." Its tone was that of the liberal opposition of the early years of Napoleon's rule, and condemned his absolutist rule in covert terms, while praising popular sovereignty and parliamentary government.[163] The royalist Right could not complain of Napoleon showing political favoritism. Nicolas de Bonneville had been a leading Catholic royalist during the Directory, and one of the founders of a royalist front organization, the Philanthropic Society of the Revolution. He was soon in trouble with Napoleon for comparing him to Cromwell. In October 1810, Napoleon ordered his arrest and wanted him banned from producing books and engravings because he was printing Louis XVI's testament: "After that, throw them in a State Prison (high security)." There was, he added, "a small group of malcontents in the (official) Publications Press who are trying to disturb the peace, (and who) must be not be allowed to print or sell books or engravings."[164] "Even-handed" repression, balancing the repression of Left and Right, had been a cornerstone of Napoleon's policy from the outset, but these two examples denote a marked shift: de Bonneville was a recidivist, but the harsh swipe at Paganel's pamphlet signaled that even moderate republicanism was no longer acceptable, because the regime was increasingly unacceptable to it.

Then there were those who could not speak out, but as Thierry Lentz has sagely noted, "The silence of the people does not always denote their loyalty."[165] Mollien believed that even if the momentary crisis had been contained, the deeper malaise of the continental system remained, and the masses of granite knew it:

> If one considers how long this political measure continued . . . (and) the disorder it brought to . . . commerce, one must regard that coup d'état which never took place as quite extraordinary; and one must see as even more astonishing . . . the resignation, the submission of all those interests that suffered from it.

Still, he concluded, the French bourgeoisie had long done its muttering in the safety of the family.[166]

Napoleon conserved a healthy respect, bordering on fear, for the common people. Calm returned by the spring of 1812, but Napoleon's awareness of the capacity of the French to revolt when their survival was threatened proved astute, and it brought out a residual populism in him, if only in extremis. The Church, royalists of all classes, and even the masses of granite, could be affronted, but not the sans culottes or the peasantry in times of dearth. Richard Cobb, that incomparable historian of the French people, caught it best:

> Napoleon's regime was . . . made safe from the grain riot, not only by repressive legislation and the use of troops, but also by a combination of the charity of the bazaar, the pillage economy of conquest, and by the existence of a European grain market that stretched without barriers from the Atlantic to the Ems, from the Channel to the Adriatic.[167]

The common people of France had been saved by Napoleon's hegemony. For a brief moment, he could claim to be their savior. Beyond the Trianon line, though, it was a different story.

2

THE GREAT EMPIRE,
1810–1812

❧ ── ❧

B y the summer of 1810, Napoleon had almost completed the series of
annexations that brought his own empire—exclusive of the territories
under the satellite kingdoms and his allies—to 130 departments, as opposed
to the 83 that composed France in 1790, when they were first created by the
revolutionaries, and the 112 of 1809. Most of them had been stripped from
his siblings: the suppression of Louis's kingdom of Holland and Jérôme's loss
of the entire North Sea coastline of his kingdom of Westphalia accounted for
fifteen of the new departments.[1] Four more were being readied for annexation in Catalonia, confiscated from Joseph at the outset of 1810, while all
Joseph's other provinces north of the Ebro—the Basque country, Navarre,
and Aragon—were under French military rule. Only the two departments
carved from the rump of the Papal States—the result of Napoleon's deposition of the pope—were conquered. The "French" Empire now reached from
Rome to the Baltic.

The map of the "Great Empire" looks imposing, but in reality it was born
of exasperation, disillusion, and ultimately of weakness: Its tentacles spread

along the North Sea coasts and into central Italy, arms flailing, punching thin air as smuggled British goods floated in from huge contraband bases in Heligoland in the north, and Malta in the south. Its geography was really a testimony to British power, power that was all the more enraging to Napoleon for being indirect—economic and financial—as much as naval. The seizure of the Papal States was only partially spurred by the failure of Pius VII to enforce the blockade, however. It masked another profound weakness at the heart of Napoleon's hegemony. When Pius excommunicated Napoleon in the summer of 1809, he shrugged it off, but everywhere he turned there were scattered signs that he had roused an old enemy, the Catholic faith, into subtle, insidious rage. Even if the mass of French Catholics and their bishops did not openly oppose the regime, the consensus created by the Concordat of 1801 was badly eroded, while a small but determined network of real opposition took shape.[2] Napoleon dealt with it by trusting only himself and those he could rely on in the face of danger. They no longer included most of his family.

Naples: A Family Affair

Napoleon came to believe that his brothers had failed him as the guardians of his most dangerous imperial marches. They were now replaced by trusted, French henchmen. Only in his sister Caroline, Queen of Naples, did Napoleon feel he had a reliable lieutenant among his siblings. Caroline's mixture of serpentine court politics, crude assertiveness, and unflinching determination to survive were the exception that proved the rule as Napoleon set about dismantling the system of family vassalage he had so recently created.

Since the advent of their joint rule in 1808, Murat increasingly followed the pattern of behavior that doomed Louis. He consistently advanced Neapolitans for high office, and the general interests of his new kingdom, and did so with a bluntness that bordered on the naive. He challenged Napoleon with a brazenness that the emperor's own brothers never dared vent. Late in 1810, he chided Napoleon that "You don't know this country very well," even going so far as drawing a crude cartoon of a starving mother and child in the margins of a missive from Paris, demanding he enforce the blockade more rigorously.[3] Napoleon always suffered from the delusion that the kingdom of Naples was economically advanced and wealthy, confounding potential with reality, making his demands for revenue unfeasible.[4] Murat's disastrous invasion of Sicily in 1810 further undermined his credibility with Napoleon, but their relationship, and so the survival of the kingdom, only reached crisis point over the course of 1811. The fate of Louis held no more terror for Murat than the Russian guns at Eylau. As soon as he returned from Paris following the imperial marriage, and after several stormy meetings with Napoleon, on June 7, Murat abolished the post of governor-general of Naples, which had always been held by a French officer. Napoleon struck back. On June 24, he ordered his minister of war to inform Murat that, "I have dissolved the army of Naples and formed an observation corps (exclusively of French troops) under the command of General Grenier . . . it will be fed, maintained and clothed by the Neapolitan Treasury," and was exclusively under Grenier's orders.[5]

In the meantime, under the influence of his leading minister Antonio Maghella, Murat ordered all foreign nationals in his service to become naturalized or leave their posts. Napoleon knew all about it in advance, and countered Murat's decree with one of his own, asserting that "in so far as the kingdom of Naples forms part of the Great Empire . . . all French citizens are citizens of the Two Sicilies (the official name of the kingdom)."[6] Napoleon asserted a core principle of his vision of hegemony: the all-pervasive, if not actually superior, place of the French beyond the borders of the empire proper. Severe orders were sent immediately that two French officers in Naples whom Murat trusted were to talk him out of the "false position" he had gotten himself into. They duly did so, and Murat backed down. The climate in Naples was not so easily soothed, however, and there was brawling between French and Neapolitan troops. Nor did Murat stay calm when amorous correspondence between Caroline and his French minister of war fell into his hands. The French members of the government felt his wrath, losing their posts to Neapolitans. In his rage, Murat brandished two pistols, howling that he would use them on Caroline. It did not stop a furious Caroline from demanding the reinstatement of Daure, the minister of war in question.[7]

Queen Caroline had been well out of range a great deal of the time. She remained in Paris after the imperial wedding, consolidating her favorable position with Napoleon. She began by being the only Bonaparte to welcome and befriend Marie-Louise, escorting her to Paris; she was the sole sibling to treat her with respect at the wedding. She organized the new empress's household. Once returned to Naples, Caroline almost immediately persuaded Murat to let her go back to Paris to plead their cause with Napoleon. She arrived on October 2. The other person closest to Napoleon was undeniably Hortense, Josephine's daughter and the estranged wife of Napoleon's brother, Louis. A clear sign of how well Caroline had cultivated her friendship and won her confidence at this time came when Hortense confided her angst about attending the baptism in the same cathedral, Notre-Dame, where her mother had been crowned empress in 1804, and where her own son lay buried. Caroline persuaded her that she needed to be there.[8] In a very significant moment in her ascent, Caroline became godmother to the King of Rome, although she stayed away from the ceremony, to avoid appearing in open defiance of Murat, who refused the invitation. Their mutual infidelities notwithstanding, she still exercised influence with Murat, and she used it—and Napoleon's trust—carefully.

By the summer of 1811, tensions between the two men had reached the point where Napoleon preferred to communicate indirectly with Murat. This was always a sign when he knew his temper was at breaking point; it was his way of averting confrontation, as when he made Louis-Alexandre Berthier communicate his rage with Bernadotte over his presumed cowardice at Jena, or when he kept out of direct contact with the negotiations with the British at Amiens. Napoleon let Murat know his mind through Berthier in early September, who told his old comrade that Napoleon said of him: "Murat has rendered me great service, but he contrives to weaken the workings of my system. The king of Holland lost his throne by forgetting France and the French, to become Dutch."[9] Caroline sensed her brother's preferred methods, and took it upon herself to approach Murat in this indirect manner. She did not rail at him or threaten him by siding with Napoleon. Rather, she gave the impression she was interceding for him, trying to avert a crisis. In November she, in her turn, recalled Napoleon's words for Murat's sake:

> Should the king, above all, furnish a naval contingent, and come into the French system, I would regard him as I do the kings of Bavaria and Westphalia, as a great vassal; but I do fear that your dynasty will not reign long in Naples, although I desire that very much . . . but the king has gone down an evil path . . . I fear that . . . he will force me into a reunion (the official term for annexation to France) I do not want.[10]

Her turn of phrase had many layers, revealing as much about her own political acumen as it does of Napoleon's political vision. In June, Napoleon had asked Murat "to build . . . two ships-of-the-line and the same of frigates each year . . . otherwise I declare our treaty as void."[11] Caroline saw clearly that building a fleet was central to Napoleon's concerns, and remembered vividly that this had been a major cause of Louis's downfall. If she drew the parallel for Murat, it came as a plea to save their positions, not a threat. She also understood what a "model vassal" should be: someone like Jérôme, who took orders sent from Paris, via the French ministers imposed on him or, better still, Max-Joseph of Bavaria, who needed no such promptings, and carried out Napoleonic reforms of his own volition. She made her own point at the end of the letter: "The Emperor does not want to be king of Naples; but in his capacity as the Emperor of a great Empire, he will never permit the kings of his empire to treat him as an equal."[12] There could be no more penetrating a definition of Napoleon's "Carolingian" vision than this. It worked. Murat quickly dismissed both Antonio Marghella, who Caroline simply regarded as treacherous, and Giuseppe Zurlo, a leading reformer. The "French party" had won in Naples. When Napoleon recalled Murat to active military service early in 1812, Caroline became the effective sole ruler.

Securing the Marches

Napoleon's new, centralized hegemony faced dangerous borders everywhere. As with Trajan's empire, if Napoleon's bestrode its world, and if "every day the astonished senate received the intelligence of new names and new nations, that acknowledged his sway . . . and rich countries . . . were reduced to the state of provinces," this seeming power brought with it fresh perils, "and it is justly to be dreaded, that so many distant nations would throw off the unaccustomed yoke, when they were no longer restrained by the powerful hand which had imposed it." [13]

Each of his frontiers posed different problems for Napoleon, all of them brought into sharper relief by the rejection of the satellite kingdom as the linchpin of his system. Napoleon moved swiftly to make his new order a reality. Exactly a week after Louis's abdication, Napoleon told Charles-François Lebrun, ". . . I have need of your services in Holland. Pack your bags for the trip and come to see me as soon as possible . . . to get your instructions. It is indispensable that you leave Paris for Amsterdam, tomorrow." [14] They were ready for him the next day, clear and detailed as promised. [15] The same day, he quashed all rumors that Louis's son, Napoleon-Louis, the Grand Duke of Berg, would succeed his father, with Napoleon as regent. Holland was to be annexed:

> Make it known to the people of Holland that the (present) circumstances of Europe, their geographic position and the intentions of our common enemies make it my duty to put an end to the provisional governments which have tormented this part of the empire for sixteen years.

He then ordered a deputation of "distinguished" Dutch worthies to Paris. [16] The next day, to underline the reality of centralization, he ordered Napoleon-Louis to be brought to live in Paris. [17] On July 11, he began the practical steps to remove much of Hanover from Jérôme's kingdom of Westphalia and annex it to France. [18] He set to work refortifying the artillery batteries the whole length of his hegemony with particular attention paid to the newly annexed North Sea coast: "I want to know how much a company of coast guard artillery costs, and if they might be deployed in the service of better, and better organized troops," as the existing coast guard batteries were not staffed with good personnel.[19] This was work he knew. Later that day, he sanctioned a judicial commissioner for the new Illyrian Provinces, Joseph Coffinhal-Dunoyer (who was currently serving in the same capacity in Rome), and set out the levels of revenue he expected from Illyria.[20] The empire was being gathered ever closer around Napoleon and his most trusted team.

Spain: The Ineradicable War

The most perilous of Napoleon's marches was Spain, for only here did open war persist after 1809. The embers at the Austrian embassy were still smoldering as Napoleon set about dismantling his "Carolingian experiment" there. In Catalonia, his two judicial commissioners, Joseph-Marie Degerando and Bernard-François Chauvelin, were already at work, with four young auditors of the Council of State soon to follow, to become the de facto prefects of the new departments. Aragon was already under the military command of Marshal Louis-Gabriel Suchet. In the course of that summer, Suchet won a series of victories over Joaquin Blake, notably at Bechite, and secured most of Aragon and southern Catalonia. Suchet soon proved an effective ruler, keeping his troops under strict discipline, cooperating with the local authorities and persuading some Aragonese to form their own local militias to contain the guerrillas. By the time he advanced into Valencia, early in 1810, Aragon had become a secure base, and remained passive longer than any other Spanish province. His moderation as a civil governor, and his ability to use his whole corps of over twenty thousand men for policing—a dividend of the end of the war in 1809—marked him out as the most successful military governor in Spain by 1810.[21] It was not without tensions, however. Napoleon raged at Suchet's initial abandonment of his advance on Valencia—under orders from

Joseph—to return to the siege of Lérida. On April 9, Napoleon exploded to Berthier:

> He has compromised the honor of my arms, and contravened not
> only my express orders, but the first principles of war. His retreat
> from Valencia can only be considered (throughout) Europe as a
> great victory (for the Spanish) and can only revive revolt.[22]

Napoleon was still very nervous about this sector, but Suchet's judgment proved correct. The way to Valencia was opened by Suchet's seizure of several important towns in southern Catalonia, of which Lérida was one.

On July 3, 1810, Napoleon ordered a trusted aide-de-camp in several campaigns, Honoré Reille, to Navarre. Reille had recent experience of pacification in the newly annexed Tuscan departments,[23] and he would have need of it. Napoleon warned him: "Things in Navarre are so badly managed that I want you to go there immediately . . . as soon as you get to Navarre, use all means necessary to repress brigandage."[24] The guerrilla leader Espoz y Mina commanded large swathes of the region, captured or destroyed French convoys, and engendered despondency among the French troops, not least their commander, Georges-Joseph Dufour, who "had taken to skulking in Pamplona" when he was not executing prisoners randomly at dawn in vain efforts to lift his spirits.[25] Reille arrived on July 27 with eight thousand troops, and faced a daunting task. After initial humiliating defeats, Reille drove Mina out of Navarre by the autumn. By September, his forces numbered fifteen thousand men and "Mina's men became so hard-pressed that they scarcely stopped running from August to December."[26] It was 1812 before Mina truly had the upper hand again.[27]

In Andalucía, Nicolas Soult showed impressive resourcefulness, adapting to mountain fighting and taking the offensive against the patriots in their strongholds, even though by the end of 1810, he only properly controlled the lowland regions. Nevertheless, he trained his troops in mountain fighting, and deployed small, collapsible field howitzers—all built locally in Seville—which could be transported across the hardest terrain, confining the Spanish in their remote holdouts.[28] The successes of General Bonnet in Asturias, Leon, and Galicia were especially worrying for the British. Driven from Oviedo in March, Bonnet retook it quickly, and established a base there. By May, he was on the offensive and recovered most of Asturias and Leon, mainly in pitched battles but, like Soult, he developed effective counterinsurgency tactics. By July, he had driven into the Anglo-Spanish stronghold of Galicia, and although unable to take its western coasts or its major port, Vigo, he now occupied almost all the good agricultural land of the province, denying the allies local supplies.[29] On July 6, Napoleon authorized the organization of Gendarmerie brigades for all the northern provinces.[30] Freed from war elsewhere, Napoleon's new ability to concentrate on Spain produced the high tide of French success in the peninsula by late 1810.

In every case, the military governors either co-opted Joseph's *comisarios regios* dispatched from Madrid only a year before, or swept them aside.[31] In Catalonia, the organs of local government were specifically ordered to ignore the *comisarios regios* altogether, and those who stood by them were swiftly removed.[32] Military rule in Spain did not always spell a harsher regime than Joseph's. Indeed, the most successful commanders proved remarkably effective practitioners of the core Napoleonic policies of *ralliement* and *amalgame* among the local elites. Soult, Suchet, Reille, and Bonnet all drew on the need to restore and preserve civil order with considerable success, turning many terrorized communities away from the guerrillas and the Patriot government in Cádiz, which sanctioned them. The restoration of order was the oldest weapon in Napoleon's political arsenal, and it acquired new potency here. The military commanders approached their task with more sensitivity to regional diversity than was often displayed by French civilian officials across the empire. Jean-Marc Lafon has shown that Soult made significant progress in "rallying" important sections of Andalucían society because here, in an area of large feudal estates—the *latifundi*—the great noble landlords backed the guerrillas, who directed their raids on the rural bourgeoisie and the towns. Soult drew on this local knowledge and possessed enough influence to enforce those of Joseph's policies that attracted the rural bourgeoisie, mainly through the opening of the property market to them by the sale of Church lands. Soult carried out important projects of urban renewal in the major cities and reopened the port of Malaga for trade with France. The result was collaboration widespread enough to allow the emergence of local militias that fought with the French against the irregular Spanish forces in the region.[33] During his brief tenure in Aragon, Suchet proved an honest and able administrator.[34] When he reentered Valencia, he found socioeconomic structures broadly similar to those confronting Soult in Andalucía, but the political allegiances of the feudal nobility and the peasantry were reversed. Suchet protected the feudal landed elites and helped them suppress peasant revolts to ensure his troops were provisioned and their properties were secured. Effectively, he practiced appeasement of the feudal nobility in the countryside, parallel to very different policies in urban areas, centered on Napoleonic reforms of taxation, property rights, and the sale of confiscated Church properties.[35] In Asturias and Leon, in very a different society of small-holding peasants, Bonnet profited from the increasing ruthlessness of the Spanish resistance in its search for supplies. Peasant communities often cooperated with the French against their incursions. By early 1811, the morale of even the most determined Spanish patriots was very low.[36] Reille made similar progress when he set up a civilian deputation to administer Navarre in August, which proved very efficient and relatively fair in raising revenue. However, Espoz y Mina proved a formidable opponent, and by winter, Reille was resorting increasingly to terror—marked by mass hangings along the main roads—which ensured Mina's support would revive in time.[37]

The real problem was clear: the British grip on the West. Napoleon's reach still did not extend to the western commercial entrepôts of Portugal and Galicia. If one commander could be singled out for his excellence in the Wagram campaign, it was André Masséna, and it was to him that Napoleon entrusted yet another invasion of Portugal. On April 17, Napoleon created a new Army of Portugal, composed of about sixty-five thousand men drawn from troops already in Spain, and put Masséna at its head,[38] with Michel Ney and Jean-Andoche Junot—both disgruntled by this—under his command.[39] Masséna reached his new army at Valladolid on May 10. The campaign began well, when on July 10, the French finally took the fortress of Ciudad Rodrigo, after a siege of over a month. A key point on the western extreme of Estremadura had been secured, and Napoleon rewarded the men Masséna singled out for valor, a sign of his pleasure.[40]

Napoleon saw this campaign as twofold: not only to seize Portugal, but to bring the British to the large engagement he always regarded as definitive. He knew he had a likeminded commander in Masséna, whose strategy was to inflict just such a defeat on Wellington.[41] Masséna was given this task because Napoleon needed free hands elsewhere. His major preoccupation was now the enforcement of the blockade along the North Sea coast, and the growing tensions with Russia, which required massive concentrations of forces in central Europe. By spring of 1811, there were clear signs his patience could snap easily when failures occurred on what he regarded as secondary fronts. When the guerrillas in Navarre seemed to be resurgent in April, he lashed out about Reille to Berthier with his usual lack of comprehension, but with marked intensity:

> . . . Write to Reille to let him know my displeasure at his lack of energy . . . Write to him with orders to arrest the relatives of the brigands and send them to France, *to hit the towns which harbor brigands with taxes, to burn the houses of their relatives* . . . It is all quite simple, for the brigands will punish any lack (of severity) they are shown: If General Reille leaves them unpunished, it all works in favor of the brigands.[42]

Reille already had a well-established reputation for brutality—at one point in 1809, he had threatened to decimate the entire male population of Tudela over the death of a single French sentry[43]—of which Napoleon seemed unaware or now deemed to be insufficient. This was not an isolated outburst. That same day, Napoleon exploded over unrest among Dutch sailors, raging at Lebrun:

> This is a serious business. Send in a high ranking police official with the necessary armed force. The 500 sailors have to be arrested . . .

and sent to France. Who is the general commanding this department? Who is the Gendarmerie commander? Why didn't they do anything to suppress this rabble? Give the order to execute three or more of the mutineers publicly . . .[44]

When an officer in Segovia failed to carry out his orders regarding troop movements correctly, Napoleon's response was disproportionate, to say the least. On May 1, he wrote to Berthier:

Let General Belliard know that I am most displeased that my orders were not executed, and that the next time this happens, I will have him up before a court-martial: this is the first time I have seen so formal a disobedience, when your orders were clear . . .[45]

This was the state of mind his commander was in when Masséna took the field in what had previously proved a near impossible front.

Masséna soon felt himself in so difficult position that he worried Napoleon was deliberately seeking to disgrace him out of jealousy, and that the campaign was a "setup." In contrast to Masséna's paranoia, the usually cynical General Paul Thiébault—known as "the nastiest tongue in the army"—said Napoleon believed Masséna could work miracles.[46] In fact, Napoleon put great faith in Masséna when the campaign began, telling Berthier that Masséna was always free to "make whatever changes he judged indispensable" to his initial orders,[47] investing in him the same latitude and trust he did in all his best commanders.

Transport made supply almost impossible; the terrain was rugged, the roads poor and unmapped; the British and Portuguese had, not for the first time, resorted to a ruthless scorched-earth policy. Guerrillas harassed Massena's supply trains and when Masséna dispatched his aide-de-camp on a direct mission to Napoleon to alert him to the magnitude of taking Torres Vedras, his baggage was pillaged en route, for which Napoleon had to reimburse him six thousand francs.[48] Nevertheless, the army pressed on into Portugal.

Napoleon remained stubbornly oblivious to the logistical and geographic perils of fighting anywhere in Spain, and on the border of Portugal and Estremadura, above all. No miracle was coming; no setup possible. The lessons of 1808 and 1809 had been learned by the marshals, but not by Napoleon; his personal experience of the north in 1808, or what had reached him from the front during the Talavera campaign of 1809, and even his hard-won lessons of the fighting in the equally hostile environment of Lithuania in 1807, seemed to bounce off him. Napoleon showed his complete ignorance in equal measure to his confidence in his directive to Berthier of May 29, compiled while on "honeymoon": After Ciudad Rodrigo and Almeida were taken, Masséna was not to proceed "by expedition"—that is, piecemeal, striking here and there—"but methodically" to Lisbon, which he did not want him to enter until September, "after the summer heat and above all, not until after the harvests." Estremadura and western Portugal were barren places at the best times, without Wellington's ruthless policy of scorched-earth, as the Talavera campaign should have taught Napoleon. Wellington's redoubtable defensive preparations held Masséna up in any case, but Napoleon's timetable sent his men into terrain that was daunting enough without the late summer rains. Napoleon put the Portuguese at twenty-five thousand men, and believed Wellington had a mere twenty-four thousand "assorted English and Germans."[49] His intelligence was not too wide of the mark, the Portuguese numbering twenty-six thousand regulars—not counting the local militias—while Wellington had about thirty-one thousand British troops with him.[50] But Napoleon utterly failed to grasp how this army had changed since the Talavera campaign. That was for Masséna to find out. The newly made Prince of Essling was the first to learn there was a fell beast on the western march, for he, too, had a poor opinion of the British and Portuguese—until he faced Viscount Wellesley's men.[51]

Masséna's first brush with the British at Côa did little to shake his prejudices. The engagement was the result of the impetuosity of one British officer, Robert Craufurd, who was ignorant of the effectiveness of Masséna's troops. Losses on both sides were heavy, but Craufurd was forced from his positions back to the safety of Almeida, a well-fortified, provisioned fortress built on steep, rocky ground. Masséna should have been held up, but luck favored him when a random shell hit the main powder magazine that "atomized" the castle that housed it and reduced the fort to ruins. The dazed, confused Portuguese garrison simply surrendered.[52] Masséna continued his advance, which was governed less by seeking to engage the enemy than finding a route to where supplies might be found. Although his immediate goal was Coimbra, Masséna did not follow the retreating British along the main highway to Lisbon, but turned north, on a much worse road, hoping so remote an area had escaped Wellington's scorched earth.[53] His hopes were forlorn; the poor roads only delayed his supply trains further. "All our marches are across desert; not a soul to be seen anywhere; everything abandoned," he told Berthier in mid-September.[54] Wellington turned north to meet them at his well-fortified position at Serra do Buçaco, a steep, wide north-south ridge nine miles long that blocked the way to Coimbra.

Masséna knew about the ridge, but not how well it was defended: Wellington had been able to concentrate fifty-two thousand men and sixty guns on it; below, the ground was rocky, crisscrossed by gullies and scrub. It had one weak point, a very poor mountain path that joined the main road to Coimbra. Wellington was very concerned about this, knowing that he could only spare a small Portuguese force to hold it, which could not contain a concerted French advance down even such a narrow defile.[55] A man imbued with a classical education would all too readily recall the fate of the Spartans at Thermopylae. Overall, however, this was too good a position for Wellington to reject battle, and he hoped he could halt the French here. He need not have feared a Thermopylae. Masséna did not even seek a way around the ridge: On September 27, he launched a full frontal attack on it and, predictably, was beaten back with heavy losses of forty-five hundred men. Not only had the British fought well, the Portuguese contingents also distinguished themselves.[56] This was where Masséna got his first real lesson in the new military reality Wellington had created, in both fortifications and in men. Cut off from Spain by local Portuguese units, and in a countryside bereft of provisions, Masséna had no other choice than to break off the battle, but he did not retreat as Wellington had assumed. Instead, the French found a small mountain road to the northwest, and marched on, hoping to outflank Wellington and take Coimbra from the north. Despite his emphatic victory, Wellington had no choice save to fall back on Coimbra, his troops' morale plummeting. However, this was not 1809. Much had changed, as Masséna now discovered.

Wellington now withdrew to well-prepared positions, with a disciplined, better supplied, and now battle-hardened army, its current mood notwithstanding. The army that fell back into Portugal after Talavera in August 1809, was bedraggled, exhausted, and riddled with sickness. If they were the victors, as Wellington claimed, with enough success to win his first title, they neither looked nor felt the part. Wellington "did not believe his own publicity," and left the fighting to the Spanish in the months to come. He knew his army had to be rebuilt, and he did so. As soon as the news of Wagram reached him, he knew Napoleon would turn again to Spain. Although far from perfect—and there were some in the British high command who agreed with Napoleon's assessment that a French victory was likely—Wellington and his fellow Anglo-Irishman, William Beresford, who commanded the Portuguese, spent the winter of 1809–10 in the manner Napoleon had used his enforced leisure at Boulogne, to forge a deadly weapon, unsuspected. The British, well supplied by sea and better funded than Wellington liked to admit to the government, recovered over the winter of 1809–10, their commander noting by spring that "The troops are becoming again very healthy and strong, and the army is more efficient than it has ever been." The sick fell from almost a third of the total to less than 12 percent. Many officers were still skeptical of the whole endeavor, but they were battle-ready.[57]

The Portuguese, on whose effective contribution Wellington's strategy hinged, were a different matter. Beresford had to work something akin to a cultural revolution within the Portuguese military, to transform an officer corps based on aristocratic standing to one based on merit; to instill notions of precision and strict adherence to orders among men long used to doing things in their own manner. Such indiscipline was inevitably reflected in the ranks.

Beyond the regular army, throughout the winter, spring, and early summer of 1810, Beresford put tremendous effort into turning the militia regiments into effective support units for garrison duty, and the local semi-regulars, the *ordenanças*, into threatening guerrilla fighters. Rory Muir has attributed this metamorphosis to ". . . the promotion of those who showed promise; endless drill; and the growing assurance that the British would stay and fight."[58]

Wellington fell back on the finest defenses imaginable, the lines of Torres Vedras, which Beresford and he had expended titanic efforts to create. The lines were not a solid wall; indeed, many of the engineers who built them did not grasp their real purpose, and felt they could be easily bypassed, because they did not see the whole project.[59] Rather, the "lines" were composed of a series of 59 mutually supporting strong points and field fortifications, containing 232 cannons, which ran across the Lisbon peninsula for 22 miles, backed by a shorter line of fortifications behind them, a last line of defense. The lines were not impenetrable, but to take Lisbon, the French would "have to fight their way through the first line, defeat Wellington's army in a position of his choice, and then repeat the process with the second line."[60] The hard, physical labor was done by six thousand Portuguese peasants and militiamen at an astonishing pace, driven by a collective desire to prevent another brutal French occupation. The expertise and money was British; its chief engineer was Lt. Col. Richard Fletcher. Begun in earnest in late 1809, the work was completed by the time of Buçaco.[61]

Masséna had no inkling of its existence. Now, he ran right into it. The siege of the lines of Torres Vedras lasted into the early spring of 1811, and Masséna came off worst. Having wrong-footed Wellington, he now found himself stranded. While the allies were regularly supplied by sea, the French, with their lines stretched to the breaking point, could only forage an already devastated countryside and endure the harassment of the *ordenanças*. Heavy rain compounded the army's plight. Reduced to only forty thousand effectives, Masséna raised the siege on March 5, 1811, reaching Spain by March 22. His army was still formidable, but it had lost half its horses, many of its guns, and almost all its baggage train. Wellington might have finished him, had he taken the offensive, but as it stood, Masséna lived to fight another day, just not before Lisbon. Allied casualties were minimal, but the mutual damage done to much of rural Portugal by both armies was lasting; eighty thousand civilians lost their lives.[62] A new military culture had emerged from nothing, but a dead zone had been created to protect it. Beresford pursued the French and laid siege to Badajoz in April, while Wellington clashed with Soult for the first but not the last time, in indecisive actions at Fuentes de Oñoro, all of which proved what formidable opponents the new Anglo-Portuguese forces had become.

Masséna felt he had been abandoned during the campaign, and that his six badly weakened divisions could not relieve the French besieged at Almeida or bring Wellington to a decisive engagement there. Nevertheless, desperately short of supplies and of the artillery he needed to break the siege, Masséna resumed the offensive on April 25, 1811.[63] His divisional commanders protested that the offensive was doomed, and begged him in vain not to advance. Some, indeed, arranged transfers for themselves elsewhere as the march began.[64] He had about forty-two thousand infantry, forty-five hundred cavalry, and thirty-eight guns, but they were in very poor condition—"the second corps is not in a fit state to do anything" he told a subordinate[65]—and many in his ranks were convalescents from the military hospitals in Salamanca, who had volunteered to help save their comrades at Almeida.[66]

Masséna slightly outnumbered Wellington, whose forces were stretched by the sieges of Ciudad Rodrigo and Almeida, but the British were dug in very securely along a steep ridge near the village of Fuentes de Oñoro, which barred the way to Almeida. Rory Muir has rightly described Masséna's frontal assault as a crude plan, probably based on the unlikely hope that Wellington would fall back. As late as April 28, he hoped Bessières was coming to his aid, which would have tipped the numerical balance well in his favor. However, news reached him on the 29th that Bessières had halted his advance under the assumption that Masséna himself intended to halt. Masséna reacted with incomprehension and anger: ". . . if the Army of Portugal meets with a reverse, you will have much to reproach yourself for . . . We all have the same master;

all the troops in Spain are of the same family."[67] Stranded, Masséna attacked Fuentes de Oñoro on the night of May 2. His tired troops fought with great verve and briefly held the village; it took considerable British numbers to push them out.[68] The spirit and leadership shown by Masséna's troops at Wagram lived on, as witnessed by a British private:

> How different the duty of the French officers from ours. They, stimulating the men by their example, the men vociferating, each chaffing each until they appear in a fury, shouting to the points of our bayonets. After the first huzza, the British officers, restraining their men, still as death, "steady, lads, steady," is all your hear, and that in an undertone.[69]

They were well matched, for a truce was not called until May 4; Masséna gained little ground for the loss of over six hundred men, but had not been pushed very far back. On May 5, Masséna regrouped and struck the southern end of the British line, forcing Wellington to fall back on Fuentes de Oñoro. From a different angle, Masséna resumed his frontal assault and was bombarded by the British from their defensive positions. Nevertheless, Wellington's army was too battered to advance, just as Masséna was now too weak to hope to relieve Almeida. As Rory Muir has put it, "Fuentes de Oñoro was a clear victory—Wellington achieved his objective and Masséna failed to achieve his—but it was not the sort of victory which left the defeated army fleeing the battlefield in panic."[70] As if to prove as much, Masséna managed to evacuate the garrison. He organized its withdrawal by blowing up the town: "At midnight, a deafening, prolonged explosion told the French army that, at last, Almeida was no more."[71] It also marked the end of Masséna's career.

The French now withdrew behind the Agueda, and Masséna ordered his aide, Jean-Jacques Germain Pelet, to convey to Napoleon the news that Almeida had been successfully evacuated, and that Wellington could not now hope to lay siege to Ciudad Rodrigo. Masséna himself, fully aware of the weakness of his army, was proud of what had been achieved.[72] He had a point.

Napoleon's assaults on western Spain and Portugal ended in costly failure, yet the Anglo-Portuguese were still confined to the defensive. A protective shield had been created on both sides.[73]

Masséna had not calculated on Napoleon's frame of mind, perhaps a sign of how odd his behavior was now becoming to those who thought they knew him best. The reversal of Almeida shook Napoleon to his core. He ordered the suppression of the news of Masséna's retreat that had been reported in British dispatches. More tellingly, it led swiftly to one of the most ruthless, unjustified, and self-defeating decisions of his military career. On April 9, he coldly ordered Berthier to make sure Masséna received a copy of the official government publication, *Le Moniteur*, his way of informing his oldest comrade that he was dismissed not just from his present command but, effectively, from active service.[74] By doing this through Berthier, Masséna was treated in the same way as Bernadotte at Jena. The man he created a prince of the Empire and to whom he gave a rich *dotation* after his heroics at Wagram less than two years earlier, the same Masséna whom he urged Eugène to trust, despite all his faults, was faced with these words from Berthier:

> Prince, the Emperor asks me to convey to you that he expected more energy from you, and from the opinion he had formed of you as a result of the glorious exploits in which you have so often taken part in the past.[75]

Masséna was ordered to Paris, where Napoleon kept him waiting for several weeks. There is no reliable account of their meeting, but it was clearly very bitter. Napoleon is said to have "welcomed" him with "Ah, Prince of Essling, you are Masséna no more, it seems."[76] If true, this was followed by a tirade against which Masséna had no chance to defend himself. Whatever the truth, Masséna's career as a field commander was over. The general who assembled Masséna's correspondence in the French army archives attributed Napoleon's behavior to news reaching him from the front haphazardly, usually poisoned against Masséna by Bessières, whose reports were more useful to Napoleon, according to Berthier, who himself had disliked Masséna since they first served together in the first Italian campaign of 1796.[77]

The aides Masséna sent to explain the situation to Napoleon strove to make the emperor see sense, but to no avail. One of them, Pelet, warned Masséna:

> The Emperor cannot believe that an army commanded by you let itself be intimidated, or that the officers and men, whatever privations they endured, were not as His Majesty has always known them, and even more so before the English, our eternal enemies.[78]

Nothing could have been further from the truth. Yet, Napoleon still refused to believe the Anglo-Portuguese army was a match for Masséna; he could not understand how difficult western Spain was to fight in. Napoleon's obtuseness and the poisonous behavior of Bessières and Berthier were obviously significant in Masséna's shocking demise, but it also fits a more worrying pattern of Napoleon's behavior at this time.

Bessières's poison carried a particular potency for Napoleon. Napoleon had trusted and valued Bessières implicitly since the first Italian campaign, and made it clear that when he showed an interest in his favorite sibling, Caroline, he would have much preferred Bessières for a brother-in-law to Murat. Bessières often commanded the guard cavalry, and was wounded at Wagram. On his return from Spain, Napoleon entrusted him with what he held dearest: ". . . go to see the King of Rome often; to see Madame de Montesquiou, and take all necessary measures for her safety. Let her know that, should anything untoward happen, she should turn to you, and you are the one she should forewarn."[79] He had known Masséna just as long, and just as well, but in a different way, and that difference had seemingly come to be decisive for Napoleon. The circle of the faithful narrowed. The confidence he had so recently placed in Masséna evaporated and turned to loathing almost out of nowhere. He had forgiven him previous reverses in western Spain, but he now needed success everywhere, and the strain told on everyone. The real casualty was Napoleon himself. The only real interest Napoleon showed in the man whom he first met—and had to impress—on the eve of the first Italian campaign—was to investigate his possible involvement in the failure of a prominent bank.[80] Masséna was overlooked when Napoleon assembled his army for the Russian campaign a year later, nor did he call upon him in the campaigns of 1813 or 1814. In that respect, Almeida may have been one of the key battles of the Napoleonic Wars.

Masséna was replaced by Auguste de Marmont, who soon regrouped the exhausted army, abandoning the corps structure in favor of smaller concentrations of troops better suited to the region, and finally sent Jean-Baptiste Drouot south to reinforce Soult, who feared a British attempt to lift the siege of Cadiz, a move Napoleon had come to suspect and fear himself.[81] Ultimately, when Marmont swung his entire command south, Wellington was constrained to raise the siege of Badajoz. In all this, Marmont proved himself a good strategist,[82] and his boast—reminiscent of Napoleon's in 1796 about the disheveled army he inherited in the Alps—that "A month before seemingly so disorganized, so discouraged, so incapable of taking the field, the army . . . has recovered its vigor, its élan, its confidence"[83] was not unfounded. Nevertheless, unlike Masséna, he had not tried to crack the nut of Torres Vedras. Nor would anyone, ever again.

Napoleon's control in Spain had very clear limits and the lines at Torres Vedras marked them out for all to see. Nonetheless, within those limits, the French commanders were tightening their grip on the Spanish march. Napoleon's solution to Spain was unique in many ways. It was the only time he ever invested his commanders with significant civil powers, to the point that he allowed Soult to become a veritable proconsul, behavior he had reprimanded him for in Portugal only two years before. Napoleon tacitly sanctioned Suchet's virtual protection of the kind of feudal order he was bent on destroying in most of his realms. Suchet's ability to adapt to local circumstances—anathema to Napoleon—enabled him to be the only commander in Spain able to send funds to Paris, and to Joseph in Madrid.[84] While according him powers equal to Soult's, Suchet did not flaunt his position with the same swagger as Soult, "a haughty and imperious satrap," who behaved as a king in his province, surrounded by pomp and a servile, well appointed court.[85] Suchet kept a different if not lower profile. In keeping with the wealthy bourgeoisie from which he sprang, Suchet and his wife—the daughter of a mayor of Marseille whose presence with her husband contravened regulations—scandalized the local elite by the social equality they accorded women, but this did not dent the important levels of collaboration Suchet achieved. For all the unique character of Napoleon's response to the conditions of Spain, it bore one hallmark of the "new order" he proclaimed at the end of 1810: Spain was now, in great part, in the hands of Frenchmen he trusted, which was neither his brother nor his Spanish ministers.

As these events unfolded, although Napoleon did not communicate directly with Joseph, Joseph continued to badger him. When he wrote to his wife, Julie, who never left Paris, that he wanted to abdicate and settle quietly on his French estates, Jean-Baptiste de Nompère de Champagny, then foreign minister, informed Julie dryly that he could not do so without permission, as he was a French commander, in charge of the Army of Centre. Napoleon calmed Julie's nerves, telling her he would allow him "a sort of permission," if he really wanted. It was the first of several wholly duplicitous promises he made to Joseph.[86] Joseph hoped the birth of Napoleon's son would break the deadlock. His pleas to be relieved of his throne—to follow Louis's example voluntarily—continued while en route to Paris. From Santa María de la Nieva, he wrote:

> Since I have been on the road, my health has returned, far from the ever-recurring spectacle of misery and humiliation I have had before my eyes in Madrid, this last year. I have watched my respect as a king crumble, my authority reviled or eluded by the soldiers under my orders, on the pretext of orders they get directly from Paris. I dare to hope Your Majesty will not send me back, but allow me to retreat into complete obscurity.[87]

Needless to say, it remained unanswered. The two brothers met at Rambouillet on May 16, when all the official ceremonies were over, and spent six amicable hours together. Or so it seemed to Joseph. Napoleon agreed to send one million francs a month to the Spanish treasury for "political and military operations," and to confirm, without nuance, that Joseph commanded all the French armies in the peninsula. Finally, Joseph was to be allowed to appoint Spanish officials to work with the military governors general, north of the Ebro. It was all a lie: Before Joseph even left for Madrid, Berthier informed him that the agreed monthly sum was 500,000 francs; a circular was soon sent out to the military commanders to ignore Joseph. Berthier authorized them to raise their own revenue, again, without recourse to Joseph.[88] Joseph learned of this last directive on his way back to Madrid, in Burgos, and wrote to Napoleon: "I am firmly convinced of success by speaking to the people (of Spain) in their own language and (by) repressing the disorders of several (bandit) chiefs. If Your Majesty does not have sufficient confidence in me . . . it only remains for me to ask to be allowed to live in retirement with my family."[89] Napoleon returned to his policy of silence, and kept it.

Napoleon's grip on Spain was hardly secure. Important pockets of increasingly well-organized guerrilla resistance remained and were consolidating around Espoz y Mina in Navarre and in La Mancha, not so very distant from Madrid; a Spanish army in the far southwest under Francisco Ballesteros still harassed Soult as best it could.[90] Cadiz, safe behind the British fleet—as well as the Balearic islands—were centers from which innumerable raids were made along French-held coasts and guerrilla groups were supplied, these bases likened to modern aircraft carriers, in the apt analogy of Agustín Guimera.[91] Above all, the British grip on Portugal and maritime Galicia had become unshakable. Nevertheless, these centers of resistance were scattered. Napoleon's delegation of power to "his men," civilian and military, was yielding impressive results, epitomized by the marshal's baton he awarded Suchet on July 8, 1811. Charles Esdaile, in his masterly survey of the Peninsular War, concludes that "it was still entirely reasonable to think in terms of a French victory" in Spring 1811.[92] Napoleon certainly felt so, declaring to the *Corps Législatif* on June 16:

The insurgents have been beaten in a great number of open battles. England has begun to understand that this war is reaching its end, and that intrigue and gold are not enough to sustain it. It has found itself constrained to change the nature (of the war); and from being an auxiliary (in the war) it has had to become the principal (agent). All this has come about because it has had to send regular troops of the line to the peninsula: England, Scotland, Ireland are undefended . . . This struggle against Carthage, which seemed to have been decided on the battlefield of the Ocean or beyond the seas, will now be decided on the plains of Spain![93]

He was wrong.

The Illyrian Provinces: The Perils of a Balkan Frontier

When Napoleon and the Habsburgs connived to destroy the ancient Republic of Venice in 1797, all its territories passed to the Austrians, including a long strip of the Dalmatian coast, along with the city-state of Ragusa (now Dubrovnik in modern Croatia). Napoleon stripped Austria of this area in 1806, putting it under the supervision of the Kingdom of Italy, but never actually annexing it outright. The War of 1809 saw Dalmatia transferred to direct French control but, again, without making it a formal part of the empire. He then stripped Austria of the northern Adriatic coast, around Trieste, and the Alpine provinces of Carinthia, Carniola (the core of modern Slovenia), and sections of the Tyrol, together with areas of inland Croatia comprising part of the Habsburgs' military border with the Ottoman Empire. They were amalgamated with Dalmatia to form the "Illyrian Provinces," a name drawn from antiquity to denote a heterogeneous, wholly artificial creation. Its highly diverse population numbered about one and half million, spread over fifty-five thousand square kilometers.[94] It owed its creation to the mixture of spite and defensive pragmatism that characterized most Napoleonic imperial expansionism: The birth of "Illyria" was one of the last shockwaves of the trauma of 1809, in its goal of denying the Habsburgs of the last coastline they possessed; equally, the seizure of modern Slovenia was meant to place a direct French threat on their southern border, like the Duchy of Warsaw to the north. This was driven home when the capital of the provinces was moved from the Dalmatian coast to Ljubljana, even though Trieste was the most logical city to accommodate it.[95] Illyria's other main raison d'être was to deny the British entry to yet another portion of the European coastline, as Venetian Dalmatia had always included the Ionian islands, which were now in theory under French control. It was also hoped that by acquiring this part of the Balkans, the empire might better secure its overland trade routes with the Near East, where so much of the cotton relied on by both French and Italian industry originated, which led to extensive road building across the provinces.[96]

Once "on-the-ground," however, more complex ramifications emerged. Illyria was never properly pacified, and remained a theatre of numerous local rebellions, particularly after the imposition of conscription. Dalmatia was a region traditionally known for lawlessness in the valleys of the Dinaric Alps; in contrast, the orderly society of modern Slovenia was quickly transformed into a region of endemic, collective resistance to conscription, and so a source of unease in the very area Napoleon intended to use to cow Austria.[97] Its very existence began to complicate Napoleon's cherished hopes for a Russian entente, in that henceforth he felt he had to warn the Russian tsar, Alexander, not to advance south or westward in the Balkans, to keep him away from his new march. When the tsar asserted traditional Russian interests in the Ionian islands, and in Corfu in particular, the alliance came under further strain. Relations were further aggravated by Alexander's support for the Serbian rebellion against the Ottomans, which impinged on the Illyrian hinterland. In 1807, the British had seized the island of Vis—"the Gibraltar of the Adriatic"[98]—only forty kilometers from the Dalmatian coast. Direct French rule soon turned the Adriatic into a genuine nightmare for Napoleon. Its complex archipelago proved impossible to police; its islands—beyond the reach of the meager naval power the French could muster—became havens for whole mainland communities evading conscription, and bases for smuggling on a grand scale. British naval power was swift to assert itself in the Adriatic. From 1809 onward, they exploited their position ruthlessly, aiding resentment to French rule and providing a naval screen to protect the Ionian archipelago; a French attempt to retake Vis in March 1811 was easily beaten back.[99] The judgment of two Croatian scholars, that "[t]he Illyrian provinces had to juggle too many roles" within the empire, appears more than valid.[100] In truth, they were a liability to Napoleon.

Napoleon had intended Illyria to be a bargaining chip in his relations with Austria, initially as part of a swap for the Austrian rump of Polish Galicia. Even as late as March 1812, he dangled their return to the Habsburgs in return for support in a war with Russia.[101] Yet, this deeply ancien régime realpolitik stands in sharp contrast to the manner in which he sought to rule the Illyrian provinces. "The new order of things," the Roman template of a uniform empire under one law and one civic sphere, was to be implanted in the Balkans. This will was epitomized by the dispatch of a judicial commissioner, the redoubtable Joseph Coffinhal-Dunoyer, who had imposed the Code Napoleon on Rome, to do same in Ljubljana. It is doubtful if his mission achieved any significant results—his reports are marked by their sheer exasperation[102]—but the intent was clear enough. Marshal Marmont, whose tenure as governor-general had been marked by concerted efforts to integrate the local elites as provincial magistrates and administrators, was terminated. He was replaced by General Bertrand, who held the post from 1811 to 1813, and Marmont's appointees were swiftly replaced by young French auditors of the Council of State, shipped out directly from Paris and named "Intendants," rather than prefects, in a small nod to the temporary nature of the occupation. In April 1811, Napoleon issued a definitive "Organisational Decree" of 271 articles for the provinces, described by one scholar as "in effect their constitution," which brought the Code Napoleon into full, official force; the Criminal Code had been decreed a year earlier, a tacit recognition of the almost ungovernable state of the region.[103] The introduction of the Code had powerful implications for "Illyria," where truly feudal conditions persisted in much of inland Croatia and the Slovenian provinces, and the principle of equality before the law was alien. If successful, these reforms promised genuine social revolution. These were regions where the first battles of the Revolution remained to be fought, and a new generation of French administrators, many from aristocratic backgrounds, showed themselves eager to wage them. The young French Intendant of a Croatian province, a scion of one of the oldest noble houses in France, castigated "the feudalism in all the severity of it origins" he found around him, while a French magistrate complained that "the feudal system still exists here, as it did in France in the fifteenth century"; they all pinned their hopes on the introduction of the Code Napoleon.[104] These policies fell on stony ground, however. Illyria symbolizes the contradictions and frustrations of the wider empire created after 1810.

The Channel: The Oldest March

Napoleon always wanted war during this period of relative peace, just not the one he got in 1812. In 1810, he cultivated Alexander more assiduously than ever, often to his cost. Rather, he chose to take what passed for his "honeymoon" on the Channel coast, concentrating his thoughts on whether it was now possible to pass from the reactive methods of the Continental Blockade, to open warfare to defeat Britain. The planning began in what Nicola Todorov terms "the strategic summer" of 1810, when Napoleon sought the construction of twenty ships-of-the-line annually, when he began the systematic application of conscription for the navy, and created the new naval colleges.[105]

That war was projected for 1812, when Napoleon hoped to have amassed a fleet capable of invading England. In the course of three years, Napoleon sought to lift the French fleet from its paltry 37 ships-of-the-line to 104, a number he knew could not outnumber Britain's 124, but hoped would be formidable enough to get his army across the Channel. His thinking was clear, if not necessarily feasible, but in some respects Napoleon showed more realism than in the past. He always needed 200,000 men to guard against a

British invasion, as his coast now included Holland, and they were wasted on garrison duty;[106] he rejected the plans of 1804 to ferry his troops across in the small *briques*, which he now knew to be death traps. His new plans provided for proper vessels. His strategy was "to paralyse a large part of the British naval and military forces, to enable (him) to strike at certain nerve centres."[107] To this end, he planned his invasion for the winter equinox of 1812—during the worst of the weather and the longest nights—"to confuse the enemy's vigilance."[108] Napoleon's senior naval commanders—the long-suffering Decrès and Ganteaume—were very skeptical, and the budget he accorded the project in 1810—200 million francs per annum—seems far from adequate.

Nevertheless, such projects are not always best judged objectively by their feasibility; chances of success do not help to explain the actions of those at the time, who calculated in different ways: Napoleon now felt that what had proved unrealistic a decade before, with lessons learned, might work in 1810.[109] The British knew all about these plans—a long memorandum drawn up in 1811 for the naval building program appeared in *The Times*[110]—and they continued to take invasion seriously, particularly the threat to southern Ireland,[111] that is until Napoleon's army was destroyed in Russia, in 1812. A 235 page report in January 1811 asserted that 400,000 militiamen were still needed in case of a French landing. The reporters read Napoleon's mind perfectly:

> These considerations must be too strong upon the mind of every reflecting Man and the disasters of successful Invasion too evident to need any illustration . . . irresistible evidence from long experience that till Invasion has been attempted He will never be at rest.

The only calculation they got wrong was that Napoleon had only sixty to seventy thousand troops available, which "could never subjugate the Country . . . nothing short of five times the number . . . could hold the probability of even temporary success."[112] As the British scholar Roger Knight observed, the number for success was exactly the size of the Grande Armée Napoleon led into Russia in 1812. Undistracted by wars elsewhere, Napoleon might ponder his options. This all hinged on harnessing the resources of his hegemony to the task, which in turn hinged on peace with Russia.

The North Sea Coasts: From the Hansa to the Humber

Napoleon's plans for Holland sprang into action as soon as Louis fled his throne—"[he] is in Bohemia, and it appears he has no idea what to do"[113] Napoleon gleefully wrote to Josephine about the fate of the man for whom they had developed a mutual loathing for his ill treatment of Hortense, as much for his failure as a vassal.

Napoleon's orders to Lebrun were clear and stark: "My intention is to govern this country myself. My lieutenant general (Lebrun) will be there to oversee everything, to gather information, to inform me of everything, and to receive my orders and execute them."[114] On July 10, a further note to Lebrun advised him not only to rid himself quickly of Louis's minister of police—"[who] seems to me very bad"—but to "thank the foreign minister for his services" because he was now redundant; finally, "All maps of the country, passes, drills, marine charts, reports on the colonies and countries belonging to Holland must be brought to Paris."[115] These are the details of state-death, and the starkest manifestation of the "new order of things."

In the middle of it all, there was also personal business. On July 8, he wrote with relief to "my friend," Josephine:

> I have reunited Holland to France; but this act has the happy effect of emancipating the Queen (Hortense), and this poor girl can now come to Paris with her son . . . That will make her perfectly happy. My health is good. I have come here (Rambouillet) for a few days hunting. I shall see you with pleasure this autumn. Don't doubt my friendship. I don't change.[116]

Indeed.

Napoleon's reactions to what he found in Holland reveal the gap he felt existed between the realities of a satellite kingdom and those of his own empire, and how he intended to correct them. Initially, however, his first actions in the nine new Dutch departments drove home the importance of enforcing the Continental Blockade. Lebrun's first task was to dispose of the foreign and colonial merchandise Louis had allowed into the country, and to appoint French customs' officials to do so. There was to be as little Dutch involvement as possible. In the following months, his judicial commissioner for the new departments, Joseph Beyts (a Belgian who had rallied to Napoleon very soon after Brumaire), saw his lists of proposed candidates for the new customs tribunals rejected en masse because they contained Dutch nominees, even though Beyts had been careful to choose men who were known for their aversion to the British. Napoleon had come to see the Dutch elites as opposed en bloc to the blockade. Most important posts on these very busy, much detested courts went to Frenchmen. Eventually, they were dominated by Gendarmes and regular officers.[117] Napoleon tackled enforcing the blockade in instinctive manner. True to his own military training, he dispatched one of his best cartographers, General Louis d'Albe, to travel the most exposed parts of the Dutch coast to map them and make careful notes about all that he saw: "These observations and reports must be made carefully, and be solid, not done in haste . . . (G)reat care will be taken in the course of his mission, to gather only sure and exact information, and to find the best maps. . . ."[118] No orders could have reflected his own approach to a new campaign more, harking back to his work on Liguria in the 1790s.

The imperative of making the blockade a reality accelerated the drive for centralization in the Dutch departments and exaggerated the gulf between Louis's concept of government and Napoleon's. The need for d'Albe's mission pointed to a wider sense that Louis's rule had lacked precision; that he did not know where to begin understanding the territory he ruled, because he did not appreciate regularity. Several pro-French Dutch administrants shared Napoleon's vision of conformity to the French model of the public sphere. Cornelis van Maanen and Isaac Gogel—who were akin to the Dutch versions of Cambacérès and Lebrun, respectively—had been driven to distraction trying to work with Louis, but rallied readily to his brother. Napoleon had marked out Gogel, who Louis had badgered into resignation as minister of finances in 1809, as one of the men "best versed in the affairs of the country" during the annexation crisis.[119] Now, he was recalled to help Lebrun, as was van Maanen to assist Beyts in introducing the French legal system, devoid of the nuances preferred by Louis. Two decrees of September 13 and October 18, 1810, imposed the entire French administrative and judicial order on the Dutch. The enormity of the shift from satellite kingdom to imperial departments—and, thus, the differences between Louis's rule and his brother's—were in the details: All variation in municipal government, which Louis had retained, was swept away, to be replaced by the single office of the *maire*; all towns of five thousand people or more received a police commissioner, thus abolishing local bodies; all local and provincial courts were abolished to make way for the French judicial system. Lebrun reported to Napoleon with some satisfaction that the last vestiges of the old Republic were gone by August 1811.[120] Gogel and van Maanen played vital roles in this, and continued in Napoleon's service.

With direct rule came conscription, a more ruthlessly enforced blockade, misery, and unrest. Napoleon sought to ameliorate this by making Amsterdam "the third city of the Empire," envisioned as the financial hub of Europe. The reality for his three million Dutch subjects was different. Before the work of annexation was even finished, he felt the need to tell Lebrun to meet with the police and security services and Gogel "to deliberate about what to do to assure the peace in Amsterdam":

> There is no doubt nothing to fear from the propertied classes; but there are a huge number of indigent people. They must either be arrested or turned over to the navy, put into the poorhouses, or set to public works. These four methods, together, should rid Amsterdam and the other towns of this rabble. Another method is to create military commissions and make examples of the first

one to make trouble. There are many indigent people, order must be restored.[121]

Direct rule did not bring about a better grip on local realities. Amsterdam collapsed, economically and socially, because of the blockade. The net result was an ever-increasing police force, headed by Frenchmen, which ". . . was basically designed to control the nation itself," in the words of its historian Johan Joor.[122] As a result, the Dutch were contained, but not appeased. Louis had faced collective, popular unrest from the outset—his coronation had been met by rioting—but widespread, violent tumult increased after annexation. The departure of the first Dutch conscripts, in April 1811, sparked fighting across the city; it began when a girl trying to kiss her boyfriend goodbye was brutally shoved away by a Gendarme. At least twenty serious revolts against conscription occurred over 1811 and 1812; when the regime began to falter by 1813, small, localized revolts in villages around Rotterdam spread into a chain of serious unrest, and finally engulfed the great cities.[123] When the prefect of a Dutch department was manhandled by a large crowd during the conscription process, Napoleon's response was ruthless:

> My intention is that the 500 men who composed the crowd which
> beat up the prefect all be sent to France, to serve in my ports . . .
> (T)he prefect represents me; those who stood aside, indifferent to
> the bad treatment dealt out to him are guilty . . . The houses of
> those who got away must be burnt, their relatives arrested, all their
> properties confiscated, and those individuals condemned to death
> in their absence. It is essential that many of those who were present
> be shot . . . Blood and chastisements are needed to wash away this
> outrage to the government.[124]

With the return of the "Roman model" came signs of tyranny. Napoleon's blood was up, as old demons returned in new places. The new Dutch departments were militarily secure, but the Roman model inspired the same hatred in its populace as it had among the ancient Batavians, who revolted in 69 B.C.E., crushing two legions, when Rome attempted to tighten its control over them. For all their defiance, the Dutch were now under the Napoleonic model of the state, which its future rulers retained after 1814.

The annexation of the entire North Sea coast, between the new Dutch departments and the Danish border, in December 1810, was very much of a piece with the reasoning that drove imperial expansion in its last stage. The four new imperial departments embraced three very heterogeneous regions—the coastal part of Jérôme's Kingdom of Westphalia, which was the former British kingdom, and the then-Prussian territory of Hanover; the three great maritime, commercial city-states of Hamburg, Bremen, and Lübeck; and a collection of small principalities, the last true vestiges of the Holy Roman Empire, which formed the immediate hinterland of the Hansa ports. From Napoleon's vantage point, they had one thing in common: they leaked like a collective sieve as far as the blockade was concerned. Following the defeat of Prussia in 1806, he imposed a harsh military occupation on them all, under the most ruthless and competent of his marshals, Davout, who lived up to his dour reputation and was hated throughout the region for his determined efforts to stamp out smuggling. Commander of all the French forces in Germany, he signaled his determination to enforce the blockade by moving his headquarters to Hamburg, in December 1810.[125] He uncovered vast corruption at the very apex of the French administration. The most senior French civilian administrator in the region was Louis Antoine Fauvelet de Bourienne, a school friend of Napoleon who had been expelled to Hamburg because of his involvement in a financial scandal in 1802, in which Josephine was also implicated. It was a gross miscalculation, if exile was meant to neutralize him, for Bourienne—who Napoleon described as "a man with the eye of a magpie"—soon found himself in his element, as the Hansa ports entered a period of a clandestine prosperity, once the British seized the Danish island of Heligoland in 1807, and directed their smuggling activities from its vast wholesale depots to the Hanseatic coast. In the six months following the Berlin and Milan decrees of November 1806, 1,475 vessels without French authorization docked in Hamburg alone, leading an exasperated French official to tell Paris the next year, "Trade with English goods in the city continues as prior to the decrees."[126] The ports were only the beginning, as contraband goods spread across Europe through the small states of the hinterland; the Duchy of Oldenburg "has always been a center of smuggling for England," Napoleon told Tsar Alexander, as he seized it in December 1810.[127] The small principalities of Salm, Lauenburg, and Amberg met the same fate for the same reason.

When Napoleon confiscated the coast of the former state of Hanover, however, it was a family matter, as much as one of grand strategy, for in the first month of 1810, Napoleon transferred it from French occupation and nominal Prussian rule to Jérôme. The "model kingdom" needed a coastline, and it was intended as part compensation for the loss of revenue Jérôme suffered through the creation of the *dotations* in his territory, although it actually left Westphalia with indemnities payable to the empire and liable for a larger military contingent than previously.[128] Nevertheless, Napoleon had now made his brother's realm the second largest in the Confederation of the Rhine (after Saxony), with a population of 796,000 and an extent of 497,000 square kilometers.[129] It did not last long. The real liability for Jérôme was direct responsibility for the maritime blockade, and his failure to stem the tide of contraband only added to Napoleon's increasing distrust of a ruler he perceived as frivolous and irresponsible—"You make a lot of chatter about yourself from the way you have of holding women standing up when you dance. A king does not dance, even at twenty (years old)."[130] In late August, Napoleon ordered in his own troops to occupy the coasts. Jérôme replied as did his older brother, in Spain: "If the French generals in my state can appropriate to themselves rights which properly belong to the state . . . if they can dispose of territory at their will . . . there is no guarantee for my subjects that they know where they belong . . . and every act of government will be paralyzed."[131]

A few months later, when he saw the extent of the annexations Napoleon was ready to make at his expense, Jérôme told him that "I would be reduced to nothing."[132] He was not mistaken. By the end of the year, the personal and the political congealed, and Jérôme's coastal departments went the way of Joseph's kingdom north of the Ebro a few months before. The seizure "was reduced to the minimum of politeness required" and with the less consultation the better, to hasten the process.[133] Jérôme learned of it only through his ambassador in Paris.[134] He lost the most populous and potentially the most prosperous parts of his kingdom: Close to a quarter of a million of his subjects were now "French," and he soon expressed his fears that he would go the way of Louis directly to Napoleon.[135] He did not, but from that point onward, Napoleon tightened his grip not only through direct annexation but in the governance of the rump of Westphalia. "(T)he model state became a satellite," in the succinct words of Jérôme's biographer, Jacques-Olivier Boudon.[136]

The diverse composition of the territories of the new departments was reflected in their experience of direct French rule. Coastal Hanover was the "political football" of Napoleonic Europe, passed from its autocratic native rulers to the Prussians, then to Jérôme, and finally to Napoleon, in the space of a few years. The Hansa cities lost their economic prosperity and their unique form of republican liberty, ruled by their patrician elites, a political culture based on commercial interests and civic engagement by a wide spectrum of the urban populations. It was a form of liberty as alien to French revolutionaries as to enlightened absolutists, Napoleonic and non-Napoleonic alike, possible only in such localized conditions that could not long survive in an era of conflict. Napoleonic rule here was a step backward in time. In contrast, the immediate hinterland of the Hansa ports was dominated by social structures that seemed almost medieval to the French. Direct rule meant the abolition of feudalism and decided attempts by French magistrates to enforce this often won them a degree of popular support among the peasantry.[137]

Nevertheless, the fate of the different regions of the four new "Hanseatic departments" was dominated by the blockade. French customs officials seized contraband more effectively than before, punished smugglers with greater brutality, and publicly burned confiscated British goods from the very outset of annexation. Nocturnal raids became normal.[138] There seems little doubt that, in this case, annexation worked. Large-scale contraband became too dangerous by 1812. Smuggling now became a guerrilla war against the French, but it was not a war the smugglers could hope to win, for "even black market trade could not replace steady employment for the mass of the population."[139]

The entire region was crushed by this. In the judgment of a contemporary Hamburger in 1811:

> This hardship is not simply felt by one area of commerce, rather all trades on land and sea are coerced, destroyed, and restricted . . . The merchant is not alone in his decline, those who depend on him—brokers, agents, accountants, sailors and boatmen, loaders and all kinds of laborers—have their existence threatened.[140]

The people of these highly sophisticated, law-abiding cities were transformed into an increasingly violent, lawless, defiant mass, impotent for the most part in its collective protests centered on the city gates.[141] The French were storing up a powder keg for themselves, should their rule falter. Napoleon admitted as much in March 1811, when he asked his minister of the navy if work could be found for the mass of unemployed sailors in Hamburg—"the hundredth letter I have written to you about this"—by building small vessels to patrol the rivers: "That would be a useful way to give work to the poor and set the country in movement. These idle sailors are all going to take off for London, otherwise. . . ."[142] The occupation of the Hansa ports is a poignant example of the blockade as "Napoleon making war on his own empire," in the resonant words of Paul Schroeder.[143]

Until annexation, the British believed Napoleon was losing, and with some justification. In March 1810, a British secret agent in the region wrote to his superiors:

> I am far from believing that this measure, even if applied in full, will seriously damage Great Britain's commercial interests . . . [T]he French government must have learned from experience that it would be difficult to find a general or commissioner in the French army who would enforce French measures or defend its interest, real

or supposed . . . [T]his measure can only have been conceived as
[a way] to furnish the generals of the French army with the means
to enrich themselves . . .[144]

This view was shared in London. In July 1810, the royal speech from the
throne declared with a hubris surpassing anything Napoleon ever uttered in
public:

The country's resources manifest themselves through every possible
proof of prosperity . . . and by commerce which is expanding in
every possible direction . . . which the enemy has tried in vain to
destroy . . .[145]

Pride comes before a fall. In this case, it came before the year was out.

The blockade had been nothing but a bad joke to the British, but this
was about to change dramatically. They had no inkling of the ruthlessness,
loyalty to the regime, and professionalism of Lebrun and Davout. In a matter
of months, they made the blockade a reality. As early as August 1810, a
whole cavalry regiment under the trusted Charles Antoine Morand, who
had served under Napoleon during the coup of Brumaire, now patrolled the
whole German coast as far as the Baltic, while Davout was ordered point-
edly to send "an intelligent officer of you[r] headquarters to reconnoiter the
whole of the . . . coast in detail and report to you."[146] Jean Rapp, Napoleon's
own aide-de-camp, was made governor of Danzig (modern Gdansk), and
tolerated no further corruption, "because everyone there is on the take,"
and "taking money there is like taking it from the enemy." Napoleon was at
last catching up with Bourienne in Hamburg, "who is suspected of making
a large fortune in contravention of my orders" (it is tempting to add "as
opposed to under them"): "Are there large stores of colonial merchandise
in Hamburg, and how much?"[147] Davout was given the troops to make
the blockade work, and command over all branches of the security
forces—the coast guards, customs agents and police, as well as the regular

army—to this end: "The two divisions I keep in the north have no other purpose than to achieve this end, and it is very important," Napoleon told Davout in September 1810, ending, "You have to busy yourself with repressing the abuses (committed) by the customs service, make sure that the merchandise seized is confiscated and that all is done according to my intentions. I want the troops to get a share of what is taken."[148] Napoleon had long fired off such missives, but now he had direct control through men he trusted. In early October 1810, a record seizure of British cotton goods was made in Frankfurt. The success of the operation was a tribute to Davout, but what mattered more was that this time Napoleon's order to burn it all, made on October 8, was carried out in full. Davout prevented pilfering and resale.[149] The realization that such success was now possible led Napoleon to issue a new decree on October 18, authorizing that all confiscated goods either be burned or sold off for the profit of the government. When a large seizure was made in Hamburg, Napoleon entrusted the contraband "to several auditors (of the Council of State) and inspectors whose probity can be counted upon" together with gendarmes; they were to escort the goods to Cologne, and then to Paris, where they were to be sold for consumption in France, for the profit of the Treasury.[150] In the wider context of the continental system, this was the sharp edge of the ever more blatant policy of "France first," but in the particular context of the blockade, it was a practical demonstration that repression now worked.

The ruthlessness of Davout, Rapp, and Lebrun—bolstered by secret funds of six thousand francs each Napoleon put at their disposal[151]—soon made itself felt in Britain and, for a moment at least, it seemed as if the blockade might achieve its real aim. Napoleon was adamant to Mollien that "this fund is to remain known only *to me* and you."[152] As in his intervention to save the textile merchants of northern France, Napoleon had now developed a penchant for secretive financial practices.

Heligoland was soon paralyzed. In April 1810, its British naval commander reported: "In spite of our naval power, there is little traffic, because the whole coast is garrisoned by French troops"; by June, the British commercial agent made a dire assessment: "The news coming in from every part of the coast is extremely worrying . . . and I fear that our island may have seen its most prosperous days . . . The commercial prospects on the coast become more somber each day," while a British merchant house noted gloomily, "the insurmountable difficulties which exist at present to transport (goods) on the Continent or to sell them, in consequence of the measures adopted by the enemy."[153] By July, commerce out of Heligoland had virtually ended. By November, even the spy network had ceased to operate, and the British commander admitted that the French had effectively ended commerce from the island, which was now full of four million pounds sterling worth of British goods that could not be sold. The great days of Heligoland would return, briefly, at the very end of the Napoleonic Wars,[154] but from the summer of 1810 until late 1812, Napoleon's dream of an iron grip on the coast proved real enough.

The cruel new broom that swept through the North Sea coast in 1810 coincided with an economic and financial crisis in Britain, more severe than that facing France in the same years. This reinforced the French—and Napoleon's—view of Britain as "Carthage," an inherently unstable society, its materialism built on sand and doomed to falter. Mollien felt Napoleon listened to bad advice about the success of the commercial war against Britain—"Bankruptcies were numerous in London, (but) people exaggerated the consequences to him"[155]—yet there was plenty of hard evidence for Napoleon to cling to: The pound sterling had known marked inflation from 1808–10, which at first benefited British exports, but then led to a run on specie that the Bank of England responded to with an injection of currency, causing further inflation, and a rise in the illegal export of gold out of the country. None of this, of itself, posed a grave danger to the British economy, although it was driven in part by the success of the Napoleonic Blockade. The depreciation of the pound was not felt by the public; it did not dent the government's finances; but Napoleon thought it hampered the British war effort. Grand coalitions were, for the moment, hard to fund. "Pitt's Gold," so feared and loathed by all French governments since the wars began, saw its assets shaken in these years.[156] For a brief moment, the new success of the blockade stirred nautical hubris in Napoleon. In March 1811, he chided Davout:

> . . . [D]on't speak to me any more about Heligoland . . . You have
> a good flotilla. Set yourself to threaten this important place . . .
> Can't you find one or two good bricks (light craft) in Lübeck or
> Hamburg and arm them for me?[157]

Reality soon dawned on him when he admitted to Davout that it was useless even to build frigates in Hamburg, as clearly they could not slip past the British, and that his prospective sailors, who were deserting the flotilla in droves, had to be caught and shot.[158]

Napoleon's actions were significant for his enemy's woes, but they were not the sole or main cause of them. Nor, indeed, were Britain's efforts to imitate him: The Orders-in-Council were first issued in January 1807, to prohibit legitimate British trade with France and subsequently to force all neutral commerce with France to pass through British ports and pay British tolls. It antagonized the Americans, in particular, and they were deeply resentful of the ruthless and efficient stop-and-search tactics of the Royal Navy, which often led to the impressment of both vessels and men into its service. This whole policy of mirroring the blockade drew ferocious opposition from free-trade and mercantilist politicians and merchants, alike. William Eden, 1st Baron Auckland—a president of the Board of Trade—raged against Napoleon's and his own government's tactics alike: "Such conduct could only be compared to the insanity of two maniacs . . . cutting each other with knives across the veins."[159] For all his fury, the grave crisis now facing Britain did not arise from either, despite the ability of the Royal Navy to police maritime commerce far more effectively than even Davout, Lebrun, or Rapp.[160]

The fundamental causes of the crash of 1810 were, in the words of François Crouzet, "the ransom England paid for becoming the emporium of world commerce."[161] The collapse of Spanish imperial rule in Latin America—coupled with Napoleon's impotence at sea—opened these new markets to British commerce, which responded with overoptimistic investments in exports to a macro-region still too underdeveloped to absorb them, paired with over-importations of colonial goods. However, partly through the ruthless work of Lebrun, Davout, and Rapp, it became ever harder to reexport these goods to the continent.[162] By the last months of 1810, the coffee trade had all but collapsed.[163] From the summer of 1810 onward, a series of bankruptcies brought down major firms specializing in colonial trade. The government itself was threatened by the financial collapse when on September 28 "its financier of choice and its principal agent," Abraham Goldsmid,[164] died by suicide by shooting himself in the garden of his London home, threatened by creditors he could not pay and deserted by his friends. One journal reported:

> Never had the death of one person unleashed such a commotion across the capital. Business all but ceased, and the Exchange and all the streets around it were full of people of all sorts, desperate to learn the details of such a fatal catastrophe . . .[165]

The government quickly took steps to rescue Goldsmid's creditors, but confidence in lending to the government was shaken.[166] The official committee of inquiry into the economic crisis determined in early 1811 that it was in no small part aggravated by the ability of "the enemy" to prevent the reexport of colonial and Latin American goods.[167]

The human tragedy of one man soon spread. Numerous bankruptcies and the surplus of raw materials like cotton that were now un-exportable brought manufacturing to a halt in many sectors of British industry, textiles above all. By late 1810, the commercial and industrial sectors were in crisis. This was all compounded by a bad harvest. The result was social unrest that the government interpreted as ripe for conversion into political sedition. "New sources of anger and resistance . . . with deep roots in society and economy, were already stirring," in the words of the British scholar David Andress.[168]

The period between late 1810 and the spring of 1812 was the nadir for Britain during the Napoleonic Wars, and contemporaries knew it. The general crisis forced the pace of the erosion of the livelihoods—and whole ways of life—of the self-employed framework artisans of south Lancashire and the West Riding of Yorkshire. The militarization of society that had begun in the 1790s gave their recourse to violence a new effectiveness and resilience: "In a country so long at war, it was unsurprising that (unrest) took on so many contours of an armed insurrection."[169] Attacks on mills were often by groups of disciplined, well-armed men, leading the *Leeds Mercury* to compare the current climate to the days of the English Civil War.[170] By early 1812, there was revolt in the West Riding of Yorkshire "with the full panoply of . . . military array," its rank and file drawn from a highly literate, long politicized artisan workforce, not afraid to make open references to the deeds of the sans culottes, threats made real in April 1812, when William Horsfall, a mill owner who had sworn to "ride up to his saddle-girths in workers' blood," was gunned down in a well-organized ambush. Only a few days earlier, a disciplined force of about three hundred men destroyed a mill near Wakefield. They were driven off by the owner, William Cartwright, but only with the help of regular troops.[171]

As if to mirror the fate of his people, George III descended into his last and longest psychological collapse in November 1810. In February, the Prince of Wales was reinstalled as Regent, but his long-standing links to the Whig Opposition made Alexander Perceval's cabinet wary of him, and he was given only limited caretaker powers in the hopes the king might recover. Even the most inner sanctums of authority were not untouched. The British state unleashed military repression on a scale and of an intensity equal to Napoleon's. Supported by Yeoman cavalry, three thousand troops flooded into the East Midlands in early 1812, "a larger force than had ever been found necessary in any period of our history to be employed in the quelling of a local disturbance," declared the Home Secretary. By May, Lieutenant-General Thomas Maitland had more men serving under him—mainly regular troops—across the Midlands, Lancashire, and Yorkshire than did Wellington.[172] Maitland was a tough colonial soldier, a clear sign of how seriously these revolts were taken.

The embattled British establishment had found in Perceval a most unlikely rock in the crisis. A mild mannered, deeply pious man—". . . with his skeletal frame and skull-like face, he looked like something out of Golgotha"[173]— "the Evangelical Prime Minister" proved ruthless and calm, as the waves of rebellion broke over him. Whereas Napoleon was daunted by the specter of mass unrest and widespread bankruptcies, the British government did not yield to popular pressure. Where Napoleon resorted to public works and token bailouts to preserve jobs, the British sent in troops and took the blows.

The most prominent casualty of the crisis was Perceval himself. The only British prime minister ever to be assassinated, he was killed on May 11, 1812, in the lobby of the House of Commons by John Bellingham, a Liverpool merchant driven mad by the collapse of his livelihood. The government regrouped under Lord Liverpool, with Viscount Castlereagh as Foreign Secretary. His year as a caretaker monarch over, the Prince of Wales emerged as an unexpected supporter of Liverpool's administration. This most steadfast but flexible of ancien régimes responded to the mounting chaos around it with its own blend of clear-eyed, stonehearted, cold-blooded, steely-nerved pragmatism. Its leaders needed all these qualities in abundance. All the signs pointed to an ever-mounting crisis. In the spring of 1812, the Whig opposition in Parliament, led by Henry Brougham, led a skillful campaign to repeal the Orders-in-Council to revive maritime commerce. In an effort to head off an outright defeat in the Commons, Liverpool rescinded them on June 26. It was too late. On June 18, the United States declared war on Britain. Nevertheless, the resolution of the center to hold fast was not dented.

Sweden: The Improbable Crown

Scandinavia stood on the periphery of Napoleon's hegemony, but it was far from immune to the ills of the Napoleonic Wars. Denmark and Sweden were bombarded and badgered by France, Russia, and Britain from the outset, and drawn into the wider conflict. In 1809, events in Sweden took a startling turn, even by the standards of the age.

Swedish high politics had long been volatile. In 1772, a violent coup had brought the determined absolutist Gustavus III to the throne, who was succeeded by his son, Gustavus IV, a prince who showed a deep fear of the French Revolution and a personal loathing of Napoleon. He was easily persuaded into the Third Coalition of 1805, and stayed in the field until 1807, when an armistice was forced upon him by Napoleon's entente with Tsar Alexander of Russia. He was the first victim of the free hand Napoleon offered the tsar when, without any declaration of war, Alexander invaded Finland—a Swedish possession for centuries—and swiftly conquered it. When Bernadotte's attempt to seize Norway from the Danes also ended in defeat, Gustavus was overthrown in a military-led coup in March 1809, and imprisoned, simply to prevent what many sensed was the collapse of the kingdom. Peace with Russia was concluded by September, which entailed the definitive annexation of Finland to Russia. Sweden subsequently made peace with Denmark, by then a firm Napoleonic ally, in December—clear evidence of the effectiveness of the Franco-Russian alliance in this part of Europe.

The rebels' choice of Gustavus's successor was his childless, aged brother, crowned Charles XIII, but this only postponed the succession crisis. The new regime in Stockholm made it clear that the deposition of Gustavus also spelled the end of his absolutist system of government. The Swedish parliament, the Riksdag, seized back many of its traditional powers, drew up a new constitution, and made it clear that it alone would choose an heir apparent to Charles XIII. Peace with Denmark opened new possibilities for cooperation in the region, and Christian Augustus, a Danish prince, accepted the Riksdag's offer to become Crown Prince. Forty-two and in good health, he died suddenly of a seizure while reviewing his troops on May 28, 1810. It initiated the second succession crisis in a year. What followed was remarkable by any standard.

In the words of the Danish and Norwegian historians, Rasmus Glenthøj and Morten Ottosen, by 1810, Napoleon's power "left virtually no European government . . . with the courage to make a decision of this importance without (his) consent."[174] When Frederick VI of Denmark showed interest in the throne, Napoleon let it be known he did not oppose it, but nor he did endorse him, which unsettled many in the Riksdag. The most likely candidates became the older brother of Christian Augustus and the heir to the Danish throne, Christian-Frederick, who many hoped would win Napoleon's direct support, because of the Danish alliance. Napoleon indicated that Christian-Frederick might be the better of the two,[175] but expressed no clear support for anyone for fear of unsettling Tsar Alexander with any endorsement that might produce a united, more powerful Scandinavia on his borders.[176] His stated priority was to "maintain harmony between Denmark and Russia," but he warned Champagny that "I intend not to meddle directly in Swedish affairs," even though "I would prefer it to be Prince Christian."[177] This oblique approach cost him dearly.

The original crisis was the work of the Swedish military, in response to a Russian invasion and the growing likelihood of a Danish one, supported by France. They still hoped for a reconquest of Finland, which was impossible without a firm French alliance. In recognition of the aura exerted by the Grande Armée, and with no clear lead from Napoleon, the Riksdag and Charles XIII resolved to go after one of "his men." The ambassador to Paris, Count Möerner, went "headhunting," and over the course of June 20–21, 1810, met with—successively—Eugène (who rebuffed him brusquely), Macdonald, Masséna, and finally Bernadotte, who was the king's declared preference.[178]

Napoleon's was not the only extraordinary life in these exceptional times. After his disastrous conduct at Jena-Auerstadt, Napoleon ordered Bernadotte on a "punishment detail," to pursue the remnants of the Prussians in their retreat to the Baltic ports, to link with their Swedish allies. When Bernadotte entered Lübeck, he impressed the Swedes with his bearing—his nickname in the army was *Serjent Belle Jambe* ("Sergeant Pretty Legs")—apparent military experience, and intellect. Bernadotte displayed an ability to "sell himself" since his political rivalry with Napoleon during the Directory. Napoleon's attempt to chastise Bernadotte produced improbable consequences. The impression he made in 1806 had not dimmed in 1810. Bernadotte saw his chance and took it. He immediately launched what amounted to a PR campaign targeting the Riksdag deputies, using massive bribery—and assuring them, against all evidence to the contrary, that he had Napoleon's unequivocal support and a glowing military record.[179] This from a man who had been relieved of command on the field of Wagram for incompetence, then stripped of his command on the Belgian coast. Even his difficult relationship with Napoleon became an advantage, giving him more independence of action than other marshals.[180] "This was, to put it mildly, a highly improbable outcome," in the words of the election's most recent historians.[181] Napoleon agreed. Following Bernadotte's election he was very open with Charles XIII:

> I was hardly prepared for this news since Your Majesty let me know that he proposed to elect a brother of the late royal prince. However, I appreciate the views of the Swedish nation to render such esteem to my people and to my army. I authorize the Prince of Pontecorvo (Bernadotte) to accept the throne . . .[182]

However, Napoleon was almost desperate to make it clear to both Alexander and the Danes that this was the last thing he wanted. Soon afterwards, in the small hours, he ordered his ambassador in Saint Petersburg to make it known to the Russians that:

> I had nothing to do with all this, that I could not resist a unanimous will (in the Riksdag); that I wanted to see named the Prince of Augustenburg (Frederick-Christian) or the king of Denmark. You will press on that which is the exact truth . . . that if any doubt is raised, to hold to this line, because it is the truth . . . [A]ssure them that the Prince of Pontecorvo is old, and only wants to live in peace; that he will only care about quelling the anarchy which is ruining this country, and that I don't think this is a matter which should worry Russia.[183]

There could be no clearer evidence of how important the Russian alliance was to Napoleon. It verges on the pathetic. Bernadotte was only six years older than Napoleon, who was forty-one.

Napoleon got his wish that Bernadotte's arrival in Stockholm did not unsettle Alexander, but not the way he meant. Bernadotte had been in intense, secret talks with a Russian envoy, Prince Alexander Chernyshev, with whom he had established good relations long before he sought the Swedish throne. Chernyshev followed Bernadotte to Sweden in the winter of 1810, and he had reassured the tsar that not only was Bernadotte anxious for good relations with Russia, but that he bore Napoleon no goodwill. Bernadotte resigned himself to the loss of Finland; he saw that Russia, not the Napoleonic Empire, would always be the permanent power in the Baltic. Suddenly, Alexander was freed on his imperial march, but he behaved with courteous caution for some time, keeping one eye on Bernadotte.[184] For his part, Napoleon noted worriedly that the Russian divisions in Finland were "on the march" south, into Lithuania in the spring of 1811.[185]

There was a new "satellite kingdom" of sorts, but it revolved around Alexander, not Napoleon. Worse, it was under someone Napoleon loathed more than many of his avowed opponents. Their mutual dislike had roots as deep as their acquaintance, exacerbated by Bernadotte's mistreatment of his wife, Désirée, the Clary sister who was his first serious girlfriend. As recently as 1809, Napoleon had told Fouché, "This man's vanity is excessive . . . He has only mediocre talents. I have no faith whatsoever in him." On his election, Metternich claimed he told him, "I see in him no talent as a ruler."[186] Even as he wrote to congratulate Bernadotte on his election and authorize his acceptance, he added one clause: "which is that, personally, you may not bear arms against France . . . it fits your inclinations, and does not even contradict the duties you owe to the throne you now ascend, which should never, even in madness, find itself at war with France."[187] The dread irony of these words lay in the near future. In the meantime, Napoleon had to cope with a new ruler—Charles XIII was not long in ceding all real power to his heir—on a strategically important throne, who was as undesirable as the siblings he was busy deposing or neutering.

The peace with Denmark in 1810 had already forced Sweden into the blockade and the continental system, and Napoleon put pressure on Bernadotte from the outset to make it a reality, but to little avail. Bernadotte quickly took up the mantle of the Bonaparte siblings in trying to protect his people, and with rather more success. He also knew that Napoleon would never support an attack on Russia to regain Finland, and in this respect, he proved a useful ally to Napoleon, but that was as far as it went. However, Bernadotte quickly perceived how popular hopes were for the acquisition of Norway among those who had placed him in power, and offered Napoleon sixty thousand troops—an illusory number—to invade Britain, in return for his support in taking Norway from Denmark. Denmark was a reliable, valued ally, and Napoleon rebuffed this with the contempt it deserved, but in language that betrayed their old enmity:

> There is too much restlessness and muddle in the mind of the prince
> of Sweden, to the point that I attach no importance to (this) . . .
> I am too powerful to need anyone with me . . . (A)s long as the
> alliance with Denmark endures, France will not countenance any
> harm coming to Norway.[188]

He stood on his position as a head of state to refuse to communicate directly "with a regent" in their official dealings.

Bernadotte's election bears the extraordinary hallmarks of the era. The son and grandson of legal clerks in a provincial town on the Spanish border, who had risen slowly through the ranks until the Revolution made him a general and politician, he was now the heir to an ancient throne. His wife had a more secure throne than her older sister, even if she did not leave Paris for her new country until 1822. Bernadotte had certainly duped the Swedes about his military prowess, but his family rules there to this day. Napoleonic bugle calls still ring out when the guard is changed at the royal palace in Stockholm.

The Baltic: The Blockade's Weakest Link

Napoleon never really tightened his grip on the Baltic. Initially, with Russia and Sweden in the blockade, the French had been able to disrupt a large British convoy in October 1810. When many of its ships were driven ashore by bad weather, Rapp moved swiftly, and the losses to British merchants were a "veritable disaster" at the time.[189] This did not last after the open defection of Alexander and the covert desertion of Bernadotte. Despite constant harassment by Danish privateers, Napoleon felt the Baltic "is going to be inundated with British ships" as a consequence of Russia's withdrawal from the blockade.[190] In March 1811, he told Decrès, "I want plenty of privateers in the Baltic . . . Eight to ten ships for them should be built in Lübeck and Danzig. They will be armed with cannon . . . These privateers will be the terror of the Baltic . . . (and will) do great harm to the enemy."[191] Nothing of the kind happened. Lübeck remained a dangerous center of smuggling out of Russia,[192] and the Royal Navy soon had a stranglehold, spurred by the fact that some of the most serious losses to London merchants early in 1810 were exactly to those specializing in trade with the region.[193] Admiral James Saumarez's British fleet of sixty-two ships and sixteen thousand men sat on the island of Anholt, at the mouth of the Baltic, and were covertly supplied by Bernadotte from 1810 onward.[194] Only the outbreak of the war with America reduced his presence by 1812.[195] Napoleon's frustrations increasingly pointed to Russia.

Prussia: A Dagger Sharpened for the Back

Early in September 1808, Napoleon wrote to Champagny, "I am forwarding you a most extraordinary letter, in so far as I can understand it. Get it translated and . . . report back to me first thing tomorrow. . . ."[196] The letter in question was sent by Heinrich Frederich Karl vom und zum Stein, the new Prussian chief minister, to Prince Peter Wittgenstein, and appeared to compromise him in a plot against the French. Napoleon reacted swiftly: He ordered

Stein brought to France for "detailed interrogation." "[T]hese Prussians are miserable people,"[197] he concluded. He then ordered Jérôme to confiscate all Stein's property in Westphalia, where his family originated.[198] Stein eluded Napoleon, fleeing first to Vienna and then to Russia, where Alexander quickly took him into his service, but not before Napoleon demanded he be dismissed from his post, "without which the king of Prussia will not be allowed to come home."[199] (The Prussian Court was still in Konigsberg, now Kaliningrad, where it had taken refuge after Jena, and returned to Berlin only in 1809.) Paul Schroeder has observed that Napoleon did not know what to do with Prussia,[200] but he could certainly do as he wished with her. He could threaten Prussia with Davout's large army whenever he chose. This was the brutal reality of Franco-Prussian relations.

This did not mean that the Prussian elites were idle. Immediately after the crushing defeat of Jena-Auerstadt in 1806, and with the court-in-exile, a cadre of energetic, reforming civil servants and army officers stepped into the breach and set about an ambitious, if piecemeal, series of reforms bent on modernizing Prussia. In reality, few of their far ranging plans—for the reform of landholding, the phasing out of serfdom, for mass education, and the centralization of the administration—came to much. They were often thwarted by conservative noble interests in the localities, and traditional elements in the higher echelons of government; they were always constrained by Napoleon's ruinous war reparations.[201] This was made starkly clear in 1810, when Napoleon, his own expenses mounting, demanded full payment of the war indemnity. So cowed was the ministry under Karl von Altenstein that it was prepared to accept Napoleon's offer to write off the debt if it ceded him part of Silesia. This was too much for Frederick-William, however, who dismissed von Altenstein and replaced him with the experienced diplomat Karl August von Hardenberg, who appealed to the Prussian provincial elites to support extensive fiscal reforms, including the abolition of many privileges, to pay off the indemnity and pave the way to a more efficient and equitable system of taxation. He was unsuccessful, and the Assembly of Notables he called soon turned into a forum for traditionalist opposition to all reform, particularly where their rights over the peasantry were concerned.[202]

Partial exceptions to this litany of frustration were the reforms of the state apparatus and the army. Stein, von Altenstein, and von Hardenberg all felt that the root of Prussian failure in 1806 had been leadership; that the executive, based on the cabinet of ministers run too loosely by the king, had created muddle and infighting that paralyzed the state in a crisis. Before he was forced from office, Stein persuaded a very reluctant monarch to abolish the cabinet and replace it with an executive of five ministers, each with a specific brief, and direct access to the king. As Christopher Clark has put it, "it was difficult to counter this argument in the emotionally charged environment of post-Tilsit."[203]

The desperate need for thoroughgoing military reform was clear to all, and even Frederick-William accepted that "the fate of Prussia should not depend on whether the monarch himself was a gifted strategist,"[204] which put Prussia well in advance of Napoleonic France. The debate over reform was not new in the Prussian army, but in the wake of so crushing a defeat the need for change was desperate. A group of dynamic reformers, clustered around Gerhard von Scharnhorst and August Wilhelm von Gneisenau, became the dominant voices in the Military Reorganization Committee set up by the king in July 1807. They met little opposition in tearing down the old edifice. Nothing short of a purge of the officer corps followed: 208 officers were removed following a thorough investigation by the Military Commission; of the 142 Prussian generals, seventeen were simply dismissed from service and another 86 honorably discharged. Barely a quarter of the pre-1806 officer corps remained. The new corps was now purely meritocratic; in the words of the official order of August 6, 1808: "All social preference that has existed is henceforth and hereby terminated in the military establishment, and everyone, whatever his background, has the same duties and the same rights."[205] New dedicated schools were created for the artillery and engineers. More emphasis was placed on developing light infantry tactics and training, and there were crucial changes in weaponry and training at all levels.[206] The more savage corporal punishments of the old army were abolished, among them running the gauntlet. The Napoleonic model had won yet another victory over the Prussians.

These reforming impulses had their limits, however. Frederick-William, like Francis in Austria, would not countenance mass conscription when it was proposed in 1810, and was even more dismissive of the idea of a citizens' militia: "Good—as poetry" was his withering response.[207] Tsar Alexander egged on the reformers to attempt a Spanish-style guerrilla war in the spring of 1811, when he was considering an offensive against Napoleon. He urged Frederick-William to set up camps near the coast where his militias could be supplied by the British navy, as was happening in Spain. All this was music to the ears of the military reformers. Gneisenau, possibly caught up in the spirit of Spain, urged a popular uprising to support a Russian advance, with the clergy at the head of their communities. Even if it caught the imagination of the intelligentsia, most of the officer corps treated this with contempt.[208] Alexander also urged a "scorched-earth" policy on Prussia—"the system . . . which has brought victory to Wellington in wearing down the French armies"—in the event of the Russians being beaten in the field by Napoleon and having to retreat. Hardenberg and the king were one in rejecting this. Prussia's earth had been scorched enough.[209]

There was one reforming measure that was adopted, despite the reservations of many commanders and the king: the "Krumper system." Napoleon had limited the size of the Prussian army to forty-two thousand men (some estimates put it at thirty-six thousand)—in reality, it usually stood at about forty-five thousand—a constraint all felt had to be circumvented without provoking the French. The Krumper system sent five men per unit each month on leave, and replaced them with five raw recruits, thus creating a reserve of well-trained troops who could be recalled to the colors at will. In practice, many officers resented the loss of good men and did not always comply, but even so, the army had increased to about sixty-five thousand men by 1812.[210] Frederick-William also sanctioned the reinforcement of key fortresses and improving infrastructure to facilitate troop movements.

This was not lost on Napoleon. In May 1811, he wrote to his foreign minister:

> Is it true that the troops which were in Silesia are being moved
> to the coast? And what is the purpose of the new bridge being
> built between Stettin and Custrin? . . . these measures can only
> arouse suspicion, the use of the *semestries* (the French term for the
> "Krumper" reservists) has to be prevented, and the ranks not aug-
> mented . . . I think it would be useful to send several secret agents
> to Berlin and Prussia . . . under the cover of businessmen to see
> what is going on . . . It is all too clear that they are arming on the
> coast . . . I am assured that they are raising many *semestries* and
> have recruited a great number in Prussia.[211]

There is in this a hint of fear, as well as aggression. It is impossible to know,
but Prussia's determined revival, however limited, was unique among Napoleon's
vassals. It was the country of Frederick the Great, and had the will and the
way to fight again. Even the Berlin bourgeoisie was in arms, in its own way: In
1811, the Turnbewegung, or gymnasts' movement, sprang up in the suburbs,
to ensure the young men of the urban middle classes would be physically fit to
turn into "citizen-soldiers" when the time came. Their "uniform" of a loose-
fitting jacket and wide, gray linen trousers and their mass calisthenic displays
drew derision from Prussian officers, but they betokened a widespread will to
resist if circumstances changed.[212] Napoleon may or may not have known of
this, but it would not have changed his innate fear of Prussia. More than once,
Frederick the Great had seemed beaten, his country in ashes, only for Prussia to
rise again like a phoenix. He was Napoleon's hero, and on Saint Helena he spoke
to the Marquis de Montholon of a Prussian monarchy "made so imposing in
the reflection of the victories of the great Frederick."[213] His ghost often haunted
him, and perhaps the summer of 1811 was such a moment.

The bully soon swung into action. By August, Napoleon felt he knew
enough to confront von Hardenberg, and threw down the gauntlet: If rearmament did not cease, he would replace the French ambassador to Berlin

with Davout, at the head of an army of occupation.[214] Frederick-William had no firm assurances of British support; Metternich advised him to look to Russia,[215] this at the very moment when Alexander changed his mind about an offensive war. Even as Alexander approached Frederick-William with his plan for a Prussian "uprising," he confessed that, his entreaties to the Poles having failed, "I have decided not to begin war with France."[216] In truth, Metternich feared Napoleon's promises to Prussia of territorial expansion if it agreed to an alliance would be at Austria's expense.[217] Such hypothetical promises meant nothing to Frederick-William. Davout was reality. The king complied with Napoleon's demands. Consternation among the reformers followed: When Gebhard von Blücher—one of the heroes of 1806, and among the few to avoid the purge—protested and urged the king to flee to Russia, he was removed from his command; Scharnhorst withdrew into private life; Gneisenau and several others took service with the tsar.[218] They left a much-improved army behind them, and its first beneficiary was Napoleon, the very man who tried to strangle it at birth. He imposed a humiliating treaty on Prussia in December 1812, obliging Frederick-William to take the offensive with him in any future conflict. Worse still as that war would be with Russia, Prussia was now ordered to support a massive French military presence during the buildup: The Prussian ambassador to Paris was told that the Grande Armée could enter Prussia as a friend or a foe.[219] Ironically, although the military reformers constituted a new "war party," whose aim was to build an army to revenge Prussia on Napoleon, Frederick-William and von Hardenberg had a quite different purpose for it. Just like Murat in Naples, Frederick-William hoped that a better army would make him a useful ally to Napoleon, and so his kingdom might be spared the worst.[220]

Instead, the horrors of the post-Jena occupation returned. The brutal, costly occupation of the eastern provinces began in early 1812—in winter, and after a bad harvest—and made the worst fears into reality. "(T)he mood gradually shifted from resentment to a simmering hatred of the Napoleonic forces" in the stark words of Christopher Clark.[221] That hatred would not boil over just yet, so tight was Napoleon's grip, but it was there, waiting and seething for its chance.

The Duchy of Warsaw: The Crucible of the Empire

Of all Napoleon's troubled marches, none carried the potential for catastrophe more than the Duchy of Warsaw. He had hesitated long over its creation, and only accorded the "Prussian" Poles their state after his direct talks with Alexander at Tilsit in 1807. Even the name of the new polity underscores the dangers its very existence created for Napoleon's cherished entente with Russia: The word "Poland" was studiously avoided.[222] Two things always frightened Alexander about this new state on his western border: One was, quite simply, that it was a formidable military presence, for the army of the Duchy could swing on a hinge against the Habsburgs or Russia at will; it could give Napoleon a springboard for invasion, or a daunting first line of defense. There was a deeper problem, however. Many Poles considered the Duchy only a rump of the pre-partition Polish Commonwealth, which had been one of the largest states in early modern Europe, stretching from Lithuania in the north, across modern Poland, east into modern Belarus, and south, incorporating the western half of the modern Ukraine. Henceforth, the specter of this "greater Poland" was alive in many minds, Alexander's chief among them.

The short-term advantages of the Duchy were soon obvious to Napoleon: the Poles had shown themselves loyal and superb soldiers well before 1807, almost twenty thousand of them serving with distinction in the Eylau-Friedland campaign. The Duchy fulfilled its obligation to maintain a peacetime army of thirty thousand, if not without great financial strain, and its contribution to the 1809 campaign was striking. Józef Poniatowski, the minister of war, worked wonders with his forty-seven thousand troops. He ejected a larger Austrian force from the Duchy and conquered Galicia, the Polish portion of the Austrian empire, along with its capital, Cracow, the second city of Poland.[223] Nor did the Duchy's contribution end with the war. By 1812, the "home" army numbered seventy-five thousand, with still more serving in Spain.[224] The bulk of the army was raised by conscription on the French model, made much easier in time of war by the continued existence of large estates, still feudal in essence, which allowed the Polish aristocracy to mobilize their peasants. There is considerable evidence that, once in the ranks, Polish conscripts "imbibed at least some of the general motivation . . . felt by their commanders," helped by the nature of their enemies: Russians and Austrians were long considered invading oppressors.[225] The problem was never recruits, but the money to sustain them; even in September 1812, demands for an extra seventeen thousand men did not worry the authorities.[226] By that year, the Duchy had raised over 100,000 men for Napoleon, and the Poles comprised the largest national contingent in Napoleon's service, after the French.[227] The Poles were rewarded well for their efforts in 1809, whereas Alexander had made only a token show of support for Napoleon. They were compensated proportionately, in accordance with Napoleon's mathematical reasoning: the bulk of Austrian Galicia went to the Duchy,[228] by which its size grew from 104,000 square kilometers to 151,000, an increase of over a third; its prewar population of 2.6 million rose to 4.3 million, and Cracow was, again, "Polish."[229] By comparison, Alexander received a paltry county. This was fair, but hardly sound diplomacy on Napoleon's part.

Despite the financial burdens of mass conscription and the blockade, or Napoleon's ambitions to impose the Civil Code on them—which carried the twin dreads of the abolition of serfdom and the threat to Catholicism in so deeply pious and feudal a society[230]—all but a minority of the Duchy's elites failed to be drawn into Napoleon's orbit. Their loyalty is all the clearer, because Alexander tried to tempt them on several occasions. The majority of the ruling class saw that, for all the constraints he placed on them, Napoleon remained their best hope of independence, helped by a tradition among them of dependence on a foreign protector, and a political culture that did not interpret national sovereignty in terms as absolute as they later became, as the Polish scholar Jarosłav Czubaty has incisively observed.[231] Those who supported Alexander were a minority, but in Adam Czartoryski, they had a formidable advocate. A former diplomat in Russian service and a scion of one of the greatest families of the old Commonwealth, he was a plausible link between Alexander and the elites of the Duchy, particularly those serf-owning nobles who cast envious eyes toward their fellow Poles under Russian rule, whose way of life was not threatened by the imposition of the code.[232] Czartoryski's influence was crucial in convincing the tsar that he had to "beat Napoleon at his own game," as it were, by offering to recreate a larger "Kingdom of Poland"—under himself—which would reunite the Duchy with "Russian" Poland, excluding what is now Belarus and Ukraine. He first broached this with Czartoryski in January 1810. Just over a year later, Alexander let it be known that "as long as I cannot be sure of Polish coopera- tion, I have decided not to start the war with France," but that "if the Poles back me up, success cannot be doubted."[233] It is not known who Czartoryski approached, but he replied in discouraging terms on both occasions. In March 1811, Czartoryski reported emphatically that the Polish elite could not, at present, be swayed. It is probable that Czartoryski's approaches were oblique. Perhaps he was not, himself, convinced of Alexander's sincerity, and so confined himself to asking those he contacted to keep open minds about the possibility of Alexander's proposals. Poniatowski seems to have known something of all this, and reported it to Napoleon.[234] Many among the Polish nobility were disgruntled and unnerved by the character and consequences of Napoleonic rule, but they showed singular loyalty to Napoleon at the moment when his entente with Alexander was breaking down. Moreover, perhaps they had worked out for themselves the price of changing sides: Alexander wanted to spare Russia the ravages of war by fighting in Poland and, if possible, "combined with the exasperation that ferments against (Napoleon) in Germany."[235] Nevertheless, Alexander's very attempt to "turn" them reveals starkly how great a liability this outpost of his hegemony had become for Napoleon.

In the context of a Franco-Russian alliance, the Duchy of Warsaw rapidly became a victim of its own success. It had made itself militarily invaluable to Napoleon, and in 1809, it had also fulfilled his hope that it would serve as dagger pointed at Austria, its formidable army only a few days' march from Vienna, but it frightened Alexander. The Duchy proved itself on the field of battle in 1809, and Napoleon could no longer think of using it as a diplomatic pawn, while Alexander gradually learned he could not bring it into his own orbit, particularly after the Duchy acquired Galicia: acquiescence to this would definitively alienate Austria.

Metternich was among the first to grasp both how useful and how dangerous Poland was for Napoleon. On September 20, 1810, he had a long conversation with Napoleon, kept secret even from Champagny, and communicated only to Emperor Francis, according to notes he made immediately afterward (and not found in his "creative" memoirs). Napoleon was aware that war with Russia was probable, and that Poland was central to it. In this eventuality, Napoleon's preferred method of coercing Austria into supporting him was Poland. Echoing his arguments to Alexander in February, he told Metternich he could not guarantee controlling the Poles, but if Austria at least remained neutral in a Russian war, he would not "revolutionize" them—meaning in this context, prevent them from seizing the southern part of Galicia still under Habsburg rule. However, if his Polish allies chose to do so, he would not be able to prevent them, with consequences for Austria. It bore immediate fruit: Napoleon said he did not want war over Poland, or an expansionist Polish revolution; Metternich promised to supply an Austrian corps of thirty thousand men for any Napoleonic army sent against Russia. The Duchy now served its original purpose for Napoleon: a stick with which to beat the Habsburgs. Metternich predicted in these notes that 1812 would be the crucial year for determining the course of events.[236] He was right. Both emperors felt they had no choice but to prepare for a struggle that Alexander had been waiting for cautiously since at least the meetings at Erfurt in 1808. If Napoleon took longer to see his hopes were in vain, he still moved ruthlessly to harness his hegemony for war, from mid-1810. Poland was, if not the spark, then "one of the cankers eating at the heart of the alliance."[237] The Duchy had become an immoveable object in the path of useful relations between the two emperors. The events of 1811–12 transformed this impasse into conflict.

3

LURCHING TO WAR: NAPOLEON AND ALEXANDER: POSTURING AND POISE, 1810–1812

N apoleon could never read Alexander, although he thought he could. The diplomatic circumstances Napoleon had created by late 1810 made this flaw in him fatal. He left his series of meetings with Tsar Alexander at Erfurt convinced he had cemented their alliance, when the exact opposite was the case. Alexander returned to Saint Petersburg determined to turn on Napoleon at the first clear opportunity, but he was prepared to bide his time. Napoleon was guided by hope; Alexander by faith. Napoleon hoped he could defeat Britain with the blockade, and that he could either persuade or bully Alexander back into it; he hoped he could salvage their alliance; he hoped he could impose a French vision of civilization on his empire. He hoped his son would succeed him. Hope requires action, and Napoleon was incapable of approaching life in any other way. Alexander had to adapt to survive, to become what circumstances dictated, but beneath it, he had patience in abundance. He had faith he would survive the machinations of his own court. If he vacillated over the particular, he still clung to a greater purpose. Alexander had faith that Napoleon would break his neck, a conclusion he had drawn after closely observing him at Erfurt. It meant he could wait; that he could bear defeat or miscalculation. When faced with this, Napoleon was out of his depth.

Even Paul Schroeder, who sees Napoleon as a warmonger, concedes that in 1810–11, although Napoleon and Alexander both seemed to be preparing for war, "in fact, both were trying to avoid it by warning and intimidating the other."[1] The sequence of warnings and intimidations might better be described as a "seesaw": Napoleon's initial troop movements in northern Germany were actually meant to intimidate Prussia, but Alexander could not assume this. As Napoleon ordered Davout to the Prussian border, Alexander planned an offensive strike through Poland; at the point he drew away from this, Napoleon began to shift from the defensive to the offensive. He was, for once, reacting to events; Alexander was used to this. Schroeder is closer to the mark in his belief that Napoleon "was seeking peace through bullying,"[2] hardly a new tactic. He wanted peace, but did not know how to achieve it. His commitment to the alliance was clear in 1809, when he virtually overlooked Alexander's refusal to join him against Austria, and again in his muted reaction to being rebuffed over his proposal of marriage to Alexander's sister. Napoleon's crushing, if costly, victory in 1809 confirmed Alexander in his opinion that challenging Napoleon at this stage would be suicidal.[3] Vengeance could wait: Alexander retained a foreign minister, Nikolay Rumiantsev, whose priority was challenging the Ottomans in the Balkans and was unperturbed by antagonizing Austria.[4] Rumiantsev worked hard with the Marquis de Caulaincourt, the equally pro-alliance French ambassador to Russia, to calm mutual tensions over Poland in 1810,[5] and this partnership continued when further sources of conflict emerged over the course of 1810–11. They were averted because Napoleon sought peace and Alexander was not yet ready for war. Nevertheless, relations worsened between the two emperors. As 1811 opened, Alexander wrote to his sister, Catherine, "I will trace out the lines for you with a wounded heart . . . Everything is taking on a dark hue . . . It seems that blood must flow again: at least I have done all that is humanly possible to avoid it."[6] His approach soon changed. Napoleon bore no such malice, although his "track record" as an aggressor by nature and much of his personal behavior hid this from view. These years exposed his inability to conduct benign diplomacy on any terms but his own. By contrast, Alexander skillfully played a double—indeed, triple—game with Napoleon, with his own "war party" at court, and even with Rumiantsev. Multiple "flash points" arose in 1811, all of which underscored Napoleon's inability to understand Alexander, and tested Alexander's patience to its limits.

The Blockade: Realpolitik

The first jolt to the alliance that Napoleon perceived came when Alexander opened Russian ports to neutral shipping in December 1810. This was a reaction to a longer-term crisis. It became painfully and progressively obvious since Russia joined the blockade in 1807 that its economic needs were profoundly incompatible with French priorities. Politically, Alexander kept Russia in line with the blockade and the continental system for the better part of three years in the face of growing anger and resentment at home, believing that doing so would be the surest way to avoid war with France. By late 1810, however, Alexander knew he had to do something to arrest the collapse of the ruble (partly brought about by his own reckless printing of paper money to meet the costs of military expansion) and even more by the collapse of business confidence. He took drastic measures: the printing of new money was halted; taxes were raised; the import of luxury goods was either banned or had prohibitive tariffs placed on them.[7] This was all to little avail, and Napoleon's initial reaction was negotiation. He asked the Russians if they wanted a revised treaty, and ordered one to be drafted for their consideration.[8] Soon, however, it was subsumed into the larger, critical issue of Russia's place in the blockade.

Napoleon's introduction of the licenses against neutral shipping, which applied to all countries adhering to the blockade, Russia included, was the point when Alexander felt he had to refuse to cooperate. He introduced an edict, a ukase, which opened Russian ports to neutral shipping. Technically, this did not actually mean he had withdrawn from the blockade, because direct trade with Britain was still prohibited. Even so, Napoleon resented this, and became suspicious. His reaction to the restrictions on the import of luxury goods bordered on the paranoid, and he was quick to accuse Alexander of deliberately targeting France, an utterly false assumption.[9]

His second complaint was more founded: Neutral ships were being used as cover to bring British goods into Russia and ship Russian raw materials to Britain. At the political level, Alexander only enacted what Louis Bonaparte had sought in vain to do for Holland earlier that year. Like Louis, Alexander rejected only the licenses, a new aspect of the blockade. Indeed, Alexander did not formally leave the blockade until the outbreak of war in 1812. On February 10, 1811, Caulaincourt made it clear that although Alexander found the new system banning neutral shipping profoundly unjust, particularly when applied to a friendly power, he remained committed to the anti-British alliance.[10]

When he replied to Alexander directly on February 28 (in a letter held in the Russian State Archives and not published until 2014), Napoleon could no more control his bullying instincts with the tsar than he could with his younger brothers. Napoleon enumerated his grievances in very plain language: "The latest ukase was directed especially at France":

> In earlier times, Your Majesty would have let me know before taking such a measure against my commerce and I would have suggested other methods to him which, still fulfilling its principal aim, would have not appeared to French eyes a change to the whole system. The whole of Europe sees it thus; and our alliance already no longer exists in the opinion of England and Europe . . . Might Your Majesty permit me to say to him frankly: he has forgotten the good he has drawn from the alliance . . .

He had annexed Oldenburg only to buttress the blockade. Attempted conciliation gave way, in a breath, to indignation. England was at the root of it: Napoleon
had made clear he did not intend to restore Poland, as this would have risked war
with Austria, but Alexander would not believe him. Alexander's actions could only
be interpreted as moving toward rapprochement with England, through the ukase
above all: "I am struck by the evidence of these facts that Your Majesty's thoughts
are well disposed . . . to come to terms with England: this is the same thing as
igniting war between the two empires. Your Majesty, once abandoning the alliance
and burning the conventions of Tilsit, it would be clear that war would follow a
month later." In a crescendo, he exploded: "I was the master at Tilsit: twelve days
after the battle of Friedland, I could have been at Vilna."[11]

Alexander replied calmly on March 25, in almost lawyer-like measured
terms, to all Napoleon's complaints. The French had no right to interfere in
his actions in Moldavia and Wallachia, because Ottoman territory was not
included in the Tilsit agreements, and Russia had been under attack; the ukase
had not transgressed the blockade in any way and, echoing Louis's pleading
for Holland the previous year, Alexander said he had been forced to admit
American ships to save his economy, so much damage had it endured for the
cause of the blockade. The tsar reserved his most poised, composed riposte
for the question of Oldenburg:

> A tiny corner of land, held by the only person who was a member
> of my family, who complied with all the formalities asked of him, a
> member of the Confederation (of the Rhine), and as such, under the
> protection of Your Majesty, whose territories find themselves guaran-
> teed by an article of the Treaty of Tilsit, finds himself dispossessed,
> without Your Majesty saying a word (about it) to me in advance. Of
> what importance can this little corner of land be to France?

Alexander quietly reminded Napoleon that he had acquiesced to his many
sweeping annexations in Italy, Germany, and the whole of Holland. He was
at his most disarming, when referring to his own rearmament:

Your Majesty is too much a soldier not to recognize that when one established fortifications on the scale of the frontier between Paris and Strasbourg (as he had, along the Polish border), these are certainly not aggressive measures, but purely defensive . . . Thus, my fortifications serve as conclusive proof of how little disposed I am to aggression . . . Russia has no need of conquests . . . The superior genius which I recognize in Your Majesty for war leaves me under no illusions of the difficulties of the struggle that might arise between us.

Only over Poland did the mask slip: "The armament of the Duchy of Warsaw proceeds without respite. The military (establishment) of the Duchy has been augmented out of all proportion to its population." He recovered himself in his concluding remarks. The French alliance had become his amour propre, so hard had he worked to get it accepted by his own court, so much opposition to it had he to overcome: "If war comes, it is Your Majesty who will have wanted it, and having done so much to avoid it, I will know to fight and sell my own existence dearly."[12] For all his bluster, Napoleon did not cross his own red line into war. At this point, he placed more good faith in the tsar than his own brothers. Instead, he demanded that his customs officials be given the right to operate in Russian ports. Alexander ignored him.[13] He had that sort of power, to match his poise.

Alexander was far from all-powerful in his own home, his official title of "the Autocrat" notwithstanding. The ukase's opening of the ports to neutral shipping gave little relief to the Russian economy,[14] and never enough to satisfy those powerful Russian interests that shared Britain's goal of breaking the alliance on economic grounds. The Russian economy was in the hands of the great court families, the same men who had murdered every tsar since Peter the Great. This was no ordinary commercial interest group. The court nobles were now richer than ever, some of their number were families far older than the Romanovs, closely knit by webs of marriage alliances, all of which gave them great power.[15] Yet Napoleon's near hysterical reaction to the ukase had rational roots. The

British navy had long depended heavily on Russian raw materials—pitch, tar, timber—and Russia's adherence to the blockade of 1801–02 had done much to bring Britain to the conference table. Napoleon obviously hoped this would happen again after Tilsit, and Britain's own economic woes in 1810 gave him cause for optimism, but at that very moment the ukase came into force. It was a clear sign of how close and natural the partnership between the Russian nobility was, as well as who controlled these industries and the royal dockyards, to the point that the British government itself almost feared this dependence and sought, with limited success, to find alternative sources of supply.[16] Britain was the chief market for Russian exports, and the most powerful and wealthy at court believed that continued adherence to the continental system and the blockade would see these markets lost for good, among them the influential economic expert Admiral Nicolai Mordvinov.[17] Mordvinov was a long-standing advocate of social and economic reform and an opponent of serfdom,[18] and so he was often at odds with the majority of the great nobles, but not over the French alliance. This gave the British a much hoped-for entrée into the Imperial Court.[19] Napoleon had not been wrong when he asserted that "Insinuating men, encouraged by England, weary Your Majesty's ears with calumnious proposals."[20] For the moment, however, Alexander chose not to be provoked by these issues, and Napoleon chose not to press them. Napoleon soon told Champagny to be more directly conciliatory, that "I will never make war over the tariff . . ."[21] and soon after, that he was to reassure the Russians that Napoleon's reinforcement of the garrison at Gdansk was in response to a British naval buildup in the Baltic.[22] He repeated all of this to the Russian ambassador to Paris in early April, "in the context of *How it is seen in Paris*."[23] The ukase had tested Napoleon's will; Oldenburg was Alexander's turn to struggle to hold his nerve.

Oldenburg: Wounded Pride

In December 1810, just as Alexander issued the ukase, Napoleon swallowed up the small Duchy of Oldenburg in his efforts to tighten the blockade. Such annexations had become almost routine by then for Napoleon. However, Oldenburg's ruling family had close ties to the Romanovs. It was a sign of how crucial the blockade had become to Napoleon, because he had spared the duchy in 1806, specifically on these grounds. In the first instance, Alexander did not make the annexation easy by withholding information on the duchy held in Saint Petersburg.[24] Caulaincourt felt strongly that Alexander would not let such a matter compromise the peace of Europe. It was a matter of how it was handled, he argued; Napoleon should avoid making the annexation definitive. Alexander's commitment to peace would allow him to swallow this. Napoleon chose a different route. He did make the annexation definitive, and he compounded the offense this gave Alexander by refusing to offer the duke compensation elsewhere in Germany, so enraged was he by his flagrant defiance of the blockade.[25] Napoleon had adopted the mechanics of ancien régime diplomacy, making and unmaking the map at will, but its essence was lost on him. The Romanovs had married into the families of the small German states for over a century; all four tsarinas—Alexander's redoubtable grandmother, Catherine the Great among them—were minor German princesses, and Alexander renewed this as recently as 1809, when he married his sister Catherine to the duke's nephew,[26] a warning sign Napoleon or, at least, Champagny, should have read. Caulaincourt saw this, but still felt that Alexander could be placated. The tsar expressed his displeasure in terms that escaped Napoleon. Caulaincourt reported his conversation with Alexander thus:

> The Tsar added that his familial ties to the prince of Oldenburg are known, that the reunion of this small state, which forms only a quarter of a (French) department is unnecessary to Your Majesty, neither as regards his commercial interests, nor for the security of his new frontiers, and thus there being no motive here for the public interest, it is evident that the plan behind this is to do something offensive to Russia.[27]

Alexander went on to tell Caulaincourt that ". . . the whole of Europe bears witness to the manner in which my uncle (the Duke) has been treated; it can see how little regard is shown to an allied power, to a friendly prince."[28] Caulaincourt then lost access to Alexander for two weeks. The French ambassador was stupefied by this. His biographer, Olivier Varlan, believes he had badly underestimated Alexander's amour propre.[29] It was less amour propre, perhaps, than deep anger at an insult to a proud dynasty. Even though a marquis of the ancien régime from a military family,[30] Caulaincourt could not quite penetrate how deeply the tsar was wounded. Yet Alexander had also shown craft and guile. He turned the deposition of his uncle into a calculated propaganda coup, portraying Napoleon in the worst light possible: a Jacobin who enjoyed dethroning princes; a land-grabbing despot; an unpredictable, treacherous rogue leader of a rogue state. It drove Napoleon into a corner: Faced with this, he could not now compensate the duke, of which Caulaincourt seemed to have persuaded him; he had French public opinion to face.[31] Napoleon could not understand Alexander's rancor, and Alexander then appeared to "see sense" by his inaction. He swallowed this and it seemed to have blown over by March 1811, but Caulaincourt knew better by now—even if "the government affects calm," the harm was done.[32] There was no war, but only because Alexander was not in a position to wage it. The Poles had seen to this.

Poland: The Potential War Zone

During the Oldenburg crisis, Caulaincourt and Rumiantsev held out hope that concessions over Poland would get the affair in perspective for Alexander. They negotiated a draft convention by January 1810 that banned any restoration of a Polish kingdom; that is, any further expansion of the duchy was to be prohibited. Napoleon refused to ratify it, on the flimsy excuse that, although he might agree in principle, he could not guarantee to control any Polish efforts to change the status quo.[33]

Even as the ambassador and the foreign minister shook hands, Alexander was making overtures to the Poles: "If the Poles back me up" he told Czartoryski, "success cannot be doubted because it would be founded not on a hope of counterbalancing the talents of Napoleon but solely on the lack for forces in which he will find himself." Through Czartoryski, he offered them "a union of all the lands that formerly comprised Poland" but with himself as king. As has been seen, Czartoryski correctly warned him of the confidence the Polish elites now had in Napoleon. "As long as I cannot be sure of Polish cooperation, I have decided not to start the war with France" he concluded early in 1811.[34] The Duchy of Warsaw had become a new Malta, the rock—literally—upon which the Anglo-French peace had crashed in 1802. Britain could not give up its strategic advantage in the Mediterranean, and Napoleon could not tolerate that advantage. Whereas there was no love lost between Napoleon and Albion, he continued to reassure Alexander he did not want war over Poland. In April, Napoleon told Champagny, "I will never make war for Poland," but concluded that, "As for Poland, the question must be put from this point of view; that the Emperor (Alexander) has made it impossible to remove all suspicion from his part . . ."[35]—words that seem to indicate that Napoleon was now aware of Czartoryski's mission probably through Poniatowski. Napoleon did nothing; Alexander chose to draw back from the brink.

In tandem with his initiatives for an invasion of Poland and Prussia, Alexander began preparations for a defensive war: Mikhail Barclay de Tolly presented his full report to Alexander in March, and by the summer Alexander was developing military and diplomatic strategies, as well as efforts to create internal consensus in the face of war.[36] This was made all the more imperative, because following the rebuffs by the Polish nobility and the Prussians for alliances, Alexander sent a secret letter to Francis of Austria, asking him to remain neutral in the event of war with Napoleon. Instead, Austria signed a treaty with France. Although Metternich assured Alexander it was done with reluctance, and the Austrian troops would pose no threat, Alexander now stood alone against Napoleon.[37]

Diplomacy: The Rapier and the Saber

Part of Caulaincourt's brief was to spy on the Russians and provide information about troop movements and the military buildup. He had a marked distaste for this, and simply sent Paris general, anodyne lists, devoid of any reference to the actual effective fighting capacity of units. He searched for indiscretions in the salons of Saint Petersburg, but found none of value, despite being so popular a figure.[38] He admitted as much to Champagny in January 1811: "As for the more detailed information (you seek) . . . it is impossible to procure it at present. . . ." Caulaincourt had some reasonable excuses. He noted the linguistic barrier and the extremely tight security the government exercised over the military, made all the easier by the vast extent of Russia. Above all, "the Russian officers are very reserved and if a few of the younger ones are indiscreet, they know nothing."[39]

In stark, almost comical contrast, Alexander conducted a subtle, oblique war at the heart of Napoleon's empire. Russian diplomats faced no language barrier in France; they could converse as freely with a chambermaid as with a councillor of state. Now, the French "soft power" of cultural dominance acquired in the eighteenth century was turned against itself. Whereas Napoleon retained the pro-Russian Caulaincourt in Saint Petersburg until the spring of 1811, Alexander staffed his Paris embassy with very different men. The Russian embassy had an effective spy network as early as 1806, which had even penetrated the Council of State. From 1807, it was honed by the calm, tactful Karl Nesselrode and the extroverted soldier Alexander Chernyshev, and widened considerably after 1808, with the compliance of Talleyrand and Fouché.[40] Nesselrode was the scion of a distinguished family of professional diplomats; his father, from a small Rhenish state, had served both France and Prussia before becoming Russian ambassador to Portugal, where Karl was born. His poise often "led some observers to miss his intelligence, subtlety, and determination."[41] He worked directly for the tsar, not Rumiantsev. Chernyshev, who worked for the army through Barclay, had been Alexander's aide-de-camp, and was a notorious seducer and a dancer of repute. The Duchess d'Abrantes remembered him thus:

[The women] looked at each other like wild cats when the Northern
Lovelace appeared among them . . . Everything about him, even
his attire, that waspish way of being enclosed in his suit, his hat
with its plume, and hair thrown in big tufts, and that Tartar face,
his almost perpendicular eyes—everything was of an original and
curious type.[42]

A better balanced team could not have been imagined, and the young
diplomats moved in Parisian society like fish through water, able to report
accurately on Napoleon's ill health and increasing forgetfulness. Even Saint-
Cloud was not safe from them. How this aided Alexander directly is hard to
know with precision, given what Caulaincourt called the "acquired sovereign
dissimulation" he possessed,[43] but Caulaincourt did not stand a chance against
the Russian team in Paris. Although he came to know Alexander well on one
level, he could not supply Napoleon with the sensitive information, personal
or military, that flowed to Alexander. Caulaincourt, a thoughtful, cultivated
aristocrat of the old school, strove to fathom the soul of the man known as
"the sphinx of the north."[44] Nesselrode knew Napoleon's bowel movements,
to say nothing of those of his troops.

Nesselrode and Chernyshev proved remarkably adept at amassing military
intelligence, and Chernyshev, in particular, had a deep knowledge of Napoleon's methods of waging war. His last report to Barclay drew on leaked documents, but also on conversations with French officers "who have no affection
for the head of the French government." Chernyshev's analysis of Napoleon's
strategy proved entirely correct: "Napoleon's goal and his hopes are all directed
toward concentrating sufficient strength to deliver crushing blows and decide
the matter in a single campaign. He feels strongly that . . . he would be lost
if this war lasted for two or three years." This was why the Russians had to
adopt tactics not unlike those Wellington was employing in Portugal.[45] The
details were exact and proved invaluable when war finally came.

The disparity in the flow of intelligence between Napoleon and Alexander
is indicative of deeper currents. The disaffection of Talleyrand and Fouché

opened the breach as early as 1808, but the willingness of lesser officials and officers to "volunteer" sensitive information to the Russians, consciously or not, speaks volumes for the ebbing away of support for Napoleon among those closest to power. The exact identities of these men, or their motives, nor their numbers, cannot be known with any certainty, but they existed. Alexander had no such problems.

By spring 1811, there were signs that Napoleon was about to fulfil Russian fears. Predictably, it turned on Poland. On April 17, Napoleon replaced Champagny as foreign minister with Maret, one of his oldest, closest collaborators and the head of his personal office since Brumaire. "The changed circumstances of external affairs are such that I have felt it necessary to employ you elsewhere," he told Champagny.[46] This brusqueness marked two sea changes. It broke the last vestige of Talleyrand's influence in the foreign ministry; Champagny was his protégé, and adhered to a very traditional ancien régime French policy of trying to hem in Russia through alliances with Sweden and the Ottomans and now, if possible, Austria. By spring 1811, it was clear that Russia had gained the upper hand against the Turks, concluding peace with them in May 1812, with British mediation. It was soon evident Bernadotte was not to be trusted. Prussia never could be relied on, even before its harsh treatment after Jena. The duchy, however, had proved itself the only effective bulwark Napoleon had east of the Elbe. The appointment of Maret has rightly been seen as "the docile functionary Napoleon wanted," particularly as his principal task would be to prepare for war.[47] Maret was not only "Napoleon's man" to the core, he had vigorously supported the territorial expansionism embodied in the Peace of Schönbrunn, and was an outspoken advocate of a strong, independent Polish state to counter both Russia and Austria,[48] to the point that Napoleon's chaplain, the acerbic Dufour de Pradt—a close associate of Talleyrand—remarked, ". . . he might have been taken for a descendant of the Jagellons (the dynasty that ruled late medieval Poland), rather than the son of a scalpel wielder from Dijon."[49] Napoleon had chosen one of his own, at last, but also a man dedicated to securing the outposts of the empire.

Caulaincourt was recalled in March; he had asked to be replaced after his failure with Alexander over Oldenburg, and with Napoleon over the Polish accords. His pretext was the usual claim of ill health.[50] Caulaincourt was a poor information gatherer, but he caught the essence of the tsar:

> He is thought weak, but that is a mistake. No doubt, he can bear much contrariness and hide his discontent . . . But this facility of character is circumscribed: he will not go beyond the circle he has traced; this circle is made of iron and will not bend because . . . there is a stubbornness that nothing can vanquish.

What Caulaincourt could not penetrate was the cause of this stubbornness, what was within this "iron circle." He believed Alexander's goal to be "the general peace" that "he hopes . . . to reach without violent crisis."[51] He was wrong.

Yet even Napoleon's changes of personnel did not quite spell the end of his hopes to preserve the alliance. When Napoleon replaced Caulaincourt, he asked him which of his three candidates for the post "would be the most agreeable to Alexander . . . not wishing in this, as in all things, to do anything that might prove disagreeable to the Emperor." This was more than diplomatic platitude, for Napoleon finished the letter by asking Caulaincourt to meet with Alexander and his foreign minister before he left:

> . . . and to declare to both of them that I persist with the alliance; that I do not foresee making war on Russia in any possible circumstances, the only excepted case being if Russia throws in with England; that I have no alliance with any other power, and that my political situation is the same.[52]

A week later, he told his new ambassador to Denmark "to be on good terms with the Russian minister (to Copenhagen); to continue to reject any idea of hostility to Russia."[53] Soon after, his ambassador in Berlin was ordered to

"make it known that the situation in Europe is not as one might believe relative to the possibility of a break between Russia and France, without trying
dissimulate that there does exist a cooling (of relations) between the two
powers."[54] Prussia was the first to know, officially, that there was trouble and,
indirectly, that she was an ally of France.

Caulaincourt arrived home to rumors that Napoleon was furious with him,
and that disgrace awaited.[55] Napoleon did, indeed, lambast Caulaincourt in
public and private for being taken in by Alexander. At a soiree in the Tuileries,
he "joked," "M. de Caulaincourt has become Russian—It's true isn't it?" When
Caulaincourt took offense, Napoleon tried, in his way, to apologize: "I know
you're a good chap, but the cajoling of Emperor Alexander has turned your
head, and now you're a Russian!" Caulaincourt added that he said it with a
smile, not in anger.[56] Perhaps a case of pots-and-kettles—but Napoleon was
not wrong.

This was as far as Napoleon's ire went. On August 15, 1811—Napoleon's
birthday and a national holiday—Caulaincourt met him for a marathon
debriefing. He was received amiably, and Caulaincourt spoke plainly:

> . . . I see only two ways to go: reestablish Poland . . . to have the
> Poles on your side . . . or maintain the Russian alliance, which
> would lead to peace with England and the end of your Spanish
> business . . . Maintain the alliance, Sire. It is the path of prudence
> and peace.[57]

Caulaincourt saw the deeper problem clearly. Alexander would always think
of the Duchy of Warsaw as a springboard to something worse. Yet, only a few
months earlier, the loyalty of the Poles was what had stood between Napoleon
and a Russian invasion of Germany. Caulaincourt defended Alexander from
Napoleon's accusations that the tsar had always been playing a double game,
particularly over Russian military movements on the Polish border, but Napoleon was right when he replied that "Alexander is ambitious; he has a goal he
is hiding when he says he wants war; he wants it . . . He has a secret motive:

have you been able to find out what it is?"[58] Napoleon refused to see that his own actions had led Alexander to fear him as an aggressor: "I did not hide from the Emperor that if he wanted war, his cabinet had done everything possible to get it," a point Napoleon did not try to defend. Caulaincourt was deeply worried by Napoleon's repeated conviction that he could defeat Alexander: It would have to be an offensive war on Russian territory, Caulaincourt argued, reading Alexander correctly: ". . . all the advantages are on the Russians' side, the climate, the hard winter, and more than all that, the emphatic desire of Emperor Alexander to prolong the struggle and not to show the weakness of other sovereigns, by signing a peace treaty in his capital." Napoleon based his hopes on his belief that the key to Alexander's character was weakness, which would count against him in a crisis. Caulaincourt came away with the impression that Napoleon equated weakness with deviousness.[59] If so, it ranks as a fatal flaw in his view of human nature.

In the course of the meeting, Napoleon accepted direct, hard criticism without anger. Caulaincourt was clear in his account that Napoleon still appreciated honest, intelligent argument. At the height of his clashes with the clergy in these same months, the aged Abbé Émery challenged Napoleon's claim that the pope had to obey him because he was responsible for Europe, its "sole master": "What exists now cannot always exist." Napoleon did not arrest him or chastise him. Rather, when other clerics apologized for him, he replied "Your are mistaken. I am not irritated by him. He speaks to me as a man who knows his subject. That is how I like being spoken to."[60] Caulaincourt emerged from the meeting convinced his career was over, but Napoleon had come to value him all the more. This did nothing to deflect him from his course. His immediate reaction to Abbé Émery was the same as his conversation with Caulaincourt. He changed the subject.

The timing of this meeting shows that it had taken Napoleon some time to see through Alexander. His recall of Caulaincourt showed that he was now in a belligerent mood, if not yet ready for war. However, there were other issues between the two emperors that aroused some of Napoleon's worst nightmares. Napoleon's personal letter to Alexander on February 28 covered a great deal of ground, as it outlined in almost colic outbursts all Napoleon's grievances, ranging far beyond the blockade and Oldenburg. In Napoleon's view Alexander had also broken the Treaty of Tilsit by occupying the Ottoman provinces of Wallachia and Moldova—"one third of the Turkish empire in Europe . . . and, one might say, annihilating this empire, my oldest ally." It was a gross exaggeration, but his fear was palpable. Nevertheless, Napoleon did not contest it, just as he raised no objections to the Russian seizure of Finland from Sweden, also an old ally.[61] He made it clear he would do nothing as long as Alexander did not try to expand south of the Danube, but ordered that "even this ultimatum is not to be pronounced" to the Russians.[62]

An older vision of hell was emerging in Napoleon's mind that spring: the aggressive Russian expansionism Talleyrand had long warned him was in the nature of the beast. Although by the terms of the Treaty of Bucharest, Russia only received a small portion[63] of the two Ottoman provinces she had occupied during the war, and although Napoleon had not reacted, he noted the tendencies that Alexander's initial demands to acquire the whole of Moldova and Wallachia seemed to reveal. Even as the two emperors sat down at Tilsit, Talleyrand had spoken of "the Russian invasion that began with Catherine the Great's conquest of Ukraine in 1770, and has only grown since." Expansion had become Russia's raison d'être:

> (Russia) has so sought to meddle in all the affairs of other peoples
> that it is easy to analyze its resources, its views, its position. This
> is not the work of simple interests and circumstances: it marks a
> remarkable period in history. It is since 1770 that the weakening
> or disappearance of parts of the states neighboring Russia begins.

He listed them: Crimea (1783), Bessarabia (1784), the subjugation of Moldavia and Wallachia (1807), the dismemberment of Poland, the annexation of Georgia, the invasions of Persia, the establishment of the Russians in Corfu.[64] Talleyrand still whispered in his old master's ear. There seemed concrete grounds to listen. Since 1807, Serbia had been in revolt against Ottoman rule, fueled by

Russian aid.[65] However, there were also signs that Alexander was learning from Napoleonic imperial ideology: Finland's incorporation into the Russian Empire in 1809 was not accompanied by any specific justification but by tacit right of conquest. Even in the Balkans, Alexander had seemingly abandoned his role as the protector of his fellow Orthodox Christians, for the "civilizing mission" of driving out Turkish barbarians from a "enlightened Europe."[66]

The end of the Russian war now freed the Ottoman Porte to deal with the Serbs and the revolt soon collapsed, but Talleyrand's vision stirred fears in Napoleon that Alexander's goal was to advance his presence to within easy reach of the Adriatic and Napoleon's new Illyrian Provinces directly or indirectly through a Serb client state. Paul Schroeder argues that, "Trying for everything, Russia gained nothing."[67] Perhaps, but Alexander obtained his short-term objective of closing the Turkish front and freeing a whole army he could now use against Napoleon. Nevertheless, the collapse of the Serb revolt checked his influence in the region, and Russia gained little territory from the Treaty of Bucharest, but no alliances. Napoleon saw it differently, feeling that Alexander had shown his hand, and could still "envisage Mediterranean expeditions."[68] Juxtaposed to Alexander's fear of "greater Poland" was Napoleon's of a Russian empire that knew no bounds. It was a nightmare that stayed with him all his life. On Saint Helena, he told Bertrand:

> Russia is a terrifying power and seems determined to conquer Europe. She can put thousands of cavalry everywhere, with her Cossacks, Tartars and Poles. There aren't enough horses in the whole of Europe to resist her. Three powers tried to stop her in the past: Sweden, who can now do nothing since the loss of Finland; Poland, which is now part of the Russian Empire. The Turks are nothing.[69]

In the spring and summer of 1811, Napoleon remained impervious to the fact that his own actions made Alexander feel the same about France. In August, Napoleon exploded to the Russian ambassador, in a characteristic attempt to "win peace through bullying." He was not fooled, he thundered, this was really about Poland:

> . . . I am starting to believe that you want to take it away. Well, no, you will not have one village, not one windmill of the grand duchy (sic). Even if your armies were camped on the heights of Montmartre, I would not give you an inch of Warsaw territory![70]

Within three years, he was badly disabused of this.

There was a more concrete fear aroused by the end of the Russo-Turkish war: the involvement of the British, who brokered the settlement. Just as Maret's appointment signaled a new course for Napoleon, so did the return of Castlereagh to the British Foreign Office. He leaked the secret clauses of Tilsit to the Porte, revealing Napoleon's willingness to partition the Ottoman Balkans with Alexander,[71] thus helping end a war the continuation of which Napoleon said "would be advantageous to France."[72] Napoleon had always insisted that only an alliance with Britain would persuade him to wage war on Alexander, and the peace concluded at Bucharest—and the manner of its brokerage—seemed to bode exactly this.

As summer drew to a close, all the tensions between the two emperors festered into personal rancor. Napoleon's emotions are the easier to trace—his outbursts were open and blunt. Marie-Pierre Rey noted that it was from the summer of 1811—and not before—that Napoleon evoked "the war which is readying itself" ever more openly.[73] That Alexander should write to Napoleon in his own hand in the terms Napoleon used with him in his missive of February 28 was unthinkable. However, each time each man set aside a perceived breach of their alliance and seemed to move on—or, more often, draw back—the bad taste lingered. The grievances Napoleon enumerated to Alexander in February emerged again, unabated, in his conversation with Caulaincourt in August. Each perceived violation of the terms of the Treaty of Tilsit came as an angering revelation for Napoleon, a betrayal by someone he hoped he could trust. This finally placed Alexander among the ingrates he saw all around him, and it resounds in his language. When Napoleon told the tsar he had "forgotten what he has gained from the alliance," his feelings about his brothers, Talleyrand, Fouché, Masséna, Broglie, and even Portalis, were now affixed to Alexander. Betrayal was all around him. For Alexander, the same confrontations confirmed, rather than revealed: Napoleon was deaf to all interests but his own over the blockade. His behavior over Oldenburg—the point where the tsar's personal feelings came closest to the surface—revived the hatred of Napoleon he formed over his treatment of the Hohenzollerns at Tilsit. The deposition of the Spanish Bourbons led him to believe that Napoleon would do the same to any monarch he could. It was over Oldenburg that Alexander came closest to lashing out at Napoleon, seeking an offensive war, and only stopped in his tracks by his failure to find allies. From then on, he braced himself for a defensive war. Napoleon's frame of mind is best caught by Michel Kerautret: "to boot Russia out of Europe was no more than to bring her back within the limits of the partition of Tilsit. A strange paradox of a war fought to force an adversary to become a friend again!"[74]

The diplomatic formalities continued to be observed. The certainty of war was found in quiet asides. In November, Napoleon, then in Düsseldorf, asked Cambacérès to visit "the Queen of Spain" (Julie, Joseph's wife) and tell her to pass on quietly to her sister, Désirée, now the Princess of Sweden, that she ought to leave Paris and go to Stockholm because ". . . it is probable that the measures being taken by the Swedish government will lead to war between Sweden and ourselves, and it would not do if the Princess were found here at that moment; so I think that the Princess ought not to delay a moment."[75] In January 1812, Napoleon's frustrations over Sweden's failure to enforce the blockade, and Bernadotte's ever warmer relations with Britain, gelled with the ancient rancor between them. Davout's troops marched into Swedish Pomerania. If this was meant to cow Bernadotte, it failed miserably.[76] By April, a Russo-Swedish alliance was concluded.[77] Désirée, née Clary, was now at war not only with her old boyfriend, but with the rest of her family, that warm, gentle, cultured home that first taught Napoleon his love of France. It was not only his own family his ambition threatened to tear apart.

4

THE ORDER OF BATTLE: AUTUMN 1811–JUNE 1812

The Bleak Midwinter

Napoleon traversed the Channel coasts and northern Germany relentlessly in the early autumn of 1811, inspecting the defenses and assessing his garrisons there, returning to Saint-Cloud on November 11. He then proceeded to bombard Henri Clarke, his minister of war, with missives about the inadequacies he had detected on his travels. He immediately told Clarke he had sacked General Jean-Baptiste Solignac for failing to provide the accounts of his command, ordering him to go home and stay there.[1] A few moments later, he informed Clarke that his Swiss allies were falling foul of him, and "owed" him three thousand conscripts: "The Swiss cost me a lot of money and give me no service. I have been badly duped up to now." A war with Russia should matter to them, for "in the case where France did not succeed, Switzerland would be compromised," and these recruits were a small price to pay.[2] Next, in a matter of minutes, ". . . the captain of the third mounted artillery regiment at Bonn is absent. The lieutenant is a young fool . . . It is very important to send a good captain there."[3] He told Clarke in detail about the deficiencies of the coastal batteries in Germany and what to do about them; about the worrying state of several regiments quartered near Maastricht and the need to break them up;[4] he stripped General Jean-Baptiste Dumonceau of command of the 25th Division—"one of the strongest in France"—as unfit to lead it, and gave it to General Louis Henri Loison[5]—all before he had lunch with his wife and son on his first day home. So it continued for months on end.

It was not all irritated impatience. That same day he found time to praise, of all people, a company of British prisoners of war. While repairing a pontoon bridge, several of them had exposed themselves to real danger in the rough water. Napoleon wanted their "zeal and activity" rewarded with new, dry clothes and money to get them to the Transport Office, where they were to be set free for their courage.[6]

That same November, Tsar Alexander wrote to his sister:

> Never have I led such a dog's life. Often in the week I get out of bed to sit at my desk and leave it only to eat a morsel alone, and the go back until I go to bed . . . You say I am lazy not to come and see you—ah, if only I could . . . We are on continual alert: all circumstances are so thorny, things are so tense, that hostilities may commence at any moment. It is impossible to leave my center of administration and activity.[7]

On the first day of December 1811, Napoleon left Saint-Cloud and returned to Paris, definitively. His domestic idyll was over, just as Alexander confessed that a visit to his beloved sister Catherine would have to "wait for a more propitious moment." The tone was set.

The Imperial Court in Paris swung into high gear in the first months of 1812. Two balls were held at the Tuileries in February, where Hortense and Caroline "dazzled on the dance floor" as Cambacérès remembered it. Cambacérès played his own convivial part, holding salons every Tuesday and Saturday, where ambitious provincial notables and all those who "wanted to stay in the corridors of power" came to hobnob.[8] Deputies from the newly annexed departments of northern Germany and Holland flocked to Paris, the official expectation being that the grandeur and glamour of the court would overawe them. But their journeys took them across a France ravaged by famine and infested by brigands. On arrival, they were greeted by an ailing emperor with an overweight body but a ravaged, gaunt face, who often needed helped into the saddle. Rather than being impressed, many confessed to Cambacérès that they were horrified by the costs of the festivities.[9] Napoleon had, it seems, overlooked the frugal culture of these Protestant commercial elites, or how ruthlessly he had exploited them.

It was all underpinned by the coming of war. Berthier was back in Paris from Spain, and holding salons and soirees of his own, even though he was increasingly ridden with gout.[10] Napoleon had recalled him from command of the Spanish armies on January 16 to become the major-general and chief of staff of the Grande Armée.[11] There was no clearer sign that a new campaign was coming, but the high command was now far removed from the lean, young wolves who had swarmed over and up the Rhine, and down the Danube, in 1805.

There was an old book doing the rounds in Paris that winter, Voltaire's *History of Charles XII, King of Sweden*, first published in 1731. Napoleon ordered a copy of it for himself, hoping to glean practical information about Russia from it.[12] Others read it for very different reasons. Voltaire's book told the tale of the young, dynamic—and often deranged—king of Sweden whose military reputation rivaled Napoleon's own in the first decades of the eighteenth century. Until, that is, he invaded Russia where his small, if excellent, army was crushed by the massive, untrained levies of Peter the Great at Poltava, in 1709. Charles returned to Sweden only after a long exile in Turkish captivity, and may have been murdered by his own troops when he tried to lead his country into yet another war. His military adventurism left Sweden in ruins, and saw his absolutist system of government dismantled forthwith.[13] Among those who read it with a burgeoning sense of foreboding was Cambacérès, who raised the subject with Napoleon, stressing that the lesson of the story was that "even the best organized states can be shaken to their very foundations by the disasters of one campaign, above all when their ruler is not universally recognized," a subtle reminder to Napoleon of his own admission that he could not afford to lose a battle. Napoleon's reply shook Cambacérès to his core: "I am not as daft as Charles XII," assuring his old friend that his invasion would not go as deep into Russia as that of the Swedish king. "(Had Napoleon been) misled by false assumptions or driven on as much by the thirst for conquest as by the mania to dictate terms to every part of Europe?" he jotted in his notes. Cambacérès did not flinch. He first appealed to reason: There was much to fear from so long an absence for both the present and future of the regime, all for a war that posed real dangers, and offered only chimerical advantages. He did not mince his words, if his notes are to be believed: "The love of glory is only ambition disguised. Pride is the basis and the principle of both these feelings." He also remembered that his words came to nothing. Yet, he elicited from Napoleon, perhaps, the real reason driving him. War with Russia, he told his most trusted collaborator, was inevitable, and it had best come soon, "while I can still mount a horse, which may not be the case tomorrow," and when his son was not yet old enough to lead an army. "The danger? I have to put all confidence in giving myself up to destiny."[14] Napoleon did not sack his old friend for speaking his mind; far from it. He became Napoleon's virtual regent again once the war began, but he was not heeded any more than Caulaincourt. Cambacérès was not alone. Mollien, his treasury minister, worked even more closely with Napoleon than Cambacérès, and he noted a similar, worrying pattern: Napoleon feared the coming conflict as much as anyone, and his solution was to take refuge in minuscule, detailed planning, but his calculations, however careful, were constructed to give him the answers he wanted. Mollien observed in his memoirs, compiled from copious notes and written soon after the event, that ". . . [Napoleon] believed that there was only one more war left to fight, that one last effort would assure the domination of the continent from Moscow to Madrid." He was convinced he could win, and that Russia was possessed of such vast resources that the war could pay for itself. When Mollien took Napoleon to task over this fundamentally erroneous assumption, he replied:

If I am obliged to undertake another war, it will probably be of great political benefit; but it would also be in my financial interests, and precisely because (those interests) are showing the first symptoms of trouble: is it not through war that I have always reestablished (my finances)? Isn't that how Rome conquered the riches of the world?

This was the moment, like Cambacérès, when Mollien felt certain Napoleon was going to endanger the foundations of his own power.[15] As always, they were all allowed to speak their minds, but none were heeded.

Taken together, the reflections of Cambacérès and Mollien reveal the paradox of Napoleon's state of mind in these crucial months. He was deeply conscious of the magnitude and dangers of an invasion of Russia, but his answer was to take refuge in the particular, and so avoid considering the general. His declining health drove "the clock," for he must have sensed—even if he left it unsaid—that the younger, healthier Alexander had time on his side. Taking the great risk had come to be construed as caution; the window to destroy the only army capable of defeating him was ever narrower, and had to be seized while he was still fit to do so. This was the point when "probability" slipped into "destiny," when "necessity" was overtaken by delusional "advantageousness." Napoleon, who had devoured geographical information all his life, now assumed Russia to be rich, when his armies were about to traverse some of the most barren lands in Europe. Mollien recalled that nothing struck those involved at the time more than "the grandeur of the preparations, and the even greater disasters of the events."[16]

Napoleon still found time to return to other preoccupations, often in worrying ways, some characteristic, some not. As he set himself to creating the largest navy in the history of the world to date, he wrote to Vice-Admiral Decrès, his long-suffering minister of the navy, in the last weeks of 1811, that "I have 16 million trees in France, or 480,000,000 cubic feet (of wood), or 4,800 vessels. Thus, with one order, I can, between now and February, cut enough wood in my empire to build 4,800 ships . . . And if I wanted to use the same wood as employed by the Dutch in their building . . . I could have an infinite quantity . . . The overviews I have established are the results of observations made over many years . . ." So it went on, outlining which forests could be used best for each naval base. It bordered on the mathematics of the madhouse.[17] Attention was soon diverted to more pressing matters, and the magnificent forests of *la France profonde* flourish still. Nonetheless, there were other signs of a worrying mind at work. Legacy bore down ever more heavily on Napoleon. On the last day of November 1811, he wrote out of the blue to Berthier—still trying to hold things together in Madrid at this point: "As major-general of the Grande Armée, you must produce a history of all the events of the campaigns of Ulm, Austerlitz, Jena, Friedland, and those of Eckmühl and Wagram . . . You must set yourself to this without respite . . . it is your duty to do so without delay . . . and we will see if it can be published."[18] Suddenly, Napoleon wanted a full history of his greatest deeds in print, before he marched into Russia, the fact that Berthier was probably the most embattled man in his empire not withstanding. Whether this sprang from hubris or a deep, unspoken dread that his legacy was now the prisoner of history cannot be known. However, this was not the only uncharacteristic instance of Napoleon "racking over the past." One of his watchwords in life was that "what is done is done, move on." Yet, in the first days of January 1812, he ordered Cambacérès to reopen the inquiry into the catastrophic French defeat by the Spanish at Bailén in 1808. After pointing out many practical problems—among them that many crucial documents had been destroyed—Cambacérès turned Napoleon's own principles on him: "This system of retroactivity is not in the least among Your Majesty's principles, nor in those of a well organized society." Above all, such a procedure could tarnish the image of the army at this crucial time.[19] Napoleon finally conceded that it should be given to a commission to investigate,[20] another way, both men knew, of forgetting the whole idea. Cambacérès still knew his man, at least in this instance, but it is arguable that Napoleon no longer always knew himself.

On the last day of 1811, Napoleon penned a rare letter to Joseph, thanking him for his good wishes for the New Year, and concluding that "Under no circumstances will I withdraw any troops from Spain, and I will even send new ones."[21] As Napoleon's lies went, it was not a big one. He did withdraw troops from Spain as the buildup for the Russian war began: In the following weeks, close to twenty-five thousand men were pulled out, including many Polish units and all the troops of the Imperial Guard serving there.[22] Most of the guards were made up of the Young Guard, usually spread thinly over the many fronts in Spain, but all now bloodied veterans who had taken heavy losses throughout 1811. Some of them served with a distinction run through with ruthless determination at Astorga, where a Spanish rearguard was cut to pieces, of which Napoleon took note.[23] They were sorely missed, as were the Poles. Charles Esdaile has described the departure of a Polish division from Andalucía as a grievous blow for Soult, whose campaigns had been very successful up to 1812. Henceforth, however, "the French presence in the countryside dwindled away."[24] Dorsenne soon lost two full infantry divisions and most of his cavalry from the Army of the North, while Soult and Suchet lost about six thousand infantry each.[25] Seen in numerical terms, the initial troop withdrawals were damaging in terms of quality more than quantity. However, they came at a time when Wellington was receiving impressive numbers of reinforcements by sea and had forty-five thousand men fit for duty, supported by thirty-three thousand Portuguese regulars.[26] Nevertheless, Napoleon never left his brother with less than 260,000 French regulars in Spain throughout 1812[27] (there were 320,000 there at the start of the year).[28] As 1812 dawned, they had enough to do.

Napoleon continued to disparage the threat of the guerrillas. Even before he withdrew troops for Russia, he had weakened Dorsenne's forces in Aragon, Navarre, and the Basque country considerably to reinforce Suchet's assault on Valencia in 1811, taking his best troops in the process. Over these months, the guerrilla forces in the north, under Espoz y Mina, grew not just in numbers but in expertise; and were increasingly better armed and supplied, both from ruthless control of large swathes of the countryside and from increasing contacts with the Royal Navy.[29] Weakened French garrisons, now often staffed by raw recruits, soon felt the force of this new power in their midst. Mina defeated a French force at Rocaforte, near Sangüesa, on January 11, not by ambush but with a bayonet charge under which the raw recruits crumbled and six hundred were killed. A Spanish regular officer initially assumed Mina's men were deserting to the French when he witnessed this revelation. The American scholar John Lawrence Tone has underlined the importance of this seemingly minor engagement: "The battle of Rocaforte initiated a new phase in the guerrilla war . . . After Rocaforte, the French were the quarry rather than the hunters." Mina took no prisoners that day.[30] Henceforth, the French drew back from the countryside, while finding it ever harder to control the major towns and cities. Pamplona was now under siege by Mina; his men controlled the pass into France at Roncesvalles—the place where Roland had made his heroic, semi-mythical last stand against the Moors—and Mina's grip on the north enabled him to enforce his own brand of terror on the civilian population if they defied his demands for supplies or support. Suspect ears and noses were cut off galore; VIVA MINA was branded on recalcitrant foreheads, although as his grip became surer, fewer people were actually executed. His intelligence network had no rival among the French.[31]

Napoleon did not leave this unanswered. He recalled Reille from the western front, reorganized the northern command and poured fresh troops into the region, bringing about twenty-five thousand men under Reille's command, although most of them were new recruits, a sign that he still failed to appreciate the true threat of guerrilla forces. However, the local populace knew by now that "this wave of French pressure would recede and the guerrillas would remain."[32] So it proved. Even the fall of Valencia to Suchet failed to free up substantial troops to root out Mina.[33] One crack unit was sent into Navarre under General Jean Antoine Soulier, in early February—the "Infernals," proven bandit-fighters. They fared as badly as the raw levies at Rocaforte, and were defeated decisively at Sos del Rey Católico on February 5. Soulier told Suchet, ". . . I confess to you . . . in all honesty that the brigands of this kingdom merit the name of veteran soldiers. They can compete with the best of our armies, for the continuous battles and victories have made them lose their fear of us."[34]

As Charles Esdaile has noted, "the logical conclusion . . . was that the French armies in Spain could maintain a defensive posture" with the forces available, but were at full stretch. The proof of this was that Suchet could only take and hold Valencia by risking the loss of Aragon. Instead, Napoleon chose to resume the offensives in the west and south, leading Esdaile to conclude, not unreasonably, that Napoleon was becoming detached from reality.[35] When it came to Spain, it is tempting to rejoin that he never had a reality to become detached from. The need to withdraw troops for the coming war, combined with Napoleon's preoccupation with Suchet's advances in Valencia (which forced Marmont to divert troops there and away from the western front) had "destabilized the whole position of the French forces in Spain."[36] Marmont's depleted Army of the North was soon ordered to prepare for a new campaign. With Berthier also withdrawn, Napoleon made Joseph the nominal commander in Spain, with Marshal Jean-Baptiste Jourdan doing the real work. It amounted to letting the regional commanders go their own ways.

"At this moment, nemesis struck."[37] In early January, Wellington took the offensive and laid siege to Ciudad Rodrigo. He did so in dreadful winter weather and difficult terrain. One veteran remembered "terrible snow on the ground, and rain and sleet falling, with a high wind," and the army's supply train took ten days to cover as many miles. Five men died during the advance from "the inclemency of the weather and the badness of the roads."[38] Hardened by continuous fighting with the best French troops in Spain, and well drilled during the lulls, the Army of Portugal was now a formidable weapon. Wellington's men were well rested, with good billets to retire to. Combat duty was carefully rotated in the coming campaign. The long march to the front was followed by a day in combat, but then by two to three days rest back in their own quarters before resuming active service.[39] Although Wellington outran his supply train at times, the supplies were, in vast quantities, never too far behind. The British maritime logistical effort was staggering: Supplies flowed into Portuguese harbors not only from home but from North Africa, the Baltic (a sign of the breakdown of the blockade), and even from America. Some 800,000 barrels of flour reached Portugal from the United States in 1811, and the trade was not interrupted by the outbreak of war in 1812. Wellington's cavalry had more than doubled in the course of 1811, and over half of its horses' fodder arrived by sea.[40] Wellington's campaign of 1812 is a striking example of what Mollien meant when he concluded that "England made war the modern way; Napoleon in the old."[41] Wellington was about to prove that the days of the dynamic "war of movement"—that of living off the land to move quickly and travel light—which had powered the French armies for twenty years, were over. Nevertheless, getting these supplies to the army in the mountainous interior was far from easy, and local requisitioning was still necessary,[42] but however rugged, Wellington's lines of communication were not long. Above all, Wellington had learned from the mistakes of the previous year. He had been hampered by an inadequate siege train in his earlier assaults on fortified positions, and this had been rectified. When he attacked Ciudad Rodrigo, he had a better grasp of its defenses, and made his plans accordingly.

Knowing how thinly spread were the French, Wellington laid siege to Ciudad Rodrigo on January 8, 1812—the same day Suchet took Valencia—and promptly drove them out of their forward defenses. Within six days, Wellington had twenty-seven guns in place and began bombarding the walls to open breaches. Always looking over his shoulder for Marmont, he pressed the assault vigorously. On January 19, the infantry attacked the walls. They were met with heavy fire; the French booby-trapped the rubble as they fell back, and massed what guns they had in the breaches to sweep the advancing British infantry. Wellington had concentrated his assault on parts of the wall he thought were weakened in the previous siege, and gaps were created easily. However, the French fought tenaciously in the narrow spaces between the two breaches; one breach opened onto a sheer sixteen-foot drop the French had dug. It was to no avail, however, and the British stormed into the town, as the French regrouped in the main square and surrendered. They had inflicted eleven hundred casualties on the British, but the entire garrison was either killed or captured.[43] The whole siege train of the French Army of Portugal was now in Wellington's hands.[44]

Then all hell broke loose. Plentiful supplies and rotated combat service had done nothing to curb the savagery of the British troops in a captured town. One officer felt that the breakdown of discipline began even before the fighting was over: "Our troops, as soon as the breach was gained, more eager for plunder than their duty, broke and ran in defiance of their officers . . . and committed shameful excesses . . . (There was) not a soul that was not rifled, and the dead were scarcely cold when they were inhumanly stripped." The horrors had only begun, however. Another officer recorded:

> Scenes of the greatest outrage took place, and it was pitiable to see . . . the inhabitants half-naked in the streets . . . while their homes were undergoing the strictest scrutiny. Some of the soldiers turned to the wine and spirit houses, where, having drunk suffi- ciently, they again sallied out in quest of more plunder; others got so intoxicated that they lay helpless . . .[45]

Wellington was commendable for the swiftness with which he restored discipline, where it would not have occurred to a Napoleonic officer even to try. These scenes bore lurid witness to the truth that even "war waged the modern way" could not curb the ferocious atavism of the soldiery.

Guerrilla cavalry had been so effective in preventing French patrols from getting close enough to Ciudad Rodrigo that Marmont did not even know the siege had begun until January 14. He began to organize a counterattack, but soon saw that he had no hope of reinforcements. It was painfully clear to him that he was helpless, so dispersed was the Army of North. Marmont could only hope that Wellington did not strike into central Spain. Wellington, for his part, feared the Army of North would simply concentrate against him further east and perhaps push him out of Ciudad Rodrigo in a counterat- tack. Instead, he turned south against Badajoz. Marmont saw this coming, and wanted to move to its defense. Napoleon thwarted him: His plan was to retake Ciudad Rodrigo and push on to Lisbon, with Wellington distracted.[46] Although daring, Napoleon's plans were not outrageous[47] but they showed his habitual inability to grasp the difficulties of the terrain in western Spain or the harshness of the season. Behind this lay his inherent belief that a big, single engagement was the only way to win a campaign. In this case, it was to take Lisbon, and leave Wellington stranded. It all emerged in a letter Napoleon ordered Berthier to send Marmont on February 18. It began with complaints about Marmont's conduct that bore a worrying resemblance to those hurled at Masséna a year before:

> His Majesty is not pleased with the direction you have given the war: you have superiority over the enemy, and instead of taking the initiative, you wait to receive his. You complain about the tiredness of your troops. This is not the art of war . . . your army is strong and well enough organized not to fear the English . . . This advantage cannot be lost by waiting for the harvest . . . Once this resolution is taken, there is no going back on it, no "ifs ands or buts"; you must choose your ground below Salamanca and win or perish with the French army on the battlefield of your choosing . . . In so doing, you will be the master of the movements of the English army. If Wellington wants to advance on Badajoz, let him.

The time to strike was now, in winter, Napoleon concluded, but Marmont had to make Wellington believe he was waiting for "the first shoots" of spring to enter Portugal. And he was to do this without the troops from Asturias under Jean-Pierre-François Bonnet, who were needed to hold the north.[48] Marmont, like Masséna before him, dispatched an aide to Paris to try to apprise Napoleon of the dangerous realities of the situation, and the importance of holding Badajoz to protect Andalucía. Colonel Jardet was met with the same courteous capacity to listen as Napoleon had shown Caulaincourt and Cambacérès, but with the same result. Marmont recalled in his memoirs:

> It was something truly inexplicable. The emperor completely ignored the question . . . Many long conversations with the emperor had the air of convincing him, but they did not bring any change in the . . . orders that had been given.[49]

Marmont duly set about preparing to retake Ciudad Rodrigo and attempt to advance into Portugal. It was Jourdan who countermanded this, and ordered him to support the troops at Badajoz, for Joseph and he grasped the danger to Soult in Andalucía that Napoleon could not see. Napoleon agreed too late, Marmont's new orders reaching him only on March 27. When he did so, hoping to draw at least some of Wellington's forces away from Badajoz, it was in haste, without a supply train. He was too late. Badajoz fell on April 15.

Wellington did not have it easy, however. He began the siege on March 16, and it took him a month. Badajoz had been refortified heavily since the previous year, and the French were as ready for him as possible. Still, he had learned from his earlier mistakes. Wellington changed his main point of attack to the southeast, not on San Cristobal. He had a fine siege train, although heavy rain did not allow the guns to be in place to bombard the walls until March 30. The British took very heavy losses, as the French were able to fire directly into their trenches, and the real damage was done to them not by the artillery but by the British riflemen of the 95th, who picked off the French gunners with deadly accuracy. It was only then that the massive British siege train wreaked havoc on the French. On April 6, Wellington judged the breaches in the walls big enough to launch an infantry assault. This was probably premature, but he knew Soult was moving on him, and feared Marmont was doing the same. Charles Esdaile describes what followed as "a terrible affair."[50] As at Ciudad Rodrigo, the French had booby-trapped the rubble, mined parts of it, and dug a deep canal beyond the breach. Incendiaries of all kinds were hurled down on the British as they scrambled out of the ditch. It was all made worse because Wellington ordered a night assault—a rare occurrence in the Napoleonic Wars—which saw his men lost and tripping over each other; many drowned in the ditch, and five hundred were blown apart when the French detonated their mines. The attack ended at midnight when, unable to climb their ladders to the top of the walls, Wellington saw his men had had enough. After the loss of two thousand men, Wellington switched his attack to the San Vicente bastion, knowing the French had become thinly stretched there. It fell easily and, with the British inside the walls, the French were forced to surrender.

The horrors of Ciudad Rodrigo were repeated on the people of Badajoz. One British officer recorded with a chill:

> There was no safety for women even in churches, and any who inter-
> fered or offered resistance were sure to get shot. Every house repre-
> sented a scene of plunder, debauchery and bloodshed committed
> with wanton cruelty . . . and in many instances I saw the savages
> tear the rings from the ears of beautiful women . . . Men, women
> and children were shot . . . for no other reason than pastime . . .
> The infuriated soldiery resembled . . . a pack of hellhounds vomited
> up from the infernal regions for the extirpation of mankind . . .[51]

The temper of the army had darkened since Ciudad Rodrigo, where few people were actually killed. Its savagery had increased in proportion to the horrors of battle, it seemed. Badajoz had cost Wellington 4,670 casualties, of whom 3,713 died in the assault.[52] He was in no position to attack Soult, who had isolated himself by advancing into Estremadura, and soon pulled back. Instead—as Napoleon said he would—Wellington left a small holding force and swung back to protect Ciudad Rodrigo. In the meantime, a small British force under Hill had seized the strategic point of Puente de Almárez, which bridged the only good road between Madrid and the Portuguese border, cut-ting off Marmont from Soult.[53]

With Joseph "in command," and Napoleon now so distracted with the coming Russian campaign that he barely cast his eye over the reports from Spain,[54] the marshals showed some common sense. Marmont ceased any attempts to advance into Portugal, and when Joseph sent an emissary to him with orders to renew the offensive, Marmont simply had him run out of camp. He would choose when the time to fight again was right. Soult had already made clear his intentions to consolidate his "satrapy" in Andalucía when he withdrew from Estremadura; he simply refused to obey Joseph's orders, telling him that he did not wish to engage in any "adventurous movements" at present. Suchet did the same, tightening his grip on Valencia, but no more.

Dorsenne dug in, where he could, against Mina, parrying Joseph by claiming he was acting on Napoleon's orders, as did Suchet.[55] Left to themselves, they saw clearly that there was no purpose, and every danger, in trying to extend French control anywhere in Spain. What they did not grasp in full was just how much the tide had turned against them. The status quo would not be so easily maintained now, unlike in 1811, if it could be maintained at all.

This was the military position Napoleon found himself in as he prepared for war with Russia. Whereas Alexander has secured himself by careful diplomacy through the Treaty of Bucharest and cultivated his alliance with Bernadotte, thus releasing almost all his forces for the oncoming invasion, Napoleon was as embroiled in the Spanish quagmire as much as ever, faced with ever more formidable foes on almost every side. Napoleon's only attempt to secure his rear in Spain and the Mediterranean bordered on the ridiculous. In mid-April, he wrote to Castlereagh offering to restore the Braganza as rulers of Portugal—a territory he did not control, in any case—if Murat were recognized in Naples. Spain was to be ruled by the Cortes "under the existing dynasty." When Castlereagh replied that if he meant the Bourbons, talks could begin; if he meant Joseph, however, his proposals were inadmissible. Napoleon did not respond.[56] It may have been that Britain, still in the throes of economic crisis, might have been ready to consider peace, for Castlereagh was under pressure from the Opposition to seek exactly this.[57] It was an old Napoleonic ruse gone stale. Napoleon had often tried to play this game with the British on the eve of a major offensive, and it was all he could come up with now. It was not long before he was complaining to Caulaincourt that the ever-loyal Maret had "let slip" his chance to "square" the Swedes and the Ottomans.[58]

Napoleon had not defeated his enemies, nor even really contained them. In the course of the fighting in Spain in 1812, he revealed how little he had learned about campaigning in barren country where "the war of movement" was a liability, nor could he grasp the dangers posed by well-armed guerrillas, nor how they could mutate into proper, formidable soldiers. The bloody clashes of these months only underscored how hated in France the war Napoleon already had on his hands was. Mollien and Cambacérès repeatedly raised this in their attempts to caution him over Russia. Mollien argued that Spain was seen as "a wasteful, pointless drain on France," and people were not afraid to say so.[59] Napoleon did not disagree in principle. Since 1809, he had known Spain was proving intractable, and by 1812 was said to be "disgusted by the Spanish business."[60]

Unlike Alexander, he had no one to negotiate with even had he chosen to do so. The emergence of the Liverpool government after the assassination of Perceval in May, with Castlereagh as foreign secretary, confronted Napoleon with an implacable foe who, coming into office on the heels of Wellington's successes, was no more inclined to think of peace when winning than Napoleon. This was apparent by November, in the ease with which Castlereagh brushed aside criticism in the Commons of Wellington's withdrawal into Portugal.[61] For all its bitter internal divisions, a genuine national government had come into being in the Cortez of Cadiz. Protected from Soult by the British, its decrees and fractious debates were diffused across Spain via the Royal Navy. Whether obeyed or not, its authority was acknowledged by every element of the scattered, splintered resistance. Wellington's success won him such prestige with the Cortez, that he was soon the de facto commander in chief of the Spanish forces, and was formally named their Generalissimo later that year.[62] Napoleon knew no more how to extricate himself or his realm from Spain than how to avoid war with Alexander. The Spanish war and the preparations for one greater still went ahead, relentlessly.

"The Army of Twenty Nations"

Those preparations reached into the very bowels of *la France profonde*, into every village and family of Napoleon's sprawling empire, and engulfed the coffers and manpower of every ally, loyal or reluctant. The Grande Armée would, in the end, total just over 640,000 men[63] of whom 350,000 were "French," including those drawn from all the 130 departments of the Grand Empire. Something like 140,000 to 150,000 of them were new recruits. Conscription had been relatively light, if ruthlessly enforced, after 1809. In February 1811, Napoleon asked for only 40,000 recruits, but in December, he sought no less than 120,000.[64] The careful research of Alan Forrest has shown that perhaps over 80 percent of these men were actually conscripted, so well oiled had the Napoleonic system become.[65] Likewise, Isser Woloch has described 1811 as the annus mirabilis of Napoleonic conscription.[66] The new French conscripts accounted for less than a quarter of the army that invaded Russia, but the manner of their conscription showed the brutal reality of the Napoleonic state. The impact of these levies was traumatic for countless communities across western Europe. The tools of repression were nothing new, but now they were applied with a new intensity and ruthless precision.

Because levies had not been heavy when Napoleon was at war only in Spain, there had been little need for heavy-handed enforcement of conscription, save for habitually recalcitrant regions such as the mountainous departments of the Massif Central or those along the Spanish border, and local officialdom had become somewhat lax in granting exemptions. The state had noticed this and tightened up the administration of conscription since 1809, but this was largely procedural. Marriage was a common way to avoid conscription—only bachelors were mobilized automatically—but in 1811, new restrictions were introduced to curb the "marriages of convenience" that could pair young men with women in their seventies and eighties. All unions of men of conscription age with women over fifty were now carefully scrutinized before any exemption was granted.[67] More ruthless, still, from 1809, only married men with children were automatically exempted. All this led peasant communities to feel that their private lives had been invaded by the state.[68] In 1810, a year of peace and relative optimism, the number of marriages actually fell, whereas in the following years, it rose steadily, in response to the heavier levies: In Angoulême, in western France, for example, it rose by 5 percent in 1811, and 12.6 percent in 1812, reaching 19 percent the following year.[69] Whereas in the "real world," rising rates of marriage are seen by demographers and economists as a sign of stability and prosperity, in the perverse world of the Napoleonic war machine, the reverse was true. Naturally, police surveillance tightened in the search for successful draft dodgers. At times, it became Kafkaesque. In 1811, a soldier named Pierre Carrette, who had deserted from his unit some years earlier, died of a fever in his home town of Tourcoing in Flanders: when the notice of his death appeared, his father was hauled before the courts.[70]

In 1811, the regime turned to open repression the moment heavier quotas were imposed, to scotch serious rebellion before it began. "From then on," in the words of Alan Forrest, "the government set itself . . . to destroy the last cores of resistance. Indulgence gave way to blows," and the success was tangible.[71] The process was aided by the fact that the forces of order, the Gendarmerie above all, were already on high alert because of the subsistence crisis that had gripped France since 1810 and left many communities and individuals too exhausted to resist.[72] Napoleon ordered the dreaded "flying columns" into action in February 1811, in tandem with the first levy. Their success was stunning. The mobile forces of gendarmes and reservists achieved more than intimidation of the new recruits of 1811. There were about one hundred thousand men abroad before the levy of 1811, who had either escaped the call-up or deserted, but over the course of the year, more than 78,000 such men were rounded up: Where the arrival of the flying columns in a given area did not produce immediate results, villages were "garrisoned" by troops billeted on the families of draft dodgers and the wealthiest residents until they were produced.[73] This was the revival of some of the most ruthless practices of the late Directory and early Consulate. The regime had never liked resorting to it, and the Council of State only legalized it in 1807, and it was applied only to very violent, difficult areas. From 1811, however, it was in use all over France, and whenever a commune had more than one in eight of its conscripts absent, "the prefects imposed it implacably."[74] Wealthy landowners offered rewards to draft dodgers who turned themselves in, or to anyone who captured them, to avoid the presence of the flying columns; parents even sought to persuade their children to come out of hiding. These tactics risked shattering the carefully constructed *ralliement* of the early years among small communities where it had usually been fragile at the best of times. It was now a time of often desperate dearth. The policy of occupation and billeting deliberately set rich against poor to provoke people into denouncing their own. The reality was often more complex, and still more dangerous for civil peace: Local notables who turned over draft dodgers had to live with the enmities this produced, and could face reprisals.[75] Nevertheless, by February 1812, after a year of the government "harrying" its own country, only nine thousand draft dodgers remained in France.[76] It was a sign that the regime was as desperate in its own way as the peasantry.

The other great victory won by Napoleonic ruthlessness in 1811 was geographic. The flying columns managed to enforce the new levies and flush out generations of evaders in parts of France that were hitherto bastions of resistance. The most dramatic humblings of regional defiance were in the Massif Central. There were four thousand known draft dodgers in the mountainous department of the Corrèze in 1810, some dating back to 1806, and one tenth of whom had defied the call-up in 1810; in 1811, there were only eleven left. In the Lot, there were on average four hundred evaders a year until 1811, when only seven were reported. In the Tarn, the draft of 1807 lost 200 of its quota of 616; in 1811, there were only 31, most of whom were quickly caught.[77] The flying columns of 1811 had finally completed the internal "pacification" of France begun in 1800. They halted their work in February 1812, but conscription continued successfully thereafter. Although desertion rates from serving units remained high from 1811 onward, the "bumper crops of conscripts" from 1811 offset this.[78] The state now had the power to keep these communities permanently intimidated. Isser Woloch has seen this breakthrough as "the cumulative impact of bureaucratic pressure . . . An instinctive and by now traditional resistance to conscription was giving way to a grudging compliance."[79] Certainly, the sea change of 1811 would have been impossible without the decade of state-building that preceded it. However, resistance crumbled suddenly, and only after brutal coercion. The judgment of Alan Forrest catches the climate: "Submission . . . was not the fruit of patient politicization, but the result of a more repressive attitude on the part of the state . . . (I)t was neither patriotism nor respect for the Emperor that incited the conscripts to submit, but fear."[80] The scars of war were already burned into the common people of the empire before a single shot was fired. Some of these new conscripts went to Spain, mainly to the Army of North and Portugal,[81] and a few were integrated into the frontline corps of the Grande Armée, but the bulk were organized into a reserve of 165,000 men in Marshal Claude Perrin Victor's IX Corps.[82] There was scarce time to train them.[83]

There were two other components of the new Grande Armée of 1812: the hardened veterans of previous campaigns in the Imperial Guard and the regular units, and the troops of the allied and satellite states. The guard had been expanded to over 55,000; then there were the 200,000 veterans of the three corps of observation under Davout's overall command in northern Germany.[84] The effective fighting power of the guard in the field was over thirty-six thousand; the rest of its men formed support and logistical units, and part of Napoleon's personal retinue. It had become a self-contained army unto itself in the buildup to 1812, under the joint command of Marshals Adolphe-Édouard Mortier (infantry) and Bessières (cavalry). It had three infantry divisions: two of the Young Guard, and one of the Old Guard—*les grognards*—suitably given to Marshal François Joseph Lefebvre, the most grizzled of the Marshals. Attached to them was the elite Legion of the Duchy of Warsaw, with its own command structure, a clear indication of the high regard in which Napoleon held his Polish troops. There were also small contingents from the Dutch departments—formed from Louis's former guards that became the second Grenadier regiment of 2,100 infantry; its 740 horses were dispersed throughout the guard cavalry.[85] Although units of the Royal Guard of the Kingdom of Italy were incorporated into the Imperial Guard in 1812, they were composed almost entirely of French troops.[86] The First Division was under Henri François Delaborde, a baker's son from Dijon and a soldier in the royal army, who had known Napoleon since Toulon and held a general's commission longer than his emperor. The *grognards* of Lefebvre's Third Division were aging, if still formidable. Claude-Joseph Rouget commanded the Second Division, deemed the best in the whole army: This was the Young Guard, the hardened "Spaniards." Rouget was a "blue," a volunteer in 1793, from a bourgeois background, who had fought in every major campaign under the Republic and Napoleon. It was the clearest example of the resources Spain could offer Napoleon, in terms of fighting quality, but it numbered only sixteen thousand by foot and four thousand on horse.[87] When first withdrawn from Spain, one hundred were chosen as the King of Rome's bodyguard, but quickly seconded to "instruction battalions" at Fontainebleau, so valued was their hard-won experience.[88] They made a vital contribution to training the raw conscripts of 1811, who now entered the new nine "pupil" battalions formed by Bessières, eight thousand strong and carefully selected from orphanages in France and Holland, starting in 1810. Most of them were now used to garrison the Channel coast.[89] Even the reserve of the army now had its own reserve.

Beside the guard, no other unit of the Grande Armée matched Davout's I Corps, the line descended from the "fighting III," whose men had held the right so bravely at Austerlitz and defeated the Prussian army single-handed at Auerstadt. His divisional commanders were his own *grognards*—Charles Antoine Morand, Louis Friant, Charles-Étienne Gudin, Louis Jean Desaix—a roll call of heroes who were trusted implicitly by men who knew them well, were used to fighting together, and to strict discipline.[90] Now expanded to almost seventy thousand effectives—larger than the whole French force that fought at Austerlitz—it was the most important component of this vast army, all of them French, but even in the I Corps, the term "veteran" had become relative. About half of the I Corps were the conscripts of 1809, bloodied, but with only one or two campaigns behind them. Most of the veterans of earlier campaigns were now in the guard. They did relatively little training during 1810, but when the new recruits of 1811 arrived, Davout swung into action. Training began with real intensity and enthusiasm, and by the outbreak of war, they were well drilled.[91] I Corps remained "the model of administration and discipline"[92] that had emerged from the Channel camps. Napoleon obsessed about detail in the preparations for the Russian war, and Davout was, perhaps, the only one of his commanders to follow his lead properly: Their knapsacks were scientifically packed with ten kilos [c. 22 lbs] of rations, cartridges, and musket balls;[93] each regiment was as self-sufficient as possible, leading one observer to remark "his army was like a colony . . . He had anticipated their every want."[94] The most recent historian of I Corps catches its importance to Napoleon poignantly: "It was not by chance that I Corps was going to find itself part of all the important actions of this campaign."[95] Even so, Davout saw new problems. The huge battalions Napoleon had created, often of more than one thousand men, would be difficult to direct in combat; Davout wanted smaller, more flexible battalions,[96] although there was already a shortage of experienced officers in the army to lead them.[97] He was also worried by having to break up experienced units, to disseminate veterans throughout the large numbers of new recruits, so diluting the fighting capabilities of I Corps as a whole.[98] Even the very bastion of the army had its weak points.

They were supported by II Corps under Nicolas-Charles Oudinot, numbering thirty-seven thousand men drawn from the Observation Corps of the Elbe, and III Corps under Ney, numbering about thirty-eight thousand, a mixture of French troops and a division from Wurttemberg, under a French general, Jean Gabriel Marchand.[99] Ominously, David Chandler noted that "The number of men in these formations ranged . . . according to the Emperor's estimates of their commanders' capabilities."[100]

Oudinot was the son of a brewer from a small town in Lorraine, and carried more wounds than any other marshal. He ran away from home to join the old royal army, but was bought out by his father, who wanted him to be a bookkeeper. He joined the "blue volunteers" at the first opportunity in 1791. His unruly reputation notwithstanding, Oudinot was elected the captain of his local battalion in 1793. "How I loved those men," he recalled in later life—he lived to eighty-one, despite his wounds—"I loved them so much I got them all killed!"[101] Wounded by a saber cut to his throat in 1793, and hit by a bullet the following year, Oudinot rose to brigadier in 1797. He was known as "bullet head" to his comrades and troops, possibly as much for his wounds as his premature baldness. He fought in all Napoleon's major campaigns, save Spain, but Napoleon had a scathing opinion of him, if always tinted with affection. "A decent fellow, if hardly bright," was his verdict on Saint Helena.[102] Oudinot was a capable commander, but his normal role was to lead the Grenadier Division, an elite—but small and specialized—unit. Napoleon always kept him on a tight leash, as part of the reserve. However, he had emerged as a leader at Wagram, where his quick thinking and moral courage led him to disobey orders and seize the Wagram heights from well-entrenched Austrians, for the loss of an ear and his horse. Napoleon told him he deserved to be shot, but made him a marshal a few days later.[103]

Michel Ney was the son of an army veteran turned cooper from Alsace. Poorly educated, he joined the old royal army at nineteen. His red hair gave rise to the legend that he had Irish ancestry, and he played up to the part, gaining a reputation as being difficult, proud, and easily led, but fearless, as he rose up the ranks in the 1790s.[104] A general at thirty, he paid for his career with five wounds, one very serious, and a spell as a prisoner of the Austrians.[105] Known for his own irascible indiscipline, he imbued his VI Corps with it in the Channel camps and in the 1805 campaign.[106] While on mission to Switzerland, he made the acquaintance of the Swiss military theorist Antoine-Henri Jomini, but little in his future conduct was marked by his influence.[107] Ney had not served at Austerlitz or Jena-Auerstadt, and distinguished himself only at Friedland; his record in Spain was questionable, where he had proven himself headstrong and selfish. Napoleon said of Ney on Saint Helena, ". . . it was impossible for . . . Ney to be anything but brave"; he could improvise, react to sudden changes, but he lacked decisiveness when he had time to think.[108] Whatever else, Michel Ney was "an original." Much would pass between Napoleon and these men in the months and years ahead, but on Saint Helena, Las Cases felt his opinion of them had not changed from the day he put them in Davout's charge: "Oudinot, Murat, and Ney . . . common . . . who possessed nothing only personal bravery."[109]

Murat's cavalry benefited most in the years immediately before 1812. After the French gained control of the great stud farms of Prussia and Poland in 1807, it entered a true golden age.[110] It suffered terrible losses in the 1809 campaign, where the heavy cavalry was used repeatedly in murderous charges. Nevertheless, at the outset of the Russian campaign, Napoleon had fifty-four thousand French horsemen and twenty-one thousand from his allies, mainly the Poles. Some of its units were dispersed throughout the corps, but two divisions formed a reserve of forty thousand under Murat, comprised mainly of heavy cavalry, the big men on the big horses used as shock troops in combat.[111] Napoleon was able to muster eighty thousand well-trained horses for the cavalry and another thirty thousand for the artillery of the Grande Armée in 1812.[112] Nothing surpassed the magnificence of the mounted Grenadiers or the Chasseurs of the Guard,[113] and many frontline units were well mounted.[114] Napoleon had purchased 170,000 horses in France alone. Many were of good stock, but it took almost two years to train horses for the chaos and terror of combat, and time was lacking, particularly for the heavy cavalry.[115] The state of the horses mirrored that of the soldiery. In 1812, Napoleon devised a variant of his corps system for these divisions. Now, he attached a regiment of light cavalry to each division to act in the manner of his light infantry—skirmishing, scouting, and for pursuit after a victory.[116] Polish light cavalry formed a significant part of almost every unit in the Grande Armée.[117] Napoleon continued to wear the uniform of a colonel of the Chasseurs on many occasions.

There was nothing new about the use of non-French troops in Napoleon's armies. They had been present in sizeable numbers since 1807; the ranks decimated at Eylau were partly replenished by levies from the allied and satellite states amounting to just over 18 percent of the whole by Friedland.[118] The "foreign" troops amounted to almost 48 percent of the Grande Armée by 1812, a striking increase from the 28.32 percent used in 1809, and a far cry from the mere 15 percent—largely from the Kingdom of Italy—who served in 1805. Only six of the eleven corps into which Napoleon organized the Grande Armée were predominantly French.[119] They varied in quality from the eighty-three thousand Poles, who were the equal of the best French line troops and by far the largest foreign presence in the Grande Armée,[120] to troops from the smaller states of the Confederation of the Rhine, who were openly acknowledged to be fit for little more than escort duty or guarding the interior lines of communication. The states of the Confederation had a collective population of fourteen million, capable of supplying almost 120,000 troops,[121] but Napoleon knew they were of questionable quality. Indeed, Napoleon integrated only a small number of them into his frontline French corps explicitly on these grounds. He told Davout so in no uncertain terms: "You have for escort duties the troops of Mecklenburg and other German forces. You should therefore not give these duties to French troops, frittering them away."[122] Bavaria, Saxony, and West-phalia formed their own divisions; the rest of the troops of the Confederation were organized into "national" brigades of their respective states, and their battalions scattered about, usually serving with French battalions. They were almost all under French officers.[123] The Neapolitan army, so cherished by Murat, was butchered in Spain. Altogether, about nine thousand Neapolitans served in Spain during the Napoleonic Wars. Although the first levies sent to Spain in 1808 were mainly freed convicts and rejected by Napoleon as unfit for service,[124] and the "class of 1809" was little better—many of the criminals and amnestied bandits simply melted away into the lawless mountains of the Abruzzi when marched north in 1809.[125] However, those who eventu-ally fought in Spain often did so with great courage, led by excellent French officers carefully chosen by Murat.[126] Spain bled Naples dry. As soon as the Wagram campaign ended, in December 1809, twenty-one hundred conscripts were sent out; within a month, eight hundred of them were dead or wounded. Murat's request to withdraw his contingent was rebuffed by Napoleon. When the huge demands for the Russian war came a few months later, Murat balked: Napoleon sought ten thousand men of his brother-in-law. Murat pleaded he had only thirty thousand men in all, and four thousand were needed to guard the coasts against the British in Sicily (to say nothing of Spain). When the two men met face-to-face in May 1812, Napoleon seemed to relent, lowering the total from the 1812 levy to four thousand, plus those regular troops Murat had at his disposal.[127] The fifty-five hundred regular Neapolitan troops sent to Russia were also under French officers and integrated into the XI Corps under Charles-Pierre-Francois Augereau, which formed part of the reserve.[128]

In total contrast, the troops of the Duchy of Warsaw formed an inte-grated command under their own officers, and were mainly in V Corps under Prince Poniatowski, as were the sixteen thousand men of the four

Swiss regiments.[129] The twenty-two thousand Prussians of X Corps were under the overall command of Marshal Étienne Macdonald, but the officer corps was Prussian, and General Ludwig Yorke was their effective field commander.[130] The Austrians, although under overall French command, retained their own structures, and their thirty-four thousand men under Karl Philipp zu Schwarzenberg—Napoleon desperately wanted Archduke Charles in command but he refused[131]—were obliged only to serve as a protective shield.[132] The ten thousand Danish troops were detailed to guard the coasts against possible British incursions.[133] The troops longest under French command or longest allies to Napoleon, the Bavarians and Italians, were lumped together into the first auxiliary army, a force of almost forty-five thousand, a clear question of quality over numbers.[134] The Italian army made up half of IV Corps, and was largely under its own commanders by 1812,[135] but its headquarters was staffed mainly by the French.[136] Its problems were more basic, and starkly reveal how much Spain had truly cost Napoleon in his hour of need. The Italian army suffered a similar fate to that of the Kingdom of Naples, on a larger scale. The Kingdom of Italy had sent over twenty thousand men to Spain since 1808, where many units served with great distinction, particularly in Catalonia, under the discerning eye of Suchet. By 1811, only eighty-seven hundred of them were still on active service. Few of these veterans seem to have made their way into the almost twenty thousand men who went to Russia in 1812, and there were not even enough to train the new recruits properly.[137] The Bavarians, by contrast, had performed so appallingly—and least in Napoleon's eyes—in suppressing the Tyrolean revolt of 1809 that he seriously considered stripping his oldest ally of the province.[138] In 1812, they made up the bulk of the twenty-five thousand men of VI Corps, under General Gouvion de Saint-Cyr. Charles Esdaile has astutely pointed out that this reliance on German and other foreign contingents was a direct result of the large numbers of battle-hardened, first-rate French troops he was obliged to keep in Spain.[139] Napoleon's approach to the organization of the Grande Armée in 1812 indicates that he would have agreed.

The high command of the Grande Armée was indicative of its inherent problems. Napoleon chose to organize this unprecedentedly huge force into large blocks, its army groups dwarfing any formations seen before, and their component corps as large as the whole armies of the previous campaigns. Napoleon organized the Grande Armée into three lines of advance: The vanguard of the first line was the army group composed of the guard and I Corps; on its left flank was Eugène's army group, and Jérôme's on the right. Together, this amounted to about 440,000 men. The second line, of about 165,000 under Victor, formed a reserve, to provide replacements for the vanguard. The third line, under Augereau, was the ultimate reserve of about sixty thousand men and could be helped by ten thousand Danish troops.[140] Precise figures for the Grande Armée of 1812 are notoriously hard to pin down,[141] but there is no doubt that it dwarfed anything ever seen before. There is a sense of "shock and awe" driving this, in keeping with Napoleon's gargantuan plans for his palaces. Its tactical usefulness would be tested when the war began, but two things were immediately apparent: First, these large formations, operating over a vaster front than any Napoleon had encountered hitherto, needed commanders who were able to operate independently in the manner of the corps system that evolved in the Channel camps, but writ large. Second, Napoleon no longer had enough men of proven ability to lead such an army. In the course of 1805, a "team" of marshals imbued with these gifts emerged: Davout, Lannes (dead), Soult (kept in Spain), and Masséna (in disgrace) were the only marshals unquestionably in this class. Now, only Davout was left, and it was no coincidence that he was given the largest army, with the best troops.

While it was, in so far as possible, "business as usual" for the guard and the first army group under Napoleon and Davout, respectively, Napoleon went down a new, questionable road in his choice of army commanders. The second army comprised of IV and VI Corps was given to Eugène de Beauharnais, with Junot, and Gouvion de Saint-Cyr under him. This did not bode well for Eugène. He had conducted himself well enough in the defense of the Kingdom of Italy in 1805 and 1809, but he had Masséna at his side. Junot and Gouvion de Saint-Cyr were not of his calibre. Junot was an old comrade, but his mental health was always fragile and Napoleon had seldom given him commands of real importance; his roles at Austerlitz and Wagram had been subordinate, and he did not distinguish himself in independent command in Portugal, in 1808–09. Gouvion de Saint-Cyr had never been well regarded by Napoleon—he had been given the command of the Channel camps between 1806 and 1808, the high command's answer to "sweeping out the office"— and his stint as commander of the Army of Naples in 1808 was not crowned with success in Napoleon's opinion. Although he fought well in Catalonia, his "reward" in 1812 was the command of the Bavarians. Nevertheless, this was a large concentration of men for someone who was not yet a marshal. The third army group comprised V Corps (the Poles under Poniatowski), VII Corps (the Saxons), and VIII Corps (the Westphalians). Napoleon ensured that the Poles were left largely to themselves, and he placed Dominique Vandamme in charge of the Westphalians. Vandamme had supported Jérôme in previous campaigns effectively, and was very experienced, but he had never commanded at so high a level. Napoleon obviously felt it logical to put Jérôme at the head of "his own army," as he had with Eugène. With commendable self-awareness, Jérôme had asked Napoleon to give him command of only the Westphalian corps.[142] Instead, Napoleon chose to go further, and gave him high command of what amounted to the right wing of the Grande Armée.

The "dynastic presence" formed part of his "shock and awe" policy, but it was, in reality, a sign of weakness. Jérôme was the only one of his brothers with whom Napoleon was still on speaking terms, and those terms were usually little short of badgering and bullying. Some of the worst troops in the Grande Armée—over thirty-six thousand of them—were now in the hands of a man Napoleon had berated as recently as the previous November for "your lack of experience."[143] When taking Jérôme to task in December about the state of the Westphalian army, Napoleon harped: ". . . I have not ceased repeating to you from the day you ascended the throne: fewer troops, but well chosen troops,"[144] words he chose not to heed himself. Whereas Jérôme and Eugène were thrust into the front line of the invasion, the reserves were confided to reliable commanders, Victor and Augereau. At the apex stood the unchanged unified command structure of Napoleon and Berthier, both now ailing but confronted with the greatest challenge of their inseparable military careers. The logic, as well as the men, of 1805 had given way to political and diplomatic considerations at a time when the Grande Armée was entering uncharted territory in every conceivable sense.

The French scholar Jean-François Brun felt Napoleon's political agenda for creating an "army of twenty nations" for the Russian campaign had two reasons: The first was to intimidate Alexander by showing him that the whole of Europe now stood against him, to heighten the tsar's sense of isolation. The other was Napoleon's attempt to assert his own authority over reluctant "allies," particularly Prussia and Austria, almost in the manner of feudal over-lordship.[145] The inclusion of Murat, his brother-in-law and vassal, provided a moment of high family drama, more than an exercise in imperialism. The tensions between the royal couple and Napoleon had not eased in the months of feverish preparation for the war. In September, Caroline negotiated a theo-retical mending of fences when she persuaded Napoleon that Murat would accept command of the cavalry reserve, his habitual role in the great wars.[146] Even so, given the characters of the two men—Murat, emotional and volatile; Napoleon, implacable and increasingly suspicious of his family—nothing was certain until they met, face-to-face. Murat was in a state of depression after the failure of so many crossings of swords with Napoleon by the autumn of 1811.[147] He did not reach Napoleon in camp in Poland until May 1812. Murat reported back to Jean-Michel Agar, his childhood friend and comrade-in-arms, now his minister of finance:[148] "All our interviews have been of pure affection."[149] He was, quite literally, so glad to be back in the saddle that he forgot his long-standing grudge against Napoleon for making Caroline coruler, and that she now exercised full powers in Naples. Vincent Haegele, the chronicler of the Bonapartes, comments, "The moment was right for her to prove herself at the head of an administration of which she had patiently learned the ways and the snares."[150] She seized it with both hands, the last of Napoleon's family of vassals who truly had his confidence. Convinced of the need to keep the kingdom well defended during the Russian campaign, Napoleon ordered its French Army of Observation heavily reinforced. He told Clarke that "only the great energy of the Queen will get this armament and the defensive situation to work, so that the kingdom can impose itself on the enemy."[151] There could be no greater vote of confidence, and Caroline was the only Bonaparte now worthy of it. Her time had come.

There is considerable irony that, at the very moment when the Civil Code, with its uncompromising commitment to eradicate feudalism, was finally in force over so much of the continent, Napoleon chose to exert the truly feudal concept of lordship over his siblings and allies: The test of fealty and lordship was the right of a sovereign to demand knight service from his vassals. The new Grande Armée looked imposing in these terms, but its military value was compromised as a result. Gone was the homogeneity of the early campaigns, save in the guard and I Corps. That such units were detailed to lead the assault is indicative of this weakness, as much as their own particular excellence. As Alan Forrest has put it, with judicious restraint, "The largest army in modern history was not necessarily Napoleon's best."[152] He knew it himself.

There remained two very fundamental questions: Where was Napoleon's behemoth to go, exactly, and what was it meant to achieve when it got there? One thing remained as always: the campaign was to be swift, three weeks in all, and its aim was to bring Alexander to one large and decisive battle, to crush his army. "(There was) no doubt in his eyes that the schema of Austerlitz, Jena and Friedland was about to repeat itself," in the words of Marie-Pierre Rey, the most recent historian of the campaign.[153] This was to be done without advancing into the Russian heartland proper: Napoleon would drive toward Moscow, but with the objective of fighting the main Russian army under Barclay, near Vilnius, the capital of modern Lithuania. He was aware the Russians could well retreat eastward, as in 1807, but at the very worst, Napoleon was sure he could catch them somewhere around Smolensk, the gateway to "Holy Russia." He had no intention of marching further than this.

There were two possible routes to his objective, with the vast, impassable Pripet Marshes between them. The route to the south of them was the fertile countryside of Volhynia, but Napoleon chose the northern way, a barren plain interspersed with lakes and marshes. The decision was military and political, in equal measure. It led, first, through Lithuania and Courland, parts of the old Polish-Lithuanian Commonwealth, and likely to be welcoming. Above all, choosing the northern route would split the Russian armies, dividing the main force under Barclay, in the north, from Pyotr Bagration's army, which was just north of the Pripet Marshes; it would also cut most of both armies off from Saint Petersburg.[154] The northern route also gave Napoleon the possibility of swerving away from the Moscow road, turning on Saint Petersburg, instead.[155] However, the lack of clarity discerned by Alan Forrest emerges in the fundamentals of the plan.[156] The three armies of the advance guard—Macdonald and the Prussians to the north; Napoleon, Davout, and Murat's cavalry reserve in the middle; Eugène and Jérôme to the south—were stretched over a front 650 kilometers wide. Further south still were Swarzenberg's Austrians. Napoleon had never attempted such a sprawling advance. The precision of his earlier campaigns had depended on concentrating forces in one place, after careful, tight linear advances along well-defined routes, under experienced commanders. Even before the nature of the terrain or the dispositions of the Russians were taken into account, the three army groups had their unfamiliar work cut out for them. Napoleon had obsessed over detail to an almost worrying degree, as Mollien never ceased to point out to him. Now, it began to emerge that he had focused too much on the particular, and not on the fundamental problem he had set himself.

Nevertheless, the details were important. Napoleon could not be accused of thinking his army could live off the land in such barren country. This much he had absorbed from the experience of 1807, telling Eugène on the last day of 1811, "without adequate transportation, everything will be useless."[157] In May 1812, he told Davout, "The aim of all my moves will be to concentrate 400,000 men at a single point. We can hope for nothing from the countryside and accordingly must take everything with us."[158] These two observations encapsulated all the contradictions inherent in the enterprise. The army would need a huge baggage train to provide for itself, in a region where roads were numerous enough, but usually in very poor condition.[159] Napoleon sought a quick victory, as he always had, but knew he had to abandon the cardinal principle of the "war of movement." In his words to Davout, Napoleon pointed, almost inadvertently, to his other great difficulty: how to concentrate a huge number of troops, moving in different columns, in one place, over so wide a front, when moving slowly. He sought the result of the "war of movement," within the timescale of the "war of movement," but with a different kind of army, in terrain wholly inappropriate for complex coordination. Such maneuvers might have been possible had Napoleon decided to attack across the more fertile, less rugged country to the south of the Pripet Marshes, but he chose the northern route, hoping to meet friendly locals and to secure shorter, better protected lines of communication—and withdrawal—by sticking closer to the frontiers of the Duchy of Warsaw.

Accordingly, the Grande Armée went to war with a baggage train that would have made the eyes of even the commanders of the previous century water. Twenty-five thousand transport supply wagons and ammunition caissons advanced with it.[160] They were manned by twenty-six transport battalions, comprising almost six thousand officers and men.[161] The largest wagons—252 of them—were pulled by four-horse teams, capable of carrying 1,500 kilos [c. 3,000 lbs], which soon proved too heavy for the poor roads. There were large herds of cattle to provide fresh meat; draft oxen were also "earmarked" for the pot as the need for transport became reduced as the supplies were consumed.[162] The vast number of horses with the Grande Armée could only be provisioned with hay seized locally, and they would need a staggering nine hundred tons of it, daily, however deep in forbidding enemy territory.[163] To anticipate this, as much as the conditions for marching his men, he timed his invasion for the spring. Napoleon's personal train comprised no less than fifty-two carriages and wagons, for a staff of six hundred.[164] They carried 422 bottles of Chambertin—the imposing red Burgundy that was Napoleon's favorite wine—55 kilos [c. 340 lbs] of Gruyère cheese, nine sacks of coffee, and 36 kilos of chocolate.[165] All for three weeks. Napoleon, himself, remained frugal, but times had changed since 1805, when the stunning victory of Austerlitz was toasted at headquarters with captured Hungarian Tokaji, guzzled straight from the barrel.

Napoleon had confidence in his plans, whatever the doubts of so many around him, and his example coursed through the ranks of the guard. "The

Russians?" scoffed the *grognards* of Austerlitz and even Friedland, "we've beaten them, smashed them . . . The Tsar? Just some guy the Emperor outwitted at Tilsit. Now we're off to Russia where the Cossacks eat candles!"[166] Caulaincourt noted with apprehension the same bravado among the officer corps, and felt it fostered an atmosphere little short of delusional at General Headquarters— "The general sentiment was, one may say, patriotic; one would have blushed to show any other."[167] The Poles shared this attitude in full measure. "The Poles all want war very badly," noted one French infantryman.[168] The fighting spirit of the Poles, backed by their fearsome, proven reputation, seemed to spur the French from bottom to top. The triumphal welcome they gave Murat on taking up his command, and the very sight of their splendid cavalry, galvanized him. Roused from his torpor, Murat's spirits were again soaring: ". . . (e)veryone seems driven by the best of spirits, and ready to do whatever," he wrote to one of his ministers, "The Emperor's preparations are immense, his army is superb . . . and everything points to it not lasting long," to another.[169]

The verve of the Poles was all the more striking because no part of Napoleonic Europe, save eastern Prussia, felt the brunt of the preinvasion occupation more. The region was already the victim of a poor harvest in 1812. On top of this came 200,000 imperial troops bent on supplying themselves by any means they could. The Westphalians were the worst, "a new plague," who assumed that dubious mantle in local eyes from the dreaded Bavarians of 1807. Of its heavy cavalry, a Polish garrison commander complained, "It treated the local inhabitants in a way that the enemy could not . . . It was not just that (the people) saw no discipline . . . but that no authority was respected even by its commanders,"[170] which did not bode well for any pretentions Jérôme was rumored to have to assume a new Polish throne. The Poles found his demands for etiquette and "creature comforts" verging on the comical.[171] There were far more serious, draining demands on the Polish people, however. The refortification of the duchy, so dreaded by the tsar, came at a terrible price. The work at Modlin alone swallowed up ten thousand civilian laborers, as well as one thousand artisans, and by late 1811, disease spread through their squalid, makeshift camps. For all that, the progress was impressive. By spring 1812, the state's finances were imploding; Poniatowski, the minister of war, and his counterpart at finance, were at daggers drawn. The whole cost was unparalleled and Jérôme's pretensions provided much-needed comic relief in all this. For all that, most of the supplies demanded were proffered. The mass of the people bore it, and the elites did so with the underlying patriotism the French detected. Hopes were high that Russian Poland—mainly modern Lithuania and the western Ukraine—would be reunited with the duchy, and that a new Polish kingdom would emerge as their reward.[172] These hopes were bolstered by the presence of nineteen thousand Lithuanian volunteers in the ranks of the Grande Armée.[173]

The diversity of the Grande Armée seems to have been reflected in its morale, however. General Bro noted that as they advanced, troops from the Confederation states kept looking behind them, and some of their officers "complained bitterly that they had been dragged so far from their country to serve a cause that meant nothing to them."[174] Napoleon was not worried about the outcome, however much he fretted over the organization. It was a punitive expedition; each solider needed only twenty-one days' rations. Davout's decision to give his men twenty-four days' worth was just a sign of his innate caution.[175] Davout knew a forbidding foe awaited.

The Russians

The French regarded Russia as an innately primitive country, possessed of raw, brute strength, but barbaric and unable to harness its power. Napoleon did not quite share this prejudice. Eylau had taught him great respect for the Russian soldier, and a healthy dread of the Russian climate in winter. All his punctilious preparations spoke to this. His military intelligence—unlike that of his diplomats—was good, and he had a fair idea of where to find his enemy and how strong he was, numerically at least, but there was much about Russia, its ruler, and its people that escaped him.

The tables had been turned since the war of 1807, when Napoleon and Alexander last clashed. Napoleon knew how improved the Russian army was;

he found out the hard way at Eylau, but he did not realize that these improvements had continued apace, nor did he grasp the political forces driving them. Alexander now had three clear advantages over Napoleon: He had never really believed in the alliance, and so had prepared for war for far longer, in more coherent and consistent ways than Napoleon; Alexander braced himself for a defensive war, which gave his plans a clear focus. He had disentangled himself from his other wars, real—with the Ottomans—and potential—with Sweden. Napoleon was still being bled slowly by Spain. While Napoleon had to boost his numbers with heterogeneous, often substandard troops from all over Europe, Alexander possessed a homogenous, tightly knit professional army, its rank and file fighting on home ground. This gave the tsar his third, most intangible but greatest advantage. His political elite, usually so dangerous it could prove deadly for a male Romanov, stood united behind him, and exhorted his people to do likewise. Napoleon's regime was never loved by the mass of the people. French revolutionary regimes, his included, trumpeted patriotism because little of it actually existed. Napoleon and his men were about to learn about a different breed of patriotism they could scarcely credit to an ancien régime dominated by serfdom and the Church. Alexander held many other particular advantages over Napoleon—an endless supply of good horseflesh; a crude but efficient system of conscription based on the *mir* that tapped into his vast reserves of manpower; the fact that the Russian summer could be as deadly for armies as its winter. He did not have to look over his shoulder, at home or abroad.

The defensive war was conceived early as one of gradual retreat, to draw Napoleon further from his bases, stretch his supply lines to the breaking point, and deny him the great, decisive battle all knew he sought. The governor of Moscow reminded Alexander that his loyalist allies were "(Russia's) vastness, the immensity of its territories, and its climate," which would make Alexander the more formidable the farther east he withdrew.[176] The military command was less sanguine. Just how far the retreat should go was a moot point. Most of Alexander's generals—among them his best field commanders, Alexander Suvorov and Nikolay Rumiantsev—and the whole officer corps were imbued with a belief in offensive war. This was rooted in concepts of personal honor, as much as by purely military considerations. Even supporters of a staged withdrawal felt that to fall back as far as the Russian heartland was very different from luring Napoleon only as far as the interior of Lithuania. As Dominic Lieven has expressed it, "To retreat before the enemy was almost as shocking as failing to defend one's honor in a duel when challenged."[177] The ethos of the two warring officer corps differed little.

However, Barclay and others had been developing plans based on a controlled retreat from Lithuania since 1810, partly because the region was too barren to support a large army for long, partly because they feared the army would be trapped by a pro-Napoleonic uprising there. Such concerns had to be weighed against the hope they all shared: that Napoleon could be stopped on the western borderlands. Alexander feared a situation where Napoleon actually penetrated into the heart of Russia proper—that he might get beyond Smolensk—yet Barclay pointed out that this was where Napoleon might prove most vulnerable. Alexander rallied to this view in the face of "traditionalist" opposition and the intermittent influence of his Prussian aide-de-camp, Karl Ludwig von Phüll, who encouraged Alexander to quibble with Barclay over details.[178] Barclay had deeper currents of distrust running against him, and Alexander kept faith with him against them.

Barclay was a Baltic German, and his ethnicity did not help him convince his Russian colleagues of his defensive approach, for it was seen by many as the theoretical ponderings of a "German staff officer."[179] Moreover, he was a Lutheran, at a time when anti-French patriotism was increasingly associated with protecting the Orthodox faith from alien ideologies, which could include Barclay almost as easily as Bonaparte. He was always cold-shouldered at Court.[180] Barclay was the most prominent Baltic German in a high command full of resented "outsiders." In 1812, only 60 percent of Alexander's generals had Russian surnames; one in three were not Orthodox, whether Baltic Germans, German émigrés, or simply German relatives of the Romanovs. There was no coherent "Russian party" opposed to them, but that did not prevent an all-pervasive climate of loathing among Russian officers.[181] As soon as the strategy of retreat went into operation, Barclay, in particular, was the target of vilification from his own staff. Poems and songs against him abounded. He was a traitor, a coward. One poem, ironically in French, declared "Barclay avoids battles, hoping to hide out in Siberia."[182]

In 1808, Alexander appointed Aleksei Arakcheev his minister of war.[183] Arakcheev was born in the provinces, in 1769—the same year as Napoleon—the son of an impoverished nobleman, and arrived at military academy with only one pair of riding breeches he had to wash every night. His father could not raise the money to register him in the Artillery Cadet Corps, but its commander waived the fee and made him tutor to his sons.[184] He rose through sheer ability and the patronage of a powerful court faction. An artillery officer by training, he was made a colonel in 1796, four years after graduation,[185] the same year Napoleon took command of the Army of the Alps. A very reactionary figure, devoted to the concept of autocracy as the spirit of Russia's unique political culture, he detested the Lutheran, Germanic Barclay as much on principle as on policy.[186] Deeply Orthodox in religion, hostile to all foreign influence on Russian culture and society, he told Alexander bluntly at one point, "I thought I was serving the Tsar and my country, but in reality, I serve Barclay. I swear to you that this is impossible."[187] He continued to serve his tsar, nonetheless, as did Barclay. Napoleon was not the only ruler in Europe who could keep bitter rivals in harness.

All knew that the danger and the risks were enormous. The strategy of defensive retreat, of the kind of scorched-earth policy used by Wellington and Beresford in Estremadura and Portugal, but on a vaster scale, would test troops even as well-disciplined as the Russians, and could undermine civilian morale, points driven home by General Bagration, an ethnic Russian, "fiery and charismatic,"[188] deeply imbued with the fighting traditions of the army, who opposed the whole concept of retreat: This approach handed Napoleon the initiative, its main hope being to make him fight the kind of war he was not good at. Barclay and Alexander always understood all these risks, and debate was not stifled, but it was no coincidence that these discussions were kept a very tight secret, nor that the two years over which they took place were a time of wrangling and second thoughts for all concerned. The immense advantages Russia had over Napoleon could be easily turned against her. In the end, Alexander felt that the unprecedented size of the Grande Armée left him little alternative but to concentrate on a defensive strategy that could well entail retreat.[189]

Alexander let the debate swirl around him, deeply aware that he was no soldier. Like Napoleon, he disliked "yes men"; unlike the Napoleon of 1811–12, he listened. Ultimately, Alexander realized, as many of his commanders may not have grasped, that the Franco-Austrian alliance meant that any Russian advance into the Duchy of Warsaw might well unleash an Austrian offensive on the Russians to defend what was left of their Polish territories in Galicia, and attack him from the rear. Whatever Metternich's protestations, this was a real possibility if Russia became the aggressor, and it confirmed Alexander in his natural inclination to wait and defend.[190] He also drew on his knowledge of Napoleon, of how he fought, and the nature of his regime. As Dominic Lieven has put it, all this "made a strategy of sustained patience unlikely."[191] He had Napoleon's measure once again. Nevertheless, Alexander had much to do. Above all, he had to prepare his people, of every rank, for war, and a war that would not bring quick victories, but was predicated on immense sacrifice.

This was just as well, because as war drew near that spring, it was all too clear that Russia faced Napoleon's juggernaut alone. The alliance with Sweden was on paper, its real value being Sweden's renunciation of its designs on Finland, which freed up battle-hardened Russian troops.[192] Beyond that, Bernadotte took no active part in the war, nor could he be expected to. From Alexander's point of view, it was "benevolent neutrality."[193] Austria and Prussia had attempted to "cover" their participation in the invasion by assurances to Alexander that they were not willing participants. The Austrians assured him to "only act out of form, and gently." This may have made the Franco-Austrian treaty "null and void"[194]—and Metternich kept his lines open to London even after the conclusion of the French alliance[195]—but it did little to help Alexander. An Austrian corps still stood between him and any chance of sweeping around through easy terrain to take Napoleon behind his right flank. Likewise, over twenty thousand fine Prussian troops were moving on Riga.

The British had helped Alexander broker peace with the Ottomans, but their commitment would not stretch beyond this. Britain never really cared about the political map of eastern Europe, save when it impinged on the Mediterranean. She did not share Alexander's nightmare of the "greater Poland," or even the emergence of a militarily effective new satellite state in the East. It was all very far away. After 1809, British ministers were openly reluctant to think in terms of another coalition. The lesson of a succession of failed wars was, for many, that "the Continental Powers could only hope to prevail if they knew they were fighting in their own interest and to the utmost of their power."[196] Austria was a broken reed; Prussia elicited more sympathy and, at times, useful intelligence, to the point that the government tried to send her military supplies when there was hope of Berlin joining Alexander in an offensive war in early 1811, in the mistaken belief that the war party had prevailed in Berlin. Such hopes were soon disabused.[197] So were Alexander's attempts to coax monetary subsidies out of the British. "Pitt's gold" had been the bugbear of every French government since the outbreak of war in 1792, and Napoleon's was no different. More often than not, for Alexander and his Austrian and Prussian counterparts, it had proven a chimera and source of bitterness. Lack of British support had left Alexander livid with London in 1807.[198] Although Alexander had reneged on his own promises to help Austria in 1809,[199] he watched warily as the British first encouraged the war, and then reacted coolly to Vienna's requests for financial help. Even if Canning eventually conjured one million pounds through his own efforts, in dribs and drabs, no regular subsidy ever transpired.[200] At least this time the British were frank with Alexander. In May 1812, Richard Wellesley set out his arguments clearly in cabinet that it would be wrong to incite Russia to oppose Napoleon, as Russia would be "encouraged . . . to make demands of money and armies which we could not satisfy . . . it is certain we can give Russia no money, and it is probable that it will not be in our power to give her military assistance . . . Aid may perhaps be afforded . . . by supplies and stores."[201] Arms and supplies were forthcoming—101,000 rifles arrived from Britain,[202] 50,000 of which came before the outbreak of war[203]—but Wellesley was heeded. Alexander did not even ask for money.[204] Russia stood alone.

Alexander now showed a steely, unwavering side of himself that was the antithesis of his approach to statecraft, and quite possibly ran against his personal and political instincts. Mikhail Speransky had been a leading minister and adviser to the tsar since 1803, and by 1809, he had grown as close to Alexander as anyone could. An open advocate of reform—increasingly so after the threat of Napoleon grew starker after Wagram—Speransky, the son of a priest who had been taken up by one of the powerful court factions,[205] was loathed at court. His political beliefs were rooted in conservative enlightenment thinking about a state controlled by the rule of law, and he regarded Whig England as "the norm toward which . . . society is moving,"[206] but he was perceived by most of the nobility as "a Jacobin, a worshiper of Napoleon and a traitor."[207] He was also regarded as far too close to Alexander, and the tsar was too shrewd a politician not to see that he had to sacrifice his favorite to win the voluntary support of the nobility at court and in the provinces for the struggle ahead.[208] On March 29, 1812, he summoned Speransky to a two-hour private meeting—a direct confrontation of the kind he loathed. In a shocking, cynical exercise in realpolitik, Speransky was accused of treason in a dossier fabricated by Alexander Balashov, the minister of police. Speransky was really only guilty of imprudence verging on ingratitude. In intercepted correspondence, he had denigrated Alexander for his prevarications and, in disrespectful terms, even his competence to govern. He had also withheld diplomatic correspondence meant for the tsar only. This was spun into treason. Alexander flew into hysterics and threatened to have Speransky shot. This may have been "the performance of the brilliant actor letting off steam"[209] or that of a friend and benefactor "deeply upset by this treachery (if not political, then at least moral),"[210] so unknowable was the man. Whichever, it led to Speransky's arrest, the sequestration of his property—something an autocrat like Alexander could do, but which was beyond Napoleon's powers—and he was exiled that night from the capital. The charges should have led to his prosecution, but Alexander left it at this. He was deeply uneasy about his actions and confided to his close friend and fellow Freemason,[211] Alexander Golitsyn, "If someone cuts off your arm, no doubt you should shout and cry in pain; last night I was deprived of Speransky and he was my right arm . . . You will examine (his) papers but you will find nothing; he was not a traitor." He soon tried to justify himself to another old friend, Nicolai Novosiltsev, a member of what he liked to call "my own Committee of Public Safety":[212] "He is really guilty only toward me alone, guilty of having paid back my confidence and my friendship with the blackest and most abominable ingratitude."[213] The sentiments, indeed the very words, could be Napoleon's in these same, wearing times, but Alexander kept them private; Napoleon hurled them across council chambers.

Speransky's fall was but one small action in a greater "culture war" Alexander now unleashed. Propaganda, not just political, but cultural and religious, rained down on Russians of all classes. Napoleon was, literally, demonized, as was the French national character and their Godless culture. Alexander had deployed such terms in 1805 and 1807, dampening them after Tilsit, but in 1811 and 1812, he portrayed the coming war as one of "liberation." The term is deeply significant on several levels: Implicit in it was the admission that this would be a defensive war; that Russia would suffer invasion and occupation; that Napoleon would have to be pushed back, and that sacrifice and suffering were inevitable. The import was wider and deeper than a call to arms during a humiliating retreat. As the Russian scholar Liubov Melnikova has put it, 1812 was a crusade, driven by "the idea that Providence itself was calling on Russia to stop the atrocities of the godless Napoleon, and to free Europe from his grip."[214] This left many among the upper classes adrift, not in their hatred of Napoleon, per se, or in their patriotic commitment to the war effort, but culturally. An elite whose first language was more often French than Russian, whose very domestic habits—to say nothing of cultural tastes—was now forced to learn Russian from their servants, to change their dress code and "de-refine" their cuisine. It was far less difficult to reach the masses. Alexander had the unwavering, wholly enthusiastic support the Orthodox Church, of which he was the official leader. Sermons spoke openly of Napoleon as the

Antichrist sent to punish Russia for her sins, for falling into Western ways, and there is evidence that they made a powerful impact on the populace. The Bishop of Smolensk issued an appeal that was prophetic. He urged the people of the region not only to abhor fear or flight, but:

> . . . (of) how much their duty and the Christian faith demand that they band together, try to arm themselves as best they can, give the enemy no quarter, pursue him wherever he is, and instead of fearing him, cause him great injury and terror.[215]

Such calls to arms came from every pulpit in the vastness of Russia. When the moment came on July 6, 1812, Alexander called directly to his people: "Unite, one and all: with the Cross in your heart and a weapon in your hand no earthly force can defeat you!"[216] If any aspect of the Napoleonic Wars bore a resemblance to the "total wars" of the future, it is here.[217]

Appeals to popular sentiment were one thing, those to arms were quite another in many eyes. Serf rebellion was not a specter in Russia, but a recurrent and widespread reality, particularly should Napoleon announce emancipation by instituting the Civil Code, as he had elsewhere. This was a very real prospect in Lithuania and modern Belarus, but the fear of revolt in the Russian heartland caused the greatest unease. This same promise from pretenders to the imperial throne had provoked huge revolts in the past. The tsarina herself admitted that "although I am convinced that our people would not accept the gift of freedom from such a monster, it is impossible not to worry."[218] The dilemmas of weighing official sanction for popular resistance—particularly when faced with the strategic need to disrupt Napoleon's internal lines—against its consequences for the established order inevitably troubled the high command and the court. When Alexander decreed the creation of a national militia, these apprehensions are all there in the details. The state-owned serfs of the Russian heartland were excluded from it—they became the fresh conscripts of the regular army—and only privately owned serfs were eligible; the noble landlord decided which of his peasants could be enlisted. They were under officers of the regular army.[219] This was the cautious reality behind the brave words of Alexander's rousing proclamation:

> We now appeal to all our loyal subjects, to all estates and conditions both spiritual and temporal, to rise up with us in a united and universal stand against the enemy's schemes and endeavors.[220]

Nonetheless, however carefully he had to tread over the ever-hot embers of serf revolt, Alexander would soon find he had two precious advantages in rallying popular support. The defensive war was a real and present danger; no one could accuse him of reckless adventurism, of a "vanity project" at the ends of the earth. Even more, Alexander drew from the deep well of a shared history and culture that cut across class. He spoke the language of his people, and he knew how to reach them, through the Church and the faith they all shared. Napoleon could only dream of such devotion beyond his guard.

Stirring "holy war" did little to change the ideological or cultural predilections of a Freemason, educated by a philosophe, whose preferred language was French, and who was known to be open to the reform of serfdom and the modernization of the state, so much so that he had accepted Speransky's project for a Council of State and many of his ideas for the governance of Finland as recently as 1811, in the face of outspoken opposition from his trusted advisers.[221] Yet, 1812 may have seen the beginning of a sea change in Alexander. Charting the inner life of such a man is all but impossible, but Marie-Pierre Rey, in her astute biography of the tsar, believes that Alexander "had completely internalized his combat against Napoleon." This only became obvious when the war was over, when he emerged as a genuine believer in the faith he officially led.[222] If he evoked Orthodox mysticism in 1811 with "the usual pragmatism," the struggle of 1812 proved transforming for the tsar.

For all the patriotic fervor, no Russian serf volunteered, any more than would a French peasant. When it came to raising and commanding his armies, Alexander emerges as a true feudal overlord. Unlike Napoleon, he could demand military service from the people of Great Russia, for they were, in law, all his serfs, from the most powerful court noble to the most miserable peasant *mir*. As the French threat loomed ever larger, he did so. Alexander mirrored Napoleon exactly, as he increased his conscription quotas heavily throughout 1811 and 1812. By 1812, over a million men had been conscripted to fight not only the French, but the Ottomans, and by 1811, losses in the Turkish war that had to be made up were in the order of 20 percent, to say nothing of the need to swell the ranks further.

As in France, mass conscription did not equate with war-readiness. Barclay saw only regiments composed of raw recruits, "unused to the trials of life on campaign," where once were "strong and valiant troops."[223] All Barclay could do was raise still more such raw recruits, and he did so: 285,000 more men were put under arms between 1810 and 1812. Barclay was clear in his own mind that the standing army had to be doubled to meet the French threat.[224] However, he knew, as did Napoleon, that the new recruits conscripted to fill this void were fit only for a strategic reserve until properly trained. Many of them had to be hurled into battle in 1812 but a considerable proportion of them were able to remain in barracks for proper training. Even though replacements often arrived late to the front line, arrive they did, and units were usually able to remain at proper strength. This reserve was not exhausted in the campaign, and by its end was still supplying replacements—ever better prepared—well into 1813. At the end of the 1812 campaign, the Russians were able to bring their ranks back up to full strength with well-trained men, in a way Napoleon could not.[225]

The Turkish wars were Alexander's equivalent to Napoleon's "Spanish ulcer," but on a greater scale. The Ottoman army remained particularly formidable in siege warfare. At Rushchuk, in 1810, the premature storming of its fortress cost the Russians eight thousand casualties from a force of twenty thousand.[226] This level of casualties made Alexander's decision—and ability—to cut his losses and make peace all the more important. Nevertheless, the forty-eight thousand to forty-five thousand troops freed up by this under Alexander Tormasov (a seasoned soldier and the most senior field commander,[227] if "something of a martinet"[228]) were battered more than battle-hardened. In August 1810, Barclay—minister of war since March as Ara-kcheev moved into Alexander's inner circle—wrote of their general state: "This prolonged war blunts the heroic, hereditary virtues in them, and the national spirit, like any physical force, begins to weaken under the burden of a hard and cruel war." Poor infrastructure meant that this army would not reach the main theatre quickly. This, combined with its debilitated state, meant that it formed a separate "Army of Observation"—the III—based south of the Pripet Marshes, well to the south of the heart of the fighting. It remained the weak point of the Russian forces.[229] The III Army was virtually cut off from the rest of the front, and its main role was to try to outflank the French as they advanced.[230]

To the north, where it was clear Napoleon would strike, Barclay himself took command of I Army, centered on Vilnius, guarding the approaches to both Moscow and Saint Petersburg. By far the strongest Russian force, it numbered about 136,000. The elite guards regiments of all arms—infantry, cavalry, and artillery—were mainly with I Army. In general, like their opponents under Napoleon and Davout, these troops and their horses were in excellent condition, well fed, well quartered, and well trained. Indeed, Dominic Lieven has argued that, at the outbreak of hostilities, I Army was more battle-ready than even the best of Napoleon's units, which had been exhausted by their long marches to the front, and poorly quartered in East Prussia and Poland, where food was becoming scarce.[231] To the south was II Army, under Bagration, positioned just to the north of the Pripet Marshes, whose fifty-seven thousand men bestrode the road to Minsk. Bagration and Tormasov commanded forces little bigger than French divisions—or Russian corps, for that matter—and overall, Alexander's combat-ready forces were sorely outnumbered by those of the Grande Armée. Although possessed of considerable reserves and excellent light cavalry in the Cossacks—who were of little use in set-piece battles—Alexander's three armies together prob-ably numbered just over 240,000.[232] The fighting quality of the Russian soldier—the grim determination of its infantry, the skilled horsemanship of its cavalry—was never in doubt, as the French had learned the hard way at Eylau, when they faced them in well dug in positions. Barclay was always clear in his own mind about their superiority in hand-to-hand combat.[233] Nor did their numerical inferiority deter the high command. Suvorov, the hero of so many wars against the Turks under Catherine the Great and against the French in the 1790s, asserted from experience, "Beat the enemy not with numbers, but by knowing him."[234]

Neither Barclay, nor Arakcheev before him, were complacent, and the gathering storm found the Russian military establishment in the midst of intense reforms. Not only did the horde of raw recruits need to be trained, the veterans needed to learn the lessons Napoleon had taught them so often, and this reached from the battalion to the high command. The process began in January 1808, with Arakcheev's appointment as minister of war, made against the preponderance of opinion at court—"only *both* empresses, Count Lieven . . . all the imperial aides-de-camp, the Tolstoys, in a word, everyone who had weight here" objected, observed the Savoyard émigré Joseph de Maistre.[235] Alexander stood by him with the same quiet resolve with which he had brought down Speransky. Frugal, abstemious, at work by four in the morning, he cut an unwelcome, almost belligerent figure at court, a walking riposte to the elegance of the Hermitage and the sparkling world of the salons that swirled around it. Resentments cut across the Russo-German ethnic divide. Dominic Lieven may well be right when he speculates that Alexander exercised the subtle diplomatic skills that were his forte, by moving Arakcheev "upstairs" to his inner council in 1810, to put a buffer between a man with a chip on his shoulder, given to vendetta and petty cruelties, and the field commanders.[236] Arakcheev's vindictiveness distinguishes him from Napoleon. Even so, there were so many echoes of Napoleon in the threadbare noble's son from the forested northern province of Novgorod as to make him an almost eerie nemesis created to shadow Napoleon, to become the specter of his past, dynamic self, as his powers waned. Arakcheev might have been fashioned by Goethe as a dread warning to Napoleon.

Arakcheev may have been committed to the principles of Autocracy and Orthodoxy, but it did not blind him to the need for drastic, practical reforms of the kind certain to ruffle the established order. The first was his demand, as the price for his services, for complete control over the army, and the emasculation of the office of the Tsar's Chancellery, which ousted the powerful Lieven family. "Fascinated by mathematics and technology, his mind was entirely practical. In modern jargon, he was a problem-solver and an enforcer," in the words of Dominic Lieven.[237] "Geek," an equally modern term, would also do. Even his enemies respected his work as Inspector General of Artillery from 1803 onward; his outstanding success was based on careful analysis of Napoleon's own reforms, and of the French victories of 1805–07. Napoleon felt the full force of his work at Eylau, in 1807, where the interspersing of artillery in the infantry lines, manned by well-disciplined gunners, had wrought carnage on the French. In the intervening years, Arakcheev continued to hone "his" arm into a fearsome weapon. He began with the guard artillery, instituting rigorous exams for artillery officers and professional training, then rotating them with units from the line regiments, using the guard as a laboratory, and making it the "gold standard" for the rest of the artillery. By 1812, his efforts had made the Russian artillery "a redoubtable part of the Tsar's forces," numbering forty-four heavy, fifty-eight light, and twenty-two horse batteries.[238] On the eve of 1812, the Prussian military reformer Gneisenau told Alexander that "the Russian artillery is in wonderful condition."[239] Right down to the parade ground, Arakcheev shared the passions of the man he devoted his life to destroying.

Arakcheev also shared the attitude to authority and organization of the man he saw as the Antichrist. All communications from generals to the tsar now passed through him; regulations were to be obeyed to the letter; misconduct by any junior officer was to come to his desk. The supply and equipping of the army was tightened up and corruption and sloth were dealt with severely. By 1810, empty arsenals were full, with 162,000 muskets in reserve; proper budgets had replaced ad hoc cash payments to suppliers. New and better muskets were manufactured and issued, Arakcheev having seen how superior French firepower had proven itself, although Russian industry was still incapable of mass production of such advanced firearms. Nor was Russia's textile industry capable of turning out good uniforms in the vast quantities needed. These were things beyond Arakcheev's control, but he made one fundamental change to the training of new recruits, which crucially began in 1808, before the mass levies of 1811: Russian conscripts had always been sent straight to their units, but henceforth, they received nine months' training in the new Reserve Recruit Depots, where disoriented peasants had time to adapt to military discipline and routine, develop skills in weaponry, and be free of regimental duties while they did so.[240] Arakcheev invigorated the army inspectorate, and took steps to soften the harsh discipline that pervaded the army:

> The usages of the army are well known: all the science, discipline and military order are founded on cruel corporal punishment; there are even cases when officers treat their men inhumanely, admitting neither their feelings, nor their reason . . .

Arakcheev declared openly that such brave, loyal, dutiful men deserved better. He pressed for better quality rations and better barracks, and above all, that better means be found to keep discipline than cruelty.[241] Again, the words and sentiments could be Napoleon's. Even more, they could be those of Marshal Pétain in 1917. Just as the legacy of the Channel Camps began to fade in the Grande Armée, Arakcheev replanted it in very foreign soil, and a new, equally great army was forged. The depot system was disrupted during the war crisis of 1812, but at the moment hostilities began, many relatively new Russian troops were better trained than their French counterparts, save those who had learned in the "school of hard knocks" that was Spain.

Barclay's bitter rival left him a good legacy when he took over in 1810, but there was still much to do, and Barclay set about it with an energy equal to his predecessor's. He was no courtier, any more than Arakcheev—"awkward, wooden and insecure," if respectful. Carping always dogged him in these quarters but, again, Alexander firmly stood by his man, at least for the moment.[242] Like Arakcheev, Barclay also turned to lessons learned from Napoleon, particularly in the basics of battle tactics. The depot system he inherited did much to help him. There was a long, often heated debate in the Russian officer corps about the relative effectiveness of the bayonet charge and musket fire, which

endured until the First World War. "The bayonet party" had the immeasur-
able support of the great Suvorov, whose firm view that "the (musket) ball is
mad; the bayonet knows what it's doing" carried most officers with it, to the
point that marksmanship was almost criminally neglected in favor of mass
charges, with the ghastly casualties they entailed. Barclay steered a middle
course between the two factions, but with time against him, he concentrated
his efforts on the weakest points in his men's expertise, and that meant intense
target practice. In 1812, he made clear that "Target practice must become
the principal occupation of the soldier . . . this art can only be acquired by
continuous emulation," and recommended they practice in groups of about
ten, to lessen the likelihood of boredom and drowsiness. Like Arakcheev with
the artillery, Barclay began this process with the guard and spread it to the
depots.[243] He had studied French battlefield tactics closely, and adopted much
of the essence, but never slavishly. The use of columns for an army used to
the bayonet charge (so beloved of the French revolutionaries, ironically) was
retained, but integrated with the infantry to support the column; the better
maneuverability given it by Arakcheev also made it possible to support the
dispersed line more easily. Mobility in the field was a guiding principle, and
Barclay fundamentally reorganized the infantry to this end. As rooted in
the light infantry as Arakcheev was in the artillery, he changed the balance
of the army, increasing the light infantry considerably at the expense of the
line regiments: In 1810, fourteen regular line regiments were transformed into
light infantry, and twenty-two new light regiments were raised between 1810
and 1812. They were easier to train, as the crisis mounted and time ran short.
The adoption of the dispersed line formation also made maneuvering in the
field much easier and clearer. To this end, the proportion of line regiments
to light infantry was established at two-to-one, a much larger proportion of
light troops than Napoleon used. The expansion of the light infantry was
one of the few things Barclay and Bagration agreed on, both having begun
their careers in this arm, but this seminal change did not go unopposed. The
light infantryman needed skill and initiative, qualities many senior officers
felt the Russian peasant lacked. At the other extreme, the Prussian Gneisenau

felt their training under Barclay was too rigid, formulaic, and overcomplicated.[244] If Barclay sought quantity from his light infantry, he demanded higher quality among the grenadier units, which were reduced in number to about 25 percent of all infantry. By 1810, all infantry regiments were composed of three battalions and, as in the Grande Armée, the battalion became the basis of most battlefield tactics. Unlike Napoleon's reorganization, although regiments became bigger, battalions did not.[245] His organization of the cavalry was less successful. Although blessed with some of the finest horsemen and light cavalry in the world in the Cossacks, the heavy cavalry was no match for the French at the outset of the campaign. The Russian cavalry was a heterogeneous mix of genres, and its effectives were scattered about the corps and divisions; no large reserve existed comparable to Murat's. The closest Barclay came to this was the arrival en masse of twenty-six regiments of the Don Cossacks, which simply could not be integrated.[246] They found themselves cut off from the main army once fighting began, and had to serve with Bagration's II Army most of the time.[247]

As a senior field commander, however, Barclay had different preoccupations to Arakcheev's. Barclay diverged considerably from many of the reforms of the army undertaken since 1805, and even more from the path Napoleon took for the 1812 campaign. He seems almost to have heard Davout's complaints about the unwieldy size of the new, large battalions Napoleon had foisted on him, and read the problems inherent in the huge corps and army groups facing him, even before they manifested themselves. The division as a unit had not been a success in 1805 or 1807, because it attempted to ape the comprehensiveness of the Napoleonic Corps by bringing together diverse arms of infantry, cavalry, and artillery, but in too chaotic a fashion for it to work on campaign, or for the relative strengths of each division to be known accurately. Barclay brought some order to this, but the real problem was the lack of any real tactical entity above the division. Barclay created corps to try to correct this. In 1810, he had organized six corps on the western front, composed of two or three divisions each; in 1812, the corps were grouped into the three armies that faced Napoleon—Barclay's, Bagration's, and Tormasov's—although they remained vastly uneven in size. For all that, Barclay and Arakcheev had forged a much better organized, manageable military force by 1812 than any previous Russian army. Its units were more suited to adopting the new lessons of the Napoleonic Wars than in the past. Compared to the Grande Armée, the Russian battalions were better balanced, smaller, and more adaptable to changing circumstances. Napoleon had allowed his to become too unwieldy; their composition now lacked uniformity. Napoleon's infantry was now less easy to direct in combat than the Russians'. Russian corps—if not the army groups above them—were also more uniform; Napoleon's were not only too big, but comprised large non-French units with their own structures. Homogeneity, the key to so many Napoleonic victories, was now Alexander's preserve.[248]

The real problem for Alexander was his high command. It was dogged by the snobbery and vindictiveness directed toward Barclay and Arakcheev, by the powerful influence of court factionalism on appointments and personal relationships, and by other, long-simmering animosities among the generals acquired since the difficult campaigns of 1805 and 1807. Then there was Alexander's truly feudal relationship with his commanders: Alexander knew his limitations. Although a thoughtful strategist, he was not a field commander, delegating this to his generals, but when he was present, at least de jure, his writ overrode theirs, and it caused awkwardness. This was particularly the case when difficult and potentially unpopular decisions had to be made, and there was none more so than the staged retreat of 1812. He disguised his influence well, most of the time, but the idea of a unified command remained anathema to Alexander—he had been brought to the throne in a bloody military coup—and so he preferred to play his generals against each other. His tact and opacity—so useful so often—had its problems, none more so than in the spring and summer of 1812. Alexander effected real *ralliement*, of that there is no doubt, but he did not match Napoleon in forging *amalgame*.

Given the rancor among the commanders, fostering rivalries was potentially a dangerous, if easy, game to play. Alexander made this worse when he recalled a number of older generals, who had often been retired in disgrace following the defeats of 1805 and 1807, and who carried the baggage of perceived injustices. As the scions of old aristocratic families, they had a propensity to criticize Alexander openly.[249] The accumulated venom of past failures was not confined to the Russians. Levin August von Bennigsen—"able but selfish"[250]—returned to active duty from disgrace in 1812, feeling he had been made a scapegoat for Eylau and Friedland, where he had been in command.[251] In such circumstances, the lack of a centralized high command may have been as well, although Alexander's insistence that Barclay's and Bagration's chiefs of staff write directly to him, as well as to their own commanders, was a cause of confusion and delay. In the early part of the campaign, the three army groups had to operate independently of each other, which eased matters, but this was hardly by design. Indeed, it has been suggested that the relative stability and coherence of the command of Tormasov's III Army was because the key staff officers were drawn from the same client-patron network.[252]

Great as they were, these faults were not insurmountable, but in the fraught spring of 1812, this was far from certain. The Russian generals were beset by personal rivalries and rancor of all kinds, but they were all eager to fight. At the very top, Barclay was four years older than Berthier, but at the height of his powers, not burdened by gout. That Bagration, Arakcheev, and Napoleon were all exactly the same age exposes starkly that Napoleon was old before his time by 1812. More rested on his shoulders than Alexander's in this war, and those shoulders were now sagging.

The Last Imperial Triumph

Napoleon had always held an imperial Roman triumph after a campaign. Now, he chose to do so beforehand. He let his prey know he was coming in spectacular fashion. With Marie-Louise at his side, and a swollen entourage of three hundred carriages and wagons in tow, Napoleon traversed the lands of his German allies in the manner of a feudal overlord "visiting" the manors of his great retainers. The German princes had already witnessed—and endured— the passage of hundreds of thousands of imperial troops across the lands of the Old Reich. Finally, they beheld their commander coming to join them, in splendor.

Napoleon spent most of April and the first week of May organizing the government for his absence in the now usual way. Cambacérès became the effective regent, presiding over the council of ministers, which was to meet every Wednesday and whenever else was necessary. Cambacérès did not have full powers; Napoleon was to be kept constantly abreast of business by special couriers chosen from among the auditors—he was undeterred by the vast distances now involved—and reserved all major decisions for himself, as in the past. Marie-Louise was charged with all audiences, as his representative, but no more.[253] On April 25, Napoleon issued his final ultimatum to Alexander, who had already joined Barclay's army at Vilna. On the last day of April, the tsar replied to Napoleon in kind. "The new order of things" was about to test itself.

And yet. Napoleon paid homage to the heritage of the Revolution in his very brass-tacks manner: On April 19, he imposed "the Napoleonic Maximum" on grains prices. Sans culotte Paris remained the friend he loved and feared in equal measure. There was another old friend to see. He went to visit Josephine in the first week of May. It was the first time he had gone off to war without her as his wife. He now had no infidelities or spending sprees to fret about on campaign, but it probably seemed very odd. In his risibly unreliable memoirs, Louis Constant—Napoleon's valet—said Josephine implored him to look after Napoleon.[254] Perhaps. No one can truly know what passed between them in the two hours they spent together at Malmaison, but it could only have been a deeply emotional moment for both of them. Deeply personal, without doubt. To what extent the intense feelings they shared were tinged with nostalgia for the early days, for the sun of Austerlitz, is impossible to say any more than if they shared an unease about what was to come. That they met at all was as in character as it was romantic.

On May 9, the imperial couple left Saint-Cloud and the imperial progress began. In the next week, Napoleon met with the grand duke of Hesse-Darmstadt and the kings of Baden and Württemberg, some of his oldest and most loyal allies. These were men Napoleon knew and respected. From Mainz, he wrote to Fredrick of Württemberg:

I thank you for the good wishes you give me for the happy conclusion of the events that seem to be coming. I hope that they will furnish me with further occasions to offer proof . . . of the interest I take in the aggrandizement of your House.[255]

The old allies were to be rewarded. At the expense of whom, we may never know.

The imperial couple arrived at their destination, Dresden, on May 16, the capital of his ally, Frederick-Augustus, King of Saxony and Duke of Warsaw, who had been constrained to vacate the best rooms in his palace for Napoleon. Frederick-Augustus met the imperial party on the edge of the city at night, and Napoleon entered his temporary capital by torchlight, to thundering cannon. Dresden was a city of about thirty thousand inhabitants, the capital of a small, wealthy state that had prospered under the continental system. It was a Baroque jewel of central Europe, until reduced to cinders by the Allied air forces in 1945. Napoleon held court here for the next week. Every morning, he received the minor German princes and Frederick-Augustus himself. His father-in-law, Emperor Francis, was summoned from Vienna and duly came, as did Fredrick-William of Prussia, but only after some cajoling. After receiving them, Napoleon led them all to observe the toilette of the Empress. Banquets and balls buzzed around this, and the Imperial visit all but bankrupted Frederick-Augustus,[256] as was meant to happen to retainers on such occasions. Luigi Mascilli Migliorini sees in this whole spectacle more than Napoleon making a show of force to Alexander, of showing him how alone he was. Rather, Migliorini argues with considerable insight, "the subtle need to prove to himself that . . . he was no longer alone, and that all his tribulations, his costly victories and his marriage . . . had lifted him from the precarious condition of the parvenu who remained tied inexorably to his past."[257] This was doubtless the conscious design. Yet there was still something of Figaro in Napoleon. He could not resist humiliating Francis and Fredrick-William. He openly called the Prussian king a "blockhead" to Caulaincourt.[258] He had humbled Francis in the cruellest manner imaginable, and now did so again, making him watch his own daughter's toilette as a courtier. It was not what was called for.

Napoleon looked over his shoulder to a still older enemy. On May 21, he wrote to his governor-general in Turin:

> Having learned that there are English ships around Savona . . . get the Pope and his people out . . . Precautions will be taken to ensure he crosses Turin by night, that he will only halt at Mont Cenis (a small pass over the Alps), that he will cross Chambéry and Lyon by night, and thus he should arrive at Fontainebleau . . . The Pope must not travel in a papal habit, but only in an ordinary clerical habit, and in such a way that nowhere along the route, save at Mont Cenis, can he be recognized . . . I want this kept as the greatest secret.[259]

The tight secrecy was a measure of the dread he felt for Pius that he no longer had for the Austrians and Prussians. Paris was secured, and Pius would now be "secured" there, "at the center of the Empire." Caution mingled with hubris that week. On May 27, Napoleon appointed an "ambassador" to Lithuania.[260] The next day—Napoleon's last in Dresden—the peace between Russia and the Ottomans was finally sealed.

On May 29, Napoleon headed for the Grande Armée, while Marie-Louise went first to Prague and then Vienna. Napoleon reviewed Davout's I Corps en route and reached the banks of the Niemen—the Russian border—on June 18. On June 22, Napoleon issued a proclamation to the army:

> Soldiers! The second war of Poland has begun. The first ended at Friedland and Tilsit: at Tilsit, Russia swore an eternal alliance and war with England. Today, it has violated these oaths . . . Russia is fatally doomed! It must meet its destiny! Do they think we are degenerates? Are we not still the soldiers of Austerlitz? . . . Cross the Niemen![261]

The world would soon find out.

5

INTO THE ABYSS:
THE MARCH ON MOSCOW

❧ ——————————————————————— ❧

The Advance to Vilna

On June 22, 1812, small patrols of Polish light cavalry gingerly crossed the Niemen to scout for Russian forces. They were soon joined by Napoleon, who chose the place for the crossing of the main army himself. That night he crossed the river again, disguised in a Polish hussar's cloak and cap, with only an officer of engineers as escort. The next day, at ten in the morning, the main army—the guard, Davout's I Corps, and the Reserve Cavalry—crossed over cautiously. They found nothing. "It appeared the door to Russia had been left obligingly ajar."[1] Kovno, the first designated center for operations, was occupied without a shot being fired. Nevertheless, word soon spread that Napoleon had been thrown from his horse when a hare dashed under its hooves.[2] "The reflection occurred" to Caulaincourt that this was a bad omen, who recounted that Berthier seized his hand and told him, "We should not cross the Niemen," while the talk among the staff at Headquarters was that the Romans would have taken this to heart and would have called it all off. "People are superstitious despite themselves in such moments," Cau-laincourt remarked with the benefit of hindsight. Napoleon, he recalled, tried to laugh it all off and remained outwardly serene, but he was irritated by the climate of gloom it had stirred up.[3]

On the night of June 24, when the news reached him, Alexander was at a ball at Bennigsen's country house, where the roof of the marquee had collapsed and the guests danced on, unperturbed, under a clear, starry sky. The elegant calm prevailed beyond the ballroom floor. Alexander and Barclay had long ago agreed what to do, and the orders for a strategic withdrawal to the fortress of Drissa, on the River Dvina, went out. Their intelligence was good as to Napoleon's posi-tion and numbers, and for the first two weeks of the invasion, most of Barclay's First Army withdrew to prepared positions in good order. There were problems with requisitioning carts and supplies, and many units—even the guards—soon found the pace of forced marches hard in the summer heat. Nevertheless, the first phase of the campaign went well for the defenders.[4]

There was no such calm in the French ranks. It took nine days for the Grande Armée to cross the Niemen. Napoleon's host had come to resemble that of the Persian king, Xerxes, as it crossed the Hellespont to invade Greece, an army "far greater than any other in recorded history . . . There was not a nation in Asia that he did not take with him against Greece . . . there was not a stream his army drank from that was not drunk dry,"[5] as described by Herodotus. The Grande Armée was no longer akin to that tightly knit band of thirty-five thousand Macedonians Alexander had led in the opposite direction, the men who, according to Arrian, Alexander the Great enjoined to: "Remember that danger has often threatened you and you have looked it triumphantly in the face . . . Our enemies are . . . men who for centuries have lived soft and luxurious lives; we of Macedon . . . have been trained in the hard school of danger and war. Above all, they are slaves and we are free men."[6] Napoleon knew these words well; he may have modeled his own declarations on them, but they had little relevance to the army that crossed the Niemen. He had a lingering belief that free citizens would fight better than serfs, but too many of his men were not really free. All that remained of the link between Alexander's army and Napoleon's, in the words of Plutarch, which Napoleon knew so well, was Alexander's method of "binding them together and leading them on . . . by giving them provisions for only thirty days,"[7] rather more than had Napoleon.

It looked impressive at first glance. A young French lieutenant recalled a scene "my eyes could barely take in the spectacle before me . . . ": "All was in movement, infantry, cavalry, artillery, wagons of all sorts, herds of cattle and sheep . . . all . . . crossing the bridges pell-mell . . . lit only by the fires of the bivouacs, which made it all look exactly like a Chinese shadow light show."[8] It was soon seen to have feet of clay. Even in the face of barely token resistance, the advance was unraveling. When it became clear that the Russians would not offer battle at Kovno, as Napoleon had anticipated, the main army was unable to push forward to Vilna, so far behind were Eugène's corps, which had to close up with Napoleon to protect his advance.[9] It was as well for the men. Ney's infantry, among the best troops in the whole army, were already malnourished and exhausted by the march. More worrying still, Murat's surviving horses—the equestrian elite—were ill and malnourished, and simply unable to race ahead to Vilna as the advance guard.[10] Alexander did not have to rush the second phase of the retreat. When the French did reach Vilna, on June 28, they found the city abandoned by Barclay. Having prepared for battle, Napoleon had seen Barclay elude him yet again as he had in 1807. Napoleon was enraged, and it was at this point he seemed to realize that he would not gain the quick victory he had planned. His orders to his corps commanders emphasized consolidation and regrouping: Oudinot was ordered "not to wear out his troops, to rally them, to organize their supplies and establish good order."[11] It may have been as well, as the supply convoys—carrying ammunition as well as victuals—lagged still farther behind. In a letter to Berthier on June 30, Napoleon inadvertently revealed how desperately short of ammunition the army was, when he ordered two million cartridges and twenty thousand cannonballs to be brought up quickly—to an army that had hardly fired a shot. The uselessness of the roads was underlined by his orders to bring them by river, the Niemen now being navigable after the floods.[12] The

Russians showed no signs of playing into his hands by standing firm and giving battle. The absence of any Russian forces made Napoleon "a trifle uneasy."[13]

The absence of everything else—of towns, villages, people, food, and fodder—worried his men, whichever of the "twenty nations" they came from. No support was forthcoming from the population. "The Poles hereabouts are not like those in Warsaw," Napoleon remarked to Caulaincourt with a wryness that was increasingly deserting him.[14] Nor was the land. "The terrain was not so precious as to yield him (Napoleon) much by ceding it to him," noted Caulaincourt in his memoirs.[15] Napoleon harbored the hope that the policy of scorched-earth would turn the great landowners against Alexander, their property in cinders,[16] but Caulaincourt spoke for the whole army when he remembered, "We were in the heart of inhabited Russia, and yet . . . we were like a vessel without a compass in the midst of a vast ocean, knowing nothing of what was happening around us."[17]

As the poor roads turned to mud in the spring rains, the long supply trains either stalled or got lost, bereft of maps. Davout informed Berthier a few days into the campaign that he had only six maps of Russia, which he had given to his divisional commanders, "but I don't have enough for the artillery or engineer commanders, nor for the generals commanding the light cavalry (that is, the advance guard), nor for the brigadiers." "I might say," he added with stinging understatement, "that without this aid, most of the generals will continue to suffer problems which are very prejudicial to the good of the service."[18] The army was soon short of basic supplies in a barren wilderness. All of Napoleon's calculations took no account of the glaring heat of a Russian summer, which even he admitted to Marie-Louise "is excessive."[19] The combination of raging heat, ever more tangled supply trains, and empty fields—they came too early for the harvest—took a rapid, terrifying toll on the army. It has been estimated that over sixty thousand men went down sick while the crossing was still underway.[20] "(T)his evening at six, when the intense heat will have fallen, I will be on the march," Davout told Berthier on June 24, with just a whiff of misgiving mixed with defiance.[21] Pillaging and its attendant horrors engulfed the region on a massive scale. Whole communities fled to the forests, "with sorrowful screams and invoking divine mercy" as a Polish officer recalled.[22] This befell the people of a region Napoleon chose because it was meant to be well disposed to the French, it should be recalled. Worse still befell many of the one hundred thousand horses of the army. With their forage now far behind them, the cavalrymen allowed their mounts to graze on raw, green grass, which usually proved fatal, the horses dying in the thousands in throes of agony. Caulaincourt, part of whose remit was logistics, estimated that some ten thousand horses died of exhaustion, want, and "the piercingly cold rain that fell at night" before the army had even reached Vilna on June 28.[23] They were among the most prized possessions of the Grande Armée, and their loss would prove disastrous for Napoleon, and far harder to replace than men.

Men died just the same, and many of them were crack troops. "Many of the Young Guard died on the road of fatigue, cold, and hunger," Caulaincourt recorded. "The chiefs wanted these young men to rival the veterans . . . and the youth of the army was the victim of their misplaced zeal."[24] These were the veterans of two hard years in Spain, who had lost sixty-three men en route from Burgos to Poland. By the time it reached Vilna, the whole guard amounted to only sixteen thousand infantry and four thousand cavalry without facing action; Napoleon ordered men from the National Guard to replace them.[25]

When burning sun gave way to rain, it made things worse still. The official report of the army bulletin of July 6 records that rain fell for thirty-six hours without interruption, turning unbearable heat to cold very quickly. The impact was dreadful: "Several thousand horses died through this sudden change. Artillery convoys ground to a halt in the mud. This horrible storm that so weakened both men and horses, necessarily slowed our march."[26] Hundreds of men died in the floods; Murat's horse artillery lost eight thousand horses. Dysentery and desertion followed.[27] At the first moment he had to draw breath, Napoleon ordered Berthier to requisition forced labor among the troops and the local population to bury all the corpses of men and horses, and all wastage from the butchers shops in Vilna and over a circumference of two leagues around it: "This work must proceed unceasingly until it is finished."[28] The Cossacks were dogging the army; plague was, potentially, in its midst.

The loss of the horses was soon felt, not only for the cavalry, but in transport. On July 2, Napoleon realized that the ovens he had ordered set up to feed the troops in Vilna had not been built because there were no cart horses to carry the bricks to the city.[29] Discipline crumbled even among his best troops. The guard was put on half rations as of June 27, for six days.[30] The less reliable troops were almost out of control. Napoleon took it upon himself to write to the Prince-Royal of Württemberg that the seventy-six hundred men under his command—part of Ney's corps—"were conducting themselves appallingly"; even their officers were "expressing the worst sort of opinions"; a general had called his own king a tyrant and threatened to change sides; the colonel of the Salm unit was no better:

> It is the officers who have to be punished . . . (You) must imprint upon your corps the same spirit and zeal, as to leave no difference (between them) and the French . . . It is the way of things that an allied corps is either very good or very bad . . . You must reign over Württemberg: you can only do so by and for the Confederation.[31]

Württemberg was among Napoleon's oldest allies. The core of the empire was crumbling on the edge of Europe. It is hardly surprising that the army went on a rampage of pillage and rape when it entered the capital of Lithuania, a part of Russia that Napoleon hoped would welcome him. A young woman of the local nobility, Sophie de Tisenhaus, recounted, ". . . unimaginable disorders," ransacked churches, women violated, "even the cemeteries were not spared." Napoleon publicly admonished his officers, but it was all too predictable.[32]

In the face of this, the arrival of an emissary from Alexander only stiffened Napoleon's resolve to seek battle. Alexander's note was an exercise in serenity. He said he took Napoleon at his word that the flimsy pretext for the invasion was the withdrawal of the Russian ambassador from Paris. "If Your Majesty does not intend to spill the blood of his peoples for a misunderstanding of this kind, and if he consents to withdraw his forces from Russian territory, I shall regard what has happened as without consequence . . ." An accommodation over the terms of Tilsit was always possible; it was up to Napoleon.[33] Napoleon replied that he did not want war, and was prepared to talk, but the trouble went back to 1810 and was more deep-rooted than the tsar cared to admit.[34] As soon as the emissary, Count Balachoff, had left, Caulaincourt recounted that Napoleon exploded, "I have not come here to negotiate a trade treaty." What followed, according to Caulaincourt, was more profound:

> I have come to finish off, once and for all, the colossus of the bar-
> barians of the North. The sword is drawn. They must be thrust
> back into their snow and ice so that for a quarter of a century at
> least they will not be able to interfere with civilized Europe . . . We
> must seize the chance and teach the Russians an unpleasant lesson
> about their say in what happens in Germany . . . Since Erfurt,
> Alexander has become too haughty . . . If he must have victories,
> let him defeat the Persians, but don't let him meddle in the affairs
> of Europe. Civilization rejects these people of the North; Europe
> must settle its own affairs without them.[35]

It had taken Napoleon the experience of invading Russia for himself before he grasped what Talleyrand had warned of—and resigned over—at Tilsit: the innate aggression and power of Russia was an intractable danger to the rest of Europe. If Napoleon meant these words, the object of the exercise was no longer to bring Alexander back into the entente as an equal, to but crush him before he crushed the West. There are also echoes of this thinking in his avowal to Cambacérès in the buildup to war that he had to defeat so dangerous a power as Russia while he could still mount a horse.

Caulaincourt is generally regarded as a very reliable chronicler. As Jacques-Olivier Boudon has wisely observed, Napoleon was all too aware that history was on his shoulders in 1812, but could not know how it would judge him, and so "he did not seek out a 'yes-man' to report his words (for) he was already thinking of posterity."[36] Caulaincourt was no such animal, and an upshot of

Balachoff's visit underscores this. Napoleon teased Caulaincourt—not for the first time—that Alexander had made a good Russian of him, but Caulaincourt took real offense at this, as it was said to Balachoff. He raged at Napoleon, and asked for a transfer to Spain, as he had long opposed the Russian war and had seen no reason to change his mind. Napoleon smiled and said quietly, "Who is doubting your fidelity? I know you well enough to know that you are a man of worth. I was joking. You're too touchy." It did not calm Caulaincourt, who started packing. Napoleon sent for him the next morning, as he was ready to set off on early patrol. He tugged Caulaincourt's ear—always a sign of good humor—and asked, "Are you mad in wanting to leave me? I esteem you . . . and had no wish to hurt your feelings." He galloped off, then wheeled his horse and gave Caulaincourt orders. It was business as usual. "I could come to no other decision . . . except that it was impossible to leave him," Caulaincourt concluded.[37]

The Pursuit of Bagration

In the midst of this mess Napoleon transformed a complex grand plan into an evermore intricate set of maneuvers. His initial strategy was based on the enveloping "hinge" he had used to trap Mack at Ulm, with Davout on the right, Jérôme as "the hinge," holding the center, while Napoleon swung around in a leftward arch, to concentrate 400,000 men across a narrow front and so drive Barclay and Bagration into a pocket where they could be defeated in one blow. He now saw that Barclay was pulling back, northeastward, as Bagration moved east, along the northern edge of the Pripet Marshes, toward Minsk, with the ultimate aim of linking with Barclay further east. Napoleon decided to keep them apart rather than drive them together and concentrate on crushing Bagration. This meant dispersing the central army, sending Murat, Ney, and Oudinot north to contain Barclay (and catch his rearguard under Wittgenstein if they could), while Davout's exhausted, depleted corps was, effectively, to race Bagration to Minsk and head him off there, before he could join Barclay.

Napoleon would remain at Vilna with the guard. This split the central army into disparate components and depended on coordination to an even greater degree than before in the face of deteriorating communications and logistics. Napoleon was aware of this. Even the relatively straightforward operations of the northern sector against Barclay called for constant cooperation between Murat, Oudinot, and Ney, three of his most impetuous commanders even when under his nose. He told Berthier as he sent them off: "Advise the commanders of these three columns to correspond frequently with you, so that I might be able to take steps to support them (from Vilna, with the Reserve) . . . At the least, we ought to have a useful idea of the enemy's position, and of what is going on, (for) it is essential not to tire out the troops."[38] It was almost pathetic.

This new plan depended even more heavily on Jérôme, who now had to take the offensive, rather than standing firm as the hinge; his corps now had to keep up with Davout, to close the trap on Bagration: Davout from the north, the king of Westphalia from the south. The need for haste became obvious when Napoleon received reliable intelligence on July 1 that Bagration was heading toward Vilna; his intention to link with Barclay was now clear. Napoleon ordered Davout to move south at pace to hit Bagration head-on, while Jérôme was to hem him in from his rear. Davout fulfilled his orders, getting to Minsk. His badly depleted forces—three of his best divisions (those of Morland, Friant, and Gudin) had been seconded to Ney and Oudinot, compounded by losses to sickness—worked a minor miracle, reaching Minsk in less than a week. "Davout had executed the first part of the plan with clockwork precision" in the apt words of his biographer, John Gallaher.[39] It came at a dreadful cost, however. This unopposed march cost him thirty thousand men of the elite I Corps, 45 percent of its strength at the start of the campaign.[40] This was the force Caulaincourt felt "could rival the Guard" as they crossed the Niemen only a few weeks earlier.[41] He was belatedly reinforced by fifty thousand men from Eugène's corps that arrived in Vilna well behind schedule, much to Napoleon's ire, but they were not of the same quality, composed mainly of Italians and Bavarians.[42] Eugène's late arrival was not due to slough or incompetence. He had halted at Piloni because a large Russian force was close to him, ready to attack. It was actually "a figment of General Rouget's imagination,"[43] but he felt he could not take any risks. Eugène was yet another victim of the poor intelligence gathering that bedeviled the campaign. Despite the many hindrances, Davout and Eugène, with almost fifty-five thousand men, were converging on Bagration's mere forty-five thousand Russians from the north. It all now depended on Jérôme's fifty-five thousand, his Westphalians, soon reinforced by the troops of the Polish contingent of V Corps under Poniatowski. They were still some distance from Davout, as he forged forward with only Jean Dominique Compans's infantry division. However, Murat took some of Davout's cavalry when he thought, wrongly, he had found Barclay's main army; he lost more cavalry support when Grouchy ran into a Russian corps he had not known about, and lost contact with I Corps. Davout's advance was vulnerable from the outset.

Jérôme did not match Davout's endeavor, but he had suddenly been handed a daunting task. He had considerable ground to make up, switching quickly to hanging back in defense, and now thrust into a long forced march, away from his supply trains—which had little hope of keeping apace with him—through countryside already stripped bare by the retreating Russians. Having found no trace of the Russians, Jérôme halted in Grodno for two days, entering the town on June 30. Jérôme's men had been marching at pace for over three weeks. The Polish V Corps was a striking example of this. Its thirty-two thousand men were mainly recent conscripts, some inducted only in 1812,[44] and they had been weakened by poor rations and garrison conditions, together with hard forced labor on fortifications even before the start of the campaign. Disease and malnutrition were already rife before the long forced marches began. The main body of the corps had not fired a shot by the time it finally reached Davout's at Mogilev on July 24, but it had lost over 30 percent of its men and 35 percent of its horses.[45] Bagration's men were more than a match for Jérôme on every level. Retreating toward their own depots, they were mostly veterans who outpaced Jérôme.

This was not helped by poor reconnaissance, nor Napoleon's orders. Jérôme complained they were not clear, first ordering him to shadow Bagration—who

Jérôme believed to be to his south—and then to head for Davout, hopefully at Minsk, to the northeast. If he followed his own intelligence, he would risk being cut off from Davout; if he took Napoleon's, he would, from what he knew, lose Bagration. His delay arose from genuine confusion, but his real mistake with his brother was failing to inform Napoleon of his position for two days, even after Berthier had made it clear he was to march for Minsk with all speed.[46] It was not until July 4 that Napoleon received the news that Jérôme had not advanced an inch, and his response was furious. On July 5, he told Berthier:

> You will let him know that I am extremely unhappy . . . that he did not harass (Bagration's) corps and stop his march; arrived at Grodno on the 30th, he was supposed to attack the enemy immediately and pursue him energetically. You tell him that it is impossible to maneuver worse than he did . . . that by having drifted so far from his orders, he has allowed Bagration all the time he needs to make his retreat, and to do so at his leisure . . . he can be at Minsk on the 7th, and what matter that the king (Jérôme) gets there on the 10th, since Bagration has gained four days' march on him? . . . You tell him that all the fruit of my maneuvers and the best chance that war can offer have been lost by this singular neglect of the basic notion of war.[47]

In an ominous sign of what was to come, when Jérôme's advance guard finally caught up with the Cossacks and regular light cavalry protecting Bagration's retreat, six regiments of Polish lancers were cut to pieces at Mir on July 10, ensuring that Jérôme kept a safe distance between Bagration and himself henceforth. This was the first major clash between the rival cavalries, and as Dominic Lieven has noted, "The superiority of the Russian light cavalry . . . was to grow ever more pronounced over the next two years of the war."[48] Napoleon did not take it well. He lashed out at Victor Latour-Maubourg, who commanded these units: "The business of the 10th (of July) . . . does not match the confidence placed in him. Since when does a general who has already fought in Poland (in 1807, at Friedland) send one light cavalry division against an enemy rear guard he knows is composed of . . . 11,000 cavalry?" The report Napoleon received was deemed "oblique and insignificant." Napoleon decided that, ultimately, it was Jérôme's poor organization of the advance that was really at fault—"it is the only (army) which has not done its duty"—and that Latour-Maubourg would have done better with proper support, but this did not excuse his lack of communication with Napoleon, nor the fact that he had been ten days in the vicinity of Bagration and not sorted himself out better.[49] Latour-Maubourg had distinguished himself at Friedland, and fought well at Austerlitz and in Spain.[50] Now, lost in forbidding terrain and ill directed by both Napoleon and Jérôme, he stumbled into a costly defeat, which was not his fault. The loss of confidence Napoleon had long felt in his family and civilian collaborators was extending to trusted commanders under the strain of Russia.

When Napoleon became aware that Jérôme was moving slowly, it only enraged him further, concluding that his brother was simply too soft and lacking in energy for command. On July 6, he told Jérôme that he was being placed under Davout's command.[51] Jérôme did not get this letter for several days, but another bitter rebuke from Napoleon, of July 8, did reach him:

> [I]f you had the slightest notion of this job, you would have been on the third where you were on the sixth and . . . the results of my calculations would have been a good campaign. But you know nothing, and not only have you consulted no one, you have allowed yourself to be guided by petty motives. Know well, that all is now clear. I will give you justice when you merit it. But until that time, I am very angry about all the petty motives you allow to direct you . . . Act vigorously and energetically, and don't be embarrassed to ask about what you don't know. Raise yourself . . .[52]

The "petty motives" Napoleon referred to were the fact that Davout had unilaterally seized command of the sector and put Jérôme under his own orders, several days before Napoleon ordered the same thing, an action Jérôme put in the context of Davout's high-handed, often aggressive behavior toward him the previous winter, when he commanded the French forces in Westphalia.[53] He now flatly refused to obey Davout, and told Berthier, when he learned that Napoleon confirmed Davout's action, that Napoleon had "a firm desire" to humiliate him.[54] Napoleon virtually admitted that he needed his best corps commander to carry out so daunting a task. Jérôme had shown himself a poor leader of men from the outset. The Westpahlians had broken down in the Duchy of Warsaw, even before the campaign began, and Jérôme had never been able to exert control over them. As for the men under him, Poniatowski had no doubt that he had been forced to lead V Corps "like a poisoned rat" through punishing forced marches in ferocious heat and pounding rain, into illness and hunger, because of Jérôme's muddled head.[55] Caulaincourt said simply, "Such was the support given to the Emperor in sore straits by the brothers he had made kings."[56] Indeed, but it had been the emperor's mistake and he had himself to blame. As John Gallaher has put it, Jérôme "had been miscast by his all powerful brother."[57] He might well have added that Louis, too, had been miscast. It was part of Napoleon's character—of his ego—to look for himself in his brothers, but at least in the case of Louis, his failure in Holland had come as a shock. He had long distrusted Jérôme.

The same day, Davout's bedraggled men entered Minsk unopposed, to find some welcome stores of flour and working ovens. Bagration had seen the danger, and swerved south. Between July 14 and 16, Davout set himself the goal of keeping Bagration on the south bank of the Dnieper. He gave chase, the battered state of his force notwithstanding, with only Compans's twelve thousand men. Both Latour-Maubourg's cavalry and Poniatowski's Poles were too far behind him, even if he could command them. As at Auerstadt, he was on his own when his reconnaissance force ran into Bagration's advance guard on July 21. It was badly mauled and fell back with heavy losses, but Davout drove ahead, and occupied Mogilev, near a ford on the Dnieper. He dug in on a high ravine, with the river on his left, and waited for his opponent. Bagration had close to forty thousand men available, but threw only twenty thousand into the battle. With typical bravado, he offered Davout terms if he "stood aside," but got short shrift. On July 23, Bagration launched his infantry at the ridge, and was driven back; Davout attributed this to his light artillery, which deployed quickly to a good defensive position. Its "murderous fire" killed five hundred Russian infantry within an hour, according to his official report. Davout counterattacked and was checked, in turn, by a battery Bagration brought up with some speed. It was a long, hot, bloody day in every sense. "The fighting became very lively," in Davout's wry words. Davout fought a purely defensive action; all he had to do was hold the ridge—which he reported General Fredericks did "with great vigor"[58]—whereas Bagration had to break through Davout and seize the crossing for his action to be worthwhile. When he saw this could not be done except at huge cost, Bagration, so often the loudest voice for attack in the high command,[59] saw that Davout's men were too dangerous to risk his army against, even in their battered state. He swung further south, away from the river. He knew Davout had reinforcements coming, but not, fortunately, that they were a four days' march away.[60]

For a time at least, Davout had prevented the juncture of the two main Russian armies. His men were exhausted, but they had driven on, alone and unsupported, against a bigger opponent and achieved what had looked impossible to Napoleon only a week before. This only forestalled the juncture of Barclay and Bagration—Jérôme had seen to that—but forestall it Davout did. Mogilev was a bitter but small action, a skirmish when set beside Austerlitz or Auerstadt—Davout lost over 1,000 of the 20,000 men he threw into the battle to hold the ford across the Dnieper; Bagration, 2,500 of the 16,500 he had in the field.[61] These were some of the finest troops of the Grande Armée, and they were shrinking in number by the day. It was a triumph of discipline, endurance, and no small amount of courage. Davout reported with glowing pride:

> I owe the greatest praise to the conduct of the troops . . . No soldier quit his post to help the wounded[62] and the young (troops), just as the old, showed the greatest valor. The old soldiers gave their

young comrades the greatest honor there could be, that they were conscripts no more.[63]

The "fighting third" of Auerstadt lived on.

Jérôme abandoned his army on July 16, and returned to his capital, at Kassel. Napoleon ordered him to do so ten days later, but for once, Jérôme took the initiative. Even the handover to his chief of staff cost the advance a day.[64] Jérôme was no loss to the campaign, and operations improved, in so far as they could, when Davout took over the consolidated command of the right of the main army. However, it represented the collapse of a whole system Napoleon had already lost faith in. Jérôme's cashiering—far more brutal than anything Napoleon had done to a commander, even Bernadotte—was yet another nail in the coffin of the concept of a dynastic order in Europe. A family unfit to bear arms could not hold sway over his hegemony. The contrast with Davout and his men was, perhaps, too stark for him to bear. His actual reaction to the victory of Mogilev was not to accord some respite. Instead, on July 26, only three days later, he ordered Davout north to join him against Barclay.[65] Davout set out as soon as the order reached him, on July 29.[66]

Vitebsk

Napoleon had watched most of these events unravel from Vilna. Such immobility was new, and not in keeping with all his behavior on previous campaigns. Adam Zamoyski has astutely observed that, whereas Napoleon had always been "out and about" among his troops, seeing their condition for himself, this was impossible in Russian conditions, and so he regarded many adverse reports as scaremongering.[67] He tried to direct operations from a central point, not the front. This is not to say he was idle. Caulaincourt—who had to endure them—recalled the long hours Napoleon put in at his desk.[68] It was desk work, nonetheless. His decision was also an indication of a deeper problem. His choice to stay put was rational, but only because he had allowed his front to fragment to the point there was not one, consolidated, forward position. Murat, Ney, and Oudinot had been dispatched to the northeast to harass Barclay; Davout was well to the south, pursuing Bagration. Napoleon and Davout both assumed he was heading for Barclay at Vitebsk, but instead, he pushed farther east to Smolensk, a miscalculation that allowed him to cross the Dneiper on August 3.[69] There was no forward position to direct from. Napoleon saw this happening as soon as he reached Vilna. On July 6, he told Berthier the ultimate goal was now driving on to Smolensk, in the hopes of catching the Russians as soon as possible en route, and force the Russians to concentrate their troops in large garrisons to protect Moscow and Saint Petersburg "instead of (fighting) a small war of rearguard actions and ruses."[70] It was an admission, if not in so many words, that the front was disintegrating.

Nor were his interior lines at all secure. He ordered the creation of a new Gendarmerie brigade on July 10, to deal with pillaging soldiers of one of Davout's units—the 33 Light Infantry under Desaix—around Voronovo, "who are doing all sorts of damage in this area." On the pretext of marching to join the main body of I Corps at Minsk, they "went off route" and were "pillaging this superb valley . . . Tell the Viceroy (Eugène) to create a military commission and to round up all these stragglers."[71] Incidents of this kind were rife, Napoleon's response was a straw in the wind, but this one carried terrifying import: Desaix's men were among the best troops in the army. They were part of Davout's I Corps, a unit that drew unstinting, universal praise for "the order and harmony which prevailed . . . the happy result of this severe discipline . . . (which) caused them to be the acknowledged as the model of the whole army" as Ségur was able to claim, even on the last stages of the advance to Moscow.[72] The behavior of Desaix's men shows that order could only prevail under Davout's direct gaze, Napoleon's problem in microcosm. It revealed how far the rot had spread.

However, when it seemed that the situation had changed, so did Napoleon. Convinced the Russians would give battle, Napoleon—literally—sprang into the saddle. Barclay was now the main target; he was pulling back and consolidating around the fortress of Drissa, and Napoleon ordered Oudinot,

Ney, and Murat to react accordingly. These forces had not been subjected to the same ordeal as those of Davout or Jérôme, but Napoleon, now mobile, soon saw that they were in anything but good condition. Ney's artillery train of about seventy cannon was far behind him, and Napoleon had to order him to halt his advance on July 4, to let it catch up: "Without artillery, his corps will be very vulnerable." There was more to it, though. Ney needed to get organized, to build ovens to provision his men properly and, more worryingly still, "he must organize the police." Cavalry detachments had to be sent to the rear, commanded by reliable officers from headquarters, for ". . . there are many (drivers) who commit crimes, and who will end up being captured by the Cossacks." Ney's reputation for recklessness and tolerating indiscipline were increasingly evident and costly. He told Berthier to remind both Ney and Oudinot that they owed him detailed reports about the condition of their corps.[73]

With his forces in so disorganized a state, Napoleon ordered the guard and those of Eugène's troops not with Davout forward from Vilna to join the general advance on Drissa and the other Russian positions along the line of the River Drina. Only when Murat reported signs that Barclay might be taking the offensive did Napoleon leave Vilna for the front, on July 17. As has been seen, as soon as Davout had barred Bagration's passage of the Dneiper and forced him south, his men were also called to the Dvina line. Bagration's retreat eastward could not be halted indefinitely, and the roads he was on were better. This meant, simply, that there had to be no Barclay for him to join. Napoleon wanted to avoid a direct assault on Drissa if at all possible, and hoped to outflank Barclay from the south and sweep around his rear, moving northward, cutting him off from Saint Petersburg. This would, Napoleon hoped, either force him to fall back on Moscow, away from Bagration, or make him fight. Barclay wrong-footed Napoleon by sticking to his strategy: Neither Barclay nor Alexander had actually inspected the state of the fortifications at Drissa,[74] which Napoleon had assumed to be formidable,[75] finding himself yet again the victim of poor intelligence. Faced with furious opposition from most of the general staff, Alexander stood by Barclay's wish to abandon Drissa and the Dvina line, and retreat to Vitebsk. Alexander saw both sides of the argument: This was a blow for morale—an ill-judged, bombastic proclamation had been issued to the troops, proclaiming in Napoleonic fashion that this was the last, great stand, that retreating was over[76]—but it also made it difficult to organize another line of defense or organize reserves. However, in letters to Barclay and Bagration, he made his thinking clear. To Barclay, he wrote "I entrust my army to you. Don't forget this is the only army I have. Keep this always in mind." To Bagration, "Don't forget we are still opposed by superior numbers . . . [W]e need to be cautious and not deprive ourselves of the means (to fight on) . . . by risking all on one day." He reminded Bagration how outnumbered the Russians were,[77] obviously not aware that Napoleon had lost approximately one hundred thousand men from this army group to illness and straggling by the time he reached Vitebsk.[78] Even so, Alexander read Napoleon like a book. On June 17, the Russians slipped out of Drissa in good order, and two days later, aware of the risk he had taken, Alexander left the front for Moscow, to steady his "second city" for the worst.[79]

Napoleon assumed that Barclay was striking south toward Polotsk to find Bagration. He was wholly wrong; his intuition had deserted him. Barclay was, indeed, heading for Bagration, but not by the route Napoleon thought. Napoleon rapidly saw his error and moved from Vitebsk, where Barclay intended to stand, and he had assumed Napoleon would guess this from the outset.[80] Napoleon had recovered his energy. Undaunted by Drissa, he was now even more convinced that he could soon force Barclay into battle, without Bagration to support him. He joined his men on the forced night marches. "We were always in bivouac or under canvas," Caulaincourt remembered, but Napoleon did not rest long in these days. He remained in the saddle all night on July 27–28, and was always pressing forward, "urging and encouraging the troops." He was very quickly on the scene when a unit of light infantry held off the Russian cavalry of the rearguard, congratulating "you brave lads" and awarding several Légions d'honneur.[81]

Barclay intended to stand at Vitebsk, arriving there on July 25, still hoping Bagration would make it to him. That day saw the first major clash between

Napoleon and Barclay at Ostrovo, and it proved that Barclay had many of the same problems of command as Napoleon. Barclay's IV Corps had been entrusted to the charismatic but wholly inadequate command of Alexander Ostermann-Tolstoy, who kept a pet bear he dressed in military uniform and went on campaign with his pet eagle and a white crow. Like so many of Napoleon's commanders on this campaign, he was effective only under close supervision, and incompetent in charge of larger forces under independent command. So it proved at Ostrovo. He was ambushed at considerable cost advancing on the French, reacted with a bayonet charge of the kind that had undone the Russians at Austerlitz, did not take the adequate cover available, and crashed into the main French force. A dragoon regiment meant to cover him then stormed out of the forest to save him, and straight into the French. It spent the rest of the war on police duties behind the lines. For all his lunacy, Ostermann-Tolstoy's bravura—he ordered his men to "stand or die"—delayed the French for a time, before he got his orders to pull back. He was relieved of his command, nonetheless.[82]

When the news of Davout's victory at Mogliev reached Barclay, his first instinct was still to fight, but wiser council prevailed upon him. Once more, the Russians withdrew in good order. It was no easy operation, however. The Russian rearguard under Pyotr Pahlen had to fight bitter defensive actions to cover the main army, as it began to pull out on July 27, and he had to continue to do so for several days, until Barclay was safely to Smolensk. Napoleon drove Pahlen hard, still convinced Barclay would turn and fight. The ploy by the Cossacks to keep the Russian campfires burning long after the withdrawal did not fool the French for long, but many experienced officers were unnerved. Berthier remarked on ". . . the admirable order in which the Russian army had made its retreat . . . without abandoning a single cannon, cart, or sick man." Ségur saw "nothing left behind, not one weapon . . . no trace, nothing, in short, in this sudden nocturnal march." There was more order, he observed, in the Russian retreat than in the French victory.[83] Caulaincourt agreed: "For some hours we had to act like huntsmen and follow up in every direction the track they had taken. What was the use?"[84]

At least Napoleon had his main army together again. He halted at Vitebsk for eight days, in another attempt to regroup and allow his supply trains, such as they were, to reach him. In the meantime, he watched discipline crumble as the exhausted troops "slept, ate and plundered."[85] Napoleon now started to realize the real state of the army, and it began with the Imperial Guard. Its men were the "spoilt children of the army" no more and soon became as unruly as the rest in the face of the appalling conditions they were under. They had marched harder than most—nearly twenty-five miles a day through forests[86]—but their rations had not reached them, any more than any line regiment composed of raw conscripts. It came to the point that Napoleon appointed Caulaincourt's younger brother, Auguste, to distribute what supplies there were, and try to handle the NCOs. This meant that "often he had to stand sword in hand at the depots."[87] Napoleon showed no favoritism over their indiscipline. Severe examples were made of a few; the majority were set to work renovating the governor's palace in the glaring heat. Order was restored, but it was sorry business.[88]

Napoleon made it clear to Berthier on July 29 that his main aim was to rest the army for eight days and get supplies organized.[89] He ordered Ney's III Corps—the advance guard, at this point—to do the same, and to ensure his troops were well supplied with reserves of rations to last twenty-four days, having procured these supplies "by legal means, through the local authorities."[90] The need for rest was clear to him, but he was convinced, he told Cambacérès, that the Russians were now terrified of him, and that—despite having burned all their supply stores as they retreated—"the country here is the best we have seen; the harvest is very good."[91] The black earth region of central Russia was indeed more fertile than the country between the Niemen and Smolensk, but the Russians had been there first, and in great number. There was no other hope than to live off the land now. Caulaincourt saw the destruction of the horses as the key to it all: ". . . their death meant the breakdown of the service." Without horses, there was no supply chain, "There you have the secret and cause of our earlier disasters and our final reverse."[92] There is much in this, but not all. Napoleon had counted on commandeering wagons and horses that were not there, and so the service was damaged, the artillery, supply, and ambulance corps alike.[93] That he could not pursue Barclay when he had good cause to think he could catch him, brought this home.

In David Chandler's judgment, a lack of experience of the disastrous impact of long convoys on the "war of movement," and the vast distances involved, were the keys to understanding the calamitous state of the invasion.[94] This is not really the case. The vastness of Russia was certainly wholly new, but lessons had been pouring in from Masséna especially, and many other commanders in Spain, about the problems of supply and the obstacles inherent in campaigning in barren, remote terrain. Ney and Oudinot had experienced this firsthand, yet remained seemingly oblivious to its application in Russia, particularly the need to maintain good communications with other formations. This is to say nothing of the hard lessons of the Eylau campaign of 1807. None of it registered with any of them.

The Grande Armée was a shadow of itself. Even Murat had come to see this. Almost blissfully ignorant of the ruin his forced marches were doing to his undernourished mounts in the first phases of the campaign, and consistent in his habit of shifting his reserve from one point to another en bloc,[95] he now saw he could push his cavalry no further. "Always at the forefront of the skirmishes, and eager to thrust his plumes and bizarre uniforms beneath the very noses of the Cossacks . . ." the man who had ruined the cavalry "and ended by causing the loss of the army" in Caulaincourt's judgment,[96] now saw that with the Russian army really massed before him, he was in no position to fight. He left Belliard, his chief of staff, to confront Napoleon: "Your Majesty must be told the truth. The cavalry is rapidly disappearing."[97] In a short note to Clarke, his minister of war back in Paris, Napoleon had to admit as much: "I fear you ought not to put too many (new conscripts) into the cavalry. The losses of horses surpasses those of men."[98] The same fate had already befallen the Young Guard, and the ranks of Davout's I Corps were ever thinner. Hunger, the elements, and illness made no distinction between the elite of the army and its poorest troops.[99] Ultimately, Napoleon's obtuse refusal to listen and learn was to blame for the desperate state of the army under his direct command by the time it reached Vitebsk. Worse was to come.

Smolensk

Caulaincourt felt that the Russian strategy of retreat had "opened his eyes to the possible consequences of this war." Perhaps, but he was thoroughly right that "the one and a thousand things that ought to have opened his eyes to his position vanished before the slightest incident which might revive his hope."[100] On August 3, Barclay and Bagration finally joined forces at Smolensk. This was more than a "slight incident." Although Alexander had been steadfastly loyal to Barclay's strategy, it had aroused powerful resentment from the outset, and not just from frontline soldiers of the "old school" like Bagration. At Smolensk, even Barclay was prepared to make a stand. There was, in the phrase, "history here."

Smolensk was no mere provincial capital like Vilna or Vitebsk, in borderlands of recent acquisition and dubious loyalty. It was the historic western redoubt of the Russian heartland. Although an economic backwater by 1812, Smolensk was something close to a sacred place for Russian patriots. It first entered the historical record in 863 C.E.; it had been assailed and seized many times by the Polish-Lithuanian Commonwealth in early modern times. In the process, the city had become a fortress, and stood as a warlike challenge to all comers from the West, the walls of its Kremlin—the largest in Russia, built by the ferocious Tsar Boris Godunov in 1597—reared up from the banks of the Dnieper as a marker to European invaders: this far and no further. In 1812, the walls worried Barclay because they could not bear modern cannon, but much of them remain, surviving even the battles of the Second World War. The very name of the river that gave Smolensk its name—the Smolnya—was said by some to derive from the black soil of its banks, the black soil that itself defines the Russian heartland. Its cathedral housed the icon of the Virgin, an image so potent it traveled with the army throughout the 1812 campaign. Now she had come home.

Great hopes and fears swirled around Smolensk, bringing to fever pitch the many tensions that had mounted during the weeks of endless retreat. Napoleon now stood on the threshold of the heartland. The troops gathered there felt all this deeply. Ivan Paskevich, commander of Bagration's 26th Division, brimmed with emotion when he recalled that "(N)ow we are fighting in old Russia, as every birch tree standing by the side of the road reminded us." Luka Simansky, a lieutenant in the Izmailovsky Guards, was deeply moved when he saw the icon of the Virgin actually in Smolensk, and felt its saving grace in times of national peril.[101] The pressures on Alexander to make a stand were intense. They were first felt when he reached Smolensk on his way to Moscow, when many of its nobles made offers of supplies and money for its defense. Nikolai Mikhailovich Kalichittsky was not unique in volunteering his three sons for "either a determined defense or a glorious death" and supplies of such quantity they would have ruined him.[102]

Alexander's visit to Moscow brought this home to him with even more force. Aware of how deeply unpopular Barclay and his whole strategy were in the old capital, Alexander snuck in quietly in the dead of night, hoping to avoid the nobles. Instead, they had already gathered at the Kremlin, while crowds of all classes followed his coach; peasants clutching candles, their priests lining the roads. When he entered the gates, the crowd unharnessed his horses and hauled him to the Kremlin, while others knelt as he passed. The next day, he was blessed with an icon of St. Sergei by the Metropolitan, to cries of "Lead us . . . we will die or conquer." When he met the merchants later that day, their will to fight was almost hysterical. "They struck themselves on the head, they tore out their hair, they raised their hands to heaven, tears flowed down their faces . . . I saw one man grinding his teeth," one observer recalled.[103] It was, in its way, Alexander's equivalent of the vigil the Imperial Guard gave Napoleon on the eve of Austerlitz. Both were born of the hope of a great victory, but Alexander's aim was not quite that, as yet. He did not present them with a clear plan of action. Rather, he spoke in general terms of the sacrifices they would all have to make, and made a hasty exit, leaving them to ponder his meaning for themselves. They remained fanatically determined.

Alexander returned to Saint Petersburg just as Barclay and Bagration joined forces. His perceptions had changed, for he now saw he had to bow to so powerful a manifestation of public opinion. His trusted sister, Catherine, took the chance to tell him his thoughts of resuming command, in person, were ill-conceived, and that his vacillations had undermined Barclay.[104] Yet, back in his capital and now surrounded by a high command driven by Arakcheev, Alexander was rudely reminded of how deeply hated Barclay and his whole strategy remained. Alexander may have left Moscow a "changed man," filled with resolve to defeat Napoleon,[105] but he reacted to this dilemma in typical, hedge-betting fashion. He did not abandon Barclay, but he did order him to stand and fight in a position Barclay felt, rightly, to be unsuitable for a major battle. On August 9, he told Barclay, "I now hope with the help of the Supreme Being you will be able to take the offensive and thereby stop the invasion of our provinces."[106] Alexander's change of course may have been sincere, in that he had never expected the retreat to reach Smolensk, but Dominic Lieven's judgment that he was now driven by the fear of public opinion[107] is in keeping with his wary character. Mixed with the determination of so many to fight in Saint Petersburg society was deep anger at the succession of retreats. As early as July 6, Varvara Ivanova Bakunina told a friend "They write about our successes, about the slow pace of Napoleon's advance, about his lack of confidence in his forces, but the facts show us something quite different; we have been successful only in retreating . . . the enemy . . . has helped himself to entire provinces . . . despair and fear grow by the hour."[108] Alexander would be blamed if the heartland fell. Adam Zamoyski puts it starkly, "he could not forget what had happened to his father and grandfather."[109]

The "exploits" of Barclay's army left the French in awe as it slipped away in good order time and again, its cavalry besting them in retreat, its Cossacks hitting them on the run at will. In fact, it was the perfect example of the old adage of the swan—grace and poise on the surface, frenzied thrashing about below. Once joined at Smolensk, now aware of Alexander's change of heart, the ungainly, uncoordinated flailing came to the surface. Any semblance of unity of purpose between Barclay and Bagration quickly evaporated, the intrinsic incompatibility of "the fiery Georgian and the cerebral 'German'" there for all to see.[110] Their fundamental disagreement of what to do was now exacerbated by the tsar's specific order to make a stand. Bagration had nearly the whole high command with him in wanting to strike hard and fast at the French, because he believed—wrongly—that Napoleon's troops were scattered, and—rightly—that the retreat to Smolensk had been too hurried to allow their position to be secured. Barclay was no longer in a position to argue, but he went on the attack in a very half-hearted manner, halting continually. He held to the view that seeking a big battle was playing into Napoleon's hands; it was one thing to do so in a well dug in position and wait for Napoleon's assault, it was quite another to try to outmaneuver him on the offensive. Barclay told Admiral Pavel Chichagov that he had no reserve organized in the rear, and only buying time could change this.[111] Moreover, Bagration badly underestimated Napoleon's concentration of forces: he had close to 180,000 men in the vicinity by mid-August, even if only 156,000 were battle-ready. By contrast, the combined forces of Barclay and Bagration came to barely 125,000,[112] and they were operating at odds with each other. The stuttering nature of Barclay's advance produced confusing orders and counterorders to Bagration; when the third "about face" reached him, Bagration exploded to an Arakcheev who was "all ears," as it were. "For the love of God get me a posting anywhere away from here . . . I just cannot stand it here any longer; headquarters is so full of Germans a Russian can't survive there."[113] In fact, Barclay's own staff was rapidly losing confidence in him. "Germans" were muttered about in headquarters; there was even talk of a "German" spy ring.[114] This confusion soon led many junior officers to question if their superiors were fit to lead; in the ranks, the iron discipline of the Russian soldier began to crack, as desertions and looting multiplied.[115] When Barclay virtually ended the advance, fearing a major French thrust, Bagration simply defied the agreed plan. Instead of halting his retreat at Smolensk, he continued eastward, and consolidated his men along the Dnieper behind the city. Bagration had brazenly defied Barclay, but he had also effectively blocked any attempt by Napoleon to sweep around Smolensk from the south. By about August 13, the "offensive" had all but petered out,[116] and there were signs that the Russians, too, were on the verge of imploding.

While the Russians were dithering, Napoleon struck.[117] He quickly changed course from his initial plan to prepare for a Russian attack; by July 10, he sensed it would come to nothing,[118] and four days later he drove on to Smolensk, sweeping aside the poorly led seventy-two hundred Russians in his path. That they escaped at all and made it into the city was because Murat failed to act without a semblance of military competence, a worrying sign of what was to come.[119] Bagration now rushed a division to Smolensk that brought its garrison up to a meager fifteen thousand men by August 16; by the next day, Barclay had about thirty thousand troops in the western suburbs and on the walls.[120]

Napoleon did not move fast enough to take advantage of Smolensk's weakness. Effectively, he took his birthday—August 15—off, to review the guard.[121] In about forty-eight hours, the Russians were, if not prepared to crush a major assault, then certainly ready to do him damage if he launched any frontal attack. Napoleon could have bypassed Smolensk easily, leaving it cut off and forcing the Russians to retreat in disorder. This would also, in all likelihood, have driven a wedge between Barclay and Bagration, which had been his intention for so long. It was a missed opportunity.[122] In two letters to Cambacérès on August 12 and 15, Napoleon confided that "a big battle" was likely, and Cambacérès was to keep it to himself.[123] Napoleon believed he had the main army in his grasp. This was, he hoped, the decisive engagement his original plan of campaign was based on, and in the place he had regarded as the last acceptable limit of his advance. As so often, his reasoning—however flawed—might be found in his words to Cambacérès. It would not have been the first time he confided his real thoughts to him. Ney had only eighteen thousand infantry before Smolensk by August 15, and was not ready to attack. If this were to be the decisive engagement, it had to wait for Napoleon to concentrate his forces. That took time, and it was only late on the 16th that Davout and Poniatowski arrived in force to encircle the western approaches to Smolensk and provide the numbers needed for a serious assault. Barclay's main body was now arriving on the high ground to the northwest and Bagation's to the east of the suburbs.[124] Their orders were, after all, to give Napoleon what he wanted.

This still need not have entailed a frontal assault by the French, however. Napoleon chose to try to trap the Russians in Smolensk by an elaborate operational plan of envelopment that David Chandler has likened in its theoretical brilliance to Jena-Auerstadt.[125] In reality, the "maneuver of Smolensk" was an exercise in grandiose delusion. Bagration's insubordination had already seen to that. Instead, Napoleon fell between two stools.

Napoleon drew up Ney's III Corps in front of the city with Murat's massed cavalry immediately behind them; Davout and Eugène were in support from the southwest, but it all went wrong from the start. On August 16 Ney probed the suburbs and was beaten back by well-entrenched Russian infantry. The next day saw furious and costly fighting in the western suburbs. Both sides fought with a determination that often bordered on fanaticism. It turned on house-to-house fighting, as often as not with the bayonet. In bitter irony, after months of stumbling through the wilderness, when the major engagement came, it was in the nasty form of street fighting. The French were thrown back time and again, only to regroup and charge again. Davout's men got closest to the Old City. When he saw that the Russians could not use their artillery properly in the debris, he pressed his attack. He reported the Russians as spread out in houses they had fortified, and supported by artillery from the walls. "The attack was very lively, and the defense decided," as Davout put it in the laconic manner that personified him in every sense.[126] However, his own twelve-pound field guns could not broach the medieval walls,[127] even though the French had reduced the houses of the suburbs and much of the Old City to rubble.[128] The Russians were prised out of the suburbs by Davout,[129] but Ney and Poniatowski had less success.[130] The Russian infantry, although eventually driven back behind the walls, fought like wolves. A Russian staff officer recalled that officers had to curb the urge among the men to launch almost suicidal counterattacks, and that wounded men often refused to leave the line for attention. Volunteers for dangerous duties were never short.[131]

The courage of I Corps, and the endurance of the esprit de corps of the Channel camps so many years ago, was shown in its senior commanders, as much as in the ranks. After the battle, Davout wrote with pride and emotion to Berthier:

> I cannot praise enough the conduct of the troops . . . Generals, offi-
> cers, soldiers of all the arms (of the service) have rivaled each other
> in zeal and bravery, and devotion to the service of His Majesty.

He accorded special mention to the men of the 127th Line Regiment, ". . . who, finding themselves under fire for the first time, conducted themselves in the finest manner possible. I hope His Majesty will accord them their eagle, which they could not deserve more."[132] The excellence of the French command was seen best in the number of senior officers who were wounded: General Alexandre Dalton was hit by a stray bullet; Friant—a divisional commander—by a "dud" shell. Of his "old team," Davout spoke glowingly: "Morand, Friant, Gudin, have given still more proof of their ability and their valor in this business."[133] Davout singled out "the brilliant and energetic part" played by the officers of Gudin's 3rd Division. General Étienne Maurice Gérard took command of the division with "great bravery and ability" when Gudin was wounded.[134]

Nor was Davout's corps alone in distinguishing itself that day. Ney said he regarded the attack by a battalion of his 16th Line Regiment as "the bravest feat of arms" he had ever seen.[135] No praise could be higher from the marshal dubbed by Napoleon "the bravest of the brave." The performance of I and II Corps was almost to be expected, but other, far less likely reputations were made or redeemed that day. As the day ended, several units stormed over a broken bridge, waded over the river, and breached the walls under heavy fire, and it took ten of Bagration's regiments to halt them. These were the same Württembergers who had been so mutinous only a few weeks before, together with Portuguese units, who had been forcibly incorporated into French ser-vice.[136] Poniatowski's Poles shined just as brightly. They had arrived on the field in bad odor with Napoleon. He blamed them for many of the failures of Jérôme's ill-conceived pursuit of Bagration, and greeted Poniatowski with an onslaught of gross, loudly proclaimed accusations of laziness and cowardice, among them that all V Corps was good for was chasing whores in Warsaw.[137] On August 17, nineteen hundred of their fifteen thousand men fell; they were the first into the Old City the next day—Napoleon ordered them out, to allow French troops to take formal possession—and on August 21, Napoleon—realizing his own gross error—reviewed them, awarding eighty-eight Légions d'honneur to V Corps, and spoke to many of the men personally.[138]

Smolensk was a needless battle, certainly in terms of a frontal assault. It was fought in gruesome conditions, recalling Wagram. "(T)he heat is excessive and there is a lot of dust, which tires us a bit" Napoleon admitted to Maret when it was over.[139] If his point needed making, it was reported that Napoleon collapsed on his bed as soon as he had dictated it, the secretary's explanation to Maret as to why it was unsigned.[140] Smolensk cost Napoleon about ten thousand casualties, the Russians between twelve thousand and fourteen thousand,[141] all in the course of less than two days. It displayed poor strategic thinking on Napoleon's part, poor coordination between a petulant Bagration and a dithering Barclay. Yet, it had shown deep reserves of pent-up courage, resilience, and loyalty among the ranks of two armies on the verge of disintegration. Despised units had risen to the chance to fight, just as much as the elite; raw conscripts fought as bravely as hardened veterans on both sides. Blood was up, Napoleon's just as much as his men's. Russian cities made of wood burned like no others the French had seen. As he saw his staff sickened by the sight—and doubtless, the smell—of charred ruins, Napoleon chided them, "Remember, gentlemen, what the Roman emperors said, 'the corpse of a dead enemy always smells good'." Caulaincourt recalled how they were all silently shocked by a remark so out of character in its ghoulishness.[142] Pent-up aggression ran from top to bottom that day. This made its final outcome all the more angering for the soldiers on both sides. After resting his men on August 18, Barclay defied his tsar's command, and ordered yet another retreat. The holy icon was put back on a gun carriage and hurried along the road to Moscow.[143] Napoleon's poor judgment let him get away with it. The French had battered Smolensk ruthlessly, even if they failed to breach the walls, which may have been as well, given that no one had issued them with ladders.[144] The mortar and cannon shells crashing into the wooden city created a conflagration the French found almost hallucinatory in its beauty and horror as night fell on the 17th. "Dante himself would have found inspiration for the hell he set out to depict," recalled one erudite French officer.[145] For the Russians, it was an inferno, fled in haste, great fear, and confusion. The French entered a living hell. People had been burned alive in their homes, and few buildings remained standing. The intense heat had shrunk many of the corpses so badly that French observers took dead soldiers for children. Those few who had not fled were, literally, cowering in the ashes. Napoleon detailed sixty doctors and other staff to organize hospitals in the stone buildings that remained, mainly monasteries and warehouses.[146] Lack of clean bedding and basic medical supplies, combined with the intense heat, soon led to the spread of disease. Having surveyed the battlefield in blazing heat, Napoleon issued an order to Berthier, chilling in its very crispness: "It is necessary to take measures for the corpses. The best method would be to order *corvées* (forced labor), and to burn them; if we don't burn them, it would not be well and would cause great trouble during this season.[147] It is also necessary to take steps to deal with the Russian dead, who are around the town."[148] The French could not wait for long, however.

Napoleon's decision to stake everything on a frontal assault allowed Barclay to concentrate his main force on the east bank of the Dnieper, and retain control of the main road to Moscow. He used the gap Napoleon had left him, and in so doing faced the opposition of his whole general staff. Entreaties to stand soon escalated into accusations of incompetence, at best, and even treason. Grand Duke Constantine, the tsar's brother, went so far as to shout aloud that "it isn't Russian blood that flows in those who command us."[149] It got worse: "You German, you sausage maker, you scoundrel; you are selling Russia . . . I refuse to remain under your orders!" "Let everyone do their duty, and let me do mine," Barclay replied,[150] with a composure worthy of Alexander himself. There was shock and bitterness throughout the army. They had fought bravely and the French had not breached the walls. It was Napoleon who broke off the action at dusk on the 18th. Barclay took the right decision, one that he knew would probably destroy his career. For Dominic Lieven, it was an act of selfless moral courage.[151] Barclay had saved the army, if not himself, by seeing sense, and not for the first time. Inadvertently, Bagration's petulant defiance had made Barclay's retreat possible, his march eastward preparing the way for the withdrawal and preventing a French encirclement. Two acts of defiance had allowed the Russians to fight another day, but it was by chance, not design.

The Russian withdrawal was a mess. Barclay had ordered it in haste, his staff lacked the time and expertise to chart the roads, establish depots and rendezvous points, or issue clear directions. The result was mayhem, compounded because the retreat began in the dead of night. Only a handful of units managed to leave on time, but were soon held up by poor roads made for peasant carts, not heavy ordnance. Ostermann-Tolstoy got hopelessly lost, going in complete circles—one of his units wound up so close to Ney's men, they could hear his bands playing "Reveille" at dawn, after a whole night's marching, at a place called Gedeonovo. Purely by chance, Barclay turned up in person, saw the danger, and organized the defense.[152] Ney should have made mincemeat of the three Russian regiments against him, but he was as taken aback as Prince Eugen of Württemberg, the young, inexperienced Russian commander. Ney moved too slowly, while Barclay and Eugen dug their men in, in the woods and the improvised trenches the Russian solider was renowned for. Eugen's small force held off the ever-swelling ranks of Ney's corps for several hours, and gave Ney so much trouble Gudin's division was detached from I Corps to help him. Eugen showed as much personal courage as any French commander, "fighting hand-to-hand like any hussar."[153] Both sides lost between seven thousand and nine thousand men in this chance encounter, among them Gudin, "one of the truly fine divisional commanders of the army."[154] It was an agonizing death, as Davout—his friend and comrade since the Channel camps—told his wife the next day:

> He had one leg amputated and the muscle on the other one shattered by a cannonball which exploded near him. There is little

chance he will survive. He took the amputation with rare courage
. . . it was he who tried to console me . . . I cried like a child.[155]

Gudin had a literate, famous friend to record his agony. Few others did, but Davout's unflinching clarity, together with his genuine, undisguised grief, give a grim example of what befell so many. Barclay ordered a retreat at nightfall, through the forest to the main road. Ney was so battered that Davout took over the advance, with Murat ahead of him. However, confusion and delays still reigned. Barclay was still there for the taking.

Napoleon was in his own state of confusion. Initially, he was unsure whether Barclay would head for Saint Petersburg, which meant swinging north and then west, or continue east toward Moscow. Murat set off down the Moscow road, with Ney behind him. When it was clear what Barclay was doing, Napoleon entrusted Junot and the Westphalians he had taken over from Jérôme with the flanking movement to cut off Barclay's retreat, while Murat and Davout pressed his rearguard. Napoleon remained in Smolensk, desperately trying to organize the rest of the army. He put his trust in these three old comrades. At this point, the French command fell to pieces, almost mirroring the Russians. Junot failed to take the ground fast enough, and took considerable time to get his men over the Dnieper. Yet, so great was the Russians' disarray that he found Tuchov's three thousand men at his mercy. He froze, and the moment was gone. Junot had displayed a lack of energy for some time. Davout had had cause to chide him during the advance on Smolensk[156] and he had a long history of mental instability. Napoleon's choice of Junot for such a crucial operation has been widely criticized and with reason.[157] He was one of his oldest comrades, and Napoleon knew his faults. Although often a corps commander, Napoleon never made him a marshal. Murat, whose cavalry had struggled through marshy, treacherous terrain to get close to the Russians, only to find Junot had not come, felt badly let down.[158]

Napoleon's "personnel problems" had only begun, however. Murat was furious at Junot, but it was as nothing compared to the loathing he now developed for Davout, which was reciprocated in full. Napoleon observed to Davout that, oddly, he was not in close enough contact with him on August 22, and he had explicitly ordered Murat "not to tire out his troops in this extreme heat, only to engage the rearguard."[159] Davout felt Murat's harassment of the Russian rearguard was too fragmented and undisciplined, and that he was still running his horses into the ground to no good end. Davout argued he could not support him properly, particularly as he was trying to spare the battered I Corps hard marching if he could. "It was not surprising that . . . two contrasting soldiers found themselves in complete disagreement" as John Gallaher observed.[160] Murat and Davout soon clashed bitterly as their pursuit of Barclay came apart. There was more to it, however. Davout now had Napoleon's orders to Murat in his hands. Each time Murat called on Davout for support, as he was entitled to do, Davout saw it as a drain on his men for a lost cause. When Murat rashly took on well-entrenched Russians on August 27, one of Davout's artillery commanders flatly refused to obey Murat. Davout finally ordered him to comply and he did, but the following day, the two went to see Napoleon and had a shouting match in front of him. Davout said he could do nothing to stop Murat running his cavalry into the ground, but he was not going to do it to I Corps; he threw out the disparaging nickname the Russians had for him—"The General of the Highways"—while Murat stood on his dignity as a king, over a marshal. Napoleon listened in silence.[161] Murat stormed off first, after Napoleon told them simply to get on with it. Then Napoleon turned to Davout and said they both had their strengths and weakness—that Davout was a superior commander in the field, but he reminded him that Murat knew how to harass a rearguard. John Gallaher has argued that it was now obvious one or other of them had to be replaced, and someone given undisputed command of the vanguard.[162] This makes sense, but Napoleon simply expected men he had trusted for so long to "get on with it," and not to need constant control. That was the point of the corps system, honed so long ago. It was coming apart. People had changed. Murat was a king now; he resented all authority, that of Napoleon most of all. Davout had taken command of Jérôme's army and organized the government of Minsk without awaiting orders.[163] He had grown used to ruling Germany, King Jérôme included. Napoleon missed this, and held on to past certainties—there had been bitter rows before, and he had calmed them. Caulaincourt recalled that as the campaign dragged on, Napoleon complained ever more frequently of people letting him down.[164] Sometimes this was more than justified, as with Jérôme; at others, Caulaincourt noted, it was grossly unfair, the result of illness, stress, and, perhaps, the realization gnawing away at him that he was in over his head.[165] Although Davout was doubtless correct in his row with Murat—the King of Naples may by now have realized he could not cope with a pitched battle, but did not make the connection when in pursuit—Napoleon still had a right to feel disappointed in both of them, simply for failing to cooperate on their own and to pursue a retreating enemy as the Grande Armée had done with such success since Austerlitz. Murat and Davout reached him quickly enough to have their "inopportune" falling out, as David Chandler wryly put it.[166]

Even before he reached Smolensk, Napoleon's front had widened beyond control. It now stretched from Riga in the north to Ukraine, but it was fraying. Napoleon detached Oudinot's II Corps from the main army in late July and sent it north, to shadow Wittgenstein's twenty-three thousand strong First Corps. Oudinot's brief was to ensure Wittgenstein did not reoccupy the valley of the Drina or the forts at Drissa.[167] He was then to occupy Polotsk, and use it as a base to harry Wittgenstein.[168] In words he soon regretted, Napoleon told Berthier that Oudinot "alone will decide what should be done; that he has, thus, carte blanche; but that he must take proper steps to correspond promptly with us."[169] It should have been straightforward enough, particularly as II Corps was one of finest units in the army. It still stood at something close to its original forty thousand strong; its core was Lannes's old Corps that Oudinot took over at Wagram after Lannes was mortally wounded. It also contained some Swiss units of good quality. Oudinot had always fought well when under Napoleon's direct control—as commander of the elite Grenadier Division, he was often part of the reserve—but he soon proved unsuited to the carte blanche Napoleon gave him. The first reports to reach Napoleon seemed good: Oudinot seemed to have routed Wittgenstein in the last days of July around Polotsk in "fairly hot actions,"[170] but it was soon clear that Wittgenstein was outwitting him. Oudinot had been reinforced by St. Cyr's exhausted Bavarians—now only thirteen thousand of the twenty-five thousand who began the campaign[171]—but Napoleon reminded him that he still outnumbered the Russians considerably, and was in a good position: Why then did he keep falling back on Polotsk?[172] Wittgenstein had utterly confused Oudinot with hit-and-run raids, his combination of light infantry and cavalry, and the hard experience of forest warfare acquired in the recent war with Sweden on the Finnish border. Alexander had made a formal treaty with Sweden on April 5, but, with his typical caution born of suspicion, he put little store by it initially. However, on August 27, he met with Bernadotte—now Charles John, the Swedish Prince Regent—at the Finnish city of Åit. There the two men learned to trust each other. Alexander was disabused of any fears that Bernadotte was yet another Napoleonic "satellite monarch," and one of the most important partnerships of the era began. Only now did Alexander unleash the "Finnish army" on Napoleon, sure in the knowledge that Bernadotte would not attempt to retake Finland, although there were many at his Court who urged it.[173]

The results of Alexander's careful diplomacy were soon felt on the battlefield. Fresh troops reached Wittgenstein, who proved increasingly impossible for Oudinot to fathom[174]—although Napoleon reminded him that such units were never large and could be checked[175]—and he failed to concentrate his forces. Napoleon was uneasy, but on August 10, was still under the impression that Oudinot had Wittgenstein "on the run," that he had inflicted heavy casualties on the Russians—he had not[176]—that Wittgenstein himself had been wounded—he had not[177]—and that "this enemy army seems to be in consternation."[178] When Wittgenstein struck at the combined forces of Oudinot and St. Cyr at Polotsk on August 17, it came as an enraging shock. Whereas the Russians were organized and concentrated, many of the French were off foraging. Oudinot had his shoulder shattered by grapeshot the night before the attack, when—in an act typical of him—he had rushed forward to steady a company of light infantry caught unawares by the Russians.[179] It was St. Cyr who saved the day and pushed Wittgenstein back—albeit in good order—noting how well the Russians had fought.[180] He won his marshal's baton. Oudinot—wounded or not—was berated by Napoleon:

> You shouldn't ever have let yourself fall into such gross traps. The Russians are publicizing everywhere and beyond, the stunning victory they have won over us, since you allowed them to camp down on the battlefield . . . Go find Wittgenstein and attack him wherever you find him . . .[181]

Oudinot's organization was so poor, Napoleon had yet to know how seriously he had been wounded. St. Cyr continued the chase; Wittgenstein fell back to a well-fortified position, and this sector soon degenerated into a stalemate of raid and counterraid, but the Russians had sound interior lines and remained better supplied and reinforced than St. Cyr.[182] Above all, Wittgenstein had neutralized one of the few good units Napoleon had left. This once proud corps was worn down over the coming months by sickness and hunger, as it tried to contain Wittgenstein in a barren countryside. By September, it was weakened enough for the Russians to resume the offensive.[183] Oudinot had remarried just before the campaign and, in the manner of the new Napoleonic womanhood, his eighteen-year-old aristocratic wife, Eugénie de Coussy, raced to join him in Vilna, against explicit orders that wives were not allowed on campaign. Oudinot was back in the saddle by October, before she even got there.[184]

Fortunately, Napoleon's commanders on the furthest-flung wings of the front proved much better. The Prussians and Austrians fought with a skill and distinction his other, older allies often lacked. The westernmost flank of the front was in the hands of Macdonald. His almost wholly Prussian corps proved very effective in the limited actions required of it. He drove up the Baltic coast fairly easily, forcing the main Russian force under Essen into Riga, where they remained bottled up for the rest of the campaign.[185] These most reluctant of Napoleon's allies sowed more panic among the Russians than anyone else. Hundreds of refugees flooded into Saint Petersburg where their tales spread "grief, fear and despair" according to one observer.[186] The reform of the Prussian army post-Jena bore its first fruit in Napoleon's service. Macdonald's advance might indicate how easy it would have been for Napoleon to threaten Saint Petersburg; it underlines emphatically that his aim was always to destroy Alexander's army, not to seize his capital or his territory.

The situation was far more serious to the south, where considerable Russian forces freed up by the end of the Turkish war were arriving in force to threaten Napoleon's extreme right flank. Napoleon considered Tormasov's army of forty-five thousand too scattered to pose a real threat, and had assigned a mere nineteen thousand Saxons under Jean Reynier to hold this sector. However, once chided into action by Alexander, Tormasov thrashed the Saxons at Korbin in late July, taking two thousand prisoners and forcing Napoleon to send Schwarzenberg's Austrians into action against them. On August 12, Schwarzenberg inflicted a heavy defeat on Tormasov at Gorodeczna, proving the unsuspected worth of the Austrian contingent in battle. This threw Tormasov back on the defensive, blunting any threat to the central army from the south for the moment. However, the definitive peace with the Ottomans in late July at last released Admiral Chichagov's fifty thousand battle-hardened Army of the Danube for use against Napoleon. It took fifty-two days for Chichagov to reach Tomarsov in mid-September—just as Napoleon was advancing from Smolensk to Moscow—and it was only then did Napoleon see how threatened his southern sector had become. Until then, Schwarzenberg proved an effective check on Tomarsov.[187] Only when it was too late, and Napoleon had plunged irreparably into central Russia, did the twin menaces of Wittgenstein and Chichagov emerge clearly.

Smolensk was a tipping point for Napoleon. He was now plunging farther into Russia than he ever envisaged. Even a few days before Smolensk, Napoleon mused to Eugène, "If a peasant revolt took place in old Russia, it would be a very advantageous thing and we could draw great advantage from it . . . let me know what sort of decree and proclamation would stir the Russian peasants to revolt and rally them to us."[188] No more. His supply lines were stretched beyond the breaking point; his men—and his horses—were thinning in number by the day, to the point that he now ordered conscription imposed on the provinces of Vitebsk and Mogilev—"since they are Poles and speak Polish" he told Maret—to fill the ranks of Poniatowski's battered V Corps.[189] If ever there was a sign of desperation and delusion from Napoleon, it was this: He ignored the reality that the peasants of these benighted provinces had long fled into their impenetrable forests; his own experience of empty towns and villages was forgotten in his growing realization of the weakness of his army as a great battle loomed. That army was venturing into the unknown, soon to be surrounded by a hostile population whipped into a fanatical, determined resistance at least the equal of the Spanish. Caulaincourt put it best: "In Poland (Lithuania and Belarus) everything had been lacking . . . at Smolensk, by searching the countryside we had found standing crops . . . After Dorogobonje all was in flames."[190] The further they advanced, the emptier the country became—not only did the army leave no stragglers or transport behind, "not even the old folk or the sick were to be found."[191]

Napoleon did not stop to reflect for one moment about any of this. He drove the army on, and was soon in the midst of the advance. That neither man nor beast could sustain the war of movement mattered not a jot.[192] The Russians were now concentrated and still within his grasp, and the decisive battle Napoleon craved now appeared closer than ever. This was the world Napoleon continued to live in, but it was not for want of dissenting voices. He continued to allow all those close to him to speak freely, and they spoke with one voice: Turn back. Bessières—joint commander of the Imperial Guard[193]—was among the most outspoken,[194] but even the man to whom Napoleon entrusted the well-being of his son was not heeded. "Never was the truth so dinned into the ear of a sovereign to no effect," Caulaincourt recalled.[195] It was almost blind faith, as so little information reached the French. Spies had been scarce from the start, so it was no small matter when two very different men were captured in these days. One was the Black servant of a Russian general, who proved incomprehensible and was utterly baffled.

He steadfastly refused to believe he was speaking to Napoleon, for no Russian general, never mind the tsar, would risk themselves by being in the vanguard of the army. More than a little of the old spirit was still alive in Napoleon, when seen from the outside. The other prisoner was a Cossack, who proved very forthcoming once Napoleon bribed him. Napoleon now learned that Barclay had been sacked for abandoning Smolensk, and replaced by Mikhail Kutusov. This showed how poor Napoleon's intelligence was, but it also convinced him that the Russians would finally give battle. His first thought was of Kutusov's incompetence at Austerlitz.[196] In the knowledge that the Russians had their own problems, Napoleon saw his prize before him at long last.

Borodino

The order of the Russian retreat astounded the French. The military strategist Antoine de Jomini, serving with Napoleon, felt it "highly deserving of praise" not only for the generals behind it, but "for the admirable fortitude and soldierly bearing of the troops who performed it."[197] It did not look like that to the Russians. The troops who had fought so bravely at Smolensk—and had been agitated to do so by their superiors, military and clerical—were sullen and, if not by now surprised, certainly made uneasy by the streams of refugees who followed their march and the results of the scorched-earth policy all around them. There was remarkably little indiscipline, for all that, but frustration mounted as Barclay and Bagration selected positions to dig in to face the French, only to change their minds and fall back ever closer to Moscow. They were at one with most of their commanders in blaming Barclay.[198] Not surprisingly, the appointment of Kutusov was hailed from top to bottom in the two armies. His arrival at headquarters, at Tsarevo-Zamishche on August 29, was described by one young officer as "an outpouring of joy . . . a universal rebirth of morale among the soldiers."[199]

Kutusov's appointment caused Alexander as much angst as his dismissal of Speransky. Kutusov's failure at Austerlitz smacked of incompetence born of his disheveled personal conduct. The tsar's dislike of him came partly from a sense of being hounded by public opinion into demoting Barclay, in whom he had faith, but also by his lingering suspicion that Kutusov had played a part in the assassination of his father. Nevertheless, the abandonment of Smolensk left Alexander little alternative.[200] He found a compromise, true to his nature: Kutusov was given overall command, with Bennigsen—now brought out of semi-disgrace—as his chief of staff. The two men were good friends, which gave the new arrangements a chance of success, even if Alexander probably saw Bennigsen as a brake on Kutusov and a source of information. For his part, Bennigsen expressed a "reluctance to serve under the command of another general after I had previously served as commander in chief."[201] Tensions grew as the campaign progressed, but initially their partnership worked well. Barclay and Bagration kept their respective armies; they were not dismissed but, rather, subordinated to Kutusov, a "fudge."[202]

For all the differences of personality between Kutusov and Barclay, the blustering "Russian" firebrand of the old school continued the retreat favored by the cautious "German." However, Kutusov continued looking for a suitable position to make a stand. By September 3, he felt he had found one, near the village of Borodino, 124 kilometers west of Moscow. The northern part of the Russian line ran along the river Kolocha, which itself flowed parallel to the main east-west highway, the New Smolensk Road, from the village of Maslovo in the northeast, to Borodino. Barclay's army took over its defense. It was the best-protected part of the front, formed of rolling countryside, broken by streams and ravines, and patches of woodland. Just south of Borodino stood the Hill of Kurgan, just over two hundred meters high, which Barclay set about turning into as formidable a position as he could; it became known as Raevsky's Redoubt, after the general who commanded it. The houses and hamlets around it were destroyed, providing more cover among the rubble. Barclay's men were well positioned in the woods and brush along the Kolocha, where his light infantry found a perfect place to shield the main infantry and cavalry units, with the earthworks behind them as the last line of defense. South of Borodino, however, the terrain was more open and offered much less protection to Bagration's men. Indeed, Bagration pulled back from his original line, feeling the countryside was too vulnerable, to a line between the village of Semenovskoe in the north to Utitsa in the south, where the front ended, anchored by the marshes south of the villages, and the Old Smolensk Road. This, too, was relatively open country, where troops risked being decimated by artillery fire. To counteract this as best he could, Bagration quickly threw up flèches ("arrows")—simple wooden stakes, sharpened at the top—on the crests of three small hills in the middle of his line. Bagration's twenty-five thousand men were badly overstretched. The Redoubt and the flèches were not well constructed, as they had been built by the Moscow militia, who did not have the same experience as the regular troops, whose skill in such work was well proven. The speed of the French advance meant all the frontline troops were needed on active duty. The Redoubt also had a natural weakness; it was built on a small hill that could hold only eighteen guns.[203] Kutusov remained indifferent to the initial complaints of Barclay and Bagration about this; it was only brought home to him when Bennigsen returned to headquarters with similar views of the vulnerability of the southern sector. Kutusov was showing himself at his worst: having chosen the battlefield and briefly inspected it on September 4, he spent most of his time in his tent, in his disheveled green dressing gown and nightcap, issuing vague orders in his native language—impeccable French. He happily informed Alexander on the strength of his forward positions on September 6, and assured the governor of Moscow, Fyodor Rostopchin, that Napoleon would be routed and the ancient capital saved.[204] His rosy picture had already been exposed the previous day, when Compans's division attacked the 27th Russian division and, bolstered by Poniatowski, forced Bagration to pull back, although both sides took very heavy losses in the region of five to six thousand men each.[205] Over September 6 and 7, Kutusov poured more troops into this narrow salient, and the field commanders packed men rank-on-rank behind the outer defenses and the flèches, in an effort to counter the lack of natural obstacles with raw manpower. Estimates of the total Russian strength varies—David Chandler puts it at over 120,000[206] while more recent research brings it to between 155,000 and 157,000[207]—but it seems clear that about 90,000 men were poured into the very narrow salient Barclay and Bagration had created.[208]

Kutusov's inactivity was typical of him, but Napoleon was behaving in similar fashion, which was completely out of character. The French moved speedily along the highway from Smolensk in something close to the normal, compact formation for Napoleonic armies. Murat's cavalry provided the screen for the advance, with Davout, Ney, and Napoleon with the Imperial Guard in the center, with Eugène on the left and Poniatowski on the right. Junot brought up the rear. Murat's cavalry reached the monastery of Kolotskoie early on the morning of September 5, where he could see the Russians digging in around Borodino and the Redoubt. Napoleon arrived about midday, wished the monks a good lunch in bad Polish, and did a reconnoiter.[209] Compans's clash on the southern fringe of the front also brought him clear information. Napoleon spent the whole of September 6 in the saddle, trying to work out the Russian positions, but he did not seem to be processing it well, having been ill the night before. By the end of the day, he was exhausted, his bladder complaint had recurred, and his legs were badly swollen.[210] Although he saw how well Barclay's men were dug in north of the Rebout, and determined not to confront him, he thought there were only two flèches. He failed to see the third, which stood behind the others.[211] Above all, he badly underestimated the strength of the Russian left, or Kutusov's ability to reinforce it quickly. He actually thought the Russians were weakest around the flèches, rather than to the south of them, on the open ground. This decided him on a frontal assault on the Redoubt and the flèches, led by Ney and Davout. Eugène was to hold down the Russian right, while Poniatowski drove up their left back as far as far as possible.

When he summoned the marshals to set out his battle plans, Davout saw the true nature of the Russian front, and argued that its extreme south was actually the weak link, and that he and Poniatowski should try an even wider flanking movement with forty thousand men, to envelop the Russians completely from behind overnight, while Ney simply pinned their center down. Napoleon thought it over, but finally rejected the plan because it would take too long and divert him from his main objective. Davout was not satisfied and argued back until he saw Napoleon would not shift, finally saying it was simply too dangerous. Davout confessed he was perplexed by Napoleon's newfound prudence.[212] When pressed, Napoleon was frank: Night marches were rare and challenging; Davout's plan demanded a confidence in the men that Napoleon no longer had; he doubted their very physical ability to carry out a forced march anymore. He knew his numbers had thinned badly, that he was outnumbered—it is doubtful the figure of 128,000 in the field given to him by his commanders was accurate[213]—but more important, the Russians were in better condition. The French were tired and hungry; despite the disheveled retreat from Smolensk, the Russians were now generously supplied from Moscow and had gotten to whatever there was to pilfer on the road before the French. However, the Russians now eclipsed the Grande Armée in exactly those vital respects on which a frontal assault depended: Murat's cavalry was clearly no longer a match for Kutusov's superbly mounted seventeen thousand regular cavalry, supported by about seven thousand Cossacks.[214] The Russians surpassed Napoleon's artillery. Kutusov had 640 guns[215] to Napoleon's 587.[216] The Russian cannons were of better quality and better positioned. Most of Napoleon's guns were light artillery, ill-suited to attacking entrenched positions.[217] The only thing that helped the French was the tightly packed deployment of the Russians, so dense and immobile that they were very vulnerable to any bombardment, but Napoleon could not know this before the battle. All this urged him to a caution unthinkable in the early years. He stuck with a frontal assault on the Redoubt and the flèches, led by Davout and Ney, supported by Murat's cavalry. They were all drawn up on the open plain before the Russian earthworks. The Russians waited behind them. Now, at long last, both sides—from the ranks to the high commands—were going to get what they wanted. The self-styled unstoppable force hurtled ever closer to the self-designated immovable object. The result was carnage.

The night before the battle, in the quiet before the storm, Kutusov and Napoleon did something eerily similar. September 6 was a Sunday, and Kutusov ordered the Virgin of Smolensk taken around the Russian positions on a gun carriage, accompanied by a procession of monks with incense, and his own staff. Prayers were said and blessings given to the ranks all along the line. The troops had already displayed great calm, and this gesture reinforced it. Hardened veterans handed over their last coins as offerings, and held out their own crucifixes to be blessed. ". . . (It) seemed as though after praying for a while each of us gained in strength," recalled one officer.[218] Phillipe-Paul de Ségur may have been an aristocrat, but this touched a Jacobin nerve in him. When a Russian general spoke to his men of heaven, Ségur sneered that it was "the slaves" last remaining refuge: "In the name of . . . religion, he called upon these serfs to defend the livelihood of their masters." When he asserted that the French had no such nonsense in their ranks,[219] he was not quite right, however. The same evening, a portrait of the King of Rome reached Napoleon that he "considered very beautiful."[220] It had been commissioned for the Salon of 1812—the last of under the empire—from François Gérard, a pupil of David who became one of the foremost portrait artists of the regime.[221] Bassuet—an unreliable source, it must be said—recalled only "the regret that he could not clasp his son to his heart" clouded the sheer joy he felt on seeing it: "His eyes expressed a true tenderness."[222] It is, however, well documented that Napoleon put it on display for the Old Guard.[223] The officers mocked the Russian "mummeries" as Napoleon himself is reported by Rapp to have called the procession,[224] but the hardened *grognards* filed past it with a sense of reverence not so unlike that of their adversaries for the Virgin of Smolensk.[225] It is impossible to gauge, but the troops' response to the image of the King of Rome may reveal a deepening dynastic loyalty among them, now further removed France than ever, a bonding with the leader alone. It is certain that Napoleon kept it before him at all times from then on. He had told both Cambacérès and Caulaincourt more than once in the prelude to the war that its purpose was to secure the future for his son. The timing of its arrival was poignant. It had the whiff of "destiny."

The night of September 6–7 was foul, cold, and damp, a sudden change from the blistering heat of the previous months, and a taste of things to come.[226] Napoleon was encamped in the midst of the guard, as ever, near a copse of trees, north of Eugène's corps on the extreme left of his front lines. From there, he issued a call to arms to the army: "Soldiers! Here is the battle you have so long desired! Henceforth, victory depends on you; we have need of it. We will win ourselves abundance of supplies, good winter quarters, and a prompt return to our Motherland." He went on to remind them of the great victories of the past and the pride they should feel for having fought well under the gates of Moscow,[227] but he knew what they all desperately needed was respite, of the most basic kind, and said so. Alan Forrest has remarked that "Napoleon's words managed to stir [the troops'] emotions and fuel their self-interest in the same breath."[228] It echoed his appeal to his first command, the Army of Italy in 1796, an army in rags he exhorted to fight for food and gold. Early in the morning, he moved to the hill of Shevardino, as good a vantage point as any. Napoleon sat on a folding camp chair to observe as much as he could. He did not move from it all day. As day broke, a ray of sun emerged. "The Sun of Austerlitz!" he remarked.[229]

At 6:00 A.M., the artillery of I Corps, III Corps, and the guard opened up on the Russians. Ney and Davout's lead divisions moved forward in the center. On the left, Eugène's IV Corps stormed into Borodino and took the village, helped by the cover of an early morning mist. Eugène pushed on to take the high ground near Gorki, but was unprepared for the fury of the Russian response. By 7:30 A.M. he had pulled back to Borodino. The main force withdrew further still, leaving only one division to protect the morning's gains. On the right, Poniatowski took Utitsa. However, the Russian counterattack came swiftly and in force. Poniatowski was halted by a hail of fire from light infantry shielded in the woods north of the villages, "showing a courage (they) did not always and everywhere display" for one German observer.[230] His retreat was only halted when reinforcements from Junot's Westphalian corps arrived.

The real fighting came, as planned, in the center. At 7:00 A.M., Ney and Davout attacked the two forward flèches; Ney attacked the northernmost one, Davout that to the south. The Russian fire was murderous, and casualties heavy. Compans was wounded before he even got to the Russian lines. His men were badly shaken, and Davout himself took over the division, rallied the men, and took the flèche along with Desaix's division. Napoleon's misreading of Russian strength led him to hold Friant's division in reserve, which meant that Davout and Desaix were too weak to repel the Russian counterattack, which was not long in coming. Napoleon had counted on Poniatowski reaching them, but he was actually in retreat, and had to be bolstered by the Young Guard.

Ney fared better, and took the northern flèche, which meant Bagration had to divert his men against him, allowing Davout some respite to regroup and launch a new assault on the southern flèche. Ney then divided his corps, diverting two divisions to help Davout, and took it upon himself to order Junot's VIII Corps to help Poniatowski, farther south. This crucially weakened the concentration of forces needed to take the main objective, the area behind the flèches around Semenovskoe. In the process, the troops of I and III Corps got mixed up and, as officers fell wounded, command structures became tangled at the most basic level.[231] I Corps needed all the help it could get, just the same. Davout's horse was shot out from under him; briefly knocked unconscious, he came to and refused to leave the field. Desaix was so badly wounded he had to be carried from the field.[232] Napoleon sent in Rapp from headquarters to take over, and it was Rapp—one of the most versatile of all Napoleon's men—who retook the southern flèche and held off another Russian counterattack, at the price of his twenty-second combat wound.[233] This was only the beginning of the horror. These two flèches were now exposed to the full fire of the big Russian guns on the third flèche. Whether in Russian hands or their own, the flèches were death traps for the French. Following this heavy bombardment, Bagration threw his whole might against the flèches and retook them. Napoleon saw the gravity of it all, and threw in not only Friant's division, but Latour-Maubourg and General Etienne Nansouty's cavalry, which had been exposed to heavy Russian fire all morning, simply waiting for orders on open ground. In the course of less than two hours, the flèches were taken and retaken seven times.[234] Davout, by now unable to ride after his abdomen was hit by a cannonball and his thigh pierced by a bullet, led his men on foot.[235] Ney was everywhere on his white horse, resplendent in full dress uniform, a clear target who was obviously born lucky. Murat, too was at the forefront and highly visible, as always. Even Bagration was moved to cheer the French for their courage on the flèches.[236] The Russian commanders were no less brave: Prince Vorontsov was severely wounded leading his Grenadiers against Rapp, but the worst loss was Bagration, who was mortally wounded in a moment of temporary triumph, at about 10:00 A.M. After retaking all three flèches he was hit in the leg, his thighbone shattered, and fell from his horse. Insisting nothing was wrong, he was carried from the field, dying. His last words were to commend his army to Barclay: ". . . let him look after my army, and may God help us all," a grudging admission of his rival's competence.[237] Shattered by the news, the Russians on the flèches were soon driven off, but it had taken everything Napoleon possessed to do so, and only this moment of luck actually turned the tide. Ney and Davout wasted no time. They drove the Russians back over the ravine of Semeonovka, and turned them northward toward the village of Semeonvskie, using their light cannon to advantage, as they had at Friedland. Semeonvskie's houses collapsed in ruins "like theatrical stage sets," one Russian officer observed.[238] The Russians rallied, and met the oncoming French with real fury. The struggle for the ruined village descended into bestial, atavistic combat. A Russian officer, Captain Lubenkov, remembered it with a shudder that can be felt even now on the page of memoirs written twenty-five years later: "It was a fight between ferocious tigers, not men, and once both sides had determined to win or die where they stood, they did not stop fighting when their muskets broke, but carried on, using the buts and swords in terrible hand-to-hand combat, and the killing went on for an hour and a half."[239] Ney was wounded four times. The commander of the Russian artillery, Aleksandr Kutaisov, was killed, his body never found.[240] These were men now isolated from superior orders, left to their own instincts, two armies that still wanted to fight; their privations and loss of direction counted for nothing in the face of the enemy. The French won.

This was the first clear moment in the battle when Napoleon's inertia thwarted his commanders. Ney and Davout now saw the tide had turned for them. They had opened a gap behind the Russian lines and could drive north, behind the Redoubt, and begin rolling up what was left of Bagration's forces.

They could no longer do so on their own, and implored Napoleon to send help. He did not respond, unaware of how his position had changed because he did not ride out to see for himself. Nor was he taking in the reports he received from exhausted riders from Ney and Davout. Davout saw immediately that the battle was bereft of any central direction. Napoleon has been much criticized, and Davout and Ney were doubtless right that had the guard come to their aid, they could have isolated the Redoubt from the rear, caused havoc among the Russians, and forced a result. Louis-François Lejeune, Berthier's aide-de-camp, recalled that Napoleon was on the point of committing the guard when "a timid counselor remarked to him '. . . that Your Majesty is at present moment 700 leagues from Paris, and at the gates of Moscow.'"[241] Lejeune felt this is what swayed him. By the same token, Napoleon knew Kutusov still had reserves and he did not. The real fault was, perhaps, in his sluggish approach to command. Napoleon should have listened to Davout and Ney, simply because they were there, and he was not.

Kutusov was equally inert that morning, as was his wont. Kutusov, unlike Napoleon, lacked any coherent strategy, he was "simply reacting to appeals for help and alarming reports."[242] At least he did react. The original eighteen thousand defenders of the flèches rose threefold as he poured men from Barclay's units into the ever narrowing salient to hold the Redoubt.[243] Seeing the danger for themselves, units now under Aleksey Yermolov fought their way through the French onto the Redoubt.[244] Kutusov was using up his reserves at a worrying rate, but Napoleon had none left by late morning, except the guard, and he held it back. It was his only remaining unit intact.

Instead, he threw all his forces at the Redoubt. This has been seen as proof of how little coordination Napoleon exerted on even the center of his front because Ney and Davout had no inkling of this.[245] Napoleon sent Eugène's men and Morand's division against the Redoubt in a head-on assault. The first attack, by Eugène, at about 8:30 A.M., was thrown back in a bloodbath. This was the first example at Borodino of how the quality and training of the Grande Armée had declined, and its ghastly results in the field: The well-drilled infantry of the early campaigns could deploy from the column into the line easily, even under fire, before an attack. This made them a less easy target. It was a complex maneuver that even the best French troops now found difficult. Eugène did not risk it, but the result was columns of densely packed men, who were simply cannon fodder for the Russian guns.[246] The Redoubt, however hastily built, proved formidable early on. By now, Yermolov had organized the rest of his forces in a defensible position near the Redoubt to check Davout and Ney. Eugène, Davout, and Ney, supported by the cavalry, flung themselves on the Redoubt as "a formidable array of (Russian) guns spat forth death in every direction."[247] An assault by Morand's division at last ousted the Russians, but by then he was isolated and an easy target. The Redoubt was retaken by a mixture of luck and the quick thinking of several Russian commanders left adrift by the listless Kutusov. Units under Yermolov, who had been ordered further south to stop Poniatowski, saw what was happening literally as they passed by, changed course, and hit the French almost from the rear. The French fell back into the undefended rear of the Redoubt, pursued by Yermolov's men. General Bonamy, of Morand's division, was badly wounded and captured; French losses were devastating: Of the 4,100 men of the 30th Line Regiment who attacked the Redoubt, only 268 made it back to Eugène's lines.[248]

To relieve the Redoubt, Kutusov authorized a cavalry assault on Napoleon's extreme left, and temporarily drew off Eugène. Eugène beat back this ill-advised attack with ease, but it seems to have convinced Napoleon still further to retain his last reserves in case Kutusov attempted something more serious in this sector.[249] The attack on the Redoubt resumed in earnest. No fewer than four hundred guns were brought up to support Eugène's renewed assault. At 2:00 P.M., his infantry again charged the hill head-on, while the heavy cavalry, composed of Saxons, Poles, and French cuirassiers—the true shock force—now led by Caulaincourt's brother, Auguste, tried to batter its way through the Russian lines to the south of the Redoubt to get behind it, exactly what Davout and Ney wanted to do when it was there for the taking. Eugène's assault was bloody but checked. When he asked Napoleon to send in the guard, he was rebuffed with a curtness the emperor reserved only for family: "I will not demolish my Guard."[250] When Caulaincourt's cavalry poured into the earthworks, they found them almost full to the top of Russian and French corpses. Further on, they rode into the breastworks, where the Russian infantry was waiting. Those who crashed through the musket volleys were met with a sea of bayonets, as many of which plunged into the horses' bellies as into their riders. Auguste Caulaincourt lost his life somewhere in the midst of this, but his men drove on up the hill, the infantry charging behind them. When they reached the top, the center of the Redoubt, uncontrolled slaughter broke out, hand-to-hand fighting in a very confined space—"a frenzy of slaughter" to one Saxon officer[251]—as mounted Frenchmen hacked at the gunners with their swords, and the gunners fought back with their ramrods, their bayonets, their fists. Grouchy's cavalry and horse artillery had watched this from afar, cheering their comrades on. "It would be difficult to recall our feelings as we watched this brilliant feat of arms . . . and a roar of joy resounded . . . as they became masters of the redoubt," one officer remembered.[252] Now it was their turn. Grouchy's men led the sweep into the area behind the Redoubt, but Barclay had arrived and taken command. While Davout and Ney were checked around Semeonovskoie, Barclay formed what was left of the infantry into squares, and stopped Grouchy's horsemen in their tracks. He was remembered as "a beacon in the storm."[253] He called for the reserve cavalry division to launch a counterattack, as Grouchy reeled backward, only to find that Kutusov had ordered it elsewhere. Rallying what horsemen he could, Barclay, himself, led a charge that drove the French back into the Redoubt. Many scholars feel that, knowing disgrace awaited him, Barclay was courting death. He exposed himself to danger, astride his horse in full uniform, while his staff were butchered by French artillery fire.[254]

Farther south, around Lieven, three elite Russian Guard regiments were devastated in their exposed positions by Ney and Davout's artillery fire, while their light infantry held back French attempts to break out of the forest to their left. When the French unleashed the cavalry, they, too, formed into squares that blunted Ney and Davout's final assault. If less spectacular than the fighting behind the Redoubt, these actions were equally costly—two of the three guard regiments suffered sixteen hundred casualties. Dominic Lieven asserts that "their steadiness was the rock around which the Russian defense coalesced."[255] With the arrival of Russian cavalry, it was clear to Ney and Davout their men could go no further. Again, they pleaded with Napoleon to commit the guard; again, he refused, although he did agree to release eighty guns to bolster the new lines.[256] But the eleven thousand men of the Old Guard, and their almost five thousand horses,[257] did not fight. Twice that day, the guard heard the order to advance, only to be told to halt after a few paces.[258] It was as close as that.

On this occasion, it seems to have been the influential voice of their own commander, Bessières, who, according to Caulaincourt, advised Napoleon of the Russians that, "far from being in disorder, had retreated to a second position where they seemed to be preparing for a fresh attack."[259] The belief that the guard would have won the battle hinges on the assumption that Davout and Ney's assessment was correct. Murat is reported in conversation with Ney as supporting Bessières's view that the Russians retreated in good order; Ney asserted that their losses were too great for this: "How could they after such a pounding?"[260]

The cavalrymen were half right. Russian losses were heavy, but true to form, Barclay withdrew in good order to a stronger position, and the fighting spluttered out. Kutusov, in blissful, blustering ignorance, ordered preparations for a fresh attack in the morning, and foul-mouthed a member of Barclay's staff who informed him of the dreadful Russian losses, and that the new positions represented the loss of crucial ground: "Where did you invent such nonsense? You must have spent all day getting drunk with some filthy bitch!"[261] In this context, Napoleon's decision to preserve the guard does not seem unreasonable. He knew Kutusov. What he had not counted on was the ability of cooler heads to prevail on him. Kutusov may not really have intended to fight again, but it was only when accurate reports were shoved under his nose that he could not avoid the reality that he had only forty-five thousand men in arms left; Kutusov was told his losses came close to 50 percent. These figures may not have been wholly accurate, but they came from the front. Bennigsen, on his own initiative, had covered as much of the combat zones as he could, and

Kutusov accepted his word.[262] Because Napoleon had left the Russian right alone in the battle, the main road to Moscow was still open, and Barclay now made good use of it.

From start to finish, if disaster at Borodino was averted, it was through the initiative and intelligence of individual Russian commanders, and the steadfast courage of the Russian soldier. Napoleon had, at least, tried to stay in view of the fighting. Kutusov made his headquarters at Gorki, well away from the action, and almost never left it. Kutusov did not even bother to replace Kutaisov when he fell, leaving the Russian artillery—perhaps their strongest arm—rudderless: batteries went unsupplied to the point that the Russians fired no more rounds than the French; reinforcements arrived piecemeal when the French overran batteries; the reserve was never used.[263] Bennigsen and Kutusov redeployed large units of Barclay's forces to bolster Bagration's sector without his knowledge.[264] The Russian high command was as flawed as it had been at Austerlitz, seven years earlier. The blustering over, Kutusov wrote to Alexander and had the decency to extol the courage of his troops, but admitted he had too few men left to hold the present front. He still intended to destroy Napoleon, and to this end he was pulling back a few leagues. He retreated all the way to Moscow, with Barclay handling it with his usual competence and, at least outward, calm.

Napoleon awoke on September 8 to the usual disappointment, but the road to Moscow was at last open. Borodino, Adam Zamoyski has said, was the "greatest massacre in recorded history," not to be surpassed until the first day of the Somme in 1916.[265] Napoleon picked his way through the battlefield late on September 7, to behold a sight that made Eylau pale, yet something had changed in Napoleon. Whereas the aftermath of Eylau had genuinely shaken him, he told Maret, "This battlefield is the most beautiful I have ever seen."[266] An officer of the Vistula Legion who observed Napoleon measuring out the dead on the Redoubt recalled that "Napoleon's face was quite impassive, but he did look a little pale,"[267] perhaps as much—or more—due to illness as horror. As at Smolensk, this sadism—as quite opposed to callousness—was new. He beheld an obscenity. Mangled corpses covered the plain below the

Redoubt and the flèches, a zone where little real combat took place. The dead were victims of the Russian guns raining down on massed ranks simply awaiting orders. Dying horses wandered the field, sometimes collapsing on dying men trying to get up. Men and beasts staggered about in search of some kind of relief. The area around the Redoubt excelled even this horror, its earthworks crammed with the dead. A Polish officer spoke of a depth of six to eight men in the ditches. Inside the Redoubt, the Russians had fallen in formation; lying in neat lines, looking as if they had been scythed down. The living French were less stoic. Many cried in agony, soaked in their own blood. Few cheers greeted Napoleon as he rode out.[268] This squalid butchers' yard was the reality behind the huge numbers: between forty-five thousand and fifty thousand Russian casualties according the most recent estimates, against about thirty-five thousand French. Bagration's army was almost totally destroyed, having borne the brunt of the fighting: over twenty-one thousand in all, including their leader. The loss of senior officers was "crippling."[269] The roll call among the French commanders was just as stark. In I Corps, Gérard alone emerged unscathed among the divisional commanders. Friant, Morand, Desaix, Compans, and Rapp—who had replaced Compans—were all seriously injured. Davout badgered Napoleon in the weeks to come in their favor.[270] Davout, himself, was a physical wreck. His chief of staff, Jean-Louis Romeuf, died of his wounds. Gudin had already been killed. This was but one corps. The bravery of the commanders on both sides matched that of their men. Their courage was all the more evident because their respective leaders were nowhere to be seen among them.

Borodino has been called "an imperfect victory" by David Chandler; inconclusive by John Gallaher.[271] Perhaps, but the army would never be the same again. Nothing could bring back the cavalry. Many veterans were no more.

Far from the battlefield, Wittgenstein had had his part to play. It is often forgotten that his skillful campaign tied down Oudinot's II Corps, as well as St. Cyr's Bavarians. Had the French veterans of II Corps been present, using the guard may not have become as crucial. Napoleon saw the threat, and badgered St. Cyr "to attack and batter him, and turn him" with the superior forces of II Corps.[272] He remained just as worried by the ever-closer Chichagov. He told Maret soon after the battle he was sure Chichagov was heading for Moscow, and that Schwarzenberg was "not let the enemy fool him . . . if the enemy who is close to him falls on me, he must follow him and fall upon him. That is well understood."[273] It was an admission, however oblique, that Borodino had not delivered him from danger. Behind them all stood Arakcheev, patiently training and mobilizing Russia's huge numbers of new conscripts and militia for the reserve.[274] The dead of Borodino bought him precious time.

It was all the more reason to dissemble and lie. Immediately after the fighting, Napoleon referred to the "Battle of Borodino" but by September 9, he rechristened it "the Battle of Moscow"[275] (as it is still known in France); that he was still over one hundred kilometers from Moscow was neither here nor there. He was very selective in who he wrote to after Borodino. As always, he lied, but this time he lied to Cambacérès, as he had never done before. "The battle was hot," he conceded, but "at 2:00 P.M. the victory went to us." Only ten thousand Frenchmen were lost.[276] When he wrote to his father-in-law, Francis of Austria, French casualties had dropped to between eight thousand and ten thousand.[277] By the time he wrote to Maret, he had settled on nine thousand.[278] The official Bulletin, issued on September 10, saw the figure back up to ten thousand.[279] The lies were set against the very thorough examination of the battlefield by Napoleon on September 8, asking details of the officers present and applying mathematical formulae—measuring out the area in squares and counting the corpses in them—to arrive at an estimate of the slaughter.[280] He told Marie-Louise he was very well, save for a bit of a rotten cold after too many hours in the saddle.[281] He told everyone he had a very bad cold. The truth seems to be far worse. That Napoleon lied was normal. It was to whom he lied that is most revealing. On September 10 came the order to Clark to fire a one hundred–gun salute for "the victory of Moscow"; the French bishops were commanded to rally the people to church to give thanks for all the battles since the crossing of the Niemen.[282]

He told the truth about some things. He put Russian losses at between forty thousand and fifty thousand, and told all and sundry that it was getting colder.

The "tent is chilly of an evening" he told Cambacérès. "What a climate!"[283] Far away in Saint Petersburg, Alexander's sister, Elizabeth, wrote to the Dowager Empress, "Each step he takes into this immense Russia makes him approach the abyss. We will see how he bears the winter."[284]

As it was, the army gathered itself up and marched to Moscow. Davout incarnated them all. He was hoisted on to a litter, and led I Corps on, not taking to his bed for two weeks.[285] On September 20, he wrote to his wife he had suffered a great deal, but was mending in Moscow: "The inflammation disappeared at the end of forty-eight hours. The scabs have fallen off . . . and now the wounds are healing."[286] He was one of the lucky ones. The French soldiers had a saying they repeated when telling tales of heroes at the start of a long journey, "March today, march tomorrow, by dint of marching one goes a long way."[287] On September 9, 1812, the Grande Armée set off for Moscow. It was the last forward march they ever made.

6

HELL IS A VERY COLD PLACE: MOSCOW

The Race to Moscow

The horror of Borodino soon descended into farce. As the two rival commanders responsible for the bloodbath noisily claimed victory—"I have won the battle against Bonaparte!" Kutusov told his wife[1]—their battered armies staggered to their feet and faced facts. Barclay's initial consolidation of the Russian forces and his careful withdrawal from the combat zone quickly disintegrated, in no small part because so many officers had been lost in the fighting that units were directionless. As Adam Zamoyski has pointed out, this fragmentation may actually have helped Kutusov, even though it hindered the retreat: The ranks did not really know the wider picture, and so no one really appreciated how weakened they all were.[2] The exhausted troops got no respite, and a great many wounded were simply abandoned in the rush to retreat. The rearguard was placed under Matvei Platov, the Cossack commander, but he proved unable to slow the French down sufficiently and was replaced by a regular cavalryman, Mikhail Miloradovich, which improved matters, but not enough to buy time to make another stand.[3] Kutusov continued to bluster, particularly to the genuinely belligerent Rostopchin in Moscow—who liked to claim descent from Genghis Khan[4]—to whom he announced that "the loss of Moscow entails the loss of Russia, itself."[5] Rostopchin replied that the Muscovites would defend their city with pitchforks and "a hail of stones."[6]

For all that, Kutusov continued to fall back and Rostopchin continued to evacuate the inhabitants and as much of the supplies he knew Napoleon needed. Both men did so at a fast pace. To disguise his army's plight, Kutusov got Rostopchin to visit headquarters at Fili, and asked him to bring the Metropolitan of the city with two icons of the Virgin and a host of clergy to inspire the army. Rostopchin was not fooled, noting the unease at headquarters, and was at last disabused by "all the baseness, the incompetence and the poltroonery of the commander of our armies." Barclay took him aside and said it was madness to stand.[7] Alexander still had no firsthand information, and simply believed Kutusov's claims of victory, for all his dislike of him. Ironically as "in the dark" as Napoleon's Council of State in Paris, he ordered the bells of Saint Petersburg to ring out and began preparing for victory celebrations, believing Kutusov's news that the Cossacks were in pursuit of the enemy. The awful truth only dawned—hazily—when Kutusov's short note reached him that heavy losses had compelled the army to retreat eastward. It was the last letter he sent the tsar for some time.[8]

While Rostopchin went back to Moscow and prepared for the worst, Kutusov held a council of war at Fili, on September 13. All the anger and frustration exploded, as Kutusov stood aside and let his subordinates draw the battle lines. Barclay argued that to stand and fight was tantamount to suicide; the army was so battered that both it and Moscow would be destroyed. Others, notably Yermolov, had expressed similar views beforehand, but now kept quiet, as Bennigsen was cholic at the very idea of surrendering the city. This may have been to save face, as he was the one who had chosen the ground where a stand might be made, which Barclay claimed was inadequate. Now he blamed Barclay for the ignominy of abandoning the city.[9] Soon no one would believe they had won at Borodino.[10] He had his supporters, but Kutusov already knew that Barclay's was the only realistic path to take. The divisions within the high command were bitter, and this decision only made them worse, but as the Russian scholar Viktor Bezotosnyi has pointed out, they did not really follow the "German-Russian" ethnic divide.[11] The course of the campaign had produced enough venom of its own. Kutusov broke into the debate after half an hour and announced they would, indeed, abandon Moscow.[12] When Rostopchin was informed that evening, he was, by his own admission, "in a fury . . . outraged," but admitted there was nothing he could do.[13] Kutusov then took what Adam Zamoyski believes to be "the only brilliant decision he made during the whole campaign." He withdrew through the city, not around it. No commander of the era relished urban warfare; Napoleon was no different from the rest. This was the only way to slow down the French advance, for Kutusov rightly judged that "Napoleon is like a torrent which we are still too weak to stem."[14]

In what ensued next, it all seemed too true. Barclay had done his best to ensure an orderly passage of the army through Moscow, but the mass of troops, their wounded and the baggage train, were soon engulfed by a civilian exodus swollen by panic as Muscovites were now certain that the French were descending on the city. A staff officer envisioned "the relocation of whole tribes from one corner of the earth to another,"[15] as tens of thousands fled, stopping only to hurl abuse and even paving stones at the retreating troops.[16] Rostopchin was manhandled by a mob, and ran into Kutusov, himself in full flight. There is no reliable account of their encounter, but it was scarcely amicable.[17] Discipline disintegrated as the troops broke ranks to loot in the chaos. The retreat was in tatters, and it took something quite extraordinary for the army to survive the passage through the city it had sworn to hold to the death.

As he ordered the retreat, Kutusov predicted that "Moscow is the sponge that will suck (Napoleon) in."[18] So it proved. The first of the French to be "sucked in" was Murat, who led his cavalry into the city from the west on September 14, just as the Russian rearguard under Miloradovich covered the retreat. This led to the meeting of two of the most colorful soldiers of the era. Seeing for himself that Polish lancers were already riding deeply into the city, Miloradovich knew that his confused, straggling troops would soon be cut to pieces, and the main body of the army threatened by Murat, unless a way could be found to delay him. Never lacking for courage or aggression, Miloradovich instead chose a mixture of guile and bravado to check Murat. He dispatched an aide to speak to Murat directly, asking him to show mercy to the Russian wounded, and for a truce to allow the Russians to leave the city with their baggage and artillery intact. He added the brazen bluff that if Murat refused, he would "fight to the last extremity." When an aide ventured that "it was not brave to speak thus to the French," he snapped back "It is my business to be brave, yours to die."[19] Confronted with this, Murat at first said he had to ask Napoleon, but then changed his mind and agreed. It emerged that Miloradovich wanted to meet him. Murat was delighted, and they rode together alone for a few hours.[20] Murat had been outwitted, for he detected no guile in this kindred spirit. The truce was extended for another twelve hours—Napoleon agreed to listen to his commander in the field—and so the whole battered army, not just its rearguard, lived to fight again thanks to what Dominic Lieven has aptly called Miloradovich's "cheeky initiative."[21]

Returning to the Kremlin to oversee the last stages of the withdrawal, Miloradovich took part in the last act of the farce. In the midst of the mayhem, the garrison of the Kremlin marched out, its band playing. When a bewildered Miloradovich asked their commandant, "What swine ordered you to play?" he was told it was Peter the Great's regulation. Miloradovich retorted "And what do the regulations of Peter the Great have to say about the surrender of Moscow?"[22]

When the main body of the Grande Armée reached the hills west of Moscow, its men stood in awe of a sight none of them, even the oldest *grognards*, had ever imagined. Behind them lay the privations of the long march and the charnel house of Borodino, a place so ghastly that Junot's Westphalians took a month to gather and burn the hordes of corpses.[23] Before them lay their longed-for prize, but no one—not even their leader—had envisioned what spread out before them. It was a clear, sunny day. Ségur remembered that "The sun caused this great city to glisten with a thousand colors." The troops began to cry "Moscow! Moscow!" just as sailors shouted out "Land ho!" Napoleon gasped: "There, at last, is the famous city. It's about time!"[24]

"The city is as big as Paris," he wrote to Marie-Louise, "There are 1,600 church spires and more than a thousand beautiful palaces, the city has everything."[25] Moscow contained over 275,000 people in 1812. There were said to be 9,151 buildings—2,367 of them made of stone, 6,584 of wood.[26] The great building projects of the tsars in the eighteenth century had transformed it into an impressive sight. "(T)he architects were chiefly Italian but the style is Tartarian, Indian, Chinese, and Gothic, Here a pagoda, there an arcade! . . . Taken altogether, it is a jumble of magnificence and ruin . . ." remarked an English visitor.[27] On that sunny September 14, the brightly painted onion domes of its many churches, surmounted by golden crowns, glittered and sparkled before the awestruck French. Adrien Bourgogne, a hard-bitten sergeant of the guard, had the perspective of the well-traveled veteran: "Many capitals have I seen—Paris, Berlin, Vienna, and Madrid—had produced an ordinary impression on me. But this was different and the effect was to me . . . magical."[28] Their entry was no less surprising.

Moscow: The Sponge and the Oven

The great city met the jubilant conquerors with silence. Their fairyland seemed a ghost town. The streets that had thronged with fleeing Muscovites and soldiers only a day before were deserted. Roughly two thirds of the inhabitants had gone; the rest cowered in their homes as the guard marched in, resplendent in their dress uniforms, to the music of their band playing "To us the victory!" Bourgogne recalled "The solitude and the silence which greeted us . . . calmed down, in a disagreeable way, the frenzy of happiness which had made our blood race a few moments before." Lejeune remembered François Haxo—chief of Davout's headquarters—muttering to him "This means we'll soon be defending Paris."[29] Napoleon was more worried by the Russians he could not see. Murat was quickly dispatched to shadow Kutusov—who was now headed southwest toward Tula[30]—but not before wringing a dinner of salt cod and a good bed for the night out of a wealthy manufacturer.[31] Napoleon was nervous of a counterattack launched by stragglers, insisting to Berthier, on September 14, that it was essential to have "detachments (of troops) continually busy with rounding up the Russians who are to be found in great numbers on all sides." He ordered Bessières to send dragoon patrols into every part of the city to find the Russian stragglers and hand them over to Davout, outside of Moscow.[32] No one could be found to make a formal surrender of the city, or take charge of its civil administration, so Mortier was quickly appointed its governor; Rostopchin had made sure government officialdom had left in its entirety.[33] There was simply no one to deal with, to organize the occupation or help billet the army. This was unprecedented in Napoleon's considerable experience, and it unnerved him. "The barbarians, do they really mean to abandon all this? It's not possible," he blurted out to Caulaincourt.[34]

Once inside the city, unrestrained by any real authority other than their likeminded officers, the army ran wild in an orgy of pillage. Rostopchin had done his best to deny the French as many supplies of food and alcohol as possible but, as Napoleon said, the city had everything, and his men soon found it. The plunder of churches began and the streets were soon full of soldiers laden with sacred silverware; officers—even generals—allowed their men to loot at will, so short of supplies were they; fighting broke out even among I Corps, as individual units sought to keep their newfound plenty to themselves. A lucky artillery battery stumbled upon one of the finest and largest wine collections in Moscow. For the most part, their needs were more pressing and more mundane. One artillery officer, François Pion des Loches, admitted to helping his men batter down doors to seize flour and warm clothes, although once inside, they were soon after gold. The empty houses and shops in which Moscow now abounded were easy prey and comfortable billets for the ravaged army.[35]

Napoleon did not enter Moscow on September 14, staying instead in a small wooden hut just outside the gates. He entered the city the next day, quietly. He was the first foreign conqueror to do so in two hundred years. He had a bad cold and a urinary problem.[36] Napoleon made straight for the Kremlin, which he made his headquarters, and found a magnificent but emptied palace. Rostopchin had stripped the Kremlin almost bare, carrying the doctrine of scorched-earth into the very sanctuary of "the Third Rome." His guard, sent on to occupy it on September 14, had seen to the rest before he got there. Bourgogne confessed that, despite clear orders that no one was to leave his post on arriving, "an hour afterward . . . the whole place (around the Kremlin) was filled with everything we could want. We went into houses . . . asking for food and drink, but as we found no one in them we helped ourselves." A sergeant of the Guard Fusilier-Grenadiers, the "elite of the elite," did not balk at allowing his men to "go out marauding"; they returned with wine, champagne, sugar, flour, and "excellent beer." Men from the same unit even set upon one of Napoleon's own orderlies, the Polish count Roman Sołtyk, when he tried to stop them plundering the wine cellar of a Russian aristocrat.[37] Inside the Kremlin, the guard battered down doors and ransacked at will, but Rostopchin had left little for them. The throne of Ivan the Terrible was still there, but the state bedroom had no curtains or shutters. Napoleon camped on his mobile bed; he had a desk, and that was enough. He hung Gérard's portrait of his son in a prominent place. Sufficient discipline had been maintained to allow General Mathieu Dumas to secure the stores of flour from pillage.[38]

Beyond the Kremlin's walls, the soldiers' binge was short-lived. On the evening of September 15, massive fires broke out and spread rapidly.[39] Nowhere was safe and soon the whole vast city was engulfed, even as Napoleon tried to get his first night's sleep in his hard-won prize. The first large blaze began in the commercial quarter, Kitay-gorod, probably in its Merchant Court, known colloquially among the French as the "bazaar" or "bourse." Kitay-gorod was comprised of narrow, crowded streets with shops and warehouses full of potentially inflammable goods. It is hard to know when the fire began, but it was raging almost out of control by 8:00 P.M., when about one hundred men of the Young Guard arrived to try to quell the flames at the Merchant Court. Only then did they discover that Rostopchin had dismantled the water pumps. As the fire spread, it became terrifyingly clear that he had done so systematically across the whole city.[40] They saved the Merchant Court after a four-hour struggle that left them exhausted. "Everyone hoped that this would be the end of our troubles . . . Alas, we soon became witnesses to a spectacle more horrible than anything we could imagine," their commander recalled.[41] The fire had spread further, and as the French tried to reach it, they ran into Russian stragglers. Fierce hand-to-hand combat resulted, as the fire threatened the Foundling Home, which housed 586 children—275 under age eleven among them—and 500 staff whom Rostopchin had refused requests to evacuate. Its director made his way to the Kremlin to beseech the French for help, and twelve gendarmes of the guard arrived to protect the building. Together with the staff, they kept the fire at bay because Rostopchin's orders had been ignored, and the firefighting equipment was in place. At about 7:00 P.M., Russian troops blew up a powder magazine in the Yauza River area. An actress of Moscow's French theatre company recalled seeing "a flaming sword" rising into the sky as it went up; a priest of the French church of in the city remembered "a fiery ball . . . an ominous sign." A Dutch captain of the guard assumed it was a firework display to welcome Napoleon, "but we were mistaken." The Württemberger troops feared it was meant as a signal to begin a deliberate general arson attack on the whole city. No such plan was needed. Later that night, a strong wind arose and carried burning wreckage and sparks everywhere. A Muscovite recalled in stunned awe that "the entire horizon . . . had turned into a bright and fiery sea! The cupolas of the nearby churches appeared like some shadowy giants rising against this blazing background." The spread of the fire actually intensified pillaging, as the French began feverishly to seize as much as they could before the fire robbed them of supplies.

Napoleon's initial response was almost nonchalant, blaming them on drunken troops causing accidents, and went to bed. That night, the wind changed direction three times, ensuring that no part of the city remained untouched. To Ségur it seemed as if the flames were "obstinately bent on the destruction of the imperial quarters (in the Kremlin)" as the wind shifted to the north. Duroc and Caulaincourt allowed Napoleon to sleep on, knowing he was exhausted and ill, but even when he was roused—or wakened himself, it is hard to know—he remained unperturbed and went back to bed. Still in discomfort from his urinary problem the next morning, he refused to see it as more than a few accidents caused by soldiers trying to bake bread near wooden houses. At this very moment, a powerful new wind began—"a hurricane of terrifying strength"—and the fire rose to full fury. Nothing was visible from the Kremlin save thick clouds of black smoke. Napoleon changed in an instant from complacent torpor to a man suddenly aware that he was faced with a catastrophe he could not control. Pacing about, peering from the windows incessantly, his first reaction was to see it as a planned attack on him: "It is their own work! What extraordinary resolution! What men! These are Scythians indeed!" On Saint Helena, he recalled the terrible impression that remained vivid in his mind of a city in flames and admitted to being "struck with terror and consternation."[42] At 9:30 he mounted up and set out from the Kremlin to see for himself.

Even before getting out of the courtyard, his belief in a Russian policy of deliberate arson was confirmed by the declarations of captured Russians, that their officers had ordered them to set fire to the city. All the while, the fire swelled in intensity, as the wind continued to pick up. It was not long until the Kremlin became an island in the midst of a fiery ocean. By late morning, the clock tower over one of the gates caught fire and sparks began falling into the courtyard—a courtyard filled with artillery and ammunition, for a whole battery had been stationed directly under Napoleon's own windows. He was going nowhere. While groups of soldiers remained happily inebriated in the surrounding taverns, their commander and their own loot perched on a lethal tinderbox. The roof of the kitchens and the stables were only saved from destruction by the heroic efforts of guard artillery and the grooms. Even Caulaincourt and generals of the guard lent a hand. "(E)ven the fur on the Grenadiers' caps was singed," Caulaincourt recalled. Napoleon went first to the stables and then to the arsenal, exposing himself to great danger if it went up. His great coat on fire at one point, he rebuffed his staff's pleas to leave. Instead, he climbed to the top of the tower of Ivan the Great to try to get an idea of the situation. He saw only an inferno and exclaimed, "The barbarians, the savages, to burn their city like this! What could their enemies do that was worse than this? They will earn the curses of posterity!" When he came down, he still had no idea what to do. By 4:00 P.M., the fire was close to the arsenal and only one route out of the Kremlin remained. What actually seems to have convinced Napoleon to leave the Kremlin was being isolated from his commanders outside Moscow if the Russians sought to exploit the chaos and counterattack, which Berthier pointed out forcefully.[43] At about 5:00 P.M. Napoleon mounted one of his Arabian horses and escaped by a tower on the southern side of the Kremlin, leaving only one guard battalion in the fortress.

His destination was the Petrovsky Palace, to the immediate north of the city. "Many an old moustache was singed on this infernal journey" one guard officer recalled. The atmosphere was stultifying by all accounts, and the horses hard to handle. Myths abound, however. Ségur's account of an emotional chance meeting between Napoleon and Davout was roundly refuted by General Gaspard Gourgaud, and seem unlikely as neither Napoleon or Davout mention it. Nevertheless, the journey was most certainly fraught with danger and they did not reach the Petrovsky Palace until about 7:30 P.M., according to Caulaincourt. Napoleon lay awake all night, it seems, but wrote to Marie-Louise that all was well, and described a beautiful city that was no more.[44] Others felt the same macabre fascination displayed by so many at Smolensk. Henri Beyle, the future novelist Stendhal, actually enjoyed the sight of "the most beautiful fire in the world that formed an immense pyramid."

The fire raged for three more days, as the wind did not abate, always changing direction. Muscovites and French troops wandered the streets searching for shelter, but even many stone-built structures—the churches and cathedrals among them—were starting to collapse by September 17. The troops, maddened by the loss of their plunder and supplies, often abandoned by their officers, ran amok, pillaging what they could and exercising ferocious violence on the remaining population. The guard, holding the Kremlin, was among the worst, robbing not just unlucky civilians but other soldiers. Other troops were forced to pay a five-franc "toll" to enter the Kremlin with their booty, and then robbed of it once inside and chased off. It was discipline of a sort. The cellars and their contents survived more often than not, and the troops were experienced in finding them. When Dumas—the intendant-general of the Grande Armée—rushed into a cellar being looted to stop the disorder, sword drawn, he collapsed in anger and consternation when the first man he seized turned out to be his own cook—drunk, blood-spattered, and clutching three bottles of wine.

Rain at last began to fall early on September 18, and Napoleon took advantage of it. Returning to the Kremlin, he remembered passing bivouacs piled high with looted furniture, gilded doors, and even windows. The troops were eating rotten black bread off silver and gold plates. Napoleon spent the afternoon riding about the city and saw the devastation for himself. "This was a beautiful city. I say it was because today half of it is destroyed," he wrote to Cambacérès.[45] For once, he did not exaggerate. It was worse than this. Eighty percent of the stone buildings and 68 percent of the wooden houses had been destroyed.[46] Some streets were gone, altogether. A rancid smell of the burning, rotten flesh of humans and beasts borne on the wind was what most people remembered. Napoleon returned to the Kremlin about 4:00 P.M., glum and worried.

Napoleon had been contemplating pulling out of Moscow soon, to attack Saint Petersburg; a Moscow in ruins was no longer a bargaining chip with Alexander, it was no longer bait. The devastation he saw and the collective counsel of his marshals soon dissuaded him of it. Agathon Fain, a member of the headquarters staff, recalled, "they managed for the first time to make him doubt the superiority of his own assessment."[47] As the fires abated by the 20th, it was time to start picking up the pieces. Discipline had disintegrated along with the city. The troops of the line alternated between pillage—interspersed with rape—and simple foraging. Luxuries were in plentiful supply; wines, spices, furniture, furs. There was still enough food—the fields around the city were full of vegetables and potatoes—but it was disappearing fast, and by early October troops had to venture four to six hours' march beyond Moscow to find anything. Meat was in very short supply.[48] The line regiments who did the foraging were, in their turn, robbed by Davout's I Corps while their commander was incapacitated by his wounds, and by the guard, while their *Tondu* ["the shorn one"] was out of the city.[49] It was an army utterly unfit to march or fight, but as the fires flickered out, Davout, the iron disciplinarian, roused himself. His wounds were now healing and his inflammations gone he told his wife on September 20,[50] and he ordered an end be put to the pillage, confining his men to barracks "until order and discipline are restored," making his generals personally responsible for this, who were to lead patrols themselves, "to arrest of whatever corps who are taken in contravention (of these orders)."[51]

Napoleon cracked down on the guard with an ironic eye. He posted them around the Kremlin gates, but then ordered them to divest their comrades of their plunder as they returned to their barracks from the city. "It was quite a sad sight to see all those piles . . . of precious items left there in the mud," recalled one officer.[52] It took over a week, but fifty barriers, each manned by ten soldiers, were set up around the city; supply depots were at last set up to control the distribution of resources. Nonetheless, pillaging persisted into the first weeks of October. On September 29, Napoleon's orders of the day bluntly stated his displeasure that his elite troops, his own guards, "had forgotten their sense of duty" and were still looting.[53] A few days later, Mortier reported that some guardsmen had even sacked the flour stores of the Foundling Home and a major of the Horse Chasseurs of the Guard—Napoleon's own escorts—had been robbed of his wallet while guarding the emperor. They were severely dealt with by Marshal Lefebvre, who noted that "a soldier of the Guard who cannot appreciate the honor of serving in the Corps does not deserve to belong to it."[54] For all that, they were always immaculately turned out for the daily midday parade on what is now Red Square. Napoleon noted after the thorough reviews of the guard on October 7–8 that the infantry had regained its strength and health. To a degree, the rest of the army mirrored this.[55]

There were far fewer of them to feed or police, however. Of the huge army that had crossed the Nieman three months earlier, just under one hundred thousand were left. One line regiment that marched into Russia with twenty-eight hundred men could muster only nine hundred in Moscow. Four army corps—Davout's, Ney's, Eugène's, and Junot's—could muster only fifty-five thousand among them.[56] Junot's was so diminished that he asked Napoleon to reduce it to a division. Napoleon agreed.[57] The weakness of the army after Borodino was all too apparent. Napoleon's attempts to rebuild it pointed in two directions: Retreat was now unavoidable and had to be prepared. It was also to be reinforced, but Napoleon was deluded in thinking reinforcements could reach him from Poland—and as far away as France—in good time. He sent out patrols to secure the roads back to Smolensk,[58] and ordered troops from Hesse-Darmstadt and the Illyrian Provinces and several cavalry regiments up to Moscow.[59] A fresh conscription levée was ordered of 140,000 from France and 30,000 from the Kingdom of Italy. Maret was cajoled to pressure the Duchy of Warsaw and the states of the Confederation of the Rhine to raise their own levées, as well as to find much-needed horses and artillery, without delay. A hard truth was exposed in his tirade against the Polish ministers, "who do nothing," whose "bad will has made me very discontented."[60] "What are these petty nobles doing?"[61] They were trying to cope with the catastrophic state of the duchy's finances, in the wake of the pressures of the campaign, which made it impossible to raise more troops.[62] Levées were ordered throughout Lithuania, and troops were sent to guard the depots along the roads there, a sign that withdrawal was coming.[63] It was all couched in the language of victory; the real state of affairs masked from his allies: "The circumstances of the battle of Moscow (Borodino) and the taking of Moscow must not lessen the zeal of the allies, nor (allow them) to sleep. While informing them of the great levées I am raising everywhere, impress on them the need to fill their corps."[64] No honest admission could better expose the desperation of his position. As September ended, he told Cambacérès bluntly, "There is nothing new to report here."[65] He was right, but not as he meant it to be understood.

Trapped and isolated as never before, Napoleon grasped at straws: seizing and melting down precious objects from churches, private houses, and public buildings for currency. The smelting was done in Upenski Cathedral, a sign that Napoleon's revolutionary anticlericalism was alive and well when under pressure.[66] He told Berthier to press his director for remounts that he was counting on fourteen thousand new horses from northern Germany and the eight thousand Prussia still owed him to remount the troops in Russia.[67] Finding such numbers of horses after the great levées already raised for the invasion was doubtful; to get them to Moscow intact, all but impossible across a devastated country.

Delusion mingled with hard truth as Napoleon barricaded himself in the Kremlin. Reality was literally closing in on him as winter approached. The ramshackle municipal government he had corralled together from those few reluctant notable Muscovites to be found managed to clear the streets of corpses and debris, but did little else, strapped of resources and fearful of being tainted with collaboration.[68] Simply finding supplies increasingly showed the French that the noose was tightening around them. The peasants bringing food to sell in Moscow were set upon and robbed by the troops within the town and harassed and intimidated by Cossacks who came ever closer to the city. Most rural communities destroyed their crops, rather than supply the invaders. French foragers now had to risk the Cossacks and range as far as thirty miles to find anything.[69] Behind them, Kutusov was closer at hand than Napoleon initially thought. For a week after Borodino, Napoleon believed Kutusov was in full flight eastward; he told Marie-Louise the Russians were falling back on Kazan, almost four hundred miles from Moscow.[70] In fact, he mustered on Tarutino, only one hundred miles southwest of Moscow. It was a strong position; the arms works at Bryansk and Tula were close by and safe from the French, and the army was easily supplied from the fertile provinces to the south. Men and horses recovered their strength and began raiding deep behind the French lines, as far as Smolensk. There was now no chance of Kutusov being cut off from Chichagov and Tormasov, to the south.[71] Napoleon's line of retreat was increasingly threatened: To the north, Wittgenstein now faced Oudinot and Gouvion St. Cyr's seventeen thousand men with forty thousand troops near Polotsk. To the south, Tormasov's Third Army had been reinforced to sixty-five thousand strong, to whom Schwarzenberg could oppose only thirty-four thousand. The thirty-seven thousand French troops at Smolensk were increasingly hemmed in by Cossacks and partisans who threatened the rear all the way to the Polish border.[72] Napoleon soon got a taste of this closer to home. On September 24, a force of regular Russian cavalry and Cossacks cut the main road to the west near Mozhaysk, and then captured all the elite troops—the Dragoons and Chasseurs of the Guard—sent to dislodge them. A larger force soon reopened the road, but this did not auger well among the ranks.[73]

Napoleon placed his all hopes on negotiating with Alexander, playing on the loss and destruction of Moscow and believing this would goad the tsar to try to retake it. "The beautiful and superb city of Moscow is no more: Rostopchin burnt it . . . I think it impossible that, given his principles, his heart, the justices of his ideas that he would authorize such excess, so unworthy of a great ruler and a great nation."[74] Alexander was, indeed, horrified—"My God, so much misfortune" was his first reaction[75]—and Rostopchin was quick to distance himself from it. Only after 1814 did he start to take credit for starting the fire when conservative circles praised him for it.[76] Nevertheless, Alexander's repugnance at the fate of Moscow was not enough to lure him into Napoleon's trap. He did what he did best; he waited. Put another way: Alexander stood firm. When Napoleon's letter finally reached the tsar after two weeks—its carrier, a Russian civil servant, having been beaten up as a spy en route—he found Alexander deeply immersed in his newfound religious faith, "my only consolation, my sole support." When he received the news of the fall of Moscow, he told Kutusov's messenger:

> I will make use of every last resource of my empire . . . But even if Divine Providence decrees that my dynasty should cease to reign . . . then I will grow my beard down (to my waist) and will go off and eat potatoes with the last of my peasants rather than sign a peace that would shame the fatherland . . . I have learned to understand (Napoleon) and he will not deceive me.[77]

Napoleon's hopes were dead in the water. He asked Caulaincourt to go to Saint Petersburg, but he replied flatly that it was hopeless. Instead, he sent General Jacques Auguste Jean Lauriston, the commander of the Gendarmerie of the Grande Armée, who was received politely, but firmly rebuffed.[78] Napoleon treasured the image and thoughts of his son. He kept Gérard's portrait of him before him constantly, and delighted at the news he received about him. There can be little doubt that "making the world safe" for Napoleon-Francis was one of the reasons that drove him to war, and finally, all the way to Moscow. With Alexander's rebuff, these hopes were gone.

Napoleon seldom read "the Sphinx of the North" aright, but he did grasp a current at his court. Alexander's brother, Grand Duke Constantine, his foreign minister, Rumiantsev, and his own mother, Maria-Feodorovna, all implored him to seek talks with Napoleon, even before the fall of Moscow.[79] In stark contrast, opinion in Saint Petersburg reviled the tsar for surrendering Moscow without a fight. "Violent discontent swirled round the capital," one observer recalled, as his sister, Catherine, reproached him for having abandoned the city when he should have led its defense. There were dark rumors of a coup to depose Alexander and replace him with her.[80] Fortunately for Alexander, there were those in his capital who rallied to him. Most were foreign exiles, fugitives from Napoleon's wrath, and each of them incarnated vendettas Napoleon had accumulated over the years: Joesph de Maistre, the ambassador of the House of Savoy in Saint Petersburg since 1804, whose own ruler languished on the island of Sardinia; Stein, the reforming Prussian minister and leader of the "war party" in 1809; Charles-André Pozzo di Borgo, a scion of one of the few remaining families of the "insular" nobility of Corsica, whose enmity to the Bonapartes went back at least to their rift with Pasquale Paoli in 1793. Hurrying to join them from his lengthy American exile came Jean-Victor Moreau, by Napoleon's own acknowledgment the finest general of the Directory, who had narrowly avoided the guillotine in 1804, for his presumed—and false—part in Georges Cadoudal's plot to kill him. They never formed a coterie akin to that around Germaine de Staël in Vienna before 1809, but they were far more determined and useful. Each had their part to play in forming a chain that would help to choke Napoleon.

Napoleon's staff believed he could winter in Moscow; there were resources enough for the army for six months, and waiting for spring would avoid the horrors of the retreat from Eylau in 1807.[81] However exposed his position was militarily, it was all too obvious that Alexander did not intend to attack him. Instead, Alexander hoped to use his fresh troops in the south and Wittengstein in the north, to cut Napoleon's retreat off far to the west around Minsk. It was an overly ambitious plan, but it did not involve marching on Moscow.[82] On October 18, Napoleon ordered his corps commanders to be ready to leave Moscow in two days.[83] He had been defeated by patience.

7

THE GAUNTLET:
THE RETREAT FROM MOSCOW,
OCTOBER–DECEMBER 1812

The moment Napoleon knew the loss of Moscow would not bring Alexander to the negotiating table, he decided to pull out. He did not "dither" as is often argued. He took Moscow for diplomatic reasons; when these proved a chimera, he withdrew. He may have fared better militarily to have left Moscow much sooner, after two weeks rather than six,[1] but this would have left him only the smallest of windows to negotiate with Alexander. In truth, the futility of the whole venture was now exposed. Alexander had "outfoxed" him yet again. Napoleon had challenged him to a "game of dare" but "the Sphinx of the North" lived up to his nickname. As a result, Alexander's armies recovered and grew in strength, even as Napoleon's withered. The stark truth was that Napoleon had no good options left to him.[2]

There were several routes west Napoleon had to choose from, all of them fraught with dangers. The way to avoid hunger was to strike south toward the as yet unplundered, fertile plains of Ukraine, or to head for Smolensk by an indirect route, also swinging south through Yelna, another unspoiled region.

Going south at all risked direct confrontation with Kutusov's main army. What food and fodder that remained in western Russia had to be fought for. Napoleon rejected this course of action, and not without reason: The army in Moscow numbered just over ninety-five thousand; although it had been reinforced with men, it had had little respite thanks to the fire, and no fresh horses.[3] By contrast, food and supplies flooded into Kutusov's headquarters at Tarutino, even eggs and pies brought by peasants of their own free will, while new winter coats, gloves, and fur lined boots were made for the army. The troops rested, bathed in traditional Russian steam baths—*banyas*—and felt human again, feasting on beef stew and fresh vegetables, a world the French could only dream of.[4] Yet Kutusov still did not feel strong enough to risk battle if he could help it, and held out against it despite being surrounded by disgruntled, warlike subordinates.[5] Among them was Bennigsen, who feared the arrival of Victor's corps from Smolensk.[6] Only about fifty thousand of his eighty-six thousand infantrymen were trained veterans in early October, and now was not the moment to risk them against Davout, however bedraggled, or the guard—still 21,000 strong with 176 guns[7]—which had not fought at Borodino. Nevertheless, Kutusov held powerful superiority in cavalry: Many fresh horses had arrived for his ten thousand cavalry, in stark contrast to the state of the French cavalry, most of whom were now without mounts at all. Cossacks numbering twenty-eight thousand arrived in these weeks. They were soon set to work harassing the Grande Armée. Kutusov's 620 pieces of artillery far exceeded Napoleon's, drawn by strong horses, with plenty of shells. Taken together, Kutusov's army may not have been ready for the offensive, but it was more than a match to defend good positions against a French assault.[8] Kutusov thus began constructing a well-fortified camp the area around Tarutino.[9] Fewer troops stood between Napoleon and Saint Petersburg, but the terrain was barren, forested, and uncharted; it was the surest way to make Alexander fight, but such a march would weaken the Grande Armée even further.[10]

Napoleon hoped to avoid the war-ravaged road to Smolensk by swinging south toward Kaluga, before turning northwest. In a letter to Maret on October 16, long in private hands and only published in 2012 by the

Fondation Napoléon,[11] he announced his intention to leave Moscow in three or four days' time. Napoleon set out his reasons for choosing his route very clearly. Moscow, he said, was "no more than a military position" for him, and was now of no further value as such, particularly as it was now nothing but a ruin. Marching on Saint Petersburg, 190 kilometers west, would oblige him to go through Vitebsk, which was not practicable. He said he intended to winter at Smolensk, which was relatively friendly country, and prepare for a move on Saint Petersburg in the spring. His immediate plans, as set out to Maret, were exactly those he followed:

> I intend to leave on the 19th for Kaluga, (and) to fight the Russian army if it wants, as it claims, to block this strong point (the way to Smolensk) and, allowing for the weather (I will) march for Toula and Bryansk (south into the fertile zone), or head straight for Smolensk, Minsk and Mogilev in the first week of November (the route of the advance on Moscow).

He added that Maret was to be sure to couch his report to the ministers in exactly these terms. It was meant for public consumption. It is exactly what transpired.[12]

To do so he had to outthink and outrun Kutusov. In hopes of drawing Kutusov off from blocking the main road west through Kaluga, Napoleon sent out feelers for an armistice to the Russian camp—which Bennigsen feared Kutusov might accept[13]—while telling his troops that this was not a retreat, but a reopening of hostilities by an attack on Kutusov's left flank.[14] He had no idea that Kutusov no more wanted a big battle than he did himself, so much had their normal instincts changed after Borodino. Thus, Napoleon thought he had to outrun the Russians. This set his men on the most daunting march any had faced, but he set off in such haste that they could not have been worse prepared for what lay ahead. As Dominic Lieven has put it, "Just to list what needed to be done more or less describes what did not happen."[15] Napoleon's meticulous attention to detail had evaporated. The army clung to its hard-won spoils, and Napoleon had not the will to deprive it of them, which meant that vital food supplies were dumped and even burned to make way for plunder. As the plunder-laden army lumbered out of the city, carrying some of it in wheelbarrows,[16] Segur likened it to "a horde of Tartars."[17] Even the guard was no longer immune to this. Sergeant Bourgogne of the Young Guard confessed in his memoirs to carrying a Chinese silk dress, two silver framed paintings, and a lady's riding coat in his knapsack, and a large bag slung over his shoulder laden with silver and porcelain.[18] Not all of the spoils were inanimate objects. Moscovite women who had attached themselves to French soldiers—"involuntary captives" as Segur dubbed them[19]—fled with their new friends, doubtless knowing the vengeance that awaited them should they remain. No army was less prepared for a quick getaway, and none of the commanders, not even the fastidious Davout, did anything to correct it.[20] No effective system for distributing rations had been organized. The horses—now so precious a commodity—had not been shoed against winter ice. No new winter coats or boots were to be had. Caulaincourt's verdict was damning: "The glorious habit of always marching forward made us veritable schoolboys when it came to retreating. Never was a retreat worse organized."[21] There would be no more glorious advances.[22]

The march began badly for both commanders. The first stage of the French withdrawal was protected by Murat's twenty-six thousand cavalry, spread out almost haphazardly to the southwest of Moscow around Voronovo and Vinkovo. They were in a ghastly state. Camped in the open, increasingly afflicted by the first frosts, they could neither forage nor expect regular rations from Moscow. Only about eight thousand of them were still actually mounted but even these horses were dying, one trooper remembering that "when a soldier dismounted, you could see the horse's entrails."[23] This weakness was compounded by an attitude to the Russians David Chandler called "somolescent," a sense that they would not attack.[24] Although true of Kutusov, Bennigsen and his staff, now backed by Alexander, and well apprised of Murat's condition, increased the pressure to strike at Napoleon's weak point,[25] while Napoleon, himself, remained blind to Murat's reports of all this, even as his men lived mainly on their dead mounts.[26] When the attack came, it mirrored the hatreds and divisions within Kutusov's command, and almost balanced out Murat's weaknesses. Left to himself, Kutusov would probably not have attacked,[27] but he ordered it for October 16. When the officer charged with passing on the orders disappeared to dinner, it had to be postponed by a day, which threw Kutusov into his worst rage of the war, and with good reason.[28] It all reflected the festering enmity between Kutusov and Bennigsen, further compounded by changes at headquarters motivated by rivalry and distrust, not utility. Finally, the Russian cavalry struck at Murat on October 18. They crashed through an ill-defended wood to Murat's left flank, with the aim of cutting him off from Moscow. The first wave, composed of Cossacks, got through the forest at night with ease. They scattered the French, but Murat rallied them and stood firm. The Cossacks found themselves alone. Their infantry support was ill-coordinated, some units got lost on the night march. This led to a violent row among the field commanders, ending when one of them, Karl Gustav von Baggohufvudt, resigned his command and stormed off the field. Despite the disarray in the French ranks and the heavy losses inflicted by the Cossacks, Kutusov called off the whole operation, allowing Murat to slip away. To the Russians, the battle of Vinkovo—sometimes called Tarutino—had been a catastrophe that further embittered the commanders, yet the French saw it as a Russian victory. Murat could easily have been annihilated; he lost three thousand men and many cannon. Above all, it sent him packing back toward Moscow and spread panic in the French ranks. Napoleon, fearing Kutusov would follow up such a success, brought forward his withdrawal by a day, and left Moscow on October 19, exactly four months after the start of the "three week" campaign. Napoleon still hoped Kutusov thought he was going to attack the Russian left and the Kaluga road would be clear long enough for him to get through, but he was too slow. It rained heavily for the first two days of the march, slowing the army still further. It took it five days to cover sixty miles, shadowed by Kutusov's cavalry all the way. Kutusov's horsemen supplied him with ample information about French movements, while Napoleon remained largely in the dark.

As the French withdrew, there was one last act played out in Moscow. Now, it was Napoleon's turn to wreak havoc on the unfortunate city he found gleaming and left in ashes. On October 20, Napoleon told Berthier that he had ordered Mortier to blow up the Kremlin, to place powder kegs at the foot of all its towers, and then to leave Moscow immediately, and join Ney's III Corps as the army's rearguard.[29] Napoleon wanted to make Alexander shudder, even in his hour of triumph. The dull thuds of Mortier's work were heard by the retreating army on the morning of the 23rd, and the 26th Bulletin of the Army crowed to the French public that "This ancient citadel, which dates from the foundation of the monarchy, this first palace of the Tsars, no longer exists!"[30] As with so many of Napoleon's plans in Russia, it was not quite the case. Despite his precise orders that "the fuses must be broken into small pieces" to keep them short and accurate, most of them failed. The damage was extensive, but the Kremlin still stands.

Maloyaslavets

The day before, Kutusov ordered a corps to shadow Napoleon, following along himself the next day with the main army. The immediate goal was to outrun the French, occupy a bridge at the important road junction at Maloyaroslavets, and thus stop Napoleon's advance on Kaluga. Eugène's Italians got there first, on October 24, but Dmitri Dokhturov's corps arrived soon after, and drove him out of the town. In bitter hand-to-hand fighting thirty-two thousand Russians took on twenty-four thousand Italians, seeing the town change hands several times. The Russians were able to charge downhill, causing heavy casualties, but the Italians regrouped behind the thick walls of a monastery and put up determined resistance. Napoleon praised the courage of the Italians and Eugène's generalship to both Maret and Marie-Louise. "This combat did the greatest honor to the Viceroy and his troops," he told Maret. "He carried himself well, tell the Vice-queen,"[31] he told Marie-Louise.[32] Many of the Russians were relatively raw militiamen, the Italians often underrated by the French, but both sides fought with great courage and ferocious determination.[33] By the end of the day, the

French held the town, the Russians the high ground across the river, where they established a powerful artillery battery. About seven thousand men were lost on both sides. Napoleon lied about his own losses, as was his nature—"Our loss is about 2,000 men," he told Berthier—but he could not disguise the death of General Alexis Joseph Delzons, one of Eugène's most experienced commanders, who had served with Napoleon since his first major battle, at Montenotte, in 1796.[34] The town had been reduced to cinders; many of the wounded on both sides were burned alive, unable to crawl away from the flames. The narrow streets were a mass of rotting corpses of men and horses, stuck together by congealed blood.[35] It was a cameo of the whole campaign. The next day, to the fury of his staff, Kutusov ordered a withdrawal to Kaluga before Poniatowski's Poles cut him off,[36] but when Napoleon arrived with the main body of the army, he, too, ordered a halt.

Early on the 25th, Napoleon went out on a personal reconnaissance of the southern bank of the river, from which the Russians had recently withdrawn. Suddenly, a Cossack unit charged out of a wood and took him and the chasseurs of his escort, under Rapp, completely by surprise. One Cossack got within twenty yards of Napoleon. His sword drawn, Napoleon turned to fight, along with his men. In the mayhem, a chasseur who had lost his sword and was fighting with a lance he grabbed from a Cossack, was nearly run through by a Horse Grenadier, who mistook his green tunic for a Cossack's. When reinforcements arrived—including the Mamelukes—they all charged the Cossacks, who took flight and easily outran the French. Napoleon had almost been taken, and seemed perfectly happy to get himself killed in the brawl, but that the Cossacks had managed to spend the whole night camped not three hundred paces from a whole French battalion, and then sprang out of nowhere, was a chilling lesson.[37] After that colorful personal reconnaissance, Napoleon held a council of war almost as acrimonious as Kutusov's.[38] This was small wonder, for although he could now have driven on and taken his chosen route to Smolensk through the easier country to its south, Napoleon decided to avoid any chance of an engagement, and made the army retrace its steps along the main road.

This small action was among the most influential of the wars. Napoleon had wasted time and a hard-won victory he could have exploited, probably through fear of small roads and Cossack raids,[39] in favor of known hardship. Kutusov pulled back to his base, and left open the road into a fertile, unspoilt countryside, but Napoleon spurned it. Napoleon had foreseen this. In his report to Berthier after the battle, he hid behind a barrage of knowing—or self-deluding—lies on the one hand, and his initial calculations on the other. He denigrated the quality of the Russian forces in blatant disregard of the facts: "the enemy infantry has diminished greatly since the battle of Moscow; it is composed of 15,000 old soldiers . . . they have recruited their Cossacks . . . this cavalry, hardly dangerous in reality, tires often."[40] It is tempting to think that he was trying to hide his own fears about the men who had nearly killed him and the fighting spirit and ability of the raw militiamen who had nearly bested Eugène. His dismissive remarks about the Russians flatly contradict his subsequent course of action: If true, it was all the more reason to press on, but he was warier of Kutusov than ever. His decision looks more rational when he turned to the weather and the need for haste: "The cold and the need to dispense with the large number of wounded who are with the army has decided the Emperor to head for Mogilev."[41] The onset of the cold had preoccupied him from the outset, first on leaving Moscow, as he told Cambacérès on October 24: "We have beautiful weather here, hot even; the local people think it is extraordinary. . . . We are taking advantage of it to get to our winter quarters, as it is probable that in a fortnight, the weather will be severe."[42] With Kutusov's power now clear to him—however he tried to hide it—he reverted to his contingency plan. He had lost precious time, however, by failing to make a clear, decisive choice between a quick march through a wasteland or swinging wider, in search of supplies. The dithering was not in Moscow, but on the march. Now, he had to outrun the weather, not the Russians. For David Chandler, it "doomed his army to extinction."[43] "Napoleon's star no longer guided his course," remarked General Robert Wilson, a British observer with the Russians. As the skies turned a flinty gray, it was no longer visible.

Almost immediately, the march threatened to disintegrate. By October 28th at Vereya, just north of Maloyaroslavets, Davout moaned to Berthier that the supply wagons of Eugène's IV Corps had tangled themselves up with his own logistics train so badly that three of his divisions did not reach their assigned positions until 9:00 P.M. that night. Davout chided not Eugène, but Berthier—and by implication, Napoleon—for the crisis being created:

> Orders must be issued that the troops who march ahead of the rearguard (Ney's III Corps) must take precautions not to burn villages which have resources which the rearguard needs very badly. It (the rearguard) alone must be allowed to burn the villages it abandons, and which the army of the Tsar would find very useful to it.[44]

Thus did the military mind interpret and describe the second round of the rape of rural Russia. Napoleon seems to have given no such order. The closest he came was in ordering Davout to wait for Eugène to cross the river Dukhovshchina before crossing himself five days later.[45] He then ordered Davout to assume the rearguard of the main body of the army and to hurry up and close the gap between himself and Eugène by making between seven and eight leagues per day, to reach Smolensk in three days, a pace Kutusov's staff felt was destroying the French troops.[46] "I imagine his corps is short of supplies," Napoleon remarked to Berthier.[47] His understatement was breathtaking. It underlines the yawning gap between Napoleon and his men on this campaign. From Smolensk, one of Ney's officers told his mother that the army was now living on the meat of its dead horses—"and I can assure you that a slab of horsemeat cooked in a pan with a little fat or butter makes a very reasonable meal"—that was when they were lucky. On the march, he had "enjoyed a very good cat stew, and they were really excellent."[48] Caulaincourt—who saw it for himself—reported that Napoleon ate well in Russia: mutton, beef, white bread, and lentils—his vegetable of choice—washed down with Chambertin, the majestic emperor of red Burgundies.[49] It was a long way from his frugality at Austerlitz.

Russian reports showed the ruthlessness with which the Grande Armée abandoned not only its baggage trains, but its own. The roads were littered with its sick and wounded. Stragglers abounded.[50] Ammunition was discarded to lighten the load for exhausted horses, now more valuable than men. The artillery, desperately short of horses to pull their guns, not only seized those pulling wagons full of plunder from Moscow, but carts full of wounded men, left to die on the road. "They called out to us (as we passed) in heart-rending tones that they too were Frenchmen, that they had been wounded fighting at our side, and they begged us not to abandon them," recalled one veteran.[51] The Cossacks and wild Baskir irregular cavalry, who shot arrows at the enemy, stopped the French from pillaging what little was left to take.[52] At least between Maloyaroslavets and the main road there was still something to pillage. No longer.

Predictable chaos soon gave way to stunned horror. There was now only one way home, through the swathe of destruction Napoleon had cut through Smolensk—his first supply base—to Moscow. The armies had made of it the valley of the shadow of death. It was strewn with rotting corpses, most of them probably French; the Russian police later calculated that over 430,700 burned corpses had been found along the advance march of the Grande Armée, while many more had certainly been buried by their comrades.[53] Mogilev was a devastated town surrounded by half-buried, rotting corpses, not a haven. No one was buried at all on the field of Borodino. When the Russians reached it weeks later, one officer recalled:

> . . . (the corpses) had lain as victims of the elements and the changing weather. Few still had human form . . . maggots and putrefaction had made their mark . . . wolves had come from every corner of Smolensk province. Birds of prey had flown from nearby fields. Often the beasts of the forest and those of the air fought over the right to tear apart the corpses. The birds picked out the eyes, the wolves cleaned the bones of their flesh.[54]

To General Marbot, it was "an immense tomb," which made even hardened veterans shudder when they furtively glanced at the Golgotha they had made.[55] They were the only human forms over much of this denuded countryside, in a barren landscape long abandoned by its peasantry, save for peasant guerrillas and regular partisans, there to spy on and harass the French as the darkness of winter drew in. The only protection this hell gave the French was its very barrenness. The corridor was too bereft of food to lure the Russians into it.

Kutusov was not free of these problems, either. Although the meticulous work of Barclay and Arakcheev ensured his army was well supported, the poor roads and the weather of late autumn frustrated his troops as much as Napoleon's in these weeks. The Russians were now three days behind Napoleon, and for all the logjams on the way, he was still too fast for Kutusov to catch him without exhausting his men. Whatever pace Kutusov chose to move at, his army could only live off what it could carry amid such devastation. As early as September, he had begun creating a mobile magazine of supplies and ammunition, with the full support of the local nobility and peasantry. Even with these advantages, it still had to cope with poor roads, and the privations created by its own army as well as the French, thus being forced to consume the supplies meant for the army. The supply trains were badly directed, often got lost, and even fell into French hands. Kutusov had more reasons to avoid combat than fear of the French.[56]

There was only one sizeable engagement on this stage of the march, at Vyazma, on November 3, when both armies finally made it to the main Smolensk-to-Moscow road. The French were strung out over fifty kilometers along the road, which tempted a Russian corps under Miloradovich to try to cut off Davout's rearguard from the main body. Kutusov was reluctant to allow this, and did not hurry any of his own main body to support him. Eugène's Italians swung back to help Davout, along with Ney. Davout had to run a veritable gauntlet to escape, with heavy losses. There was plenty of fight left in the Grande Armée, for men now living on horseflesh,[57] but for the first time in a direct engagement, the French took more losses than the Russians. The Russians now knew their superiority in cavalry and artillery.[58] The weather was still mild, but the Grande Armée had been battered well before real winter began.

Napoleon pushed on quickly from Vyazma, this time making Ney's III Corps the rearguard to spare Davout. Emboldened, the Russians lunged at Ney, trying to cut him off as they had Davout. Badly mauled, they fell back, but only an arduous march reunited Ney with the main army by nightfall.[59] It was just as well. Davout's I Corps—once the bedrock of the army—and Eugène's Italians were now at the end of their rope. Discipline and morale were disintegrating.[60] Ney and his men now assumed the heroic role they played until the bitter end. On November 6, the first heavy snows began to fall. When Ney caught up with a unit of Württembergers camped ahead of him on November 7, he assumed they were still asleep in their tents. They had frozen to death.[61]

Smolensk

By November 9, when Napoleon finally reached Smolensk—now seen as almost a haven of plenty by the army—winter had come. Along with the snow, a plethora of news just as chilling poured down on him from every side. In the last days of October, Napoleon got reports that the northern flank of his proposed retreat was in peril. Wittgenstein had defeated Victor and St. Cyr, first at Polotsk, in mid-October, and again at Chashniki, on the last day of the month, which separated the whole Bavarian corps from the front and cut it out of the campaign. Wittgenstein won through superior numbers and artillery, but that did not stop St. Cyr from blaming Victor for not supporting him.[62] Napoleon exploded on November 7, ordering Victor to drive Wittgenstein back. His fear was palpable: reunite your troops, meet the enemy without delay, push him back, retake Polotsk:

> This movement is important. In a few days your rear will be inundated with Cossacks; the army of the Emperor (the main body) will be at Smolensk, but very tired . . . Take the offensive, the well-being of the army depends on it; any delay will be calamitous. The cavalry is on foot, the cold is killing all the horses. March! That is the Emperor's order, and it is essential.[63]

The renewed assault failed, but Wittgenstein halted his advance for another three weeks, and the road stayed open as he was resupplied locally, growing stronger by the day. This was meant to be the first phase of Alexander's plan to encircle Napoleon before he reached Poland. Chichagov was meant to close the gap to the south, and take Napoleon's main food depot at Minsk, before closing the gap with Wittgenstein at the river Berezina by mid-November. He moved swiftly, drawing off Schwarzenberg and pushing north, while the Austrians were forced back toward the river Bug, a move Napoleon thought almost duplicitous, better suited to defending Warsaw than protecting his southern flank. In fact, Schwarzenberg had turned back to protect Reynier's Saxons, and so lost all initiative.[64] Chichagov was forced to halt for two weeks, to await his supply train, hindering Alexander's grandiose pincer movement. Alexander's plan for enveloping Napoleon looked perfect on paper, but its vast scale and tight timetable showed he understood Russian geography and logistics little better than Napoleon. Time was now on Napoleon's side, as he could probably reach the Berezina before Chichagov, and certainly before the Russians could fortify the crossing point.[65] But Napoleon was now exposed and the need to drive his exhausted army intensified. With Schwarzenberg pushed west, Chichagov now had the way clear to his north and Napoleon, eased further by the need for Victor to contain Wittgenstein. Contingents of light infantry made it to the Berezina crossing at Borisov, but the main army was far behind them. Despite Kutusov's ponderous advance and Chichagov's frustrations, Napoleon received news as he entered Smolensk of just how tight the net was closing in on him. The reinforcements he hoped to find there, under Baraguey d'Hilliers, had been intercepted by the Russians southwest of Smolensk and cut to pieces. The Grande Armée was now cut off from all help, and there was precious little of it left, as its columns staggered into Smolensk over the next four days. Of the ninety-five thousand who left Moscow, only just over forty thousand were combat ready: the guard had fallen from seventeen thousand to fourteen thousand, but they had fared best. Davout's I Corps stood at barely ten thousand, and Eugène's corps at half that number. Ney's rearguard numbered only three thousand. The Poles and Westphalians were the most battered of all. In truth, the real strength of the army was now the twenty-five thousand men under Victor and Oudinot holding down Wittgenstein. That the five thousand men of the dismounted cavalry were one of the army's larger units spoke volumes for the scale of the catastrophe.[66] They were all starving. Napoleon had counted on Smolensk's stores of supplies, but the retreating support units had depleted them badly; Victor had also been drawing on them, as had the fifteen thousand sick and wounded quartered there, while the surrounding countryside offered scant food.[67] As so often during 1812, the Grande Armée fell upon what was left like hungry wolves in an orgy of desperate greed and indiscipline, the guard included.[68] In the meantime, Wittgenstein managed to seize the other major supply stores at Vitesbk. The city was now in Russian hands.[69] The last straw came when Napoleon ordered Eugène to retake it, but after attempts to build a bridge over the small river Vop failed, Eugène's men had to wade through it in freezing cold and driving snow, all the while harried by Cossacks. Mud gave the Russians their victory, as caisson after caisson became trapped midcrossing. Only a handful could be pulled out, and the loss of horses was so great most of the guns had to be spiked, fifty-eight in all, while the men died from Cossack charges and more still from hypothermia. Eugène lost twenty-five hundred men in what the Italian survivors called "the night of horrors."[70] It was clear the retreat had to go on immediately; the longed-for and long-promised respite was illusory and morale fell to its lowest ebb. The guard got there first, and got more rest and food than the units who arrived in its wake, causing bitter divisions. On November 12, the temperature fell to −75°C.[71] Two days later, Napoleon and the guard struck out west for the Berezina, the rest following quickly behind.

Krasnyi

Napoleon was deeply worried that the road west could be barred, despite the slowness of Kutusov's advance. He sent out each of his corps at twenty-four-hour intervals from Smolensk, which eased road jams, but made them all vulnerable to being cut off from each other, and Kutusov promptly exploited this. Between November 15 and 18, Napoleon launched a series of small attacks on Kutusov, known collectively as the second battle of Krasnyi (the first being a cavalry engagement during the advance). The village of Krasnyi nestled in a narrow gorge leading west to the Berezina. Napoleon had to pass that way, but a Russian battery barred his way, and only the guard could break through. The guard artillery was hoisted by its gunners up the steep slopes to the plateau above Krasnyi, but it took almost a whole day, and the Russians dominated the gorge. Napoleon took charge of "his children" in person, "I count on you, as you can count on me, to perform great feats . . . I have played the Emperor long enough. Now it is time to play the general."[72] The guard formed its squares and withstood both the Russian guns and repeated cavalry charges, but at one point a Russian horse battery outflanked the French, trapping Mortier, and opened fire directly on Napoleon and the Old Guard. Napoleon ordered the Chasseurs of his bodyguard to drive it off, and so save Mortier. The stubborn stand of the Old Guard allowed first Eugène, and then Davout, to join Napoleon[73]—Napoleon himself led the attack by the guard that scattered the Russians in terror and briefly cleared the road for Davout to slip through—but Eugène had his own adventures in getting there. Eugène's men fought a daylong engagement and were saved only by nightfall, when they slipped away through woods and small trails to bypass the Russians, only because a Polish officer told Russian sentries that they were troops from Kutusov's headquarters on reconnaissance and was believed. Napoleon could have been easily captured, and henceforth wore a small vial of poison around his neck. Victory was accomplished by a series of bayonet charges, one of which killed 464 of the 500 Dutch Royal Guards, troops disparaged by Napoleon when his brother Louis created them, but who he now lauded—too late—as "the glory of Holland."[74]

Napoleon then had to make the difficult decision whether he could afford to wait any longer for Ney or leave him stranded from the rest of the army. Ruthless realism prevailed as always. Napoleon was too afraid to wait, believing Kutusov's main force was on its way, although he blamed Davout for leaving him in the lurch.[75] Ney now had his finest hour. Having been reinforced in Smolensk, his six thousand men and six cannons were still hopelessly outnumbered, but rebuffing an entreaty to surrender—"A Marshal of France does not surrender"—he launched a full frontal attack on the Russians barring his way, then three more, his ranks thinning all the time. "Whole ranks fell, only to be replaced by the next," remembered an awed Wilson.[76] As night fell, like Eugène, Ney resorted to guile. He dug in giving the impression of standing firm for the night, but he took his remaining two thousand men and slipped into the woods to the north. Soon lost in the dark, Ney himself guided them down a streambed in driving snow, in hopes it led to the River Dnieper, cursing Napoleon all the time for abandoning him. They found the river frozen, but able to bear only small groups at a time—the wagons plunged into it, the guns were all left behind—but most of them made it across, Ney himself saving one man from drowning as the ice crumbled beneath him. They rested in a well-provisioned village the next day, and another night march brought them at last to Eugène's picket line.[77] Only eight hundred remained.[78] A Russian partisan commander may have remembered the guard as passing through "our Cossacks like a gun ship through a fishing fleet,"[79] but the reality was the end of Davout and Eugène's corps as fighting units. A campaign that began as an exercise in "shock and awe" descended into a game of "hide-and-seek" as Ney and Eugène slunk through the woods in dead of night. For all that, "Napoleon's men" fought like lions. Their losses make the blood run cold. Perhaps as many as ten thousand of the best troops in the army had been killed, and double that number wounded or captured. Two hundred guns were lost.[80] The Grande Armée had become a rump of its former self, but not yet a shadow.

Still ignorant of Ney's escape but resigned to losing him to save the main body, morale received a much-needed boost when this news reached the army. It did not last long. The previous day, November 17, Napoleon learned that Schwarzenberg had captured Minsk and its stores.[81] Interpreting this as Schwarzenberg was near to closing the gap, Napoleon made haste, burning still more wagons and stores to lighten the load, among them—to set an example—some of his own coaches, and most of his papers, but also, in a supreme act of carelessness and stupidity, the pontoon bridges.[82] Two days later, Napoleon told Oudinot that his corps could not reach Borisov fast enough. He was still determined to march on Minsk, his main supply base, presumably still thinking Schwarzenberg held it.[83] It was too late. On November 25, a Russian division from Chichagov's vanguard reached Borisov and seized the French bridgehead over the Berezina, destroying both the bridge and the pontoon train Napoleon had left there. Although Oudinot was able to recapture Borisov—and some much-needed supplies—the Russians simply withdrew to the western bank of the river and burned the bridges behind them. Then an unseasonal thaw broke the ice and flooded the banks.[84] Hot or cold, the weather was against Napoleon even as the jaws of the Russian bear seemed to have closed on him at last.

However, Kutusov's own supply problems and the mauling Napoleon had given him made him wary to coming too close, too fast—reservations shared by Wittgenstein and Chichagov. Victor and St. Cyr, despite their bickering, had rendered Napoleon a great service by hindering Wittgenstein, however much Wittgenstein had weakened them and cost the French Smolensk. Kutusov, meanwhile, was resting his men and reprovisioning.[85] There was continual jealously and suspicion among the three Russian commanders, and misintelligence: Chichagov was "operating in the dark," and had only the sketchiest notion of what Kutusov wanted of him or where the main army was.[86] Wittgenstein—who disliked the thought of linking with Chichagov in any case and finding himself under his command[87]—was loath to advance further and risk being caught between Victor and Napoleon.[88] None of them really acted as required. It was not helped by Friedrich Oertel, the commander of Chichagov's vanguard, who did not risk encountering the French, which meant the western bank remained lightly defended. For all that, the Russians destroyed the one bridge over the Berezina for miles, at Borisov.

The Crossing of the Berezina

Napoleon had one, last, desperate hope of escape. He seized it, according to Caulaincourt, with an energy that had been notably absent in recent weeks.[89]

He was helped by a stroke of fortune when one of his scouting units captured a peasant who showed them a small ford over the river some miles north of Borisov, near the village of Studzienka.[90] It was a very dangerous gamble—the crossing was not really fit for an army even as reduced as his—but it was his only chance, although crossing to the north of Borisov meant abandoning all hope of reaching Minsk. Chichagov had no way of knowing this, and Napoleon gambled correctly when he assumed as much. A small diversionary movement convinced Chichagov that Minsk was still Napoleon's goal. This bought him time he sorely needed.

The Berezina is a tributary of the Dvina, flowing north to south. It is only about two meters deep and twenty meters wide at Studzienka. Its steep banks made it necessary to build a longer bridge than that.[91] Bereft of their pontoons, and with a whole army—however shrunken from the bloated horde of June—it must have seemed as wide and insurmountable as the Channel to Napoleon and his sappers. Oudinot was placed in overall command of the crossing. His first step was to install a battery of forty guns on the eastern bank, while five thousand men of guard covered the crossing of Oudinot and his infantry, who had to ford the river on horses' cruppers or flimsy rafts, dodging ice floes all the while.[92] What followed was one of most heroic and murderous feats of Napoleonic arms. The heroes were mainly Dutch engineers, often the butt of Napoleon's derision; the conditions they faced were horrific cold, a fast-flowing river full of ice sheets, driving snow, and the dark, so relentlessly did they have to work. Napoleon envisaged building three bridges from scratch, but there was time to construct only two: one was designated for the artillery, wagons, and carriages; the other for the infantry and the remains of the cavalry. Studzienka was systematically dismantled to provide wood for them, the logs cut to precise measurements; nails were forged at breakneck speed. Fortunately, in the midst of the wanton destruction of the pontoons, their commander, Jean-Baptiste Eblé, had held on to six wagons of tools, two of charcoal needed for smelting iron for the nails, and two field forges.[93] Once the construction began, the Dutch sappers had to work stripped to the waist in the freezing cold, in fifteen-minute relays. Even so, many died of hypothermia. When finished, they had to make frequent running repairs to prevent them collapsing, particularly on the bridge carrying vehicles. Napoleon stayed with the sappers, watching the whole operation. There were moments of detachment but he often came to the river bank to encourage and salute them. Above all, he enjoined the men to take pride in their eagles.[94]

Most of the army had assembled at the bridges by October 26. David Chandler realized that exact figures are hard to come by. Although now reinforced by Oudinot and Victor, and by a handful of newly arrived garrison troops from Poland, the Grande Armée mustered only about forty-nine thousand men under arms, and almost the same number of stragglers, military and civilian, who now began to arrive at the crossing. Among them were 5,500 still-mounted cavalry, and about 250–300 guns. This was minuscule compared to the Leviathan of the spring, but it all still had get over two makeshift bridges in haste. Between them, Chicagov and Wittgenstein had about seventy-five thousand men.[95] Kutusov remained too far away to influence events, but coming he was. The French began to cross on the morning of November 27. Gendarmes guarded the entrances. The guard moved at dawn. Oudinot was next over, with those of his corps who had not crossed earlier. As Napoleon watched, they cried, *"Vive l'Empereur!"* which had been seldom heard on the march. Oudinot's men wheeled south immediately to face Chichagov's advancing troops. Napoleon established his headquarters on the western bank by midday; Davout, Ney, and Eugène followed. Victor dug in on the eastern bank as the rearguard, awaiting Wittgenstein. It was often nerve-wracking, as the makeshift bridge swayed and its planks—often little more than tree branches and straw—gave way.[96] There was pushing and shoving, a few fights, but on the whole discipline held until about 4:00 P.M. when the "vehicle" bridge started to give way when three of its trestles collapsed. While the Dutch sappers risked life and limb below them, the orderly column suddenly turned feral. Men stampeded to get off and tried to push their way on to the other bridge, with considerable loss of life, men and horses. Both bridges were now blocked with corpses and Eblé's exhausted sappers now had the grisly task of hacking their way through the dead and pushing them over the bridges to clear the way for Davout and Eugène to cross.[97] In spite of everything, now only Victor remained on the eastern bank. The crossing must count among Napoleon's great successes, if in the spirit of Dunkirk, rather than Austerlitz.

When Napoleon first announced his plan, Ney reportedly scoffed to Rapp, "If Napoleon succeeds . . . he is the very Devil."[98] Hell soon followed in his train. An exhausted, relieved calm fell on the army as it camped for the night, cold as they all were. Snow began falling, hardening into frost, and the next day it was overlain by more thick snow.[99] It had all exhausted Napoleon, too. The rekindled energy of Kraskyi and the crossing gave way to lethargy. He ceased overseeing the bridges personally, once the main army was over, leaving it to Victor and Eblé. Even more worrying, the forty thousand stragglers mirrored his mood. Eblé tried repeatedly in the course of the 27th to persuade them to cross in small numbers in the gaps between the army corps, but few did so, preferring to rest on the eastern bank, possibly feeling safe under Victor's protection. Their mood changed when Wittgenstein got close enough to shell them on the morning of the 28th. The hapless, defenseless mass of civilians, many women and children, were butchered. Panic broke out among the living, who now hurled themselves toward the bridges in a mad frenzy, or plunged into the river. A kitchen girl from a Polish regiment seized a horse and tried to ford the river with her baby son in her arms, only to be swept away by the current, halfway across; another mother, her leg shattered by a shell, kissed her infant, strangled the child with her garter, and lay down to await death. With the bridges packed to bursting, every Russian shell found its mark until Victor pushed them back. This only intensified the panic. Eblé and Victor made one last effort to clear the bridges.[100] The next morning, Victor received orders to begin withdrawing to the west bank and to destroy the bridges by seven that night. He cajoled the remnants of the stragglers to take their last chance, but the horrors of the day had again reduced them to apathy. Loath to abandon them, Eblé delayed obeying orders for an hour and a half, until Wittgenstein's Cossacks appeared. The last, desperate surge ended in death for those who reached the bridges, being crushed to death in the crowd, or drowning.[101] The carnage was the result of mental and emotional disintegration, the culmination of weeks of privation, as much as Russian shells.

Victor's men did escape, and none had fought more bravely. Largely composed of Poles, Hessians, Saxons, and men from Berg, they put the lie to the fabled uselessness of troops from the Confederation of the Rhine. Their losses are hard to know, so mingled were they with the stragglers, but they were not small.[102] These eight thousand men—outnumbered almost four to one—fought without respite for twelve hours to hold the ridge ahead of the bridges.[103] The congestion on the bridges meant that only one brigade of Badenese troops arrived to help them. They fought with great courage, but Victor's only real relief came from artillery fire Napoleon directed from the western bank.[104] By daylight on the 29th, Victor's men were safely over the river and the bridges were no more. The Berezina was clogged with frozen corpses for weeks.[105]

Nor was it long before the western bank had to be fought for. It did not take long for Chichagov to see he had been duped and he quickly turned north to check the crossing, His advance guard on the western bank was now under Eufemiusz Czaplic, an energetic soldier who had replaced Oertel, "a timid commander," and made good progress.[106] On the opposite bank, Yermolov drove his men ferociously and reached Borisov on November 27, just as the French were crossing the river a few miles to the north.[107] Ney and Oudinot could muster only between twelve and fourteen thousand exhausted men, whereas Chichagov's thirty thousand were all fresh troops who had not fought major engagements.[108]

At this point, yet more unlikely heroes emerged. The pan-European character of the army now showed itself as a force to be reckoned with. Almost three quarters of the troops who turned and faced the Russians were not French. Half of them were Poles, but the rest comprised four Swiss regiments and handfuls of Croats, Italians, a few Dutch grenadiers, and—the most unlikley lions of all—a Portuguese regiment that had been forcibly incorporated into the French army by Junot in 1808. The guard had shown its teeth at Krasnyi. Now it was the turn of the runts of the litter. The Russians arrived quickly and in force. Czaplic's vanguard was reinforced by two divisions and a battery of artillery. As Ney's Poles advanced into the woodland from which they had just driven Czaplic, the Russian guns opened up, showering splintering pine trees among them. Then the Russian infantry charged, and bitter hand-to-hand fighting in the woods led to three senior Polish officers being wounded. Ney sent in what he had, badly weakened men who fought with true élan until Polish lancers and French heavy cavalry threw the Russians into panic and drove them out of the woods. The infantry steadied behind them, and held the line. After their ammunition ran out, the Swiss made seven bayonet charges that day. The Russians did not give up until just before midnight, but at last fell back. "It was butchery," one French soldier remembered, "There was blood everywhere on the snow."[109] Chichagov had been checked and the crossing at last secured, but the cost had been high. The French lost almost thirty thousand good troops over the three days. The worst-hit units were those of Oudinot and Victor, who began the crossing as the strongest Napoleon had left; Victor's corps now had but sixty cavalry and three thousand infantry.[110] The Russians has lost roughly ten thousand, a heavy blow,[111] but one they could well absorb with Kutusov's main army not even engaged. The Berezina showed, too late, the fighting quality of the prodigals of the Grande Armée, and also the effectiveness of often wayward commanders like Ney and Oudinot, once the scale and scope of the war had narrowed. The Berezina had narrowed it further, but Napoleon escaped with forty thousand men, when he should have been crushed. Indeed, had the Russian commanders not been so negligent, they could have still cut him off, for the road west to Vilna led through marsh land, crossable only by a narrow causeway. As it was, Davout and Eugène had reached Zembin, at the far end of the causeway.[112] The ordeal of the army was far from over, however. While the Russians halted, the Cossacks and their powerful ally, winter, took over the pursuit.

Winter now came on relentlessly as the French recrossed a region considered barren at the best of times, an area Napoleon called "a very pretty place" in his 29th Bulletin to Paris. The guard went first, over a corduroy road of pine logs lain across the marshes.[113] It was that same stretch of pine forest and bog they had crossed in summer, but it was covered in snowdrifts. Vilna now assumed the mantle of Moscow and Smolensk as a land of milk and honey at the end of their ordeal. The Cossacks snapped at their heels. Oudinot—still wounded and moving slowly—was nearly captured, but fought them off ferociously with a handful of troops.[114] It was a dire warning to stragglers of all ranks. Unrelenting cold was now the real enemy, however. Temperatures remained constantly below −30°C during the ten-day march, at one point reaching −37°C.[115] Frostbite struck many down as ears, noses, and fingers froze and fell off bodies already badly weakened. A Swiss officer only had his penis saved by an old peasant woman, who threw cold water on it and rubbed it back to warmth as the blood returned. "I have more than once given thanks to God for this good and worthy woman," he recalled.[116] It was not a typical encounter for a Napoleonic soldier on the march.

The Russians who trailed the Grande Armée were horrified by what they found: The main road was blocked by the corpses of men and horses; abandoned wagons were strewn across it, as were many wounded Russian prisoners. In the woods to either side could be seen the fires of French stragglers, already half frozen and awaiting death.[117] There were almost twenty thousand of them.[118] That the French were largely safe from the Russians was because they had deprivations enough of their own. Hunger, cold, and a new threat to both armies, typhus, struck at Wittgenstein, Chichagov, and Kutusov—and it came mainly from the malnourished, exhausted French stragglers they captured. They clung to the edges of the French advance, knowing that only worse hunger and disease lay in the corridor along the main road.[119] The Grande Armée struggled into Vilna on December 8–10, but by then they had a new commander, Murat. Napoleon left the army to hurry to Paris on December 5.

The Coup d'État of General Malet, October 22–23, 1812

On October 22–23, there was an attempted coup against the government in Paris. Its instigator and leader was an angular personage, the discharged general Claude-François Malet. Malet had "a chaotic" military career under the ancien régime. He reenlisted in 1792, and rose to brigadier by 1799, under Moreau and Bernadotte, irritating everyone he served with.[120] Forcibly retired in 1808, he played a prominent role in the attempted coup that year. At first detained in prison of Sainte-Pélagie, he was transferred to a sanatorium run by Louis-Paul Dubuisson, a doctor with royalist connections. There, Malet seems to have forged a devil's alliance with the abbé Jean-Baptiste Lafon, who was there for having disseminated the pope's circular condemning Napoleon for his seizure of the Papal States. They fabricated a *sénatus-consulte*, announcing Napoleon's death in Russia, and proclaimed a provisional government by Senatorial decree. This was followed by a more widely diffused proclamation aimed at the Parisian Municipal Guard. Both documents were firmly republican, and show no trace of royalist influence. Malet's "provisional government" was headed by Moreau, Lazare Carnot, and Augereau, none of whom could have had any knowledge of the coup. The sentiments of the proclamation were far more worrying for their content than their impact, at least for Napoleon:

> Bonaparte is no more! The tyrant has fallen under the blows of the avengers of humanity . . . If we should blush at having supported for so long a foreigner, a Corsican at our head, we are too proud to suffer a bastard (the King of Rome) there. [121]

However ephemeral in reality, Malet struck right at Napoleon's greatest fear, the legitimacy of his dynasty, yet this was not immediately clear to him in Russia.

Malet and Lafon escaped the hospice with ease on the night of October 22. Supplied with the garrison's password and dressed in a general's uniform, Malet made his way to the barracks of the 10th Cohort of the Municipal Guard, where he convinced their commander, General Jean Antoine Soulier, that Napoleon was dead and a pro-republican provisional government was in place. Malet then liberated two of his allies in the 1808 coup from the La Force prison: generals Emmanuel Maximilien-Joseph Guidal and Victor Lahorie. They managed to arrest Savary and Pasquier, the Parisian chief of police, and intended to seize Cambacérès and Clarke. When Soulier informed the prefect of the department, Nicolas Frochot, of the coup, Frochot believed him and put a room at the Hotel de Ville at their disposal. Two commanders of the Municpal Guard, Colonel Jean-François Rabbe—who sat on the Military Commission that condemned the duc d'Enghien to death—and Captain Georges Rouff, accepted the conspirators at their word and put their men under their command. They next tried to persuade the governor of Paris, General Pierre-Augustin Hulin, to join them, but were opposed. Hulin saw it for the hoax it was, and was wounded by Malet, who fled the scene. Hulin's subordinates—one of whom knew Malet—swung into action by 9:00 A.M. on the 23rd. Lafon simply vanished, while Hulin's office informed Clarke, but Cambacérès had begun the fight back two hours earlier.

A bemused Cambacérès was disturbed at his desk at home by his colleague on the Council of State, Pierre-François Réal, who asked him—pale, agitated, and confused—if it was he who had ordered Savary's arrest. "You're mad my dear Réal, and I don't know what you're talking about." Réal had been a radical, rabid revolutionary, a veteran of the Terror, and did not frighten easily. Cambacérès collected himself and told Réal to tell Clarke to come to the house without delay. He also sent word to Bon-Adrien Jannot de Moncey, the commander of the Gendarmerie, and to the commandant of the Imperial Guard. A detachment of the guard was sent to Saint-Cloud to protect the imperial family. While this was going on, Lahorie had managed to rally some of the Municipal Guard, but Clarke was on his way to intercept them.[122] Cambacérès then took one further measure on his own initiative: He ordered the Senate to be locked, and had the keys brought to him, personally. He knew the potential powers the Senate could wield. If it met, it could change the constitution should enough senators believe Napoleon was dead.[123] He acted as he did, because he feared that indeed they would. More than the coup, itself, this action revealed how fragile the regime had become in the eyes of its loyalist and most senior servant. By the time the Council of Ministers met at 9:00 A.M., the coup was over and its leaders under arrest. The ministers were as one that the conspirators needed to be dealt with quickly and severely. They were shaken, as emerged in the investigation of the coming weeks, but they presented it all to Napoleon as they did to the people of Paris: a minor incident.

Napoleon swallowed it. When he got the news, as distilled by his ministers and Cambacérès, his only reactions were to tell Clarke to give Rabbe's regiment to a more energetic and reliable commander,[124] and to berate him for sending an ill-informed aide-de-camp to alarm Marie-Louise unnecessarily about "this slimy mess."[125] The next day, on reflection, he ordered the arrest of all the officers of the 10th Cohort, and ordered any others involved out of Paris.[126] For the moment, he told Cambacérès, the most important thing was to hold a solemn, "religious-like" ceremony at the Invalides, to assert that he was not dead, but above all to make clear that the Senate did not have the right to change the constitution.[127] His arch-chancellor knew better, at least on the latter point.

Most of Napoleon's subsequent orders to Paris on the Malet coup were intercepted by the Russians,[128] which left the Council a free hand to deal with the investigation. Malet, Lahorie, Guidal, and Soulier were promptly executed on October 29, in front of the disarmed men of the 10th Cohort. Rabbe was spared, possibly because of family connections,[129] but it was just as well, given Napoleon's initial reaction. Initially, Napoleon did not argue about it, remarking merely that he would probably find the reasons in a report from Savary at some stage.[130] The distance between the emperor and Paris aided the swift, ruthless work of the military commission, and enabled Cambacérès to impose his will on the Council, wary of how Napoleon might react to such ruthlessness. To await his orders "would be to recognize there was an absence of judicial power" in a moment of crisis. Minds were further concentrated when queues formed at the Banque de France, and a run on the franc seemed likely.[131] On the very eve of his departure for Paris, Napoleon appeared more worried about the "pitiful, unjust and impolitic" wrangling between Savary and Clarke than anything else, over their relative culpability for letting the coup happen.[132] These were views he stuck to on the two-week trip home, telling Caulaincourt—his only interlocutor and our only source for this period—that Clarke's insistence on mass arrests—"he sees Jacobins everywhere"—was an overreaction, and that Savary was closer to the mark in seeing the plot as just something "hatched in the minds of idiots."[133] Malet, he concluded as he crossed the Rhine, "had to be a lunatic if the thought he could overthrow the government with a few officers and a prefect for a few hours. He is a man who wanted to get himself shot to get himself talked about."[134]

If it was not the Malet coup—the serious implications of which only dawned on Napoleon when he reached Paris, if at all—something prompted him to head home with such haste in the last days of November. From Smolensk, on November 14, he made it clear to Cambacérès that "I am getting closer to Poland, to find the quietest winter quarters possible."[135] Napoleon does not seem to have confided what impelled him to change his mind about this in the space of three weeks, and he remained confident of the army's ability to rebuild and hold Vilna; nor did he seem to share—or even be aware of—the general unease about the political climate in France that so wracked Cambacérès. In the much-cited letter from Napoleon to his viceroy, in which he berated Savary and Clarke for their "spat," he said he was sure Cambacérès has seen the 29th Bulletin and knew of "our position and what has happened." He added, "Your worries must have been acute."[136] Cambacérès's biographer, Laurence Chatel de Brancion, has challenged the usual interpretation of this letter as Napoleon simply wanting to subordinate and frighten Cambacérès. Rather, it should be understood as Napoleon trying to blunt the scale of his own disaster as news of it reached the government.[137] On his voyage home, Caulaincourt makes frequent reference to Napoleon's worries about the timing of the publication of the 29th Bulletin, and how unnerved he was to learn that it appeared two days later than Napoleon wanted, his plan being to calm things immediately as the news broke.[138] These were shades of Egypt twelve years before. He was also conscious how quickly he had to rebuild the army after the Berezina, especially as he intended to hold the line in Poland, and this could only be coordinated from Paris. Malet was a minor matter at this point, but speed was of the essence, for whatever reason. The snow obliged Napoleon to travel by sleigh, and he traveled light. His toilet, his library, his Chambertin, and even his shaving kit were left behind. Napoleonic decisiveness was much in evidence.

The Ninth Circle of Hell

Napoleon's departure was announced to the guard on the evening of December 5, at the village of Smorgoni, where they were all camped. The drums beat, the bugles sounded, and the sleigh carrying Napoleon and Caulaincourt, followed by a small escort of lancers, disappeared into a −30°C night.[139] He turned the army over to Murat. Two days earlier, from the village of Molodechno, Napoleon issued one of the most extraordinary documents of his career, an army bulletin—the 29th of the campaign—that told the truth, in a manner of speaking. Napoleon spoke only of the events between leaving Smolensk and the crossing of the Berezina. He did so truthfully, although he issued no casualty figures. He did not hide the horrors of the last days, but never revealed those of the previous months. It was truth built on lies, encapsulated in the phrase "This army, so beautiful on the 6th (of November) was very different by the 14th, without cavalry, without artillery, without transport." It dwelled on the death of so many horses and how this made so much else dangerous and difficult, but gave the deliberate impression that all the woes of the campaign stemmed from the freezing cold of November, and so Napoleon engendered a myth that still persists—that the onset of winter alone defeated him. Nevertheless, the admission that the army now needed to "reestablish its discipline, remount its cavalry, its artillery" and that "rest is its primary need" were not admissions the French public was used to seeing in print. All things are relative, and perhaps the clearest admission of disaster came two days later in a letter to Marie-Louise: "You will have seen from the bulletins that (things) have not gone as well as I would have wished. It is violently cold."[140] He left for Paris almost as soon as the ink was dry. It was seven years and three days since Austerlitz.

As Napoleon sped for Paris, the army still had ten days of horror to face before it crossed the Niemen again, to the safety of the Duchy of Warsaw. Maret commanded Vilna, and Napoleon warned him that vast stores would be needed for the troops, but according to Caulaincourt, Napoleon was still convinced Vilna was well provisioned and the army would have time to recover there, and equally certain that the Russians would halt and go into winter quarters.[141] There were provisions in place—rations of meat, dry biscuits, and warm clothing[142]—but Napoleon had been outflanked by his oldest enemy, the corruption of the army administration, for whom Maret was no match. Typhus, too, had preceded them, in the form of the sick and wounded evacuated from Minsk. When the temperature suddenly rose, corpses began to rot, making it worse. Discipline broke down completely when the desperate troops fell upon the stores, often killing themselves by gorging on food their shrunken stomachs could no longer cope with. In the face of this, Murat began pulling out of Vilna as early as December 10, just as the last units staggered in, far from the long period of rest Napoleon had ordered, leaving Ney to command the rearguard. Murat had gone ahead on the road to Kaunas on the 9th. Ney had cleared the town by the 10th, but he left five thousand sick and wounded, and another ten thousand men incapable of keeping up. They were massacred with great savagery by the Cossacks.[143] Increasingly, the French had to abandon their wounded, losing huge numbers of men who could have been restored to service with better care and, above all, more time to recover in safety. The Russians took gruesome losses, too. Of the ninety-eight thousand men Kutusov marched out of Tarutino, more than half were wounded by mid-December, forty-eight thousand in all, and that was only his command. Nor was Russian medical support in the field of good quality. However, they were fighting at home, and most of the forty-eight thousand wounded were in hospitals. These were well organized in Russia, but less so as the army advanced into Lithuania. Nevertheless, most of these men, veterans by now and the equivalent of two army corps, regained their health, returned to the colors, and became the core of a new army, ready to fight by spring.[144] Napoleon had no such reserves now.

By December 10, Murat had only seven thousand men under arms, among them the sixteen hundred of the guard. Almost all the baggage and guns were abandoned in the last days, as the army raced for the Niemen. They had once swatted the Cossacks away with contempt, but now Platov's light horsemen were a real threat. As the Cossacks closed in at the Niemen crossing, Ney gathered together about six hundred men to hold them off in a heroic action that allowed the pitiful scraps of the once "Grande Armée" of Twenty Nations, to cross into Poland on December 14. The Russians did not risk an invasion. On December 13, Kutusov told the tsar flatly that if the army did not get rest now, it could disintegrate entirely; he could not afford to lose his veteran troops or his experienced officers. A few days later, he admitted to Alexander that his losses had been so great since November that he had been obliged to hide them not just from Napoleon but from his own officers. Alexander was not pleased that his commanders had failed to catch and destroy the French, or that they had allowed Napoleon to escape,[145] but he had to accept the real price of limited victory. The Russians, too, had enough of winter war. It was respite by mutual exhaustion.

There was one more blow to come, another straw in the wind for the future. Murat was not the best organized commander. He was appointed partly because Berthier favored him, and because he was senior to Eugène.[146] Paperwork was not his forte, and so Macdonald, who had been besieging Riga with a mainly Prussian force, did not get his orders to fall back on Poland until December 18. He set out in two columns for Tilsit but one, under the Prussian general Johan David Ludwig Yorck, was trapped by the Russians. By the Convention of Tauroggen, Yorck's seventeen thousand men with their sixty guns pledged neutrality and went free.[147] In fact, they soon joined the Russians.[148] Yorck did this without his king's permission, in direct contravention of Prussian policy. He justified himself to Frederick-William in such brazen terms—claiming to act in defense of "the nation" and soon becoming an advocate of popular insurrection—that the king was left with little choice but to strip him of his command and order his arrest,[149] although powerless to effect either. The rest of Macdonald's men reached Königsberg on January 3, 1813. The campaign was over. Russia had stood alone, and liberated herself.

8

FROM DELUSION TO DETERMINATION, DECEMBER 1812–APRIL 1813

❧ ———————————————————————————— ❧

O n the night of December 18–19, a carriage entered Paris, and drove under the Arc du Carrousel—an honor reserved for Napoleon, alone—and into the courtyard of the Tuileries. Two unkempt men got out and tried, at first in vain, to gain entry to the palace. When challenged, the taller of the two—by his own admission his face barely visible behind his untrimmed beard—told a bewildered porter he was Caulaincourt, the grand equerry of the emperor. The porter summoned other personnel to vouch for this before accepting his word, and he was led inside and met by a group of officials. He told them he wanted to see Cambacérès, who was not there. He was asked, "Where is the emperor?" and replied "In Paris." With that, he was admitted. A smaller, scruffier man followed behind, having the same arguments, until he, too, got past the porters. When they finally convinced all and sundry of their true identity, the weary travelers made their way to the Empress's apartments, where her ladies-in-waiting gave them a warmer, less wary welcome. Napoleon said to Caulaincourt, "Good night. You need some rest."[1] Napoleon was right. They had returned to confront the country with the only genuine disaster it had faced since 1799. Napoleon set to work the next morning on a plethora of tasks, all of which stemmed from the unmitigated catastrophe of Russia.

Napoleon had had almost two weeks in total isolation as he made his way home, a remarkable interlude in the busiest life imaginable. Over thirteen days, he had only Caulaincourt to talk to, and talk he did, ranging over all that had happened, and what he believed, hoped, and feared would happen next. Caulaincourt, a reliable witness, left a very full account that serves as a poignant template by which to judge both the past and the future of the regime, and offers a window on the most influential mind in Europe. The journey itself was eventful in its way. Beset by blizzards, interspersed with floods, they spent a great deal of time bailing out the sleigh as they traversed Lithuania and Poland, its windows broken, its joints rotten and weak.[2] Axles broke and had to be repaired. They entered Warsaw unannounced and in secrecy, staying in a hotel. Napoleon was determined to "have it out" with his ambassador, Dufour de Pradt, and did not feel right staying under the roof of a man he intended to sack. After a blazing row, he did so, in what words we cannot know, for Caulaincourt deemed them "unprintable." Napoleon accused him of slough and of currying favor with the Poles, of not supporting French interests. De Pradt told Napoleon that his expectations for Polish mobilization were impossible without funding, and that the cavalry he thought were ready to act as a screen for the retreat had not even been mustered. When Napoleon asked de Pradt what the Poles wanted, he told him "To be Prussian." "Why not Russian?" Napoleon snarled and broke off, but when de Pradt dared to disparage the French army, Napoleon went into a genuine, not a contrived, rage. It dawned on him, even in so colic a state, that no one in Warsaw knew the scale of the disaster, and when he met a delegation of Polish notables the next day, he simply lied about the state of the army, telling them he still had 150,000 men under arms. Napoleon and Caulaincourt did not tarry long after this, and struck out for Saxony. Prussia was the more direct route home, but Napoleon chose to go through Poland and Saxony, because, for all his

official declarations that he could still count on Prussian arms, he wanted
to avoid the kingdom, but a small part of it had to be crossed. Napoleon
tried to make a joke of being captured—they might try to ransom him and
ruin France as a result, or they might turn him over to the English.[3] For
all his brave face, Caulaincourt remembered that Napoleon was deeply on
edge, "more than (during) all the rest of the journey."[4] He had good reason.
As news drifted in of the catastrophe in Russia, there were spontaneous
attacks on French personnel across Prussia, but the real hatred emerged
as the defeated Grande Armée made its way into Prussian territory. The
sight of ragged, starving columns made them easy prey for the peasantry,
so ruthlessly exploited for their benefit for so long. A local Prussian official
reported that the peasants "permit themselves in their fanaticism the most
horrific treatment of these unhappy wretches . . . in the villages and on the
country roads, they vent all their rage against them." Stragglers were often
no safer than in Russia.[5] Napoleon sensed this before the event, and sped
on. His return to Dresden stood in stark contrast to his departure from it
a few months before. They snuck in, late. Napoleon dealt with his post and
saw his great ally, Frederick-Augustus, for three quarters of an hour, while
still in his hotel bed. He was soon off again.[6]

The Empire Contracts: Defeat in the East

Napoleon worked under the false assumption that Murat could hold out at
Vilnius, and would be bolstered by the Poles. He knew nothing of the horrendous loss of life and health the army had endured since he left it. For over
a week, he received no dispatches, and so it was the army of the Berezina he
saw in his mind's eye.[7] Both illusions were pricked before he reached Paris.
His eastern march was collapsing all around him. Two days after he lied to the
Poles, the remnants of the army struggled across the Niemen. Kutusov entered
Vilnius in triumph the same day. Although the Berezina had not broken the
army, the marches to Vilnius, and then to the Niemen, had finally reduced it

to a starving, half-emaciated rabble, led by a bewildered, incompetent commander. Its core had been hollowed out. Of the 70,000 men of Davout's elite I Corps, only 2,281 were fit to fight by mid-January; the guard had fallen from 50,000 to a mere 1,300 in arms, with over 200 true invalides—amputees—the victims of frostbite. Of the Old Guard, the elite of the elite, 823 remained. The Young Guard—itself largely reconstituted from veterans of Spain—had all but ceased to exist.[8] Two days after Napoleon reached Paris, Murat reached the Prussian fortress city of Köenigsberg, where the news of Yorck's defection reached him.[9]

Two days later, Alexander returned to Vilnius, not with the "bored and squabbling band of courtiers"[10] who had come with him almost as a lark that spring, but with the core of his war cabinet, hardened by conflict. Nesselrode, his Parisian spymaster, now foreign minister in all but name; Petr Volkonsky, the soldier without whose hard work the Russian general staff would have imploded,[11] and now the tsar's right-hand man in military affairs; and Arakcheev, the Russian Carnot, the "organizer of victory." Alexander meant business. Napoleon usually spoke well of Alexander to Caulaincourt on their journey, describing him as able and intelligent, but "his misfortune lies in being so poorly seconded." "He is not master in his own house," he told Caulaincourt.[12] No more. He assumed Alexander had not evolved since Tilsit. He was still an intelligent, charming prince—"just the sort of king the French would like. Gallant with women, flattering with men . . . his fine bearing and courtesy are very pleasing."[13] Napoleon knew nothing of his sense of mission, of the steely determination born in him through religious awakening and sense of duty, that led him to tell a courtier as he left for Vilnius, "the only true and lasting peace would be signed in Paris."[14]

For the moment, Alexander's determination to pursue the French was tempered by the state of his own army, which he now saw for himself for the first time. He was shaken by what he beheld in Vilnius: "One single lamp lighted the high vaulted room, in which they had heaped up the piles of corpses as high as the walls. I cannot express the horror I felt, when in the midst of these inanimate bodies, I suddenly saw living beings," he recalled.[15]

One third of Kutusov's main army came down with the typhus already rampant in Vilnius.[16] Nesselrode and Stein continued to press for the invasion of Germany in the first weeks of 1813, while most of the commanders argued that their exhausted army needed rest. Kutusov and his staff won the argument and most of the army remained in quarters until March. Napoleon was right: The Russians were, indeed, reluctant to advance before spring. He told Caulaincourt, "There will only be Cossacks."[17] At the end of January, Kutusov and Wittgenstein launched three columns of Cossacks, supported by regular cavalry, to harry the French. They numbered barely six thousand men, but they caused havoc because there was only a paltry excuse left of Murat's once proud horsemen.[18] This was enough to panic Murat into flight, but it did not amount to an invasion.

For a brief moment Murat's army of wraiths won some time to keep running, and so they did. Murat began pulling out of Köenigsberg on January 3, for Elbing. Best placed to know, Murat thought he had about thirty thousand men fit to fight, three thousand horses, and sixty guns. He was finding it difficult to consolidate the smaller units scattered about the region, while his hopes of establishing depots evaporated, so rapid was the retreat. The Grande Armée, even with all its garrison troops and scattered units taken together, probably numbered only ninety-three thousand as the new year began.[19] The withdrawal was so disorderly that it verged on mass desertion, Murat checking it only by bribing as many men as he could with new gloves.[20] That same day, Napoleon held a small meeting in the Tuileries of his closest councillors, where he and Maret, newly returned from Poland, stood firm against the entreaties of Caulaincourt, Cambacérès, Talleyrand, and Admiral Decrès to accept an offer by Metternich to negotiate an armistice, fulfilling an urgent appeal Metternich had made to Emperor Francis in December, as soon as he learned the extent of Napoleon's disaster.[21] Napoleon and Maret took the stance that it would be "an admission of weakness."[22] It was an attitude Napoleon persisted in henceforth, but never was it more divorced from reality than on the day Vilnius was less evacuated than abandoned.

By January 12, the Russians had besieged Danzig, denying Murat its garrison. Less than a week later, Murat had fallen back behind the Vistula. For all intents and purposes, he had abandoned the duchy. Warsaw was evacuated on February 4. Murat handed the army over to Eugène on January 16, without Napoleon's formal permission. His biographer described it as "nothing more and nothing less, than desertion"[23] in the eyes of his colleagues. Napoleon had no choice but to confirm the fait accompli. He wrote honestly and warmly to Eugène, "My son, take command of the Grande Armée. I am ashamed not to have left you in command on my departure . . . The wrong that has been done is without cure."[24] Napoleon now saw Murat—and the eastern front—for the shambles he and it were, and he did not forget it. On January 26, he wrote to his brother-in-law:

I can hardly find words for my discontentment with your conduct, which is diametrically opposed to your duty. This proves once and for all, the weakness of your character. You are a good soldier on the battlefield, but away for that, you have neither character nor energy. You committed an act of treason, from fear of giving me good intelligence. I counted on you . . . You have done me as much harm as could be since you left Vilna (Vilnius), but we will speak no more of it. The title of king has turned your head; if you want to keep it, conduct yourself well, and keep your word.[25]

Murat joined the ever-lengthening list of "ingrates." Whatever else, Napoleon told Murat exactly what he said to so many others, Caroline included, to whom he wrote two days before Murat:

Your husband is a very brave man on the battlefield, but he is more cowardly than a woman or a monk when the enemy is not in sight. He has no moral courage . . . Make him understand his stupidity . . . However, I am happier with the message he sent me

through you. If he is truly sorry . . . I can still pardon him for the
harm he has done me.[26]

Nor did he censor his official organ, *Le Moniteur*, when it publicly castigated
Murat. It seemed to work, for Murat immediately threw himself into creating
a new National Guard and fresh regiments in his kingdom.[27] Caroline's star
rose still higher in Napoleon's firmament as a result.

Murat's behavior had become erratic, to put it mildly. Optimism alternated
with black rages, none of which was helped by the illness that now debilitated
Berthier.[28] Eugène continued the retreat to the line of the Oder, which drew
Napoleon's ire because it stretched the front too thinly. Eugène, like Napoleon,
had been deceived by the weather, thinking the Oder was defensible because
the ice was melting, but, in a risky operation, some Russian cavalry did cross
on very thin ice. A few reached Berlin, with Wittgenstein's light infantry not
far behind, convincing Eugène to leave the city to them, and fall back on the
Elbe. The Russians entered it on March 4. Any French counteroffensive would
now have to begin deep in Germany, while the Russians now controlled much
of Prussia and its resources. To what extent they controlled the Prussians was
a more complex issue, but help was at hand.

Metternich now reentered the game, quietly determined to remove Austria from the French alliance by sleight of hand. Schwarzenberg's twenty-five
thousand troops were the best Austria had, and Metternich wanted them out
of harm's way, not confronting Kutusov on Napoleon's behalf. Napoleon left
Schwarzenberg to defend Poland, but diplomacy, not Kutusov, was now on the
march in the East. Francis and Metternich helped their commander engineer
an armistice with the Russians at Zeycz, on January 30. It was his first small
step back into the "great game," and a clear signal to Alexander that Austria
would not oppose him. Schwarzenberg duly withdrew to Cracow, claiming
to the French he had been outmaneuvered.[29] The Russians took it on February 9.
The first "satellite state" had vanished.[30] Napoleon still believed—or so he
told Caulaincourt—that "the Russians should be viewed by everyone as a
scourge," and this would bind Austria to him, and that Prussia would follow

Austria's lead.[31] Alexander was "shifty," no one trusted him.[32] By contrast, "Schwarzenberg is a man of honor. He will keep his corps in readiness."[33] He declared repeatedly that one of his main reasons for returning to Paris was his conviction that he could control Austria and Prussia better from there. "The Emperor journeyed to his capital cherishing illusions such as these," Caulaincourt reflected.[34] Nor did they disappear, so adept was Metternich's game. "Austria, Denmark and Prussia (will) not change sides," Napoleon wrote to Emperor Francis soon after his return. "I believe I have grounds to hope that Your Majesty will give me the 30,000 extra troops I have asked of him."[35]

While Napoleon had had no information at all for most of December, framing his plans on what might be termed "office memory," Metternich emerged as the best informed man in Europe. Napoleon was not entirely mistaken in believing that Metternich and Francis feared a resurgent Russia.[36] He had no idea, however, that Metternich—alone among the European policymakers—had kept lines of communication open to all the other great powers during the Russian campaign. Indeed, Metternich was so well apprised of the war's progress that he knew when to supply and reinforce Schwarzenberg better than the French.[37] He also knew enough to fear both Napoleon and the tsar. Napoleon was the source of all his woes, but Alexander had proved a fickle ally in 1805, and territorially aggressive, as shown by his seizure of Galicia in 1809. Napoleon was weaker than ever before, but still master of vast resources, and he had hobbled Austria militarily and financially after Wagram. Metternich was realistic enough to know that Napoleon could only be driven out of Germany by force, and that there could be no real peace, otherwise, but also Austria was militarily the weakest of the powers, and any war with France would mean a war on two fronts for Austria, not just in Germany but in northern Italy, a region Napoleon was determined to hold. The assiduous research of Wolfram Siemann has confirmed that, far from being an opportunist with no real plan in 1813,[38] Metternich had evolved a subtle, complex set of policy goals first set in motion with the armistice of Zeycz, and then by cautiously exploiting the networks to all the potential members of a new anti-French coalition. By coaxing Russia, Prussia, and Britain into closer cooperation, he hoped to foster the emergence of a coalition it would be safe for a weakened Austria to join. The time had not yet come to take the field, but Metternich felt he could create such a moment, and maintain the semblance of the French alliance in the meantime.[39] It was a very dangerous game, but it worked. Indeed, he was still able to regain the Illyrian Provinces, and their coastline, from Napoleon on February 3, as an incentive to remain loyal.

Although hatred of the French was as widespread as in Prussia, Napoleon was not entirely wrong when he told Caulaincourt that he could still control Berlin while Murat held Lithuania. He wrote two letters while in Dresden both on December 12. One was to his father-in-law, Emperor Francis of Austria, saying that, in the light of "all the events that have taken place since my departure from Moscow" it was essential that Francis mobilize all his troops in Galicia and Transylvania, thus doubling his contingent, and put them at Napoleon's disposal.[40] He did no such thing. Simultaneously, he wrote in almost identical terms to Frederick-William of Prussia, saying he needed "fairly numerous" troops from him, meaning a new army corps of thirty thousand.[41] "Berlin meekly complied," as Christopher Clark aptly put it.[42] Scharnhorst's *Krümprsystem* made this easy, and Frederick-William had close to seventy thousand troops on a war footing.[43] That did not mean he wanted to use them in the interests of either side. He remembered all too well Alexander's failure to support him in 1806–07, and knew the Russian high command was deeply divided about advancing further. Although Alexander was strong enough to bully Frederick-William, it was most uncertain he could defeat Napoleon, as yet. The Prussian leadership feared popular unrest as much as Napoleon. Even the warlike Prussian military balked at the propaganda Stein was issuing from Alexander's headquarters, still bent as he was in 1809, on inciting a proto-Spanish general insurrection against the French. Both factors made them hesitant to change sides.

The French retreat, more than the Russian victory, began to shift the king's position, if not his attitude. His capital and eastern provinces were in Russian hands; Stein was the effective governor of East Prussia, convening its estates—whose members obeyed him—dismantling the Continental

Blockade, elevating the "rebel" Yorck to his military commandant, and levying conscription to the point of having twenty thousand men under arms and ten thousand reservists.[44] All this, but in whose name? His official title was "Plenipotentiary of the Russian Emperor."[45] The Estates claimed to speak in the name "of the nation"; all professed loyalty to Frederick-William, but the king dared not acknowledge them. Napoleon still controlled the western provinces of his kingdom and could take dread revenge, as he had in 1806. Yet, would the monarchy lose control of everything to a popular rising, the elemental basis of which was all too evident? Frederick-William, as so often, was a prisoner of events. He was presented with two choices, in three memoranda from his councillors on Christmas Day 1812: two of them advocated breaking with Napoleon and throwing in his lot with Alexander. The third, to which he gave his support three days later, felt Napoleon and Alexander must reach a new détente, mediated by Austria; even if this failed, Prussia would only join Russia if Austria also changed sides. Its essence, for Christopher Clark, was "live and let live."[46] There were many outward similarities with Metternich's strategy, but they are in the details. Francis controlled his realms; Frederick-William manifestly did not. While Frederick-William was on the brink of having to "ride the tiger" of a Prussian guerrilla war that terrified him in the first months of 1813, good intelligence and management by Metternich enabled Francis to scotch well-honed plans by his brother, Archduke John, and other high-level councillors, to raise the Tyrol in revolt, as in 1809. The whole plan was wiped from the official record so successfully that it was only brought to light by Wolfram Siemann in 2016.[47]

Events moved swiftly in Prussia, but none of them were of the king's making. Fearful the French would take him with them as a hostage when they left Berlin, and aware that Napoleon, now back in Paris, was regrouping, the king and the government fled into Silesia, to Breslau. Public faith in Frederick-William was shaken in western Prussia now, as well as in the East, when reports arrived of anti-French unrest west of the Oder, and calls for revolution if the king did not join the Russians.[48] In the first days of 1813, Frederick-William sent Karl von dem Knesebeck as an envoy to Vienna, where he stayed for almost three weeks. Metternich conceded nothing concrete, save that Austria would not turn on Napoleon, but both Francis and Metternich gave clear assurances that Austria would be "bought" if Napoleon offered them Prussian territory to take the offensive, and hinted that Prussia would do well to ally with Russia. Knesebeck returned to Breslau in early February having read Metternich aright: "(S)ooner or later, Austria will go to war with France because the peace terms she wants . . . are unobtainable without war."[49] This may have shaken the king out of his characteristic vacillation—"he appears not to know what he wants" lamented Hardenberg just before Knesebeck returned.[50] One clear policy did emerge: the government's collective determination to channel popular resistance into proper military formations, under the control of the army. A call went out for all Prussians to take up arms, but they usually did so as "free companies" recruited and commanded by regular officers.[51] This temporized, even if it did not extinguish, Stein and Alexander's long-nourished hope for mass popular uprisings behind Napoleon's front lines.

Negotiations began with Alexander in mid-February and were concluded as the Treaty of Kalisz on February 27–28, just days before the Russians formally occupied Berlin. It was far from an easy process. Now very much "master in his own house," Alexander drove a hard, almost Napoleonic bargain with his old friend. Russia promised to protect Prussia and advance quickly westward—being supplied by Prussians all the way—and to work together to bring Austria into the war. There was much talk of restoring the balance of power in Germany, and of territorial compensation for Prussia, at this point from Saxony, perhaps further west. However, whatever Prussia might gain would have to be fought for; its potential spoils all still lay in Napoleon's hands. Indeed, they would come, if they came at all, as compensation for all of Prussian Poland—save a corridor linking East Prussia to the rest of Prussia—which Alexander took for himself. Prussia was promised castles in the air. In the meantime, Alexander demanded eighty thousand more Prussian troops in the field, a point with a very Napoleonic ring to it, which forced Frederick-William to resort to the dreaded mass conscription in mid-March.[52] Breslau became the center of operations for both armies. The Prussian alliance made it possible for two Russian corps to occupy Silesia and rebuild at its expense. Huge supplies of flour greeted them; bathhouses were built; muskets repaired.[53] A contemporary remembered, "the streets were agog with preparations for war . . . virtually everyone, from tailors to swordsmiths, cobblers and harness makers, hatters and saddlers is working for the war."[54] Prussian volunteers flocked in and were put under military discipline; some Russian regiments could be seen drilling every day, although few Russian reinforcements arrived. Arakcheev's vast reserves, garrisoned deep in the Russian hinterland, would not arrive for several months. When Napoleon took the field next, the Russian units he faced were in "a thoroughly reduced, even in some cases skeletal condition."[55] The first fighting had to be carried by the Prussians.

Napoleon had already begun a frantic reorganization of his forces to confront this change, but he made no mention of it directly, only that the enemy seemed to be concentrating around Breslau. Nothing could mask his fears, however. He could see only his own weaknesses, not those of his opponents. On March 5, he made a devastating, desperate confession to Eugène:

> My son, I don't know enough about the condition of the army to direct it . . . I am in such ignorance that I do not know the state of the garrisons of Stettin, Cusrin and Glogau. I don't know what has become of the corps that was in Swedish Pomerania, or of the garrison of Spandau, or the formation of your divisions; and don't know where the Poles, the Lithuanians or the Poles of my Guard actually are. I don't know about your artillery or its provisions. How many men *have you* lost around Posen?[56] How many infantrymen have been left behind in the retreat? . . . I don't know why you don't send me detailed reports . . . Who commands the cavalry? . . . Who is actually in command in Stettin? . . . Who is in command of Glogau?

Of course, he lambasted Eugène and the corps commanders for lack of information, but Napoleon admitted he was in the dark. He ordered Eugène to hold Berlin and the Elbe line as long as he could. He concluded by telling Eugène that, if he had to abandon Berlin and the Elbe, he had to maintain communications with Magdeburg, the new headquarters.[57] Eugène had already withdrawn, and the Russians had taken the city the previous day. In the three months since he left it, Napoleon was none the wiser about the state of the eastern front. The same day, he warned Jérôme that Eugène might have to yield Magdeburg, and to expect the army in his territory: "Thus, it is necessary to prepare this theatre."[58] Jérôme had much to lose, and little to fall back on. Once back in Paris, Napoleon had to confess to his brother, "Nothing at all remains of the Westphalian army . . . and everything points to crisis in the coming spring."[59] There was more to worry about than "holding the line," and not just in Germany.

The Empire Contracts: Spain

On October 10, from Moscow, Napoleon informed Clark he had received his letters written in early September, bringing bad news from Spain. "Being so far away, I can do nothing for the business in Spain," was his first reaction. The way his commanders and Joseph had allowed garrisons to become scattered across northern Spain—exactly what he, himself, had done in the East—was "disastrous." "Tell the king this must not happen again"; these forces had to be concentrated because "if we lose this frontier it could only be retaken with difficulty."[60] The "disaster" was Wellington's invasion of northern Spain, begun in late June, with forty-eight thousand Anglo-Portuguese troops that led to a heavy French defeat at Salamanca and the subsequent occupation of Madrid.

By the time Napoleon was on his way home his mood had brightened, and his opinions on Spain had returned to his usual mixture of insight and folly. "We are winning," he told Caulaincourt; it was now only a matter of "scattered guerrilla contests, and the English would soon be driven out, once the Spanish saw the benefits of a code more liberal and better suited to the times in which we live than the . . . Inquisition."[61] Those "scattered guerrilla contests" grew more like pitched battles by the day, as British arms reached Mina's bands and he remained blissfully unaware of the competing claims to enlightened reforms emanating from the Cortez of Cádiz, among them the abolition of the Inquisition.[62] On one point, however, he had learned much: "In Wellington, my generals have encountered an opponent superior to some of them."[63]

While Napoleon thrust ever deeper into Russia in the summer of 1812, at the other end of Europe, Wellington had held the upper hand in western Spain since he took Badajoz in April. He certainly showed better prescience than Napoleon when, soon after learning the invasion of Russia was imminent, he wrote, "If the Emperor of Russia has any resources and is prudent, and his Russians will really fight, Buonaparte will not succeed."[64] He also saw, more prosaically, but sharp-eyed, that the French could hope for no reinforcements from then on. They still had about 300,000 men in Spain, but they were thinly spread. If concentrated against him, he had little chance of success, but Napoleon—and Joseph even more—saw that Wellington had less to worry about here than he could know. His marshals were incapable of cooperation, Napoleon told Caulaincourt.[65] It was now a question of which French army to attack, Soult in Andalucia, or Marmont in the center. Wellington's initial reaction on finally taking Badajoz, was to strike at Soult, his satrapy around Seville being far the greater prize, and if he raised the siege of Cádiz it would make a better impression on a British Parliament that was then without a stable government. Soult had about fifty-eight thousand able-bodied men but they were hard-pressed and pulled in many directions—containing "scattered guerrilla bands" and besieging Cádiz chief among them—which meant he could muster barely twenty thousand against any invasion.[66] Yet, advancing south would stretch Wellington dangerously should Marmont decide to help Soult. Marmont was well placed to attack Ciudad Rodrigo and Almeida, and so threaten Portugal, if Wellington let his guard down. Wellington thus struck into central Spain with about fifty thousand men on June 13, 1812, forcing Marmont to fall back on Salamanca. Marmont had about forty-four thousand troops, but they were widely scattered and he needed time to regroup. Wellington shared with Napoleon an unfortunate knack for missing the best campaigning season. By waiting until June, he sent his men—many newly arrived in Spain—into blistering heat. Nevertheless, the bulk of his infantry were now battle-hardened veterans, and the arrival of two brigades of heavy cavalry gave him superiority over the French in horsemen he had not held before. Wellington entered Salamanca three days later, its beautiful plaza—the largest in Spain—filled with cheering crowds, but Marmont had left three well-fortified convents, held by good troops, who threw down a marker to Wellington: It took the British ten days to reduce them, at the cost of 99 dead and over 300 wounded.[67] Besieging the French, even on so minuscule a scale, was no easy matter.

Both commanders were "stranded": Marmont did not know that Joseph had answered his call for help, stripped the garrison of Madrid to a paltry fourteen thousand, and was rushing north. Bonnet had defied Napoleon's orders and heeded Marmont's call, but it took him until mid-July to reach Marmont. This made Marmont wary of launching a frontal attack on Wellington, although their armies were of almost equal size.[68] Wellington's advance had been carefully planned; he was meant to be supported by simultaneous thrusts by Francisco Javier Castaños to his north, from Galicia, and Ballesteros, to his south, driving into Andalucia. Castaños was delayed, and Wellington actually had to draw Marmont away from him, instead of the other way around; Ballesteros was crushed by Soult at Bornos, and withdrew. Although other diversions—an Anglo-Sicilian amphibious invasion of Murcia and a naval incursion on the Basque coast—tied down potential French reserves, Wellington was still alone.[69]

Marmont made up for the difference in quality and concentration between the two armies by a series of clever maneuvers. He made a series of flanking movements that threatened Wellington's line of retreat to Portugal and forced the British to pull back from their forward positions to a line of small hills southeast of Salamanca. By July 22, the French held the highest ground around a hill called Arapil Grande; Wellington held the smaller one, Arapil Chico. Bonnet had finally arrived. Wellington awoke that morning "to the knowledge that his campaign was on the brink of failure."[70] Marmont then made his major mistake. He assumed Wellington's movements were defensive, to protect his line of retreat, and that his cast of mind was not aggressive. In fact, Wellington was looking for a gap all day. Marmont provided it. He swung the bulk of his forces right across Wellington's lines, his goal still being to shepherd Wellington into a retreat and avoid battle.[71] As Charles Esdaile has observed, Marmont was breaking a cardinal rule of the age—marching across the front of an opponent.[72] It came down to a misjudgment of character. Wellington delivered hammer blows to Marmont in the next hour. Legend says the Irishman was munching on a chicken bone when he saw Marmont's mistake and leaped into action, tossing the bone aside. In truth, he said himself, he had been straining his eyes all day when he saw that the French left was now almost cut off from the main force, which itself was dangerously strung out in front of the British lines. Marmont saw his error, but as he rushed to take personal command of the left, he was badly wounded by a shell while mounting his horse. Bertrand Clauzel, his second-in-command, had already been wounded and was having his heel stitched. Bonnet took over, but only for a matter of minutes before he was hit in the thigh. Wellington dashed off to the French left and took control. Pushing his troops hard to get ahead of the French line, they reached a ridge, drew up behind it, and then burst over its crest in full cry, overwhelming the lead French division under Jean Guillaume Thomières, who was mortally wounded along with so many of his men. Wellington then hurried back to the center of his lines, and launched an assault on the rest of the French left. It was destroyed by one of the greatest cavalry charges of the Napoleonic Wars. Led by Major-General John Le Marchant, the British heavy cavalry stormed out of the haze of a blazing summer sun into a field enveloped by musket smoke, shattering an already disordered French infantry. The charge then splintered, its left crashing into the French second line; the rest—"disordered but full of impetus"—literally smashed into the lead regiment of the hindmost French division, which was left with only forty-seven officers and men out of one thousand when the heavy cavalry had done with them. Le Marchant lost a mere 108 men, a reward for élan more associated with Murat than the British.

Wellington's assault on the Arapil Grande proved a sterner test. After a long exchange of fire, Clauzel's men charged and broke the British line, and were soon supported by Bonnet's division, coming around the side of the hill where a British staff officer remembered how his men "gave way like a wave of the sea." It was made worse when a Portuguese brigade charged up hill in the burning sun. Exhausted by the time they reached the French lines, they were easily thrown back, losing almost 18 percent of their strength. Although the fighting was now very confused, Wellington deployed his well-positioned reserves, while the French were now half destroyed. Wellington was now leading from the front, and was almost wounded in the process. When a ridge to the south—behind Marmont's lines—was taken by exhausted British troops as the light drew in, all that was left for the French was to salvage what they could from the wreck. In the first hour of fighting, the French took 13,500 casualties[73]—plus 2,500 prisoners, twelve guns, and two eagles[74]—compared to 5,220 Anglo-Portuguese, 694 of them killed.[75] Nor did the retreat go well. The dragoons of the King's German Legion harassed the French rearguard the following day, breaking a well-formed square of infantry that cost the French one thousand men, a rare feat of arms.[76] Once clear of the battlefield, however, the French retreat was so well organized, and their marches so swift, that the exhausted British gave up the chase after a week, Wellington expressing astonishment at their speed.[77] Marmont, fell back first on Valladolid, and then on the well-fortified stronghold of Burgos, securing the quickest route back to France. "Salamanca was the greatest French defeat in open battle since the dark days of 1799," Rory Muir rightly notes.[78] The road to Madrid was now wide open, and Wellington entered the capital in triumph on August 12, but there were still a quarter a million of French troops in Spain under the excellent generalship of Soult and Suchet. Wellington was no fool. "I must still expect that they will collect upon me in all directions and I shall have another battle to fight yet."[79]

Faced with seeming mayhem, in a quiet act of defiance while he was thousands of miles from Paris, Cambacérès reappointed Masséna to command the Army of Portugal in place of the wounded Marmont, to hold the line of the River Duero against Wellington at all costs. Masséna hastened back, but was taken violently ill at Bayonne, and pronounced unfit for active service by his doctor.[80] Not all in the corridors of power agreed with Napoleon's handling of Spain, and knew a mistake when they saw it. Until Salamanca, repeated appeals for help to Soult and Suchet were ignored or swept aside with predicable contempt. Suchet claimed to have orders from Napoleon to stay put in Valencia: "The king (Joseph) has his instructions. I have mine. If he insists I send him a single regiment, he will also get my resignation."[81] Until the facts were in his face, Soult fobbed Joseph off with his theory that Wellington's real target was Seville, not the North.[82] Now the game was up. They knew Joseph did not have the men to hold Madrid. He made it clear that he was going to fall back to Valencia. Soult's first reaction was to propose Joseph come to Seville, and make it the new pivot of the counteroffensive. As Charles Esdaile has shrewdly observed, the plan had its merits: Wellington would have been forced to go after them and fight both armies in a pitched battle he may well have lost. The risk to the French would come if they were beaten, and Andalucia lost for good. When Joseph rebuffed Soult, the plan was scotched, but Andalucia was lost in any case. Soult saw he would now be isolated. When Soult got the news of Salamanca, he ordered all his units to concentrate in Seville and Cordoba, as a prelude to complete evacuation. Over the coming weeks, the siege of Cádiz was lifted, small garrisons bade their Spanish girlfriends goodbye, blew up their fortifications, and fell back. Soult left with a dash, celebrating St. Napoleon's Day (August 15) in Seville with fireworks, a banquet, and a ball.[83] He withdrew gradually eastward, into Valencia. The scenes of Joseph's departure from Madrid on August 11 were almost pathetic. Filing out of the city were twenty thousand civilians and thousands of wagons, with Joseph in their midst, his face hidden under and large white hood. Dozens of trunks, filling over forty coaches, were needed to transport his looted treasure of paintings, silverware, porcelain, paintings, clocks, and chandeliers.[84] As they staggered on, parched by the summer heat, with the shadow of the yellow fever rife in Murcia stalking them,[85] General Joseph Léopold Hugo observed the scene and expressed himself almost exactly as his comrades would a few months later, as Napoleon fled Moscow: "Our journey resembled rather the migrations of the (nomadic) peoples of Asia."[86] It was the first such scene of the collapse of a "satellite kingdom" in Napoleonic Europe, but it would not be the last.

Wellington had actually read Napoleon's men better than he. Forced from his "kingdom," with little to lose, Soult began to coordinate with Marmont and Suchet, and even Joseph. Vast swathes of Spain were now lost to the French for good: Estremadura, Andalucia, and New Castile had all fallen. However, as Esdaile discerns, "with every step that Wellington advanced, the French had less territory to garrison."[87] Joseph soon shifted from Valencia to Zaragoza, the capital of Aragon, which was better placed for a counterattack. Soult continued to argue for the reconquest of Andalucia, his reasoning obvious in the pile of looted treasure he, too, had brought with him. This, at least, was Joseph's opinion. He put it bluntly in a memorandum to Clarke:

> . . . you must understand the extent to which the repugnance of (Soult) to abandon Andalucia has caused most of our problems, and how the strong desire he has, and cannot contain, to return there . . . could work to the profit of the enemy.[88]

Real enmity developed between Soult and Clarke, who had forced his hand over talk of retaking Andalucia, but they both agreed that Joseph had to fight back. Joseph buried himself in detail and the arms of his mistress. He showed no leadership; "he bit his fingernails." It was October before a council was gathered of Joseph and all the marshals, and a plan of attack agreed. Even then, Joseph and Soult clashed so fiercely over the details that only the threat of dismissal brought Soult to heel. They were saved from themselves.[89]

Wellington paused for three weeks in Madrid over what to do next, and chose the wrong option. His initial decision to abandon chasing Marmont made sense, given the exhaustion of his army and the threat Soult still might have posed if he had moved north sooner. He captured considerable stores in Madrid—his men, even more, in an orgy of violence and looting—but he had bought the French time to dig in at Burgos. Clauzel had left two thousand good troops there. The castle stood on a 200-foot rock above the town, daunting for any direct assault, but well within the capabilities of a siege train. Wellington had left his siege train well to the rear, however. He rested his men in Madrid, as Napoleon would in Moscow, assuming Soult would come north to fight him. Suchet and Soult, along with Joseph's troops—concentrated between Zaragoza and Valencia—were too powerful for him now. With so many options closing, he struck at Burgos, against his own original judgment. He moved north on September 1, with twenty-eight thousand men but without a siege train, not even taking the Spanish artillery he had captured in Madrid. Salamanca has been called "Wellington's masterpiece." His quick thinking and sheer energy and leadership, his decisiveness, were breathtaking. What followed was quite the reverse. Rory Muir's judgment is damning: "No mistake in Wellington's military career was as wilful or as inexcusable as his failure to ensure he had sufficient means to undertake the siege of Burgos." Years later, with an honesty Napoleon seldom summoned, Wellington admitted his folly, and attributed it to his experience of capturing similar fortresses in India.[90] The siege began with an unsuccessful assault to scale the outer walls on September 22, that led to between six and seven hundred casualties, and led to arguments among the officers. Wellington then tried to tunnel his way in, but it was slow work, worsened by the increasingly poor morale and sluggish behavior of the Portuguese, but they were not alone. One officer wrote home that even "our friends in the Guards are not very stout."[91] The outer wall was taken by October 8, but the mood of the army grew darker when a night assault was repulsed on October 18, with the loss of two hundred men. Wellington was of two minds throughout the siege, deliberately using small assault parties to keep casualties low, but leaving them too small to succeed. With his morale deteriorating and wet weather eroding it further, Wellington raised the siege on October 21, having lost two thousand men.[92]

Despite their internal animosities, the French now showed a unity of purpose unprecedented in Iberia. For all Joseph's fears that Soult's only goal was the recovery of Andalucia, the marshal put forward a plan in early October that set this aside, and was adopted: The campaign hinged on uniting as many French troops as possible for a drive into central Spain, to force Wellington back into Portugal, thus retaking Madrid and reopening the roads to Burgos and France. Soult needed between fifty and sixty thousand infantry, nine to ten thousand cavalry, and eighty guns to do so. Concentrated in Aragon, the French had them, even without Suchet's army, which was guarding Valencia. Soult was the man to organize the counterattack.[93] By mid-October, Soult and Joseph pushed into La Mancha in force. Wellington had no choice but to begin a sullen retreat. Mirroring events in Russia, neither he nor Soult really wanted to fight, so thin were their resources: Wellington was exhausted and overstretched, and when he learned how outnumbered he was, it was clear to him Madrid had to be abandoned, as it was on October 30, and that he would have to retreat at least as far as Salamanca. Soult was strong in central Spain—he had sixty thousand men with him, and fifty-five thousand more north of Burgos[94]—but knew there was no help coming from France. Joseph reentered Madrid on November 2, to a sullen city and silent crowds, more fearful of French vengeance than British rape and pillage. "I could see on all the faces, more than ever, stubbornness. The king arrived during the day; it caused no sensation at all," one of Soult's commanders told him.[95]

The foul weather lashed Wellington's men with rain, and as supplies dried up, many broke from the columns to forage, or simply collapsed from hunger, French cavalry harassing them all the way. The troops from Madrid reached the main force around Salamanca. Soult caught up with them on November 14, in misty, cold conditions neither commander wanted to fight in, but Soult captured about two thousand prisoners and much-needed stores.[96] On November 19, Wellington trudged back into Ciudad Rodrigo, with good billets and supplies for the winter. Soult, too, was relieved to call a halt.

This was the position in Spain that greeted Napoleon on his return to Paris. It offered false hope, even if Wellington himself was dissatisfied with his troops' ill discipline and the lack of support he felt the Spanish had given him, which led to long and bitter recriminations. After Salamanca, he was offered by the Cortes, and accepted, supreme command of the Spanish armies.

It proved a poisoned chalice.[97] For all his own failure, the unease he caused ousted the French from vast territories and raised the siege of Cádiz, exposing the frailty of Joseph's regime to the whole of Europe. Napoleon's main source of information in Paris, Clarke, showed an almost imbecilic optimism. He spoke of Wellington's "remoteness, his lack of transport" and the unlikelihood that he would take the field again.[98] In fact, Wellington's strength rose between November 1812 and May 1813, from just over thirty-three thousand men to almost forty-eight thousand as reinforcements arrived—among them a brigade of the Household Cavalry—and his sick and wounded recovered. His men now slept in tents, although their Portuguese allies still roughed it under the stars.[99] By May, when the Spanish and Portuguese were counted, Wellington had almost one hundred thousand men, well-fed and trained. The French numbered over 200,000 in the same months, but they were no real match for this new army by spring. Napoleon accepted the fait accompli of territorial retrenchment. Soult and soon Bessières were on the ground to talk sense to him. For once, he listened. He soon shook off Clarke's complacent advice when he set in the context of his own collapse, telling him on January 3:

> Let the king (Joseph) know, secretly, that in the current circumstances, I think he ought to make his headquarters in Valladolid: the 29th bulletin will have made him aware of affairs in the north, which requires all our attention and efforts; that he would do well to make Madrid one of the extremities of his line . . . and I want him to take advantage of the inactivity of the English to pacify Navarre, Biscay, and the province of San Sebastian.[100]

Joseph duly complied. At the head of another wagon train, he left Madrid on March 17. Napoleon's orders to Joseph—still sent through a third person—signaled another, belated shift of opinion. For the first time in almost five years, Napoleon took the guerrillas seriously. Bessières was dispatched to Navarre almost as soon as he returned to France, and left Napoleon with no doubt about the serious threat Mina posed. With Wellington in winter quarters, he was now the most active and dangerous military threat in Spain. He possessed enough strength to besiege Pamplona and push it to the brink of starvation that winter. Bessières added that Mina was now "so numerous and war-hardened that (the French in Pamplona are) incapable of facing (him)" in a letter to Clarke that was, poignantly, intercepted, proving his point that French ability to administer the province was "absolutely nil."[101] Even as Bessières wrote, the British landed two large siege guns for Mina, who used them to reduce Tafalla, a well-fortified position, and took it after a bloody siege, won in reality by Mina's crushing defeat of the relief force sent from Pamplona. The French poured nineteen thousand troops into Navarre that winter, but to no avail.[102] Whether brought about by Bessières's good advice or his own growing respect for the Cossacks, Napoleon was now alert to the power of the guerrillas. It was a deathbed conversion. The balance had tipped away from him, and much of that was Napoleon's fault.

France, December 1812–March 1813: An Improvised Army

Napoleon returned to the Tuileries fearful for his army and his son. He set to work to secure both. Without a new army, there would be no empire for Napoleon-Francis. There was little time to find one. The Russians drilling on the walls of Breslau wallowed in their bathhouses and lived off the fat of a Silesian countryside as yet unravaged by war. Alexander's hesitancy had gone. Across Europe, Wellington's redcoats slept in their new canvas tents, all their needs provided in plenty by the Royal Navy; new shoes and uniforms arrived, as did proper tin kettles to replace their cumbersome old cauldrons. Like Napoleon in the Channel camps, Wellington drilled them incessantly.[103] A Tory government committed to the war was firmly in power, and Liverpool assured Wellington that the Opposition's castigation of the retreat from Burgos would fall on deaf ears in cabinet.[104] Hard cash flowed to the army more freely as spring came.[105] Alexander and Wellington had gathered useful allies around them, the Prussians and Portuguese respectively. From their bathhouses and new tents, the hard-bitten veterans watched as Navarrese bandits and Brandenberger schoolmasters became real soldiers. Behind both front lines, the awesome, if very different, resources of Britain and Russia were set in motion to support the coming onslaught.

Napoleon rose to the challenge. "I never saw him younger, more active, more patient, less the emperor, really," Cambacérès recorded.[106] "He transformed (France) into a vast workshop," said Caulaincourt.[107] His attention to detail flooded back when it was needed most; his energy at his desk, at least, was clear to all. The sluggish, ill Napoleon of Russia had evaporated. Caulaincourt recounted a rare flash of honesty from Napoleon about Russia as he began forging the new army: "Well, gentlemen," he told his small council, "fortune dazzled me. I let myself be carried away . . . I had thought to gain in a year what only two campaigns can achieve. I have made a great blunder, but I have the means to retrieve it."[108] Napoleon wanted a new army as large as that lost in Russia—of almost 650,000 men—and he almost got it. His administration responded to the challenges he threw at it to redeem his "great blunder."

No Napoleonic enterprise was as titanic as that of the first months of 1813. The timing could not have been more difficult in terms of the "calendar of conscription." The class of 1812 was all but exhausted, having been drawn upon ruthlessly for the Russian campaign: less than 2,000 could be mobilized, while 137,000 conscripts of the 1813 levy were only now entering the depots.[109] Napoleon had to resort to "exceptional levies," in the words of official euphemism, and on January 11, the Senate gave him permission to do so.[110] In other words, the Senate allowed Napoleon to break the law. As Alan Forrest puts it, "the rules . . . were deliberately ignored." Boys of lower than legal height were sent to the depots and men over thirty-eight to the reserves.[111] Men with widowed mothers, orphaned siblings, or brothers already with the colors who would normally be deferred, were conscripted. Many who had been deferred on medical grounds were reexamined.[112] The demographic statistics on which departmental quotas were based were torn up. So were standards.

The prefect of Seine-Inférieure reported frankly that some conscripts were unfit for service because they had been deprived all their lives: "The doctors are agreed that their weak constitutions go back to the time of their birth, and have no doubt that the political troubles and the privations of 1793 have had a powerful influence on their physical condition."[113] The replacement system was strangled on paper, but the rich still managed to get exemptions on spurious health grounds; some recruitment officers made small fortunes that year. Local authorities proved neither efficient nor trustworthy, their lists of conscripts often at odds with longer ones drawn up by the War Ministry,[114] although military doctors were now much less ready to listen to conscripts' complaints.[115] The clergy increasingly preached against conscription, despite the dire warnings of their bishops. The bishop of Mende exhorted his clergy to refuse communion to the families of deserters, a step even the government would not sanction.[116] By the time the levy was over, Savary reported a marked rise in criminality; desertion and avoidance had grown "at a speed and to a proportion hitherto unknown."[117]

Yet, Napoleon came close to meeting his seemingly fantastical target. The well-practiced partnership of the clammy hand of the bureaucrat and the iron fist of the gendarme once again reached out into the four corners of France. In January, official estimates put the number of "hard core" resisters in France and the annexed departments at fifty thousand and probably more.[118] Most of them were too cowed to fight; rebellions were few, but "the tribute paid was no less real."[119] When the mobile columns sallied forth, Clarke insisted they were led by high-ranking officers, to overawe not only local communities, but the prefects.[120] Napoleon had mused to Caulaincourt about a postwar world: "We shall spend four months of the year traveling about our own frontiers . . . I shall see the cottage firesides of our fair France. I wish to visit the departments which lack proper communications."[121] On his return, these remote firesides of "fair France" received only the brutal attentions of the mobile columns and ruthless bureaucrats.

Even so successful a levy as 1813 was not enough. The Senate let Napoleon break another law, and it proved very valuable. National guardsmen, who were supposed to be for local service only, were "temporarily mobilized" and sent directly to Magdeburg. Added to the ranks were ninety-two thousand men—the "cohorts" of the National Guard. Most were drawn from the veterans' companies of the departments.[122] With them went approximately twenty thousand naval gunners and marines;[123] three battalions of the gunners had served previously at the siege of Cádiz.[124] Eighty thousand men drawn from those who had escaped conscription in earlier years (also named "cohorts")—the "strategic reserve" of the male population—were incorporated and deployed for garrison service in France, thereby releasing tens of thousands of regular troops for active service.[125] There was one very powerful reserve. As in 1811, Napoleon turned to the army in Spain, less for raw numbers than to skim off its best men, because they were now the best troops he had. Every battalion in Spain—infantry, cavalry, artillery—had to send a certain number of its best men north. The numbers were not great, about twenty thousand in all, but Napoleon looked only for the best.[126] They served two purposes: The Imperial Guard was reconstituted by the outstanding soldiers, while others stiffened the ranks of many line regiments. However, whereas for the Russian campaign the Spanish veterans reconstituted the now-extinct Young Guard—and usually had three years' service—they were often the levies of 1810 or 1811, and went into the Old or Middle Guard. Some of them were so out of touch they thought they were "going to dance with the Russians"; one hoped so, assuming it would be his last campaign before retirement. In 1813, the Young Guard actually had "promising" conscripts in its midst. Its core was its reserve battalions, which Napoleon had left in Paris in 1812. By these means, Napoleon had twelve thousand men in the I Division of the Young Guard by February 15, when they left for Mainz, but some were going there to be trained, a stark sign of how the army had changed since Russia.[127] His last expedient was to mobilize the departmental *gardes d'honneur*, young men drawn from the masses of granite, whose very creation had shaken *ralliement* to its core. Pleas and subterfuge to avoid the "honor" of joining the military elite inundated prefects.[128] Boundaries were being pushed. The correspondence and the inventories show the Guard was as spoiled as ever, showered with new, expensive uniforms.[129] Napoleon accorded his "children," even the youngest and least tried, a vanity he never displayed himself when in uniform. He took more than good troops from Spain. He took Soult and Bessières. "The army of Spain is an inexhaustible nursery," he told Clarke.[130] It had proved so in 1811, and the Spanish front survived, but by 1813, Napoleon was bleeding a battered army. "[T]here is no more money to send to this army," he told Clarke in late January.[131] The next few months would show if his empire could still fight on two fronts.

The one hundred thousand men of the departmental cohorts had seen combat and were fit for service. Napoleon was deeply aware of the need to balance numbers with age and experience, if he could. The most exhausted survivors of Russia were sent to garrison duty to form the core of the reserve army.[132] The departmental cohorts were as crucial here as the "Spaniards," particularly to fill the critical absence of sergeants and corporals. Nine thousand of them went to the front in place of the teenagers of the 1814 levies. It was "urgent" to select from them literate men with two years' active service to become sergeants, and those with two years' service—but not necessarily literate—as corporals, twelve hundred in all.[133] This was a considerable drop in standards, compounded by the promotion of hundreds of corporals to sub-lieutenants. As David Gates notes, although immediate needs were met, "there was no cushion for wastage."[134] It was harder to replace the higher ranking officers lost in Russia. "You are sending me young people . . . who have not been to St. Cyr. They know nothing, and it is in the new regiments you are placing them," Napoleon barked at Clarke.[135] Speed was of the essence; urgency marked all his orders: Nine hundred new conscripts reached a line regiment in January 1, "dressed as peasants" and so they would remain until March 1, he was told—"that it is far too late!" came the reply. Three other new light infantry regiments were in the same state—"Is this for lack of cloth or lack of workers?" "Find out the cause of the delays," he told Lacuée.[136] Even Napoleon had to tolerate some delays: The new conscripts in the depots were not to be sent even to garrison duty until properly armed and uniformed, and until trained "that they might have the first idea" of soldiering, but the depots "must never send out conscripts . . . with less than six weeks' training."[137] When they arrived for training in the German depots, Napoleon warned Marshal Francois Etienne Christophe Kellermann, the commander of the Rhine Corps, "These troops must be kept together, otherwise the training will crush them; they are young soldiers."[138] At least the "bottom of the barrel" could still be kept in reserve.

As Pierre Branda points out, the army that went into Saxony that spring was not wholly made up of raw levies who had never seen combat. Most of them—175,000 out of 210,000 infantrymen—were French.[139] The new Imperial Guard reflected this. Napoleon began rebuilding the guard artillery and infantry almost immediately, and made clear to Clarke on January 2, 1813, that the first replacements were to come from the departmental cohorts—veterans—but care was to be taken not to incorporate Belgian, Dutch, or cohorts from the imperial Italian departments.[140] "Frenchness" was now very tightly defined. Yet, by Napoleonic standards, experienced leadership was in short supply.

So were horses. When Poland and Prussia were lost to Napoleon, so were the great stud farms that so transformed the French cavalry. The colossal losses of horses in Russia were of quality, not just quantity, and could never really be repaired. Napoleon's search for new mounts bordered on the pathetic. A national appeal was launched to each department to "donate" mounts for the army. He wrung three hundred out of the Senate and one hundred from the Council of State.[141] Napoleon calculated they would be just enough to see the guard cavalry remounted, along with those donated from the Paris region.[142] ". . . [T]he response is such, that in France, we are assured 60,000 horses from voluntary gifts alone made by the communes, cantons, and individuals," he told Maret.[143] His rough figures for Lacuée were more sobering: After all the projected "donations," together with those he presumed available in the markets, there would be 44,800 horses for 66,000 cavalrymen needing mounts. 21,200 were still needed, at least fifteen thousand of which would have to be "requisitioned."[144] Very few of the horses were "combat ready," trained for the noise and intricate maneuvers of battle. The horse artillery got priority, but draft horses were scarce; the supply trains suffered most, their heavy loads often pulled by horses not fit for purpose.[145] In the end, only fifteen thousand cavalry took the field by April.[146] There was no more time to train horses or riders than for anything else. The need for haste grew with every day.

In a long letter of January 18, reasserting that "the weather had done for him," Napoleon spelled out the growing danger to Jérôme:

> The Emperor of Russia has just named Stein as his minister of State: he admits him into his most intimate councils, him and all those men who aspire to change the face of Germany, (who) have sought for a long time to bring about upheavals and revolutions. If these men succeed, as they try to do, to gain influence in the heart of the Confederation, and spread the spirit that moved them, boundless woes without number will fall at once upon (the Confederation).

He dispatched almost identical missives to the kings of Bavaria, Saxony, and Württemberg, and to the Grand Duke of Hesse-Darmstadt.[147] The message was clear: the specter of "1809" had arisen again, in the person of Stein; the allies meant to undo the Napoleonic settlement of Germany, to "demote" them from their thrones, expel them from their territorial gains, and to resurrect the Holy Roman Empire. Fear was the spur. They rallied, but there were cracks appearing. In his letter to his confidant, old ally, and brother-in-law, Frederick of Württemberg, Napoleon remarked in a tone more hurt than angry that Frederick had prefaced his orders for the exceptional tax levy imposed after the Russian campaign with a disclaimer saying it was not his fault it was needed, and that all the blame attached to France. The real danger, Napoleon warned him, was the popular unrest Stein was stirring up, "but how can we hope to prevent them, if rulers themselves start using such language? . . . The instigators of these troubles . . . are the enemies of all the princes (of the Confederation); their hatred exempts no one. To create what they call Germany is their real end, and they want to bring it about by anarchy and revolution which, after having devastated (the princes) will leave them at the mercy of the strongest." He reminded his old friend that if the sufferings of Württemberg had been "considerable," those of France had been great, words usually reserved for his brothers.[148] On March 25, Alexander and Frederick-William issued a "Proclamation to the German Princes and People" calling on them rise up against Napoleon "through the strength of public opinion and the power of righteous arms."[149] Only one prince of the Confederation—the Duke of Mecklenburg, a relative of Alexander—changed sides. For the moment, Napoleon's warnings rang true. Revolts broke out in his own Grand Duchy of Berg at the announcement of the first conscription levy, the rebels stiffened by Frederick-William's call to arms.[150] Its commandant, General Le Marois, was ordered to send all those captured before courts-martial, shoot the five or six ringleaders, and send five thousand troops into Berg to "return the country to peace."[151] He warned the Grand Duke of Würzburg to prepare his fortress for a two-month siege "in order that no matter what, it will be safe from any surprise." "Cossack patrols can appear from all directions," he added.[152] On February 24, a riot of impoverished women and children in Hamburg spawned a mass rising that drove the French out.[153] On March 18, the Cossacks took the city.

A Fragile Throne: Old Foes and New

Napoleon was not overly troubled by the news of the Malet coup, probably because he never knew its true extent. However, his subordinates' response to it revived his deepest fears, fears he hoped the birth of an heir had laid to rest. Napoleon shuddered that it did not cross the minds of his most loyal collaborators to declare his son emperor or his wife regent, on the news of his "death." The coup exposed how fragile his legitimacy remained. "(T)his underlying theme that silently—but incessantly—followed him all his life, now returned with a bang," in the words of Luigi Mascilli Migliorini.[154] Its awakening coincided with his growing conviction, as expressed to Caulaincourt, that monarchy was the only way to rule the French.[155] His response was to ram this "truth" home, and he began with the Senate. On December 20, 1812, less than forty-eight hours after his return, he told it boldly, "'The king is dead! Long live the king!' These few words contain the greatest advantage of a monarchy." Monarchy was atavistic, not just expedient. If Talleyrand did actually say, "Behold the moment when the Emperor Napoleon decided to become king of France,"[156] he was half right. Napoleon swung into action because he knew he was no such thing, for all he had long cultivated the image of "the father of his people."[157] Nor did he return victorious, and his own prophecy—that he could not afford to lose a battle and keep his throne—now seemed all too real.

Napoleon created two types of regency: one for his imminent absences, and one permanent, should he die before his son was of age. To secure this, typically, in one breath, he delved into archaism, while shoving enshrined tradition aside. He wanted Napoleon-Francis crowned his successor in his lifetime, but had to reach back to Charlemagne for a precedent. The report of the Council of State noted dryly, "No specific regulation whatsoever has been found regarding this ceremony."[158] He also wanted Marie-Louise crowned in his lifetime. Tradition did point to regencies under the wives of dead kings, but even Louis XIV's will was discarded on his death, in favor of the duc d'Orléans, when he sought just this.[159] The omens were not good, particularly as the constitution of 1804 categorically excluded women from a regency for a minor. This had to be discarded if Marie-Louise were to assume the role Napoleon now felt was crucial to the survival of the dynasty. The creation of a provisional regency, to rule in Napoleon's absence, proved less problematic, simply because Napoleon could impose it legally. He stood by his conviction that no barrier could be placed before Marie-Louise becoming regent, any more than to his son's right to succeed him. Cambacérès was aghast at the blatant disregard of Napoleon's original oath to the nation in 1804, opposing his plans "with all the force of inertia."[160] However, he was won over because the prospect of a regency in the long term, which was all too possible, had always proved arduous for France in the past, while Napoleon's return to the front was inevitable.

In both cases, there were very personal problems that demanded discarding tradition. Cambacérès set his mind to them. Tradition dictated that Napoleon's brothers be part of any regency, but as recently as his journey home, Napoleon told Caulaincourt, "My family has never backed me up."[161] Lucien had long been a "nonperson"; Louis still held the post of constable of the empire, but now lived quietly in Rome and had no interest in affairs. Napoleon's resentment of his other brothers resurfaced when a tired, sixty-year-old Cambacérès suggested he stand aside as chair of any regency council, in favor of Eugène. "Impossible," Napoleon exploded, "my brothers would be even more furious." If tradition were to prevail, the dread specter of Joseph as regent loomed. Cambacérès had the answer, which Napoleon warily accepted: the brothers would have the formal possibility of being on the regency council, but they would be excluded as long as they remained rulers of foreign countries.[162]

In the midst of it all, Napoleon still separated family from even the highest affairs of state when he felt he could. On January 16, Napoleon wrote to Louis begging him to return to Paris, "not as a brother you have offended, but a father who raised you." He reminded Louis not of his imperial status, but that his children were growing up, and needed their father:

> Stop writing novels and poetry; think of your children who have need of you; and if the feelings you have for mother are real, they not to be found in the bottom of a glass, but by being close to her; that's how you prove it . . . return to your country, to your family, with your mother and your children; you will be useful to everyone.

Napoleon told his brother that if he did not, he would censor all Louis's writings—they were "making him look ridiculous in any case." His threats went no further. No mention was made of Hortense;[163] Napoleon's forgiveness had its limits. It fell on deaf ears.

The regency council was tight-knit. Effectively, it was composed of Cambacérès and Talleyrand. Its other members, Eugène and Berthier, would be away with the armies; Lebrun remained in Holland; the Prince Borghese—Pauline's estranged husband—stayed in Turin. Murat, Joseph, and Jérôme were "there but not there," thanks to Cambacérès.[164] In practice, little changed when

Napoleon took the field. This familiar "old team" was now underpinned by very different principles, however: Ultimately, the dynasty, headed by a Habsburg, came before the nation. Cambacérès confided to his notes that Napoleon was busily digging his own grave: Where was the patriotic, revolutionary legacy in all this, which he would soon need to rally?[165]

Yet, the benchmark of recalcitrance, conscription, ran well. The prefects reported by April that "the levies are operating everywhere without difficulty."[166] If there had been trouble, prefects normally exaggerated it, if anything. As the American scholar Isser Woloch reflected, although the prefects reported a desperate desire for peace, they were confident of public order. Their reports seem reliable, and helped "Napoleon set his course . . . he was reassured that his rear was secure," at a time when mass rebellion should have erupted.[167] The prefectoral corps emerged greatly strengthened from the strains of 1813. Aging prefects were exposed by the work of conscription. Joseph Frain, one of the first appointed in 1800, was "lifeless," according to a ministerial report, "just a nobody"; another, Pierre Montant-Desilles, was "feeble." They were invariably replaced by the young, aggressive, ambitious auditors of the Council of State. Although the army suffered from young recruits and untried officers, the prefects appointed in the last years of the empire "were the best trained ever to enter the corps under Napoleon." By 1813, 32 of the 130 prefects of the empire were auditors.[168] Napoleon's investment in the new generation, *les enfants du siècle*, now bore fruit.

The chambers seemed in a compliant mood. Just as the Senate had allowed Napoleon to ride roughshod over the conscription laws, it approved the new regency on February 5. The Corps Législatif agreed to a budget of 1,150 million francs for 1813, on top of the 1,120 million it have granted in 1812, but imposed no significant new taxes, creating a huge deficit of 232 million francs. Napoleon said two things about the Senate to Caulaincourt on their travels: that he wanted to transform it into a chamber based solely on merit, and—in the same breath—that it was "composed of nothing but spent torches and dark lanterns."[169] Perhaps with both thoughts in mind, he suggested to Cambacérès that some of the powers of the Corps Législatif should be transferred to it. It is hard to know if Napoleon recalled his own words, but his idea would have handed more authority to weak men in the short term, before better ones took their places. Cambacérès knew better and dissuaded him.[170] Napoleon read the Senate wrongly. In the course of its seeming docility, while voting as Napoleon wanted, the Senate accorded itself a new epithet: "the organ of the sentiments of the Nation."[171] The senators sensed what Napoleon did not: the tectonic plate of the masses of granite was shifting.

Napoleon reeled off nothing short of a "checklist" of the types of Frenchman he loathed to Caulaincourt. The whole revolutionary generation was "reared in disorder, with no conception of morality or religion"; "marquises . . . their only place is on the comic stage" he snorted, "present company excepted" however. A touch of Figaro still lurked behind the dynast. His marshals were all "money grubbers." Savary, with his young, spendthrift wife was the worst, but Ney and Oudinot were not far behind: "They never finished a campaign without coming to me for cash." And the real enemy, the ingrates:

> Who makes an outcry in France? A few salons; a few people who have forgotten their debt to me for the position or fortune they now enjoy; others who I have brought back from exile and restored to their property, which they would never have recovered but for me; a few obscure lordlings who are discontented at no longer being sprinkled with holy water on Sundays; a number of self-centered shopkeepers who are under a cloud at the moment because they can find no scope for speculation; some army contractors, veritable blood suckers whose ill-gotten gains I have made them disgorge. These are the people who cry against me.

It was a list of the old enemies, the "usual suspects," and Napoleon treated them with contempt, never a sensible attitude to opponents, particularly when at so low and ebb as now. Conscription may be hated, but at least it was equal and fair.[172] His thoughts went no further. He saw the mobilization of the *gardes d'honneur* in this context, not in that of the erosion of *ralliement*.

Nor did he blanch from conscripting law students in their final year at the Imperial University, a hitherto protected species, the pride of the masses of granite.[173] At times, the residues of Jacobinism blinded him more than his burgeoning faith in monarchy. He did not seem to notice that *la France profonde* had not offered him his horses. Horses were for the wealthy, and their procurement caused more consternation than that of manpower.[174] The great cities had no choice—Paris with 500, Lyon with 120, Strasbourg with 100. Even Amsterdam and Bordeaux, decimated by the blockade, gave 100 and 80, respectively. But from his "heartland," very little. The real proof of loyalty came from Cambacérès, who gave 200,000 francs of his own fortune to the Treasury and did so anonymously to avert a financial panic by drawing attention to the shambles of the war debt.[175] There had long been resentment. Now, there was a loss of confidence when Napoleon needed it most. The political opposition to Napoleon—the clergy, the Chevaliers de la Foi, the *chouans*, the diehard Jacobins, communities angered by conscription and brigands born of it—had always been too scattered and weak to pose a real threat. He had grown used to them, and could handle them. So it remained, but quiet defiance, voiced subtly by the Senate, and palpable fear for the future were the new enemies, and he did not sense their strength. On reading the last words of the 29th Bulletin of the Grande Armée that "His Majesty's health has never been better," François-René Chateaubriand quipped "Families, dry your tears. Napoleon has never been better."[176]

Napoleon had deep misgivings about the return of Talleyrand to the corridors of power, suspecting he would try to insinuate himself with the Empress.[177] Napoleon is said to have called Talleyrand "shit in a silk stocking" on their journey. Even if true, this memorable drop of venom bore no comparison to Napoleon's reflections on Talleyrand during the journey. "I was wrong to be angry with Talleyrand (after Tilsit)," he starkly admitted, "he would have handled Poland better," perhaps avoiding antagonizing Alexander.[178] He all but parroted his ex–foreign minister at one point: "The Russians should be viewed by everyone as a scourge. The war against Russia is a war . . . of old Europe, and of civilization . . . Metternich knows this full well."[179] His rehabilitation comes as no surprise in light of such remarks. Talleyrand was always a telling straw in the wind with Napoleon. Napoleon's grasp, or lack of it, of his circumstances was reflected in his handling of him, now as ever. By rehabilitating Talleyrand, Napoleon acknowledged the value of the Austrian alliance at the very moment it was slipping away from him. Talleyrand, along with Cambacérès and Caulaincourt, had urged Napoleon to engage with Metternich's initial offer of mediation in January, which he ignored, believing he could still bind Austria to him. Yet, Talleyrand continued talking to Schwarzenberg, now the Austrian ambassador in Paris, stressing that Austria could make Napoleon see sense, but only from a position of strength it did not yet have. He told Schwarzenberg, "Napoleon has to become king of France . . . he lost the empire when he lost the army."[180] Metternich, as always, knew better. On March 3, Emperor Francis appointed Metternich as Chancellor of the Order of Maria Theresa, the highest dignity the monarch could bestow, and a major sign of trust in a servant. In other words, Francis openly avowed his willingness to edge away from the French alliance. Metternich moved fast, "because every moment (is now) irreplaceable." On March 14, he proposed Austria become the broker of an "armed mediation" between Napoleon and the allies, a move to "redefine the politics of foreign relations" as he told the council. It was subtle but clear: Austria was still neutral, no longer Napoleon's ally. At the same time, Austrian troops were deployed not only along the Galician border, near the potential war zone, but along the borders of southern Germany and northern Italy, in preparation for war with France.[181] Metternich now had little need of his old informant in Paris, "Monsieur X." The real momentum lay with the Russo-Prussian alliance, possessed of a powerful army and the will to fight.

Just as Napoleon went to his grave never knowing of "Monsieur X," he had no idea that Talleyrand, the great survivor, was gingerly seeking out a new "pen friend," Louis XVIII. As always, Napoleon's misgivings about Talleyrand were far worse than he suspected. From his well-upholstered exile in England, Louis showed how acutely he sensed the unease of the masses of granite, issuing a proclamation promising "unity, respite, peace, happiness" and more to the point, the retention of the Napoleonic administrative and judicial edifice, and the abolition of conscription. In a telling phrase, he lauded the Napoleonic Senate, where sit "men so justly distinguished by their talents," wording that was "very adroit . . . to reassure the imperial elites" in the judgment of Emmanuel de Waresquiel.[182] "Louis now appeared as the chief guarantor of the status quo the emperor was wrecking by his mania for conquest," in the words of his biographer, Philip Mansel.[183] Talleyrand's behavior mirrored Metternich's. He was far from ready to change sides, and Molé was not foolish when he reassured Napoleon in March that he was "the natural enemy of the Bourbons" as much as of the republic—Talleyrand did stress to Schwarzenberg that he wanted to keep Napoleon in power—but historians are skeptical of his claim to Napoleon that he knew nothing of Louis's proclamation, which circulated widely in Paris. Indeed, Emmanuel de Waresquiel thinks he recognized "his hand behind the praise directed at the Senate." As early as January, Napoleon had his suspicions, and said so, but he did nothing. Not only Cambacérès, who shared Talleyrand's views, but Savary spoke in Talleyrand's favor. Talleyrand could easily have made contact with the court-in-exile, and may well have, but no correspondence has been found.[184]

Everywhere, at home and abroad, Napoleon's enemies were growing in confidence and strength, but his intelligence told him that one old foe was weakening, vulnerable and ripe for the taking. The journey from Savona to Paris had nearly killed Pius—he narrowly escaped a hazardous operation for bleeding on the bladder though the intervention of a local medical official at a hospice on the Montcenis pass—and arrived at Fontainebleau on June 19, exhausted, if cured.[185] Informed of all this, Napoleon wrote to Marie-Louise from Vilnius in early July asking her to "write (Pius) a little letter" asking for his news and how he was keeping.[186] She was his "cavalry screen." Napoleon had pressing, unfinished business with Pius left over from the National Council of the previous year, above all filling the twenty-six vacant sees. He now opened his artillery bombardment. No sooner installed in the imposing apartments created for him in 1804 for the imperial coronation, Pius was assailed by Bigot de Préameneu, the minister of religion, presenting Napoleon's complaints. He was followed over the coming months by repeated visits from Napoleon's loyalist bishops, Jean-Baptiste Duvoisin, the bishop of Nantes to the fore. Napoleon saw to it that the "red" Cardinals were also installed in Paris, a gesture that at one and the same time, mimicked and mocked the College of Cardinals. With their "black" colleagues either in prison or in internal exile, they were Pius's sole clerical company. [187] Believing the ground had been softened up for him, Napoleon turned his own attention to Pius VII as soon as he got home. On December 29, he wrote to the pope in lulling tones eerily like those in which he wrote to Josephine just before he demanded a divorce. Napoleon declared himself very happy to hear from Duvoisin "of the good state of His health, for I had a very alarming moment this summer, when I learned He was seriously indisposed." This would mean they could soon return to business, "and I can wholeheartedly say . . . that, despite everything that has happened, I have always retained the same friendship for Him personally. Perhaps we can now reach the conclusion, so hoped for, of ending all the differences between State and Church." [188] Now, Napoleon unleashed his clerical heavy cavalry: Duvoisin paid Pius a visit in early January, accompanied by cardinals Barral, Ruffo, Dugnani, and Bayanne. For Ambrogio Caiani, Duvoisin was "the perfect emissary from Napoleon"; although an émigré during the revolution, he rallied quickly to the regime, and was an ardent Gallican. Pius and Duvoisin had faced each other many times in Savona. [189] He presented the pope with fresh articles that toughened the terms put to the National Council. There were four points that struck Pius like a dagger: There was no change in how the vacancies would be filled; if the pope did not agree to Napoleon's choices within six months, they would be filled by candidates chosen by the metropolitan bishop or the senior bishop of the area; henceforth, the College of Cardinals would be restored, but Pius could select only one third of future cardinals, the rest would be named by "the Catholic princes of Europe," in other words, by Napoleon; Pius and the College would remain in Paris for there would be no return to Rome. In buffered language, it was made clear that Pius could retain those of his territories "which had not already been alienated." [190] Napoleon knew Pius would not agree immediately.

Rather, he hoped to unnerve him, and Duvoisin reported to Bigot on January 13 that this had seemed to work:

> The Pope is extremely agitated, he can't sleep, his health has changed. At present, I don't think he is in a fit state to enter into any discussions. He has very little trust in any of the people around him. He persists in saying that . . . his honor and his conscience will not allow him to pronounce (on the terms) alone, a prisoner, without council.[191]

Napoleon saw his best chance. On January 19, he sent in the Imperial Guard—himself.

Diverting from a hunting expedition in the forest of Fontainebleau, Napoleon rode to the palace and burst in on Pius and the red cardinals. He greeted the pope obsequiously, but then began five days of entirely private "discussions." There were no witnesses, but eavesdroppers recounted much shouting behind closed doors, usually by Napoleon. Chateaubriand concocted a libel that Napoleon had actually whacked Pius at one point, something the pope categorically refuted in September 1814, although he did remember vividly that "one day in the heat of the moment when discussing the subject of the renunciation of the Papal States he grabbed me by one of the buttons of my cassock and shook me so strongly, by pulling it, that my entire body stirred. It is probably to this incident that most are referring."[192] Napoleon's temper did not extend to striking an ill old man, but his relentless, militaristic approach to Pius was marked by cruelty. Violence was too much; psychological cruelty was not.

For one, fleeting moment, Napoleon's pitiless pressure seemed to work. Throughout his seven months at Fontainebleau, ill as he was, Pius studiously ignored the material temptations Napoleon laid before him. All financial offers were refused—he was often seen darning his own clothes—nor was his attitude softened by the red cardinals or the frequent presence of Marie-Louise and her female retinue, with their overt displays of piety toward him.

Pius knew an iron fist in a velvet glove when he saw one. Yet, soon after their prolonged harangue, Pius gave in to Napoleon and signed the accords. Ambrogio Caiani, in his thorough account of these days, observes of Pius "(For) an exhausted and isolated seventy-one-year-old . . . his reserves of determination and his resolve had been remarkable. For over three years he did not surrender the church's prerogatives and demonstrated an iron will."[193] Now, at last, on January 25, Pius signed the accords, now called the Concordat of Fontainebleau. Pius was assured this would all be kept secret; Napoleon also agreed to release the thirteen black cardinals—even the hated Bartolomeo Pacca and the insufferable Ercole Consalvi—and allow them to join the pope and their red colleagues at Fontainebleau. Napoleon made the mistake of keeping the second part of the bargain, but not the first. Marie-Louise wrote in glowing terms to her father that the great dispute had been solved, stressing to him how happy Pius was with the result,[194] in the hope that this news might salvage Austria's alliance with France and stop its slide to the allies. Sextius de Miollis, the governor-general of Rome, was ordered not to publish it, "but he can refer to it in conversation," and was to let it be thought that Pius would reside in Avignon, former papal territory absorbed by France in 1790, rather than at Fontainebleau.[195] Inevitably, however, the news got out, and was greeted with great relief by the public.[196] Napoleon also wrote immediately to Pius, to reassure him that the articles did not include his "implicit" renunciation of his claim to the Papal States, because the document related only to clerical matters, a gauche sidestep, but a sidestep, nonetheless.[197] It was to no avail. Pius had doubts as soon as his signature was dry. When Pacca reached Fontainebleau, on release from the grim prison of Fenestrelle in the Piedmontese Alps, he found Pius in the throes of a nervous breakdown, often gazing blankly at the wall.[198] Then, Napoleon overplayed his hand. On February 13, in the same session in which the Senate allowed him to flout the laws on conscription and hand the regency to a Habsburg, it approved the text of the new Concordat. Napoleon published it the next day.

Suddenly, Napoleon found himself outflanked and at war on two fronts with the Church. At the center, in Fontainebleau, the black cardinals rapidly reassembled to give Pius the comradeship and support he had sorely lacked for so long. Consalvi was on hand to play Cambacérès to Pius's Napoleon, and advised the pope that what had been signed were only articles forming the basis for further talks, and so he could retract them. The publication of the concordat and the registration of the accords by the Senate made the agreement null and void. Consalvi's counsel was hardly surprising, but all the cardinals—red as well as black—fell in behind him.[199] This unanimity embraced Fesch, Cardinal Archbishop of Lyon, Primate of Gaul—and Napoleon's uncle. A letter of support from Fesch to Pius had been intercepted a few months earlier, for which Napoleon had threatened him with Fenestrelle and the deprivation of the considerable revenues he held from the archdiocese of Regensburg, which he administered. Fesch kept a low profile and returned to Lyon before the vote was taken, but he did not oppose Consalvi at any stage while there.[200] Napoleon's brothers were not the only "ingrates" in his family. Thus bolstered, Pius retracted his signature on the grounds Consalvi proposed, on March 24.

In the meantime, Napoleon pushed ahead at full speed with his main aim, to fill the vacant dioceses as soon as he had Pius's signature. On March 9, he wrote to Bigot, "There will be a council meeting tomorrow. I beg you, please bring along the work for the nominations for all the bishoprics vacant in France."[201] Even as the regime set to work, rebellion arose in the dioceses. The cardinals were emphatic that Napoleon's candidates would not get papal investiture, and that they could not take oaths of loyalty to the regime required of them. As early as March 13, Napoleon was driven to distraction, exploding to Bigot:

> All the pretentions of the cardinals are ridiculous . . . if ever the Pope does become a temporal ruler, we will break with him . . . Since the Pope only takes counsel from Di Pietro and Litta, you will make it known to him that there will be dire consequences . . . The French bishops have to stand firm; soon they will organize the taking of oaths, give canonic institution (to the new bishops) and we will name bishops.[202]

What followed sheds a piercing light on Napoleon's actual grip on his realm. All of his nominees were "political," men chosen for proven loyalty to the regime, and all went to their sees without papal investiture. However, once there, none dared ask their Metropolitan to invest them. Most tried to come to some working arrangement with their clergy, with varying degrees of success. Cussy, in Troyes, and Baston, in Séez, were able to negotiate the powers of Vicar-Capitular with their chapters, although these truces were short-lived when Pius clandestinely started appointing his own men. The two great Belgian dioceses of Tournai and Ghent—long centers of defiance—simply refused to acknowledge Napoleon's appointees, and were run by canons who withdrew from their chapters. Napoleon finished by arresting several canons.[203] Jacques-Olivier Boudon, the leading modern historian of the Church under Napoleon has rightly noted, "For the first time, Napoleon was thwarted in the interior (of the empire) by the refusal to apply the measures he had decided."[204] There is a difference between obedience and loyalty, a distinction that Napoleon needed to gauge more than ever, but he could not. Such is the price of too effective a dictatorship.

There was nothing Napoleon could do in the face of this, nor could his new bishops, who were now left dangerously exposed to popular opprobrium in the months to come. But at Fontainebleau, he lashed out. The velvet glove was now ripped off, in one case quite literally. Antoine Lagorce was a distinguished elite gendarme, who had been Pius's personal guard since Savona and at Fontainebleau. In the flush of goodwill that followed the signing of the accords, he was ordered to put on a fashionable court livery, in place of his uniform. Now, the uniform reappeared. The host of servants dispatched to attend Pius also withdrew, not that he had ever called upon them. Pius's celebration of daily Mass had become a focal point for the faithful; ordinary people from the immediate area and beyond flocked to it (while Lagorce took the chance to search the papal quarters). Now, Napoleon closed it to everyone except Pius' attendants.[205] This was less a case of history repeating itself than the latest skirmish in a long war between the French state and the Church, begun in 1789. Transferred forcibly from Versailles to the Tuileries in

October 1789, Louis XVI had used his attendance at daily Mass as an overt affront to the revolutionary assembly, allowing the public to attend. He pulled in crowds so considerable as to unnerve the government.[206] Napoleon soon sent the black cardinals packing back to their places of exile or imprisonment. Plans to release the priests from the Roman departments, jailed in Piacenza, Bologna, Pinerolo, and Corsica were aborted.[207] Needless to say, the bulls of investiture promised by Pius for Napoleon's appointees did not materialize.[208]

Napoleon had been fought to an uneasy draw with Pius, his interior lines insecure, his major objectives achieved only technically. The two western departments of Mayenne and Sarthe were long noted as havens of royalism, traditional Catholic piety, and of *chouans*. In his moment of seeming triumph, Napoleon ordered their bishops to make their parish priests help the mobile columns in their dioceses against "the brigands who take refuge in the woods and commit outrages" by supplying information to the authorities.[209] If Napoleon's hubris drove this order, it did not last long.

Napoleon's frenetic energy after his return from Russia was driven by fear and desperation. Everything could be snatched from him. It hardly mattered now if "the weather did for me, the chances of war." The tables were turned. On his way home from Russia, he told Caulaincourt, "I shape my policy as a torrent shapes its course."[210] The torrent was now heading for him.

Alexander I, Tsar of all the Russias, was Napoleon's nemesis. Urbane and charming, at times vacillating and indecisive, he possessed an iron will. Known as "the Sphinx of the North," Alexander had a religious conversion during the 1812 invasion and drove the coalition to final victory. *From the Bridgeman Art Gallery.*

TOP LEFT: After serving as Secretary for War, Robert Stewart, Viscount Castlereagh, became Foreign Secretary in 1812, and played a key role in building the Fifth Coalition. He died by suicide, exhausted, in 1822. TOP RIGHT: Klemens von Metternich became Austrian Chancellor after Wagram. He cautiously but determinedly steered Austria into the Fifth Coalition in 1813, and brought the princes of the Confederation of the Rhine into the allied camp. *Images from the Bridgeman Art Gallery.*

CENTER RIGHT: Joseph Fouché was of questionable loyalty to Napoleon. Immensely powerful, but ousted as minister of police in 1811, he served Louis XVIII in 1814 but joined Napoleon in the 100 Days, only to betray him, and served Louis again, briefly, after 1815. BOTTOM LEFT: Imprisoned first at Savona in 1810, and then at Fontainebleau, Pope Pius VII was subjected to intense harassment by Napoleon over 1811–13. Pius, in worsening health, defied Napoleon, and was allowed back to Rome in January, 1814. *Images from the Bridgeman Art Gallery.*

ABOVE LEFT: Arthur Wellesley, Duke of Wellington, came from an Anglo-Irish family. By 1811, he was commander of all the allied forces in Spain, and inflicted a series of defeats on the French across northern Spain, culminating at Vittoria on June 21, 1813. He defeated Napoleon at Waterloo on June 18, 1815, and went on to play a crucial role in governing France during the allied occupation. ABOVE RIGHT: Gebhard, Prince Blücher von Wahlstatt, was Napoleon's most ferocious opponent. Known as "Marshal Forward!" for his relentless approach to combat, Blücher was over seventy in the last years of the wars, but fought tenaciously in 1813, 1814, and in the Waterloo campaign. Abrasive and courageous, he became a "cult" figure among the allies. BELOW LEFT: Field Marshal Mikhail Kutusov had a reputation as a brave, if reckless, commander who was sixty-five when he took command of the main Russian army in 1812. Disliked by Alexander, he proved cautious in 1812, but masterminded the pursuit of Napoleon. He died in 1813, on campaign, and became an icon of Russian resistance. BELOW RIGHT: Field Marshal Karl von Schwarzenberg was known for his caution as a commander and infuriated the allied leaders and his own generals in the campaigns of 1813–14, but his approach was in keeping with Metternich's foreign policy, and he was concerned about keeping the fragile Austrian army in tact at the end of the war. *All images from the Bridgeman Art Gallery.*

LEFT: Marie-Louise gave birth to Napoleon-Francis, "the king of Rome," after a horrendous delivery, on March 20, 1811. She proved, unexpectedly, a tenacious, loyal defender of the dynasty in the crisis of 1814, but had to surrender to her father. Separated from her son, she became an effective, much loved ruler of Parma-Piacenza after 1815. Napoleon-Francis lived out his life a captive of the Austrians. He became a rallying point for Bonapartists as "Napoleon II" and died in 1830, under suspicious circumstances. *From the Bridgeman Art Gallery.*

BOTTOM LEFT: Marshal Michel Ney, "the bravest of the brave," was a reckless field commander, known for his short temper and valor in equal measure. Made "Prince of Moscow" for his heroic command of the last stages of the retreat from Russia, Ney was much loved in the army. He deserted Napoleon in 1814, but rallied and led the army at Waterloo. Unwilling to compromise, he was executed by the Bourbons on December 7, 1815. BOTTOM RIGHT: Auguste Marmont, Marshal of France, Duke of Ragusa, where he was governor-general, 1810–11, was a favorite of Napoleon, highly regarded for his service in Spain, where he was wounded in 1812. He served with distinction in the Saxon campaign of 1813, and in 1814. Napoleon often entrusted him with the Imperial Guard and the protection of his family. His defection in 1814, and loyalty to Louis XVIII in 1815, earned him Napoleon's enmity and his name became a by-word for treachery. *Images from the Bridgeman Art Gallery.*

ABOVE: Napoleon received the portrait of his son, "the king of Rome," by Gérard, just before the battle of Borodino against the Russians, on September 7, 1812. He displayed it to his Old Guard the night before the battle, almost mirroring the devotion of the Russian troops to the Madonna of Smolensk, at the same time. Napoleon hung it in the Kremlin, and took it with him everywhere thereafter. BELOW: The crossing of the River Berezina, in the last days of November 1812, was one of the most heroic and grizzly episodes of the Napoleonic Wars. His depleted army almost trapped by the Russians, Napoleon threw a makeshift bridge across the river. The work was done by Dutch marines in freezing conditions. The bridge eventually collapsed, leaving many trapped or drowning as the Cossacks closed in and the French fought a fierce rearguard action. *Images from the Bridgeman Art Gallery.*

ABOVE: The battle of Leipzig, October 16–19, 1813, was a major turning point. The Austrian, Prussian, and Russian armies, fighting together for the first time, defeated Napoleon in a three day battle, which saw them force their way into the city. Napoleon fled in haste westward, leaving almost a whole corps trapped as he did so. BELOW: The three allied sovereigns, Tsar Alexander, Emperor Francis II of Austria, and King Frederick-William III of Prussia, were all present by the end of the battle, and entered Leipzig in triumph together, to signal of the power and unity of the new coalition. *Images from the Bridgeman Art Gallery.*

ABOVE: Waterloo culminated in desperate assaults by French heavy cavalry on the British infantry atop Mont St Jean. The British were assembled in squares, their bayonets fixed to ward off the French horses, as Ney's cavalry circled them, trying to break their ranks. Ney's failure to do so helped decide the battle. BELOW: The Old Guard were Napoleon's best troops, and his last reserve. He only used them as a last resort, and when their advance was checked by the British, the rest of the army panicked. The Imperial Guard regrouped and shielded Napoleon as the retreat began. *Images from the Bridgeman Art Gallery.*

ABOVE: So swift was Wellington's counter attack, and so anarchic the French retreat, that Napoleon had to abandon his famous coach and all its contents, and flee for safety on horseback. The coach and its treasures were captured by Prussian advance units. BELOW: Napoleon arrived in Paris exhausted and disoriented. Within a day, he had been hounded into abdicating for a second time. This painting captures his dejection, and hints at the ill health that dogged him in his final years. *Images from the Bridgeman Art Gallery.*

9

THE STRUGGLE
FOR GERMANY,
APRIL 1813–AUGUST 1813

❧ ———————————————————————— ❧

A New Diplomacy

Napoleon was riding on shifting sands when he left Saint-Cloud for Germany in the early hours of April 15. With allied armies on their doorsteps, the loyalty of all Germans, princes and peasants alike, was in the balance. The military campaign soon ran parallel to nothing short of a "bidding war" for the support of princes Napoleon had always counted on as unshakable allies. Only clear victory in the field could guarantee this now. Metternich was teaching the Allies new lessons in diplomacy, however, capable of trumping even a second Austerlitz.

Frederick-William and Alexander had openly exhorted the "German people" to rise in revolt in support of the allies in March. Peasant revolts became more menacing with a powerful Russian army within reach, but this was the "old politics" that had backfired disastrously in 1809, when the German princes drew closer to Napoleon. The real menace to Napoleon emerged quietly, in February, when Nesselrode, Hardenberg, and Metternich reached an understanding that opened the way to a new approach to the Germany Napoleon had shaped. The fruitful, if cautious, exchanges between Metternich and Hardenberg led Nesselrode to argue in a memorandum to the tsar that the princes had to be courted, not intimidated by Stein's appeals to chaos; only the promise of stability could draw them away from Napoleon. There would be no more talk, as in 1809, of restoring the mediatized rulers or divesting the princes of the Confederation of what Napoleon had given them. It said nothing about deposing Napoleon, but Jérôme's fate was sealed. This was how to eject Napoleon from Germany, and concentrate minds on that.[1] When he reopened the prospect of Austrian mediation with Napoleon, Metternich obliged the allies to be open about their military and diplomatic aims,[2] and Nesselrode had paved the way for him. Hardenberg and Metternich revitalized their relations in April, on the basis of their shared belief that these tactics were in the interests of both their countries, but it went beyond an Austro-Prussian entente. Wolfram Siemann's insight is of fundamental importance here for the months ahead. The old diplomatic order had shown scant interest in the independence and well-being of the lesser states, seeking only equilibrium among those of the first rank.[3] Metternich's emphasis on the role of the princes of the Confederation in unhorsing Napoleon was a major step in a new direction. The first concrete sign of this "new politics" came when the allies took Dresden in the last days of March. The king of Saxony, Frederick-Augustus, one of Napoleon's loyalist allies, fled his capital not for Eugène's lines on the Elbe, but for Prague, in Austrian territory, where he signed a convention with Austria adhering to Metternich's policy of armed neutrality.[4] It was now clear to Napoleon that Metternich's strategy was to destabilize the Confederation, not by "a German Spain," but through its rulers.

Napoleon countered this by halting at Mainz and summoning the princes to him. The atmosphere was very different from the triumphalism in Dresden a year before. The host of that exercise in hubris, Frederick-Augustus, was now the target of unveiled threats. After repeated requests that he supply his contingent for the imminent campaign, Napoleon ordered his ambassador on April 20, to tell the king that "I would consider a refusal (to do so) as the beginning of a change to the system"[5] and broke off diplomatic relations.[6] Napoleon did not yet know that Metternich had insisted on exactly this—that Saxony leave the Confederation—as part of their pact. He was also anxious that Frederick-Augustus's defection was not known to the other princes: "The speculations about the loyalty of the king of Saxony are absurd: (they are by those) who know neither the feelings nor the probity of that prince," he told his ambassador to the Grand Duke of Würzburg.[7] By April 24, however, he had to admit to Frederick of Württemberg that "it seems there are many intrigues around this respectable prince . . . Perhaps it would not be untoward if Your Majesty and the king of Bavaria made a few approaches to the Court of Saxony to engage him to continue within the system of the Confederation."[8]

Napoleon's tone to the other princes was very different. The requests were the same, however, for men and, above all, horses, and to move as quickly as possible to the front, all of which made his parade of the guard before them[9] ring a little hollow. Napoleon was caught between the hard realities of resources so thinly stretched they could not be hidden, and the need to reassure. The muddled tone emerged in a letter to Frederick of Württemberg:

> I attach great worth to having (your) 2 and 4th cavalry regiments. The Prussians have raised a lot of "bourgeois cavalry" *(landwher)* who do not ride well, but are a worry nonetheless . . . (A)s soon as general Bertrand gets to Coburg . . . there will be not the slightest shadow of fear for the states of Your Majesty . . . The reason why I have so accelerated my movements is my desire to protect Your Majesty's states and Bavaria.[10]

In the same letter, he boasted that "there is a great quantity of cavalry on its way from every part of France," but he could not quite hide his anxiety two days later when he told his ally, "please send me all the cavalry at His disposal: it is the only aid I can hope from Him, and it is the best thing He can do, to save his state."[11]

As always, Napoleon's wrath fell on Jérôme, but so did his deepest fears. When Prussia changed sides in March, Westphalia became the empire's front line. On March 2, even before the Russo-Prussian alliance was formalized, Napoleon agreed to Jérôme's request that Queen Catherine be sent to the safety of France. She left the next week for the palace of Compiègne, Napoleon fearing that if she were seen to arrive in Paris, it would be "wrongly interpreted" or, more likely, correctly so. The fall of Hamburg and the presence of the Cossacks to his north, who plundered the countryside at will, forced Jérôme to defend his own territory, and he received little aid from his brother to supply the French troops flooding in to his kingdom. By late April, Jérôme's unpaid, unwilling conscripts disappeared en masse, and he feared for the safety of his capital at Kassel. The University of Halle was closed in the face of student unrest fomented successfully by Stein's pan-German nationalism.[12] The "model kingdom" degenerated into a helpless, impotent police state. Napoleon saw this before him from Mainz, and he was quick to blame his brother. He regarded reports of rebellions as merely "partisans"; Jérôme's Westphalian commander, Hammerstein "sees just ghosts and lets his spies dominate him."[13] The same day, Napoleon told his ambassador Kassel to tell Jérôme that his decision to have a personal guard of native troops "was madness":

> If, right now, he had of 600 French horse, 3,000 French infantry and one or two companies of French artillery, he would be the master of his kingdom, and safe from it all . . . The king's rule is contested by all the old sovereigns and has never even been recognized by one, England; how, in such circumstances, could he not have adopted what I advised and formed a sure guard which would not betray him? . . . Had he done so six years ago, the Westphalian guard would be superb today, instead of being made up of conscripts. The king of Westphalia will always be unsteady

on his throne. The kings of France always had Swiss guards . . .
The great defect of a king is not to know enough history . . . And
here's the result: he has an army of 15 to 20,000 men, but is on the
verge of being chased out of his capital by a couple of squadrons
of poor troops . . . fallacious ideas were put in the king's head that
he could win his independence . . . As if independence was more
a right than a fact![14]

In the ever-changing circumstances of that spring, some things remained
unaltered. Napoleon berated Jérôme as ever, but when he recalled in the same
letter that Joseph and Murat, and himself in Italy, at first, all had French
guards, Napoleon inadvertently drew attention to how fragile his edifice had
always been.

The next day, Napoleon arrived at Erfurt, his headquarters. He did so still in
two minds, militarily. His initial plan had been to strike north, using Eugène's
line on the Elbe as a springboard to retake Berlin and drive into Poland, to
outflank Alexander. The British scholar, Munro Price, posits that Napoleon
hoped retaking Berlin would shatter Prussian resolve to fight on.[15] It was the
same mistaken assumption Wellington had made in Spain, but the allies had
to save him from himself. Solidly dug in around Dresden, and nurturing their
strength, they left Napoleon little choice but to set aside the march on Berlin
and seek them out where they were. Napoleon did not abandon his initial
plan, returning to it twice later, but he saw quickly his first priority was to
engage the new allies in a major battle, as was his wont, impress his allies
with a crushing victory, retake Dresden, and entice Frederick-Augustus back
to his capital, and into the fold.

On April 24, Alexander entered Dresden at the head of his guards to
celebrate the Russian Easter. The religious services provided "a moment of
exaltation" for the massed regiments, roused by the liturgy's culmination in
the cry "Christ is risen," as one officer in the guard cavalry recalled.[16] "The
time for picnics and prayers was drawing to a close."[17] Napoleon was soon
upon them with the speed of old.

The Saxon Campaign, April–May 1813
Lützen

Napoleon made straight for Dresden from his base in Erfurt on April 30, his main force consisting of about 140,000 men: Ney's III Corps; Marmont's VI Corps; Bertrand's IV Corps; Oudinot's XII Corps; and the Guard, together with about forty thousand men from Eugène's forces. Citizens of Hamburg did the allies a great favor when they took back their city from the French in mid-March. They forced Napoleon to divert his best commander, Davout, to deal with them. Davout took command of the northern sector of the Elbe, from Magdeburg to the sea and, as John Gallaher has put it, he would "have to fight his way into his new command."[18] His subordinate, the ruthless Vandamme, did so by April 29. The rebels hoped they would be supported by the Swedes. Bernadotte had brought thirty thousand men into the former Swedish territory of Stralsund in northern Germany, supported by a generous British subsidy. He had also brought himself, however. More concerned with preserving his army until the peace, when he intended to use it to conquer Norway, which the British had promised him to punish the Danes,[19] Bernadotte behaved as a neutral, despite his agreement with Russia and Britain to take the field against Napoleon. He left the people of the city to their own devices, thus depriving Davout of his chance for revenge for Auerstadt.

The allies were taken aback by the speed of Napoleon's advance; no one had expected him to move until early June. This did not deter them, however. So politically charged had the campaign become for both sides that the allies were unanimous: they had to confront Napoleon, even though this risked allowing him to retake Dresden and cut them off from their line of retreat over the Elbe. To shy away from battle at the first French advance could unsettle Metternich's cautious but clear intentions to support them, and convince the German princes that they had best stay loyal to Napoleon. They were outnumbered. Together, the Prussians and Russians could summon about eighty-eight thousand regulars and five thousand Cossacks. Kutusov, old and ill, died at Bunzlau, on April 28. It did nothing to alter allied plans. He was succeeded by Wittgenstein, who had won stunning victories over the previous year, and spoke German, which eased communications with the Prussians. He was junior to the other commanders, which stored up problems, but he was "brave and bold," an inspirational field commander, and ready to fight, the most necessary quality at this point.

Napoleon wanted battle for the same reasons. He pressed ahead to Leipzig, but his lack of light cavalry gave him poor intelligence about where the enemy was. Wittgenstein was no better informed. He knew what Napoleon was up to, but had no precise information on his deployments, and assumed the French were strung out thinly along the main road to Leipzig, and this erroneous assumption formed the basis of his strategy: His main attack would come from the south, and hit the middle of the French march, cutting Napoleon's forces in two while he was crossing the River Saale, and vulnerable.[20] Napoleon had no idea of this; Wittgenstein had no idea that Napoleon had sent Ney's whole corps to occupy and dig in, around four villages to the south of the road, near Lützen: Grosse Görschen, Klein Görschen, Rana, and Kaja. This was directly in Wittgenstein's path, but he assumed Ney's men were only a small rearguard. The ensuing battle of Lützen was a battle of escalation, so impromptu that Napoleon could only muster seventy-eight thousand men in all for action, and Wittgenstein but seventy thousand, roughly equally divided between Russian and Prussian troops. It was what they all wanted, however, and on May 2, they got it.

Napoleon ordered Ney to occupy the villages, which he did, and to scout to the southeast, which he did not. Wittgenstein was conscious that the Russians were short of manpower, if not of combat experience, and placed Blücher's corps at the forefront of the assault, supported by Yorck and Berg's Russians; the main Russian contingent was in the rear. Blundering by the allied general staff led to a confused night march, and a dawn attack proved impossible. Blücher was not able to strike until nearly midday, but when he realized how strong Ney was, he halted and bombarded the villages, giving Ney time to form up around Starsiedl. When Napoleon heard the guns, he turned off the main road and headed for them, sending Marmont to support Ney's right, and Bertrand to bolster his left. The guard was rushed to Lützen as the reserve.

Blücher halted the bombardment after forty minutes and attacked the villages at 1:00 P.M. They now became the center of ferocious fighting, changing hands again and again, escalating into a bloodbath. The allied troops got a shock in the villages. They were unaccustomed to stone walls and buildings, which could be used as little fortresses, whereas the wooden villages they knew were useless. Ney's men were relative novices on the battlefield, but understood this kind of terrain, used it, and fought valiantly, doubtless drawing confidence from the protection the stone walls offered.[21] Napoleon was deeply impressed, telling Cambacérès, "Above all, nothing equals the valor, the goodwill and the love all these young soldiers have shown me; they are full of enthusiasm."[22] In less than an hour, Blücher had committed his last reserves, which pushed Ney's line close to collapse. Marmont had been attacked by Berg's Russians and was barely holding Starsiedl; the last reserve of Russian infantry had stopped Bertrand. Then, Blücher was wounded and Napoleon arrived on the field, about 2:30 P.M. Yorck took command of the Prussians, but Alexander, who was with the army, refused to let him unleash his guard, convinced victory had been won. No Russian reinforcements arrived for another two hours.

Napoleon raced from one crisis point to the other, encouraging his men and appraising the situation. Marmont said of these hours in his memoirs, "This was probably the day, of his whole career, on which Napoleon incurred the greatest personal danger on the battlefield."[23] By 5:30 P.M., a Prussian counterattack retook Klein Görschen and Rana, but Macdonald's corps had arrived on the right, and Napoleon was now ready to drive at the allied center with Ney's corps and the guard. At 6:00 P.M., Napoleon placed the eighty guns of the guard artillery in the countryside between Starsiedl and Kaya, and ordered the Old Guard to defend them: "You will defend these batteries, and if the enemy attacks them, you will give a good account of yourselves." Just then, a Prussian volley smashed into the grenadiers, killing two and shattering the thigh of another. "We will give him a good pension," Napoleon responded. As the hail of fire grew, he called out to the Chasseurs, "Does the Guard duck?" They did not, and when the barrage ended and the Russian charge came, the guard caught them at close range. Napoleon remained in the midst of "his children," throughout, in the center of an infantry square, near the guns, under fire all the while. Supported by the eighty guns, the Young Guard under Mortier and Ney drove forward.[24] The allies were driven out of the villages, but regrouped, and their retreat was orderly. They fell back first, to Dresden, and then to well-prepared positions at Bautzen. "The Russians had by now no equals in Europe when it came to rearguard actions and withdrawals," Dominic Lieven observed, adding, "It would have taken far better cavalry than anything Napoleon possessed in 1813 to shake them."[25] They practiced the same scorched-earth retreat as in Russia in 1812. The French found Pegau deserted, its houses plundered by the Cossacks, its church burned to the ground.[26] Even Napoleon had to admit to Frederick of Württemberg that "the enemy army had burnt all the bridges . . . All the villages along the route are full of the wounded and the dead."[27]

Up to this point, all the strengths of the French, and of Napoleon, were to the fore. Now, on the cusp of a crushing victory, the weaknesses were exposed. Wittgenstein had been close to complete envelopment, but Napoleon lacked cavalry to pursue the allies, and Marmont's attempt to do so ended in near catastrophe, when he was almost killed himself, as nine Prussian cavalry squadrons fell on him, broke through, and almost got to Napoleon. Berg fought a spirited, well-disciplined rearguard action, and enabled the main force to escape. The American scholar, Michael V. Leggiere, has said without exaggeration, that at Lützen, "the Sixth Coalition came within hours of being destroyed by a double envelopment that would have been so crushing it would have ended the war."[28] It was not to be. Either way, Lützen was a bloody affair. Losses were horrific, when it is remembered that the battle lasted only eight hours. Estimates of allied casualties vary wildly between eleven and twenty-two thousand, but the Prussians bore the brunt of them, with fifty-three officers killed, among them the military reformer, Scharnhorst, who has some right to be called the father of the Prussian army that fought that day. He died of his wounds in Vienna a few weeks later. The French lost between twenty and twenty-two thousand, fifteen thousand of them from Ney's corps; the Young Guard lost over a thousand of its carefully reconstructed ranks; the

Old Guard was thinned by fifty-five. That either were even used revealed the arduous shape of things to come. Two French generals killed, nine more wounded, and thirty colonels dead or wounded further weakened the officer corps. Napoleon could bear these losses far less than the allies. He had no well-trained levies on their way, unlike Alexander.

There was one loss, in particular, that hit Napoleon hardest, even before battle commenced. At midday on May 1, Bessières was reconnoitering the advance and encountered Cossacks and a Russian battery. Just before 1:00 P.M., a Russian shell hit a stone wall, ricocheted, and killed him instantly, striking through the heart, throwing him under his horse's hooves. His body was only just rescued from the Cossacks. "Such is our fate," muttered Ney, who was nearby.[29] For once, an army bulletin did not lie when it reported, "Few losses could affect the Emperor more deeply."[30] Few had known Napoleon so well, for so long; fewer still remained so trusted. Now he was gone. His first official reaction was to Berthier, and typically hardnosed, on the morning before the battle began: "(It was) an isolated death, and has nothing in common with the train of events . . . the Emperor has a formidable army,"[31] but he opened up to Marie-Louise the moment the battle was over: "I have felt much grief over the death of the duke of Istria (Bessières); it has been a real blow for me . . . Please speak to his poor wife."[32] It broke a mournful silence that fell over him, before the battle.[33] Four days later, Napoleon told his widow:

> Your loss, and that of your children, is doubtless great, but mine is just as much again. The duke of Istria died a beautiful death, without suffering. He leaves a stainless reputation: it is the best heritage he can pass on to his children. My protection of them is assured; they will inherit the same affection I had for their father. Please find in all these considerations some reasons for consolation to soften your grief, and never doubt my feelings for all of you.[34]

Napoleon's friendship for Bessières survived the latter's disapproval of the divorce and his seeming failure in Spain. Perhaps the greatest witness to their friendship was the enmity it inspired in others. "If Bessières could be a Mar-shal, so could anyone," snarled Marmont in his memoirs.[35]

The service Bessières had tried to render Napoleon many years before, when he had sought in vain to steer Caroline away from Murat, would have been his greatest. As intrigue swirled in Naples, Murat had not followed his brother-in-law to war in 1813. Rather, he stayed in his kingdom for fear of being ousted by Caroline and "the French party" around her, who had Napoleon's confidence while he saw his own reputation eviscerated publicly. His abilities as a commander were questioned openly in *Le Moniteur*, the official government newspaper. His long letter to Napoleon of April 12, asking to be listened to, was left unanswered.[36] It was becoming just as clear to him, that the allies would restore the Bourbons to Naples, should they win. The French ambassador concluded in early April, that "I think his secret thoughts were the fear of seeing himself abandoned in any definitive nego-tiations, he was contemplating his self-preservation."[37] On April 22, Murat sent a trusted aide to Sicily, and proposed to the British that he would turn forty thousand Neapolitan troops against the kingdom of Italy, "stabbing Eugène in the back," in return for being recognized as king by the allies. The British replied that his throne would be safe if he handed the Bourbons Gaeta as a sign of goodwill and declared war on Napoleon. Murat refused these terms, but discussions continued, nonetheless. He sent out "feelers" to Metternich, and made approaches to the Carbonari, a secret society intent on expelling the French and uniting Italy, all while refusing to send troops to Eugène and Napoleon. Napoleon remained unaware of all this until news of his talks with the British appeared in the *Morning Chronicle* in May.[38] From Dresden, he told Maret that his ambassador in Vienna was angry that Murat's aide-de-camp, Cariati, "conducts himself very badly, and sees only our enemies," and to tell Murat that he was "very displeased with all the bad connections the king (Murat) has." Cariati was to be recalled and this "bad system" had to end, otherwise "it will be the ruin of the king of Naples."[39] On Saint Helena, Napoleon told Gourgaud, "Bessières was a good cavalry officer, if a little cold: he had less 'of' that Murat had more 'of.'"[40]

The immediate irony was that Bessières, perhaps a greater cavalryman than Murat, had no cavalry to lead when he was cut down.

Lützen was a much-needed victory, just the same, and Napoleon milked it for all it was worth. An hour after the battle, Napoleon told Savary there was no need for the journals to "over-egg" events; reporting had been well intentioned, but maladroit. "It is better to let events take their course . . . A mere word—a thing is true or it is not—suffices."[41] On May 4, Ney was told to "enter Leipzig with his troops and as much pomp as he is able."[42] The same day, Caulaincourt wrote to the French ambassador in Vienna, "His Majesty was once again the general-in-chief he had been in Italy and Egypt," adding "make good use of these details."[43] Napoleon took the direct route to his father-in-law, telling Emperor Francis, "I am pleased to announce . . . the victory Providence has rendered my arms on the field of Lützen. Although having directed my army's maneuvers myself, and having found myself under fire a few times, I have not had any mishaps."[44] It was all true. The new confidence Napoleon felt after Lützen was real. He now partially reverted to his original strategy, sending Ney north with forty-five thousand men, soon swelled to eighty-four thousand, to retake the fortress of Torgau, held by Saxon troops, while on May 3, Napoleon took the main army and drove east after Wittgenstein, entering Dresden on May 8. This did not stop him from lying. He told Frederick of Württemberg that he had defeated an army of 200,000 infantry and 30,000 horses; that the Prussian royal guard had been annihilated and the Russian Imperial Guard "suffered badly"; the Russian heavy cavalry had been crushed: "I will chase them; this will take us to the Vistula. Behold how many hopes of change and upheaval have been annihilated!"[45] The most emphatic effect of Lützen had been to knock Frederick-Augustus off the fence he had been sitting on. He promptly rejoined the Confederation, ordered the garrison of Torgau to surrender to Ney, and returned to his capital, now French headquarters. More important, still, the victory of Lützen cleared his kingdom of the allies before they milked its rich resources; its fat fields now belonged to the French for the rest of the next six months, who soon stripped Saxony bare while the allies foraged on the march.[46] Napoleon had ordered as much on May 8, telling Frederick-Augustus to get his troops out of Torgau, put "all the resources of his country" at Napoleon's disposal, send all his cavalry—"without exception"—to Dresden—and that he declared openly that he will not make treaties with enemy powers, otherwise he would be declared "a felon, outside Our protection, and will cease to reign."[47] The relationship had changed. So had others. On May 11, he wrote to Fouché that, in light of the victory at Lützen, the reoccupation of Prussia was likely: Fouché was now summoned to head its administration: "I am more than happy to have occasion to receive your services again, and to (have) new proof of your loyalty."[48]

Lützen had shown the allies had their problems. The two sovereigns were now both firmly with their armies, and while Frederick-William stayed out of things—observing with a shudder[49] how few Russians there actually were in Saxony—Alexander had worryingly begun to acquire the same taste for generalship that cost him so dearly at Austerlitz. His presence allowed the other Russian commanders simply to ignore or bypass Wittgenstein, as of old. Reinforcements, however strong, were still far off; Lützen had shown how raw many of the new Prussian recruits still were.[50] At this point, the French still had a clear advantage in combat. Nevertheless, although buffeted, the allies were determined to fight on. This came as much from Metternich's diplomacy as anything else. At the point when military success floundered, Metternich launched a diplomatic initiative that bolstered the alliance, while still keeping Austria neutral. Metternich was genuinely consternated by the speed of Napoleon's advance into Saxony, but he had no illusions about the potency of French arms, even after the disaster of Russia. He held out some hope in April that Napoleon would accept Austrian mediation, but after Lützen, he saw this was vain.[51] He knew Austria was in no position to fight, at this stage, but at the end of April, he convinced Francis to create an "Anticipation Fund," to strengthen the army. When Napoleon got wind of this, he scoffed at the sums involved as utterly inadequate.[52] Metternich's subsequent actions reveal that he probably agreed. However, his first step was to send General Bubna to Dresden on May 16, to explore the possibility of mediation with Napoleon. Bubna was rebuffed, Napoleon arguing that Metternich's agreement with

Frederick-Augustus—however defunct—showed that Austria was no longer his ally, and more to the point, no longer neutral. On May 12, he ordered Eugène back to Italy to organize an army of observation in the Veneto, to intimidate Austria to stay out of the war, and to defend his cherished kingdom if it did not.[53]

Napoleon was acutely aware of something else, even if he did not actually know the full facts. Metternich may have learned a great lesson in Germany, that nothing could be achieved if the princes of the Confederation felt threatened, but he had learned nothing about Italy. A week earlier, Metternich had outlined his specific plans to the allies, which included the loss of all Italian regions under French control and Napoleon's renunciation of the kingdom of Italy.[54] This mirrored the demand that he renounce his leadership of the Confederation of the Rhine, but took no account of how differently Napoleon viewed his relationship to Italy, or that there were no Italian princes in place to counterbalance him. The kingdom was intrinsic to the French economy and Napoleon always saw it as "the jewel in the crown," his personal creation. There was no "new politics" in Metternich's vision for Italy. Rather, his proposals represent an atavistic, aggressive reversion to traditional Habsburg ambitions. Tellingly, Bubna was ordered not to disclose any of this. Instinctively, Napoleon knew Austria would press for the restitution of Lombardy and Venice, at the very least: "How can I accept a power which has an interest (in Italy) and losses there as a mediator?" he demanded. Napoleon's fury grew as he ticked off his objections. "I won't hesitate to sacrifice my life . . . I will perhaps perish and my dynasty with me. You want to tear Italy and Germany away from me. You want to dishonor me!" This left Bubna so shaken that, despite Napoleon's willingness to allow the Duchy of Warsaw to be dismembered, he was too afraid to raise the issue of Napoleon renouncing his leadership of the Confederation. Instead, Napoleon waved the wholly fictitious vision of a resurgent, Jacobin France rising from the ashes of his defeat to take bloody vengeance on Marie-Louise, as it had her aunt, Marie Antoinette.[55] It was hyperbole. Napoleon knew whatever threats he faced at home, they were not from the left. When he told Bubna, "I do not want your armed mediation," he saw through Metternich. Indeed, Napoleon had sought to bypass Metternich from the outset of the campaign, treating instead with Francis, preferably through Marie-Louise: "Write to Papa Francis every eight days; give him the military details and speak of my attachment to him."[56] She did so,[57] but Lützen soon provided detail enough. Napoleon at first accepted the idea of an armistice and a peace conference, but when he met again with Bubna the next morning, Napoleon did not mention it. If Metternich's terms were, indeed, a ruse to provoke Napoleon into rejecting peace overtures,[58] there was no need. That same day, Macdonald's scouts confirmed the allies were concentrated around Bautzen, within his grasp. He had them on the run.

On May 18, Napoleon sent Caulaincourt to try to open talks with Alexander, behind Metternich's back. Alexander replied that he was inspecting his troops, and unavailable.[59] The tsar may have lost his common sense in matters of command, but not his mixture of languor and sang froid. Frederick-William was understandably fearful for Berlin, but Napoleon underestimated him. He ordered the whole army to go with Alexander to Bautzen, leaving only Bülow's thirty thousand men to concentrate around the approaches to the capital.[60] For a man so contemptuously dismissed by Napoleon at Tilsit, it was a sea change.

Metternich sent Johann Philipp von Stadion to set out his plans to Alexander and Frederick-William. It set out the dismemberment of Napoleonic Italy just as Napoleon had foreseen, and also demanded the independence of Holland from France, and Napoleon's withdrawal from Germany east of the Rhine (although he could keep the left bank, which had been in French hands since 1797). Austria was to regain everything it had lost to Napoleon, at one stage or another.[61] Metternich made it clear to Stadion that he was to get some kind of firm idea from the allies as to their own plans. He also sought to assure them that Austria would not rejoin the French, whatever the military circumstances, but equally, that Austria was in no position to take the field. Somewhere in his talks with Nesselrode on May 18, Stadion seems to have given a guarantee that Austria would enter the war if Napoleon failed to agree to accept the conditions Bubna offered him. As Dominic Lieven has pointed out, Nesselrode was an experienced diplomat of some ability, while

Stadion would never have misled the Russians, but whoever was to blame
for this, Nesselrode's account to Alexander did not represent Vienna's real
position. The belief that Austrian support would be forthcoming played an
important part in deciding to stand and fight at Bautzen.[62] It no longer mattered. With his usual decisiveness, Napoleon struck while the allies talked. On
May 16, he ordered Ney to turn back south and join him. Even as Nesselrode
and Stadion met, even before Alexander insouciantly rebuffed him, Napoleon
marched out of Dresden with the guard and about 122,000 troops, to make
his own arrangements with them all.

Bautzen

The battle of Bautzen was governed as much by politics as by military necessity. Napoleon sought a decisive engagement that would break the coalition
and end the war before Austria could join it. It was a decision made quickly.
On May 13, he still thought in terms of being in Berlin to help Davout deal
with Hamburg;[63] five days later he wrote to his father-in-law, assuring him
he wanted a peace congress and to negotiate, that he should remain loyal to
France and not become "the laughingstock of the English" or destroy their
friendship built up since 1809 or "renew the hatreds of the past which plunged
Europe into interminable convulsions and wars."[64] But he could not let the
main allied army elude him again. He set out to encircle the enemy, and then
drive the allies south, to the edge of the Austrian border: If he won a crushing
victory, Metternich would be too intimidated to join the coalition, remain
neutral, and leave the allies in a vise, caught between Napoleon and a border
they dare not cross. The allies badly needed a clear victory over Napoleon to
coax Austria into the war, if for no other reason than they needed the resources
of Silesia to maintain their troops.

On the face of it, Bautzen appeared a good defensive position, and the Russians wanted to fight on their own terms, firmly dug in, and awaited Napoleon.
At eight miles, their front was too long to be well defended with the numbers

available, however, even though Barclay had now arrived with seven thousand much-needed reinforcements, for in their haste to confront Napoleon, they found themselves outnumbered almost two-to-one. Nonetheless, its center was a line of bluffs running southwest to northeast behind the River Spree, which the Russians had prepared well, but the hills were cut through by several streams, which made maneuvering behind the front line difficult. It did not help things when Alexander shunted Wittgenstein aside, and took command himself. Alexander had no fears of fighting near the border because he read Napoleon's military intentions as poorly as he read his diplomacy well. The tsar was convinced Napoleon would try to drive him northward, to cut his line of retreat to Poland, which was just what Napoleon wanted him to think.[65] Ignoring Wittgenstein—who knew what Napoleon was about—Alexander concentrated his forces on his southern flank, convinced Napoleon would strike there. In his memoirs, a Russian commander estimated that twenty-five thousand men were needed to hold the northern flank properly. On the eve of battle, only Barclay's seven thousand stood between Ney's eighty-four thousand and the allied rear.[66] Napoleon had ordered Ney to send part of his force back to Torgau to form his northern wing, a powerful corps that would drive Alexander to the Austrian border, while Bertrand and Soult—newly arrived from Spain—and the guard hammered at the line of bluffs in the center, and Oudinot kept the allies pinned in the south.

Whereas the allied generals' problem was their deluded commander in chief, Napoleon's was Ney's inability to pay attention to his orders properly. Napoleon prepared intensely for Bautzen, his sappers laying trestle bridges across the Spree to facilitate Soult and Bertrand's war of attrition on the bluffs, while Oudinot, Marmont, and Macdonald held the south, but the whole plan depended on Ney, in the northern sector, who was to drive the enemy back. Napoleon had not chosen his man well. Typically, Ney had not kept in touch with Napoleon, and Napoleon was not clear where Ney actually was before he ordered him to Bautzen.[67] The task proved too complicated for Ney, and this time he did not have the excuse of poorly mapped wilderness to fall back on as in Russia. First, Ney brought his entire force with him, not a portion of it as ordered, which took time to move, thus arriving late and delaying the attack. The rest of the army spent the morning of May 20 simply marking time. The bombardment of the bluffs began at 3:00 P.M., the sappers manning the trestle bridges with great courage as the first attacks went in. The allies were driven out of Bautzen and back to the bluffs by about 6:00 P.M. Oudinot's assault in the south so rattled Alexander that he committed part of his reserves. Fortuitously, it also went well for Napoleon to the north. When he did arrive on the northern flank, Ney positioned his men defensively, facing east, not south.[68] Even as he reached the front, Ney still had no idea what his role in the battle was, despite clear orders, which Napoleon ordered sent to him by "*by an intelligent officer and in clear writing.*"[69] The italics were Napoleon's. The key player remained muddled, however. Fortunately, so was Alexander, who miscalculated Ney's strength and continued to ignore the buildup.

The main French assaults began on May 21. The first day was a war of attrition as Napoleon hammered at the south and center of the allied front, forcing them to commit their reserves there. Only then, on May 22, was Ney to begin his sweep from north to south and roll the allies up, completing their envelopment. Napoleon's thinking was almost "classic" by his standards. It was what had worked so many times before—first at Castiglione in 1796, and most recently, at Friedland, in 1807. However, the quality of his troops was not as of old. His young conscripts had, indeed, exceeded expectations at Lützen, but the hard marching thereafter had exhausted them. Napoleon ordered Mortier specifically "not to tire the Young Guard to no good purpose . . . it will be important to get them to Bautzen."[70] Only Bertrand's corps was fresh, and most of the French formations were worn out before the battle began. For all that, there were plenty of them. Apart from Ney, Napoleon had 115,000 men in the center and the southern flank. The allies had barely ninety-six thousand ill-distributed troops: the Prussians under Blücher, Berg, and Yorck, ready to bear the brunt in the center, the Russians under Miloradovich facing Oudinot to the south. Ney was still too out of position to attack until late morning, but the central sector, under Soult's overall command, resumed storming the central bluffs. The fighting was ferocious, and part of the Young Guard had to be deployed, but by early afternoon, the French had fought their way up the bluffs to the plateau behind them. Napoleon then let loose an intense bombardment by sixty cannon that forced Blücher out of his fortified positions, but Soult could not press on; the artillery could not be redeployed on the captured ground. Without its support, Soult took terrible losses and had to halt. To the south, Oudinot met very fierce resistance, as this is where Alexander thought the real blow would come. Napoleon refused point-blank to send him support, and his corps gave ground, but this suited Napoleon as it lured Miloradovich out of his fortifications.[71] Now, the Russians regrouped, their lines of infantry holding steady for hours, along with the cavalry of the Russian imperial guard. The Young Guard went forward, again, with all the cannon Napoleon could spare. So ferocious had the fighting become that Napoleon now thought Ney was fully engaged, and ordered Soult forward, as the start of the final push in the center. By 5:00 P.M., Alexander authorized a limited withdrawal. Oudinot renewed the offensive, but his men were exhausted, his ranks too thinned, to pursue the retreating allies.

It all depended on Ney and his subordinate, Lauriston. He had met so little resistance in the early morning, that all Barclay could do was mount a skillful retreat that, at least, saved the allied guns, while Blücher had done the same with the Prussians, who then took on Soult. Even in such favorable conditions, Ney and Lauriston muddled their movements. Ney took until midmorning to untangle things and mount an attack on the Gleinau redoubt. He was well behind schedule. He reached the well-defended village of Preititz by late morning, with Lauriston well behind him. Ney now compounded one blunder with another, and then another. Instead of bypassing Preititz, masking it, and pressing on into the allied rear, now open before him, he pigheadedly—in the forthright judgment of David Chandler[72]—besieged it at great cost in time and lives. He was saved from disintegration only by the swift arrival of Reynier's corps, which brought Ney up to strength. Preititz fell at 3:00 P.M., and Lauriston's fresh troops could have swooped in on the allies' main line of retreat, but Ney decided otherwise. He now heard the fury of Soult and Blücher around Kreckwitz on his right, and turned toward them, ordering Lauriston to support him. Soult had the Young Guard with him and Bertrand's corps, and was in no danger of being overrun, however fierce the fighting. Only Barclay was holding the road at this point. The real fighting was between Soult and Blücher, who was exhorting his men to fight to the last like the Spartans at Thermopylae.[73] So tenacious was he that Napoleon paid him the highest compliment possible: he threw in the twelve hundred *grognards*, who marched forward implacably but imperturbably on Blücher's left, at last forcing even that old warhorse to quit the field.[74] He joined the rest of the army, which slipped away—yet again—shielded by the Russian Imperial Guard and the heavy cavalry.[75] A Saxon officer on Napoleon's staff watched them in awe: "the Russians retired in the greatest order (and) made a retreat which may be considered as a *chef d'oeuvre* of tactics."[76] Ney had allowed the Russians to play to their traditional strength. Drained and without effective cavalry, pursuit was useless, its futility driven home to Napoleon when a violent thunderstorm burst at 10:00 P.M.[77] Ney never made it to Soult. He was diverted, again, attacking the fortified inn at Klein Burschwitz, and just missed capturing Blücher and the tsar.[78] It summed up the day.

There was another bitter sting left in the tail for Napoleon. He was infuriated that the allies had escaped yet again, this time from almost certain annihilation, and the next day, May 23, he assumed command of the pursuit, in person. This did not stop him telling his father-in-law that Providence had given him yet another triumph, the only letter he wrote that day.[79] He caught up with the Russian rearguard, first at Reichenbach, where even a traffic jam in the town did not prevent a stout action that held up Napoleon, and then at Markersdorf.[80] Napoleon and his staff were pressing through the village toward the Russian position when a round of cannon shot from the Russians ricocheted off a tree, came close to Napoleon, and disemboweled Duroc. It barely missed Caulaincourt and Mortier.[81] Napoleon had made Duroc his aide-de-camp on the first Italian campaign, and he rose to be Master of the Palace, one of the most trusted men in the regime. He served with Napoleon on every campaign, and in varied, vital roles beyond the battlefield. Carried to a farmhouse, he died in agony after several hours. Napoleon stayed a considerable time, and tried to give him some hope, but Duroc just asked him for some opium. Someone reminded Napoleon on Saint Helena that after he left Duroc's side, he paced up and down in front of his tent, and no one dared come near him. When he spoke of Duroc, Las Cases remembered, "He affected to speak with a stoicism that one easily saw was not natural."[82] Napoleon broke off the action, a rare occurrence.[83] The next morning, he wrote to Marie-Louise, "You can judge my grief! You know my friendship for the duke of Friuli."[84] Duroc had controlled almost every aspect of Napoleon's daily life and, when in Paris, the workings of the Tuileries. His death changed the delicate equilibrium he had fostered since 1804. Caulaincourt took his place.[85] In the interregnum, Madame Lannes seized control of protocol, and the problems she created soon reached Napoleon's ears, causing him to tell Marie-Louise:

> The duchess is handling the invitations badly, which is making a poor impression. She is inviting people who have been away from Paris for a month, for three, even, which provokes mockery and makes people think the work for invitations is done by a committee, and so people are no longer flattered to be invited.[86]

Clearly, Caulaincourt had his work cut out for him on his return. A few days later, from that same palace, a slender ray of humanity, or normalcy, shone for a moment. "I see with pleasure that my son has begun to speak and pronounce words," he replied to Marie-Louise, "All that you tell me about his roguishness makes me long to see him."[87]

The fighting at Bautzen was horrendous, as the French had to storm entrenchments, and the allies protect them. Mass artillery fire produced genuine horror, as was becoming the norm. Estimates of the allied casualties vary wildly between eleven and twenty thousand, but the French lost between twenty and twenty-five thousand.[88] Napoleon was shaken by many things, the allied escape, the death of Duroc, the fact that he had had to deploy not only the Young Guard, but the Old, as well, the surest sign that the enemy was of high calibre. Its losses were made good by stripping Paris of its garrison; all the Old Guard companies were ordered to Dresden, while twenty-five hundred sharpshooters were drawn from line regiments to fill the remaining gaps in the Young Guard. The guard had lost five thousand men in all.[89] He had seen the Russians produce the kind of rearguard action that had dragged him all the way to Moscow, and the Prussians announce their return to their proud traditions in the field. Bautzen had failed to bring the decisive result it promised because of Ney. Even more than in Russia, Napoleon suffered from the absence of his great commanders. The one who was present, Soult, promoted commander of the guard afterward, had won the day for him in the center, at great cost. Napoleon had routed the allies and put them to flight, just the same, and felt confident enough to dispatch Oudinot north toward Berlin, renewing the hopes of a second front, while he led the main army toward the allies, wherever they turned.

In contrast, the badly shaken allied high command was at odds over what to do. Cracks in the alliance appeared: Alexander sacked Wittgenstein and appointed Barclay in his place, who soon argued for a retreat into Poland to secure their supply bases. He saw immediately that Wittgenstein's incompetence had left the Russian interior lines in mayhem. It would also place the battered army closer to the formidable reinforcements that were beginning to arrive from Russia. Barclay spoke from a military perspective, and that of a man who had been thrust into an almighty mess. He opposed the alternative policy, for the same reason: To turn south, and hug the Austrian border would be to finish Napoleon's job for him, to leave the armies trapped between an uncrossable neutral border and the French.[90] The Prussians had utterly different priorities: Berlin was now in peril, and would be defenseless if they followed the Russians into Poland. They had carried the brunt of the fighting in both battles, suffering heavy losses, which made them feel the need for an Austrian alliance more acutely than the Russians. Should they abandon the border, it would make Austrian intervention less likely, because the Austrians would have to face Napoleon alone and fight their way to the allies. It would imperil the political project. On June 2, it seemed Barclay's view had prevailed, but Blücher and Yorck then angrily declared that the Prussian army should go its own way, and defend its own territory, fearing that the promised liberation of their country had been jettisoned by their ally. Then Alexander showed himself at his best, "with an impressive display of statesmanship."[91] The tsar stood up to his own commander, and kept his army on the Austrian border to keep hopes of Austrian intervention alive. His calm and resilience in a political crisis stood in sharp contrast to his blundering in battle. Napoleon and Alexander, as so often, emerged as polar opposites.

Napoleon was the stronger in the field, but Alexander had a diplomatic ally of the highest calibre in Metternich, all the more so because he did not always appear to be. He knew that when Metternich assured him that the military reverses did not alter his political objectives, he did not speak for everyone. Stadion spoke directly with Alexander, and was terrified of Barclay's plans.[92] Napoleon had been right in his approach to Francis. The veteran and victim of so many defeats at his hands, Francis was firmly of the peace party. He urged Metternich to "avoid as much as possible anything that might harm Napoleon's honor." Like Stadion, Francis also believed, from past experience, that Napoleon and Alexander were more than capable of coming to terms, at the expense of everyone else.[93] Metternich had to have Francis's full confidence in his "steadfastness and tenacity" to defeat Napoleon,[94] but it was far from the case after Bautzen. Metternich marshaled his forces with as much skill and speed as Napoleon had his troops. He read the position perfectly: "In the abstract sense—if we take the monarchy (Austria) by itself—we are far from being as powerful as we once were—but as a weight added to the scales, the side chosen by Austria is the predominant one."[95] He put his finger on it perfectly, and his course of action was a territorial concentration of his forces. Seeing that Frederick-William and Alexander were with their armies at Reichenbach, and Napoleon was at Dresden, Metternich persuaded Francis to come with him to the summer residence of his mistress-in-waiting, Wilhelmine von Sagan, just on the Austrian side of the border, and almost equidistant between the rival armies. Francis was removed from the clutches of the peace party, and Metternich could maintain close relations with all the warring sovereigns at close range.

Reports from Stadion with the allies and Bubna with Napoleon now came directly, verbatim, to himself.

Metternich had to convince the allies that he was, ultimately, on their side, that Napoleon could not be negotiated with, and certainly not on the terms they all agreed were essential to a lasting peace, mainly the end of French hegemony in Italy and Germany. Metternich needed time to rebuild the Austrian forces to levels at which they had a realistic chance of surviving battle with Napoleon—Napoleon had read this military weakness more or less aright—and this formed the main thrust of his argument for delaying what amounted to changing sides. More time was required for an armistice, which Napoleon had not ruled out. In the meantime, Alexander remained serene amid "Austrian prevarication (and) Prussian hysteria."[96] Dominic Lieven speculates with good reason, that his newfound religious faith sustained him in these weeks. He had been deeply moved by the Easter services in Dresden, and spent a week on retreat with the Moravian Brothers in late April. Writing to a friend he confided, "it would be hard for me to express to you the emotion which I felt in thinking over everything that has happened during the past year and where Divine Providence had led us."[97] His feelings of optimism, whatever their source, were answered. On June 4, Napoleon agreed to an armistice until June 20.

Metternich still needed to get out of the tsar and Frederick-William what terms they would fight on, should Austria join them. This was thrashed out at a series of abrasive meetings among Stadion, Nesselrode, and von Hardenberg between June 7 and 10, which had to reconcile the abbreviated, moderate terms Bubna had given to Napoleon, with the real allied agenda. Stadion forced their hand, telling them that if Napoleon rejected the terms, Francis would fight—when ready—but that if he accepted them, Austria would not join the war.[98] Napoleon, too, had no illusions. On June 18, he told Cambacérès, "I want peace, but not a peace that would send me out in arms three months later."[99] He was relatively well disposed at this point, but not for long.

Alexander felt emotion; he left emoting to Napoleon. During his tirade to Bubna in Dresden, juxtaposed to his lurid portrait of an imminent Jacobin Terror should he lose the war, Napoleon showed, perhaps, his real self:

A man who was a simple private person and has ascended to the throne—a parvenu—who has spent twenty years hailed with bullets, is not afraid of projectiles, he does not fear any threats at all. I do not value my life above all else, nor that of others very much. I do not waver to and fro to save my own life above all else; I do not rate it higher than that of a hundred thousand people. I sacrifice a million if necessary.[100]

This is what the allies, the Austrians, and everyone else, really had to fear. Napoleon had fought his way to everything he had. It was his to throw away if he chose. There were few ties that bound him to a world in which he would always be a parvenu, an outsider. He knew France could not afford to lose Italy or western Germany, but those were France's interests, not his. This is why he said he would cling to "every village which I have constitutionally united to France." Napoleon was fighting for something else. He had nowhere else to go. He would not go back to private life; his dynasty was born of his own struggle, it was his to keep or lose, on his own terms. He did not agree to the armistice because Caulaincourt—or Berthier, no less—had urged him to negotiate for peace.[101] Napoleon did not change his attitude or his tone when Metternich came to see him in Dresden on June 26, but was blunter still: "I was brought up in military camps, and know nothing but military camps, and a man such as I am does not give a fuck about the lives of a million men." "You are no soldier, and you do not know what goes on in the soul of a soldier."[102] This was not about making "petty territorial gains" as opposed to Metternich's plans for a stable settlement—which he was now thoroughly convinced he could not hope for from Napoleon[103]—it ran deeper. His in-laws were traitors, as were his brothers. So was Murat. Bernadotte, the greatest traitor of them all, was on his left flank with an army paid for by the City of London. Caulaincourt posed a probable explanation for what actually triggered these outbursts:

The abuse of his gifts was natural to him, as the abuse of his strength is to a gladiator. The habit of being his own master at home and abroad had made him despise subtlety. Thus, he was neither adroit nor nimble in this negotiation, the first he had ever had to conduct as equal to equal.[104]

The cautious Corsican was gone. The soldier of the revolutionary wars now dominated his character. He could neither trust nor stomach peace with the Habsburgs on any but dictated terms. It was not the way of the new regime, republican or imperial. He behaved to foreign ambassadors with the same arrogance, aggression, and republican defiance as the generals sent abroad by the Directory to bully and intimidate the courts of Europe, not only because he was habituated to power, but because that was how the new regime dealt with its enemies. He agreed to the armistice and a peace congress in Prague for a soldier's reasons, because he needed time to rest and replace his troops; because he needed horses. Allied intelligence reported that Ney's corps—forty-five thousand men when the campaign began—numbered only thirty-seven hundred after Bautzen. Desertion was rife among the French, those caught by the allies confirming that they were starving, their rations drastically reduced.[105] The news of the armistice actually dispirited many, one report noting it "dashed all fortitude. One foresees only death by starvation"[106] as the troops contemplated weeks more in a ravaged countryside. The allies had these problems in even greater measure and were in no state to face another big battle, as Barclay could testify,[107] but he agreed, just the same.

Even before Metternich and Napoleon met came the crucial change. Whatever had been achieved so far had been done without the British. Russia had liberated herself; Prussia had rebuilt her army on her own. Now, recognition came as it had never come before. Serious negotiations began with Britain on April 25, when Charles Stewart, Castlereagh's brother, reached Dresden—the rebellion in Hamburg making his progress quicker than normal.[108] On June 14, at Reichenbach, Russia and Prussia signed separate treaties with Britain for a total of £2,000,000 in financial subsidies, to be made available immediately, and the prospect of another £2,500,000 in credit.[109] Two thirds of the money went to Russia, one third to Prussia, a source of acrimony, as

Prussia actually had more men in the field in June. In return, the British demanded the Russians keep 200,000 men in the field, the Prussians 100,000, later reduced to 160,000 and 80,000, respectively.[110] They also insisted there could be no peace with Napoleon if the Spanish or Neapolitan Bourbons were abandoned by the allies, while Italy and Holland had to be surrendered. The path had not been easy, not only because the British mistrusted the allies—"I fear political treachery and the machinations that are in the wind more than any evils from Bonaparte's myrmidons," Charles told his brother—but because the British emissaries, Stewart, George Cathcart, and Colonel Thornton, quarreled among themselves.[111] Nevertheless, the breakthrough was seismic.

Britain had obsessed Napoleon like nothing else on his long sleigh ride with Caulaincourt, but he was convinced it was on the verge of bankruptcy.[112] He was utterly wrong. "Pitt's gold" so often illusory in the past, now began to flow to his old enemies. Russian manpower was at last backed by British money, and the armistice made at Pleiswitz—soon extended to August 10—gave the allies time to make use of their newfound funds. The treaties signed at Reichenbach ate away at his worst fears. At his meeting with Metternich, he exploded "(England) has just signed two treaties with Russia and Prussia; has she also drafted a third? . . . You should know something about that M. Metternich; how much has she paid you for that?" It was too gross an insult for Metternich to answer, an appalling diplomatic blunder that forced Metternich to shut his mouth.[113] Yet, it was clear-eyed. Napoleon's vision of hell had come to pass. And it was laughing in his face. When told of Napoleon's agreement to the armistice, the sober-sided Barclay burst out laughing. He had begged for six weeks to rebuild the Russian army, and Napoleon obliged. A subordinate remembered, "The two of us laughed together at Napoleon's expense, Barclay, all the generals and our monarchs were drunk with joy and they were right to be so."[114]

10

THE LAST SUMMER: DRESDEN, THE FINAL VICTORY, JUNE–SEPTEMBER 1813

A Fatal Mistake: The Last Summer, June–August 1813

News of the armistice and the imminent congress at Prague raised great hopes of peace in France. The prefects' reports reveal—through the assiduous research of Munro Price—an intensity of feeling that had been mounting since the start of the campaign.[1] Never had there been less prospect of it, however. The belligerents all had powerful reasons to fight on. Of the sovereigns, only Francis genuinely wanted a peaceful resolution to the conflict, for the sake of his daughter and grandson's future. He knew his army was still weak compared to all the others, and he remembered all too well Napoleon's military prowess and Alexander's susceptibility to defeatism. Metternich remained unsure of his master, even when away from Vienna.[2] Napoleon was right to place his hopes of keeping Austria out of the war in his father-in-law and he saw through Metternich, telling Marie-Louise,

"Metternich . . . seems to me much the intriguer, and is manipulating papa Francois very badly."[3] He had no illusions. "The House of Austria is very demanding," he told Eugène when the talks about an armistice had hardly begun, "we have to be ready for war with her."[4]

Alexander remained a mystery to Napoleon and Francis both. Napoleon still held out hope of detaching the tsar from the Prussians before Austria could join the alliance, and told Caulaincourt to float this, yet again, during the preliminary talks for the congress. Although the terms he offered Alexander for a separate peace fell on deaf ears, they are an insight into what Napoleon believed Alexander wanted most. Napoleon's readiness to admit the Duchy of Warsaw had to be dismembered showed he was at least a year behind the tsar's thinking. Bowing to Alexander's fears of the duchy may have helped things in 1811, but Napoleon revealed more about himself here than about Alexander. It did not seem to cross his mind that a brutal invasion could change the agenda. Only a French evacuation of Germany could placate Alexander now. Caulaincourt made it known how weakened the French forces were in June—whether carrying out an elaborate ruse for Napoleon, or sailing close to treason to bring about the peace he openly advocated, has never been solved—but Alexander remained implacably committed to war, through his silence, not his words.[5] Alexander's spiritual awakening was beyond Napoleon. Even had he known of Alexander's sense of mission, the tsar's spirituality would have been as alien to him as the unfaltering faith of Pius VII. More prosaically, the real prospect of British subsidies at last galvanized all the allies. Everything they had accomplished up to now had been by their own efforts. Now, that was over. The next round of fighting would be different.

The armistice bought the allies precious time. While everyone wrangled over protocol, and the allied foreign ministers and Stadion argued over the terms they would present to Napoleon, the armies girded themselves. The Russian army's treasury was all but empty; its supplies almost run dry.[6] Arakcheev's huge, well-trained reserve army was based 440 kilometers east of Moscow; a new force was being trained near Minsk. Russian infrastructures had not changed, and it took fifteen weeks for advance units to reach the front, three months for the bulk of them.[7] With peace guaranteed until August, these reserves poured westward all the summer. Hard marching over vast distances took the same toll on new Russian conscripts as it did on the French. Of a contingent of 37,000 men sent to the front from Russia in March, 2,350 died on the march and 9,600 had to be left behind. There were hospitals set up along the route to help them recover, however, and most later rejoined the colors in time to fight. Unlike the French, proper care ensured those who survived had been toughened, not weakened, by the march.[8] There was time, too, to requisition horses in numbers unimaginable to Napoleon, and train their riders properly. Meanwhile, the king of Saxony's great stud farms had "changed sides," even if their owner had not. The Russians "rehabilitated" and rested tired horses, as they did their soldiers. By the end of summer, 106 new cavalry squadrons reached the army.[9] Alexander had 184,000 men at the front by the time the armistice ended in mid-August.[10] This did not come without problems remarkably similar to those Napoleon faced. Like Napoleon, Alexander had to break his own rules. The age limit was raised to forty; height and health requirements were also relaxed. Married men were taken in ever-increasing numbers into an army where enlistment was for fifteen years, war or no war. "Tens of thousands of women would never see their husbands again and had no right to remarry," as Dominic Lieven notes.[11] There were revolts that frightened provincial governors, however easily put down.[12] Moving men and supplies in the mud of summer did not discriminate between armies, and the carts employed, often pulled by oxen that devoured en route much of the grain meant for the troops, and whose surly, conscripted drivers did little to help, echoed Napoleon's experience the summer before.[13] For all that, enough new boots arrived for the whole army during the armistice; "Pitt's gold" paid the Prussian merchants for new coats and tunics for the line regiments, together with large reams of cloth, free of charge, that Napoleon had gathered for his men in Königsberg (modern Kaliningrad).[14]

The Prussians had not been idle. They numbered over 160,000 men by August, many from the landwehr of dubious quality in battle,[15] it is true, but this was the army that had borne the brunt of Lützen and Bautzen, and was led by formidable commanders.[16] It remained the allied spearhead henceforth; its formidable character was already manifest, its new levies hardening with every engagement. Bernadotte's thirty thousand Swedes were stiffened by German units normally in British service, the King's German Legion among them, to forty thousand and were moving slowly toward Berlin.[17] Francis could summon 150,000 Austrians, many new recruits. It was considerable progress in a short time,[18] but compared to the other powers, he had justification for wanting to avoid war if possible, just as Metternich was equally right that only as the key to the alliance could Austria wield real influence. Nevertheless, Napoleon continued to think they were far less numerous and more thinly spread than they were, telling Eugène, "It is the case . . . that even with every imaginable effort, Austria cannot have more than 100,000 men . . . it is obliged to split them between you (in Italy), Bavaria, and the army corps that is here."[19]

Against this, Napoleon amassed 400,000 infantry and almost 40,000 cavalry in the war zone, not counting Eugène's Italian army or the Bavarians supporting him in Tyrol, the besieged garrisons, or the army in Spain. Yet, "a very high proportion of his strength was illusory."[20] He was now close to "the bottom of the barrel." The army mustering in Saxony was already markedly different from the start of the campaign. Only 250,000 troops were now French; the rest were drawn mainly from the states of the Confederation.[21] Nor were his interior lines still secure. The Cossacks were everywhere, hindering the arrival of reinforcements and supplies, and unnerving the German princes. He told Frederick-Augustus, "It is necessary that Your Majesty take steps to repress the Cossack patrols and partisans that pillage the country and threaten the rear of the army."[22] This was part of a wider problem, far more worrying than the Cossacks, themselves, as he told Maret:

> . . . (S)end a note in the strongest possible terms to the princes . . . to inform them of my discontent about the partisans who carry out acts of brigandage in the rear of the army and are shown favor in their states; I hold them responsible; they must carry out a sweep

to purge the country . . . if this goes on, I will end up seeing bad will in their governments.[23]

Napoleon was lashing out in frustration and suspicion, inadvertently preparing the ground for Metternich's "new diplomacy." He had the Cossacks to thank, and not only them. Napoleon's German heartland was no longer safe in his own mind. He told his commandant in Magdeburg, one of the key fortresses in central Germany, "At the least [sign of] opposition from the inhabitants or the prefect (a Westphalian official), you must put the town under a state of siege and take over its policing."[24]

Napoleon's single biggest problem in the spring campaign had been the absence of his best commanders, signaled by the desperate measure of pulling Soult back from Spain. The rebels of Hamburg kept Davout from him. The city had been retaken, but as unease swirled in the Confederation, the Hanseatic coast became a dangerous, exposed flank should a better commander than Bernadotte exploit it. An example had to be made. "My intention is to deal with Hamburg very severely . . . I will fortify Hamburg . . . in a few months (it will be) one of my strongest places. I will send a corps of 15,000 men to be there permanently."[25] Much as Davout was missed at the front, he had the right man. Napoleon's initial orders reflected a savagery typical of Spain—the immediate execution of "the five most guilty of those who served the rebel government, and the incarceration in France of the rest, mass confiscations of property and the execution of all the officers of the 'Hanseatic Legion',", the rebels' "army." Davout managed to temporize, avoiding the execution of civilians, which was not difficult as Napoleon's designated culprits had all fled to the allied armies. No one was arrested or deported. He took Napoleon's revenge in other, less bloodthirsty ways, bearing the city little love from his time there trying to enforce the blockade. Davout carried out the order to levy a forty-eight-million-franc "war contribution" on Hamburg, fifteen million of which to be paid in kind, in what amounted to the price of a general amnesty.[26] Davout took out his personal revenge through the ruthless demolition of large parts of the city to fortify it, making many already desperate people indigent. He left his mark on Hamburg in that bitter summer. Davout was not recalled to the main army when hostilities resumed in mid-August because Napoleon envisaged him launching a separate attack eastward on Bernadotte, and if possible to retake Berlin, a strategy laced with the desire for personal revenge on a traitor, and forcing Prussia's hand.[27] If revenge dominated Napoleon's mind, Davout was the right man to unleash on Bernadotte, but his continued presence in the North did nothing to solve his real problems of command. There was one surprising arrival, however. On August 14, Murat appeared in Dresden.[28] The army greeted this with a mixture of incredulity and joy: "Excellent news," said one officer, "king Murat is in the city, by the side of the Emperor."[29] Incredulity, indeed. For all his conniving, Murat answered the call. It would not be the last time he oscillated between loyalty and treason.

The Fall of Spain

Napoleon's newfound respect for the guerrillas in northern Spain was well founded; they now posed a genuine military threat, but by diverting a large part the Army of Portugal against them, he left it weakened, and encouraged Wellington to advance out of Portugal in late May and head straight for Jourdan and Joseph, in Burgos. The Anglo-Sicilian invasion of eastern Spain had stalled, but it could not be left unattended. Joseph could count on no aid from Suchet's army. Wellington felt Joseph's sector to be so poorly defended that he transferred his supply base from Portugal to the Basque port of San Sebastian, on the Atlantic coast, which was actually behind Joseph's lines.[30] Wellington moved across northern Spain, keeping north of the Duero, out-flanking Joseph all the while with hard forced marches over difficult country. He wrong-footed the French by crossing countryside so rugged and barren the French had taken it for granted he would avoid it, and so left him unopposed. But supplied by sea from his new base, Wellington could afford to take the risk, while his well-fed, well-rested men proved up to the rigors he imposed on them, if not without complaint. With their line of retreat under constant threat, the French abandoned Burgos—whose defenses had been so neglected it could not long withstand another siege[31]—and then Valladolid, with Wellington always to their north. Joseph's only hope was to fall back to a defensible position and hope he could muster enough troops to withstand a pitched battle, by combining the Armies of the Center, South, and Portugal, whose very names seemed to mock Napoleon's ambitions by now. By June 19, the main French army of about fifty-seven thousand men had concentrated around the Basque town of Vitoria, in what they hoped would prove a defensible position. It was a badly weakened army, its ranks increasingly demoralized.[32] Napoleon knew as much. He ordered Clarke to concentrate the gendarmerie of the Spanish armies into one unit, "to repress desertion" but their morale had to be rebuilt, by ensuring they were paid, before they could be trusted "to form a line against desertion."[33] Close to eighty thousand allied troops—battle-hardened and self-confident—bore down on them, but from where, Joseph knew not. Neither Joseph nor Jourdan really wanted to fight, but unless Wellington's advance was halted, they faced being run out of Spain altogether. As was so often the case in 1813, Vitoria was a "political" battle.

Vitoria stands up a small valley, with high hills to the north and south, along the main highway leading to France to the northeast, which had to be defended. Joseph and Jourdan assumed that Wellington would drive at them head-on, up the valley from the southwest, and concentrated most of their troops accordingly, but they detached a whole division to protect their swollen baggage train and head for the French frontier with five years' worth of accumulated booty and a horde of female camp followers. As Charles Esdaile has pointed out, Wellington had been trying to outflank the French right for weeks, with success, and "it seems barely credible that Joseph and Jourdan failed to realize the same might happen again."[34] Only at the last moment, on June 21, did they perceive that a large British force was coming out of the hills and down the narrow valleys to their north. The Army of the South remained in position facing south, where Joseph still thought the main strike would come, but he shifted most of the Army of Portugal north, not to the passes but beyond Vitoria, to guard the line of retreat. Only the pitiful reserve of Joseph's personal guard remained as the last line. The first fighting did begin in the south, where Hill, Wellington, Cole, and the Spanish attacked the Army of the South. The fighting was fierce, especially around the bridges, and Jourdan was forced to commit most of the Army of the Center to prevent Hill outflanking him to the south, pulling the French reserves hither and yon at an early stage. Wellington moved about the field all the time, adjusting operations and encouraging his commanders. The main strike from the north came after midday, by three columns under George Dalhousie. The march had been difficult and fell behind schedule, but a local told Wellington about an undefended bridge between Dalhousie's crossing points and himself. He took quick advantage of it, when the first of Dalhousie's columns, under the impetuous General T. Picton, came crashing out of the hills, and stormed a bridge to the north. It was fiercely defended, but the concentration of Wellington's men and his own swept the French away. Wellington halted to regroup. Dalhousie's other two columns met fierce resistance from quickly scrambled French units, but by now, French resistance was crumbling, and Jourdan and Joseph thought only of retreat and saving what they could. They regrouped to fight a holding action at Vitoria, massing all their seventy guns. Wellington matched them, and "the hottest artillery duel of the Peninsular War" began.[35] By now, the French had too few infantry to support the guns, and the allies swept over them.

The French were disintegrating, but Wellington had intended Sir Thomas Graham's force to deliver the killer blow. Graham was sent on an arduous march, pushing eastward across hard country, behind Dalhousie, and was meant to cut the main highway to France north of Vitoria, thus enveloping the French with a minimum of combat. Jourdan had almost inadvertently placed the Army of Portugal in his path, however, when he miscalculated where Dalhousie would arrive. Graham outnumbered the French, but had no way of knowing this, and advanced cautiously. Nor did he know Vitoria was his for the taking and encirclement could be imminent. He stuck to his brief, enabling Joseph and Jourdan with what was left of their forces, to escape to

Pamplona by a narrow mountain road, fighting brave rearguard actions as they went. Graham has been much criticized by historians for this. For Charles Esdaile, had Graham shown "a modicum of initiative," the whole French army would have been lost.[36] At the time, Wellington actually praised him. "By God, you have had hard work on the other side. Graham hit it admirably," he enthused,[37] but his subsequent action turned Vitoria into Wellington's Ulm, not the Austerlitz it might have been. Yet, after a monthlong march of over two hundred miles from his winter quarters in northern Portugal, Wellington brought four separate columns together in good order, an achievement equal to Napoleon's march from the Channel to the Danube in 1805, "an example of strategic brilliance that is without equal in the annals of the Peninsular war."[38]

Wellington may not have had his Austerlitz, and the core of the French army at Vitoria formed the force he would soon face in France, but its power was broken. The two sides' losses were roughly equal—seven hundred dead, four thousand wounded each—but the French could afford them far less. They lost over 2,500 more as prisoners; the allies had 266 missing, probably looting and drunk.[39] All but one of Joseph's 152 guns were lost,[40] and even the sole survivor was abandoned at Pamplona.[41] Over four hundred caissons and vast quantities of supplies—boots, clothing, ammunition—had to be left behind, so narrow and steep was the only escape route left to them. Joseph's archive and five million francs recently sent from his brother were abandoned.[42] He also lost his private luggage, in which was loaded almost obscene wealth. This plunder, now scattered like litter before the exhausted British and impoverished locals, possibly did more to save his skin than Graham's rigid adherence to orders. The Hussar Regiment that actually took Vitoria ran riot when they should have pressed the retreat. Napoleon's gold weighed down the pockets of one of their officers—after an enlisted man took pity on his wounded superior, and filled his pockets with gold and silver coins, so plentiful was his own haul.[43] Joseph had looted the Bourbons' art collection—Titian, Velázquez, Murillo among them—and when Wellington offered to return them, he was allowed to keep them for his efforts. Many now hang in his London residence, Apsley House, "Number

One, London." There were also the women. If they escaped lightly, it was often because the victorious army was either too exhausted, or because the lust for gold surpassed all others.[44] Among those who made it to France was Soult's mistress, María de la Paz.[45] At least the French could move fast now, and they did. They did not stay long in Pamplona. They had gone by the time Wellington caught up with them on June 24. A few days later, the main force under Joseph slunk over the Pyrenees into France by the pass of Roncevaux, the site of the legendary deadly struggle between Roland and the Moors, immortalized by an anonymous poet a thousand years earlier.

On July 1, Napoleon then appointed Soult the commander in chief in Spain, with the ominous title of "my lieutenant general in Spain," telling Cambacérès that even if Vitoria were retaken, Joseph would remain relieved "of the command of which he is utterly incapable."[46] To Joseph, he was brutal: "I want you to meddle no more in the business of my armies."[47] The magnitude of Wellington's victory justified Napoleon's response; it left him bereft of Soult, as well as Davout. That magnitude was evident to Napoleon because he foresaw the end in Spain, and became obsessed with keeping it quiet in France: "No officer of the King of Spain or any Spanish refugee is to pass (north of) the (river) Garonne. All the refugees are to be concentrated at Auch or Agen," towns in the southwest, far from large cities, he told Clarke. Nothing about any of this was to get into the newspapers. He was almost as brutal on himself as on his brother: "All the nonsense in Spain comes from my misplaced good faith in the king."[48] His real fear was Joseph, and it went beyond incompetence: "Given the bad attitude he has shown in Spain . . . his presence (in Paris) would sow trouble in the Regency."[49] He now faced the allies without Davout and Soult.

Soult's journey to his new command was cloaked in the secrecy of a coup, which in a way, it was. He left Dresden at night, incognito under the name of one of his aides; when he got to Paris, he went straight to Clarke, and then to Cambacérès, who briefed him on the situation. He was to stay in Paris no more than twelve hours.[50] One person Napoleon trusted with all this was Marie-Louise, telling her Soult was on his way to take over in Spain "in place of the king who is no soldier and listens to nothing." She was to keep this quiet.[51] It was a level of trust and responsibility he never placed in Josephine.

The greatest result of Vitoria was not a battlefield triumph. For Charles Esdaile, in its aftermath, "the Bonaparte kingdom of Spain collapsed like a house of cards."[52] Suchet evacuated Valencia on July 5, falling back on Zaragoza. Only coastal Catalonia remained, and the besieged garrisons in San Sebastian and Pamplona. In bitter irony, Joseph now holed up in Bayonne,[53] to learn the fate Napoleon had in store for him, as had the Bourbons he had replaced five years before. This was what Soult found, when he arrived at a disintegrating front on July 12.

From Prague to Dresden

The nervous secrecy that shrouded the returns to France of Joseph, Soult, and Catherine of Württemberg revealed Napoleon's fear that Paris would see his real circumstances for itself, whispers in the wind that he was in real danger. Napoleon was anything but oblivious to the shallow foundations his regime rested on, but the insouciance with which he treated the peace talks in Prague revealed, in equal measure, that he refused to render France what it wanted, what might save him: peace. He was in a weaker position than his enemies. He feared their power, and sought the "silver bullet" of the decisive victory that Bautzen had almost given him.

The Congress of Prague convened on July 29. No monarch came in person, sending only their ministers. Metternich now made it ever clearer to the allies that, whatever its outcome, Austria would remain "favorable to them," even should Napoleon accept his minimum terms and the allies refuse them.[54] Yet, Francis insisted he had to work for peace and not provoke Napoleon against an Austria still too weak to fight him; he was prepared to cede Napoleon the Illyrian provinces permanently. This potential tightrope suited Metternich for the moment, maintaining the semblance of neutrality in negotiations to appease Francis and dupe Napoleon.[55] Napoleon now switched his tactics.

Abandoning hopes of detaching Alexander from the alliance, he concentrated on trying to keep Austria out of it. This may have worked with Francis, but he had to go through Metternich, and when Caulaincourt asked Metternich what was needed either to keep Austria neutral or to renew the French alliance, Metternich went straight to the allies, reassuring them beyond any doubt of "the loyalty we declare toward our allies."[56] Napoleon felt sure Francis would not fight him, and that he could control Metternich. The former assumption held some truth; the latter was delusion. Perhaps the best evidence of Metternich's determination to lead Austria into the war when the time was right is a letter he wrote to Elenore, his wife, at the very end of the conference on August 10, saying he was pleased by the time he had been able to buy at Prague, for by now an army of 150,000 was in Bohemia, ready to join the allies.[57] Two days later, bonfires were lit on the hills around Prague, signaling that the congress was over, and that Austria had declared war on Napoleon.[58]

This was no impromptu decision. The Austrian commanders had been concerting their military plans with the allies for weeks before the conference convened. On July 9, Frederick-William and Alexander met at the beautiful country house of Trachenberg, ostensibly to welcome Bernadotte into the alliance and brief him of their strategy. The working assumption already was that Austria would enter the war. What emerged was the "Trachtenberg plan": With Austria in the alliance, a more aggressive strategy seemed possible. Four army groups were created, the largest of 230,000 men in Bohemia, under Schwarzenberg; one of 110,000 in the north, under Bernadotte; another of 95,000 in Silesia under Blücher; and a reserve under Bennigsen, of 60,000. They assumed Napoleon would take the offensive against one of them, probably Schwarzenberg, and the others would move to his aid, surrounding the French. Whoever was not attacked was to move to the help of he who had been. The meeting place of the allied armies would be "the enemy camp." When Francis heard of this, he signaled his commitment by asking Schwarzenberg to draw up an Austrian plan for its contribution. This was entrusted to Josef Wenzel von Radetzky, one of the finest military minds of the era, who liaised with the Prussian general Auguste Neidhardt von Gneisenau. Through

Radetzky's expertise, finessed by Metternich's diplomacy, Napoleon at last lost his numerical advantage: By August, Radetzky had brought together 489,000 allied troops against him, while simultaneously raising a new Austrian army.[59]

Radetzky added a crucial element to the plan, obviously drawn from recent experience of Napoleon's key weakness: The allies were to avoid direct combat with Napoleon; rather, they were to strike at his weakest links, the marshals acting independently of the main army. In the context of the history of the Grande Armée, the corps system, without the great commanders, was now a liability, not the backbone of operations. The refined "Trachtenberg plan" marked the abandonment of many key maxims of eighteenth century warfare. No longer were armies to retire automatically behind fortresses and hold them at great cost, or to occupy strategic positions in the landscape and await attack. The allies, by perpetually harassing isolated French corps, and standing ready to converge on a major engagement should one develop, had evolved their own version of the "war of movement" Napoleon had made his own.[60] Now, they would see if it worked.

Dresden

Napoleon fixed on a plan of campaign that wrong-footed the allies' new strategy completely. He did something unheard-of, and went on the defensive to hold Dresden, with its vast military stores and his newly recovered ally, Frederick-Augustus. For reasons both political and logistical, he could not let it fall: "What is important to me is to avoid being cut off from Dresden and the Elbe . . . I will care little if I am cut off from France."[61] He had been refortifying the city for some time. Its was entrusted to St. Cyr, where the main army of 250,000 men was concentrated; St. Cyr was to harass and attack the allies wherever he found them, although it was evident that Napoleon was not sure where their main force was, but should he encounter superior forces, he was to fall back on the city. Napoleon moved his headquarters to Bautzen, east of Dresden, with the guard and cavalry reserve.[62] He then detached

120,000 men north. He told Bertrand on August 13 that "the aim is to bear down on Berlin." Bertrand was to batter his way there if he had to:

> If you find fortified villages or redoubts, above all, shell them before
> you attack . . . neither the blochaus, nor the exterior or interior of
> a redoubt and resist shelling by superior artillery . . . If you find
> Berlin well defended, choose a point in the wall and make a breach
> in it . . . and at the same time, set fire to the city by firing in forty
> shells at a time.[63]

This was clarity and determination bordering on obsession. The importance of this operation to Napoleon is in no doubt, yet it was not his main objective. This was uncharacteristic of him. His main objective was to hold Dresden, but he divided his forces and considerably weakened them. Moreover, he chose Oudinot to lead the advance, whose experience of independent command in Russia had been anything but successful. Jonathon Riley has rightly said Soult would have been the ideal choice, but this was a concrete example of how badly Spain stretched Napoleon.[64] Napoleon soon revealed himself unprecedentedly insecure. He put his plan to the marshals not for questions but for their opinions. He got them. St. Cyr felt he greatly underestimated Bernadotte's strength; Marmont disputed the wisdom of dividing the army so seriously: "I greatly fear lest on the day on which Your Majesty wins a great victory, and believes you have won a decisive battle, you may learn you have lost two."[65]

Napoleon soon found himself more confused. The day he reached Bautzen, August 17, he learned of the Russian reinforcements pouring into Silesia. He ordered all available forces east of Dresden to strike Blücher before the Russians reached him, leaving St. Cyr exposed to Schwarzenberg's Army of Bohemia south of Dresden. Change of plan followed change of plan over the next week, shifting his troops from east to south, and back again, as Blücher fell back according to the allied strategy, of which Napoleon was wholly ignorant. As late as August 24, Napoleon was still intent on sweeping south toward Prague and getting behind Schwarzenberg, leaving Dresden to look after itself. "As for the king of Saxony," he told Maret, "tell him, if the enemy presses Dresden, it will not inconvenience me if he joins me, or takes a small house in the country," presumably until Napoleon found time to lift the siege of his capital. He was looking over his shoulder, too: "Spread very vague news around Paris, leading it to be understood that there has been a big victory over the Army of Silesia, that Berlin has been taken, and of even more important events to follow."[66] Falling on Schwarzenberg's rear was the right course of action, but news reached Napoleon on August 25 that Oudinot had been checked two days before, on his march north. Eleven miles south of Berlin, at Grossbeeren, his advance units under Reynier ran into not a hesitant Bernadotte but a resolute Prussian force attached to Friedrich von Bülow. Reynier took the village after determined resistance, although Bertrand's men met with heavy artillery fire at Blankenfelde, nearby. Eventually, the road was cleared and the French bivouacked for the night. Bülow heard the guns, however, and marched toward them with thirty-eight thousand troops, a far smaller force than Oudinot's, who had left his command strung out along the march route, a failing he had not shaken since Russia. As evening and a heavy rain fell, Bülow got very close to Reynier, undetected, and unleashed a ferocious artillery bombardment on the French, in an eerie reversal of Napoleon's words to Bertrand. With their powder soon too rain-drenched to fire, the Prussian infantry fixed bayonets and charged the French. In a savage, hand-to-hand fight, Bülow's men took Grossbeeren and held it when Reynier counterattacked in like, desperate fashion.[67] It cost the small Prussian force 1,000 men to Oudinot's 3,000 and fourteen guns, a fraction of his 120,000 strong Army of Berlin, but Oudinot assumed he was outnumbered and ordered a headlong retreat to the fortress of Wittenberg, on the Elbe.[68] Napoleon's first reaction was to march north to Oudinot's aid and engage Blücher, but word reached him from St. Cyr on August 22 that Schwarzenberg was now before the city with an imposing force he had no hope of holding, alone. Napoleon scoffed to Maret, "Whenever I am absent, they exaggerate the enemy's strength."[69] Nevertheless, he swung around yet again, with the guard and all his forces bar Macdonald, who was to hold off Blücher. Even as Napoleon went to Oudinot's aid, an outnumbered St. Cyr was driven from his forward lines back upon the city. Wittgenstein got as far as the southern suburbs by the 23rd, and only a ferocious counterattack on the 25th threw him back.

Napoleon almost changed course, again, seeing a chance to fall upon Schwarzenberg's rear, but it was now clear that St. Cyr was on the point of being overwhelmed when Schwarzenberg regrouped, and that he had the main allied army before him. The news came from Murat and Napoleon's trusted aide, General Gourgaud, and was not to be dismissed lightly.[70] The next day, the guard, the reserve cavalry, and the corps of Marmont and Victory swung back to Dresden, led by Napoleon. Only Vandamme was left to attempt to cut the allied lines to the rear. David Chandler saw this as a crucial opportunity missed.[71] Writing from the allies' perspective, Dominic Lieven agrees, believing Napoleon had a victory within his grasp of the magnitude of Austerlitz or Jena, so devastated would Schwarzenberg have been,[72] but losing Dresden was too big a risk to take on many levels.

Now, it was the allies' turn to fall into confusion and indecision. Their nerve was not helped by Napoleon's sense of occasion. He galloped ahead of his men, dodging the Russian artillery fire raking the suburbs, and put himself at the entrance to the main bridge, directing operations. An unnerved trio of Alexander, Frederick-William, and Schwarzenberg watched this from the heights to the south, as the dreaded cries of "*Vive l'Empereur*" rose up to their ears. Napoleon had marched his young conscripts hard—120 miles during his four days of indecision[73]—but he arrived with 70,000 of them. None set a better example than the guard. Gone were the days of being chauffeured to battle in ox-drawn carts. The Young Guard did the last stretch to Dresden at the double, just behind Napoleon, under a hail of allied fire, often singing as they went, crossing the river on ferries manned by the guard marines.[74]

Napoleon was outnumbered—the allies mustered 170,000—but he held several advantages. Many of the Austrian troops had had a harder time on the march than the French. Johann von Klenau's men crossed rugged mountain paths, cut by streams turned into torrents by heavy rain, "drenched to the bone," many without shoes or greatcoats one observer reported, reaching the front only on August 23. "The Austrians are always late and it is their incurable slowness that constantly leads to their defeat," snarled one Russian commander.[75] Their bedraggled state led Schwarzenberg to delay any attack for a day, until August 25. The allies were strung out over fifteen kilometers, while the French were safe behind their lines, ready first to defend well-fortified positions, and then to counterattack, all of which offset their lack of numbers.[76] Above all, the allies had a dithering, uncoordinated command structure that the expanded coalition made worse. Alexander meddled, and would not keep his distance. Schwarzenberg was a "political appointment" as commander in chief, a condition Metternich demanded as a condition for joining the war. The title meant little with the tsar present. Then there were the bitter rivalries within the Russian high command.

This was obvious from the start. Observing Napoleon's arrival, Alexander wanted to break off the action altogether: It went against the agreed policy of avoiding direct battle with Napoleon; the supply trains were far off, separated from the armies by difficult terrain and their position was open to a counterattack.[77] In contrast, Frederick-William—the onetime "ninny of 1806"—was outspokenly bellicose.[78] A new voice was present that seemingly persuaded Alexander to fight, Jean-Victor Moreau. Alexander had coaxed Napoleon's old comrade-turned-foe back from America to join his staff, and Bernadotte had bequeathed him his own marshal's sword for the occasion. It was, somehow typical, that having decided on battle, they then postponed it until the next day. It did not work out this way. No one really knows who gave the order to attack Dresden on August 26. It may have been that the order to postpone took too long to reach the front lines,[79] or that Schwarzenberg was persuaded by his staff officers to ignore his orders. Recent research by Munro Price in the papers of Carl Clam-Martinic, Schwarzenberg's aide-de-camp, claims that Schwarzenberg wanted to withdraw, feeling his own objective—to draw Napoleon's main army away from Blücher—had been achieved. Clam-Martinic blamed the order to attack on Alexander's change of mind under the influence of Toll, a staff officer.[80] Whatever the truth, at 4:00 P.M., the signal to storm Dresden was given, as all the commanders stood aghast, their plans in tatters.

No such muddle hindered Napoleon. St. Cyr had turned the nearby villages and suburbs of Dresden into a labyrinth of barricaded streets, houses full of loopholes for rifles and open spaces crisscrossed by wooden palisades. Five artillery batteries covered the area, and its large walled park, the Grosser Garten, was a small fortress. St. Cyr commanded the city, the last line, covered by batteries of heavy guns. Napoleon organized three troop concentrations as the second line of defense: Murat, with an improvised corps, on the right, anchored on the Elbe; Ney in the center, and Mortier on the left, both supported by the guard. The first line, in the suburbs, was composed of some of St. Cyr's garrison.

This was what the allies launched themselves upon. Their onslaught did not lack determination. At one point, Austrian troops stormed a French redoubt held by Ney's men, by charging into the ditch in front of it, up the side and ripping down the wooden palisade.[81] Wittgenstein's Russians pressed Mortier hard, but they had to take the main bridge across the Elbe to reach the city. The closer they came, the more carnage the French guns across the river wreaked on them. St. Cyr's lines held firm: When General Friedrich von Kleist's Prussians took the Grosser Garten, it was short-lived. The French retook it in bloody hand-to-hand combat, leaving a sight as much like an abattoir as a battlefield behind them. "I went into the Grosser Garten," a Saxon officer recalled, ". . . the dead lay all around me."[82] Vandamme's corps of 40,000, holding the far left of the French line, was bearing down on a badly outnumbered Eugen of Württemberg and his 12,500 Russians, and threatening to cut off the allies' best line of retreat well before Napoleon launched his main counterattack at 5:30 P.M. He spared nothing. Led by Mortier and Ney, the guard, Young and Old, fought from the outset. Men who had, literally, run to their posts a couple of hours before, refreshed with only brandy and a shave, went into combat. Several officers were wounded in the first sally from the Prina gate; all the drummers of the sharp-shooter regiment were mown down by a burst of grapeshot,[83] but with their drums silenced, they charged Kleist's men at bayonet point. The guard then stormed on and retook the Grosser Garten by nightfall. In the center, Ney led two divisions of the Old Guard against

Schwarzenberg's Austrians, who were so shaken that he had to commit the crack Austrian Grenadiers—his most valuable reserves—to stop a rout.[84] It was now dark and pouring rain, as the French—most of the lost ground recovered—began to bivouac, when the Austrians launched a rare night attack on the Old Guard. Their commander, Pierre Dumoustier, still with them despite a shattered leg, inspired resistance that drove the Austrians off. Hundreds of allied prisoners were taken in these actions; Cambronne's Guard light infantry captured a whole battalion.[85] All this was the work of men who had marched hard all day, and fought almost immediately; the Old Guard only got their orders to march to Dresden at half past 1:00 P.M. on the 26th. Meant to arrive at 7:00 P.M., they were still intended as the reserve.[86] Napoleon stayed with the guard all day, and was always close to the fighting. Soaked to the skin, he toured all the Young Guard positions that night, before returning to Dresden.[87] Only now, in the dark of night, did Victor and Marmont's corps arrive, sodden, from Bautzen. Marmont was sent to bolster Ney in the center, Victor, to Murat, at last bringing Napoleon up to his full strength of 120,000.[88] Away from the main fighting, Eugen bravely held off Vandamme, positioning his guns and infantry well in the woods and gullies around Krietzschwitz, to keep open the Peterswalde road, but he had committed all his reserves, and knew the French would overwhelm him soon, and so envelop the allied right completely.[89] He had no hope of reinforcements. Schwarzenberg decided to concentrate his forces in the center, leaving Wittgenstein and Vincenz Frederick Bianchi, on the left, largely to their own devices.

Napoleon took the opposite approach entirely, in a rare departure from his usual preference to attack in strength from the center. St. Cyr and Marmont were left there with fifty thousand men and the Old Guard as the only reserve. Vandamme was to continue pressing Wittgenstein on the far left, and Ney and Mortier, on the inner left with thirty-five thousand, mainly the Young Guard. Murat and Victor, with thirty-five thousand, were on the right. The pouring rain continued, always the signal for bloody hand-to-hand fighting, as gunpowder became useless. Well before dawn, the word went down the line to fix bayonets and draw swords.[90] Napoleon put himself right behind Ney, close to the front

line, and gave the order to attack at 6:00 A.M. The battles on the flanks saw the
French sweep their opponents aside; on the left, Mortier drove Wittgenstein's
demoralized troops back, and was turning the allied right, threatening to cut
Eugen off from the main body. The fighting was ferocious. The village of Reick
was taken by Ney by midday, but only after horrendous hand-to-hand combat
and bombardment by the French artillery that set its wooden buildings ablaze,
where the allied wounded were burned alive.[91] On the right, Murat proved
much more than a cavalry commander, under Napoleon's eye. Supported by the
Guard cavalry, Victor's corps broke Bianchi's line by ferocious bayonet charges,
and pinned them with their backs to the River Weisseritz, swollen by the rains.
Bianchi's men were driven, literally, into it. Dead, scattered, or taken prisoner,
the allied left had ceased to exist. In the center, however, Marmont and St. Cyr
were outnumbered, and held by the redoubtable Austrian Grenadiers and the
Prussian reserves, respectively. In contrast to the allied commanders, Napoleon was immersed in the battle. At one point, while urging his men on from
the front, he took personal control of an artillery battery and landed a direct
hit. He had no idea his famed "dead eye" had found the allied commanders.
He narrowly missed Alexander,[92] but he scored a direct hit on Moreau, who
was left with a tangled left knee and a shattered right leg. Carried to a nearby
farmhouse, he had both legs amputated by Alexander's personal surgeon, and
died a week later.[93] Napoleon often regretted showing Moreau mercy all those
years ago. He did not know he had corrected his own error, nor what else his
gunner's "dead eye" had brought about. He never knew how close he came
that day to turning Dresden into a "political" victory. Schwarzenberg was so
shaken he offered Emperor Francis his resignation. Alexander jumped at this,
telling Metternich he was going to appoint himself "Generalissimo" of all the
armies, and leave effective field command to Moreau. Metternich countered
by threatening to leave the coalition if he did so. Napoleon's cannonball put an
end to the tsar's "power grab," even before news came that Francis had refused
to accept Schwarzenberg's resignation.[94]

Napoleon halted the offensive at 4:00 P.M., fully expecting to fight again the
next day.[95] He did so in triumph, leading the way at the head of one thousand

prisoners, followed by about ten thousand more. He was drenched, his hat squashed on his head, his coat covered in dust, but it hardly mattered.[96] He had mauled the allies badly: They lost thirty-eight thousand men—fourteen thousand of them killed or wounded—the French, barely ten thousand,[97] although the guard had suffered greatly. One hundred officers and two thousand men were casualties; nearly all its generals had been wounded.[98] Napoleon had spared the beautiful baroque city the horrors of bombardment, fire, and pillage. That would come to it at the close of a yet more horrendous war, in the next century. Berlin may not have fallen, but Paris could be told truthfully of another resounding victory. He did not hide his exhaustion to Cambacérès: "I am so tired, and so busy, I cannot write to you at length . . . The business went well."[99] It had, but it was the last time.

Napoleon did not appreciate how close Vandamme was to completing the encirclement, or how shaken Alexander and the others were. Schwarzenberg ordered a general retreat into Bohemia, and rushed units of the Russian Imperial Guard and Barclay's corps to help Eugen hold the Peterswalde road, one of three designated escape routes, and the only one under direct threat. Barclay did not, for reasons never made clear, follow his orders, and actually clogged the central—but narrow—Dippoldiswalde road as his men upset the carefully calculated numbers assigned to each route.[100] Nevertheless, Eugen was able to keep the road open and prepare to counterattack. Nor did Murat show the élan he was famed for in pursuing the retreating Austrian center.[101] Napoleon lied like one of his bulletins to Marie-Louise when he told her that night, "I got on my horse and got after them." There was a time—in 1805, 1806, and even in 1809—when he need not have worried. Murat and his resplendent cavalry harried almost instinctively. No more. He may have lied even more when he added, "My health is good."[102] He issued a string of disjointed orders, showing no real direction as to pursuing the allies. He told Berthier on the 28th that he would set out for Prina[103]—toward Vandamme—but he did not leave the city, and left the pursuit to his subordinates. Instead, he reviewed his "children" on the 30th, awarding one hundred of Cambronne's sharpshooters the Légion d'honneur, and another eight to the marines who manned the ferry under heavy fire.[104] He did find time to upbraid Berthier for allowing one of his aides to let Murat know too much—he feared—about his communications with the Austrians: "I don't know why you let the king of Naples know . . . So do I owe it to him to let him know my intentions? You have very poor scribes."[105] His performance on the field notwithstanding, Napoleon knew enough about Murat's own political maneuverings to make him wary. Yet, later that same day, he told Murat "This news about the death of Moreau is coming at me from all sides, I need to know if it's true. As soon as you're sure, let me know."[106] Napoleon was needed in the saddle, and he was not there. Drenched to the skin after the battle, and exhausted by his own admission, Napoleon seemed unable to retain his energy, and may have fallen seriously ill. It is impossible to know with precision, but it soon emerged that his commanders were unable to coordinate their efforts without him. As at Bautzen, a chance to encircle and erase the allied threat was missed. Despite the treacherous weather and awful mountain roads, Schwarzenberg's armies eluded Napoleon.[107] Napoleon did not get another chance.

The allied retreat was not without its blunders. Vandamme could now get behind the allies and block their exit from the mountain passes, as they emerged at the other side. Alone, Eugen stood little chance against him, but dug in to do his best around the village of Kulm on the morning of August 29. By midday, urgent cries for help reached allied headquarters. Alexander saw the danger and ordered an Austrian division under General Count Hieronymus von Colloredo to aid Eugen. Colloredo refused, telling the tsar of all the Russias he took his orders from Schwarzenberg. The day, indeed, the war, was saved by Metternich, who had remained with the armies. This most unsoldierly of men took it upon himself to order the Austrian general forward, and was obeyed.[108] In the meantime, Eugen remained outnumbered two-to-one, but Vandamme committed his forces to the assault piecemeal, allowing the Russians to survive. The village was taken and retaken in ferocious fighting where the Russians, low on ammunition, resorted to the bayonet.[109] Ostermann-Tolstoy added to his colorful reputation by having his arm blown off.[110] It rid Eugen of a nuisance who wanted to abandon the defense of the road and fight in the hills.[111] The Russians were battered, but Vandamme underestimated them badly, telling Berthier they were "in a state of complete rout,"[112] giving Napoleon a false idea of the situation and denying himself reinforcements, just as those ordered forward by Metternich began to arrive. Their first intervention came at 5:00 P.M., when Vandamme's last assault of the day was caught by surprise, seemingly out of nowhere, by the heavy cavalry of the Russian Imperial Guard, supported by lancers, who did the real damage.[113] As night fell, Alexander, Frederick-William, Schwarzenberg, and Barclay had arrived, at the head of almost fifty thousand men. The next morning, Vandamme was quickly surrounded. Only the road to Dresden seemed open, but von Kleist's Prussians had made their way to Kulm by an unmarked mountain path, behind Vandamme. Now isolated by superior forces, Vandamme failed to fight his way out and was captured, with about ten thousand of his men.[114] The allies lost about the same in casualties, but over half of them— twenty-eight hundred—were Guardsmen.[115] Kulm was a victory that far surpassed its actual military importance. It was a "mini-Auerstedt," with Eugen as Davout. The tensions that followed the defeat at Dresden now eased as a whole French corps simply ceased to exist. All the armies had had their parts to play, and the sight of a hated, exploitative French commander being jeered by the Saxon peasants—"crocodile," "poisonous snake," "enjoy Siberia!"—could only have raised their spirits.[116] Alexander's face shone with joy, one of his staff recalled, as he rode across the field of victory in which he had played a part, erasing—at least in his mind—the ignominy of Austerlitz.[117] In Egypt, Napoleon's men shot off the nose of the Sphinx, or so the legend goes, but they did not wipe the smile off his face. It was the same at Dresden.

Napoleon had not paid attention to this, relying on Vandamme for news, which was foolhardy, and reviewing the Young Guard rather than pressing it forward to support him. St. Cyr lost von Kleist as he slipped away to Kulm over the mountains. Once again, the corps system appeared obsolete. More bad news rained down on Napoleon. News of Oudinot's defeat reached him and, soon afterward, became worse. When Napoleon swung west, to confront the allies at Dresden, he left Macdonald with one hundred thousand troops to shadow Blücher, with orders to push Blücher back a safe distance, and then take a good defensive position. Macdonald halted at the junction of the rivers Katzbach and Wütende, but in disjointed fashion, his four columns scattered over a wide area. All his plans were thrown into disarray when the same weather front drenching Dresden doused the area with heavy rain on August 26, when Blücher, who had decided to chance his luck by attacking, blundered into Macdonald. For all the poor visibility, Blücher managed to occupy a plateau just across the rivers from the French. Macdonald then sent two divisions to seize the plateau, and a third to shadow a Russian corps that was actually too far away to threaten him. Blücher had concentrated his forces; Macdonald had not, and remained outnumbered, unable to bring his full strength to bear on Blücher. As at Dresden and Kulm, with their powder sodden, the armies fought with bayonets and musket butts, the deadlock broken by a Russian cavalry charge that pushed the French back over the rivers, now raging torrents, where many were drowned. With good cavalry at his disposal, Blücher drove on in one of the best executed pursuits of the Napoleonic Wars. Macdonald's rearguard formed squares to shield the main body, but unable to fire their muskets, they could not withstand the Russian heavy cavalry for long. Of the thirty-five thousand men Macdonald lost, most were prisoners. One whole corps was completely cut off and surrendered en masse, for the loss of four thousand men and sixteen guns.[118]

Napoleon was so ill-informed about Vandamme, he showed a mixture of opinionated anger and ignorance. On September 1, he confessed to St. Cyr, "This wretched Vandamme, who seems to have gotten himself killed, didn't leave a sentinel on the mountains nor any kind of reserve; he was engulfed from behind, with no idea of it."[119] Of Macdonald, he told Berthier the same day, "Tell him I have no idea about his army, since I know nothing of his losses . . . nor his present position." What Napoleon could tell him was that "the environs of Bautzen have been ruined," and he would do well to defend Görlitz, a defensive position east of Dresden, "well placed to provide the means to live."[120] Saxony, a "land of milk and honey" in July, was now becoming a wasteland. Metternich saw it, too, and took heart: "How long will he continue to play this game in a country where he is already living on horse meat, is difficult to say . . . he runs the risk of being completely worn down."[121]

The start of the campaign had handed Napoleon his dream—"the big battle"—and he won it well. But the allies had read him correctly. They were wrong to divert from their plan and offer him battle, but when they reverted to the "Trachtenberg plan," they saw the victory of Dresden slip through Napoleon's fingers. Metternich put it perfectly: "Our war, which is entirely based on the avoidance of major field battles, is very well suited to this end," that of exhausting Napoleon.[122] For all their squabbles, the allies had a plan. In contrast, a week afterward, Napoleon did not even know how badly he had lost. All he could do, as the new month began, was tell his marshals he no longer intended to advance into Bohemia, "this operation is no longer in line with my military position." All he could do was to regroup around Dresden, where a reserve would be formed "to go wherever circumstances demanded."[123] Berthier was told to be as vague as possible for *Le Moniteur*, about "the events that have taken place," and to publish only extracts from reports, not the whole text. "It is not my way to give out much praise . . . This is the way to satisfy the just ambition of the officers who want to see their names in print."[124] It was hardly Alexander's glow of joy.

11

LEIPZIG: THE BATTLE LOST, SEPTEMBER–OCTOBER 1813

A Time of Troubles: September 1813

Napoleon has often been accused of dithering indecision after Dresden, of staying overlong there as he had in Moscow, not knowing what course to take. This is not quite fair. Napoleon had a plan, the original one, to take Berlin and knock Prussia out of the war. On September 2, he told Marmont—who had turned back from the Katzbach with Napoleon to shadow the Prussians to the east[1]—"Attack the enemy vanguard . . . I await the outcome of this day to start operations on the other side. All this is thus very urgent."[2] The urgency was made clear in an order dispatched to Ney. Oudinot's defeat had caused havoc—the Cossacks were now loose around Bautzen and disrupting communications—and Ney was to sort it out. Napoleon intended to move north, making his new headquarters at Luckau, but Ney was to drive ahead to Baruth, from whence "you will be only three days' march from Berlin . . . and the attack should take place between the 9th and 10th." Napoleon had clarity, but it was based on an array of poor judgments.

He underestimated the enemy Ney faced—"This whole nest of Cossacks and that jug of poor Landwehr infantry are falling back on Berlin from all sides . . . You understand well the need to move fast to profit from the disarray of the Great Army of Bohemia." Napoleon attributed Oudinot's defeat to his own stupidity and said as much to Ney: "It is truly hard to be as brainless as the Duke of Reggio . . . (he) never took on the enemy, and he had the 'art' to use his corps separately. If he had acted properly, he would have won everywhere."[3] Napoleon's justified lambasting of Oudinot blinded him to the real situation—that Bülow was a good commander at the head of good troops. He was right about Oudinot, but in Ney he sent a man with the same proclivities to right things. It did not help when Napoleon humiliated Oudinot by subordinating him to Ney for the coming offensive. Napoleon was bereft of acumen, compounded by the lack of common sense, among his marshals. He told Marmont, "I am sending an aide-de-camp to assess the state of things on your side. Your correspondence is too laconic."[4] It was not lack of vision that confounded Napoleon but his ill-judged decisiveness.

Ney set off north because Napoleon knew nothing of the scale of Macdonald's defeat. When the news reached him, the eighty thousand men promised to Ney dropped to fifty-eight thousand, as Napoleon swung east to try to rally what was left of Macdonald's men and steel himself for an attack by Blücher, who he assumed, not without reason, to be in hot pursuit when he was adhering to the Trachtenberg plan, and falling back. The Army of Bohemia was in anything but disarray, however shaken by Dresden, because it had a plan to pull Napoleon hither and yon, and it worked. Schwarzenberg and sixty thousand men recrossed the Elbe, panicking St. Cyr into telling Napoleon another attack on Dresden was imminent. Napoleon had little choice but to heed him, especially as Barclay seemed to be marching toward Dresden from another direction. When Napoleon turned on Barclay, both he and Schwarzenberg simply withdrew behind mountains Napoleon decided not to try to cross.[5] Napoleon wound up back in Dresden where he began, and the allies had kept him well away from Ney. Napoleon usually sought to reincarnate the Hannibal of Cannae; the Trachenberg plan was reducing him to Hannibal chasing the ghost of Fabius.

Ney was heading straight for the Army of the North, under Bernadotte. Napoleon's best hope now became his treacherous ex-marshal; his worst enemy became his loyalist marshal, Ney. It spoke volumes about the past, as much as the present. Ney set out north at the head of his shrunken but grandiosely named "Army of Berlin." Napoleon's scathing criticism of Oudinot's disjointed deployment of his corps obviously bounced off Ney, whose own march was just as shambling when, on September 5, Oudinot's corps blundered into Bernadotte's advance guard—Prussians under Friedrich Bogislav von Tauentzien—at Zahna, about ninety miles north of Dresden. It was just as Bernadotte wanted, hoping he could stall Ney there long enough to bring up his main force and fall on his left flank. Tauentzien drove Oudinot back to the village of Dennewitz, where the two forces engaged the next day. Bernadotte was nowhere to be seen. When Reynier arrived to bolster Oudinot, the Prussians came close to being overwhelmed by late morning, but the day was saved by Bülow's corps. He took his own initiative and came to Tauentzien's aid just in time. There were now about forty-five thousand Prussian troops on the field, while Ney's superior numbers were too dispersed and confused to concentrate. The battle was fought in a driving wind that whipped up the thin, sandy soil around the village, making it a battle of the blind against the blind. When Bülow counterattacked, Oudinot and Reynier proved too strong for him, and Reynier was poised to surround the Prussians when Ney made a disastrous intervention. Ignorant of Reynier's progress, he plunged into the fray, sword in hand, losing what perspective he had on the battle, and then ordered Oudinot to switch flanks from left to right, which left Reynier isolated, rather than unstoppable, at the crucial moment. Oudinot, never a stickler for obeying orders, complied in full knowledge of Ney's folly. This is universally attributed to pure spite at his demotion, and to make a fool of Ney. If so, it worked. Bülow overwhelmed the isolated Reynier and rolled down on Ney's main body, with Oudinot too far away to help. Now truly routed, Ney fell back to the Elbe, for the loss of 8,000 killed and wounded,

13,500 captured, and 53 guns abandoned. The allies lost ten thousand men, and it might have been less if Bernadotte had arrived early enough to take a real part in the fighting.[6] Bernadotte began to acquire the same reputation for cowardice and self-interest among his allies that he "won" at Jena. Bülow was forced to surrender to Bernadotte at Jena, and his grudge poured over into a nasty confrontation.[7] Under Napoleon, he had nowhere to hide, but now, a sovereign prince, Bernadotte actually published a report taking most of the credit himself at the Prussians' expense,[8] which left Bülow as furious as Davout at Auerstedt. Ludwig von Boyen, his chief of staff, was emphatic when he wrote to headquarters: "I give you my word that Bülow fought and won the two victories at Grossbeeren and Dennewitz despite all sorts of obstacles and even against the actual will of the crown prince (Bernadotte) . . . Bülow repeatedly asked the crown prince to cross the Elbe, but in vain."[9] Napoleon managed to teach Bernadotte nothing about generalship, but he could, at least, "lie like a bulletin."

A pattern was emerging that was not in Napoleon's favor, but neither he nor the allied commanders quite grasped it yet. Napoleon ordered Ney to fall back on Torgau, across the Elbe, and hold it at all costs, against any advance by Bernadotte. Bernadotte advanced, now eighty thousand strong, on Rosslau.[10] Napoleon was not overly concerned by this; he saw Ney's position at Torgau as a way to block Bernadotte linking with Blücher and threatening Dresden from the north, and that he, himself, had done enough to intimidate Schwarzenberg. The allies were the gloomy ones. Alexander was convinced that Napoleon's return to Dresden signaled an advance on the Army of Bohemia, and that he would unite with Ney. Schwarzenberg, in a rare moment, agreed with the tsar that Blücher should march his Silesian Army to the aid of the Army of Bohemia to withstand a coming French onslaught.[11] When Blücher advanced, however, Napoleon finally saw real danger. He knew how thoroughly routed Macdonald's forces were, and that Blücher would cut through them. Baffling the allies, he turned east again, with the Young Guard, to rally Macdonald's men, using all his skills as a leader, and drove Blücher back east of Bautzen.[12] The Trachtenberg plan was working, almost in spite of the allied commanders. By now, Napoleon saw as much, even if they did not. His men were exhausted by countless countermarches; Saxony was now a wasteland and his army close to starvation. Nor was he alone.

The news from Spain was worse. Soult fared badly that dread summer. The only good news he had was that Napoleon allowed Joseph to retire to his home outside Paris on July 20, leaving him in peace to salvage what he could.[13] Altogether, he had just over seventy thousand men in the field, when at least one hundred thousand were needed to contain Wellington.[14] They were demoralized, unpaid for fifteen months, and discipline had all but vanished. Soult was soon stripped of some of his best troops to bolster the Saxon front. During the retreat, desertion swelled, with men simply throwing down their arms and surrendering. Many units degenerated into bands of brigands, pillaging French peasants on French soil, while their commanders placed heavy demands for supplies on the people of the frontier departments. Whole communities simply took flight. Scenes reminiscent of Russia, Saxony, and Poland were replicated in the French Pyrenees, as Frenchman turned on Frenchman. The only clear order Napoleon gave Soult was to take the offensive and push the front line back into Spain, to avoid exactly this.[15] Rebuilding the army after Vitoria needed months, but Soult had barely days. He raised morale with admirable success, convincing his men that their defeat had all been the fault of Joseph's inept leadership, and he was readily believed. He abolished the embarrassing titles of the "armies" and put them under his unified command, divided into four columns, effectively corps, under Reille, d'Erlon, Clauzel, and Eugène-Casimir Villatte. Soult's record inspired confidence, but as Rory Muir has noted, his men's morale was always brittle after all they had been through.[16] Napoleon's expectations of "Spain" were delusional. Soult's only realistic hope of a counteroffensive was a flanking movement across the Maya and Roncesvalles passes, to get between Wellington and Graham—who was around San Sebastian—get behind them, and relieve the besieged garrison of eight thousand men at San Sebastian under Rey, and lift the siege of Pamplona on the way to the coast. He knew he lacked the strength to take on Wellington directly, on the coast road. It was a daring, complex plan in the best of circumstances, and Soult's were anything but the best. His men were not fit for so arduous a purpose. His best hope was that Wellington was having problems of his own, some of them eerily like Napoleon's.

Wellington had left the siege of San Sebastian to Graham in July, more worried by Soult's maneuverings in the passes, and trusted Graham's judgment. It had not gone well. Graham launched an assault by boat across the estuary, which then meant a charge over open ground in front of the city walls. The assault was a disaster; 571 men were lost—330 of them from one regiment, the Royal Scots—as the French defenders held their ground behind the walls. The remark of one dejected officer—"things do not appear to go well, unless Lord Wellington or General Murray are on the spot"[17]—was replete with parallels in Saxony. Wellington was right to fear Soult was up to something. He ordered Cole to hold Roncesvalles "to the utmost"[18] on July 24, but Reille and Clauzel already had him under attack, while d'Erlon moved into the Maya pass. The narrow defiles prevented Soult from using his full force of sixty thousand against the outnumbered Cole. Cole held out all day for minimal losses but, in contradiction of his orders, withdrew at midnight, intimidated by Soult's numbers, and afraid of being outflanked. In almost Napoleonic manner, Wellington castigated Cole less for disobeying orders than for failing to inform him that he had done so.[19] The fighting at the Maya pass was ferocious, the French gaining the pass because they found a lightly guarded goat track. Helped by a dense fog that shrouded their advance,[20] they overran Cameron's brigade and the Portuguese. The pass was lost along with four cannon and fifteen hundred men. The French had lost two thousand, but the road to Pamplona was now open. At this point, Wellington had not even heard from Cole. It took a full twenty-four hours for Cole to tell him of his defeat. He fumed to Lord Liverpool about "these extended operations, which I cannot direct myself" and was openly insulting in a letter to his brother: "You will perceive that my Generals are *Gallant Officers* in every sense of the word."[21] It took Soult a day and a half to get his men in position to attack the allies around Pamplona, so narrow were the mountain roads, by which time Wellington had arrived. He found Soult close by, and his outward positions abandoned, but he galloped about the sector, scribbling notes to subordinates and taking in the situation quickly. His very presence galvanized the troops; he organized a strong defense and what followed was, in his words, "fair bludgeon work."[22] Wave after wave of French assaults battered the allied lines, but they just held. The next day, d'Erlon arrived, but Soult saw a further attack would be too costly—he had lost close to four thousand men in one day—and decided to disengage, to try to cut between Wellington and Graham, and make for San Sebastian. He withdrew at night, attempting to march across Wellington at close quarters and slip behind him by daylight. His men were not of that calibre anymore; battered the previous day, they could not cope with a night march immediately. Soult's columns were strung out; only Clauzel got his men to safety. Wellington was ready, having ordered batteries dragged up to the heights overlooking the French during the night. It all took place in pouring rain.[23] Soult had left his men in a position even the best troops in the world could not have won in.[24] The French offensive was over.

Soult fell back on Bayonne and Saint-Jean-de-Luz, and began preparing a defensive line on the French border, but throughout August, he remained torn between the need to be ready for a powerful allied advance and his orders to push the war away, back into Spain. He still looked to the relief of San Sebastian as the key to both objectives. Soult set about concentrating his forces around Bayonne, still at about seventy thousand, drawing on his reserves, determined to avoid a "useless defense" of the city. However, even as he summoned his strength for a counterattack, British reinforcements were pouring in by sea.[25] He was stopped at Irun, on August 31, and thrown back over the river Bidassoa. The same day at San Sebastian, after horrendous fighting watched by a large crowd of civilians, the British stormed a breach in the walls, but were cut down from well-defended positions. Only when Graham ordered his batteries to open fire—at risk to his own men as well as the French—was the siege broken. When the guns stopped, the British fought their way into the well-barricaded streets of the town, and the last round of hand-to-hand fighting took over from the horrors of shelling that had exhausted and disoriented the French. Rey and a few men withdrew to the citadel and held out until September 9, but the city was at the mercy of the allies, and they took none. Charles Esdaile called the sack of the city "quite simply a disgrace—a war crime, indeed."[26] Looting, wanton vandalism, the desecration of churches so common in the Spanish war, all followed. "Fortunately, there were few females in the place, but the fate of the few which were I cannot now think without a shudder," recalled one officer.[27] It was yet another instance of Wellington's inability to control his subordinates. He had foreseen this, and ordered Graham to keep his men in check after the fighting. Nor had he approved of the general bombardment of the city. All in vain, and it did his already strained relations with the Spanish government no good.[28] It had cost him more than his twenty-three hundred casualties—including 50 percent of the fifteen hundred men of the lead assault brigade[29]—as even deputies in the Cortes accused him of destroying the port to further British commercial interests.[30]

For all this, Wellington now had southern France at his mercy by early September, yet he halted at the Bidassoa. His main reason was the same gloom that enveloped the commanders of that other alliance after Dresden. "It appears to me that Buonaparte has the allies, including Austria, exactly in the state in which he would wish to have them," he wrote on August 18th. In mid-October, he noted that Napoleon was still at Dresden, and took this as a sign of strength.[31] He need not have worried. The allied statesmen, and Napoleon himself, were allaying his fears, even as he wrote.

September–October 1813: The Axis of the World Shifts

"While the generals wrung their hands, the diplomats at Teplitz achieved success." Michael V. Leggiere puts it perfectly.[32] When they convened there on the day San Sebastian fell to Graham, they saw the weakness Napoleon was trying to exploit, an old one that gave him his oldest advantage: divide and rule. Napoleon had systematically applied blandishments to Alexander, blackmail to Francis, and brute force to Frederick-William, to prise the alliance apart. Now, Russia, Prussia, and Austria signed bilateral treaties of alliance with each other. In the preamble, Metternich made much of restoring the balance of power by defeating Napoleon, but the real breakthrough was the promise made by all of them not to make a separate peace with France, and to come to each other's aid if attacked. Castlereagh considered this all too vague to form the basis of a lasting peace.[33] His thoughts centered on wider issues. Castlereagh wanted discussion of the restorations of the Spanish and Neapolitan Bourbons, the Portuguese royal house, and, above all, the fate of Holland. Beyond this, he sought to establish the basis of a new state system in Europe, making permanent an anti-French alliance. He foresaw a France without Napoleon. The allies did not as yet want to think that far ahead, nor did the Whig opposition, who pressed for a negotiated peace in the weeks after Dresden.[34]

Castlereagh missed the point. For the allies, what mattered in immediate, urgent context was expelling Napoleon from their midst. They had learned the hard way how firm his grip was on the once amorphous power vacuum of the old Holy Roman Empire. The terms of Teplitz set out to deprive him of what had become the real heartland of his hegemony, to cut the ground out from under him. To look too far beyond this in the autumn of 1813, with the Grande Armée and its leader still in their midst, risked provoking divisions best left buried for the moment. The secret articles of the treaties were bent on depriving him of his most powerful military and economic weapon: Germany. There was something for all the major players. Hanover and Brunswick were to be restored to their original rulers, that is, the personal link with Britain was secured; Russian influence was seen in the restoration of the Duchy of Old-enburg and the independence of the Hanseatic cities; there would be mutual agreement on the future of the Duchy of Warsaw; the lands now under "the French princes"—Westphalia and Berg—were to be restored to their rulers, mainly the Prussians and Hesse-Kassel; more loosely, Austria and Prussia were to be compensated in ways that would restore the scale of their territories to their pre-1805 status. There was one further point of profound significance: the Confederation of the Rhine was to be dissolved, but on terms that guaranteed "the full and absolute independence" of their rulers within their existing borders. How the princes of the Confederation were handled—what they were offered—was as important for the defeat of Napoleon as anything that transpired on the battlefield, and Metternich's approach to them must be understood in the context of the ridiculous attitude Austria took to them in 1809, when it tried to restore old Reich in its entirety, stripping the princes of the gains Napoleon had given them. Metternich had learned much. He replaced "reaction" with "conservatism." "The words *l'indédependence entière et absolue*[35] were like a magic spell that opened the door for Napoleon's allies to leave the Rhenish Confederation," in Wolfram Siemann's words.[36] Metternich wooed the rulers not, as in 1809, their overtaxed and brutally conscripted subjects, by letting them conserve the two precious things Napoleon had given them: sovereign independence and huge territorial gains. The first result was not long in coming. Bavaria was the linchpin of the Confederation and Napoleon's oldest ally, into whose royal house no less than Eugène de Beauharnais had married. It defected first. On September 17, Max-Joseph signed an armistice with the allies; when it expired, on October 8, Bavaria joined the coalition and seceded from the Confederation. From that moment, only an emphatic French military victory could possibly prevent the other, weaker princes from following suit. The main voice for this volte-face was Karl von Wrede, Max-Joseph's senior military commander, not his first minister, Maximilian Montgelas, a long-standing champion of Napoleonic-style reforms at home and the French alliance abroad. He remained suspicious of Austria's long-held designs on Bavaria, and argued for only limited participation in the war. Max-Joseph was more reluctant, still, and would go no further than strict neutrality.[37] Wrede, who had been entrusted with the negotiations, had commanded the Bavarians in Russia, and used the need to fall back during the second battle of Polotsk to withdraw his men into Lithuania and effectively remove them from the rest of the campaign.[38] He now saw the chance to do the same for his whole country, and he took it. Wrede knew how hopeless the situation was, and Metternich responded by putting Austrian troops under his command as a guarantee of good faith.[39] Napoleon seemed ignorant of all this, or at least acted as if he were. Not once in these weeks did he contact

Max-Joseph or Montgelas, directly or indirectly. On October 3, he ordered Maret, his foreign minister, "Put articles in the newspapers about the lies the enemy is spreading . . . on the news that is spreading everywhere about the defection of Bavaria."[40] Two days earlier, he allowed the Bavarian commander to withdraw his men to Bavaria, despite Berthier's objections.[41] Ominously, Talleyrand knew all about it well before Napoleon and went to Cambacérès with the news, asking him to tell Napoleon as soon as possible. Even Pasquier, the chief of the Paris police, did not know how Talleyrand knew.[42]

The other German states did not fall into line with Bavaria immediately. Napoleon was still a force to reckon with. Yet, as autumn came, the scales tipped inexorably against him. For all the tensions between Britain and the allies, "Pitt's gold" flowed to them as never before and, on October 3, Britain joined the alliance. The immediate beneficiary of this was Austria, despite the deep misgivings Castlereagh had about Metternich. Austria promised to keep an army of 150,000 in the field, in return for a one-million-pound subsidy, half of which had already been paid, but unlike her allies, Austria's military supplies came out of the subsidy, rather than in addition to it, a sign of British distrust over the time Metternich had taken in joining the war. In September, the Russians and Prussians received £300,000 each in cash; Sweden was being paid £100,000 a month.[43] Men flowed to the front, too. By October, the allies had all but replenished their losses—of about eighty-five thousand men and fifty guns. Bennigsen's Russian Army of Poland had more than doubled in size to seventy thousand men and two hundred guns,[44] in addition to the Reserve Army, also in Poland, of fifty thousand. By mid-September, almost 185,000 Russian troops were on the front line. Some were raw conscripts, but more were hardened veterans, some of whom had fought the Turks. The cavalry "remained impressive," and all the mounts were well shod. More kept arriving as the weeks passed.[45] As the odds shifted, there was lessening fear of another major engagement with Napoleon. The tide appeared to have turned.

The same day that Britain joined the alliance, October 3, the Illyrian provinces—so long a bargaining chip between Napoleon and Francis—were overrun by the Austrians, and Venice put under a state of siege. A few days earlier, Chernyshev, with five Cossack regiments and six of regular cavalry, crossed the Elbe and struck across the north German plain for Jérôme's capital at Kassel, hoping to exploit local resentments and foment full-blown revolt. He covered eighty-five kilometers in one day, and ran Jérôme out on September 29. The Cossacks seized the contents of the treasury, but did not stay long. Little of military value was achieved by this most colorful cameo; Jérôme returned a few days later. The chief beneficiary was Metternich. It made his case much easier to plead among the unnerved German princes.[46] There was now a real danger much closer to home. Careering Cossacks were no longer the only allied troops west of the Elbe. Early on the cold, foggy morning of that day, Blücher's vanguard, under Yorck, crossed the Elbe near a small fortified town called Wartenburg, and shook the world.

The crossing had been arduous, made before dawn, in autumn fog and the dark, on pontoon bridges. Yorck landed in marshland, under fire, his men up to their knees in water, but one brigade, under Heinrich von Horn, reached the French outworks, and broke their lines. Blücher praised "the bravery of Horn's troops" to the king, confirming the high opinion Macdonald formed of him, when fighting with him in Russia the year before.[47] The highest praise went to Colonel Karl Freidrich von Steinmetz, "(who) held the most difficult position which he maintained with his customary cold-bloodedness," standing his ground outside Wartenburg against defenders protected by a wall and a marsh, so allowing the rest of Yorck's men to envelop the town. By early afternoon, overwhelmed and outnumbered, Bertrand fell back to Kemberg.

The Elbe, Napoleon's well-fortified bulwark in the East, had been breached. The momentousness of Wartenburg was not lost on the Prussians. Frederick-William handed out fistfuls of Iron Crosses. Blücher said later it was the most important action he ever fought. Yorck's daring stands in comparison to Washington's crossing of the Delaware. General Yorck now became Count Yorck von Wartenburg.[48] Even Blücher, who loathed Yorck, admitted "there is none better than he," in the heat of battle. Privately, Yorck felt he had "been led to the slaughterhouse."[49] He lost two thousand men, one sixth of his command. Two days later, Bernadotte crossed the Elbe further north and the Army of

Silesia, sixty thousand strong, began its descent on Leipzig, from the north in two columns, the better to thwart any attempt by Napoleon to get behind them. Cossacks spread out southward, disrupting communications between Dresden and Leipzig.[50]

Napoleon was taken completely by surprise. His hand had been forced. He was in full retreat. This news forced him to order Murat forward with the advance guard to Leipzig. He confided the defense of Dresden to St. Cyr with thirty thousand men, and began to withdraw the main army west of the Elbe the next day. Up to then, he had so concentrated his forces around Dresden as to appear ready for all eventualities, but his main worry had been Schwarzenberg's Army of Bohemia, to his south. Now, he was faced with war on two fronts and the distinct possibility of the Armies of Bohemia and Silesia, and Bernadotte's Army of the North, uniting and cutting off all avenues of retreat: 64,000 battle-hardened Prussian veterans and 332 guns were now across the Elbe and headed toward him, Blücher preempting any debates within the high command by heading to Leipzig.[51] Bernadotte lagged along behind—he could do little else because the Prussians had dismantled the pontoon bridges, fearing Napoleon might use them and fall on their rear—remaining skeptical about Blücher's readiness to confront Napoleon directly, without Schwarzenberg, further hardening Prussian animosity toward him and fostering suspicions that he was a traitor, still loyal to his old master.[52] The campaign that culminated in the battle of Leipzig now evolved on two fronts, simultaneously.[53]

Napoleon's first reaction to Wartenburg was to see Blücher, not Schwarzenberg, as the main threat. He sent Ney and Marmont ahead, with the light cavalry, while he followed with Macdonald and the Guard. He intended to take on first Blücher, and then Bernadotte, and defeat them decisively before they could link with Schwarzenberg, but his decision to leave thirty thousand men at Dresden weakened him greatly in the face of such a large enemy force. The allies had already forced him to divide his forces in two; his reluctance to abandon Dresden definitively dissipated them still further.

To the south, Schwarzenberg had his own concerns. The memory of Dresden weighed heavily on him, and he had to use the same narrow passes across the Erzgebirge mountains that had made his retreat so difficult after the battle. Entering the plains from the passes in small numbers appeared daunting, as Schwarzenberg was unaware that he outnumbered Murat by four to one,[54] or that Blücher felt confident enough to think he could get across Leipzig to support him should Napoleon turn about and attack him first.[55] Schwarzenberg continued to advance, nonetheless, if at a slow pace and in appalling rain. "The horses were almost up to their knees in mud," recalled a Russian officer.[56] By October 9, Murat met only a few sporadic attacks on his southern flank, his march to Leipzig largely unimpeded, and he advised Napoleon to strike at Blücher, confident that Schwarzenberg was on the verge of pulling back into Bohemia. His thoughts seemed confirmed when part of the allied vanguard broke off an action at Borna, just southeast of Leipzig. The truth was that Wittgenstein's men were simply too tired to fight on after their march, and the main army was right behind them. Murat was utterly ill-informed: By October 11, Schwarzenberg had seventy thousand men concentrated around Borna,[57] and told his wife he had enough support to attack Leipzig, confiding "The most dangerous moments are past for now, the most decisive ones are to come."[58] Yet intelligence suggested Napoleon was still near enough at hand to rush to Murat's aid, and Emperor Francis urged caution.[59] Schwarzenberg was as wrong about Napoleon as Murat was about him.

On October 8–9, Napoleon gave Ney a clear indication that he was going to attack Blücher, giving him ample forces to lead the assault but closely supported—and commanded—by himself. Ney was concentrated around Eilenburg, with Marmont supporting him to the west, and they converged on Düben, on the river Mulde, to confront Blücher north of Leipzig. Napoleon and the Guard formed a reserve behind them at Wurzen. Napoleon committed 120,000 men to this sector, and he meant business. Despite the pouring rain, he pushed on among the troops, paying particular attention to the Saxon contingent, exhorting them to fight well in defense of their country. Surrounded by Berthier, Ney, and Oudinot, he ordered a huge bonfire to be lit, and waited eight hours in the rain as his regiments passed by to take up their positions. Only then did he enter Eilenberg.[60]

Blücher moved, too. He only became apprised of Napoleon's movements on the 8th, and this intelligence put an end to his wrangling with
Bernadotte—who sought to avoid combat—and his commanders, who
wanted to press on. Blücher sent Yorck ahead over the Mulde, his infantry
on ferries, his horsemen swimming the river. By that evening, Blücher was at
last aware of how strong Napoleon was, but was still unsure if he was going
to strike him, or to occupy Leipzig. Even Blücher now saw that to advance
further on Leipzig was too dangerous.[61] However, the advance had convinced him that three armies—his own, Bernadotte's, which was to the
west around Halle, and Schwarzenberg's at Borna—were now close enough
to each other to mount a simultaneous attack on Napoleon, whose forces
were now concentrating. Even Bernadotte agreed it was possible.[62] By the
10th, Napoleon had advanced to Düben with the guard. In the course of
that day, he set out a plan of action that Bruno Colson, the most recent and
thorough historian of the campaign, has judged nothing short of "giddy."[63]
He conceived a grand flanking movement, shifting his whole army up
the eastern bank of the Elbe, then crossing it en masse near Wittenberg
to surprise both Blücher and Bernadotte from the rear. Crossing the river
with so big an army displayed a disturbing lack of realism. His men were as
exhausted by the marching and heavy rains as his opponents. An artillery
officer watched the arrival in Düben of the young infantrymen:

> Our soldiers need rest. The weather is frightful; the rain falls inces-
> santly. The ground is nothing but mud, the roads are flooded, the
> marching gets harder and harder. Our young soldiers, full of fight
> and good will, cannot bear up to this kind of exhaustion. The
> soldiers are only pawns in Napoleon's hands that he moves around
> the chessboard of Europe. But these pawns, rendered up by an
> exhausted France, are no longer the pawns of Austerlitz, carved
> from box-wood or ebony; they are pawns made of softwood who
> cannot stand up to the sudden and perpetual movements this
> powerful hand pushes them to.[64]

Nor were the few horses of the army in any better condition. Horace-François-Bastien Sebastiani, commanding the cavalry, reported on the 11th, "The horses have suffered many privations and are exhausted . . . The rains and the bad roads have ruined their shoes."[65]

Napoleon did halt for a few days around Düben, but his own plan, however decisive militarily for all its grandiosity, was itself confused in its wider objectives. Conscious of appearing a failure in France if he abandoned Frederick-Augustus, Napoleon would not let go of Dresden, even as he planned his massive strike north. Political reasoning led him to concentrate on driving the allies back over the Elbe, which distracted him from the threat of Schwarzenberg to the south and of being enveloped himself. As the days passed, there were indications that he did not have a grip on the changing circumstances, or the impact that constant marching and countermarching had on the army. In this climate of uncertainty at headquarters, with discontent brewing among a drenched, hungry, exhausted soldiery, Napoleon's apparent willingness to risk being cut off from France to see the Elbe defended led to open confrontation between the emperor and his most senior commanders. Caulaincourt remembered the tensions created by Napoleon's plan to strike north:

> (Berthier) . . . did everything he could to get it changed, and the other commanders did, as well. Ney, whom the Emperor summoned and talked to because of his popularity with the soldiers also tried to make him understand that the state of opinion within the army demanded that he take another direction and move back toward France . . .[66]

These mounted when it became clear that the allies now held the only two roads to the west out of Leipzig. That Napoleon still held the hub to every road, in every direction, that made Leipzig so great a commercial city[67] was lost on an exhausted army. Munro Price argues with good reason that Napoleon's four-day inaction between October 10 and 14 was not due to illness or inertia but to the divisions within his command.[68]

The argument was resolved by Blücher. Ney and Marmont had accurate information that now Blücher was moving away from Halle, well placed to fall on Murat's right flank.[69] David Chandler was of the opinion that, at this point, Napoleon thought the juncture of Blücher and Bernadotte became inevitable.[70] He was dealing with a complex set of circumstances and had little to go on. The arrival of five hundred dragoons at Leipzig from Spain, battle-hardened by guerrilla counterinsurgency convinced Blücher that "Düben" was a feint, meant to distract the allies from an attack on Schwarzenberg.[71] Bernadotte, however, halted his advance on the 15th, convinced an imaginary French corps had, indeed, crossed the Elbe and was going to attack him. One third of the allied army now ground to a halt.[72]

The arrival of the "Spanish dragoons" raised Murat's morale,[73] but not for long. At 3:00 P.M. on the 11th, Murat sent word to Napoleon, "About an hour ago, I was informed that the enemy army was retreating. I must now impress upon Your Majesty, that it is completely the opposite . . . What-ever is going on, considerable forces are taking up position against me." By 7:30 P.M., he reported: ". . . I have seen 60,000 men with my own eyes . . . I have no further doubts that the great Army (of Bohemia) is before me."[74] It was closer to a hundred thousand,[75] with another hundred thousand on the way.[76] Napoleon probably did not get the news until the next morning, but he swung into action: All his forces were to concentrate on Schwarzenberg and swing south. By August 15, he had 190,000 men just northeast of Leipzig, at Taucha.[77] Napoleon saw his bluff had been called; the allies were looking for a very Napoleonic decisive battle. He was on the defensive, steeling himself for the prospect of fighting the combined strength of Schwarzenberg and Blücher to hold onto Saxony, at best, and simply to keep his lines of retreat open, if not. Napoleon was still baffled by Blücher's brilliance at Wartenburg. He did not know where his army, or Bernadotte's, really were as he turned south, and was soon convinced they had already outflanked him and joined Schwarzenberg when he saw the extent of Schwarzenberg's campfires south of Leipzig.[78] He was wrong, undone by an army that had reached higher levels of speed and flexibility than his own.[79] In his befuddlement, Napoleon went into action convinced his line of retreat was to the north and fairly secure, when in reality, his only hope lay to the west, which the allies were bent on closing. On October 13, he told Marmont that he thought Bernadotte was not on the Halle road, but further southwest, around Merseburg, where he would be able to link with Schwarzenberg, and lambasted his marshal for not having sent out reconnaissance patrols far enough: "Your corps cannot stay where it is, if the enemy attacks from elsewhere." Reports of numerous campfires around Merseburg and Markranstädt led Napoleon to assume the juncture had been made with Schwarzenberg,[80] but what he saw was Schwarzenberg's left wing. It was Blücher who was closing in from the north while Bernadotte still loitered to the north of him,[81] so far away he did not reach the battle zone for another three days. For once, Napoleon overestimated Bernadotte, forgetting his own "office memory."

The allies had their own muddles, and the biggest was Schwarzenberg's plan of action. He sought to avoid a pitched battle until all three armies had encircled Leipzig in a grand arch, with himself to the south and east, Blücher to the west, and Bernadotte to the north. His working assumption was that Napoleon would attack in force at a particular point, and that the allies would then concentrate their forces there. This meant stretching his lines wide and thin, leaving only seventy-six thousand men to face Napoleon's main force, and placing no less than fifty-four thousand men of Blücher's army, plus an Austrian corps, on marshy ground utterly unsuited to such a large concentration. Alexander, prompted by his staff, intervened usefully, for once. After a violent row, uncharacteristic of both men—"Very well, Monsieur le Maréchal, as you persist, you can do what you like with the Austrian army, but as for the Russians . . . they will go where they ought to be, and not anywhere else!" bellowed the "sphinx of the North."[82] Schwarzenberg backed down and redeployed Blücher's troops to the main road from Halle to Leipzig. That was the only concession Schwarzenberg made, however. Most of his line remained positioned over the marshy, awkward ground on the flats to the southwest of Leipzig—"a veritable aquatic labyrinth where it is difficult to operate . . . a low ground, cut through by a hundred rivulets and covered by a magnificent forests of beeches and oaks."[83] Beyond them, were the farmlands and meadows of the valleys of the Elster and the Parthe rivers, whose clay soils had been softened by the heavy rains, making movement possible only on the proper roads along them, their fields and farm tracks now impassable.[84] This formed his extreme left flank. This meant Napoleon could "let nature protect his right flank," along with the hardened Polish VIII Corps and a redoubtable, two-thousand-strong French division under Étienne Nicolas Lefol.[85] These poor decisions were most likely the result of Schwarzenberg's overreliance on Baron von Langenau, a recently defected Saxon commander, for local knowledge, of which he had little. Dominic Lieven concludes that "Langenau was better at planning battles from maps than from an eye for the actual terrain." There has even been a suggestion, unsubstantiated, that he was a traitor, "planted" by the French.[86] Traitor or not, he did Napoleon a great service. The allies were deployed "bizarrely" by October 15.[87] A spy could not have done better.

During the battle, Frederick-Augustus had abandoned his capital for Eilenburg, under French escort, and entered Leipzig with a handful of his own dragoons early in the morning of October 14. Napoleon ordered the city's French military governor to prepare his lodgings.[88] He was now more lackey than ally. A memoirist recalled that his people, who had suffered so much, received him coldly, and how "obsolete" he looked in his outdated powdered wig, arriving in his old-fashioned coach.[89] The coming days would prove whether his days were past or not.

By the time Napoleon entered Leipzig at about midday on a somber, cold, and foggy October 14,[90] he could hear the artillery duel between Murat and Wittgenstein to the south, which preceded the largest cavalry engagement of the campaign. Prussian heavy cavalry and Russian hussars clashed with Murat's men in charge after charge, their first line only a step ahead of the second, to the sound of bugles raising the pace from trot to gallop, around the battered village of Liebertwolkwitz, the French easily distinguished at close range, even in the fog, by their moustaches. Driven back, the French wheeled and reformed only a few feet from the allies, and countercharged. The "Spanish dragoons," mounted on magnificent Andalucían grays, shone out, 250 men in ranks of 50, stirrup-to-stirrup, their officers and NCOs in the front rank, setting an example. They broke the Silesian cuirassiers, scattered them, then withdrew and reformed in such good order the allies could not break their ranks, their sabers too short to hurt the well-armored "Spanish." The French then charged a Prussian battery and ran off its gunners, who were gallantly defended by the retreating Silesians in individual, almost medieval duels with the "Spanish." At last rallied and reinforced, the allied cavalry drove them into a sunken road, where at last they inflicted heavy casualties, but the Silesians were now isolated and soon driven back. "[T]he 5th cavalry corps, composed in part of cavalry arrived from Spain, made some beautiful charges," Napoleon told Macdonald.[91] At Markkleeberg, Polish cavalry clashed with Russian hussars, who were saved by the arrival of heavy cavalry, led from the front by the redoubtable Pahlen, who was nearly killed for his pains. At just after 2:00 P.M., Murat took charge, amassed as many horsemen as he could into a column, and launched a "shock" attack to break the allied line, with the "Spanish" in the vanguard. It was bloody and costly. Packed ranks charging at close range made deadly the Russian artillery fire, enabling an allied cavalry charge led by Austrian heavy cavalry, which butchered the raw infantry conscripts on the French left, as well as the "Spanish" dragoons supporting them. It was their last effort. Exhausted and scattered, the allies retreated when faced with the head of the French column, but the allied reserve—the heavy cavalry of the Brandenburg regiment—blunted Murat's final charge. It was over. Murat had used everything he had. Losses are hard to know, but Murat has been harshly judged for wasting his best cavalry in a minor engagement, and leading them into directionless, bloody charges, possibly for the simple pleasure of the fight and the chance to lead such fine horsemen from the Spanish front.[92] The allies could absorb their losses, Napoleon could not, a fact lost on Murat. All he had done was clear the ground for the real fighting.

Napoleon did not stay long in Leipzig, heading almost immediately for a forward position to the southeast of the city, at Reudnitz, where he made his headquarters in the country house of a local banker, the guard bivouacked around him.[93] The armies both rested that day, the 15th. It was seven years exactly since Jena-Auerstedt. They all knew what was at stake. For some it was saving an empire, for others, simply the road home. In the words of David Chandler, "The French formations were hurrying toward a desperate battlefield."[94]

Leipzig, the "Battle of the Nations," October 16: The Southern Front

Napoleon and Schwarzenberg both meant to fight offensive battles when the time came. Napoleon stood squarely between Schwarzenberg's Army of Bohemia and the two northern armies. Only the fall of Leipzig to the allies could unite them. Without Leipzig, Napoleon would lose all room for maneuver and have to fight his way out in whatever direction. Neither side was in a position to avoid battle. Both armies were exhausted. The night had been "so rainy, so windy and so cold that everyone . . . felt as if they had gone twenty nights" recalled a commissar of the Young Guard as he doled out potent eau-de-vie to the guardsmen at dawn. The Russian infantry—the hardest troops in the army—trembled at the thought of the Spanish dragoons of whom they now heard so much.[95]

The bulk of the allied forces were massed to the south of the city, and Napoleon placed his main force there to match them: 203,000 men of the Army of Bohemia, to 120,000 French troops. Napoleon placed sixty thousand men under Ney to guard the northern approaches to Leipzig, where Blücher's fifty-four thousand troops lurked, their exact strength and whereabouts still uncertain. Thus, the battle of Leipzig, like the campaign that preceded it, was two distinct actions: the confrontation between Napoleon and Schwarzenberg to the south, and another between Blücher and Ney to the north. Napoleon's plan depended on good communications between the two sectors, because he intended to switch troops from Ney to support his final assaults on Schwarzenberg. It proved a challenge. Napoleon calculated wrongly on Schwarzenberg having only ninety-six thousand men in the battle sector. The French were in good advance positions around Markkleeberg on their right, held by Augereau,

Wachau in the center, held by Victor, and Liebertwolkwitz, under Lauriston. Napoleon intended this line to pin the main allied force, and then to use his reserve to roll it up from his left.

Schwarzenberg, with Barclay's agreement, entrusted his central line to Wittgenstein. He sent Barclay and Wittgenstein directly against Napoleon's center, while twenty-eight thousand men under Meerveldt would have to find their way over the marshes on the allied left toward them. Schwarzenberg was cheered spontaneously by his men as he rode forward to the lines before dawn. Only Archduke Charles ever had such a reception.[96] He had set them a terrible task. "It was a foggy, lugubrious morning" an Austrian officer recalled.[97] It was still pitch dark and the ground sodden, as his men set off, but they had two advantages: surprise and powerful artillery to pierce the mists. Napoleon went to the very center of his line, between the villages of Probstheida and Liebertwolkwitz, with units of the Old Guard and the guard artillery—which he was deploying much earlier than normal—when a fusilier of the guard recalled "a general discharge of enemy artillery announced the start of a general attack."[98] When the first blow came, Napoleon was with a battery, atop a small hill, his men marching along a narrow road, all still shrouded in fog. His troops were not yet in position; Macdonald's corps had not even arrived; bullets and shells flew all around as Napoleon and Murat galloped about, rallying the guard; Murat could be heard singing as he rode. "Instead of starting a battle, Napoleon received one," as Bruno Colson dryly remarked.[99]

"The shells fell like oranges" one guardsman remembered, as Napoleon made his headquarters on the hill of Galgenberg, from whence he saw the battle developing around Wachau, where Sokolnicki's Polish cavalry were shielding Victor from a concerted attack by Prince Eugen's Russians and Kleist's Austrians. Sokolnicki saw quickly that Wachau was their objective, and alerted Victor that it had to be held. Infantry rushed to occupy the village under a murderous hail of artillery fire. Within a quarter of an hour, a battalion from Lauriston's corps lost one hundred men, killed or wounded. As a voltigeur offered his commander a piece of his apple, a shell blew off his head, along with four of his comrades.[100] At about 10:00 A.M., the fog lifted and, under clear blue skies, the guns opened up along the whole of the line. The allied bombardment was one of the most violent even the most hardened veterans had experienced. One colonel asserted that, "Never in 25 years had any of us ever heard anything so terrible"; another recalled "the whole earth shook."[101]

The French, reeling, regrouped, but the allies had a far harder time on their left, as Maximilian von Meerveldt's II Austrian corps of thirty thousand men, which set out at 5:00 A.M. in dense fog, tried to reach Leipzig over the swampy ground between the Elster and Pleisse rivers. Meerveldt could not get his ninety cannons up the narrow roads, nor could he ford the Pleisse, as its two bridges had been damaged. He was halted at Connewitz by fifteen hundred infantry from Augereau's division and a squadron of cavalry. Meerveldt gave up and dug in by 11:00 A.M. Directed by Schwarzenberg, in person, the Austrians managed to dislodge a Polish unit from the castle of Dölitz, but a Franco-Polish counterattack around the village of Markkleeberg ensured this gain meant little.[102]

Schwarzenberg watched all this from the church tower of Gautzsch. Soon, he saw large French columns around Wachau, as Napoleon took a breath, and readied to fight back. However, essential support from Macdonald's corps was yet to arrive, and so he had to fight defensively throughout the morning. He moved his reserves forward: Augereau moved up to support the Poles; Oudinot brought up two divisions of the Young Guard to the Galgenberg hill, and the rest of the Young Guard drew up behind Lauriston. As many guns as could be found were massed in the center. Even the Old Guard moved closer to the front line.[103]

He needed to be ready, as Wittgenstein was poised to attack at 9:00 A.M.—later than hoped—when his cannonade ceased. He had assembled four columns: Eugen's Russians and Kleist's Austrians, totaling eleven thousand men, to attack Wachau from the southeast; nine thousand men of Andrei Ivanovich Gorchakov's Russians and a brigade of Kleist's corps would attack Lieberwolkwitz from the south; and fifty-four hundred cavalry under Pahlen served as a link between them; the largest column of thirty-three thousand men and eighty guns, mainly from Klenau's Austrian IV Corps, were to attack Lieberwolkwitz from the east. Elite Russian units and the combined Russian and Prussian Guards formed a reserve of 24,000 men and 243 guns.[104] This was, in the parlance of a later age, "the big push." All was not as it seemed, however. Coordination along the long allied line was poor; the piecemeal early attacks had been confused and allowed gaps to appear. Klenau was slow to take up position on the allied right, and had to be hounded to move faster by his superiors, his troops occupying the undefended Kolm-Berg heights only at 11:00 A.M.[105] When the advance got onto the open ground, in the bright sun, the ranks became vulnerable, and so it proved. The Russians were decimated at Markkleeberg by the French guns. By midday, the allied columns moving on the village were in disarray, and Sokolnicki saw his chance to unleash his Polish horsemen. It was risky but timed to perfection, ripping fifteen hundred infantrymen apart and taking six hundred prisoners. A Prussian brigade was also overrun. Eugen's column met little resistance at first, but he was quickly aware that his lines had become thinned and scattered. No sooner into the open country between Wachau and Liebertwolkwitz than he was faced with the one hundred guns Napoleon had waiting. The Russian and Prussian infantry were slaughtered, and the three Russian battalions that reached the village were easily driven off. Wachau was fought over again and again that morning, but the French held the high ground behind it, and used their artillery to deadly purpose; most of the wounds it inflicted proved mortal. Their fire had also destroyed most of Eugen's guns by 11:00 A.M.[106] "We had woken a sleeping lion," admitted a Russian officer.[107] The allied effort was no less ferocious for its futility. A French major recalled he was assailed with a determination never seen before in an enemy. Napoleon had to pull back from his vantage point, so heavy did their fire rain down on him.[108] Amid the ruins of the villages, the bayonet was readily brandished with ghastly results as the fighting descended into single combat, hand-to-hand.[109] Some of the terrified inhabitants of Liebertwolkwitz took refuge in the church, and emerged from it to find ". . . a terrible spectacle. Dead and dying soldiers lay all about, and the massacre continued, particularly on the market [place] . . . while a large part of our homes appeared to us as smoking ruins." It took a year to rebuild the village. At least its people had Leipzig to flee to.[110] Not so the troops.

For all the heroism, by about 11:00 A.M., Wittgenstein's offensive had ground to a halt. Only Klenau, on the right, seemed in a position to fight on, but Macdonald's corps arrived, inhibiting further action east of Liebert-wolkwitz. Alexander sent his elite reserves to bolster the lines and urged the Austrians to do the same. More ominously for Napoleon, Bennigsen was on his way from Dresden with seventy thousand men of the Army of Poland.[111]

For the moment, however, Napoleon thought in terms of a counterattack, and promptly plugged the gap between Victor and Lauriston created by the fighting at Wachau, with 150 guns, meant to blow a hole in the allied line for his massed forces to pour through, while Macdonald was meant to drive Klenau back toward Wittgenstein and roll him up, supported by Murat's cavalry to inflict a decisive defeat. From midday, the combination of Drouot's guns and Murat's massed charge sowed terror in the allied lines; Macdonald drove Klenau off the high ground until his cavalry was checked by the arrival of Pahlen's. Crucially, the reserve support promised to Macdonald had not materialized by midafternoon. On the right, the guard cavalry literally hacked their way through Kleist's men; an attempt to stop them by the Austrian reserve cavalry was thwarted by Drouot's guns. But at about 2:30 P.M. a force of Austrian heavy cavalry and Hungarian hussars, and uhlans from the Prussian Landwehr cavalry arrived,[112] just as twenty-three hundred French cuirassiers were carving through Eugen's flank, driving so far forward they nearly captured the tsar.[113] A battle between light and heavy cavalry was normally—logically—a mismatch, but what followed was one of the most astonishing clashes of the Napoleonic Wars. Overconfident, driven by sheer momentum, the French heavy horse let the Hungarian hussars come too close to them. Driven by an almost atavistic instinct, blessed with primordial determination, the hussars turned the weight of their opponents against them. Their speed and horsemanship rocked the French. "Impulse was all."[114] Alexander's intervention decided the day. He threw in his own cavalry escort together with thirteen fresh squadrons of Russian cuirassiers, and sent the French packing by 3:30 P.M.[115]

Now, Napoleon's offensive ground to a halt. The arrival of the Austrian reserves enabled the put-upon Meerveldt to push Victor and Augereau back from Markkleeberg and, at last, force his way over the Pleisse, where a fierce engagement developed between Polish lancers and the hussars of the Russian Imperial Guard. Again, the allies held the advantage because their reserves—Austrian cuirassiers—arrived in time. They got behind the French lines when they were stopped by a well-disciplined French *carré*, "the great square," probably manned by men of the Old Guard.[116] Murat spotted a weakness in the allied lines, held by Eugen's men who had been battered earlier by Drouot's guns. Murat amassed thirty-three hundred heavy cavalry and launched into them, and the French heavy cavalry had its revenge. The Hungarians and uhlans rode to Eugen's defense, but were thrust aside by the momentum of the charge, their commander struck down in their midst. Alexander kept his nerve and threw in his heavy cavalry, to stop the rout.[117] Once again, Napoleon had to send in the Old Guard to stabilize this sector before night began to fall. The *grognards* drove the Austrians back over the Pleisse. The unlucky Meerveldt was captured in the retreat, all he got for his thankless task.[118]

As the day ended, the two armies were roughly where they had been in the morning, "a draw," for David Chandler,[119] but Bruno Colson has shown that the allies had reached a tactical level of proficiency comparable to that of the Grande Armée. Their different arms—horse, foot, guns—worked as well together as the French, and they displayed a superior resilience as a result. They did better in a battle of attrition; their reserves arrived in time, if often in the nick of it, while localized French successes were often unsupported or outweighed by the effectiveness of allied reserves.[120] Napoleon had not managed the transfer of units around the battle at all well. At the crucial moment in the afternoon, Napoleon halted the advance of Friant's guards in the center, and sent them to the right, where they were not needed, probably because he was ill-informed of progress there. Bruno Colson concludes that was the moment when he lost all hope of winning Leipzig.[121] Certainly, a golden chance to split Wittgenstein's front in two slipped away. But Napoleon remained "the master gunner" of Toulon; his sense of timing in the heat of battle was as deadly as ever, but he did not master the wider situation on the 16th. These were not the vast, unmapped, roadless tracks of Russia, but the kind of ground the war of movement should thrive on. Poor delegation and huge numbers hindered him. While Napoleon dashed about, brimming with energy, the tsar displayed the same imperturbable calm he had shown at Dresden. He took critical moments calmly in hand, sensing when and where to commit reserves, just as he knew when Schwarzenberg was talking rubbish. Napoleon did not always know where his reserves were. Souham's benighted "migratory III Corps" was sent hither and yon in the course of the battle, shifted from Ney in the north to bolster Macdonald on the left, and then diverted to help the guard stop Meerveldt, its first real contribution coming at 4:00 P.M.[122] Alexander had shed the ghost of Austerlitz; Napoleon could not summon it.

October 16: The Northern Sector

Part of Napoleon's confusion stemmed from the fierce, unanticipated fighting to the north of the city. He had not foreseen a concerted attack here, as he persisted in thinking that neither Blücher nor Bernadotte was in the vicinity.[123] He was only half right. Bernadotte was a safe distance away, and he intended to stay there, informing Blücher he could only join him the next day, "finally persuaded of the futility of his promenades, and no longer being able to reasonably explain why he would not join us," in the words of an exasperated Alexander Louis de Langeron.[124] Blücher was far from shorthanded, however. He had 54,500 troops under Yorck, Fabian Gottlieb von der Osten-Sacken, and Langeron, over 3,000 Cossacks, 310 guns,[125] and help on the way from the southern sector: Ignaz Gyulai's Austrian III Corps was moving up the difficult country on the right bank of the Elster, to close the gap between Blücher and Schwarzenberg, and cut off Napoleon's western line of retreat.[126] Moving north at 3:00 A.M., on the morning of the 16th, Gyulai was in the environs of Lindenau, astride a main road just southwest of Leipzig. Although his main columns were moving slowly along the narrow causeway, one having to abandon its artillery, his skirmishers were infiltrating the woods trying to get behind the French. He aimed to take Lindenau and the neighboring village of Kleinzschocher.[127] Blücher, however, was still not sure where Napoleon was, but he knew there were French forces nearby. As the morning mists cleared, it was obvious the French meant to stand on a ridge, near Radefeld, where they had gun emplacements and several redoubts. Blücher had two choices: to bypass the French and drive on to Leipzig, or take them on where he found them. His instinct was to head for Leipzig but, deprived of Bernadotte to cover his northern flank, he knew he had no real option but to fight, aware that he could at least pin down troops that might otherwise move on Schwarzenberg, whose guns he could already hear. About 8:00 A.M., he attacked the ridge,[128] just as Gyulai fell on Lindenau and Kleinzschocher.[129]

Despite repeated reports from Marmont that he could actually see Blücher's campfires, Napoleon ordered his old comrade's VI Corps to pull out of their well-prepared positions near Radefeld, and head for the southern sector—at the exact moment Langeron attacked. There were only about fifty-seven thousand men covering the entire northern sector, including a weak garrison of seven thousand raw conscripts in Leipzig under Jean-Toussaint Arrighi de Casanova, and Napoleon would have dealt them a fatal blow had not Marmont and Ney seen the danger immediately. Marmont halted and did his best to dig in at Möckern, but his new position was not as solid as at Radefeld. Ney then ordered up Bertrand's IV Corps to fill the gap at Radefeld, but just then, Gyulai struck Lindenau.[130] The day began with French panic and a remarkable level of coordination among the allies.

Between 8:00 and 9:00 A.M. Gyulai's corps attacked Lindenau from three sides, his own column charging up a narrow causeway directly at the French. Pierre Margaron, the French commander, pleaded in vain for sufficient troops to hold the woods, now full of enemy infantry. The French were soon driven out of their redoubts by a heavy cavalry charge, while an artillery barrage was loosed on Kleinzschocher, which was then overrun by a light infantry battalion. The only French success came in the woods. Margaron sent a battalion of raw recruits into them to flush out the Austrians. They were led by a captain, A. F. de Gauville, recently arrived from Spain. This was "his kind of action." Hardened by counterguerrilla warfare, he was alert to how scattered the Austrians were, and with six men, he cut off their retreat and forced fifteen of them to surrender. "It was no small business with new soldiers, who barely knew how to fire their guns," de Gauville reported.[131] It was indicative of what Napoleon's army had become by now: raw recruits thrown into combat, redeemed because they were well led, another of the bounties of the well of the "Spanish army," which had now run dry. The battalion pushed forward, filled with a new courage they badly needed. At the cost of twenty casualties, they reached Kleinzschocher, in the complex formation of the line, so difficult for new troops to master. The French had the advantage of walls on all sides of the village, save on the side they came in, but the Austrian guns were superior to Margaron's, and de Gauville soon encountered deadly Tyrolean sharpshooters "offering fierce resistance"; "excellent shots," he reported. They were probably the best in Europe, the same fearsome *Schützen* who fought with Andreas Hofer and drove Napoleon to distraction in 1809; the same men ready to rise again, alone, unaided, as recently as February, an insurrection only just scotched by Metternich.[132] So often in Habsburg history, it had proven impossible to get these fiercely independent highlanders to serve outside their homeland, but now they let loose a murderous, accurate fire on the French that caused heavy casualties, de Gauville among them, who collapsed, wounded and exhausted, in a cabbage patch, with only thirty of his men left standing.[133] So perilous had the French position become, that in late afternoon Bertrand threw in Morand's division, supported by cavalry and artillery. It was a classic Napoleonic corps action on a smaller scale, led by one of Davout's finest protégés. The Austrians responded by forming a *battalion carré*. The day ended there, with the French holding Lindenau, and the allies Kleinzschocher. The French had lost 1,450 men; Bertrand's were exhausted, hungry, and almost out of ammunition, but they set to work overnight rebuilding the redoubts. Gyulai was full of praise for his men, who had lost, in their turn, sixty-four officers and two thousand men.[134]

Further north, Blücher, still unaware of where the French actually were, struck out nonetheless with a large vanguard to try to find the way. It was only when he encountered a forward unit sent by Gyulai to make contact that Blücher at last found out that the main French concentration was around Möckern. Until then, he did not actually have a clear objective. He was still wiser than Napoleon. Both men had followed the sound of the guns that day, as true commanders did, but Blücher showed more sense. When it was clear Bernadotte was not coming, he knew he was not strong enough to fight his way to Schwarzenberg.[135] When Napoleon heard the guns at Möckern, about 2:30 P.M., he took his eye off the southern front when it needed leadership to exploit his cavalry's success.[136] He set off to investigate, but only by afternoon, only shaken by the salvos of massed Prussian guns, was Napoleon finally roused from his blindness to the reality of Blücher's coming onslaught, wherever it landed. When, the previous night, Captain Jean-Pons-Guillaume Viennet had pointed out the vast camp-fires of Blücher's bivouacs, General P. F. M. A. Dejean—Napoleon's aide and "parrot"—told him, as Viennet's anger swelled, "Those are forests." "So forests march, then," Viennet retorted. Dejean at last told his master, "I thought I saw only 300. There must be 80,000 at least."[137] It still did not change Napoleon's mind. Ney and Marmont begged for help throughout the morning, to no avail, a blindness to facts that is stupefying. Ney fumbled, in his turn, ordering units south and then back, and then back again, torn between commonsensical and nonsensical orders. Marmont's unilateral decision to turn back to Möckern saved the front, helped by the fact that he led some of the best troops in the army, the veteran VI Corps.[138] They were needed.

Against them, Blücher threw Yorck's twenty-one thousand battle-scarred veterans. So much for Napoleon's assurance to Marmont that he only had cavalry to contend with. In his memoirs, Marmont said bitterly, "Napoleon's opinion was no longer relevant. The enemy was there; we were face-to-face with him. It was the entire Army of Silesia."[139] Leipzig was assuming many of the characteristics of Jena-Auerstedt, of two battles allowed to develop separately because of Napoleon's unwillingness to believe reports. This time, however, the Prussian army had changed, even if Blücher remained the same ferocious beast of old. Marmont chose to stand and fight him on the hills east of Möckern.

Marmont was in a good position. He had the Elster and its marshes on his left, and the Rietschke stream on his right; the ridge gave him a good vantage point across open country, and his troops had only a narrow front to hold.[140] This was important, because Blücher could not unleash his whole force at once, and Yorck just outnumbered the 18,400 of VI Corps. He needed support, and there was none to be had. Overall, he was outnumbered two-to-one by Blücher, his 30,000 (counting the Polish III Corps) to the Army of Silesia's 60,000; his 100 guns to Blücher's 310.[141] Ney assured him Bertrand's III Corps was at hand, possibly unaware how exhausted it was by now. Ney was in overall command of the sector, but had not left Leipzig to see for himself.[142] Napoleon promised him Joseph Souham's thirty thousand men, which would have put him in a commanding position, but they failed to materialize.[143] Never during the battle were St. Cyr's thirty thousand troops, encircled in the pointless defense of Dresden, more missed. With only a cavalry unit as his reserve, Marmont counted on his artillery to hold Blücher back until Souham arrived.

Yorck's corps had fast won a reputation for itself; Marmont's VI had never suffered a defeat, a daunting record by 1813.[144] Blücher's numbers told early, when Langeron's fifteen thousand men drove Dombrowski's thirteen hundred Poles from Wiederitzsch early in the afternoon. The arrival of Antoine Guillaume Delmas's forty-eight hundred men panicked Langeron, who halted his advance. The Poles regrouped around Eutritzsch, were pushed out, regrouped again, and counterattacked furiously. Russians against Poles, the fighting was bitter—Langeron admitted at one point his men were thrown into confusion—but numbers prevailed. Their own cause and country lost, the courage of the Poles becomes as poignant as it was awesome. Their commander, Poniatowski, was named a marshal of France by Napoleon on the field that day, but the field was Langeron's.[145]

Yorck threw his men at the ridge in a series of ferocious assaults in the afternoon but Marmont held his ground. Yorck found Möckern well defended; it was fought over house by house and street by street between these two proud commands, at a ghastly price, so heavy the Prussians had to abandon it. Every window, every wall, was a sniper's haven. The bayonet was everywhere, as the Prussians did the only thing they could, try to take the village house by house. The casualties were agonizing. Sharpshooters of the East Prussian

Grenadiers counterattacked to drum rolls and cries of "God save the king!" They were supported by a landwehr battalion, now so skilled it deployed in a line, not a column, got within fifty paces of the French, halted, and fired. Although driven back, the landwehr regrouped behind a brick wall, made a stand, and were there to support the retaking of Möckern. The village was then subjected to a merciless artillery bombardment by Marmont from the ridge, which sowed mayhem and forced yet another retreat.[146] Its defense now rested with a unit of French marine gunners, who had to withstand yet another assault, and did so with such sang froid that Yorck's men took them for the Guard.[147] Like de Gauville's French conscripts, the landwehr came of age quickly, in fighting that was "nose to nose."[148] Major August von Hiller, who led the Prussians, was severely wounded.

At about 4:00 P.M. the allies were flagging, Langeron in particular, who was now too far away to support Yorck. Yorck saw his corps was in a critical condition; only his cavalry reserve had not been under fire. A further attack on Möckern was halted by a hail of bullets, and Marmont saw the chance to use his last fifteen battalions on the ridge to drive Yorck back. Marmont later said the Württemberg horsemen under his command refused to charge, an ominous sign of doings in the world beyond the battle,[149] but the Prussian reports are clear that they fought well, causing serious damage.[150] Suddenly four caissons exploded among the French, causing havoc. Yorck saw his chance. "Attack, attack!" he ordered his hussars, "If the cavalry doesn't do something now, all is lost!"[151] The Mecklenburg hussars charged into the marines, formed in a *battalion carré*, but it was the Prussian artillery that wore them down. Hammered by their fire, many of their officers killed, wounded, or shaken, their lines began to crack and the hussars hacked their way in. Marmont, close to the fighting, was wounded, too, as was General Compans, one of Davout's protégés, now leading the marines.[152] Möckern at last fell to Yorck, but to his eternal credit, the wounded Marmont rallied his remaining men and established a defensive line between the villages of Gohlis and Eutritzsch, worryingly close to Leipzig. As dark fell, the day belonged to Blücher, but at a dreadful price. Yorck's corps stood at almost 21,000 that morning; by dark, it numbered 13,150; only 9,000 infantrymen were left standing. It had already lost seven thousand men before the battle.[153] Marmont claimed VI Corps had lost about seven thousand men;[154] David Chandler put it at eight thousand, and Marmont's total losses at ten thousand.[155] The courageous marines lost their eagle, which was brought to Schwarzenberg that night, while the streams of wounded, many missing limbs, poured into Leipzig.[156] The Prussian reports praised Marmont and his men. Gneisenau wrote to his wife that his troops had beaten "the finest corps in the French army, that of Marshal Marmont."[157] Thanks to them, Napoleon's rear and the city had held. Marmont had ensured Napoleon would live to fight another day. But where?

October 17

On the night of the 16th, Napoleon ordered Bertrand to secure the western approaches to Leipzig. It was a clear indication he knew defeat and retreat were likely, but he decided to delay it until the 18th. David Chandler saw this as folly, for a hasty retreat would have saved the bulk of his army. His only reinforcements were Reynier's fourteen thousand men, while the allies had in reserve the armies of Bernadotte and Bennigsen, ten times that strength. Napoleon's army counted barely 200,000 men and 900 cannons.[158] Marmont, who probably knew best, believed the game was up. The fate of Germany had been decided, and the only thing for it was to cut and run for France.[159] The 17th was a cold, rainy Sunday. They all rested.

Unusually, Napoleon did not use the 17th to order Cambacérès or Maret to get the bulletins to lie about a decisive victory, or even to send Marie-Louise reassuring platitudes about his health. If there is a sign he knew it was as good as lost, it may be in what he did not say. Memoirists are the only sources touching directly on Napoleon's state of mind in these hours. They speak of him usually shut away in his tent or pacing up and down, in hushed conversation with Murat. It was Murat who rode out to the troops and raised morale, not Napoleon. However, in the early hours of the morning, his commanders' reports of the fighting began to come in. At 5:00 A.M., he learned from Marmont that he had lost half his men and most of his guns, and that Souham's troops, promised by Ney, had never come. Reynier's were sent to him, with the order to hold the northern sector at all costs. Blücher and Langeron were on the move, Ney reported. Even if there was no sign of Bernadotte as yet, they were going to strike in force. Poniatowski reported he was out of ammunition; Macdonald, that allied reinforcements were arriving all through the night and that "and immense line" was forming on his right. The churches and the public squares of Leipzig were filled with the moans and whimpers of pain of the French wounded, the hospitals unequipped to cope with them.[160] "I can still see those wretched figures, as loathsome as they were terrible . . . the proximity of death on their hollow-cheeked faces, dragging themselves through the streets, groaning loudly with hunger and pain," a local recalled.[161]

That night Napoleon learned definitively from the captured Austrian general, Meerveldt, not only of Bavaria's defection, but that Max-Joseph had already sent an army against him.[162] The evidence, human and written, of the irreparable carnage of the previous day lay before him. He was set on retreat, but it was not until evening that the first orders for troop movements were issued.[163] In the pouring rain, he ordered more bridges to be built at Lindenau and pulled back his troops south of Leipzig closer to the city.[164] He took time he did not have. He tried to buy some with proposals for talks with the allied sovereigns relayed through Meerveldt, which were curtly rebuffed. "We shall give our response at the Rhine," was Metternich's retort.[165]

Napoleon said often enough he could not afford to lose a battle. His actions now showed that he knew he had. It is impossible to be certain, but permissible to guess, that these oft-repeated words now weighed on him. The feeling crept through the ranks. A cavalry lieutenant recalled "an indefinable malaise" among his men, "like the approach of a great storm. We were assailed by sinister forebodings." Another officer remembered bivouacking amid the debris of battle, of "sufferings of the body and sufferings of the heart," and a veteran in their midst sighing "Where are our comrades now?"[166]

Across the lines, Bennigsen's Russians appeared about 5:00 P.M., welcomed with cries of joy by Klenau's Austrians. Wagons full of bread and eau-de-vie had been reaching Kleist's men since midday. The news of Blücher's victory raised morale across the southern front, however shattered the men were by now.[167] There were still problems, but only of their own making. Bernadotte was only sixteen miles from Möcken but refused to move further. He was only persuaded to do so by Stewart, a British envoy: "I speak now as a soldier and you will only regret it if you do not begin your march now." This may have raised the specter of Bernadotte losing his British subsidy. Whatever, it worked and he ordered the Army of the North forward at midday.[168] Napoleon's encirclement was but a matter of hours away, or should have been. Schwarzenberg sent confused orders to Gyulai, which prevented a clear liaison with Blücher and so left a western escape route open. Once arrived, Bennigsen obstinately refused to take orders from anyone but the tsar.[169] For all that, the allies now had the upper hand in every way. By dark, over 300,000 soldiers were amassed before the city, so peaceful and prosperous until so recently. This was the best position the allies could be in. Together in such close proximity, their unwieldy command structure was of little importance.[170] The fires of the bivouacs, under the relentless rain, created a strange glow in the night sky. With the dawn, came the reckoning. "This battle will decide the fate of Europe . . . It is God's will," Gneisenau wrote to his wife.[171]

October 18

Alexander, Francis, and Frederick-William all took to their horses in the early morning fog, as Barclay's Prussians and Russians advanced on Wachau, to find that the French had pulled back in the night. Napoleon had no choice but to fight defensively, as the allies advanced from all sides, their ranks appearing ever more enormous the closer they came. The mists cleared, to reveal a brilliantly bright autumn day, even if this wasn't Austerlitz, a soldier from Württemberg quipped.[172] Then began an allied cannonade even greater than that of the 16th. Old soldiers remembered nothing like it; the earth shook. A French officer recalled "an immense plain covered with masses of cavalry, infantry, artillery, the plain was black."[173] In the face of this, retreat was no easy matter.

Napoleon had shortened his lines but not shifted his units. All he could do now was to push west through Lindenau and break out, with his left and center gradually falling back to slow the allied advance, which meant complex simultaneous movements over a wide, if contracting, front, fought village by village. Bertrand had first to clear the villages on the road west. This was helped by the swift work of the Württemberg cavalry, which cut off Austrian units as his men advanced, and even more by the erratic orders Schwarzenberg kept sending to Gyulai, which actually saw his troop numbers reduced at points. When Bertrand opened the way out, Napoleon quickly sent his own maps and baggage.[174]

The best hope the allies had of checking Bertrand and cutting him off from the main army was to press Napoleon's extreme left, at the village of Connewitz, held by Poniatowski's Poles. The task of dislodging them went to Hesse-Homburg's Austrians. At first, they swept token French resistance aside. Murat spotted that if they got as far as the Pleisse and behind Connewitz, the line of retreat would be cut. He found Napoleon having a nap amid the guns of the guard artillery, and roused him. Napoleon leaped into the saddle, surveyed the situation, and sent a division to help the Poles. With help from the Young Guard, the Austrian advance was checked, but the pressure continued, and still more guard units had to be deployed at Connewitz. The Poles held it, with help from French troops from IX Corps, under furious Austrian attack. Augereau did not stint his praise: "It is hard to describe with what determination these young conscripts fought; the wounded stayed where they fell, and if a few of them were carried to the rear by their comrades, they returned to the line straight away, after having grabbed some cartridges." Their commanders conducted themselves with great distinction, "and the same praise belongs to all the officers and soldiers of the corps."[175] Augereau had seen his share of actions, he spoke from experience. As the day wore on, the guard—Old and Young—played an ever greater role in the fighting, as the line regiments tired, and their ranks were thinned by murderous, incessant bombardment. Lauriston's V Corps "counted less men than one of its regiments at the start of the campaign" one officer noted.[176]

An even more desperate struggle developed around the village of Probstheida, where the bombardment was heaviest. Here, Murat and Macdonald defended the center of the French lines, with Friant's division of the Old Guard between them. The *grognards* took heavy losses from fire so murderous that many men had to fall to the ground for cover, but the guard itself remained passive and erect under the hail of bullets. Their very presence, "this forest of fur bonnets, imposed itself on the enemy."[177] Wittgenstein, Barclay, and Kleist ground their way inexorably forward, the Russian and Prussian guards behind them. Their progress was slow, nonetheless; it had to be, to keep such long lines intact, which allowed the French to fall back in good order. The Prussians broke into Probstheida, and found it well defended. Firing from rooftops and gardens, the French drove back the Silesian Landwehr, while the guard artillery massacred the East Prussians, who had only three officers left alive after it had finished with them. Drouot's well placed batteries held back further attacks. The village itself had been held by only a handful of grenadiers, but they were well deployed and supported. Murat and Drouot commanded well, drawing on a wealth of experience. Drouot was hit in the chest, the bullet stopped by his elaborate uniform. He continued on, almost serene, polite, emotionless.[178] While Drouot was the "soul of the soul of the defense,"[179] Murat coordinated the fighting at Probstheida with rare poise and astuteness. "He was Bonaparte's rock, his shield," a Saxon officer recalled.[180] "My boys, we can't leave the village, otherwise we're all lost!" Murat told the defenders. Napoleon came, himself, and the two stood together under heavy fire, the bullets flying over their heads, displaying raw courage, leadership when it was most needed, even as the troops despoiled the corpses under their eyes.[181] Morale took precedence over discipline in such moments. "In those dreadful moments, we were more devoted to him than ever," a grenadier wrote later, "Not one of us feared death. We had seen it close up coming back from Moscow, and it didn't frighten us anymore."[182] These were men who had been under fire every other day for four days. When Napoleon returned to his post on the Thronberg hill, he sent four hundred men of the guard heavy cavalry to their aid. The fire became so intense that Drouot and General Curial could not hear each other in conversation. The Prussians launched two more determined attacks and were cut down by the Old Guard, one brigade reduced to nineteen hundred men. The village continued to be held by fifteen hundred men of the Old Guard until 9:00 P.M.

Further east, Pahlen's horsemen were stopped in their tracks at Stötteritz by Drouot's artillery. However, the sheer weight of Bennigsen's army, fifty thousand strong, soon made itself felt on Macdonald, on Napoleon's far left. In these hours, all the meticulous graft of Barclay, Arakcheev, and countless quartermasters, surgeons, and wagon drivers came to fruition. The Army of the Reserve was in action. Driven back, Macdonald made a determined stand at Stötteritz, but when Bernadotte finally arrived, the sector was pushed close to collapse. Napoleon rushed guard units to stem the tide, while Ney and Marmont organized a new line of defense. By late afternoon, Bennigsen began a brutal bombardment that deployed the sole British presence on the field to deadly purpose: the Congreve rocket brigade. The French were driven back in chaos. Then, "politics" intervened in the heart of battle. The Saxon brigades attached to Reynier's corps were so shaken by all this that three thousand of them changed sides, although 710 of them were subsequently persuaded to recant. All their batteries were quickly redeployed by the allies.[183] The Saxons did not want to fight with the Prussians, with whom little love was lost, preferring the company of the Russians. Blücher placed them to the rear of his men.[184] This was not enough to turn the tide, but it came at a time when men and guns were at a premium. Ney and Marmont got short-lived revenge, when their counterattack virtually destroyed the British rocket brigade, which took no further part in the battle. The lost ground was soon retrieved by de Saint-Priest's hardened Russians. Ney and Souham were both wounded and out of action. Their counterattack was destroyed by sixty of Bernadotte's guns for the loss of almost six thousand men. By 4:00 P.M., the circle around Leipzig's north and east had been closed.[185] There was another defection that morning. On the 16th, Frederick of Württemberg, Napoleon's confidant among the Rhenish princes, had secretly ordered his six hundred troops not to go into battle, but to try to get home. Without a word to anyone, their commander assembled his men and went over to the Cossacks, where they took no part in the battle.[186]

Marmont stood against Langeron at Schönefeld, a village of stone houses and easily defendable by his well-positioned guns, but it was almost a suburb of Leipzig. Langeron attacked about 2:00 P.M. Powerful Russian artillery drove back Marmont's men with dreadful losses. When he ordered Compans's elite division back into battle, their commander was furious. "In the blinking of an eye, it was decimated," Compans's nephew reported. Compans himself took a bullet below his right knee.[187] Everywhere, Ney and Marmont were in retreat. First Murat arrived, telling the cavalry, "My lads, I want to live a quarter of an hour longer, just to join you in a good old charge!"[188] Then, Napoleon appeared, sensing Langeron's long lines could still be broken. The French heavy cavalry did considerable damage, driving a wedge between Bennigsen and Bernadotte, but the Russian guns drove them back. Murat forced Bernadotte to take an active part in the battle, to repair Bennigsen's lines, even if he did not use his Swedes to do so. The French still held Schönefeld, and Napoleon was certain it now held the key to the battle, denying Poniatowski much-needed reinforcements to defend it.[189] The allies thought so, too. When the French repelled a Russian attack and inflicted heavy losses, Blücher, whose men had taken little part in the day, and even Bernadotte saw it was time to intervene. The village changed hands twice, but almost out of ammunition and exhausted, the French withdrew. Marmont, a wound in Spain having left his right arm permanently in a sling, had been wounded in his left hand the day before. Now he took a bullet in his left arm, after having two horses shot from under him. Ney, exhausted, was severely wounded in the arm. Behind them, the village lay in ruins. It had cost Langeron more than four thousand men. The allies now used their reserves: Yorck's heroes of Möckern and Sachen's men drove on to Leipzig.

The line still held around Probstheida when Murat brought the news of Marmont's retreat to Napoleon on the Thornburg. Napoleon learned that the whole army was almost out of ammunition; the closest depots were in Erfurt and Magdeburg.[190] He was also apprised of the defection of the Saxons and Württemberg, which he was anxious to keep quiet from the army, however calmly he took the rest of the bad news.[191] Schwarzenberg's bungled orders to Gyulai had left him a glimmer of hope for a successful retreat, and he now ordered a general withdrawal. Only nightfall prevented the allies from finishing him off. Each side lost between twenty and twenty-five thousand men, but the allies had massive reserves. Napoleon went to work organizing his army, but there was a mournful silence around him.[192] He informed Frederick-Augustus of the situation, and that he would not have time to see him.[193] Napoleon pulled back into the city, and lodged that night in the Hôtel de Prusse, where he had stayed with Caulaincourt on his return from Russia. The Old Guard bivouacked outside it. The dread day ended, but worse was to come.

October 19

The retreat began from the forward positions immediately. The whole army had to funnel through the city, toward the causeway at Lindenau, while temporary bridges were in the process of being thrown up further north and the exits from them improved. Napoleon issued orders for the statutory lies: He told Bertrand to inform Marshal Kellermann, at Erfurt, that "after a multiplicity of events, in which the glory of our arms has always remained (intact), I am heading for the (river) Saale; that the Emperor is fine."[194] Poniatowski, Macdonald, and Marmont were to hold the left, center, and right, respectively, and to fall back after, ideally, holding the city for twenty-four hours. By 2:00 A.M. they were concentrated in the nearest suburbs.[195] The ultimate rearguard of thirty thousand men under Oudinot was to be the last out, after which the bridges closest to Lindenau and its causeway were to be blown.[196] St. Cyr was finally given permission to break out of Dresden if possible, and make his way back as best he could.[197] Trapped, he held out until November 11, when he had to capitulate.[198]

None of this actually worked. There was chaos in the ill-lit streets of Leipzig, as tens of thousands of men jostled through, all heading for the one gate that led to the West. Wagons, dead horses, dead men, dumped supplies, all clogged the streets. Discipline collapsed and the wounded were abandoned to their fate in a far more callous, shambolic withdrawal even than Moscow. As one officer snarled, someone should have thought of using more than one route.[199] Units from Baden took over guarding the gates. The remaining Saxon troops were sent to guard their king, who Napoleon offered to take with him and protect. Frederick-Augustus knew that if he left his kingdom, he would never get it back, and decided to take his chances with the allies.[200]

The allies took their time about the pursuit. During the night, Schwarzenberg and Blücher both thought about cutting off Napoleon's retreat. Langeron, his corps exhausted, was simply unable to do as Blücher wanted: march to the river Parthe and block it. Schwarzenberg had a clearer view of where Napoleon was going, and ordered Blücher to block the Saale at Halle, to stop him further west. The order was only executed at 7:00 A.M., and a reluctant Yorck obeyed it only in the letter, keeping his tired men out of harm's way.[201] By morning Schwarzenberg realized Napoleon meant to defend the city, and ordered a general advance. The bombardment started about 9:00 A.M.[202]

This was the moment when Napoleon took his leave of Leipzig. After a brief exchange with Frederick-Augustus, he headed for the west gate with a detachment of the Old Guard, as shells began to smash into the market square. An angry crowd gathered, shouting insults, but it let him pass and soon dispersed, as the bombardment increased and windows and whole buildings shook. Otherwise, it was a clear, beautiful morning. A bookseller remembered Napoleon's gray great coat, spattered with mud, a face that reflected neither embarrassment nor audacity; still less, worry, only a cold, intimidating ferocity, as he concentrated his thoughts.[203] He halted at the bridge over the Elster, Oudinot's headquarters, and met with him, and Poniatowski. He made his way to Lindenau, through long ranks of retreating troops, but there were few cheers. Marbot—never wholly reliable, but perhaps to be believed here—felt the army was surly, unhappy at how poorly organized the retreat had been.[204]

Napoleon crossed the bridge over the Lupp, and made his headquarters on its bank, in a large mill.

As the allies moved across the battlefield of the southern sector, they saw Hell on earth. Thousands of corpses of men and horses filled the streets of the ruined village of Probstheida; trees had been torn out of the ground under the hail of cannon fire; corpses of men and horses were burned to ashes, unable to escape the fires. Most horrendous of all were the wounded, men without legs or arms, who the retreating French had abandoned to their fate. The allies were now less than a mile from Leipzig, as the morning mists cleared. Alexander rode out among Wittgenstein's advancing men, saluting them, encouraging them, and ordering them to spare the civilians. The commanders dreaded the prospect of street fighting in a city; the carnage in the surrounding villages had been bad enough. The French rearguard had been well chosen, and put up fierce resistance everywhere, allowing most of the army to get out, even in chaotic conditions. But at 11:00 A.M., as the gates of the city came under attack, there were still units inside the walls who had not yet made it to the river. The rearguard inflicted heavy casualties on the allies outside the walls, their sharpshooters in particular taking a heavy toll. It took a concerted effort by a large Austro-Russian force to force the Grimma Gate, on the eastern side of Leipzig. Bülow's Russians made the break through. The assault on the Halle Gate, to the north, was entrusted to the hardened men of the 39th Jaegers, Russian veterans of the Turkish wars, well used to siege warfare and street fighting. By midday, more Russian Jaegers had pushed dangerously close to the French escape route from the north.[205] Marmont's men had to fall back from the Halle Gate, and by 1:00 P.M., the allies were in the city, and as Macdonald and Poniatowski's troops were pushed into the city center, the defense descended into mayhem. Marmont was engulfed by a hysterical crowd and had to be rescued. He made it to the Elster bridge about 1:00 P.M., but was barely on the western bank when it was detonated in error—the marshal had no idea it was rigged to explode—leaving almost fifteen thousand men trapped in Leipzig.[206]

A shambles had suddenly become a catastrophe. Napoleon had delegated the detonation poorly, to unreliable officers who fled the scene as the bombardment got closer, leaving a frightened NCO in charge.[207] The truth of it all has never been clearly established, but Napoleon harbored fears that an officer of his own staff had given the order to compromise him.[208] The destruction of the bridge "has changed the whole state of affairs. Half the army is cut off," Napoleon told Clarke, for once exaggerating the negative.[209] The immediate result was panic that degenerated into "every man for himself," as the French threw themselves into the river and Russian snipers got ever closer. Twice wounded in the course of the battle, Poniatowski had been hit again, defending the city. He struggled to the bank and tried to cross on his horse. He made it to the far bank, but as his horse scrambled up it, he was shot again by a Russian patrol and fell dead into the river. He had been a marshal of France for sixteen hours. Macdonald, still in the center of the city, knew nothing of the explosion amid the noise around him. He learned of it only from the maddened faces of the soldiers. He found a small makeshift bridge over the Elster, and got some of his men over it, but he fell in, emerging drenched, and was pulled to safety under fire. Marmont came to his aid and gave him a horse. Oudinot's Young Guard, among the first to cross, now gave cover fire for those still struggling to get over, and stalled allied attempts to cross. Napoleon fell back to Markranstädt, where he got the news. At first, Macdonald was too enraged to see Napoleon, but when did, he unleashed a tirade of indignation at such incompetence, at the appalling loss of life, declaring that, since everyone else had gone mad, he would take it upon himself to get the army back to France. He reported talk of treason, that Napoleon had ordered the detonation to protect himself. Murat reportedly reproached Napoleon for not setting up more bridges. This is known only from memoirs, but Napoleon immediately mounted up and hurried to Lindenau to see for himself.[210] Little could be done. Around thirty thousand French troops became allied prisoners because of the explosion, Reynier among them.[211]

Bennigsen and Bernadotte were the first commanders into the city, cheered by the locals in the market square, as Napoleon had been a few days before. Bernadotte went to greet Frederick-Augustus, who emerged bewildered on his doorstep. Alexander soon arrived but, when invited to speak with Frederick-Augustus by Bernadotte, he simply pretended not to hear, as the king of Saxony lurked, tentatively, awaiting an invitation to join the victors, which did not come.[212] The formal surrender was left to the troops from Baden, who were promptly incorporated into the allied ranks. Barclay, Blücher, and Schwarzenberg arrived in their turn. Everyone had stayed close to the front lines. Bernadotte sought out his old friend, Reynier, and shook his hand.[213] It was a moment of triumph, when the victors could be generous. They had all earned their share of "Pitt's gold." An exhausted soldiery did not ransack the city. Alexander was generous toward the French prisoners, but not to Frederick-Augustus, who was packed off to Berlin under escort, while his state was put under Stein's administration.[214] Metternich complained about this the very next day; his suspicions of Stein's plans for the future of Germany went back to 1809, when he had threatened the princes of the Confederation. Alexander overruled him.[215] If Metternich's diplomacy was a "carrot" for the German princes, the fate of Napoleon's loyal ally was Alexander's "stick." For Bruno Colson, "At that moment and on that square, the victory emerged clearly as the last act of a drama which had reached its end."[216] Alexander saw in it the hand of Providence, as he told his old friend Golitsyn: "Almighty God has granted us a striking victory over the famous Napoleon . . . The Supreme Being has proved that before Him nothing is strong, nothing is great here below except what he wants to raise."[217] Many regarded Blücher as the hero of the hour, especially himself, describing Leipzig as "the greatest battle the world has ever seen . . . I took Leipzig by storm."[218] He had a point. His daring crossing of the Elbe had made all the rest possible, but it betided rivalry. Metternich, even in this moment, mixed glory with a sharp sense of the wrangling to come:

> Now all those who have protested will finally realize that our operations were very justified and *well* calculated. If you think about the difficulty of bringing together on one battlefield four armies coming from all corners of the world, and how much needed to be

done to arrange everything so that none of these armies could
be defeated individually and a commander like Napoleon became
caught between then all, then the merits of Field Marshal Prince
von Schwarzenberg are surely beyond doubt.[219]

Others begged to differ with his last comment. None argued with the rest.
Metternich was badly shaken by the carnage, but he judged Leipzig
"the battle of the world" in a letter to his mistress, Wilhelmine von Sagan.
He reminded her that it had been "a bloody day"—and this only by the
18th:[220] Losses are hard to calculate for Leipzig, but Michael V. Leggiere's
thorough research puts allied losses at around 54,000: over 22,500 Russians; 16,000 Prussians; 15,000 Austrians; and a mere 180 Swedes. The
French lost about thirty-eight thousand in the fighting and another fifteen thousand prisoners—among whom thirty-six were generals—about five
thousand German deserters, together with twenty-one thousand abandoned
sick and wounded. St. Cyr's thirty thousand men were stranded in Dresden.
Twenty-eight eagles were captured or lost. Three marshals were wounded;
one killed.[221] The army that reached Erfurt had only seventy thousand men
under arms and thirty thousand stragglers, and there was plenty of typhus on
the march with them.[222] No numbers can evoke the horror of those deaths
and wounds, from grapeshot, shells, the bayonet wielded at close quarters
in village streets, or the slicing of limbs by the sabers of heavy cavalry at
the gallop. The British ambassador to Vienna recorded what he saw with a
shudder discernible on the page:

> For three or four miles the ground is covered with bodies of men
> and horses, many not dead. Wounded wretches unable to crawl,
> crying for water amid heaps of putrefying bodies. Their screams are
> heard at an immense distance, and still ring in my ears.[223]

The stench of death rose from the villages and fields, and from the stones
of Leipzig's market square. Saxony was more than a ruin; it was an abattoir.

Napoleon took stock a few days later, from Erfurt. He made clear the disaster to Cambacérès in his own way:

> I am going to Mainz, and will concentrate the army on the (French) border. The treason of Bavaria, as inconceivable as it is unexpected, and upset all my plans and obliges me to bring the war to our frontiers . . . (I)n this state of affairs, the 120,000 conscripts requested will not be enough, for I am not counting much on the 140,000 conscripts of 1815 (who were only sixteen) . . . (Find the means) to procure 60 to 80,000 men, age more than twenty-two. Independently of this resource, I am counting on 100,000 refractory conscripts. Mobile columns will need to be organized to round them up.[224]

Later that day, Napoleon thanked Cambacérès for organizing the national guards of the Rhine departments in response to Bavaria's defection, "this is absolutely indispensable."[225] His old collaborator saw the writing on the wall, without being told. France was to be terrorized yet again by its own police. Napoleon saw how the conscription of older men would shock opinion, but he did not hide his desperation from his old friend: "When the whole of Europe is under arms, when men, married or not, are being conscripted, and when everyone is in arms against us, France is lost if it does not do the same."[226]

12

THE FRONTIERS CRUMBLE: THE END OF EMPIRE, OCTOBER 1813–JANUARY 1814

The Sudden Death of Napoleonic Germany

Leipzig is often called "the battle of the nations." That is to trivialize it. Leipzig was a battle that changed history. It was a battle of sound and fury, of blood and guts. Of thundering batteries of massed guns and villages transformed into slaughterhouses by the bayonet and the sniper's bullet. But it defined the future as no other. That was how Napoleon's empire fell, in a blood-soaked maelstrom, an orgy of violence, and it fell at Leipzig. Nor would there be any quiet slipping away.

The roar of the allied guns at Leipzig shook more than the battlefield. Before the battle, Bavaria alone of Napoleon's German allies was persuaded to change sides, but on November 2, Württemberg and Hesse-Darmstadt followed suit. The rest were not long about it. The combination of allied respect for their territorial integrity, naked power in the field, and the harsh treatment meted out to Frederick-Augustus saw Napoleon's Confederation "collapsed like a house of cards."[1] Jérôme did not even wait as long as his father-in-law. He fled Kassel on October 26, as soon as the news reached him, without waiting for orders from his brother, and made for Cologne, in French territory, and then for Aachen where he released his personal guard from his service.[2] Napoleon was not pleased. It seems—the letter has not survived—that he ordered Jérôme to stay in Cologne, and not to return to Paris, but made it clear that he would be arrested if he disobeyed: "One acted in this way with the king of Spain (Joseph)."[3] When he learned that Jérôme had bought a château at Stains, near Paris, Napoleon ordered Cambacérès to see if it contravened the law that no Bonaparte on a foreign throne could do so without his permission, and to annul the sale. His displeasure went much deeper: "I am angry that in such a moment when people are sacrificing their interests for the defense of the country, a king who loses his throne should have so little tact to choose that moment to buy property, and to seem to think only of his personal interests."[4]

Napoleon was in a race against time. With the allies at his back, he now faced the prospect of hacking his way through hostile country that was once the core of his hegemony. He moved fast. The army that narrowly escaped at Leipzig was already exhausted, and it was a tribute to Napoleon's own management of the first days of the retreat that it held some semblance of order. Napoleon and most of the army reached his nearest supply base at Erfurt on October 23, facing sporadic, if fierce, allied harassment from Pahlen's cavalry and destroying all the major bridges on the way. Napoleon ordered a scorched-earth policy on the lands of his erstwhile ally to deny the allies provisions, in a ruthless reversal of roles from 1812. He had begun this even before the battle, reducing this wealthy corner of Europe to a desert, and alienating the Saxon troops in his ranks.[5] As it paused at Erfurt for three days, the ragged state of the army became all too clear, and Macdonald persuaded Napoleon that he had to head directly for the Rhine at full speed; trying to stand in Germany was futile. Murat now took his leave of the army, returning to Naples, never to rejoin it.[6]

Behind him, the bickering among his enemies was in full flow. That only Pahlen's men were in pursuit was because Alexander alone among the rulers was keen to seek another battle with Napoleon so soon. Schwarzenberg, deeply aware of how battered the armies were, slowed their advance, prompting the tsar to demand he be removed as commander in chief, which Metternich refused to countenance. Bernadotte simply took his army north, toward his real objective, Denmark, to ensure he received Norway for his efforts, such as they were.[7] Of the field commanders, only Blücher shared Alexander's thirst for the fight. His vanguard, under Yorck, was at Halle, hoping for rest after being ordered there even before the end of the battle, but pouring rain, sodden roads, and general exhaustion allowed Napoleon to press on.[8] When the allies finally began to close in around the river crossings at Freyburg on October 21, the French panicked and all discipline broke down as they crowded on bridges. "Only the appearance of the emperor, himself, restored order to the chaos and regulated the flood," according to a Saxon officer on Napoleon's staff.[9] Ahead lay the arduous ascent into the Eckartsberg mountains. Blücher knew this was his best chance to catch Napoleon, and it had failed. Part of this came from the ill-coordinated movements of his subordinates, but throughout the retreat, Napoleon deployed the elite Young Guard divisions, led by Oudinot and Marmont, as the rearguard. Blücher drove ahead, using Russian prisoners liberated from the French to rebuild the bridges, but Yorck's men were too exhausted to press on.[10] Blücher drove his troops with a pitilessness and fury that matched Napoleon's. The conditions worsened for both sides. A Prussian grenadier noted "very bad mountain paths . . . over muddy, washed-out clay roads . . . indescribable misery," and deepening cold in which men froze to death; and they were all infested with lice.[11] Tensions erupted among the Prussians. Yorck protested at Blücher's fanatical resolve more than once out of concern for his troops, and was supported by the Austrians.[12] His men had not had a hot meal for eleven days, since the battle of Möckern.[13] Blücher's Silesian Army began the campaign 36,000 strong; by the time it reached the Rhine, it counted only 9,945.[14] Yet, the Prussians had help of all kinds on the way. The armies of Bohemia and Poland (the reserve) were behind them, and supplies—some from Britain—were coming.[15] With British matériel, came a stream of Russian men: forty-four thousand reinforcements arrived for Langeron, Sacken, and Wittgenstein. They reached the Rhine with barely thirty thousand men; by the new year, Langeron and Sacken had double that number. Sixty-three fresh cavalry squadrons—twelve thousand troopers—were on the Rhine, with more on the way. Many were veterans, recovered in hospital.[16] Stein was busily turning the resources of the German princes, for so long Napoleon's mainstay, to allied ends.[17]

Napoleon could count on no such bounty. Most of his new conscripts—even the older men—were raw recruits. He could only fantasize about the numbers of cavalry Alexander was mustering. Indeed, he was scrounging horses. ". . . all the saddle horses are to be seized; all horses led or ridden by infantrymen are to be seized, and any excuse that they belong to an officer is not to be accepted . . . You will send all these horses to the artillery," he barked to Kellermann.[18] By the end of the month, his army had dwindled to about sixty thousand through illness, death, desertion, and straggling. Marmont calculated that almost twenty thousand men had formed themselves into bands of full time marauders, dubbed *fricoteurs* ("the gluttons") by their comrades.[19] Toward the end of the march, Napoleon did his best to round them up, ordering them arrested by the gendarmes and the local authorities: "It will be easy for the prefect to make the communes understand they have an interest in reinforcing the army,"[20] a nod to his need for men, as well as their need to be rid of marauders. For all that, they had outpaced Blücher. By the end of October, there was only Wrede between Napoleon and his goal. In his rush to cut off Napoleon's retreat, Wrede struck north into Franconia without the Austrians, with forty-three thousand men. He engaged what he thought was a column of twenty thousand troops guarding the flank of the main army at Hanau, just east of Frankfurt. He ran into Victor and Macdonald, with Napoleon close enough to take command. Badly positioned, Wrede allowed the French to creep up on his main force in unguarded woodlands. Drouot was able to bring cannon up very close, supported by both the cavalry and the grenadiers of the Old Guard. They made short work of Wrede, who was sent packing for the loss of nine thousand men. Napoleon reached the Rhine at Mainz on November 2, with most of his army, the day his brother's father-in-law deserted him. In besieged garrisons across

Germany one hundred thousand good troops remained stranded with no hope of escape.[21] Napoleon left a ghastly trail behind him. "I shall never forget the sight: weapons thrown away to lighten their load and increase their speed; guns, ammunition wagons, carriages of all kinds . . . all clearly abandoned because the tired horses could no longer pull them," a member of Blücher's staff remembered.[22] It was not only matériel that Heinrich Steffens, found abandoned: ". . . at first we saw single Frenchmen lying among the bushes; as we proceeded the number of the exhausted, dying sufferers increased, and we found large groups of dead and dying."[23] Typhus was rife. "Nothing could be more unpleasant and disgusting than to follow in the wake of the French army . . . it was impossible to contemplate sleeping on the same spot, perhaps even on the same straw, as this fever ridden army."[24]

Napoleon was still determined to put a brave face on his catastrophe. The enemy standards captured in the Saxon campaign were to be paraded through Paris, presented to the empress in the throne room of the Tuileries, and then taken to Les Invalides, along with six British standards captured in Spain, and put where they could be seen, but without too much ceremony once in Les Invalides. "You know what I think about these military ceremonies; but in the present circumstances I think they can be useful. I don't need to tell you that each flag should be carried by a mounted officer, and must be brought to the Empress in a great cortege," he told Clarke, adding a truth he could not hide: "The forty flags I took at Dresden sadly have been left behind in that city."[25]

The Rhine

Napoleon's initial plan was to stand at Mainz, hoping for 120,000 new recruits, quickly revised to 140,000 in the space of a day. The Saxon campaign had taught him something: the conscription of older men was unpopular, but it was essential. "I need men, not children," he told Clarke, "No one is braver than our youth; but, lacking strength, they populate our hospitals and, at the slightest uncertainty, they show their age. Men are needed to defend France."

Forty thousand of them were to come from the departments of the eastern frontier—"who are those most invested in repelling the enemy"—and fifty-two thousand from the National Guard. The national guards of the Alsatian departments were to be mobilized, "this is of great importance."[26] Senior officers from the area would command new local militias along the eastern frontier, which Napoleon referred to as *levées en masse*, invoking the spirit of 1792.[27] The whole line of the Rhine—Alsace, the Voges, Doubs, and the Jura—"will rise en masse," he told Kellermann, the commandant of the region and the son of the victor of the battle of Valmy. The people of the cities of Metz, Luxembourg, and Sarrelouis were to be armed.[28] Augereau was dispatched to take command of Lyon "and boost morale; he needs to issue proclamations, organize the national guards . . . and do everything he can in his name until troops arrive."[29] The prefect of Vesoul, in Lorraine, was ordered to form not only a levée for his department, but partisan units.[30] Napoleon got his first taste of the real climate of *la patrie*, when the prefect fled at the news. He was promptly sacked, and his successor ordered to get on with it and appoint local officers to organize the partisans, "and to protect the town from all enemies."[31] Bad news of a similar ilk came from the northern border. In Belgium, the new conscripts had rebelled in Ypres and Poperinge, where there had nearly been a bloodbath when troops intervened. Other conscripts had deserted and formed armed bands that threatened local officials. "I am surprised by the bad conduct of the department of Lys. It was always the best behaved in Belgium. Has the prefect alienated the local people?"[32] No reaction more divorced from reality was possible. In the face of such evidence, Napoleon still counted on a patriotic surge among the people of the frontiers. So did Metternich. He had a long memory of how allied aggression in 1792 had galvanized French resistance to the Prussian invasion. Similar rhetoric now might have the same result; he wrote in an unpublished part of his memoirs: "In my eyes, Napoleon was the bearer of the Revolution, and the Revolution still lived through him. If the (allied) powers had given their (warlike) undertakings . . . they would have strengthened the force of the enemy when what was needed was to weaken them."[33] This was soon tested.

Napoleon returned to Saint-Cloud on November 9. His hegemony in Europe was intact, if only just, on the eve of Leipzig, but by the time he scrambled back to France, he had only four embassies still functioning: Washington, Naples, Copenhagen, and Constantinople.[34] He knew "empire" was over in Germany, and that "France" was all he had left, telling Clarke frankly that it was not safe to confide the defense of that part of the frontier to "new Frenchmen,"[35] even those who became French as long ago as 1797. When he arrived back from Russia, the front was still over one thousand miles away, and Alexander was alone against him. Now, he was on the Rhine, and anything but alone. The allied armies entered Frankfurt on November 4, Alexander and Metternich with them. That same day, the allies declared the Confederation of the Rhine dissolved, and there was nothing Napoleon could to about it. Francis arrived two days later to cheering crowds. The time and the place was redolent with significance. Twenty-one years earlier, Francis had been crowned Holy Roman Emperor in the city. "The crowned head of the Holy Roman Empire returning as a conqueror to the place that scoundrels had besmirched—never was the triumph of truth over falsehood, of good over evil, of the majestic over the absurd—so vividly displayed," wrote Metternich to his mistress.[36] The old order was not restored, Metternich had seen to that, but some vestiges of the world of "the scoundrels" were retained. Collectively, the princes, now defected, had to provide 120,000 line infantry and the same number of mobilized landwehr to fight Napoleon, and retain their national guards, as the price for not going the way of Saxony.[37] That was about as far as allied unity went, however.

They were divided about invading France. These differences were less between statesmen than between rulers and their high commands. Their only firm commitment at Kalisch was to drive Napoleon out of Germany. Having done so, a new consensus had to be sought about what to do next—pursue him into France, or sit tight and try to make peace. Beyond this, larger questions of what to do with a Europe reconquered had to wait, but they colored their immediate dilemma. The clash between Blücher and Yorck was magnified at the highest levels. While Langeron, a French émigré with his own agenda, stood by his commander,[38] senior Prussian staff officers reported to the king in no uncertain terms the exhaustion of the Silesian army.[39] They were pushing at an open door. "This wretched invasion of France . . . makes me tremble," Frederick-William wrote.[40] Alexander shared Blücher's impatience to cross the Rhine and bring Napoleon to a decisive battle on French soil. It is tempting to call this imitation, the highest form of flattery. They were not widely supported within their own camps. Alexander Chernyshev, one of the tsar's most trusted advisers, reminded him of the devastation at home, and that "only the end of the war will heal these wounds." Dmitry Gurev, his finance minister, pointed to near bankruptcy. Nesselrode was yet more outspoken: "[I]t is impossible to calculate the chances offered by a prolonged war fought for unclear and excessive goals." This view made Alexander begin to distrust him, particularly when his wife told him he had become too close to Metternich for his own good.[41] Most of his headquarters did not want to cross into France, but to seek a compromise peace.[42] Barclay was not a man given to hyperbole. In his sober assessment, made the same day as Metternich set out his peace proposals—November 9—he told the tsar, "for all our great victories, the present campaign has cost us . . . half our army." Only two of the five corps were still fit for combat.[43] No one talked of ending the war in the Russian ranks, but few wanted to invade now. Schwarzenberg said he wanted to continue the war,[44] but his military actions since Leipzig, fully supported by Francis, pointed to "but not just yet," as he deliberately slowed his march to Frankfurt to save his men, infuriating Blücher's staff.[45] Alexander firmly believed that only a peace dictated to a France shorn of Napoleon would last, but in the current climate, he increasingly kept such opinions to himself, couching them in the more moderate vein that Castlereagh's "wheel" of pressure had to keep turning.[46] The tsar understood Napoleon far better than he did his allies.

Metternich stepped deftly into the fray. On November 9, he brokered an agreement between the Prussian and Austrian high commands that the war would continue into France, and invasion routes were mapped out. Blücher was to advance from Mainz and drive toward Paris; Bernadotte was to invade northern France through the low countries; while the main army under Schwarzenberg would move into southern France, through Switzerland. Alexander objected to the last element, as it violated Swiss neutrality. Metternich began secret negotiations with anti-French factions in Berne, Zurich, and Graubünden, to smooth the way, although he could not "square" Alexander's conscience.[47] The invasion was to run parallel to peace negotiations, however, something "unique in the history of international relations, in that military engagements were accompanied by uninterrupted diplomatic exchange between belligerents."[48]

Metternich said he would give Napoleon an answer to his request for peace talks "on the Rhine," and he kept his word. He also called his bluff. His terms offered France the "natural frontiers" of the Alps, the Rhine, and the Pyrenees, so trumpeted by the revolutionaries who first provoked the war in 1791, thus leaving Napoleon Belgium, the four German departments on the left bank of the Rhine, Nice, and Savoy. It demanded the independence of Germany east of the Rhine, and the restoration of the rulers of Spain, the Italian states and Holland—but there would be no armistice and no final peace that was confined only to Europe, a telling nod to the growing importance and power of Britain in the coalition. It was dispatched to Napoleon by a captured French diplomat, Napoleon's emissary to Weimar, Nicolas Rousseau Saint-Aignan—he also happened to be Caulaincourt's brother-in-law—whom Metternich had released from the clutches of the Cossacks that had captured him. The company Metternich assembled to assent to his plan gave it the deserved suspicion of being a sleight of hand. It comprised Schwarzenberg, his right-hand man, Nesselrode—who also "stood proxy" for the Prussians—and Lord Aberdeen, only twenty-eight, who spoke poor French, "and inevitably was eaten by Metternich."[49] Castlereagh feared this was a prelude to a separate peace between Metternich and Napoleon, and he was enraged that Aberdeen had exceeded his orders and neglected the British demand that the French be ousted from the key Channel port of Antwerp. Threatening to resign, Castlereagh felt Aberdeen was far too close to Metternich, "and that he can do no wrong." After reflection, Castlereagh told Aberdeen to assure Metternich

MICHAEL BROERS

that "I shall not fail him in the long run, however much I may complain when I am not satisfied the wheel is moving."[50] Metternich read Castlereagh, too. He was buying time for British money and allied troops to reach the Rhine in strength—"to acquire weapons for the nation"—and to calm the hesitant in the allied ranks, of whom there were many. The veterans of Leipzig got seven weeks much-needed rest in the Rhineland, bivouacked in some of the richest countryside in Europe, untouched by war for over a decade. All because of Metternich's adroitness.

Metternich also read Napoleon. He sent Saint-Aignan off with a secret note for Caulaincourt: "M. Saint-Aignan will tell you of our conversation. I do not expect that anything will come of it, but once again I shall have done my duty—Napoleon will not make peace, that is my profession of faith."[51] Napoleon ignored the proposed terms, merely expressing a general desire for peace talks, but he did replace Maret—"the hawk"—with Caulaincourt—"the dove"—as his foreign minister. This came from pressure on Napoleon by some of his closest collaborators: Berthier, Savary—who knew best the climate of public opinion—and Mollien all argued that Maret had to go if Napoleon's pacific protestations were to have any credence. He returned to his old post, as secretary of state.[52] Metternich's maneuvers were well judged with a current of opinion at the apex of the French state. Maret was sacrificed on the altar of public opinion. He felt he had been made a scapegoat, and that his ousting was part of a wider plot to bring Napoleon down from within the government.[53] In truth, Maret's opponents were trying to save their master. None of this meant that an invasion did not worry Metternich. On December 4, conscious that "the wheel was moving," Metternich issued "the declaration of Frankfurt," as reassuring in tone as the Brunswick Manifesto of 1792 had been bellicose. It made reference to the "natural frontiers"—"an extension of its territories as France never knew under their kings, because a chivalrous nation does not sink because it has suffered accidents"—and made clear that the allies were at war with Napoleon, not the French people, alluding to the prospect of Napoleon's new levy of 300,000 men.[54]

Napoleon's frontiers were crumbling, and the offer of the natural frontiers looked very generous to those with eyes to see. Napoleon's were not among them, but the truth drew ever closer. Bernadotte encountered little opposition in northern Germany, where the privations of the blockade prepared the ground for him. The revolt of Hamburg foreshadowed what happened when more determined allied military support arrived. The Cossacks led the way, rough-hewn and often terrifying liberators of the urban, commercial world of the Hansa ports. At first feted, and the objects of fascination, the Cossacks and the Bashkirs soon became monsters—according to one diarist in Bremen, "a completely Asiatic people of terrible appearance," who pillaged at will and interpreted requisitioning as a hunt for booty.[55] They were the antithesis of the idealistic, highly educated local volunteers of the Hanseatic Legion, the peaceable bourgeois defenders of Hamburg.[56] The regular troops who followed them found few French forces in their way. Bernadotte used the Russians for these operations: The vanguard of Ferdinand von Winzengerode's corps raced across the coast and into the Netherlands, a small force of light infantry covering sixty kilometers in less than a day and a half, to undo a French attempt to retake the Dutch city of Breda. Bülow's Prussians followed.[57] Bernadotte and his Swedes swung north, into Holstein, pushing back the Danes and driving a wedge between them and the French by the end of November. From then on, Davout and his forty-two thousand men were trapped. Napoleon's order to fall back on Holland arrived too late. Davout prepared for a long siege, destroying much of the suburbs to build wider and stronger defenses, making many people homeless in the process. In December, he expelled from the city "all those who are unable to provide for themselves six months' food." "Not since the wars of religion of the 17th century had a German city come to hate one man as Hamburg came to hate Davout," in the words of his biographer.[58] Davout held out, but was lost to the main fighting.

Denmark had always been Bernadotte's real goal; his plan was to force Frederick VI to cede him Norway, should Metternich renege on his assurances, which he felt lay behind Metternich's brokerage of a cease-fire. Bernadotte blustered, "I will—if necessary—bombard Copenhagen and, if the king hesitates to surrender Norway, I will plough up the soil on which Denmark's royal castle once stood!" With the Danes well-entrenched in the fortresses of

Glückstadt and Rendsburg, his frustration so mounted that Bernadotte bypassed them and unleashed the Cossacks on Holstein and Jutland, which went down in local folklore as "the Cossack winter." By January 5, Glückstadt capitulated, and Frederick gave in two days later.[59] On January 14, by the treaty of Kiel, Denmark ceded Norway to Sweden, and made peace with Britain.

Bülow, with Bernadotte safely behind him, cleared the French out of the Netherlands quickly,[60] with local approval. The writing had been on the wall even before the news of Leipzig broke. Wells of hatred swirled around Lebrun, the governor-general, who wrote to his old friend, Cambacérès, "My poor head doesn't have, and has never had, the power needed to cope with the present circumstances," to which Cambacérès replied on October 16—as the battle raged—"In the present circumstances, it's quite normal to be alarmed," but admitted he had had no news from Napoleon.[61] When the news of Leipzig broke, so did the dam of Dutch restraint. On the night of November 15, a crowd of women from the surrounding area marched on Amsterdam, agitated not by economic grievances, but by rumors of a French defeat and pro-Orange propaganda. Their ranks were swelled by large numbers of the urban working classes, and within an hour, the whole city rose in revolt. Lebrun fled the next morning, followed by all the French officials. They made directly for France. A provisional government was proclaimed, and by the 17th, calm had returned.[62] Two weeks later, William, Prince of Orange, returned from his long exile in London, and was proclaimed sovereign ruler of the Netherlands by the provisional government in Amsterdam.

Napoleon learned of the revolt quickly, on November 17, by the Chaptal telegraph,[63] and swung into action: "The main thing is the security of Antwerp, Ostend, Flushing, Willemstad, Goeree, and the citadel of Bois-le-Duc, and to have troops guarding the Rhine," he told his aide-de-camp, ". . . take all the steps the circumstances demand, to form a corps to defend the Rhine and which can serve according to the circumstances, as quickly as possible." Troops were in short supply, but Napoleon sent 29,550 men to Belgium, acutely aware that Bülow's Prussians were poised to cross the Rhine and that most of Bernadotte's Army of the North was not far behind.[64] Napoleon had always left these coasts lightly defended. In 1805 and 1809, he had gambled on quick victories in central Europe to scotch any assault on them. He did so again, in 1813, but his luck had run out.

To make matters worse, Louis materialized in Paris—defying Napoleon's edict that insisted on his permission for any Bonaparte to enter the capital—and was taken in by his mother. He wrote to Cambacérès styling himself "King of Holland," saying he had returned to help rally the Dutch to his brother.[65] Louis left Bohemia for Rome when Austria declared war on France and then for Switzerland, but he had made ambiguous contacts with Francis about getting his throne back. Still in Mainz, Napoleon was unnerved when he heard Louis was in Paris, using his old title, and making the same noises he had to his father-in-law, now in arms against him.[66] "If Louis comes as a French prince . . . he can be presented to the Empress and enter into his lawful rights. If, on the contrary . . . he has come to trouble my peace, and with this mad system put in his head by Austria and the enemies of France . . . if within forty-eight hours of this letter, Louis is still in Paris and has not declared himself a French prince . . . he will be immediately arrested and led incognito to the château of Compiègne."[67] He wrote to his mother, "I hear Louis has descended upon you." Napoleon would forgive him "the lies he has spread over all the courts of Europe, as I have raised him since birth," "but if Louis comes to reclaim the throne of Holland, he will force me into a painful duty . . . If Louis still comes armed with the same nonsense, I will address myself to you, to avoid the grief of having to arrest him as a rebellious subject, to make him leave Paris and go be quiet and forgotten in some corner of Italy." He would forgive Louis everything he had done in the last ten years, because he still loved him and cherished the memories of their youth. But in the dangerous days after Leipzig, his suspicions came out, even to their mother: "He was in Switzerland: why did he leave?"[68] To Marie-Louise, he spoke his mind, "If he comes as king of Holland, it is most ungenerous of him to bother me at a time when I have so much to do; this man is mad. Poor me, for having such an awful family, me, who gave them so much."[69] Finally, in early January, he put it directly to Louis: "You are not the king of Holland any more . . .

You must stop dreaming about it . . . All Europe is in arms against me . . . If you want to . . . retain such ideas, get yourself forty leagues from Paris. Stay there . . . you will be useless to France and to your family . . . Choose quickly, and leave me in peace."[70]

They weren't all bad. Pauline offered to sell a diamond necklace worth almost 300,000 francs for the war effort; "how much pleasure this has given me," Napoleon told Cambacérès.[71] A socialite goes to war. To Pauline, his only apolitical sibling, he confessed his real thoughts:

> My expenses have been very considerable this year and will be even
> more, next, but . . . I believe that I have the means and resources to
> confront the campaigns of 1814 and 1815. If this general European
> coalition goes on beyond then, and if I cannot obtain the success
> that I have a right to hope from the bravery and patriotism of the
> French, then I shall make use of your gift.[72]

Pauline, almost alone, heard Napoleon speak of the possibility of defeat, of how dependent he now was on French patriotism for survival, not just of how entitled he felt he was to count on it. Returned to France, faced with the full figures, it seems even these slender hopes soon evaporated. He railed at Mollien, ". . . in times of penury, such as these, the Treasury cannot follow the same principles and the same system as in times of plenty, as it has done up to now."[73]

The Pyrenees

On the Pyrenees, Wellington heeded the call of his fellow Irishman, Castlereagh, put his shoulder to the wheel, and moved against Soult. His Anglo-Portuguese army crossed the Bidaossa into France. After Vitoria, the army was exhausted, worn out by warfare, even if well supplied. One quarter of the troops that crossed the Bidaossa after Vitoria were not combat ready.[74]

The Iberian alliance ran into troubles akin to those besetting the Coalition in Germany. The Spanish troops were not being paid or supplied by their own government; the British were helping them, but it was a state of affairs that could not continue.[75] The Portuguese government doubted the worth of the whole enterprise; the French were now far from their borders, and their troops, consequently, were even harder to supply.[76] Consequently, discipline was disintegrating. The troops were ravening to advance, but for reasons that made their officers shudder. William Napier told his wife:

The plains of France lie before us, cultivated, enclosed, rich and beautiful beyond description. The Spaniards, Portuguese, and I am sorry to say the British, are exulting in the thought of robbing and murdering the unfortunate possessors of what they see before them.[77]

Wellington's only solution to Spanish marauding was to leave them behind, a full 20 percent of his army:

I despair of the Spaniards. They are in so miserable a state that it is really hardly fair to expect that they will refrain from plundering . . . a beautiful country into which they enter as conquerors, particularly adverting to the miseries which their own country has suffered from its invaders. I cannot, therefore, venture to bring them into France . . . Without pay and food, they must plunder, and if they plunder they will ruin us all.[78]

Such sensitivity was unique among the commanders, French or allied. To the Cossacks and the Grande Armée, plundering was a way of life. Wellington had other reasons for hesitating to push into France, however. He shared with Metternich and Francis the fear of provoking a genuinely popular mass uprising, a return to the "spirit of 1792." One officer confided to his journal, "Invasion may stir up the strong vanity of a Frenchman, and make him forget his grievances, in order to avenge himself on those who insult his native soil."[79] The shadow of the past loomed over the Pyrenees, as it did over the Rhine. When the French garrison of Pamplona was at last starved into submission at the end of October, freeing up the besiegers, Wellington no longer had ready excuses to halt, and on November 10, fifty-five thousand troops pushed forward to engage Soult along the river Nivelle.

Soult was short of men and matériel, but he had been far from idle. He dug his sixty thousand men in as best he could along the line of the Nivelle, in a series of redoubts and trenches that made best use of the rugged terrain, but his men were hungry and had lost confidence; they were in the habit of losing, as it were.[80] They were thinly stretched. Soult had to leave the estuary of the Bidassoa lightly guarded, but Wellington learned it was passable at low tide. By now, Wellington's pontoon train had reached him.[81] While the two armies readied for combat, far away in Mainz—cut off from French, as much as Spanish realities—Napoleon nurtured hopes of reinforcing Soult: "I think it is imperative to bring the Spanish armies up to the highest strength possible over the winter." He thought he could find one hundred thousand men for Soult by February.[82] Wellington's newfound resolve made this irrelevant. Soult's men put up strong resistance, but were driven from their forward positions, and the Nivelle line was breached for the loss of forty-three hundred men and fifty-nine guns. Wellington's losses were not negligible, at three thousand, but he had won an emphatic victory, forcing Soult back on Bayonne, a well-fortified coastal town, but well within French territory. The news of this, in tandem with St. Cyr's surrender, saw the guns of the Tower of London fired twice in one day. "If Perceval or Pitt had been alive now, they would have almost died for joy," wrote a young guard officer.[83] Wellington did not join in. He halted the advance because the weather turned against him, torrential rain swamping the roads and drenching the men. Even the news of Leipzig did not convince Wellington—any more than the tsar—that some of the allies might sue for a separate peace, leaving him stranded in a hostile France.[84]

He need not have worried. Events elsewhere soon led Napoleon to strip Soult of troops, rather than bolster him. Eugène had held the Austrians well in northern Italy, inflicting a serious defeat on them at Bassano, on the last day of October, but Leipzig and the defection of Bavaria suddenly left the kingdom of Italy vulnerable, and the Austrians were quick to exploit it. Hillier's army had forced Eugène first out of the Illyrian provinces, and then to abandon Venetia, establishing his line on the Adige, about which Napoleon was not pleased.[85] Soult's reverse on the Nivelle caused Napoleon great concern, all the more because he knew so little about it—"If you have any news, get it to me immediately," he told Clarke on November 14.[86] He acknowledged the defining nature of Wellington's victory in his own way, in the detail. He told his minister of commerce upon getting the news confirmed:

> The movement of the English on Bayonne has opened this part of the frontier. I have learned that they have already landed a certain quantity of their merchandise on the coast at Saint-Jean-de-Luz. I think you should pull back your customs' lines to other points.[87]

It was a desperate week on the borders. The following day, with Johann Hiller threatening Verona, Eugène forced him to battle at Caldiero, and drove him back, but Hiller now shifted his advance south, menacing Ferrara. Napoleon's reaction was to choose Eugène and his precious Kingdom of Italy at the direct expense of Soult and the French southwest: all Soult's Italian troops were to join Eugène.[88] "It is of the highest importance: all the Italians must go to the aid of their country."[89] Napoleon nurtured hopes that he had inculcated the same spirit of patriotism in the newly made kingdom that he counted on in France. Soult saw his army weakened by the collapse of the Confederation, as well. Napoleon ordered the Nassau regiment disarmed on November 25,[90] but it was not acted upon. On December 10, on a prearranged signal sent by the Duke of Nassau, who had defected to the allies on November 25, the three battalions of his troops serving with Soult, and one from the Duchy of Frankfurt, defected—fourteen hundred men in all,[91] which prompted Napoleon to order Soult to disband his battalion from Baden. "I am astonished by the delay in carrying out the disarmament I ordered on November 25." He extended it to all ex-Confederation troops.[92] The defeat of Leipzig brought Soult still more problems, and a bizarre order from Napoleon: "Tell the Duke of Dalmatia (Soult) not to overwork his cavalry; that the loss of horses is even more inconvenient since we are no longer in Germany and cannot replace them anymore."[93] This was the state of Soult's army as it braced itself for another onslaught from Wellington.

Wellington was still cramped into a narrow coastal belt, a potentially exposed position, because Soult had managed to hold at the river Nive. He advanced on Bayonne, but had to split his forces because his route was cut by the Nive, and Soult had destroyed the bridges. On the morning of December 10, Soult struck unexpectedly, and was only held with some difficulty, as the Light Infantry Division—the sharpshooters—took cover behind the gravestones of the church of Arcangues, and Soult, who had hoped to drive a wedge between Wellington's two wings and turn on one of them, pulled back to Bayonne.[94] It was at this point his German troops deserted him. After inconclusive, scattered fighting over two days, Soult struck again, with a powerful direct assault on Wellington's lines. Wellington arrived only at midday, and Hill carried most of the fighting.[95] Soult's assault was ferocious, and Wellington had constantly to feed his reserves into the fray to contain the French, but his superior artillery did real damage and turned the tide. Soult again retired to Bayonne. He lost six thousand men over the course of the battle; Wellington, five thousand. Wellington told an officer, "I have often seen the French licked but I never knew them get such a hell of a licking as Hill has given them."[96] He was right. Soult slipped out of Bayonne, fearful that his army would be trapped, knowing all he could hope to do was hold the line of the Ardour. The first "natural frontier" had been breached. The last few weeks cured Wellington of his dread of invading "old France," as he met no popular resistance, and pro-Bourbon rumblings began to reach his ears.

> (I)f I am right in believing that there is a strong Bourbon party
> in France, and that that party is the preponderating one in the south of
> France, what mischief must our army do him in the position I have
> supposed, and what sacrifices would he not make to get rid of us?"

The considered opinion of the commander "already farther advanced on the French territory than any of the allied powers."[97]

Napoleon had mischief of his own to make for Wellington, or at least, he sought to. On November 3, in the hopes of persuading Napoleon to pull back into France and establish a defensible front there, Soult suggested he restore Ferdinand to the Spanish throne, after having lured the British into France, and cutting them off from Spain.[98] Nine days later, Napoleon wrote to Ferdinand in his well-upholstered exile in Talleyrand's château at Valençay:

> The current circumstances of my empire make me want to bring
> to a close the Spanish business. England is fomenting anarchy and
> Jacobinism there, and annihilating the monarchy and the nobility,
> to establish a republic. I can only be sensitive to the destruction
> of a nation so close to my states, and with which I have so many
> common maritime interests. I therefore want to remove any pretext
> for the English to influence (them), and to reestablish the bonds of
> friendship and good neighborliness that have existed between the
> two nations for so long.[99]

There was a grain of truth in it, shameless as it was, but the specters of doom Napoleon held out to Ferdinand were not ones he needed Napoleon to save him from. Napoleon raised the prospect of British economic domination: "The English would sacrifice every state in Europe, even the whole world, to further their own speculations," he told Caulaincourt in 1812.[100] He was right; Spain's empire was even now prey to British commercial interests, but this meant little to Ferdinand in the circumstances of the moment. He was also right when he pointed to the power of the liberals in the Cortes, who were bent on making any restoration dependent on Ferdinand accepting the Constitution of 1812. They were far from the only political power in Spain, and Ferdinand had plenty of support among the right-wing deputies, the *exhaltados*, and among the allies; Britain was pledged to restore him, and Napoleon's talk of "Jacobinal revolution" fomented by Wellington was so much bilge, despite

Whig sympathy for the liberals in Cádiz. There were no Spanish troops in France to withdraw, in any case; Wellington had left them all behind, making this clause of the treaty irrelevant. The war was not over and Ferdinand was a captive, it is true, but once in Spain, the peace treaty Napoleon demanded of him would be worthless. He harbored his new Spanish illusions for some time, nonetheless. "I have come to terms with the Spanish, which makes the armies of Aragon, Catalonia, and Bayonne available to me. I still have close to 200,000 men,"[101] he assured Francesco Melzi and Élisa, in the expectation he could transfer these forces to Italy. Only peace with Britain could halt Wellington, and here, Napoleon was chasing a red herring. It was Christmas, but Santa wore a red tunic. Cutting Wellington off from his line of retreat was the best Napoleon could hope to gain. For Soult, that seemed enough.

There was also the matter of Joseph. Napoleon went via Pierre-Louis Roederer, telling him that in a secret clause, Ferdinand agreed to marry Joseph's daughter, and that if he renounced his crown, he could come back to Paris, see his children, "kill rabbits and play hide-and-seek." Roederer argued that it was still possible for Joseph to be restored. Napoleon's reply was cutting: "A pipedream! The Spanish see Joseph as incompetent. If he accepted, Joseph could join the Regency or have a post in Italy."[102] Napoleon met Joseph for the first time since the baptism of the King of Rome, a few days later. Joseph was made to come to the Tuileries by a service staircase and felt deeply insulted, and refused the terms. Napoleon and Ferdinand bypassed him.[103] Napoleon wrote to him on January 7, in exactly the same words he had addressed to Louis two days previously, to accept his fate as a deposed ruler, remain a prince of France, or disappear forty leagues from Paris. "Is that not possible for you? Have you so little good sense? . . . Choose quickly . . . Hostility and fear are useless feelings, and out of season."[104] Joseph replied the same day, pledging his loyalty, and accepting Napoleon's orders: "In the present circumstances . . . every good Frenchman must abjure any other sentiment." He styled himself "The premier French prince, and . . . your first subject."[105] Almost as a gesture of goodwill to Ferdinand, and of contempt for his brother, Napoleon dissolved Joseph's Guard on November 26 and put them under Soult.[106] The exiled king signed on December 11. Thereafter, however, Ferdinand showed a marked reluctance to go home when he saw how determined the Cortes was to make him accept the 1812 constitution, and almost had to be run out of Valençay. Napoleonic Spain ended as it began, with a bullied Bourbon who somehow came off best, and a bullied, embittered sibling. Joseph snarled to Roederer during all this, "There was nothing in his 'homage' for the king of Spain, but it all showed how great a thing it was to be the brother of the emperor."[107]

The Alps

The Beauharnais were Napoleon's true favorites and family, and Eugène had shown himself as fine a commander as any, despite the growing odds against him. It was the one frontier that was holding on, Eugène disproving Napoleon's criticism of him yet again. His line on the Adige held so well that in early November the Austrians tried diplomacy to circumvent it. Max-Joseph, his father-in-law, sent an envoy to him, proffering a throne in Italy if he changed sides. He recounted his reply to Hortense: "an aide-de-camp of the king of Bavaria, who had been under my orders in the last campaign . . . put forward the finest proposals for my family and myself . . . There were many blandishments of esteem and all that. It would have been very tempting for anyone but me!"[108] Both Napoleon and Eugène agreed to an armistice, however, buying time for Napoleon's promised reinforcements to arrive. The Austrian threat was still very real, however, and Murat's army now took on a vital role in the defense of the peninsula. He had promised to raise a new force when he left the Grande Armée after Leipzig, and in that he kept his word. Murat counted thirty thousand men under his flag, cavalry and artillery among them, all well provisioned, and commanded by experienced, native Neapolitan generals.[109] It remained to be seen whose side they were on. Napoleon had long suspected Murat, and he was right. Murat had been talking to the Austrians since the end of the Russian campaign, but he had raised an army and fought well in Saxony, as promised. Napoleon raised no objection to him leaving the army after Leipzig, telling Cambacérès that his presence in Naples "seems necessary to me."[110] Murat halted his journey in Milan, announcing ostentatiously to all who would listen that he would be back with his brave Neapolitans to help his kinsman, but then spread venom about Eugène to Napoleon, accusing him of preparing to defect—lies quickly exposed.[111] His first acts back in his capital in early November were to dismantle the continental system and open his ports to neutral shipping. He made it clear the army would fight under his command only, and solely in the interests of the kingdom. He met the Austrian ambassador secretly, but on the same day wrote a long letter to Napoleon proclaiming his loyalty.[112] Napoleon's reaction was to dispatch Fouché, recently run out of his Illyrian posting by the allies, to Naples, "to make the king understand the urgency of marching . . . to the Po." He added:

> . . . you will also make this known to the queen, and you will do everything possible to prevent letting that country become the foyer of fallacious Austrian promises through Metternich's silver tongue. Moving the Neapolitan army to the Po is of the highest urgency. It is shameful that part of it was not there at the start of the campaign, when it would have made such a difference. They are . . . marching on France from every side. The circumstances are massive.[113]

Napoleon was living in the past, his policy resting on defunct assumptions. Fouché was not to be trusted at the best of times. That Napoleon thought he could simply rehabilitate him from humiliating obscurity, banished to the wildest frontier of his empire, to a trusted agent, was appalling judgment. Moreover, he now needed the Murats more than they needed him, and he could not help admitting it, so great were the forces arrayed against him. Murat was irascible, unpredictable, and emotional; he might be turned as in the past, but he needed Caroline to prevent this, as in the past. That had changed, too.

The duplicity and ingratitude of which he so unjustly accused his brothers was alive in the mind of Caroline. No one had worked harder to keep the peace between Napoleon and Murat; no one had made Marie-Louise more welcome; no one proved a better vassal than Caroline. No one was better placed to deliver a stab in the back. She had opposed Murat's first approaches to the Austrians in the immediate aftermath of the Russian campaign, and deeply resented being cut out of them, once underway.[114] Her two periods as regent had given her great and justified self-confidence. A French official in Naples said of her, "She turned governing into a noble apprenticeship. The application she brings to business seems to add to her strength. It is a trait of the family."[115] In the months between Russia and Leipzig, she made her own mind up: Napoleon was beaten, as many knew, but unlike most, she acted upon it. Caroline opened talks with Metternich as soon as she got the news of Leipzig, well before Murat returned, assuring him her army would not take the field against Austria.[116] If Murat returned to Naples undecided, his queen was not. She seldom was; she had just changed sides. Fouché and Caroline were the perfect combination to maintain the double game with Napoleon and Metternich, less by keeping Murat tied to their course than by allowing him to vent his oscillations—he was often depressed in these weeks, wracked with guilt about his treason[117]—and so keeping a window open to Napoleon, in case he "made his own luck," as in the past. Fouché reassured Napoleon of Murat's good intentions while he and Caroline carefully covered up the negotiations with Metternich. Their duplicity extended to Elisa. Murat told her not to trust Eugène, and to welcome his troops into Tuscany and let them occupy her forts. She saw through Murat, but warned Napoleon she could do nothing to stop him.[118]

When Murat moved his army north in November, Napoleon was convinced it was on its way to help Eugène, and he may not have been wrong. Murat had declared himself the new savior of Italy, the future leader of a new nation, but he wrote sincerely to Napoleon more than once that he was loyal, but also that peace was the only answer, and he had to negotiate with the allies: Italy was exhausted; order was breaking down; "English gold" was working against them everywhere. Fouché picked up his pen in similar vein.[119] Napoleon remained conciliatory throughout, believing he could always win over his old comrade and convinced of the loyalty of his favorite sibling, and writing warmly to Murat in mid-December.[120] At this point, the Austrians feared Napoleon would win Murat over. When they sought to force his hand, Caroline and Fouché formed a united front with them. Murat had also been confronted by his generals, who placed a petition before him, demanding a liberal constitution on the Spanish model. How he did it remains unknown, but he persuaded them to postpone their demands until a general peace was made.[121] On January 1, an alliance with Austria was agreed, and formally declared ten days later. Murat and Caroline would keep their thrones, if they renounced their claim to Sicily and would leave the Bourbons in peace; the army of thirty thousand was to take the field against Eugène and Napoleon. Murat still had vague hopes of obtaining the Papal states, if not the whole of Italy.[122] Caroline and Metternich took all his expansionist dreams in hand, agreeing they were not helpful or realistic.[123] Murat remained true to his nature. The next day, he wrote to Napoleon, "Thus it came upon me, the saddest day of my life . . . but I had to choose,"[124] and then issued a bloodthirsty proclamation to his troops, declaring, "The emperor wants only war! There are only two banners left in Europe. One reads 'religion, morality, justice, moderation, laws, peace, happiness.' On the other: 'perse-cution, tyranny, war and grieving families.' Choose!"[125]

Napoleon got the news a week later, and it was a hard blow: "The conduct of the king is infamous, and there isn't a name for that of the queen. I hope I live long enough to avenge myself and France on such an outrage, such vile ingratitude,"[126] he poured out to Fouché, betraying how ignorant he was. The great survivor escaped blame for his grossest act of treachery. Napoleon tried one last time with his old comrade, and asked Joseph, of all people, to send an emissary to Murat to dissuade him. Then, Napoleon disavowed the emissary and turned on Joseph for obeying too hastily.[127] Murat was not alone in his confusion. The truth had to be faced, and Napoleon ordered the French embassy in Naples closed, further reducing the tally of states with whom he still had relations. Together with the surrender of Denmark that month, France's diplomatic presence in the world now fell by 50 percent, and was nonexistent in Europe. By the time Murat and Caroline's defection was known, the Neapolitan army was only a few days' march from the Po, closing in on Eugène, with the whole of Italy south of it out of Napoleon's control. When Napoleon realized this, his first instinct was to tell Eugène to cut and run: ". . . it seems to me important that you get to the Alps with all your army."[128] Whether Eugène's fate was in Murat's hands was less certain. On January 30, British warships appeared in the Bay of Naples.[129]

Diplomacy After Midnight

Talks of a kind based on the Frankfurt proposals had been going on between Napoleon and the allies at Mannheim since November. Metternich and Napoleon both saw them as "window dressing"; Napoleon as a way to assuage the "peace party" within his closest collaborators, and Metternich as enabling the allies to maintain the illusion that Napoleon was the only warmonger left in Europe. Metternich did not want peace, but rather to present Napoleon with terms he could not accept. He also had to contain the increasingly dangerous behavior of Alexander. Castlereagh arrived at allied headquarters on January 24, and it was just as well. Already incensed by the violation of Swiss neutrality, the tsar soon unveiled a plan to put Bernadotte on the French throne, or—yet more provocatively—to convene local councils to elect a national parliament to "let the French people decide" on their fate. He unveiled a plan he had nurtured for some time as regards Bernadotte, although Moreau may have been his preferred candidate until his death at Leipzig.[130] Metternich and Castlereagh balked at this, predictably, and together kept Alexander in check. Both men wanted only the restoration of the Bourbons, but Napoleon had to be defeated first.[131] Until then, negotiations had to continue. "The most powerful weapon which the coalition had used against Napoleon was to rip from his face the mask of peace, under which he has piled conquest upon conquest," Metternich wrote later.[132] Alexander proved as much a threat to this strategy as Napoleon, the closer his armies got to Paris.

The British scholar Munro Price has unearthed Napoleon's instructions to Caulaincourt, drawn up in early December: Jérôme could effectively lose Westphalia, but be given Berg in compensation; Napoleon would renounce the crown of Italy, but only to Eugène; Murat and Caroline were to remain—although they do not seem to have been told as much—and although he conceded that the Confederation of the Rhine was no more, Napoleon demanded that no similar body be put in its place, the independence of its members being sacrosanct. He seemed completely oblivious to the policy by which Metternich had managed to dissolve it, unaware, even after the event, of how he had lost his hegemony. Napoleon had always believed the "natural frontiers" were not as essential to French prosperity as its wider control over northern Italy and western Germany, but he had yet to grasp that Belgium and the west bank of the Rhine were still more important. As for the Low Countries, "No sacrifice could be greater for France than to give up any part of Holland."[133] Napoleon had been drawn to the table in no small part because the British had agreed to be there. He told Caulaincourt on their return from Russia more than once that "England had fought too long and too hard to come away with nothing," and he would have to make compromises.[134] But he had no idea what compromises to make. Not only did he demand what amounted to control of the Channel coast—the issue that had dragged Britain into the wars in the first place—but the return of France's colonies as compensation for her losses in Europe.[135] It was no wonder that Castlereagh formally protested.[136]

When the talks resumed, Napoleon told Caulaincourt, "France without its natural limits, without Ostend, without Antwerp, would not be on a par with the other powers of Europe anymore . . . Do they want to reduce France to its old borders? This is vile. This state of affairs suits only the Bourbons." He was right in his fears. On January 4, he told Caulaincourt he now accepted the basis of the Frankfurt proposals; the "natural frontiers" would be enough.[137] It was too little, too late.

The Foundation Stone Cracks: The Masses of Granite Shift

As the allies crossed the Rhine, Napoleon met resistance from the quarter he least expected. His assemblies, quiescent for so long, reared up against him. It began over foreign policy. Metternich's hope, that the Frankfurt accords would drive a wedge between Napoleon and the French, had worked. Having called the deputies and senators to Paris for December 2 to vote to give him men and money, he delayed convening the assemblies until December 19, and in the interval, they had time to see for themselves that no progress had been made in the peace talks. Newly returned from their departments, they also shared the harsh realities of conscription, taxation, and the privations of an economy driven into the ground by war. In his determination to secure their support, Napoleon showed himself at his most arrogant and obtuse. He took it upon himself to name a new president of the Corps Législatif, breaking with the norm that allowed the deputies to elect him. Nor was his choice sensible. Into the chair, he cast Claude-Ambroise Régnier, his long-serving minister of justice, now old and ailing, who had never been a deputy, knew no one among them, and was unable to exert any control over them. It was, perhaps, a sign of how pliant and insignificant Napoleon imagined this body to be—one he said more than once that he wanted to dissolve—that he sent a loyal servant to it as a sinecure. Yet, as Napoleon addressed the assembly on December 19, Cambacérès recalled the snow falling from a leaden gray sky as he spoke, and the pale, glacial faces of the deputies. More ominously, the benches were almost empty.[138] It was the quiet before the storm.

Napoleon raised the old trope up: England had sought to impose its will on France for four centuries, and the threat was greater now than ever. All their energy was needed to save the nation.[139] He played an old Jacobin card, just as he revealed himself ever more a monarch. The deputies now wanted peace with England more than anything, but Napoleon was deaf to them. There is a bitter irony in this. The Peace of Amiens, far more than military victory, had opened the way to absolute power for Napoleon. Now, he needed to secure it again, desperately. He allowed the Senate and the Corps Législatif to appoint committees to inspect all the records of the negotiations before the assemblies to appease the deputies. The committees were then to draw up loyal addresses to Napoleon, which their respective chambers would approve. It was yet another plan of campaign based on poor intelligence and false assumptions. The Senate elected "experienced, cold men," Talleyrand among them. There was no heated opposition among them, but Talleyrand posed Cambacérès one sole question: "Why was so much time lost before negotiations began?" They also noted that not all the documentation was before them. Napoleon and Maret were hiding their arrogant conduct toward the allies at the Prague talks.[140] A point had been made to those with the sense to listen. Napoleon was not of that number. The Senate fell into line, but the committee chosen by the lower house signaled a fiercer attitude. Several of its five members had had brushes with the regime; one, Jean-Antoine Gallois, was a close friend of Talleyrand. It was the most self-effacing of their number, a lawyer from Bordeaux, Joseph Lainé, who emerged from the shadows to challenge the very ethos of the regime, not just the progress of the peace talks.[141] A thoughtful, erudite bachelor, Lainé was a man of moderate republican politics, and a protégé of Cambacérès (who had urged him to become a deputy in 1808).[142] The accusations of royalism that surround him have been dispelled by the careful research of Munro Price,[143] but in his private notes made over the years of empire, Lainé came to see Napoleon as a ruler who used war as a tool to foster his despotic power at home. War had allowed Napoleon to usurp the hard-won right of the assemblies, not the executive, to control finances. Accordingly, peace was essential not just to end the slaughter, but to open the way to the restoration of a liberal, parliamentary monarchy. When the committee chose him to write their report to Napoleon, it all poured out, and his companions did not try to stop him. Lainé and his colleagues presented their draft to Cambacérès and Régnier on Christmas Eve. Lainé argued that the Frankfurt proposals offered "peace with honor" because they offered France her "natural frontiers," but he went further, criticizing all the conquests and annexations carried out since 1794, not just by Napoleon, but under the Directory as well. Above all, he condemned the "illegal" levying of taxation, the blatant flouting of the terms of conscription, detentions without trial, and arbitrary, often corrupt military requisitioning.[144] Lainé singled out the rapacity of Masséna by name "for having looted the country house of a citizen of Marseille," as typical of what was going on.[145] It was, in essence, an attack on a regime that had become arbitrary. Behind it lay Lainé's privately held conviction that Napoleon used the war to tighten his stranglehold on France.[146] Cambacérès sought to calm things down, and persuaded the commissioners to remove some of the more direct criticisms of Napoleon from the text[147] but neither he nor the other councillors of state present threw it back in Lainé's face. Lainé recalled afterward, "We thought we could read in the eyes of these exalted figures that they were delighted to have found a mouthpiece through which to speak the truth and beg for peace."[148] Cambacérès was, indeed, of their mind, and knew they were patriots, not traitors—they were clear they supported the defense of the homeland—but he sensed in them a desire to pounce on Napoleon when he was defeated, "to wrest from a defeated sovereign what he had taken from them as a victorious one." He also knew they risked giving Napoleon a chance to abolish the Corps Législatif.[149] He hoped he had steered them into calmer waters, but he was wrong. When Lainé rose to his feet before the chamber on December 29, and repeated it the next day to a fuller house, his attitude was yet more blistering. No copy of the speech survives, but if the notes taken by a deputy are accurate, Lainé did not stop at calling the offer of the "natural frontiers" fair, but deplored "that aggression, that ambitious activity, that has for twenty years been so fatal for the peoples of Europe." At this point, Régnier—presiding as best he could—burst out, "What you're saying is unconstitutional!" to which another commissioner, François Raynouard, retorted, "The only unconstitutional thing here is you."[150] The belief in a French "manifest destiny," in the "great nation" and its mission to Europe, was dead.

But Lainé went further: "Let us not deceive ourselves: our misfortunes overwhelm us . . . commerce is destroyed, industry is dying, there is not a Frenchman whose family or property has not been affected. What are the causes of this ineffable misery? . . . A barbarous and pointless war . . ." This was the festering anger of the masses of granite brought into the cold light of day. The speech invoked "the odious curse" of conscription—even if it did not call it "the blood tax" as did its peasant victims—but its real cri de coeur came from the provincial elites.[151] Lainé was more than a lawyer; he was a member of a merchant family severely damaged by the blockade, and a member of the Bordeaux's charity commission. He was his class and his city incarnate.[152] The deputies rallied to a new cause. Lainé's address was voted on, a crushing 223 to 51.[153] Lainé's hopes to address a list of grievances—which would have curbed Napoleon's powers extensively—deliberately mirroring those sent to Louis XVI on the eve of the Revolution, came to nothing,[154] but the support his motion garnered foreshowed the end for Napoleon more than the might of Alexander's guards. His solid foundation of granite had been pulled out from under him unless he changed his very nature, and the events of the next few days showed he had no intention of so doing. *Ralliement* was no more.

That evening, on reading the speech, Napoleon banned its publication and had all the copies of it seized from the printers. He then closed the Corps Législatif. He had intended to abolish it, but Cambacérès, if his notes are to be trusted, talked him out of it on the most pragmatic of grounds: "The speech is a fact, you could never stop news of it getting out now . . . To dissolve the assembly would send out a signal of (domestic) discord in time of war." Napoleon got up and left the meeting without a word. The next day, in the Council of State, he said merely, "I want to dissolve the assembly, but I'll put it off." Then he turned to Cambacérès and said "I know fine well you're protecting the Corps Législatif." Cambacérès won the battle, but knew he had lost the war for Napoleon's conscience. It was the last meeting he recorded, but wrote later, "It pains me to dwell over such difficult memories."[155]

The commissioners were then summoned to Savary and lambasted, but he did nothing. Napoleon invited all the deputies to his annual New Year's Day reception at the Tuileries, where he hurled abuse at them in like manner to his treatment of the "black cardinals" as few years before. The commissioners kept away, and were not there to hear Napoleon—in the midst of the most despotic phase of his reign—lash out at the absent Lainé in a most Jacobinal way. In one breath, he bellowed, "What is the throne? A piece of wood covered in velvet; but in the language of monarchy, I am the throne! You speak of the people; don't you realize that it is I, above all, who represent them?" Then, he accused Lainé of being an English agent.[156] The spirit of Robespierre rumbled in his guts, just as that of the Sun King marked his actions. More typical of his own temperament, Napoleon did nothing to Lainé, and let him go home, along with all the other suspended deputies, each carrying the tale of what had befallen them.

There is nothing confused about Napoleon's mingling of contempt for the trappings of the old monarchy—the throne—and his increasing insistence on the atavistic nature of the monarch as the only source of unity. Napoleon had evolved a vision of the French past—uncannily like that of the Chinese emperors—that saw history as succession of dynasties whose "mandate of heaven" to rule emerged from a time of troubles, and marked them out as embodying the "spirit of the age." The Bonapartes seized the mandate from the Bourbons, because they incarnated the new age ushered in by the revolution.[157] Napoleon clung to this vision of the world while "the mandate of heaven" was being wrenched from him.

Even as Napoleon gave Caulaincourt his marching orders, allied armies had theirs. When the talks resumed on February 5, their venue said it all: the eastern French city of Châtillon, on the borders of Burgundy and the Champagne. The "natural frontiers" were the allies' to give or withhold from Napoleon.

13

THE FALL OF FRANCE: THE END OF EVERYTHING, JANUARY–MAY 1814

❧━━━━━━━━━━━━━━━━━━━━━━━━━━━━━━━━━━━━━❧

January 1814: Collapse in the East

The invasion of France from the north and the east began in the first days of January 1814. The "hawks" in the allied camp had won. In the depths of winter, along roads turned to mud and ice, exhausted troops still awaiting new uniforms and arms set out toward one of the most defensible natural frontiers in Europe. They had also acquired typhus, a sting in the tail of the Grande Armée left in its billets as it pulled back from Mainz.[1] The armies traveled fast and light, without large supply trains or forage for their horses, through barren fields.[2] It was worse than anyone imagined. Russian officers were shocked by the poverty of eastern France—ravaged by years of poor harvests—compared to the plenty they found in Saxony and Silesia.[3] "Living off the land" heightened the latent fears of the commanders, of the specter of a France in arms behind every hedgerow. Schwarzenberg saw peasant revolt everywhere;[4] Barclay, the inevitable vicious circle of poor supplies, military brutality, and popular resistance.[5] Talk of "the natural frontiers" suddenly seemed less a diplomatic abstraction than a stark reality. The Rhine was easily forded—Victor made no attempt to defend Strasbourg[6]—but beyond it loomed the rugged line of the Vosges, their passes a deadly snare for Roman and barbarian alike for millennia. To their north lay the tangled web of the Ardennes forest, a threat to advancing armies as late as the Second World War, and beyond them, the Meuse, Moselle, Marne, and the lower Rhine and its tributaries, all of which had to be forded. Only Metternich's defiance of Swiss neutrality—and of the tsar's objections—made the passage of the southern sector easier, allowing the allies access to the gap between the Vosges and the Alps around Mulhouse and Belfort. "Old France" was made to be defended. Most allied commanders balked at the prospect of driving forward so soon, if at all. Yet, the "hawks" were right to attack. Blücher, driven by a thirst for revenge, was foremost among them, believing Napoleon had to be crushed before he could regroup.[7] The greatest hawk of all was Alexander, possessed of a messianic vision of dictating peace in Paris, his instincts bolstered by Blücher's reports, even as his perverse stance over Swiss neutrality revealed how mercurial he remained.[8] "He has a *personal* feeling about Paris, distinct from all political or military combinations. He seems to seek for the occasion of entering with his magnificent guards the enemy's capital," Castlereagh recorded with a shudder.[9] Their voices in council prevailed, almost in spite of themselves. "Winter war" had always been Napoleon's prerogative. No more.

The natural barrier the fates bestowed on France was scantily defended. Barely seventy thousand men limped over the Rhine in December, many of them riddled with typhus. Marmont's IV Corps lost fifteen thousand men—almost half its strength—to the disease;[10] it stood at a mere sixteen thousand on the eve of invasion, not having fired a shot.[11] As the victims were transported to Burgundy, they carried the deadly plague with them, spreading it across eastern France.[12] Typhus took hold in Mainz, whose hospitals and supply depots were unprepared for the influx of sick, wounded, and simply hungry troops who flooded into it in the wake of Leipzig.[13] The arrival of the army in Strasbourg led to an outbreak that claimed sixty thousand lives. Just when the defense of Paris became Napoleon's priority, the prevalence of typhus in the army made it too dangerous for many of his troops to go anywhere near the capital.[14] This was a cruel irony for Napoleon, a man who had done so much to encourage inoculation throughout his public life, beginning in 1801, with the foundation of the Hospital Center for Vaccination in 1801. Napoleon had his son inoculated publicly, to set an example in his campaign to eradicate smallpox; in 1812, vaccination became mandatory for all school children, civil servants, and serving soldiers. By the Concordat of Fontainebleau, all parish priests were ordered to preach inoculation from the pulpit. By 1814, one French child in two was vaccinated.[15] The disease became all but eradicated, only for a new plague to sweep in from the East as his empire crumbled.

Desertion bled him drier still. After two years of constant retreat, the homeland came to be seen as a refuge, a land of plenty. Instead, the troops found nothing. The army administration proved incompetent; supplies were nonexistent, and the "marauding" so well-practiced abroad soon became the fate of countless villages and farms in eastern France. Desertion became all too easy; Napoleon lost about forty thousand men to it over December and January. As they slipped away, they carried typhus and "the plague of those horrors and crimes they are so practiced at," in the words of Étienne Radet, the senior gendarme commander who saw it all coming as early as November.[16] When Blücher crossed the Rhine on December 29, and Schwarzenberg approached Colmar on New Year's Day,[17] Napoleon had just over one hundred thousand men to defend the whole frontier between Strasbourg and the Channel. Those actually under arms may have been as few as sixty-seven thousand.[18] Their leadership in these weeks was left to the marshals, with no central, coordinated command structure. Isolated, Ney, Marmont, and Victor fell back into Lorraine, yielding the passes of the Vosges to Blücher. He took full advantage: his Army of Silesia advanced seventy-five miles into France in only nine days. When Victor abandoned Nancy without any kind of a rear-guard action, his troops were pelted and insulted as they marched out.[19] He allowed the allies to cross the Meuse unopposed.[20] Yet, Blücher had done this with barely twenty-seven thousand men, a feat of Napoleonic daring, aided by the capture of vital intelligence by roving Cossacks.[21]

By 1814, all the fortifications of eastern and northern France had been severely neglected by the army engineers,[22] allowing them increasingly to be shielded by troops purloined from the German princes of the former Confederation as a price for being spared the fate of Saxony.[23] This released Yorck, who entered Trier with fifty thousand veteran Prussians, to support Blücher.[24] South of them, Marmont evacuated the Sarre, while Napoleon told Kellermann to remove the depots of the guard to as far west as Reims, Châlons-en-Champagne, and, ominously, Paris.[25] On January 11, Napoleon told Clarke he intended to turn Paris into a fortress, where he would await the enemy if he had to, and would never abandon. Les Invalides was to become a munitions factory;[26] the city's plane trees, those proud symbols of urban renewal, were to be cut down to build wooden palisades to fill in the gaps in its walls.[27] There was nowhere to run now. By the time Napoleon ordered Clarke to form partisans in the vicinity of Vesoul, on the Ardennes-Champagne border, on January 2,[28] a Bavarian commander, the Prince of Thurn-Taxis, led his "raider corps" (*Streifkorps*) on Vesoul, wrong-footing its defenders with his skirmishers, while his main body—led by Cossacks—took the town without warning, collecting two hundred prisoners and supply stores.[29] That same day, Napoleon ordered Vesoul's prefect "to keep the town safe from all enemy forces."[30] Napoleon's projected muster point was now on the front line.[31] It was no different further south. Napoleon reacted with astonishment at the rapid collapse of the defenses on the Swiss border. On January 4, as Alexander and Schwarzenberg swept forward with main army, he wrote to Clarke, "I am surprised to see that this beautiful part of France has not been defended," and that the prefect of Geneva—a French territory in 1814—had fled, rather than make a stand with the national guard and the garrison. "Geneva would now be the thoroughfare of the empire; but having deserted the city twice, not even calling out the national guard, he has deserted his post and betrayed his duty."[32] He issued furious threats to the members of its provisional government who had welcomed the allies, to take them hostage and hold them in France when the town was retaken,[33] his fury mocked by his impotence. By January 12, an Austrian force seized Mâcon, having made a pact with its municipal authorities to respect law and order in return for their neutrality.[34] Mâcon is a key route center, cutting the Rhône-Saône corridor in half, and left Augereau isolated in Lyon: Thus, another large garrison, containing almost ten thousand infantry and two thirds of Suchet's cavalry, much-needed to face Wellington, was stranded. Soult saw his forces reduced by one third for no good purpose.[35] Only the people of the Chalonnais hills offered any resistance in the region, but they were quickly overwhelmed by Hesse-Homburg's men.[36] Right along the front, Napoleon seemed oblivious to the sheer power of the allied onslaught.

Thorn-Taxis's appearance as far north as Vesoul heralded just how close Blücher and Schwarzenberg's armies now were. His unit was part of Wrede's Bavarian corps, on the extreme right of Schwarzenberg's columns. It was a cardinal element of the allied invasion plan that they did not become cut off from each other, and the taking of Vesoul showed that the French could do little to prevent the two armies uniting, although Schwarzenberg continued to fear Napoleon would counterattack, knowing the strategic importance of the Langres plateau.[37] He could still not grasp how weak Napoleon had become, or that he could not fight for such vital ground. Napoleon did, indeed, try to defend it. The plateau was Napoleon's appointed muster point for the new army he was desperately trying to assemble.[38] On January 6, he ordered Clarke to send a general to prepare the town's defenses, deploy any artillery he could find, muster its National Guard, and even gather up hunting rifles—"there must be some here and there"—and if there were not enough, to find other sources, "for this is an important place."[39] It was almost pitiful, ignorant of the proximity and power of the forces converging on this "important place." The allies did not actually merge their forces for some weeks, but not because of Napoleon.

The provinces were not the only places short of guns. Behind the front line, Napoleon returned to empty arsenals that, although well provisioned with cannon, powder, and bayonets, were critically short of muskets.[40] Negligence was compounded by Napoleon's firm conviction that the allies would not advance until the spring.[41] He could not have been more wrong. Each tactical blunder, every strategic miscalculation, any bungled diplomatic gamble now hovered over him more like eagles than vultures, powerful birds of prey.

While Blücher drove into the Vosges, Schwarzenberg advanced toward Besançon, with the ultimate objective of swinging north to meet Blücher near Langres. Schwarzenberg's Army of Bohemia formed the bulk of this southern flank, but it was stiffened by Alexander's Russian guards. Charles Stewart, the British observer, was in no doubt how formidable they were:

> It is impossible by any description to give an exaggerated idea of the perfect state of these troops; their appearance and equipment were admirable, and when one considered what they had endured . . . one was lost in wonder, and inspired with a political awe of that colossal power. The condition in which the Russian cavalry appeared reflected the highest reputation on this branch of their service; and their artillery was admirable.[42]

As Napoleon virtually scrounged horses as best he could, and inducted "promising conscripts" into the Young Guard,[43] Stewart, his words tinged with fear, beheld the new military elite in Europe, and it was coming for Napoleon in his lair.

It came cautiously, however. If anyone was buying Napoleon some precious time, it was Schwarzenberg. He apportioned a powerful force under the Prince of Hesse-Homburg to besiege Besançon on January 9, containing some of his best troops, elite grenadiers, and heavy cavalry. Besançon is an imposing site, a fortress city, set on a high, steep outcrop, but it was defended almost pathetically by raw conscripts, poorly mounted cavalry, and a few customs men who had to be rounded up, having fled the city at news of the Austrian advance. It was typical of what Michael V. Leggiere calls Schwarzenberg's "senseless prudence."[44] Throughout early January, Schwarzenberg was haunted by the groundless fear that Napoleon was somewhere between Metz and Nancy with forces thought to be between 180,000[45] and 80,000 men,[46] making him the last man in Europe to believe Napoleon's publicity. On January 2, Napoleon told the prefect of Vesoul of "the arrival of an army of 100,000 which is forming at Langres, the vanguard to which will arrive (in Vesoul) on the 10th." Better informed than his emperor, the prefect fled.[47] Schwarzenberg seemed to think Napoleon really did have the huge numbers of elite troops he claimed, and panicked when he thought they had been diverted toward Langres, despite Wrede's reports that the French numbered no more than fifteen thousand in the area.[48] Indeed, so flimsy were the French defenses that Schwarzenberg reached Langres on January 17, and soon linked up with Blücher, despite poor roads and dreadful weather. The Cossacks and the dragoons of Alexander's guard looted and pillaged as they went. Even in so poor a landscape, there was always something an army could find to thieve, it seems. Their conduct embittered the locals, but did not provoke the guerrilla war Alexander feared.[49] The allies swept to their objective.

The plateau of Langres holds the sources of the Aube, Marne, and the Meuse, a position from which the allies could strike out. Napoleon hoped he could retake Langres,[50] but on January 17, he designated Châlons-en-Champagne as his headquarters and the new muster point, and ordered its fortification.[51] The same day, he ordered the city of Troyes, to the rear of Châlons, to be fortified "to protect it from Cossacks and light troops"; its defenders were to be its national guards, forest guards, field guards, and "men of goodwill."[52] On January 24, Castlereagh joined the allied armies at Langres. In every sense, they now held the high ground.

Or almost. Napoleon's only effective marshal now seemed to be Bernadotte. Bülow's corps pushed on into Belgium in the last weeks of December 1813, and found little opposition, but he did so unsupported. Bernadotte's sixty thousand force of Swedes, Prussians, and Russians remained well behind them even after the capitulation of Denmark; Bulow's only help came from a small British contingent under Graham, which landed at Tholen on December 4.[53] The Dutch were proving as hard to mobilize in the allied cause as they had in Napoleon's. They refused to adopt Prussian conscription methods, a Prussian commander noting the absence of "that energetic activity which will . . . guarantee the independence of its liberated people."[54] Bülow pushed into Belgium, nonetheless, if cautiously, assuming Macdonald's "skeleton corps" of thirteen thousand[55] to be stronger than it was.[56] Napoleon was alert to the danger, but for all his continuous promises of huge reinforcements, there was little he could do about it. He insisted Antwerp be held and not cut off from Macdonald, even as Bülow set about doing just that. Napoleon may well have deliberately exaggerated the number of men he had at his disposal to confuse the allies, and there are indications this had some effect,[57] but he was certainly as ill-informed about the true state of affairs in the Low Countries as he was everywhere else on the eastern front. Those troops Napoleon had on hand, intended for Macdonald in Belgium, were cut off when Blücher crossed the Rhine in early January: not one battalion reached him.[58] As Macdonald was forced back, Napoleon ordered Nicolas Joseph Maison to defend Antwerp, rather than link with Macdonald, and sent his Young Guard division to the city,[59] thus adding its garrison to the list of Dresden and Hamburg, of wasted manpower so desperately needed elsewhere. Napoleon thought the allies had only between twelve thousand and fifteen thousand men in the region, but Maison knew better. He was badly outgunned, but cursed being chained to Antwerp, which stopped him preventing Bülow outflanking him or moving on the Prussians himself.[60] He could not hold the city and advance at the same time. When Maison checked Bülow outside Antwerp on January 13, Napoleon's reproaches were not long in coming: "If General Maison had united all his forces and marched straight at (Bülow), he would have driven him back . . . This general still is not used to command."[61] "Why didn't he tell you the enemy was before him, and why did he take such fright? . . . Tell him there is nothing to indicate there are considerable forces there . . . (he) emboldens the enemy by his timidity . . . it is deplorable weakness."[62] It was a shocking confession of ignorance by Napoleon, more like.

The allies were not that much better informed. Bülow remained without news from allied headquarters for the last two weeks of December, and used it to badger his superiors with demands for help, and jibes about Bernadotte, jolting Castlereagh into threatening to withdraw the British subsidy to Sweden.

"We're all in arms here against the prince-royal" he wrote on Christmas Eve.[63] It did no good, and Bülow halted, convinced he was too weak to press on. He concentrated on Belgium when he actually had Macdonald trapped between the Meuse and the Rhine.[64] By January, he at last had help, when Winzing-erode's Russians arrived, but they occupied themselves with dislodging the French from their Flemish fortresses, having been reluctant to come to Bülow's aid in the first place.[65] Only Macdonald, increasingly gloomy, saw things in the Low Countries for what they were. Blücher had forced him to retreat in early January, but he had seen the hopelessness of the situation much earlier. On December 5, 1813, he told Berthier:

> I do not know where (the enemy) will stop, and we cannot stop him with our weak resources . . . It is absolutely necessary the emperor knows the truth, it is worth hearing. There is a great deal of discouragement, everyone is tired of war, the continuous marches and movements. Those who the emperor has showered with advancement and awards are the first who desire to enjoy them in tranquility and hope for nothing else.[66]

Chief among them was Murat. His defection meant Italy south of the Po was lost. On Christmas Day 1813, Napoleon warned Elisa not to give Murat's troops arms when they arrived in Tuscany, but to send them to Piedmont, for the new conscripts there. He was deeply suspicious:

> You must not in any way, let him take over the civil administration. If he comes with such intentions, send his troops back to stay in his own country. Don't let him use your funds, don't tolerate it. If the king declares war on us, France is not yet dead, and such infamous treachery, if it exists, will rebound on its author.[67]

He read his old friend right. On January 17, Napoleon told his governor-general in Turin, his brother-in-law Camille Borghese, not to send the conscripts of the Piedmontese departments south to Tuscany and Rome, but to keep them in the region.[68] The same day, he told Eugène that Murat "has joined himself to our enemies": "As soon as you have the official news, it seems to me important that you get your army to the Alps . . . having taken care to bring (from Milan) the silver and precious possessions of my Household, and its coffers."[69] These stark orders were a crushing admission that it was all over in Italy. The "jewel in the crown" of his empire, the birthplace of his sense of destiny, had been snatched from him by those he "showered with advancement and awards"—including his sister—but who now desired "to enjoy them in tranquility." Macdonald had his limitations as a soldier, but he was a prophet.

The Machine Stops: France, January 1814

By the end of January, the allies had seized large swathes of eastern and northern France, and Belgium, denying Napoleon resources in manpower and matériel he badly needed. These regions had always been plentiful sources of recruits, and their loss turned Napoleon's projections for fresh levies to dust. Most of the Southwest, admittedly always a foyer of resistance to conscription, was also in allied hands. The levies of 1814 now fell only on what was fast becoming a rump of "old France": the "exceptional" levies declared after Leipzig of 120,000 drawn from the classes of 1808–14, another levy in November of 150,000 from the years 1803–14 to compensate for Bavaria's defection, plus that of 300,000 men declared in November 1813;[70] the mobilization of the departmental legions of the National Guard, in early January (decreed on December 30, 1813); and of 160,000 men of the conscripts of 1815 on January 15 (150,000 of them had already been drafted).[71] Napoleon dispatched twenty-three "extraordinary commissioners" drawn from the Council of State and the Senate to enforce them. This echoed the notorious representatives on mission of the Terror, the clearest sign that the once well-oiled machine no longer worked. On paper, the new levies amounted to 936,000 men.[72] Barely 350,000 were actually conscripted, and only 120,000 of them took the field.[73] It was a desperate mix of "the old men and the boys," the product of Napoleon's penchant for projecting fantasy as mathematics run riot.

Napoleon's call to arms remained unheeded; no mass uprisings on the plain of the Rhine materialized; no Alsatian guerrillas lurked in the forests along the passes. The levée en masse he ordered Berthier to conjure in the Rhine departments was a phantom.[74] At first, Napoleon limited his call for partisans to veterans and national guardsmen, wary of spontaneous popular violence, but later his appeals became more desperate, more "Jacobin" in tone. For all the noise, "the partisan" of 1814 was a thing of legend, conjured after the war, the creature of the Romantic pen more than the official clarion call.[75] Behind the front, the omens for the regime were ominous and spread far beyond lack of manpower. The careful equilibrium of demographics had been jettisoned by the regime, and its human face was the attempt to take older, married men from their families and teenage boys from their mothers. It was not the first time, but the scale struck terror into whole communities. Where revolt was not possible, evasion by clandestine legal ruses often was. "Who will feed our mothers and sisters?" was the cry of rebels in French Flanders; the local authorities did not hesitate to report it. The brigands reappeared, but as Annie Crépin has put it, "A process began that led from revolt against the excesses of conscription, to one against conscription, itself, and soon to one against the regime, itself. They were not hostile to conscription because they were royalists, but they became so in resisting the call-up."[76] There was a marked inertia in areas in the path of the allied advance. One third to half of the new recruits in the southwestern departments simply refused to go; in the more dangerous western departments—those of the Vendean revolt of the 1790s—the extraordinary commissioner, François Antoine de Boissy d'Anglas, one of Napoleon's most reliable collaborators, suspended conscription altogether. Even General Caffarelli, long a "trouble shooter" for the regime in the West, and now the extraordinary commissioner for Toulouse, reported on the areas in Wellington's path, "They believe they will find things better under the enemy's yoke." At times, it seemed Wellington knew the French better than Napoleon. Napoleon sent one of his long-serving collaborators to the northeast, to steady conscription in this populous area, long known for its quiescence, but now ever more turbulent as Bülow drew nearer. Jacques-Pierre Orillard de Villemanzy was a noble, long rallied to the Revolution, who had served in the finance administration of the Army of Italy in 1796, at the Channel camps, and in every major campaign since. A senator since 1808, Napoleon put great faith in him. It did not last long. Villemanzy described the condemnation to death of three peasants by a military commission as "An error however you look at it. It is not by shooting these poor devils that one sets the tone of public morale," and commuted them.[77] Napoleon lashed out "it is vigor that is needed now, not weakness . . . It is to set the tone for public morale, not to show weakness, that I sent him on mission."[78] He noted that the powers of his commissioners did not extend to commuting the sentences of courts martial.[79] There were "loyal" areas. The departments around Paris and the Seine basin reacted badly to the levy of 300,000, but they responded to calls to defend "the homeland" when the allies drew closer. The harshness of the allied occupation gave rise to some truly popular resistance in the Vosges, Lorraine, and the Champagne, but it came too late to matter.[80] Inertia and resentment were Napoleon's worst enemies in 1814, not an incipient Vendée or the elitist royalist conspiracies of the *Chevaliers de la Foi*. Even Lebrun, now commanding Antwerp, had ceased sending him daily reports by mid-January.[81] Napoleon's inability to "read" France, to see what he sent his loyalist men into, or learn from their reports, dug his own grave. When he complained to Clarke that artillery was not arriving at Troyes, called the efforts to get muskets to the depots "absurd," and railed, "I see no activity that the circumstances demand,"[82] it was questionable who, exactly, had lost control of the situation, Napoleon or his subordinates.

On January 16, as the moment to return to the army approached, Napoleon appointed Joseph "lieutenant general of the kingdom" at a ceremony in the Tuileries. He was made Marie-Louise's counselor for military matters, but effectively Joseph now had a wide remit over economic and administrative affairs. Napoleon placed in Joseph's hands the defense of Paris, the place he wanted defended "even on its ruins."[83] With this, Joseph assumed the defense of his wife and son. Napoleon confirmed Joseph's title of "king"—of what he did not specify, but as Vincent Haegele has wryly remarked, France now found itself ruled by an emperor, an empress, and a king, not to mention Cambacérès, when it was ever more out of control. Napoleon allowed none of them anywhere near diplomacy, the thing he needed help with most. There is a bitter irony in this, for Joseph was the real architect of the Peace of Amiens and so many minor peaceful triumphs in the early years. As so often, Napoleon cast Joseph in a role he was ill-suited to, but ignored his real gifts. It may well have been ties of blood that led Napoleon to entrust his elder brother with the protection of his family; it is hard to know. The terms of the Regency obliged Napoleon to accord Joseph a role; he gave him what was most sacred to him. Joseph had his own reasons for swallowing his pride. It was hardly the empty royal title; "an army of chamberlains and courtiers means little in this context."[84] If the memoirs of Joseph's close adviser, André François Miot del Mélito, are to be believed, the suspension of the Corps Législatif led Joseph to fear a military dictatorship. He knew Napoleon better than anyone. His own instincts as a born "parliamentarian" may have been rekindled, perhaps not, but he sensed he could cultivate a following among the angry deputies if he took up their cause. Paradoxically, while Joseph was so determined to claw back his own royal trappings, he sought to use them to influence Napoleon in favor of the deputies.[85] This is the charitable view. Joseph was, he hoped, positioning himself well with the "loyal opposition" to his brother in a time of crisis, as in 1805, when he let it be known he would be more than willing to step into the breach, should anything befall Napoleon at the front.

On January 24, Napoleon sent Joseph detailed orders and information about the defense of Paris. The Guard numbered 30,000 men in thirty battalions—18,000 of them fresh conscripts—the best of whom formed the palace guard and a strategic reserve.[86] The city was largely defended by its National Guard, much reformed after the Malet affair, but Napoleon confessed "the real problem is arms . . . we don't have any . . . It will have to be armed with all the hunting rifles we can find." The men coming out of the military hospitals of the capital "offer an immense resource."[87] Joseph replied that he had ordered all the field and forest guards formed into a division under the command of the gendarmerie "to oppose the enemy before any danger can scatter them if they were surprised by enemy incursions before having received orders."[88] Joseph had no illusions. He was, nonetheless, aware of the potential of the Gendarmerie as a force to be reckoned with within the capital: there were 100 elite gendarmes and 800 more of the Paris brigade, all mounted,[89] now under his command.

The day before, Napoleon summoned the officers of the National Guard to the Tuileries, in the presence of Marie-Louise and the King of Rome, dressed in their uniforms, and told them he went to the front "relieved that they will be under your guard."[90] The next day, he met with his council, and dined with the empress and Hortense. He hugged his son before he was sent to bed, and took his own leave for Vitry-le-François at three in the morning. He never saw them again.

The Journey of Pius VII

Savary was ordered to kidnap Pius VII yet again, this time to hustle him back to Savona. He was to travel as "the bishop of Imola"—Savary transcribed it as "Dimales"[91]—and the palace staff were to say he was being taken to Rome, "where they have their orders to drop him like a bomb."[92] Pius was duly bundled into a coach at five in the morning, and packed off. The black cardinals were sent packing, too, back into exile scattered about the towns of southern France, guarded by gendarmes "so that Fontainebleau and the environs of Paris might be free of all these ecclesiastics."[93] The "road trip" did not turn out as Napoleon had hoped, any more than all his dealings with Pius.

After Leipzig Napoleon knew he had to persuade Pius to return to Rome, but on his own terms, as far as possible. Austria's adhesion to the coalition specified Francis's desire to see Pius restored to Rome, which Napoleon saw as an opportunity to divide the allies. He probably exaggerated the importance of this in his own mind, underestimating as ever their growing collective determination to crush him, but one of his first acts on his return was to dispatch Countess Anna Pieri Brignole-Sale to Fontainebleau to entreat with Pius. She was well chosen. An Italian aristocrat of impeccable lineage and known for her piety, she was also a lady-in-waiting to Marie-Louise. She got nowhere. When they met in November 1813, Pius told her that international affairs were in too much flux to enter into any talks. Pius knew Napoleon was now on his back foot, and used his soignée emissary to tell him as much.[94] Napoleon tried again, in mid-December, through Étienne Fallot de Beaumont, the former bishop of Piacenza, a French aristocrat so hated in his diocese as an intruder he was transferred to Bourges, where Pius refused to invest him.[95] De Beaumont told Pius he could go home if he negotiated, but Pius said he would only do so when he was home. By the day of the meeting, January 19, 1814, Murat had occupied Rome and joined the coalition, so Fallot resorted to an outright lie, telling Pius the allies had agreed to let Murat keep Rome as an enticement to change sides, whereas Napoleon would let Pius have Rome back, as long as he confirmed Napoleon's appointments to the vacant sees. Pius had less reason to bargain than in November, and had been well coached by Cardinals Pacca and Consalvi before they were exiled again: The return of the Papal States was a simple act of justice, the restitution of stolen goods, and not subject to haggling.[96] Pius had taken a leaf out of Napoleon's own book: why bargain when you are in a strong position? When Fallot came back empty-handed, Maret saw the game was up, and told Napoleon simply to let Pius go back to Rome, and let him reign there. It was done the next day, if in Napoleon's rough-cut way.[97] Pius was sent on a bizarre journey through southern France. No explicit reason for this was given,[98] but the most direct route down the Saône-Rhône corridor was largely in allied hands. Pius was carted about for weeks, his disguise slipping every step of the way. When they passed through Orgon, cheering crowds and bands marked their passage. As the journey went on, and the course of the war turned against Napoleon, Pius's most recent jailer—now his escort—Lagorce, gradually reinvented himself as the pope's protector, introducing him to his mother when they passed through his home town of Brive, where Pius blessed her.[99] Even an elite gendarme could see which way the wind blew that winter, and took steps toward that "quiet life" Macdonald saw as the path to treason.

War on the Doorstep

Napoleon's journey was far shorter. It was only a day's ride from the Tuileries to the front at Vitry-le-François. He had little time to collect his thoughts when he got there on January 26, but he had more to ponder than ever before. He could not fathom his enemies as they closed in on him, nor the minds of his friends as their loyalty crumbled away. He was on narrow ground in every sense. He had chosen war as his only way out, but had only his tattered army to fight it with: The day he left Paris, he ordered Kellermann to incorporate all his fresh conscripts into the guard.[100]

Napoleon came to Vitry with no clear plan in his mind, save to muster as many troops as he could in the vicinity and counterattack. The marshals were bereft of clear orders and fell back haphazardly before Blücher, casting aspersions on each other as they went, but Blücher's obsession with capturing territory rather than crushing the marshals in flight from him enabled Napoleon to rally them at Vitry, even if he was outnumbered three to one. Blücher sought a conclusive action with Napoleon, and an army that did not yet exist, but that he had now allowed Napoleon to bring into being,[101] and now paid the price for too close an imitation of his archenemy. Napoleon believed he could catch Blücher at a narrow defile near the town of Saint-Dizier, just east of Vitry, thinking Blücher numbered only about twenty-five thousand men with only three dozen guns, and that the allies were spread very thinly across eastern France: "If we can engage this corps tomorrow and thump it, this would have a great influence on affairs." He would do so by a blunt instrument: "We can crush the enemy by an immense superiority of artillery. By tomorrow I can bring together 300 guns."[102] It was not to be. His orders reached Victor too late. The marshal withdrew from the town, after a fierce engagement with Sacken's Russians, following Berthier's orders to concentrate at Vitry along with Ney and Marmont. His original orders to destroy the bridge at Saint-Dizier were countermanded, to facilitate Napoleon's counterattack, but he did remain behind to hold off Sacken, who retook the town after a fierce struggle that left Victor's corps detached from the main army.[103] Napoleon's vague orders let Blücher pour forward over the Marne, heading southwest toward Troyes, and ever closer to Schwarzenberg. He could now only "get on his tail"[104] and hope to stop them linking up.

Most of it took place over the open plains of the southern Champagne countryside, made for open warfare in the normal campaigning season. In a harsh midwinter its fields, abundant in asparagus and grapes at other times, were either frozen or flooded, even its small streams difficult to cross. "It is still sleeting hard," Napoleon told Marmont on January 29, as his unpaid, hungry troops failed to cross the Aube that night. When Cossacks captured a French courier, Blücher knew how close Napoleon was, and he quickly called up Sacken to join him, along with the advance guard of Wittgenstein's Army of Bohemia, while Victor now caught up with Napoleon. Hungry for battle, Napoleon threw Grouchy's cavalry at Blücher on the late morning of the 29th, not waiting for Ney and Victor's raw conscripts.

The first clash took place at Brienne, near the military academy where Napoleon first learned to be a soldier, and in the cold winter weather that had so depressed him in his youth. It did not go his way. Blücher was ready for him, having summoned reinforcements to bolster the small Russian forces in the vicinity, the Cossacks having yet again captured French dispatches. The first fighting was inconclusive, but that night a French force eluded the allies and seized the château where Blücher had made his headquarters, the Prussian commander and Sacken barely escaping with their lives. The Russians then did what they did best, and slipped away in the winter night after fierce fighting, south toward the main army. Napoleon followed and caught them at the village of La Rothière. Battle was joined on February 1, as Napoleon found himself along a front that was too long for his forty thousand men to hold. Although Blücher had barely fifty-three thousand under him, close to the same number were on their way, a foretaste of all that was to come.

Gyulai's Austrians failed to dislodge the raw French conscripts from the village of Dienville, which anchored Napoleon's right, until Wrede's Bavarians arrived—having simply followed the sound of the guns—and forced Marmont to retreat. The main fighting at La Rothière fell to the Russians against Victor and Oudinot who, true to form, was wounded. With a snowstorm at their backs, bayonets fixed, Sacken's men charged the French, almost unsupported by artillery, so impassable were the roads. The tsar was present, giving Sacken powerful reasons to excel. His thrust was only held in check by a counterattack by the Young Guard and Ney's reserves. It was in vain. When Alexander committed his grenadiers, Napoleon was driven out of La Rothière for the loss of five thousand men and seventy-three guns. In the following days, a great many French conscripts deserted.[105] Napoleon organized a skillful withdrawal, but allied hubris was inevitable. Sacken wallowed in the moment, declaring "On this memorable and triumphant day Napoleon ceased to be the enemy of mankind, and Alexander can say, I will grant peace to the world."[106]

Meanwhile, Blücher did a different kind of wallowing. He was nowhere to be found the next day, when the tsar called a council of war. Alexander himself went to fish him out, and found him deep in the wine cellars of the recaptured château of Brienne sampling, to his credit, the better bottles.[107] When he recovered, the pair chatted about where to quarter their troops in Paris. The allies then split their forces, with Schwarzenberg to advance on Paris up the Seine from the south, while Blücher was to drive westward along the Marne. Schwarzenberg muttered about the size of Napoleon's army, and the length of his own supply lines: "Any advance on Paris is . . . contrary to military science," he told his wife.[108] He took his time, leaving the fighting to Blücher.

It was just what Napoleon wanted. Wedged between them, controlling the key river crossings all along their march, he could concentrate his forces to strike at one or other army at will, secure in his interior lines. In the weeks to come, he did just this. Nevertheless, a retreat was still a retreat. As the battered French troops fell back through Troyes, they were met with shuttered windows and slammed doors as insults rained down on them.[109] A few days before, the prefect had obeyed Napoleon's order to evacuate the local administration, but was now sacked for deserting his post.[110] As Napoleon fell back on Arcis-sur-Aube, the enemy fell upon the area. "The enemy troops behave horribly," he told Caulaincourt, "Everyone is hiding in the woods. No peasants are to be found in the villages. The enemy eats everything, takes all the horses, all the livestock . . . they beat everyone, men and women, and commit many rapes." Napoleon was not blind to the price of his people paid as he regrouped, but still lived in the fantasy that they would take their revenge on the allies, "for the Frenchman is not patient; he is naturally brave, and I await seeing them form themselves into bands and give the enemy pause for thought."[111] Nothing of the sort happened. He had lost more than ground.

Napoleon nurtured other illusions as he rolled back from La Rothière. The same day he wrote to Caulaincourt, he told Joseph that the allies were ready to open peace talks with Caulaincourt at Châtillon the next day, February 3, not at their headquarters at Langres. He attributed their choice of venue as a sign of fear that Caulaincourt's presence among the sovereigns would "sow the seeds of disunion among them; they prefer to hold the congress far from headquarters," with only their representatives present.[112] There had, indeed, been fierce disagreements among the allied leaders. In the days before the conference, Alexander again put forward the harebrained proposal that Bernadotte should be proclaimed ruler of France by the allies or, alternatively, that the French people be asked to elect a parliament to choose a successor and draw up a new constitution. Metternich exploded: "That would be . . . a renewed unleashing of the revolution!"[113] Castlereagh was quick to side with him, and the proposal was scotched. By the time the conference began, the allied leaders had actually reached two important decisions: that Napoleon had to go, and that the Bourbons were the only viable alternative to him,[114] although Alexander continued to harbor his own ideas.[115] Metternich stressed negotiation in order to play on French war weariness, expose Napoleon as a warmonger and, ingenuously, to make it clear that the allies were not intent on imposing a new regime on France. Alexander's intemperance let him get his way and set the agenda for Châtillon. There was no more talk of "natural frontiers," but of the prerevolutionary borders, together with a demand that

Napoleon renounce all claims to influence outside those borders—to accept the loss of the kingdom of Italy, the Rhineland, and the Low Countries. "The program amounted to a complete dismantling of the Napoleonic empire," in the judgment of Wolfram Siemann. The only way Napoleon could accept such terms was to abdicate.[116] He sent Caulaincourt to the negotiating table seeking to exploit their divisions, still in the vain hope that Francis did not really wish to depose him, a view shared by Caulaincourt.[117] This was secondary. He felt sure he could rout them in the field, and set about it.

A Month of Running Wild, February–March 1814

Napoleon's ambitions for a decisive set-piece battle were over. Instead, the chase of cat and mouse with his most resilient enemy began. "The rapier of 1796 was to replace the bludgeon of 1812," as David Chandler memorably put it.[118] He had little choice but to fight any other way with his emaciated, callow *Marie Louises* pitted against far superior Prussian and Russian veterans, but he used what he had with an insight and intelligence so numbingly absent from his politics. The unity of purpose in allied diplomacy was not mirrored in the field. When he met with stiff French resistance, first at Arcis-sur-Aube, and then at Sens, Schwarzenberg's reservations seemed confirmed, and his 150,000 men pulled back southward, widening the gap between Blücher and himself, as Blücher drove hard up the Marne, rather than shadowing Schwarzenberg. With his troops now strung out along the Marne, Napoleon decided to swoop on the disorganized Blücher, and leave Schwarzenberg alone. He concentrated about seventy thousand men against Blücher's roughly fifty thousand, and Napoleon had two divisions of hardened Spanish veterans on their way.[119] Paris was now exposed, despite Napoleon's assurances to Joseph. The risk he knew he was taking emerges in the details. "Get all the valuable furniture out of Fontainebleau, especially anything that might make a trophy . . . it is useless to leave the silverware there, get it away promptly," he told Joseph. Joseph and his daughters were to get out of Paris, too, and he said he liked Joseph's idea—never implemented—of leaving Louis in charge,[120] but by the next day, as he left Troyes to its own devices, Napoleon thought, "it seems to me that the only man left in Paris should be an imperial commissioner."[121] "As for Louis, I have always doubted his judgment. He's a child playing doctor," he told Joseph, having recovered his usual opinion.[122] On February 6, the news reached him that Brussels and Antwerp had fallen to Bülow, along with confirmation of Murat's defection and Caulaincourt's report of Metternich's repudiation of the "natural frontiers." The news of Murat, however inevitable, shook him, telling Savary, "The contents of your letter seem to me utterly bereft of reason: it is proof of how much men know themselves so little, and how they are ignorant of what is meant for them."[123] Savary was not spared a tongue-lashing, either, nor Cambacérès, as Napoleon perceived defeatism and panic at the very heart of the regime:

> I see that instead of supporting the Empress, you are discouraging her. What are all these *Missere* and prayers of the forty hours in the chapel?[124] Have you all gone mad in Paris? The minister of police (Savary) is talking rubbish, instead of informing himself about the enemy's movements . . . He has agents all over France to keep him perfectly informed about what is important to know. Speak to him! This is important![125]

Joseph was of the same mind when it came to religion and the crisis, but had a clearer eye:

> I think the solemnity of the public prayers . . . will not produce a good result, spirits are too low, and people are too inclined to submit to the course of events . . . to be roused from nonchalance by religious intervention; I add moreover, that for the less credulous, this act would be only a ceremony which, itself, only proves the danger . . . As for the good Catholics . . . the government has nothing to hope from them. No Sire, there are no other religious sects in France

than those who recognize the Pope as their spiritual leader, all the rest are not Catholics, but unbelievers or Protestants . . . I don't think that any religious ceremony would work well for Your Majesty with the Catholics—this, Sire, is the truth.[126]

Joseph proved a clear-eyed informant in these days, charting the collapse of optimism in the capital that was "too confident yesterday and the day before, (but) today is too alarmed" following Brienne, until it collapsed for good after La Rothière.[127]

If Napoleon was in a state of nerves when he joined battle at Champaubert on February 9, it did not show. When he heard that Louis was "talking peace," Napoleon exploded to Joseph on the eve of battle, "I will tell you again in two words that Paris will never be evacuated while I'm alive . . . the enemy will only enter Paris over my dead body . . . If you get news of a battle lost, it will arrive with the news of my death."[128] The next day, he showed he was in deadly earnest. He struck north like lightning from his base at Sézanne and cut a small Russian corps to pieces—he claimed to have taken six thousand prisoners, a remarkable achievement because it numbered only thirty-seven hundred in total, as Dominic Lieven notes dryly.[129] He had no need to "lie like a bulletin," for he had split Blücher's advance in two; he now stood between Sacken's fifteen thousand men at La Ferté and Blücher's fourteen thousand at the picturesque wine village of Vertus, nestling under the vine-covered slopes of Mont Aimé. Napoleon now bestrode the Roman road that still links them. Blücher had no real idea what had happened, and ordered Sacken straight into Napoleon's path, where he was duly trounced at Montmirail on the 11th and fell back in the dead of night, in pouring rain, north to Château-Thierry on the Marne, lighting fires to guide his path as his men slogged along the sodden, narrow road. The sun shone the next day on a victory for the six battalions of the Old Guard who routed the allied infantry, and on the Guard cavalry, who broke the squares formed by the Russians to cover their retreat. The raw *Marie Louises* under Ricard bravely withstood the first allied assaults, and lost half their number, winning the respect of the *grognards* forever. The guard, too, had its ranks badly stricken, among them some who had served at Marengo.[130] Napoleon's pursuit was relentless, and Sacken was saved only by a courageous rearguard action by Yorck's Prussian infantry. Sacken blamed Yorck for the mess in his report, nonetheless.[131] The retreat and pursuit took place in the pouring winter rain, in which Napoleon lost his food transports. But, thanks to a rare show of local solidarity, the peasants managed to get his guns up to him.[132] His own troops were now scattered, his immediate force reduced to only a few thousand, as the rain and mud spared him no less than the allies, for all that he had won a victory through superior coordination and tactical skill, yet he had to throw in the Old Guard against Yorck and Sacken, to support the raw conscripts.

Their escape over the Marne was a bitter disappointment, as the destruction of these two formidable corps would have been within Napoleon's grasp, had Macdonald moved faster to cut off their retreat before they reached the bridges. Napoleon was thrown further off balance when Schwarzenberg launched two successful attacks that pushed Victor back over the Seine and allowed him to take Sens. Blücher now anticipated Napoleon's mind, knowing he would turn south against Schwarzenberg, and sought to get behind him. He forced Marmont out of Vertus, but his retreat was careful and orderly, buying Napoleon the time he needed to turn and face Blücher. When they clashed at Vauchamps on the 14th, Grouchy's cavalry made short work of the Prussian right, and when Napoleon again threw in the Old Guard, Blücher retreated back to Châlons, harassed by French cavalry all the way. At one point, Grouchy found a small side road and got right in Blücher's path. It was only by battering tenaciously that he escaped the trap.

Napoleon had hounded Blücher back to his original base with only thirty thousand men, battered the allies and inflicted heavy losses; his underaged army had covered 120 kilometers in five days in foul weather and won as many battles. "The six days" was a tactical triumph for him, and is still revered by military thinkers,[133] but in truth, it meant little in the great scheme of things. Napoleon could not follow Blücher further. He had to turn to deal with Schwarzenberg's army immediately, which well outnumbered his own and had seen little action, while the ruffled Blücher was soon reinforced by Winzingerode's thirty thousand Russians, who had swept down from Belgium, taking Soissons on the main road north of Paris before heading for Reims and then Châlons. To the south, Wellington was rolling the French back ever further in these weeks; Murat's defection drove Elissa out of Tuscany and then Lucca. Only Eugène stood firm on the banks of the Mincio in northeastern Italy, holding Heinrich von Bellegarde's Austro-Russians at bay. Napoleon was a nimble mosquito, a snapping flea, on the body of a many-headed hydra he had, in no small part, created.

No one knew this better than Caulaincourt, the French representative at the farcical peace talks at Châtillon, and Joseph, who had the burbling of Paris ringing in his ears. "They are six and I am alone. They are stronger," Caulaincourt wrote to Napoleon on February 9.[134] He did not know how right he was. The allies had their own internal divisions—how to fight the war, what to do with France when Napoleon was defeated, what to do with his empire—but even Caulaincourt did not guess how at one they were that Napoleon was to "go." Olivier Varlan has argued that the conference of Châtillon was governed entirely by the to-and-fro of battle,[135] but this is only partially true. The allies shifted over tactics—how to answer the French—but they were unmoved in their objective, behind the scenes. Implicit in the Declaration of Frankfurt, on December 1, 1813, was a vision of lasting peace in Europe offered to the French people, "to separate Napoleon still more from the Nation," as Metternich put it in his memoirs.[136] When the allies adhered to this, they agreed to replace Napoleon, but not to say so. As their armies rolled through France, the internal arguments increasingly turned on "with whom?"

Napoleon continued to live in blissful ignorance that his fate was sealed, clinging to his steadfast belief that he could change their minds by bayonet charges. He went into the "six days" giving Caulaincourt a free hand to sign whatever the allies put in front of him, vague orders that Caulaincourt knew better than to follow, but he believed he could steer a middle way between demanding the Frankfurt proposals based on the "natural frontiers," and a return to the ancien régime borders. He was curtly informed that the

Frankfurt proposals were no longer on offer. So confident was Alexander of a quick victory that he withdrew from the talks, causing their suspension for several days.[137] Metternich pleaded with Alexander to see sense, at one point threatening to take Austria out of the war if the tsar persisted in his plan to put Bernadotte on the throne and drive straight to Paris.[138] "A bunch of fools have taken hold of your beautiful friend," he wrote to his mistress, with just a tinge of jealousy, perhaps, "and if they continue along the same vein, they will ruin the world."[139] In the wake of Napoleon's stunning successes the next week, Alexander resumed the talks, while at the same moment, emboldened, Napoleon lost whatever grip he had on diplomatic realities. He wrote to his father-in-law, "In the present state of things, I propose that Your Majesty sign the peace, without delay, based on Frankfurt proposals, which I and the French nation have adopted as our ultimatum. . . ."[140] If one seeks to impose other conditions on France, any peace will not last long."[141] Caulaincourt knew that any hopes he briefly held of a compromise peace were dashed, and he wrote to Maret ("You, who are closest to the Emperor, you who have his confidence") on February 14—even as euphoria reigned at his headquarters—to beg Napoleon to make a compromise peace.

Meanwhile, Joseph, too, continued to whisper in his brother's ear that peace based on the old borders was the "ultimatum" of the French nation. Joseph took his duties as lieutenant-general very seriously, liaising closely with the military and overseeing the administration of an ever more nervous capital. Parisians saw for themselves, as did Joseph, the flood of wounded into the improvised military hospitals; there were twelve thousand of them lodged in Paris, a stark presence that undermined the trumpeting of Napoleon's victories. Joseph continued to strengthen the city's defenses and its national guard, the boastful bulletins notwithstanding. The troops quartered in Paris behaved badly; pillaging and violence were common. Napoleon's successes did not stop the flood of requests to the police for passports to leave the city,[142] and it was in full knowledge of the fragile loyalty of the capital that Joseph wrote to his brother, even as he was routing Blücher, "(The national guard) is of great use as a municipal force at home," not to be deployed beyond the city, a subtle hint that all was not well with the city Napoleon had always feared as much as loved.[143] The next day, as news poured in that Blücher was in full flight back to Châlons, Joseph prodded Napoleon, "it is by treating with the enemy powers that You are going to win, and how Your Majesty will fulfil the wishes of the French, and spread as much happiness across France as he has won glory."[144] Two days later, amid talk of a cease-fire and hopes of a peace treaty, Joseph's words were redolent of pleading hope and dire warning: "I don't think there is a single Frenchman who might think differently."[145] Cambacérès was more concerned with those Frenchmen who did think differently, especially those in the municipal administration of the capital: "There are among them a great many émigrés or the relatives of émigrés who, instead of being energetic, try to insinuate that the enemy is coming for the common good. It would be best . . . to get rid of all those who equivocate."[146] So died *amalgame*.

Joseph's hopes were dashed, and his fears confirmed. On February 18, flush with success, Napoleon told Caulaincourt to negotiate only on the basis of the Frankfurt proposals; the rout of Blücher told him he could regain the "natural frontiers." When Caulaincourt balked, Maret replied that Napoleon was pleased by his "firmness of purpose," by refusing to agree to a peace based on the old frontiers.[147] Napoleon continued to badger him to force the allies to concede; the allies persisted in demanding an answer about their "red line." Caulaincourt stalled as best he could. Napoleon felt his bullishness further justified when he swung south against Schwarzenberg. Schwarzenberg's advance was slow and bedeviled with supply problems; the allies were stealing each other's supplies as they withered, and the local peasantry was raiding them, too, as a harsh occupation provoked them to sporadic acts of resistance, driven more by deprivation that patriotism.[148] "If I divide up my army, I may be beaten *en détail*; if I collect it in one place, I starve to death," he said, not without reason.[149] His four columns were spread widely apart from each other, which kept them out of each other's way, but made them vulnerable to attack. Even Schwarzenberg did not seem to think this likely, and he took his time—two days, February 15–16—to decide to fall back in case Napoleon saw his rout of Blücher as a chance to fall on him. Napoleon was right when he told Joseph, "The Austrians know my way of operating too well,"[150] but Schwarzenberg had forgotten "the Napoleon of old," he who wielded the rapier and moved like the wind.

Victor, Oudinot, and Macdonald were concentrated at Guignes, and their combined strength could not withstand a concerted push from Schwarzenberg, which would have opened the road to Paris. Napoleon again force-marched the guard and Grouchy's cavalry there, transporting some of the infantry in requisitioned carts, an echo of the days when the guard traveled by oxcart everywhere. He covered forty-seven miles in thirty-six hours—one of the fastest marches of his career—and on arrival, threw his sixty thousand men at the enemy.[151] It helped that, fed up with Schwarzenberg's snail-like pace, Wittgenstein's Russians, with Pahlen's cavalry in the lead, had pushed ahead of the main advance, and were only beginning their withdrawal, when Napoleon fell on them like a wolf on the fold. Pahlen's horsemen made it clear, but the supporting infantry were massacred.[152] Wrede's Bavarians were harried south in disarray, but Victor's slow reaction to Napoleon's thrust allowed the Prince of Württemberg to collect his forces in a strong position at Montreau and hold up Napoleon's advance on the morning of the 18th. His defense was broken only when Napoleon led the guard artillery, himself, up to the ridge Württemberg had been defending, turning a careful withdrawal into a rout. A ferocious cavalry charge prevented the Austrians blowing up the bridges behind them, and it was followed by a spontaneous charge by Napoleon's own staff—Mamelukes, Chasseurs of the Guard, and orderlies—led by the grizzled Jacobin, Marshal Lefebvre, "foaming at the mouth," according to an officer[153]—that sent Württemberg in full flight back to the main army for the loss of six thousand men and fifteen guns. Napoleon had shown himself all over the field. It was a glimmer of the old days, but Napoleon knew he had only savaged a vanguard, and the cold, hard ground allowed more of it to get away than he liked. The main army may have been in retreat, but it was still there. Yet, Napoleon was far from deterred. "Now you will see how out-of-season your sermons are," he gloated at Joseph, writing in his own hand after Montreau, "and I have no need to be preached at to sign an honorable peace, if that was ever possible."[154] He resolved to retake Troyes and drive Schwarzenberg back further. The next day, he chided Augereau, at Lyon, into action:

> Six hours after receiving reinforcements from (the Army of) Spain, you were not yet on campaign! . . . You must have a hardcore of 6,000 elite troops: I have nothing like that, and yet I have destroyed three armies, taken 40,000 prisoners, 200 cannons, and saved the capital three times. The enemy is flying from all sides back toward Troyes. Be the first to fire. It is no longer a question of acting as previously, but of getting your boots on and the resolution of '93![155]

There was a short-lived offensive in the region in these days. The French briefly retook Chambéry, Mâcon, and Bourg-en-Bresse by February 20, but by the first week of March, they were back in allied hands.[156]

A shaken Schwarzenberg begged his superiors for an armistice and fell back toward Troyes, as bitter recriminations began among the soldiers, Russian and Prussian commanders snarling that the Austrians were deliberately avoiding battle to bleed their allies dry, while Schwarzenberg exercised an "I told you so" directed at Blücher, that his drive up the Marne had been a gross error.[157] Napoleon had caused serious consternation among the allies, and a major council of war was held at Bar-sur-Aube on February 25, with Alexander, Francis, Metternich, Hardenberg, Castlereagh, and Nesselrode all in attendance, along with Schwarzenberg, but not Blücher. The mood was not helped by the fact that, flushed with their own initial success, allied headquarters had been moved to Troyes, only for it to be hastily pulled back. "I cannot conceal from you, that the internal temper is very embarrassing, if not alarming," Castlereagh confided to Liverpool. "The recriminations between the Austrians and the Russians are at their height, and my patience is worn out combating both."[158] Castlereagh's close bond with Metternich notwithstanding,[159] he showed signs of impatience with his friend's support for Schwarzenberg's caution. Metternich, he judged, bore his fair share of the blame for making Austria into "a timid power."[160] A grudging compromise over tactics was agreed, engineered by Metternich in Schwarzenberg's interest:[161] There would be a return to the pre-Leipzig plan of avoiding a pitched battle with Napoleon, which allowed Schwarzenberg to continue his retreat to Langres, where reinforcements from Austria awaited him, leaving Napoleon to retake Troyes unopposed. The Russo-Prussians were granted an offensive of sorts, as Blücher was sent north to threaten Paris and draw Napoleon away from Schwarzenberg. At Soissons, on the Aisne, Bülow and Winzengerode were waiting for Blücher, who would bring his forces, alone, to one hundred thousand men, more than everything Napoleon could muster.[162] Those reinforcements had to be acquired through diplomatic wrangling. Bülow's corps was under the command of Bernadotte, whose self-interested "timidity" far eclipsed Schwarzenberg's. He was threatened in the most jocular manner by Castlereagh's brother, Charles Stewart, that he was in receipt of a British subsidy, that Britain had the Baltic and, indeed, Sweden, at its mercy, and that "he must not forget the great claims Britain had on him."[163]

Napoleon had befuddled the allies and divided them over strategy, but never over their objective: his destruction. The most important result of Napoleon's string of victories was the Treaty of Chaumont, agreed on March 1, and ratified a week later. Its terms were largely the work of Metternich, its achievement, that of Castlereagh. It placed the alliance on a firm, contractual basis, but it revealed for the first time that Britain was now a military as well as a financial presence in the war. Castlereagh pledged 150,000 men to the cause, one third of the troops in the field, and a further five million pounds sterling to the war chest. "What an extraordinary display of power!" Castlereagh beamed.[164] The allies definitively abandoned the Frankfurt proposals; henceforth, there would be no negotiation with Napoleon: there would be terms he could accept or reject and take the consequences. It also put paid to fears among the rest of the allies that Austria might, indeed, make a separate peace with Napoleon. Marie-Louise had been working tirelessly on her father for exactly this in these weeks. "I fear, dear Papa, that you have entirely forgotten me," she wrote on February 26, "the thought of which deeply angers me, all the more so because in this very moment, we are fighting for you, and in the interests of your monarchy, you ought to be helping us. I am persuaded that you will, if you would not listen to the insinuations of the Russia and England . . . I beg to you think of the interests of my son."[165] The depth of Francis's commitment to the coalition is most poignantly found in his reply: "I will never separate myself from the coalition . . . If (Napoleon) wants peace, he must do what is needed to obtain it."[166]

The treaty presaged a much longer alliance—twenty years—and a plan for postwar Europe based on containing France and diplomatic equilibrium, Metternich's long-cherished goals.[167] But that was for the future. In the winter of 1814, Chaumont showed that Napoleon's tactical brilliance had backfired on him. It created resolve and unity, however fragile, instead of destroying it.

While Napoleon continued to revel in the liberation of Troyes, where the crowds cheered him after weeks of a brutal occupation,[168] the vise tightened around him and his capital. Troyes's fate encapsulated the reality France faced in these months. No sooner had the cheers of a grateful crowd echoed in his ears than Napoleon was forced to take the allied bait and swing north after Blücher, leaving the city at the mercy of the Wrede's men, and the countryside to the Cossacks. The city was sacked for thirty hours for having welcomed Napoleon; its mayor was held at knifepoint until 200,000 rations of bread were produced for the troops. Meanwhile, the Cossacks visited rape and murder on the surrounding villages.[169] Napoleon's dazzling tactical prowess in these weeks, and the heroism of his young conscripts, too often mask the reality that he was moving in ever-decreasing circles. He was "fire fighting."

The Shadows Lengthen: March 1814

Napoleon was not clear why Blücher was going north in force, whether simply to join Bülow near Soissons, to join Schwarzenberg by a circuitous route, or to resume his advance on Paris. He soon came to think it was the last, and moved swiftly, sending Victor and Ney north with the Young Guard across the open country west of Châlons toward the small route center of Arcis-sur-Aube—the birthplace of Danton—to seize its bridges and force Blücher back on Châlons. He followed them with part of the guard, intent on placing thirty thousand elite troops across Blücher's interior lines, while Marmont and Mortier confronted his advance. He was constrained to leave forty thousand men under Macdonald and Oudinot behind, to shadow Schwarzenberg.[170] Although Blücher's ultimate goal was Paris, he intended to link with Bülow first, and was trying to outrun Napoleon to the bridge at Soissons, to get over the Aisne; Napoleon had to catch him. The roles were now reversed. Cossack patrols kept Blücher well informed that Napoleon was closing in on his rear, and he hurried his men over the Marne just in time, burning the bridges behind him. He crossed the Aisne, achieving his objective by March 3. Napoleon trailed behind, almost frothing at the mouth because, first, his bridge train had not materialized, meaning the guard marines had to rebuild the ruined bridges from scratch, and then at the news that the town of Soissons, which had held out for so long, had been bullied into surrender by Löwenstern, enabling Blücher to cross by the bridge before its banks, rising after hard rain, flooded it. Blücher was not quite sure where Bülow and Winzengerode were when he crossed the Aisne, but he soon found them. Napoleon told Joseph, "(Blücher) is in great disarray and has lost an immense quantity of men, horses, and wagons."[171] He was now convinced that the allies were in retreat, and that all he would meet was a determined rearguard action in the vicinity of Laon.[172] Napoleon did not grasp that Blücher had eluded him. As his men got over first the Marne, and then the Aisne, crossing by a stone bridge to the east of Soissons, Napoleon's confidence grew. He would sweep the retreating Prussians aside at Laon, and then "I will prepare myself to carry the war into Lorraine, where I will rally all the troops who are in my fortresses on the Meuse and the Rhine."[173] He was right about the allies concentrating at Laon, but what he found there was something quite different.

Napoleon was walking into a well-prepared position, as Blücher carefully deployed his mixed Russo-Prussian forces, first to threaten the flank of Napoleon's advance by placing Winzengerode's corps on a plateau at the village of Craonne, in the rugged hills to the west of Laon, while Kleist's

Prussians outflanked Napoleon, and Bülow shielded Laon.[174] Laon is known as "the crowned mountain," a town perched on the highest hill for many miles, its Gothic cathedral looming over the wide plains to the east. On March 6, the young conscripts of Ney's corps took on the Russian positions with great ardour, but could not dislodge them from the plateau until supported by units of hardened Spanish veterans. It had not helped that Ney struck too soon, before support was at hand. As the day wore on, Blücher saw that, although he had chosen a good position to hold, it was too difficult to reinforce, and Winzengerode's attempt to do so dissolved in soggy marshland. The Russian sharpshooters in Craonne fought bravely all day, taking their toll on the French from behind stone walls—another turning of the tables—but the arrival of "the Spanish" made further action futile, and the Russians as so often, conducted a doughty retreat toward Laon. The losses on both sides are difficult to calculate, but it seems they lost at least five thousand men each, the French possibly more. As ever, Napoleon lied like a bulletin, telling Joseph he had lost "between 700 and 800 men."[175] He knew better, of course. He had been on the front line for most of the day. Victor was badly wounded; Oudinot lost a son. The guard suffered most of all, having borne the brunt of the assault on the plateau; its cavalry "had melted away like snow," Napoleon admitted to Joseph.[176] Napoleon probably came out of Craonne with about thirty-seven thousand men in the battle sector, with Marmont on the way with about ten thousand more.[177] Whether he lost five thousand men or a higher estimate, it is irrelevant. Napoleon could no longer sustain losses on this scale.[178] The reckoning came three days later, in the shadow of the "crowned mountain."

Napoleon still believed he had fought a retreating rearguard, that Blücher was in full flight for Belgium, and that one more thrust at his rear would draw him away from Paris for some time, allowing Napoleon to swing back to the Champagne, now an undermanned, vulnerable sector. Ney went forward to probe the outskirts of Laon, followed by the entire guard on the foggy morning of March 8.[179] The road they took was the narrow Chemin des Dames, which runs east to west. In a later conflict between France and "Prussia," World War I, the little road was the scene of a French offensive in April 1917 that was little short of a massacre. That March day in 1814, it led an earlier generation of French soldiers into the jaws of disaster. When the fog lifted, Ney stood aghast. A huge army, and a city made into a fortress, stood before them, the mountain and the cathedral looming behind them.[180] Blücher's artillery covered the main roads west to Soissons and south to Reims; Kleist and Sacken occupied the villages south of the town, well supported by batteries, directly in Ney's path.[181] Blücher cast aside the agreed allied strategy and concentrated his whole army, over one hundred thousand men, ravening for the pitched battle that would decide the war. Napoleon obliged, throwing all his available forces into frontal assaults on Kleist and Sacken, still unaware of the odds against him. For once, caution got the better of Blücher. Like Napoleon at Jena-Auerstadt, he smelled a trap: surely, a bigger force lay behind the French troops before him; Napoleon quickly halted and was thus able to choke off the probing of Winzingerode. Marmont appeared to the east of Laon that afternoon, drove back the light resistance he found, and halted, retiring to bed in a château—now a luxury hotel—some distance from the front.[182] Blücher saw his chance. As darkness fell, about 7:00 P.M., he unleashed Yorck and Kleist, supported by Sacken's cavalry, on Marmont's unsuspecting men in one of the most successful night attacks of the Napoleonic Wars.[183] Swept down the road to Reims along with their commander, they were saved from complete catastrophe by pure chance. A small French force of one thousand men and 125 of the Old Guard heard the noise of battle and rushed to hold the main road open long enough to allow the bulk of Marmont's men to escape.

Napoleon was convinced the night offensive was a rearguard action to cover Blücher's withdrawal.[184] What he then saw seemed to confirm this. With Marmont at their mercy, and Napoleon trapped, the allies called off the advance and pulled back. Napoleon saw sense, and did the same, extricating most of his men, along with Marmont's. Napoleon could reason he had "his star" to thank one last time. Having driven himself to the limit, Blücher suffered a mental and physical breakdown. It was not the first time. In the wake of the debacle of 1806, utter defeat and despair drove Blücher to believe he had given birth to an elephant. With final victory in the palm of his hand, he became incapable of speech, unable to bear any light on his eyes.[185] The next hours exposed the fragility of the allied command structures, despite their strength in the field. Langeron should have taken over, but—as a Russian—Yorck and Bülow would not obey him. When the chief of staff, Gneisenau, took over, they made life difficult for him, as they outranked him. Yorck "chose this moment to act the prima donna" and resigned his command, only persuaded to return by a scrawled note from Blücher's sickbed.[186] Gneisenau was a cerebral soldier, an inspired thinker but with little sense of when boldness was needed. He also feared the Russians were deserting him. The result was that the offensive stalled not just for the hours Napoleon needed to escape, but for a whole week. One hundred thousand men and 150 guns stood idle. Napoleon used this lull to fall back on Soissons, where his losses—about six thousand men[187]—were partially made up from new recruits from Paris. Many were drawn from the unemployed workers who had taken refuge there, for Napoleon told Joseph the city's national guard had to remain composed of "men of property who will have more to fear from a proletarian revolt."[188] Napoleon now had about forty thousand men, but of the four thousand or so casualties of Laon, three thousand had been Guardsmen, their divisions now often no bigger than regiments.[189] He still had enough to catch the isolated corps under Saint-Priest, a mixture of seasoned Russian regiments and Prussian landwehr, brush it aside, and retake Reims on March 13.[190] This cheap victory and a skillful withdrawal from Laon could disguise from no one that Napoleon's actions had ended in failure, based as they were on almost delusional assumptions. He now swung south to try to check Schwarzenberg.

Behind him, things were increasingly fraught in the corridors of power. On the day Napoleon lost at Laon, Joseph made one last plea for him to accept the prerevolutionary borders: "After having saved France from anarchy and Europe in coalition, you would become the father of your people," to which Napoleon retorted, "The tone of your letters makes me weep."[191] The news of Laon seemed to concentrate minds ruthlessly. Joseph went to the Regency Council and got support for his views. This may have stirred memories of 1805, when Joseph was linked to a "peace party," ready—many felt—to be...

and head of state, in the tense days before the news of Austerlitz reached Paris. There were suggestions that a deputation of senators approached him to declare himself publicly in favor of peace, and make himself regent for the King of Rome—"Napoleon II"—if the emperor did not accept. Joseph rejected this, but he was prepared to support a petition to his brother from the senators. From Reims, Napoleon told Cambacérès, "There are things going on in Paris I do not understand at all . . . It was about sending me petitions for peace. This idea, a veritable crime, cannot have been unknown to you . . . (Joseph) does not sense the danger in all this."[192] Cambacérès had, indeed, come to believe a prompt peace treaty alone could save the regime, so great were the forces at the allies' command, but he was not the problem.[193] Napoleon was the one who refused to see the danger. His trust in Joseph remained, save in one thing. Napoleon learned of the "peace plot" directly from Marie-Louise, but not in time to stop Joseph going to her, to try to gain her support. She rebuffed him, and warned Napoleon that the plotters were trying to get the national guard, the Senate, and the Council of State to pressure him into accepting the allies' terms. "(Joseph) replied to me that I was talking like child, and he went off in a very bad mood . . . I assure you that I think less of him each day . . . I don't know what his game is."[194] Pasquier suspected worse of Joseph, and claimed to have found letters by him to Marie-Louise full of "the most odious intentions" toward her. She portrayed it to the court as simply Joseph "being Joseph," knowing his reputation as a serial seducer, a careful way to avoid exposing a plot that may have embraced Joseph, Molé—the minister of justice—and a clutch of senators.[195] Marie-Louise henceforth took Napoleon's advice to receive Joseph only in public, with full formality, as she did Cambacérès, "Be wary of (Joseph), he has a bad reputation with women." "Don't let him lecture you about your personal life or business . . . you do better than him."[196] The scandal blew over at court, in no small way thanks to the Empress. No one was more stalwart in these days than Marie-Louise. "You explain (to Joseph), who seems to be mistaken . . . about the Empress . . . whose tact is far superior to the men around her," Napoleon told Cambacérès.[197] Her letters to Napoleon were always cheerful, full of stories about their son, geared to contradict the opinions of Joseph and Cambacérès, which dwelled on her poor health and supposedly fragile morale. The former was true; the latter anything but. She set herself and her ladies-in-waiting to roll bandages for the wounded, wrote letters to the wives of the marshals, and to the people of towns threatened by the enemy. When asked by Madame Lannes how she felt about the French fighting her erstwhile Austrian subjects, she retorted "I don't lose sleep over it." She was, indeed, "the voice of Napoleon," and like any good marshal, she kept him apprised, and followed her orders, but she proved herself increasingly able to impose herself on the Regency Council. She pushed Joseph aside, to receive captured standards, and reviewed the national guard in person, in the February cold. She publicly donated her jewelry to "the cause," in stark contrast to Joseph, who was taking a nefarious interest in state finances.[198] "It is the Regent alone who can give orders," Napoleon told Cambacérès, ". . . that authority is the result of the unlimited character and good sense of the regent."[199] Napoleon did the right thing in 1810.

He needed a loyal regent. Joseph and his supporters at least made their views clear to Napoleon, but behind them lurked Talleyrand, who played whist with the Empress at the Tuileries of an evening, his face inscrutable as ministers and Bonapartes rushed around with ever more furrowed brows.[200] "It is impossible to know how many strings he pulled in the months of February and March," Emmanuel de Waresquiel has sagely admitted.[201] He had many strings, and he was not using his influence or information in Napoleon's favor. His contacts in the postal service ensured he knew the ebb and flow of the fighting as soon as the regency, if not sooner. The mass of information at his disposal led him to the informed decision that Napoleon had to be deposed. "An 18 Brumaire in reverse" as he put it, had to be effected, and the easiest way was for Napoleon to have a glorious death on the battlefield: "The man is a corpse, but he not putrid yet. There it is."[202] For Talleyrand, making peace and the internal settlement of France after Napoleon were inextricably linked.[203] At this point, all he did was watch, but he had a better sense of circumstances that he admitted moved so quickly "that the whole scene could change in twenty-four hours."[204] Aimée de Coigny, that famous divorcée of the age—successively duchess of Fleury and countess of Montrod, "as easy as she was flirtatious"[205]—was, predictably, well known to Talleyrand. She noted his doings in these weeks in her journal, "The whole of Paris came to see him in secret for a quiet chat. Everyone who went in recognized everyone who went out."[206] His style was enchanting, but it was his talent for political survival, and his wealth of information, that drew so many worried men to him. Napoleon knew very well that Talleyrand was up to no good. Responding to Cambacérès's fears of royalism in the heart of Paris, he pointed the finger at Talleyrand as the fomenter of "the bad spirit that is everywhere in the administration," but admitted, "up to I don't know what."[207] Able to calculate the possibilities, Talleyrand came to favor a Bourbon restoration, but tied to a British style constitution, a revival of 1789. His mind was collected, his thoughts were clear, but the moment was not assured. Put another way, as it was by that very different royalist, Chateaubriand, he sought "to hobble the feet of a colossus he could not bring down."[208]

Napoleon proved more than capable of bringing himself down. In the face of all the evidence, he continued to believe he was the master of Paris. Joseph's intrigues for peace were merely attempts to undermine Napoleon's popularity:

> I am the man of the Nation, no one can ever separate me from it; I know my power over it, and I scoff at these little coteries. The movements of these tiny organic molecules would have no other end than to annoy me and result in their defeat . . . The people of the *faubourgs*, of the shops will always glory in doing what I want, and the men who want to be their petty tribunes will never do anything faced with me, who is tribune and dictator!

His illusions extended to the battlefield: "It is well known that I am more than I was at Austerlitz. Those who measure me by themselves are duped by their own calculations."[209] The victory at Reims convinced Napoleon he could force the allies to give him peace on the terms of Frankfurt, but his messengers were not even allowed through enemy lines to Châtillon to deliver his demands. Blocked at every turn, Caulaincourt left Châtillon on March 19, and the charade of a conference was dissolved the next day.[210]

With his mind full of bombast after seizing Reims, it is not surprising that Napoleon misjudged Schwarzenberg's movements as badly as he had Blücher's. Assuming Schwarzenberg also to be in retreat, he decided not to strike at him head-on, but to attempt to cut off his communications and supply lines, and then swing east, as originally planned, to join his besieged garrisons in Lorraine. In truth, the fall of Reims had thrown the allied commanders into confusion. Alexander was terrified by Napoleon's speed, thinking he was everywhere, and exasperated by Schwarzenberg's slow progress, which he feared left Blücher at Napoleon's mercy. Frederick-William hurled abuse at the Austrians for betraying the coalition, yet again.[211] They had no notion of where Napoleon was. Unbeknownst to Napoleon, he was marching toward an Austrian army of about eighty thousand men intent on battle,[212] something unprecedented in the campaign. More predictably, Blücher, "the scent of victory" having roused him, was now on the move, even if he had to travel in a carriage, his eyes shielded from the sunlight by a very stylish lady's broad-brimmed, green silk hat.[213]

As he sped south from Reims with about twenty-three thousand men, Napoleon summoned Mortier and Marmont to join him, convinced his actions were drawing Schwarzenberg away from the capital. On March 20, Napoleon reached Arcis, and when he found it lightly defended, he saw it as confirmation that Schwarzenberg was in retreat, and he would face only the rearguard. Ney easily cleared the area. In fact, Schwarzenberg—exhausted and vexed by Alexander's badgering[214] and assailed by gout[215] (the two most likely connected)—had changed his route, and was concentrating his main force between Arcis and Troyes, anticipating a renewed offensive. The news of the fall of Reims concentrated his mind on the need to support Blücher and, chided by his allies, he meant to check Napoleon's advance. Only an hour after Napoleon arrived at the front, a huge enemy cavalry charge crashed into him. Disaster was averted only by the combination of Napoleon's presence on the field, where he rallied the retreating troops himself. "Will you cross before me?" he challenged them as he stood squarely on the bridge over the Aube[216]—and the fortuitous arrival of a division of the Old Guard under Friant.[217] Napoleon persisted in believing Schwarzenberg was falling back. His long experience of him could not shake of him of this, but under cover of night, Schwarzenberg deployed his entire force in arc around Arcis, and concealed most of them behind the reverse slopes offered by the surrounding terrain. By dawn, Marmont and Mortier failed to reach Napoleon, and twenty-eight thousand Frenchmen confronted Schwarzenberg's whole army. Ney and Sébastiani led the advance uphill, and almost stumbled upon the massed allied army, a truly chilling vision that must have shaken them. Napoleon saw instantly the game was up, and retreated in good order. He was able to do so because of allied wrangling. As Schwarzenberg was in the process of arraying his men, the tsar changed his tune and berated him for his rash resumption of the offensive, which delayed the attack.[218] Oudinot and Sébastiani had to fight a bloody rearguard action, where the *volitgeurs* of the guard fought hand-to-hand in the market square, to buy time for the sappers and sharpshooters to blow up the bridges.[219] Arcis cost Napoleon three thousand men, the allies, about four thousand.[220]

On the first day at Arcis, an artillery shell, smoking, buried itself in the ground near Napoleon. To dare the troops around him not to retreat, he rode his over it, blowing his horse to pieces and throwing him some feet, before he calmly got up, unscathed, summoned a fresh mount, and went about his business.[221] On March 22, his luck ran out. His personal dispatches were captured by Cossacks, among them a letter to Marie-Louise saying he intended to get behind the allies, disrupt their interior lines, and draw them away from Paris. Until that moment, the squabbling commanders had no other plan than to locate Napoleon and catch him. On March 25, after considerable argument, they agreed to coordinate the armies of Schwarzenberg and Blücher, and advance on Paris, Schwarzenberg at last conceding that his caution had driven not only Austria's allies, but even many of his own staff, to their breaking point.[222] Nothing now could stop the allied advance on Paris, but it was slowed—and Marmont and Mortier saved—when the Cossacks discovered sixty thousand bottles of wine (hardly a scarce commodity in the Champagne) on the road to Châlons, and paused for an evening.[223]

While the allies had finally found clarity of purpose, Napoleon hesitated. He reached Saint-Dizier on March 23, where he spent four days receiving bad news. On the 27th, he learned of the heavy defeat of Marmont and Mortier at Fère-Champenoise, where the Russian heavy cavalry rode down the French infantry, with a hailstorm at their backs that dampened the powder of the French muskets.[224]

It was about all the news he got in these days. "Give the order to send out local people in all directions to get news, and to give us frequent reports of the enemy," he told Berthier.[225] "I have had no news from you for five or six days," he wrote to Marie-Louise on the 28th, "These foul Cossacks are the cause of it."[226] There was no good news to be had, save from his own imagination. Augereau was halted in his tracks by the Austrians on March 20, and abandoned Lyon the same day, falling back to Valence, his disaffection mounting all the while with the old comrade he had shared rooms with in the town as young officers, while pro-Bourbon sentiment in the fought-over region grew apace.[227] Napoleon remained convinced he could strike east and rally the besieged garrisons at Verdun and Metz, or head west, and rally at Orléans.[228] He had a mere thirty-six thousand men with him, and could muster about sixty thousand all told in the area he still held to the south of Paris.[229] Napoleon's resolve to leave Paris to its fate and keep driving east was at last firmly opposed by the marshals, who convinced him to head west for Troyes and then Paris. It was too late. By the time he reached Troyes by a series of forced marches on the 30th, the allied advance had cut him off from Mortier and Marmont, whose only hope now was to defend Paris as best they could. The next day, the armies of Blücher and Schwarzenberg, 180,000 men, were in full view of the city. Napoleon raced to Fontainebleau, arriving there the next morning.

All the while, his world shrank. On March 26, the news reached the allied leaders at Dijon that Bordeaux had gone over to the Bourbons two weeks earlier, and declared Louis XVIII the ruler of France. In Dijon, the gastronomic capital of Burgundy, Castlereagh hosted a dinner for Metternich and Hardenberg, where they drank to Louis's health with some of the finest wines in the world.[230] Thereby hangs a tale. Talleyrand knew of Bordeaux before any of them, it seems. On March 17, he wrote to an aristocratic lady friend, "Today the interesting news comes . . . from Bordeaux . . . Forty-eight hours will decide a host of questions. If peace is not made, Bordeaux will turn into something very important; if peace is made, Bordeaux will lose its importance."[231] Napoleon seemed to agree, in his own way. "The first appeal made to me for peace, I will treat as treason," he told his private secretary, Claude-François de Méneval on the very day Bordeaux declared for the Bourbons, adding for good measure that this could apply even to Marie-Louise or Joseph,[232] "that pygmy who wants to puff himself up" as he called his brother to his wife, soon after.[233] "All these people (the 'peace party' at Court) don't realize that I am going to cut the Gordian knot in the manner of Alexander. They ought to know well that I am the same man I was at Wagram and Austerlitz."[234] In this frame of mind, Bordeaux was a bagatelle, unworthy of comment. His reaction to its capitulation was limited to trying to form an "army of the Dordogne," a river to the north of the city, placing it under "generals chosen among the most loyal" and officers "of pronounced opinions," formed from some of the troops he had earmarked for Augereau at Lyon, now intended to check Wellington's advance, and to drive him back to Bordeaux.[235] As so often in these months, Napoleon saw the answer to the growing catastrophe as purely military, something he was adamant beyond reason he could master by arms.

Wellington's advance over the previous month was revealed to be less military than political. Soult could do little with his small army, depleted less by casualties, than Napoleon's need for good veteran troops. It fell back in good order, first to the line of the Ardour river, then to Orthez where, on February 27, he tried to make a stand with a force now mainly composed of raw, local conscripts. His men fought well in well-fortified positions—inflicting on Wellington the only serious wound of his career—but were pushed back by superior numbers. Having fought so bravely in the field, they melted away like snow when retreating, simply going home, where Wellington promised to leave them in peace. Given the choice between falling back to Bordeaux or Toulouse, Soult chose the latter, and opened the way for the former's defection.

Once arrived, Soult had to coerce the sullen populace of a city long known for its royalism to fortify itself for an allied assault.[236] Wellington met only friendly peasants, all the more because the flow of "Pitt's gold" to his army by sea allowed his men to pay for what they took, in stark contrast to the pillaging of their own army.[237] Beresford remarked, "It is not easy to describe the goodwill we are everywhere received with, and the efforts of the inhabitants to be useful to us, even against their own army. No one has ever exaggerated the detestation Bonaparte and his government are held in."[238]

Wellington detached a small force under Beresford to take the ill-defended port, and on March 11, the prefect reported to Paris, "I must with great regret inform Your Excellency that we cannot count on the loyalty of the citizens."[239] He was right. There were two small, but well-organized secret royalist cadres in Bordeaux, the deeply Catholic and aristocratic Chevaliers de la Foi, and the larger Garde Royale, which was more bourgeois and artisanal in composition. However small, they were a cross-section of an urban population, every segment of which had been battered by the blockade and yearned for a peace they hoped would restore their fortunes, which had been so healthy before the Revolution.[240] They had two allies who reflected their widespread political support: Jean-Baptiste Lynch, the maire, the scion of an aristocratic winemaking dynasty of Irish origins, and Lainé, still detached from the royalists and ignorant of their plans, but a powerful propaganda weapon for all that—the weathervane of the masses of granite all over France. Beresford was met some distance from Bordeaux by Lynch and an escort of the Garde Royale, who all tore off their sashes of office and tricolor cockades, and produced white Bourbon ones, which they ostentatiously donned. Lynch ripped off his Légion d'honneur. They then escorted Beresford and his men back to the city, where a large, well-primed crowd cheered "Vive le Roi!" and the royal flag was hoisted over the Hôtel de Ville. A Te Deum was sung in the cathedral, in the presence of the duc d'Angoulême, the husband of the daughter of Louis XVI, and the representative of Louis XVIII with Wellington's army.[241] He was an unprepossessing man, but he had a powerful slogan: "No more war! No more conscription! No more oppressive taxes!"[242] With that, he issued a proclamation telling Bordeaux that the allies had declared for a Bourbon restoration and resolved not to make peace with Napoleon. Wellington—although personally sympathetic to this—was incandescent with rage and threatened to disown d'Angoulême, aware that Alexander was not of this mind, and unsure of what the other allied leaders thought. In the end, he did nothing,[243] and a rival pole of attraction to Napoleon was established in France. Two weeks later, showing immense prescience, d'Angoulême appointed Lainé the royal prefect in Bordeaux. He knew the masses of granite, not the Chevaliers de la Foi, were the Bourbon's keys to success, something lost on Napoleon.

Paris Falls, March 28–31, 1814

Everything had out run for Napoleon. With the allies, literally, at the gates, Joseph summoned the Regency Council under the Empress, on March 28, to decide whether she and the King of Rome should leave Paris. Clarke and Joseph knew the capital could not be defended; there were only thirty thousand regular troops under Mortier and Marmont, together with a collection of cadets, gendarmes, and the retired veterans in Les Invalides;[244] there were six thousand national guards, half of whom were armed only with pikes.[245] Joseph wanted the imperial family to go to Blois, on the Loire, producing letters from Napoleon written in February advising exactly this. Antoine-Jacques-Claude-Joseph Boulay, Savary, and Régnier thought differently: Marie-Louise and Napoleon-Francis should take refuge in the Hôtel de Ville, and appeal to the people of Paris to defend them,[246] this after Pasquier, whose father had been guillotined during the Terror, refused to arm the populace: "There is no knowing where this might go. Once roused it could easily be led astray," he warned.[247] Although convinced by the letters from Napoleon that the imperial family should leave, Cambacérès feared the impact of this, as Paris would be left without a government "faced with a municipal government which showed signs of royalism."[248] Some still felt the shadow of the past. Others had their eyes fixed on what came next. According to Pasquier, Talleyrand said nothing throughout, "only expressing his opinion by a nod of the head which said more than he wanted it to."[249] Marie-Louise demanded to stay, writing to Napoleon, "I am wholly against this idea, I am sure it will have a terrible effect on the Parisians, that they will lose any courage they may have to defend the capital . . . and when you arrive to deliver us, you will find the capital in the grip of the enemy." Hortense and Julie agreed, believing that if the Austrians found the Tuileries occupied, they would be constrained to negotiate peace based on a regency.[250] Joseph took the decision: Marie-Louise and her son left Paris in the early hours of March 29, for Blois. Napoleon's letters had swayed the council.[251] Cambacérès and most of the government followed soon after. Joseph was now the sole Bonaparte in Paris, Louis having been carted off to Blois, suffering from a nervous collapse.[252]

The allied assault began at 5:00 A.M. on March 30. The only slender defenses Paris had were the heights of Montmartre to the north, where Marmont held off the Russians. Cadets, schoolboys, and a few volunteers under Moncey, the chief of the Gendarmerie, fought furiously at the Clichy Gate, to the west. The Prussian Grenadiers were halted at the Pantin Gate, as the French turned to urban warfare, breaking up the Prussian columns amid the walls, gardens, and buildings of the suburb, and inflicting heavy losses.[253] Watching events from Montmartre, where he could see the allies massing in strength by midafternoon, Joseph—without any news of Napoleon, much less his orders—authorized the marshals to negotiate surrender of the city with Schwarzenberg, and try to withdraw to the Loire, as he did, himself, almost immediately. Joseph has been castigated for this, but he was conforming to the letter of Napoleon's latest orders, which were hardly recent.[254] It was only a matter of time. Marmont sent word to Schwarzenberg asking for a truce of twenty-four hours and to open negotiations. Hoping Napoleon was nearby, he was trying to stall, and the allies saw through him. Alexander refused pointblank to negotiate: Although the French were allowed to withdraw rather than capitulate, Paris was to be surrendered by 9:00 A.M. the next morning, otherwise the city would be "delivered to the rigors of war."[255] Marmont conceded, and the surrender was signed at Marmont's home, that evening. The fighting ceased about 2:00 A.M. on the 31st.[256] As the news spread, Alexander's guards began polishing their buttons and boots and searching for their dress uniforms for the victory parade down the Champs-Élysées, while military bands played loudly on the recently evacuated heights of Montmartre. The Russian officer sent in to arrange the truce came back to headquarters drunk, but no one cared.[257] The battle had cost the French about nine thousand men, among them all Marmont's aides-de-camp; the allies lost roughly eight thousand, most of them Russians.[258] The courier carrying Schwarzenberg's orders to Blücher got lost in the dark, and so he did not know about the attack for some hours; Schwarzenberg himself was too far from Paris to join the assault until midafternoon. It was largely a Russian victory.[259] Alexander was in no doubt of it: "Thus, Divine Providence has permitted, in Its sublime ingenuity, what has been done by me . . . By me!"[260]

Napoleon got the news at 10:00 P.M. on the 31st. He then wrote to Marie-Louise, telling her to be brave, and ordered Berthier to muster as many troops as possible, and concentrate them on Orléans to retake the capital.[261] He wrote to Caulaincourt from a relay post near Fontainebleau authorizing him to go to the allied sovereigns immediately, make clear he accepted the surrender of Paris, and "to do everything possible to negotiate and conclude a peace, promising to ratify all which will be for the good of our service."[262] Alexander received him warmly, but ceded nothing; Schwarzenberg, his next port of call, would not see him at all. Caulaincourt knew Alexander as well as anyone could, and was not surprised by his reception, but he was shaken by Schwarzenberg's intransigence, for it told him far stronger than any words that the door to Austrian support was closed. His mission, Nesselrode told him, was useless: "You should have talked at Châtillon."[263]

"The Republic of the Weathercocks"

There was a grand victory parade down the Champs-Élysées on the morning of the 31st, a bright, sunny Sunday. Alexander rode though the city with his

Cossack guards, together with Fredrick-William and Schwarzenberg, and they reviewed their elite troops together.[264] Francis had stayed behind in Dijon, possibly because he did not want to gloat at his son-in-law's and daughter's humiliation.[265] It was a well-earned, hard-fought triumph that had begun thousands of miles away, to the south of Moscow. The Parisian crowds cheered them and, as in Bordeaux, sported Bourbon cockades. But the real history had been made the night before, in the shadows. The night the surrender was signed, long dormant forces emerged from the shadows on the last night of March 1814. Talleyrand saw to it that his prediction about the unimportance of Bordeaux came true. It was now time to erect another source of authority to counter Napoleon, not in a distant corner of France, but in Paris itself. Anything but royalist, it was drawn from those same survivors of the Terror, those "immortals" of the Directory, who had placed Napoleon in power. Now, as then, Talleyrand orchestrated their coup. The political elite had a stark choice before it: to be loyal to Napoleon, or to the regime with all its benefits—that he had created. Who were the traitors? Those who confected and adhered to the provisional government, to save the republic Napoleon had sworn to uphold in 1804? Or those who renounced their oath of loyalty to him, because he now seemed a greater threat to it than marauding Cossacks or British warships? What came first? The creator, or his creation? By April 1814, the immortals, almost to a man, had no more doubts. They had done the same to Robespierre. They had done it to the Directory. Now it was Napoleon's turn. No one was bigger than the Revolution. The "republic of the weathercocks," as Pierre Serna dubbed it, was about to be reborn.[266]

Talleyrand was regarded as omniscient not only in Paris, but among the allies when it came to French affairs, so much so that Alexander took up residence with him as soon as the victory parade had finished. This suited everyone, if for different reasons. Alexander had manipulated Talleyrand at Erfurt in 1808, and thought he could do so again; Metternich had "played" Talleyrand in the past, notably as his chief informer while ambassador to Paris; Castlereagh had come to trust Metternich completely, and the two men shared Talleyrand's concern to establish a stable regime in France, post-Napoleon, and a fear that Alexander was, more than ever, a dangerous "loose cannon."

Talleyrand's first actions in the crisis showed how astute his judgment was. On the night of March 30, he feigned departing Paris to join the rest of the government in Blois without police permission, and informed a close friend in the national guard, who "arrested" him at the Passy Gate, and sent him home. Napoleon was still to be reckoned with; he had escaped from tight corners before, and Talleyrand "cleared himself" of treason by this tongue-in-cheek farce.[267] Clever as Talleyrand was, the allies found his scope for maneuver had narrowed considerably. Although he had always kept his lines open to the Bourbons, he did not harbor confidence in their willingness to accept, or ability to preside over, the kind of constitutional regime he believed France needed: all the woes of the era stemmed from the inability of the political elite to control Napoleon, and absolute monarchy of any kind was unacceptable to these "weathercocks."[268] As the opportunity presented itself, Talleyrand's preferred outcome was a regency, with himself as Marie-Louise's first minister and éminence grise to the young "Napoleon II," in the manner of Cardinal Mazarin during the minority of Louis XIV, as Munro Price has observed.[269] It seemed the best hope for a constitutional monarchy to take root in France, the experiment of 1789–92 having singularly failed in the case of Louis XVI, a ruler too fixed in his beliefs.[270] These hopes were battered badly when Marie-Louise quit Paris—Talleyrand had joined Hortense and Julie in begging her to stay—and then blown to pieces when Alexander, without any consultation with his allies, issued a proclamation, plastered all over the walls of the capital, saying the allies would not only refuse to negotiate with Napoleon, but with any other member of his family—that is, either the empress or Joseph. Moreover, it concluded that the allies "will recognize the Constitution that the French people will give themselves."[271] Talleyrand had encouraged Alexander to issue a manifesto, but did he foresee him reverting to schemes so dreaded by his allies? Talleyrand flattered the tsar on his first night in Paris, but it was a dangerous gamble.[272]

Talleyrand suddenly pinned his hopes on the Bourbons, to the consternation of some of his intimates,[273] but when he avowed his support for them in the company of the tsar, Schwarzenberg, Frederick-William, and Nesselrode, he aligned himself openly with Castlereagh and Metternich. Only Louis XVIII had the legal precedent and traditional authority upon which to base a new order.[274] It was a pragmatic, cynical, yet long-rehearsed argument, retrieved from his "bottom drawer" as it were, in a crisis. Unsurprisingly, Alexander was not won over. Caulaincourt had met with the tsar earlier, and his warnings struck a chord. Alexander played Caulaincourt's trump card: the nation and the army were strongly opposed to this restoration. "Is this the wish of France?" he asked. With that, "the Sphinx of the North" swept out of the meeting at 10:00 P.M. with the future of France still in the balance.[275]

Alexander's assertion was far from groundless. Napoleon was still at Fontainebleau with about thirty-six thousand men, and everyone's assumption was that Mortier and Marmont would join him there with another twenty-four thousand or so, a small force compared to those arrayed against him,[276] but should he strike at Paris—toward the eastern quarters of the sans culottes—there was no guarantee, if faced with the prospect of the Bourbons, Napoleon might get the popular uprising he craved. The national guards swallowed the allied occupation, but they point-blank refused to change their tricolor cockades for Bourbon white. Commanders less cautious than Schwarzenberg usually balked at the prospect of urban combat, however good the odds, and it was no surprise that he was preparing to pull the Austrians out of the city.[277] The political elite was, by definition, a corps of "Napoleon's men" for whom ending his rule was one thing, acquiescing in the return of men whose relatives some of them had once executed, was quite another. Talleyrand knew his milieu, and saw this plainly, but Alexander's persistent support for Bernadotte and constitutional referenda raised darker specters. Either way, the path to civil war beckoned. It is possible Talleyrand knew something about the army Alexander did not. Talleyrand's biographer, Emmanuel de Waresquiel, thinks it highly likely, if impossible to know with certainty, that he gave Marmont assurances that he would be safe from reprisals under a restoration.[278] If this transpired, the results were not yet evident. Talleyrand had wrung this much from the allies: all were agreed that Napoleon and his dynasty be deposed; that should the Bourbons return, they had to accept a constitutional regime; and that a provisional government should be formed. Alexander issued a new proclamation to this effect. The tsar had "authorized every audacity."[279] That being so, Talleyrand, the man of the shadows, took the fate of France into his own hands.

Late into the night of March 31–April 1, Talleyrand gathered a small group of loyal supporters to himself, and issued a call to the senators still in Paris to assemble the next day. The allies did not oppose this, for Talleyrand had seized on their promise to form a provisional government, but he had grasped a crucial lesson from the Malet coup: the Senate was the surest means of creating one.[280] Cambacérès, no fool, had issued strict orders to the senators before he left for Blois, not to attend any meeting that did not conform to the constitution. So great was the fear among them that Napoleon could return that only sixty-four, out of the ninety senators still in Paris, answered Talleyrand's call and met at the Luxembourg Palace on April 1. They accorded themselves two tasks: to give France a new constitution "suitable to the French," and to take over the government of the country on a provisional basis. Talleyrand was elected to head the provisional government, and it was soon clear he had chosen his close collaborators in advance.[281] He had done it all before in 1799, but from the wings, not at the helm. Talleyrand had stepped out of his preferred modus operandi with as much courage and audacity as guile, and it was a stroke of genius. He found the holes in the allied manifesto, and wriggled through them. France now had a pole of attraction that was not committed to a restoration, but did not exclude it. The provisional government could act of its own accord, without direct reference to the occupying forces or Napoleon, or the Bourbons. Talleyrand's own role in creating it was a mockery of legitimacy of any kind—his only claim to authority was as the only member of the Regency Council still in Paris, so thin a veil he chose not to wear it. The Senate did have the right to seize the reins of power, for the Constitution of 1804 had drawn on the Roman formula that the Republic still existed and had only been entrusted to a hereditary dynasty. The next day, the Senate duly withdrew that trust on behalf of the Republic, and deposed Napoleon.

The royalism of Talleyrand and his close collaborators notwithstanding, the French were not obliged to accept the Bourbons, nor obey the allies, only to acknowledge the legitimate authority of Senate. D'Angoulême's government in Bordeaux demanded an emphatic choosing of sides, a "turning of coats," for many. Talleyrand's construct sought no such thing; it was a banner the masses of granite and those loyal to the regime, but not its chief, could support. Alexander agreed because it avoided a Bourbon restoration; the other allies agreed because it did not preclude one; but the real winners were the political elite, "the immortals," and the propertied classes, so battered by Napoleon of late, but on whom the regime had always rested. *Ralliement* and *amalgame* were wrenched from Napoleon. On April 4, the Senate published its motion in *Le Moniteur*, the official organ of government. It was a castigation of Napoleon, and made no mention of the Bourbons, but gave them a subtle warning, as it opened fire on Napoleon: "in a constitutional monarchy, the monarch exists only by virtue of the constitution or the social pact." It went on, "Napoleon Bonaparte, for sometime under a firm and prudent government gave the Nation . . . acts of wisdom and justice; but latterly he tore up the pact." He violated his own constitution, and the decree went on to enumerate his cavalier attitude of foreign policy, conscription, taxation, freedom of the press, and his destruction of the independence of the judiciary—stressing Napoleon created the conditions for dictatorship only recently, thus justifying their own— and the nation's—long-standing support for his regime.[282] This behavior—and nothing else—justified his deposition and released the people and the army from their oaths of loyalty to him. For the moment, all the Senate demanded was a constitutional regime committed to peace, guaranteeing "the rights of man," and the security of property.[283] Everyone present voted for this text, and four more wrote to give their adherence. Only twenty of the ninety senators in Paris abstained.[284] The next day, the Corps Législatif followed suit. The provisional government stood less for "1789," than for *Brumaire*. Talleyrand applied the same diplomatic strategy toward the French elites as Metternich used to wean the German princes away from Napoleon the previous year: the status quo stripped of its creator. Napoleon said far more than he meant to, when he told Las Cases on Saint Helena, "I was betrayed in the Senate, precisely by those who owed me everything . . . I have nothing to repent about my domestic political system."[285]

The results were soon seen. Declarations of allegiance to the provisional government flooded in, becoming "an incontrovertible chain reaction" from across the political spectrum.[286] Gaspard de Chabrol, who had designed a "model town" in the Vendée baptized "Napoleonville," and was now the prefect of the Seine (Paris), told his maires that only adherence to the provisional government could preserve "the same ideas . . . the same attitudes," and stressed the need for stability and prudence. The highest court in France, Cassation, declared openly for the Bourbons, but thanked the Senate for "delivering it from its oath to Napoleon" and called for a new constitution. The clergy of Paris, Maury at their head, joined in, adding they would "render unto Caesar what is Caesar's" should Louis XVIII be proclaimed.[287] Public servants were almost jostling with each other to accept the provisional government. The key adherence was that of the Paris Gendarmerie, generally regarded as the most upright service in Paris, and an elite corps rivaled only by the Imperial Guard. Its captains affirmed their loyalty to the provisional government, "the existing constituted authority, and not a speculative one."[288] All the while, a committee was created—including Lebrun—to draw up a "Senatorial" constitution, which they quietly agreed to submit for the approval of Louis XVIII, who was waiting just outside Paris, at Saint-Ouen, readying for his entry to the capital.[289]

By a circuitous route, Talleyrand and Alexander managed to work effectively together to create a provisional government most of the political classes could rally around. Alexander's naïve, dangerous populism and liking for Bernadotte was tempered by Talleyrand, and adapted to suit the genuine demands for a constitution among all those terrified by the Napoleon of recent years. Both harbored doubts about a Bourbon restoration. Talleyrand set his aside, bowing to the inevitable process of elimination, and disguising his change of mind just long enough to establish the new leadership and keep Alexander appeased. Nevertheless, Alexander continued to talk with Caulaincourt, and did not reject his proposition of a peace based on a regency, but time was short for Napoleon to reply, while Talleyrand tried to turn Alexander in favor of the Bourbons.[290] Alexander's challenge remained, however: the position of the army. Would the soldiers accept the new government's view that they were now released from their oath to Napoleon? The Senate had released the army from its oath to Napoleon, but whether it would be listened to, no one dared say.

Abdication

"Perhaps, the great man, which he still behaved as, defied his position, lived an illusion, for he was always wrong about his resources, and his power,"[291] Caulaincourt reflected later. He knew Napoleon well, and was a constant witness during to the surreal doings of the first week of April. The events of that week saw his judgment of Napoleon confirmed. On April 1, Napoleon gathered his remaining marshals together at Fontainebleau—Ney, Berthier, Lefebvre, Oudinot, and Moncey—who advised him to fall back west, along the Loire, to join Marie-Louise. Instead, he announced to the guard, to hearty cheers, that they were going on the attack. He spent the next three days issuing orders to Berthier, deploying and redeploying his troops for an assault on the capital. On the 2nd, Caulaincourt returned from Paris, with news that a regency might still be negotiable if Napoleon abdicated. Napoleon did nothing, but everyone else took good note. On the 4th, the marshals finally confronted him. They were as frightened by the prospect of urban warfare as Schwarzenberg, all the more so as Napoleon's plan spelled devastation of their own expensive town houses and the loss of their stashes of plunder. They clustered together while Napoleon reviewed the guard, and Ney called out, "Nothing but abdication can save us!" Unruffled, Napoleon went to his study with Caulaincourt and Berthier, but Ney, Moncey, and Lefebvre followed him. Ney told him the army would not attack Paris. "The army will obey me!" Napoleon is said to have replied, to which Ney retorted, "The army will obey its chiefs."[292] Ney's words were to be reckoned with. He was a popular commander, and ready to voice their complaints, but Napoleon was in no mood to listen. By the time Macdonald and Oudinot arrived, Ney and Napoleon were close to blows. Ney injected cack-handed humor to soothe things. "Don't worry—we're not going to act out a scene from Saint Petersburg," raking up the murder of Alexander's father by his own guards.[293] Napoleon looked to Macdonald for support, but was told bluntly, "I've come to tell you in their name (that of his generals) that they don't want to expose (Paris) to the same fate as Moscow."[294] Napoleon slumped in a chair and agreed. He wrote off a quick note announcing he had abdicated in favor of his son, and sent Caulaincourt, Ney, and Macdonald back to Paris to inform the allies. No sooner had they gone than he changed his mind, but the remaining marshals stamped on him. As these scenes took place, Napoleon's fate was sealed by something else.

That afternoon, Marmont swore allegiance to the provisional government and pulled his twelve thousand men—Napoleon's front line—out of the war. Marmont had long believed the war was hopeless, and if Talleyrand had offered him a way out, the prospect of fighting in Paris probably drove him to take it. His explanation to his men was measured and powerful. They were not capitulating, but conforming to the orders of a legitimate government to cease fighting; they were doing so because the war—once so glorious—was now pointless and no longer in the public interest. There would be an honorable peace—and he would look after his men's interests, see them treated fairly. Few had served Napoleon longer, fewer still had been so well rewarded, and it was not long before the Parisian press caricatured him as "Marshal Janus-face." "What a terrible page History reserves for Marmont," Napoleon told Las Cases on Saint Helena,[295] and he was right. "Raguser"—from Marmont's title, "Duke of Ragusa"—is still French argot for a stab in the back. In the moment, his defection made any offensive against Paris impossible, and thus shattered any hope of negotiation for Napoleon.[296] Marmont suspended his "defection" and joined Caulaincourt and the three marshals, to form a common front. They came within an ace of getting Alexander—the only allied leader they met with—to agree to a regency. His own sense that the army was solidly behind it was tipping the balance away from Talleyrand's arguments. Faced with renewed fighting, he was on the verge of forcing the Senate to overturn its deposition of the dynasty, if not its chief. Then the news came, via a Russian aide, that one of Marmont's commanders, Souham, had led his corps over to the allies. The delegation stood quietly as a conversation took place in Russian, which only Caulaincourt half understood. The delegation knew of this already, but hoped they could preempt it. Alexander broke off the meeting abruptly, saying merely, "The Emperor must abdicate unconditionally."[297] Caulaincourt confessed to crying in spite of himself, "my heart swelled up with sadness and rage."[298] It was a near run thing, after all, but it was done.

The delegates returned to Fontainebleau in the early hours of April 6. Caulaincourt roused Napoleon, gave him the news, telling him that war was now the only outcome if he did not agree. "Your reflections are hard," Caulaincourt said he replied, "Well, Sire, they are true," he answered. Caulaincourt had gotten Alexander to assent to send Napoleon into an agreeable exile on Elba, but he would lose even this if he fought on south of the Loire and the army—the only thing the allies still feared—was slaughtered. "Let's go, let's go, don't fret yourself further . . . I see the justice in your goodwill toward me," said Napoleon at last to Caulaincourt, according to his memoirs.[299] He abdicated unconditionally and sent Caulaincourt, yet again, with the news. Typically, while negotiations went on over the details of the abdication, Napoleon tried to find ways of wriggling out of it, earning a rebuke from Caulaincourt, who put the shoe on the other foot, as it were, chastising Napoleon for his ingratitude.[300] Yet, Napoleon knew his world was melting away. On April 11, the day he at last ratified the terms of his departure, he told Caulaincourt, "The Empress does not appear to want to come to Elba with me as her fixed abode . . . no one wants to go to Elba except me." He wondered if the British government would "see any inconvenience in giving me refuge in England, with the guarantees of any English citizen, and with entire and absolute liberty."[301] The next day, Wellington drove Soult out of Toulouse, Augereau accepted the authority of the provisional government and agreed to an armistice in the Rhône region, and the Comte d'Artois arrived in Paris as Louis XVIII's lieutenant-general of the kingdom. Caulaincourt remembered Napoleon as being "dominated by an unnatural preoccupation" that day, telling him "life is insufferable." Nothing seemed to lift his spirits.[302] That night, Napoleon attempted suicide. He had swallowed the opium he had carried with him since he had nearly been captured in Russia, so old it had lost its potency, but it was still strong enough to make him sick, which saved him, aided by Caulaincourt, who found him and called a servant. By 9:00 A.M. he was back at his desk.[303] Caulaincourt's account of this is the only evidence of this incident, and only came to light when his memoirs were published in 1933. Caulaincourt is among the most reliable memoirists of the era,[304] but there is still doubt it ever really happened.[305] It was singularly out of character, to say the least, and had no bearing on events. Maria Walewska came to see him on the 14th. He refused to see her, but wrote to her two days later in the warmest terms:

> Marie . . . the feelings that guide you touch me deeply, they are worthy of your beautiful soul and the goodness of your heart. When you have settled your affairs, if you go to Lucca or Pisa to take the water, I shall see you with the most real and keen interest, as well as your son, for whom my feelings will always be unchanged. Carry on well, don't be angry, think of me warmly, and never doubt me.[306]

These words also show that Napoleon believed that the terms of his abdication allowed him to leave Elba from time to time, and he could visit Maria when in Italy. For this reason, too, he advised Marie-Louise to press the allies to make her ruler of Tuscany or Lucca, with their son in her custody.[307] None of this came to pass.

Perhaps the most intriguing letter he wrote in these moments was to Josephine, on the same day:

> . . . I was complaining about my situation; today, I am glad of it, my head and spirit have had a great weight lifted from them; I have had a great fall, but at least it is useful . . . I go to my retirement,

substituting the pen for the sword. The history of my reign will be curious; they have only seen my profile, now they shall see me in the round. What things I know! That men might have such a false opinion (of me)! . . . I have benefited millions of miserable souls? What have they done for me in the end? They have betrayed me, all of them . . . Adieu, my dear Josephine, be resigned as I am, and never lose the memory of the one who has never forgotten you, and who never shall.[308]

The 16th may have been his "day" for writing to exes, but the sincerity of both letters seems real enough. Napoleon's vision of retirement, possibly a reaction to surviving suicide, had to wait until Saint Helena. Maria Walewska came to Elba, but again, Napoleon refused to see her; they did meet again, during the 100 Days. Josephine was dead in just over a month, after strolling with Alexander in a skimpy frock, and then receiving his brother, Grand Duke Constantine, and the king of Prussia at Malmaison a few days later. Her atavistic instincts of self-preservation, so quick to reassert themselves, proved the death of her.

One of the reasons posited for Napoleon's attempted suicide was a lack of correspondence from Marie-Louise. He need not have worried about her loyalty.

Blois: The Last Bastion

At the start of April, France had four governments: Napoleon in Fontaine-bleau, the provisional government in Paris, d'Angoulême's royalist junta in Bordeaux, and the debris of the Regency in the medieval fortress town of Blois, on the north bank of the Loire. None of them had any real power, but each had its cause.

If anyone was ready to fight to the bitter end, it was Marie-Louise. On April 3, Easter Sunday, she called the last Regency council of the first empire, and laid

before it a proclamation so bloodthirsty it terrified her ministers, who tried to
bury it by getting her to send it to Napoleon for approval. She called for a new
levy of 150,000 men to be sent to Fontainebleau to help retake Paris, and she
wanted to pull back to Orléans, where she could fight on longer, which
she failed to carry. Napoleon and the marshals only began to think in these
terms a week or so later. Her proclamation was sent out to some prefects on
April 4, in defiance of her councillors, but it is doubtful they posted it. She
continued to issue orders, desperate to concentrate as many troops as she could
find, and issued another proclamation denouncing the treason of the provisional government when word of the deposition of the dynasty reached her.[309]
The most peaceable step she took was to write to her father, at Napoleon's
behest, to tell him "that the moment has come to help us."[310] "For Marie-
Louise, nothing was lost. She was ready to fight or negotiate from Blois," as her
most recent biographer, Charles-Éloi Vial, has stirringly put it,[311] his careful
research exploding the many myths of weakness and treachery spun around
her over the years.[312]

The young regent needed her resolve most when confronted by the treason
in her own court. Marie-Louise had no news from Napoleon over the crucial
period of April 4 to 7, and was working on the assumption that a regency for
her son was still possible, but that, equally, Napoleon was ready to fight on.
When the news of Napoleon's abdication reached her, on the 7th, she clung
to the belief that her father would not let them all be deposed. Her immediate reaction, according to the courier who brought the news, was to join
Napoleon. When told it was impossible, she retorted, "Why then? You got
here. My place is beside the Emperor." She tried to send out her proclamation
again, amended to turn it into a call to rally to her son, and pulled one last
card out of her sleeve: she appealed to her father, not to preserve Napoleon,
but to defend the rights of "Napoleon II," his grandson.[313] Marie-Louise
was no longer regent—Napoleon's own signature had seen to that—but she
refused to accept it. Something of Napoleon's own tenacity had entered her,
and she needed it all when a challenge arose from her brothers-in-law. The
next day, Joseph and Jérôme confronted her in what they assumed was a

moment of weakness and vulnerability. They were wrong. They insisted that she leave Blois to join the army south of the Loire and Soult's retreating army to launch a civil war, but Marie-Louise and her chamberlain, d'Haussonville, feared their real plan was to take her hostage, as a bargaining chip with the Austrians. She stood her ground, declaring she would not quit Blois "with a firmness out of the ordinary," an observer recalled.[314] She told Napoleon, "(Jérôme) said they would take me by force . . . I told Joseph I would not go, and everyone agreed, and that I would await orders; that enraged them, and me, too."[315] Jérôme raised his voice and became menacing, at which point she ordered d'Haussonville to call the guard together, and the brothers beat a hasty retreat. Her authority held sway over theirs in this tiny bastion. The brothers' intentions for her may not have been as sinister as she feared, but Joseph was determined to get his own hands on the imperial crown jewels, which Marie-Louise ferociously prevented.[316] It was the last stand, won by the empress commanding the Old Guard.

Marie-Louise, conscious of the need to protect her son and stunned by Napoleon's capitulation, could not hold out for long. A few hours later, she fell into a different trap, from which she could not escape. She was all but alone, the only other Bonapartes left were the deranged Louis, wandering from church to church, praying for deliverance, and Madame Mère.[317] Later that day, doubtless exhausted by her confrontation with Joseph and Jérôme, Marie-Louise was faced with a newly arrived Russian envoy and one of Napoleon's aides who said they had come to take her to Fontainebleau under safe conduct. It took her two days to agree, convinced by Champagny, who was already seeking a post from the Bourbons.[318] He argued that her best hope was to reach her father in Paris, and argue for a regency. It was a cruel trap, as the Russians later admitted. The allies, her father included, had already decided her fate: that of ruler of Parma. Cambacérès wrote to Paris on the 10th giving his allegiance to the new regime, having watched Marie-Louise disappear over the Loire. He caught up with her at Orléans, but was allowed to go no further, and made his way to Paris.[319] At Orléans, Marie-Louise was stripped of the imperial treasury, and left penniless. Her escort became less and less French, until by Rambouillet, she was in the hands of Cossacks, the very men she was promised protection from.[320] She fell ill there, and was told her father would not see her. She became confused as letters reached her from Napoleon, urging her not to hold out for a regency but for Tuscany. She and her son were now under Francis's complete control, and on May 2, she left France for Vienna, her hopes dashed. In Paris, Talleyrand spread the word that Marie-Louise was overjoyed to see Napoleon deposed, "sowing the seeds of a lasting black legend."[321] Sent first to Vienna, she departed to Parma—without her son—to rule there until her death in 1847. She turned it into a model Napoleonic state, perhaps the only Bonaparte who managed do so.

Joseph fled from the wrath of the Empress to Orléans, still in French hands, and then to his property at Mortefontaine. The allies rebuffed his entreaties for protection, and he turned to the provisional government for leave to remain in France, bolstering his case by refusing to go to Elba with Napoleon. Then came the smug "I told you so": "All that has happened justifies only too completely my old and dire predictions." But Joseph's luck had run out with his brother's. Talleyrand refused to see Miot, Joseph's loyal emissary, and made it clear he wanted France shorn of all the Bonapartes. He was given a safe conduct to the Swiss border. Only "the inoffensive Pauline" was allowed to remain, for the moment.[322] Soult and Eugène were the last to surrender. The former signed an armistice with Wellington on the 18th; the latter did so with the Austrian commander, Bellegarde, on the 16th, ending his gallant defense of Italy. They, like the empress, proved loyal even beyond the end.

Fontainebleau: April 20, 1814

By April 20, Napoleon took his leave for Elba, accompanied by four commissioners from each allied power. Only a handful of his guards and aides were left, but he turned the moment into legend. That morning, his coaches were drawn up in the Courtyard of the White Horse, as he emerged from breakfast dressed in the green uniform of the Chasseurs of the Guard and wearing his famous black tricorn hat, with Drouot and Bertrand at his side, who went with him to Elba. Guards lined the staircases he descended to the courtyard as a band played "*Aux Champs*." He was at last alone with his true family, and addressed them from the center of the courtyard. The speech was not actually recorded, but those who remembered it claimed to know it by heart.[323] It appeared thus in a manuscript published soon afterward:

> Soldiers of the Old Guard, I have come to say goodbye. For twenty years you have always followed the path of honor and glory. In these last days, as in those of our prosperity, you have never ceased to be models of courage and loyalty . . . Do not lament my fate; if I have decided to go on living, it is to serve your glory. I wish to write the history of the great things we have done together! . . . Farewell, my children! I would like to embrace you all; let me at least embrace your flag![324]

Some claimed to remember him asking them to "be loyal to the new ruler France has chosen," some not. Everyone recalled what he did next. Napoleon took the flag of the guard, buried his face in it, saying, "Dear Eagle, let my embrace echo in the hearts of these brave men!"[325] Even the allied escort was in tears. Napoleon turned on his heel, did not look back, got into his carriage, and set out into exile.

14

ELBA: A NERVOUS EXILE,
APRIL 1814–FEBRUARY 1815

Napoleon's journey through Burgundy to Lyon, was in "friendly" country, loyal in turn to the Revolution and the empire. The detachment of Imperial Guards who marched with him out of Fontainebleau came only as far as Nevers, where they awaited their own fate under the restored monarchy. A handful, under Cambronne, continued to Elba, but by a different route. He was met by cheering crowds and boasted to the allied commissioners that he did not need an escort. Along the way, Cambronne's men turned on some gendarmes, who sported white Bourbon cockades and had nailed a placard to a scaffold with VIVE NAPOLÉON LE GRAND! scrawled on it.[1] It was a sign of things to come. The crowds who cheered him at Lyon—the city whose fortunes he had done so much to raise—were the last he heard. As his cortege made its way down the Rhône valley, the mood darkened. Napoleon had refused an escort of allied troops, arguing it made him look like a prisoner, but he had forgotten his bitter relationship with the region. Long a stronghold of Catholic royalism, he had had his baggage plundered there by bandits on his return from Egypt in 1798, and the mood had not changed. The defenseless party was attacked by a crowd outside Avignon, and again, at Orgon, where Napoleon saw a dummy of himself hung, blood-spattered, in effigy, outside the inn he stayed at. A bloodthirsty crowd surrounded his coach, rattling the doors and climbed all over it, crying, "Hang him!" "Cut his head off!" One woman shouted "Give me back my son!" Napoleon was petrified, and hid behind Bertrand, "pale, desperate, and speechless." The mob was held back only by the Russian commissioner, Pavel Shuvalov, who set about them with his fists and told them they should be ashamed of themselves for bullying "a defenseless man," now humiliated and helpless. Napoleon was reduced to a nervous wreck, hiding at the next inn, at Les Calades, jumping at every sound, and virtually cowering in tears at the back of the room. He changed into an Austrian uniform from then on, and made no complaint when a detachment of Austrian cavalry arrived to act as his escort. They were part of the troops guarding his sister, Pauline, who was staying at a château near Le Luc. When the two met on April 26, she refused to hug him until he took off the uniform of the enemy. Napoleon insisted to his captors that such scenes were all the work of Bourbon agitators, but his gut reactions were more revealing than he cared to admit.[2] Only now did he confront face-to-face the people he had ruled so roughly, and they reduced him to a cowardly, quivering wretch no Cossack or assassin ever could. Two days later, having collected himself, he had a flaming row with the British that he had been promised a corvette, which was to be given to him, but found only a brig. Napoleon eventually took ship aboard a British vessel, the *Undaunted*, and set sail for Elba.[3]

The violent hatred of the people of the Rhône stood in sharp contrast to the civilized behavior of the allies. Napoleon and all the Bonapartes were treated generously. Eugène was welcomed at the court of his Bavarian in-laws, Pius VII gave Madame Mère and Fesch refuge in Rome. Jérôme was refused entry into his father-in-law's kingdom of Württemberg, as the once-loyal ally sought to sever his ties with Napoleon, but Jérôme and Catherine were finally granted leave to stay in Austrian territory, first near Graz, and then in Trieste.[4] The new French government, like many of its subjects, did not feel the same. Talleyrand ensured that the Bonapartes were driven from France, and although the treaty granted them all generous pensions, these came from the French treasury, and they never saw them.[5] Anything they got was because Caulaincourt worked indefatigably for the family's interests both before and after Napoleon's departure. If he could not get Tuscany for Marie-Louise, or prevent her separation from her son, he saved Napoleon from a fate worse than Elba. On June 2, he announced to Napoleon, "Now that I have done all I can in my power for the interests of Your Majesty and his family, I take leave of it all, and I am going home."[6] Loyalty, not real affection, infused these final words, almost those of a debt being paid.[7] By this point, perhaps his real concern was for Marie-Louise and the helpless child, Napoleon-Francis. In any case, Caulaincourt took an extreme risk in acting as the Bonapartes' protector, compromising his own position with the Bourbons.

His chivalry and fidelity obviously struck a chord with Alexander. In the circumstances of 1814, Caulaincourt's sense of chivalry—he gallantly defended Hortense and Josephine's interests against the provisional government[8]—may have impressed Alexander, conscious of his own image and desperate to be seen a generous victor,[9] but the notion of Elba seems to have come from Caulaincourt, planted in the tsar's ear.[10] Napoleon told him, "Alexander is with you; that can achieve anything."[11] The tsar stopped the royalists changing the name of the Austerlitz bridge with the quip, "It is enough that people know that Emperor Alexander passed that way with his armies." Alexander's sense of "fair play" went only so far, it is true. He ordered Napoleon's statue taken down from its column in the Place Vendôme and replaced by a white flag.[12] But dealing with the man was a different matter.

Caulaincourt was also served by lucky timing. He caught Alexander before Castlereagh and Metternich arrived in Paris. They were constrained to agree about Elba against their better judgment. Had he arrived three days earlier, Metternich told his mistress, he would have prevented "Elba": Alexander had done "many silly things and behaved like a pupil who had escaped his teacher." As prophetic as he was scathing, Metternich went on: "This is the biggest child on earth! He has begun to turn what is good into something bad. Now, we shall have to repair the lot, but we shall have to suffer from the maladies caused by the first moment when he had escaped us!"[13] Castlereagh felt the same about "Elba," and balked at Alexander agreeing to allow Napoleon to keep the title of "emperor," something the British had never even acknowledged, but he swallowed hard. Caulaincourt found Castlereagh "obliging, positive and frank," true to his—in truth, Alexander's—word in the talks. The Ulsterman bowed to circumstances, and noted on reports of Napoleon, "during the voyage . . . his mind still seemed to cherish hopes as to France."[14] Castlereagh knew that nothing drastic could be done to curtail Napoleon's liberty because of the terms of Marmont's defection, and told his friend Bathurst that the provisional government had agreed to it, to get Napoleon's army away from Fontainebleau and put an end to any risk of civil war. "Elba" was something he and Metternich wanted undone at the first opportunity.[15]

Napoleon knew all this very well, without having to be told. He was haunted at Fontainebleau by the fear that the allies might renege on the terms of the treaty even before the ink was dry, warning Marie-Louise as he set off for Elba that if she met Alexander, he "will let nothing slip" as he was very tactful, but the king of Prussia "is capable of telling you, without any ill intentions, the most disagreeable things" and to pay attention if he did.[16] He arrived in Portoferraio, the capital of his new "empire," on May 4 to a one-hundred-gun salute, but he had no illusions that even this little fiefdom might be snatched from him in the blink of an eye. He owed it all to the man who hounded him across Europe and brought him down, and whose moods no one could fathom.

The island of Elba amounted to only 222 square kilometers, containing about 12,000 inhabitants, who lived mainly by fishing and agriculture. From antiquity until the seventeenth century, it was rich in iron ore and much fought over, but the mines had largely been worked out and, by 1814, only one was still viable. Its people were generally regarded as good-natured, industrious, and peaceable. They had known many masters in the 1790s as Elba passed to and fro between the French and the British, but since 1805, it had been part of France.[17] Being part of "the great empire" had done the people of the island little good, and the British found it relatively easy to take possession of it in 1814. Discipline had broken down in the French garrison by the time Napoleon arrived: desertion was rife, and at the news of his abdication, Napoleon had been burned in effigy in one fort, and the commander of another was killed by his own men.[18] The natives' reaction was not that of its French occupiers, however. Napoleon received a warm public welcome from the people of his new capital, but behind it was "a mixture of veritable joy and secret fear."[19] Something quite extraordinary suddenly punctuated their quiet existence but, as Philip Dwyer has said, it soon dawned on them that "his presence would mean business, money, and trade."[20] Napoleon made the transition from a public figure—to put it mildly—to a celebrity on Elba. Passing tourists, people curious to meet the fallen colossus and hear his accounts of the wars and politics of his reign came to town and found a ready audience with him. He became a fixture on the Grand Tour, and about sixty English visitors—"mostly young, mostly from educated backgrounds, generally Whigs"[21]—made the trip from the Tuscan mainland to see him. Whatever trade they brought did not compensate for the two million francs the restored Bourbons failed to pay him under the terms of the treaty of Fontainebleau, nor the heavy tax load Napoleon then passed on to his new subjects to fill the gap, as he struggled to maintain a shadow of the imperial court and indulged his mania for palace-building on a reduced scale that was still disproportionate to the resources of the island. By autumn, there were serious anti-tax revolts in parts of the island that took 230 troops to suppress.[22] Napoleon had need of his "little army"—so baptized almost in mockery of his former "great army"[23]—which began just over two thousand strong, but was soon reduced to about fifteen hundred for lack of funds. Most of them were a mixture of the remnants of the original garrison, local volunteers, and a collection of Corsicans, Italians, and some Hungarians. At its core were the 610 men of the Old Guard under Cambronne, some Poles, and about a dozen Mamelukes, a few of whom were Egyptians, but by now Greeks and people of mixed-race, prisoners from the 1804 invasion of Saint-Domingue who had taken service with Napoleon.[24] They were needed, as was the small naval squadron he tried to gather. On September 14, 1814, the Barbary corsairs appeared off the island of La Pinosa. They were driven off by artillery fire.[25]

It was a foretaste of what was in store for the western Mediterranean, as the war ended and the royal navy reduced its presence.

Napoleon was never more absolute a ruler than on Elba; Drouot was its Governor, and Bertrand, Grand Marshal of the Palace. There were no elected assemblies. He sought to be an enlightened reformer, nonetheless. His new flag was sprinkled with the golden bees, the Bonaparte family's official emblem. It was associated with the Merovingians, the first dynasty of France, whose first king, Clovis, embraced Christianity and so became the harbinger of civilization to the Franks. The bee meant progress and civilization; Napoleon set himself to the enlightened "improvement" of his new realm with his usual dynamism. No sooner installed in his "palace" in Portoferraio, he set off on the first of several tours of the island. A flood of orders—many of them self-contradictory—followed. The salt and iron mines were to be reorganized and made profitable. The roads were to be improved, even if their main purpose was better to cope with Napoleon's carriages. "Make the Longone road practicable for carriages . . . I want this road usable by next week."[26] Napoleon supported a project to set up a ceramics factory in Portoferraio, giving the budding entrepreneur a locale from his domain, but "as for advances of funds, they must only be given with great prudence, so as not to expose us to loss."[27] His enthusiasm for the mines had its limits: "It appears that (the mine of Rio) is yielding nothing now, but the workers' expenses are always the same."[28] Even the court felt the financial strain: "[M]y intention is not to give the employees of the Household heat, lighting, or linen."[29] Money was a constant constraint, even when it came to Napoleon's imperial dignity. And yet, Portoferraio was still his capital, and it was to reflect the enlightened urbanism he had once lavished on Paris: "The street from the palace to the port is very dirty, and the paving needs repairing. Give orders to have it cleaned and repair the paving . . . so that the water and the smells don't run down it anymore." It was also a good idea to plant plum trees in the vicinity, to purify the air.[30] Few aspects of Elba's life escaped Napoleon's gaze, both improving and grandiose.

Straightened circumstances made it imperative that court etiquette be rigidly imposed, with Pauline presiding, and occasionally Madame Mère, who had also joined him. Etiquette had its exceptions. In April, Maria Walewska joined him, too, at her request. Napoleon obviously wanted her with him, and did all he could to keep her presence secret, sleeping—or pretending to—in a tent outside the isolated residence he prepared for her, fearful all the while that Marie-Louise would get wind of it. As Philip Dwyer said, it all smacked of comic opera. Maria Walewska's stay on Elba lasted only two weeks, for as her presence became known. Napoleon hurried her away, without much ado.[31] Marie-Louise did find out, probably at a time when Metternich was managing to separate her from her closest French friends, notably Madame Lannes. It is hard to know when she finally turned away from Napoleon, exactly, but the news could only have helped in the process.[32]

While Napoleon fussed about on Elba—a feint, a tactical ruse—the allied powers assembled in Vienna, and in a series of meetings, formal and informal, known collectively as the Congress of Vienna, set about reordering the Europe Napoleon had left them. Napoleon's real interests, hopes, and fears, revolved on the world he had abdicated, whether in hopes of his wife and son joining him, or that Metternich and Castlereagh might still engineer a far worse place of exile for him. The quiet island soon became a nest of spies. It crawled with allied agents, while Napoleon's own networks kept information and correspondence flowing to him. Napoleon's intelligence, particularly when it came through Italy, seems to have been notably better than that of the allies, which was usually slow in arriving, often contradictory, and sometimes simply false.[33] The allies always wanted to know if Napoleon was trying to escape; Napoleon was anxious to learn what they had in store for him. Both were right in their fears. Talleyrand was sent to Vienna with two specific goals by Louis XVIII: to oust Caroline and Murat from Naples and restore the Bourbons, and to get Napoleon moved somewhere further away from France.[34] To Louis, it was all part of a wider strategy to expunge the Bonapartes, so important to him that he did not quite trust Talleyrand with it, and opened parallel talks with Metternich. For all their treason, Caroline and Murat now found their fates still bound to Napoleon's. Although the Austrians had promised he would keep Naples when he defected to them, Murat was not even mentioned in the peace signed in Paris on May 30, and George Bentinck, the British governor of Sicily—now active in central Italy—had openly refused to agree to the Austrians' guarantees, calling Murat "the most treacherous of all the Gauls." Castlereagh, unsettled by Murat's refusal to withdraw from Rome after the restoration of Pius VII, spoke of his "rascality." Metternich agreed about his presence in Rome,[35] and to the deposition of Murat when the Congress ended, as well as to bar Napoleon-Francis from succeeding his mother in Parma, as part of his wider vision for Austrian hegemony in Italy.[36] Murat played gesture politics, halting the usual shipments of cattle and grain to Elba, but on the island, the British officer guarding Napoleon, Neil Campbell, was convinced that the two were in secret communication through Pauline. Some letters from Murat to Napoleon were found among Pauline's possessions in early January. They gave nothing away, but when it became known that some of Napoleon's troops on Elba had also been in contact with Murat, Talleyrand told Louis XVIII, "it would be well to get rid without delay of the man on Elba and of Murat."[37]

Getting Napoleon off Elba proved delicate. His status was confirmed by the treaty of Fontainebleau, but his presence on Elba was problematic from the start. As early as April 1814, Emperor Francis had complained to Metternich that Napoleon was too close to the mainland for comfort, and by October, he was pressing Alexander to replace the French troops on the island with an international force: Metternich and Francis saw Napoleon as just as much a danger to their hegemony in Italy as Murat.[38] The Prussians and the British took little convincing. Castlereagh had proposed either Saint Helena or the Cape Colony as a place of exile from the outset,[39] and Louis XVIII seems to have seized on this with glee. By November, it was leaked to the press that Napoleon and his whole family were to be sent there, although Talleyrand seemed to think, in October, that Castlereagh was leaning toward his own idea of sending Napoleon to the Azores,[40] a sign of how little Louis XVIII trusted him in this, so enthusiastic a turncoat had he been.[41] Louis drove home his case when he confiscated all Napoleon's personal property in France on December 18, indicating he intended to treat him as something akin to an outlaw.[42] The only person in the way was Alexander, and even he was losing interest in the niceties of the treaty of Fontainebleau—and Napoleon.[43] It seems that by November, Napoleon's fate was decided.

Napoleon was well informed of all this. News, much of it emanating from Maret and Savary reached him who, according to their memoirs, used General Evian, in the Bourbon war ministry, as a courier.[44] He knew much about the unpopularity of the Bourbons, and even of a conspiracy led by Fouché to overthrow them[45] gleaned from the loyal supporters who gathered around Maret and Hortense, and through frequent discussions between Maret and discontented generals and even civil servants.[46] However, it seems it was Napoleon's own worries, not those of France, that preyed most on his mind. Many unsettling things swirled around him that autumn: his financial worries, all of them of political import; the growing realization that his wife and son would not be joining him; rumors of plots to assassinate him; concrete news about "Saint Helena." It was the last that he feared most. By November, even Neil Campbell, the rather unobservant British attaché to Napoleon, wrote to his superiors that "I think he is capable of crossing over to Piombino with his troops or any other eccentricity."[47] Over December and January, many other reports from the French spy network on Elba gave similar warnings, but none were taken seriously. Napoleon was seen as, simply, too weak to react. They were all wrong.

There may have been deeper motivations. It is impossible to know, but the man revealed in Napoleon's outburst to Metternich, not so very long before, that "simple private person (who) has ascended to the throne—a parvenu—who has spent twenty years hailed with bullets" and did "not fear any threats at all," who did "value my life above all else, nor that of others very much," who would "not waver to and fro to save my own life above all else" and did not "rate it higher than that of a hundred thousand people," he who swore he would "sacrifice a million people if necessary," may now have been prepared to be as good as his word. By their deeds shall ye know them.

Napoleon made no secret of his pressing concerns, going so far as to tell Campbell in December that he would have to be removed from Elba by force,[48] but this was yet another feint. He was going to remove himself. The question remained only as to when and how. In Campbell, he found his answer. Neil Campbell was what later ages term "a useful idiot." He had been with Napoleon since the day he left Fontainebleau, as one of the team of allied officers who accompanied him to Elba, and remained with him on the island. Because Campbell had his own frigate, the *Partridge*, he could give chase to Napoleon if he fled. Napoleon had to find a way to rid himself of Campbell long enough to escape undetected by the British, and he did. From the outset, Napoleon by turns flattered Campbell, according him full diplomatic status at receptions and chatting to him at length, personally, but always careful to show his "weak," vulnerable side, pining openly for his wife and son, but sighing in resignation at his fate. He also filled Campbell with misinformation he duly reported to his superiors. No disinformation surpassed how Napoleon's behavior duped Campbell. "I heard him say, myself," remembered Lord Holland, "that Napoleon's talents did not seem to him superior to those needed in a sub-prefect."[49] Lulled into a false sense of security, Campbell spent long periods away from Elba, taking the *Partridge* to see his mistress, an Italian countess, at various points on the mainland. Campbell believed firmly that Napoleon might well attempt to escape, but that the Tuscan coast was his likely destination, where he would join Murat, who was on the point of war with the Austrians, where "they would throw down the gauntlet in defiance of the sovereigns of Europe."[50] Campbell did not believe Napoleon's troops would follow him to France, whereas to begin in Italy was less of a risk.[51]

Even though Campbell was increasingly persuaded that Napoleon was up to something, on February 20 he took the bait—and the *Partridge*—to Livorno, exactly when the tides were right for Napoleon's own sailing. If Napoleon were headed for Tuscany, Campbell saw no danger in getting there ahead of him, and he told Castlereagh so.[52] In his memoirs, Lord Holland analyzed it all perfectly: "Some people think that Napoleon gave Campbell a false sense of security by hiding his intellectual faculties from him . . . I think Campbell was the dupe of his own silliness."[53] One of Napoleon's officials on Elba called him "the perfection of the British type"[54]—a "chinless wonder," in other words. In his boredom, Napoleon had found something to amuse him. He became the Figaro of his youth, playing on the vanity and stupidity of Campbell's Count de Almaviva to perfection. As he sailed off for Livorno on February 16, Campbell assumed that when he saw Napoleon's schooner, the *Étoile*, escorting him out of harbor it was a local supply run. In fact, it was checking that the *Partridge* was really heading out of harm's way.[55] Under Campbell's nose, Napoleon was ready to go. An "emperor" Napoleon may have been, but the escape from Elba was a masterly trick on a dim aristocrat. The next day, for the first time, Napoleon wrote openly to Murat that he was sending a trusted servant to him with "important and pressing communications" and was authorized to sign "any convention that Your Majesty might wish, relative to our affairs."[56] The same day, he wrote to Murat again:

> My Dear Murat, Thank you for all you have done for Countess Walewska . . . and above all, her son, who is very dear to me. Colonna (Napoleon's messenger) will tell you many great and important things. I am counting on you and above all on your speed. Time presses.[57]

The old friendship was rekindled; the trust restored, and not merely politically. Naples had become the last redoubt of the dynasty, the safe haven for Maria and her son, but both men were now readying to put this at risk, as the vise tightened on them.

Napoleon did well to keep his plans quiet, but rumors began to circulate when the guard was issued with new shoes and a Marseille merchant ship, the *Saint-Esprit*, was "requisitioned" for his small fleet of five assorted vessels. The date was set for February 26, when the tides were perfect and no British ships were in the area. Even Madame Mère and Pauline were told only the night before. Pauline was greatly troubled, and gave one of Napoleon's staff her diamonds to sell, in case of financial need. Letizia was in tears, but said to Napoleon only, "Go and follow your destiny." It was only nineteen years since Josephine had worn a sash emblazoned with the same word, "destiny," at their excuse for a wedding in a Paris office.

Napoleon went to Mass on late afternoon of the 26th, and ordered assembly to be beaten, as the guard handed over its duties to local units. By now crowds had gathered as he made his way to the port along with Cambronne, Drouot, Bertrand, and about eleven hundred guardsmen and servants. He chose *L'Inconstant* as his flagship, and set sail about midnight, slipping away into the night. His ancestors had taken to the same sea centuries before, to risk all in the conquest of Corsica for Genoa. Now, he sallied forth one last time—so cautious in his planning, so reckless in his goal—the conquistador to the end. His real self.

15

THE FLIGHT OF THE EAGLE

After three days of weaving its way around French and British patrols, Napoleon's flotilla landed in the Golfe-Juan, between Antibes and Cannes, on the afternoon of March 1. Napoleon bore more the marks of Cortez than a returning hero, surrounded by a handful of men in a treacherous, hostile land, bent on seizing what was not his, against all odds. "You are looking on rich lands. May you know how to govern them well," one of Cortez's followers said as they landed in another Gulf San Juan, in Mexico. "God give us the same good fortune in fighting, Cortez replied, as he gave the Paladin Roland."[1] Cortez was in a new land, untested as a ruler, unsure of his reception. Napoleon had no such excuses, his errand yet more brazen. Roland was massacred at Roncesvalles.

Napoleon disembarked about 4:00 P.M., with the eleven hundred men under him. He gave strict orders that no blood was to be shed, which was just as well, as he was in no position to withstand serious opposition. The twenty-five Guardsmen he sent to take the fortress of Antibes were promptly arrested.[2] He ordered Cambronne to secure the main road between Antibes and Cannes, and issued two proclamations, one to the army, and one to the French people. Napoleon knew there was a distinct difference between the army and the nation, and that his only real hope of success lay with the former "ranging itself under the flags of its chief," as "the eagle will fly from church spire to church spire with the national colors, all the way to Notre-Dame." He denounced Louis XVIII and the traitors around him—naming Augereau and Marmont—who had brought the king back to Paris in the baggage train of the enemy; Napoleon had roused himself from his slumbers to sacrifice himself for the good of the country: "I have traversed the seas in the midst of perils of all kinds: I come among you to retake my rights, which are also yours."[3] His call to his men was as powerful as his appeal to the nation was shameless. The first obstacle was Masséna, who commanded the southern coast for Louis, as he had, in his disgrace, for Napoleon. Of this old comrade, so ill-treated, Napoleon had no illusions. He sent a secret, friendly message to Masséna, one hundred miles away in Marseille, but admitted on Saint Helena, "although Masséna was attached to his old colors . . . he would not act rashly."[4] Napoleon was half right. Masséna got his first clear report about the landing late on the evening of March 3, and quickly dispatched a force against him, but Napoleon had no illusions about either Masséna or the climate of opinion in Provence. He blustered to his allied captors the year before that the hostility he met with there was all a staged royalist plot, but once returned, his actions betray a clearer, furtive eye. He evaded Masséna and the Provençal national guards by doing what he did best with his men: forced marches over hard ground. As local forces stirred themselves to confront him—the prefects and commanders were anything but "mute with fear" of Napoleon, knowing Masséna was behind them[5]—Napoleon chose to avoid both the hostile population and the king's troops by taking the high, winding road through the foothills of the Alps—so high there was still snow on the ground in places—from the coast to Grenoble. And he did so quickly. He broke camp on the coast in the small hours of March 2; he was in Grasse that night; in Barrême on the night of the third, where he rested; at Sisteron by midday on the 5th, and did not pause again, until he reached Gap that night. His men made over two hundred kilometers in less than a week on roads that are often little more than a goat tracks even today. The next day, he was within a day's march of Grenoble, on whose garrison's latent affections he had placed all his hopes. It was a forced march to rival any of those in his glorious past but unrivaled in its desperation. There were some signs he had judged aright. At Sisteron, the river Durance could only be crossed by one, easily defended bridge. It could all have ended there, but the local commander, Nicolas Loverdo, did nothing. Although personally hostile to Napoleon, he did not trust his men.[6]

Napoleon had two days on Masséna from start to finish; Paris knew nothing of any of this until March 9. Slowness helped him at least as much as speed. The allies had done Napoleon a great favor when they had agreed to withdraw all their troops from France, leaving only disjointed, if determined, local levies to defend Louis. Everywhere, however, rumor preceded him. Indeed, it lay in wait for him. The rumors of a daring escape and return began as soon as Napoleon set sail for Elba. It did not abate, carried into the most remote villages by itinerant salesmen—the colporteurs so feared by the police—and by the coachmen who carried the post, the bearers of false and real tidings from time immemorial, all fanned by a new presence in village life, the disgruntled veteran. Such rumors festered during Napoleon's time on Elba, proof in itself of how naïve it was of Alexander to insist on leaving Napoleon so close to France. The head of Louis's police, Jean-Claude Beugnot—once a devoted imperial administrator—complained of the "profusion of false news" as early as July.[7] Some ears heard tales of the English seizing Lille, or that the Bourbons had restored feudal dues to the nobles, all of which sought to dispose them well to Napoleon's return. Other rumors bore uncanny resemblance to real plots, soon abandoned: Napoleon had escaped to Italy and joined Murat, and they now held the whole peninsula, poised to invade France. It was said that Napoleon-Francis would be crowned emperor at Easter. Napoleon's agents were seen everywhere.[8] When the greatest of the rumors became reality, every part of France shuddered. Speculation became calculation, whether made in fear or hope. One of Napoleon's loyalist commanders, General d'Erlon, who had been retained by the Bourbons, now moved from contemplation to action, but in halting, ambiguous fashion. On March 7, d'Erlon, the commander of the 16th military division at Lille—while Napoleon was still creeping quietly along the goat paths of the Durance valley—marched his troops on Paris, without orders, and without declaring why. This "conspiracy of the north," as it was soon called, was rapidly scotched by the appearance of Marshal Mortier, who ordered the men back to barracks, and sent d'Erlon packing to the Belgian border. The incident was just as rapidly interpreted as a sign of a widespread, well-organized Bonapartist conspiracy, a planned flanking movement to seal off Paris from the north, while Napoleon moved from the south. Careful research by Munro Price has shown that although d'Erlon might, indeed, have been trying to open a second front, it may have been in aid of ousting Louis XVIII in favor of his cousin, Louis-Philippe d'Orléans, not Napoleon, in an effort to rally potential Bonapartists to a more liberal monarchy, in time to thwart Napoleon. Napoleon certainly thought so. Shortly after his return to Paris, he remarked, "It wasn't Louis XVIII I dethroned. It was the duc d'Orléans."[9] Price makes a very convincing case, but all ambiguity was cast aside when Napoleon faced his first real test at the narrow defile of Laffrey, just south of Grenoble.

The standoff at Laffrey is the stuff of which legends are made, and Napoleon soon made this small moment into one of his greatest. General Marchand, the commander at Grenoble, intended to stand firm. He closed the gates, girded himself to face Napoleon, and on the morning of March 7, sent out a battalion of the 5th Regiment of the Line to destroy the bridge at Pontault to thwart Napoleon's advance. Finding Napoleon's vanguard too close to Pontault, the 5th drew itself up in a strong position at Laffrey, right across Napoleon's march. Here, for the first time, the little imperial army came face-to-face with troops loyal to the Bourbons. All the witnesses to this agreed that Napoleon left his own lines and went alone toward the ranks of the 5th, a few of his Guardsmen some way behind him, then halted and addressed the men of the 5th. There are two versions of what he said. The most famous is of Guillaume-Joseph-Roux Peyrusse, Napoleon's treasurer on Elba: "Behold me, soldiers of the 5th, do you recognize me? . . . If there is among you, a soldier who wants to kill your Emperor, he can!" as Napoleon opened up his great coat dramatically. The other came from a passerby, who wrote to a friend the next day:

The Emperor turned to his Grenadiers and made them promise
not to fire, even if he was fired upon, and advanced alone. Then
he cried to the soldiers of the 5th, "Oh my comrades, do you no
longer recognize your old comrade, your emperor, he who led you
so often to victory?" Then he exhorted them to join him. Silence
was all he got; then, opening his greatcoat, he said "Since you don't
recognize me, fire on me!" [10]

What happened next is indisputable: The 5th swarmed over to the *grognards*,
shouting "*Vive l'empereur!*" It was now part of the Imperial Army, marching to
Grenoble. Charles de Steuben transposed this standoff onto canvas in 1831,
creating an icon. At his trial for treason after Waterloo, Marchand denied
none of it. [11] Marchand sent for reinforcements as soon as he learned of this,
but one of his commanders, Charles de la Bédoyère, led his men—the 7th
Regiment of the Line—out of Grenoble, and over to Napoleon, leaving the
city defenseless. Napoleon promoted him to general, and made him an aide-
de-camp at Waterloo; he was executed by Louis soon afterward. Marchand
and a handful of officers loyal to the Bourbons slipped out of Grenoble by the
northern gate, as Napoleon swept in to cheering crowds from the south, having
first confronted the men on the gates, as he had at Laffrey, and led them over
to him. "Until Grenoble, I was an adventurer, at Grenoble, I was a prince,"
he told Las Cases on Saint Helena. [12] Hardly. Behind him was a hostile, if
disorganized, Provence. Ahead, a government that did not yet know he had
taken Grenoble, but was alert to the growing danger. Yet, Napoleon had read
the army aright. He paused for thirty-six hours in his new conquest, and with
his force swollen to between six and seven thousand troops, he turned east for
Lyon. Napoleon was now doing exactly what the politicians who put him in
power at Brumaire had dreaded: raise the eagle and march his army on the
capital. The history of Rome repeated itself, and the modern *pronunciamiento*,
so beloved of Latin American would-be Napoleons, was born.

The exertions of the last week took their toll on Napoleon. He dispensed
with his white Arab stallion and took to his carriage on the way to Lyon,

making his way there by the main highway, met by cheering crowds, at least according to his own account published later.[13] He came into the open in every way. Whether the advance was the triumphal procession Napoleon declared it was or not, he met no opposition, the advance guard of hussars and light infantry an unnecessary precaution. There was no one to exploit Napoleon's exposed position.

Louis XVIII had his health problems, too. Paralyzed by gout, he sensed what was coming even before news of Grenoble reached him. He convened his ministers on the night of March 5, telling them with his own brand of sang froid, "Since Monsieur Bonaparte wants to reside in France, we shall endeavor to keep him here."[14] Louis acted swiftly but, like Napoleon on so many occasions, entrusted the task to his most incompetent, unreliable relatives. He correctly saw that Napoleon's target was Lyon, and on March 6, he dispatched south an overconfident d'Artois and a sullen Louis-Philippe. D'Artois made no effort to assess the situation he was taking charge of. "He retained the greatest nonchalance in his words, in his judgments on the state of affairs, in the orders he gave," remembered one official. "I shall have to shine my boots," he quipped.[15] Louis-Philippe, in utter contrast, reacted with almost paranoid obstinacy to Louis's whole plan of action, seeing in it a ploy to get him out of Paris because he posed, possibly, a bigger danger to the regime than Napoleon. He pleaded to concentrate the defense closer to Paris, under himself. When Louis brushed this aside, Louis-Philippe next asked the king if it would be wise to keep at least one of the princes of the blood close to him, a thinly veiled nod to his immobility, to which Louis replied, "I am very grateful to you, but I have no need of anyone," and told Louis-Philippe to shine up his own boots, and get off to Lyon.[16] Louis-Philippe's military experience consisted of a brief spell with the revolutionary army at Valmy and Jemappes; d'Artois talked a good battle—frequently—but never fought one, as Thierry Lentz caustically and accurately observes.[17] Louis sent Macdonald with them to do the real work. Politically, Louis had chosen his marshal well; for all his loyalty in 1814, Macdonald had been outspoken with Napoleon about the need for peace, but he did not have the temperament to rally a wavering garrison.

One of his subordinates remarked, "The choice of marshal Macdonald (for Lyon) was not fortunate. His own valor could not inspire a single lad, he was not communicative; he could freeze the most enthusiastic."[18] These were the men to whom the fate of the throne was entrusted.

They were all in Lyon by March 9. The need to defend the city was much vaunted, but they found only two line regiments and one of dragoons at their disposal. There was almost no artillery; the guns to come were from Grenoble, but were now in Napoleon's hands. Their commandant was Roger de Damas, an émigré, who had spent the wars fighting the French and done little to win the hearts and minds of his men, or the Lyonnais, a city long loyal to Napoleon, "brave, first into the breach, but scarcely aware of reality."[19] D'Artois got there first, and assumed that it would simply be enough to show himself at dinner, at Mass in the cathedral, at the theatre, to rally all and sundry to the crown.[20] The marshal persuaded him to stay and review the troops. It was a fiasco. D'Artois reviewed the local National Guard, but was met with stony silence from all but a few young noble cavalrymen. He exhorted them to march to Grenoble, only to be told that it had fallen to Napoleon. It did not take him long, once there, to sense the unreliability of the troops, and his first instinct was to flee and leave the defense to Macdonald. Advised that Lyon was on the verge of a popular uprising, he wrote to Louis in the gravest terms and made ready to bolt, but Macdonald persuaded him to hang on. The next morning, March 9, at 6:00, Macdonald summoned the troops for review in the pouring rain, afraid to put d'Artois in front of them. He pleaded the royalist cause for all he was worth, but was met by derisive whistles from drenched men who had not had their ration of eau-de-vie. D'Artois then did show himself, tried to compliment a veteran on his bravery, but was met with glacial silence and a cold stare. No one responded to the officers' cries of "*Vive le roi!*" Macdonald saw the game was up, hustled d'Artois into a coach, and got him out of town under an escort of gendarmes and dragoons. Louis-Philippe made himself scarce, and fled north on his own. That left Macdonald. His tour of inspection was cut short when Napoleon's hussars arrived at the bridge to the east of the city, and the assembled companies simply went over to them. Macdonald rode for his life, beaten and punched on his way, Napoleon's cavalry right behind him. His thighs badly cut by saber thrusts, he eventually caught up with d'Artois, and promptly berated him for mishandling the troops and showing too much favoritism to the émigrés among them.[21] Thus, Lyon with its 115,000 people, fell to Napoleon.

Napoleon entered the city at 7:00 P.M., to huge, cheering crowds. Mixed with *"Vive l'empereur!"* were cries of "Down with the priests! Down with the émigrés! Death to feudalism!" The threat of a ruthless restoration seemed real to many, and Napoleon soon saw he had to take up the revolutionary cause in the face of these powerful rumors. By playing to these fears, by responding to them, he now felt he could reduce support for the monarchy to its hard core of intransigent reactionaries. In a series of decrees in the three days he spent in Lyon, Napoleon invoked "the people and the army," and demanded the return of national, not royal, sovereignty, a far cry from his monarchist pronouncements of only a year ago. He declared the royal legislature dissolved and called for fresh elections under the Imperial Constitution. As he did so, he caricatured the Bourbon regime in just those terms the army and the revolutionary left feared most. The Chamber of Peers, the upper house, was full of "men who had borne arms against France, who have a stake in restoring feudal rights, who want to destroy equality and"—the dread words—"annul the sales of the national lands." The lower house harbored traitors to Napoleon, who had made his fall possible. When he got to Paris, he would convoke a new national assembly to help revise the constitution, call fresh elections, and see the empress and the King of Rome returned to Paris and crowned.[22] He mingled his dream with theirs. Napoleon now knew where his own core support lay, with the army and the diehard adherents of the Revolution. He invoked exactly what he had sought to stifle in 1799: the war of extremes. He shredded *amalgame* and *ralliement* at Lyon. Once again, there were two polar opposites, and the French had to choose between them.

In his own mind, Napoleon saw the fall of Lyon as a military victory. He wrote to those he always did, after a great battle, in the usual way. He told Marie-Louise on March 11:

I will . . . soon be in Paris . . . The people are flooding to me. Whole regiments are coming over to me. Deputations are coming to me from all parts. By the time you get this letter, I will be in Paris . . . Adieu my good friend, be happy. Come and join me with my son. I hope to hold him before the end of March.[23]

To Joseph, who was in exile near Geneva, he said he was sure the Austrians would now hand over his wife and son, and told his brother that "More than 30,000 men are under my orders . . . I am sending you my proclamations to distribute. Print a great many of them and send them to Alsace and Franche-Comté . . . I landed with 600 men of my Guard, and I met no foreigners." Napoleon had heard rumors that Murat was on the march with eighty thousand men to help him, but had had no news. He must be told what Napoleon had done.[24] His hopes were castles in the air. When first told of Napoleon's return, on March 8, Marie-Louise met the news "without the least sign of emotion" according to the Austrian police, but privately, she was furious. His gamble dashed any hopes that her son would succeed her in Parma. Reviled in the Viennese press and suspected by the police, in an effort to save what she could, she put the Habsburg arms on her coach and cut all her ties with her French courtiers, even Madame Lannes. As a sign of her trustworthiness, she turned over the letters Napoleon had smuggled to her to the Congress of Vienna. As Napoleon left Lyon on March 12, she publicly placed Parma under her father's protection, herself and her son under that of the allies, and denounced Napoleon's actions. The next day, the Congress declared him an outlaw.[25]

As for Murat, his antics did, indeed, match Napoleon's news, but only as shared illusions. Still officially one of the allies, on March 17, Murat returned from Naples to his army in central Italy, but his head had been turned by Napoleon's escape: ". . . the day he touches French territory . . . the Bourbons will no longer be on the throne."[26] "It is with inexpressible joy I learned of Your Majesty's landing on the coast of his empire . . . I assure Your Majesty that my whole army is on the march and that, most certainly before the end of the month, I will be at the Po," he assured his brother-in-law on March 14.[27] He declared to his government that he would, indeed, raise eighty thousand men, even as his minister of the Treasury asked to resign, pleading that the kingdom could not fight another campaign.[28] Joseph, who had given Murat Napoleon's news, begged him in the same breath not to take the offensive, but to "stay calmly in your kingdom," lest another invasion of the Papal States give the Congress the pretext it needed to strike at Napoleon.[29] Murat heard from Joseph only what he wanted to hear, and changed sides, but his real forces numbered a mere thirty-five thousand under arms,[30] his once proud army decimated by the wars and now short of arms and money because of corruption at home. Desertion was rife, even among his guards.[31] Against him stood fifty thousand well-armed, well-led Austrians, whose commanders knew the terrain.[32] In the face of all this, Murat issued his infamous proclamation of war and liberation: "The hour has come when destiny will be accomplished. Even Providence itself calls you to liberty. Let a single cry be heard from the Alps to Sicily, the cry of Italian independence."[33] It fell on deaf ears, none deafer than Caroline's. She had no illusions about her husband's—or her brother's—actions.[34] "Isn't it enough for a peasant from the Quercy to sit on the most beautiful throne in Italy? No, he wants the whole peninsula," she lamented.[35] She did her best to keep her own lines to Vienna open, mainly through Felix Mier, the Austrian ambassador, long known for his intrigues, among them his affair with Caroline, and Metternich, whose mistress she had been, in hopes he still retained an affection for her.[36] This was the reality of Napoleon's "second front." He was equally confident that d'Erlon was still marching on Paris in his cause.[37]

There was one assumption Napoleon got right. Just before he moved north, he showed pure audacity, writing to Ney with, on one level, a routine order to a marshal—"My cousin, my major general (Bertrand) will send you the order to march . . . Execute Bertrand's orders and join me at Châlon"—but on another, he dared Ney to treason, as only he could: "I don't doubt that the moment you learn I am at Lyon, you will bring your troops over to the tricolor . . . I will receive you as I did the day after the battle of Moscow."[38]

This was beyond confidence. Ney's troops, at Lons-le-Saunier, were now all that stood between Napoleon and Paris. They had become Louis's last hope, and he placed more hope in Ney than anyone else. He was not seen as a traitor by the army, unlike Marmont, even if he had defected to the allies before the peace talks ended. His reputation as the voice of the ranks sustained him. When the news of Napoleon's landing reached Louis, he ordered him to his command at Besançon, but he stopped in Paris on his way. On the night of March 7, as Napoleon slept in Grenoble, Ney went to the Tuileries in a high state of emotion, asked to see Louis at a late hour, and swore vehement allegiance to him: "I will seize Bonaparte, I promise you, and will bring him to you in an iron cage." If there was a mercenary motive, a large payment made to Ney to assure his loyalty, no evidence of it has ever been found. Emmanuel de Waresquiel probably read Ney correctly: These words were a chivalrous, overwrought gesture of a gallant knight. They were also the words that sealed his fate. When he had gone, Louis smiled, "I didn't ask him for all that."[39] Ney learned all the bad news when he reached Besançon, and on the night on March 10, declared, "I will leave at the head of my vanguard . . . It is I who will charge and fire the first shot; it is I who will give the first blow of the saber, and we will see if, for the first time in my life, French soldiers under my orders refuse to follow me . . . We will attack the savage beast!"[40] Three days later, he ordered his men to join Napoleon. Ney knew his men, and sensed them wavering as the news of Lyon kept flooding in. One of his regiments had already tried to mutiny and join Napoleon, and he soon saw his five thousand troops were badly outnumbered.[41] Unlike Macdonald, he did not leave his men to their fate, but went with them, as they cried *Vive l'empereur!* He led them toward Napoleon's lines, but halted, himself, at Vitaux, and did not join the "imperial" ranks. He had read their minds, as so often, but his own was harder to fathom. Perhaps part of the reason for his volte-face is in a letter Ney sent to the local prefect, who berated him for his act: "I would prefer a thousand times to be pummelled by Bonaparte than humiliated by people who have never waged war."[42] Then there was Napoleon's letter. Deep resentments were welling up in Ney, and he was not alone. Napoleon did not have to play on them. For whatever reason, Ney had opened the road to Paris, and Napoleon swept north in triumph. They met at Auxerre, in northern Burgundy. Napoleon kept his word, and embraced him as if the restoration had never happened. Napoleon issued orders to Ney in the same vein as ever, chiding him for lack of attention to detail—"I do not see any infantry cartridges with your artillery. Several caissons will be needed . . . I think you have ten pieces of artillery? Send me the itinerary of the artillery battalion you sent to Auxonne"[43]—but Ney did not stay with Napoleon. He retired to his château near Paris to await events. For all the cheering crowds along the Burgundian highways, Ney chose the path of many Frenchmen in these weeks.

As Napoleon drew closer to Paris, as the crowds around him and the troops under him swelled in size, his rhetoric grew ever more Jacobinal. His first proclamations spoke of the restoration of rights, of national pride insulted. He heard the first whisper of revolution as he entered Grenoble, when a magistrate got close to him and said "Yes, *Vive l'empereur*, but *Vive la liberté!*" Napoleon turned to him and replied, "Yes, *Vive la liberté!*"[44] At Lyon, the decrees called for a liberalized constitution, deposing traitors, and protecting property. By the time he reached Autun, where he had first gone to school, he promised the people of the Roman capital of Burgundy he would hang the nobles and the priests "from the lamp posts" in good Jacobin style.[45] On the morning of March 20, he returned to Fontainebleau, and went to work in his old rooms: "We're right here."[46] He was a cat's paw from Paris, ready to pounce from the east, through the sans culotte heartland. Louis was already gone.

As Napoleon rolled north, Louis' "mood of cool, egotistical self-confidence soon changed." Prefects' reports from all across France spoke of troops in their barracks ready to change sides, checked only by their distance from Napoleon, and of soldiers in his path unwilling to fight their comrades or oppose him.[47] Many provinces were in the hands of Napoleonic marshals whose conduct was, at best, ambiguous. Asked to send reinforcements, Suchet, in Alsace, did nothing; in Lorraine, Oudinot said he had lost all authority over his men; at Orleans, Dupont—the man humiliated by Napoleon after the disaster of Baylen, then made minister of war by Louis XVIII, but stripped of it in favor of Soult[48]—now wore the tricolor cockade. The troops of the "camp of Melun," the forces concentrated to the south of Paris under Macdonald and the duc de Berry, the last line of defense, were worse, if anything. The "officers battalions" composed of veterans were hotbeds of disaffection. These were the infamous *démi-soldes*, the troops demobilized and put on half pay after the abdication who were now recalled to serve Louis on March 9, a move one aristocratic lady labeled "a passport to the enemy." The whole army was paid six francs in cash, in advance. A contemporary observed caustically that they shouted *"Vive le roi!"* when they got the money, but when they had drunk it, broke into *"Vive l'empereur!"*[49] Cries of *"Vive l'empereur!"* became ever more frequent in the camp of Melun even when the money ran out. The 6th Lancers came out openly for Napoleon.[50] The army was what mattered now, and it was a lost cause. There was an attempt to raise "royal volunteers" in Paris—students, young noblemen and about fifteen hundred law students, "a fair portion of the bourgeois liberal elite" who marched "in joyous disorder" through the streets of Paris[51]—whose loyalty was not in doubt, but they were far fewer in number than hoped for, and one commander called them "marmots, incapable of holding a rifle."[52] "To try to stop the emperor with a drum roll, what lunacy!" scoffed Germaine de Staël.[53] It would seem that dancing marmots were all that stood between Napoleon and Louis.

Presiding over all this was Soult, made minister of war in December 1814. Soult had rallied to the Bourbons on his return from the southwest after the abdication and first served as the military governor of Brittany, where he ingratiated himself with its very royalist elite, particularly the well-connected "ultra," Comte de Bruges, through whom he became a favorite of the militaristic d'Artois.[54] D'Artois got him appointed minister of war, where he proved one of the most authoritarian members of the government[55]—he was among those who opposed the idea of Louis summoning the chambers at all[56]—which was hardly surprising in the light of his behavior first in Portugal and then in Andalucía. Soult displayed considerable energy in his post,[57] and crawled to the ultras—he called Napoleon "the infamous usurper Bonaparte" on the news of his landing[58]—but he was detested at court.[59] His appearance did not help. He might have been imposing, but Madame de Chastenay remarked of him that while he might look like "a little marquis from the ancien régime from afar," he still had a "plebeian aspect" to him.[60] When things began to go wrong, he became the source of all the woes, and was accused of deliberately sending the troops most disposed to desert out to face Napoleon.[61] He was replaced on March 11 by Clarke, who was generally thought loyal for all his own services to Napoleon.[62] Soult did not go quietly, taking his sword from its cabinet and ostentatiously offering it to Louis. He departed sarcastically doffing his hat to all and sundry. His dismissal was not really political, but "with the sole end of appeasing those minds who saw treason everywhere."[63] A few days later, Louis wrote to Soult openly praising his services, adding "I have not seen the calumnies and rumors heaped upon you without pain."[64] Without waiting for Louis's permission, he went home to his family at Ville-neuve-l'Etang—a very insolent gesture—and awaited events.[65]

The government's policing strategy was wholly muddled. In an effort to influence—perhaps merely to contact—the more hardened Bonapartists in Paris, several ministers sought out Fouché, the old regicide, who had links to the duc d'Orleans as well.[66] When d'Artois saw him, on March 15, he may have tried to bring Fouché into the government, but Blacas, the head of Louis's secretariat, came out of an early meeting with Fouché convinced of the need for a crackdown, and tried to arrest him on March 16. The old fox leaped over his garden wall and escaped.[67] Blacas also "went after" Maret and Davout, or would have, but the Prefect of Police remained inert.[68] For Thierry Lentz, it was all a fiasco; for Philip Mansel, simply "pathetic."[69]

Cack-handed and impotent as the Bourbons were in the field, they showed far greater skill, and some success, as politicians. Louis laid down markers Napoleon needed to beware of even in victory. Napoleon was stirring fears not only of renewed dictatorship, but of a new Terror. As he drew closer to Paris, Louis and many around him saw where their own most useful support came from. Louis turned, not to the ultraroyalists, but set about rallying the middle ground—the "France of the extreme center," the "men of 1789"— and he was heeded. In the fraught days after Ney's defection, Louis drew the "weathercocks" to his side, and in so doing, deprived Napoleon of the very men who had formed his own original bedrock or, rather, did not let Napoleon regain the support he had lost in the last months of his rule. Louis's most effective ally was Lainé, now president of the lower house, with whom he stayed in constant touch. Legislation was considered to name new, liberal peers to the upper house and to elect the vacant seats in the lower chamber on a more liberal franchise.[70] But Louis's strongest card, which he played on March 16, when he summoned the two chambers together, was to present himself as the upholder of moderate constitutionalism—as the embodiment of the "spirit of 1789"—standing against the threat of a new Napoleonic despotism. It is easy to mock the session of March 16 as too little, too late, "throwing everything out of the windows of a burning house," as one courtier put it.[71] Louis turned to futile "gesture politics" it is true, wearing the Légion d'honneur for only the first time when he addressed the chambers—"rather too late" Louis-Philippe quipped[72]—or thanking Macdonald and Mortier for their bravery and loyalty over the last weeks. But he touched a nerve that day. Charles de Rémusat, once a supporter of the Consulate and one of the most influential liberal thinkers of the nineteenth century, emerged from the session feeling that "I took the emperor as the personification of despotism very seriously, (and) the Restoration as the condition of, or at least the chance for, liberty." The future politician Odilon Barrot, then a young lawyer, recalled "the hatred of Napoleon's despotism" that drove the enlightened bourgeoisie to which he belonged.[73] Louis made himself clear: "I have seen my country again; I have reconciled it to the foreign powers . . . I fear for France: he who would light the torch of civil war among us brings also the plague of foreign war." Then he made a seismic shift: the Charter, his constitution, was for him, "my greatest claim in the eyes of posterity, which all the French cherish, and which I hereby swear to maintain . . . Rally around it!" Neither the words of an aging, gout-ridden Bourbon, nor the support of the wordsmiths in the chambers, could stop the advance of an embittered soldiery, its pride wounded, its old loyalties reignited, but Louis challenged Napoleon in a subtler manner: Napoleon could conquer these men, but could he rally them?

Over the next two days, as Paris looked ever more vulnerable, within and without, Louis compromised the personal goodwill he had created. Fearful for himself and his family, he reneged on his original intention to stand firm, to await Napoleon in the Tuileries, defiantly surrounded by the peers and deputies.[74] He learned of Ney's defection the day after his stirring address, and that was when he probably decided to flee Paris. It was then he began giving sums of money to the royal family and sending still more out of the country, including some of the crown jewels, as he braced himself for another life in exile.[75] Louis-Philippe may have talked him out of it in his own, menacing way: "I have heard a very grim joke based on a rumor that you would not move from your armchair . . . whatever happens." When Louis asked what "it" was, he replied, "that the victim would be too big for the executioner." Munro Price speculates that Louis-Philippe relished telling his fat, old cousin the latest jape, and it may have concentrated Louis's mind on escape.[76] Louis had probably decided on his first destination, Lille, earlier—Louis-Philippe was already there, and he had to be watched, for Louis had roused his cousin's supporters on March 16, more than his own[77]—but he kept up the pretense of standing firm to the end. The chambers were called to a secret session on the morning of March 19, sent "on leave" and promised they would be summoned at a later date; Louis told the diplomatic corps that afternoon of his intention to defend Paris, and invited them to see him again the next day. He reviewed his troops on the Champ de Mars that afternoon in his open carriage; many of them thought he was sallying forth to Melun, to fight.[78] All the while, his trunks were being packed. Louis slipped out of the Tuileries on the night of March 19–20. The palace was crowded with anxious people, desperate for the latest news. Louis remained "serene and calm in the middle of the tempest." Well he might, for only he knew what came next. When the crowds had gone, around 8:00 P.M., he summoned Marmont, who commanded his guard, and Macdonald, leader of what was left of the army at Melun, and told them of his intentions. At midnight, the doors of his apartments swung open and all was clear. He made his way down the great staircase, supported by two loyal "ultras," the stair lined with weeping courtiers. He was leaving, he claimed, to prevent the needless bloodshed of civil war, and to their histrionics, he replied "My children, spare me, I need strength. I will see you again soon. Return to your families."[79] With his typical mixture of sang froid and egotism, Louis clambered into his carriage, and lumbered off into the pouring rain, leaving Paris and his "children" to their fate. They did not have long to wait.

Just after 1:00 P.M. in the afternoon of March 20, the national guards in charge of the Tuileries got a rude shock. They were peaceable men, drawn—unlike their revolutionary namesakes—from the upper bourgeoisie of the capital, "a public force composed of landowners," in the words of its commander, General Jean-Joseph Dessolles, "a refuge for honest people," there to preserve order. Their adjutant-major that day was Alexandre de Laborde, the son of a wealthy banker who was guillotined during the Terror. Their uniforms cost a fortune. They were not the sort to want trouble, having known so much over so many years.[80] They had managed the crowd that had gathered outside the gates, but from the direction of the Place du Carrousel, they heard a great commotion. Beyond the crowd gathered there, came about three hundred officers in the helmets of the heavy cavalry, their swords drawn, blades glinting. They were *démi-soldes*, Napoleon's veterans, summoned to protect Paris by its commander, General Maison, who had informed the ministers ten days earlier that they could not count on his services unless he was paid 200,000 francs.[81] He now offered de Laborde the most unreliable troops in the army, recently removed from the front line at Melun to the northern suburb of Saint-Denis. Obeying their orders, they assembled on the main square of Saint-Denis in the white cockades of the king, to await their orders and collect their day's pay. Then, as now, the square abounds in cafés, where their pay was drunk as the news circulated that Louis had fled. As the drinks went down, so did the royal cockades, and the cries of "*Vive l'empereur!*" went up. Soon, the cockades were on fire. Macdonald came out of his headquarters to try to rally them: "I was ashamed of what I beheld, seeing French officers conducting themselves thus, in full uniform . . . but most of them drunk and disheveled . . . I still blush at the thought of them."[82] He ran for it. Maison appeared, too, and was chased off in fear of his life. Drunk or not, accounts vary, they seized several cannons, and set off for the Tuileries. It turned into a triumphal march. The line regiment at the La Chapelle gate joined them. The gendarmes at the Saint-Denis gate—the last barrier before the city center—hesitated, but let them pass. Flooding into the square behind the Tuileries, their newly acquired artillery pointed at the gates, Laborde and his "honest men" stood face-to-face with their polar opposites. They parleyed. Laborde agreed to open the gates, but only the officers could enter the palace. They were all officers, and they all flooded in, followed by their cannons. The national guardsmen agreed to get Napoleon's apartments ready for him, and the two units mounted the guard together. A massive tricolor flag appeared from somewhere, and was hoisted above the clock tower, in the center of the château. Soon after, it was flying from the Hotel de Ville and from the summit of the column in the Place Vendôme, where Napoleon's statue had been toppled a few months before.[83] All Napoleon had to do was arrive.

16

THE POLITICS OF DESPERATION: MARCH–JUNE 1815

❧ ─── ❧

At about 9:00 P.M. on the night of March 20, Napoleon's coach drew up at the Tuileries, on the quai beside the Seine. The gates swung open, the coach swept in and was mobbed by the cheering *démi-soldes* to see him get out dressed in his famous gray greatcoat, and push his way into the vestibule and up the stairs, crowded with the men who had marched from Saint-Denis that morning, held back by the now ex-royalist national guards. He climbed them slowly, his old aide-de-camp, Antoine-Marie Lavalette, recalled, his eyes closed, his hands outstretched before him, "like a blind man, showing his joy only in his smile."[1] As the crowd followed him, pressing ever closer, the national guards and courtiers forced open the doors to the first floor, and Napoleon returned to his office. The great doors swung shut behind him. Before him, he found "the loyalist of the loyal": Julie, wife of Joseph, and Hortense—both still in mourning dress for their mothers—had busied themselves directing the "emblematic" aspect of regime change, as they supervised the tearing down of wall hangings and the ripping up of carpets with the Bourbon fleurs-de-lys on them, to find the imperial eagles behind them. The valets and maîtres d'hôtel donned their imperial liveries without a murmur, as one makeshift regime gave way to another in the twinkling of an eye.[2] With them were Maret, Savary, Davout, Molé, Mollien, and Martin-Michel-Charles Gaudin. One face was the oldest friend of all, Lazare Carnot, the Director—and former member of the Committee of Public Safety—who had given Napoleon his first command, but soon withdrew into the shadows after Brumaire. The very sight of "the organizer of victory" led Napoleon to name him his minister of the interior, where Cambacérès recalled that he "worked night and day to revive the nation and rebuild the army."[3] Fouché thrust his services on Napoleon, too influential to be ignored. He resumed his old place at Police, almost taking revenge for the ten years Napoleon had spent trying to prise him from it. Savary, the "incumbent" in 1814, became head of the Gendarmerie.

Napoleon sent for Mollien three times before he came to see him. "I thought I would be able to resist his orders," but he could not. Napoleon won him with frankness: "My friend, the time for compliments is over: they let me return just as they let me go"; it was a crisis: "The phrase was characteristic, and proves that, if he tried to create illusions around him, he had none about himself." Above all, "there would have been a kind of cowardice to refuse to share his danger; a sort of ingratitude to desert in such a moment . . . and I agreed."[4] If anyone was "Napoleon's man," it was his minister of the treasury. Others took more coaxing. Caulaincourt had joined Napoleon at Essonne, and rode with him into Paris, but it took Napoleon several weeks to convince—more like bully—him into becoming foreign minister, thinking his presence might be the only hope of avoiding war because of the tsar's high opinion of him. Caulaincourt was certain Napoleon's enterprise was doomed.[5] Cambacérès was of the same mind. On March 20, he openly declared he had no intention of abandoning private life. Napoleon sent for him directly three times that night, before his old friend finally came. He climbed the great staircase with some difficulty, to find Napoleon at his desk, "that imperial look" on his face. To this man, his second-in-command for so long, Napoleon confessed a truth he had hidden from all and sundry: Napoleon had let it be assumed that he

had Austria on his side when he left Elba, that Francis was now so afraid of
Russia that he had, quietly, changed sides. He told Cambacérès it was all a
lie. The futility of it all was now revealed. Cambacérès pleaded age, illness,
"an infinity of details" to avoid service, but Napoleon resolved all his issues,
said he only had to serve for two weeks, but then added that another obstinate
refusal would give Napoleon doubts about him that Cambacérès would not
want aroused, and that Napoleon would not want to nurture: "I had to serve the
emperor, or range myself among his enemies." Cambacérès had nowhere to
hide. Unlike so many others, he had never taken the oath of loyalty to the
Bourbons, and Napoleon knew it. There could be no crisis of conscience.
With that, Cambacérès became minister of justice.[6] A ministry was assembled
rapidly: Mollien and Gaudin returned to their roles at Finance and Treasury.
Davout became minister of war, having at first refused it, arguing that he
would serve Napoleon better in the field, and that he was neither popular in
the army, nor very good with people. Napoleon turned to him, as he had to
Cambacérès, and confessed: "I have let it be known, and must continue to let
it be known that I act in harmony with . . . the Emperor of Austria. It has
been widely announced that the Empress is on her way bringing with her the
King of Rome, that they will arrive any day now. The truth is this is false.
I am alone before Europe . . . Will you also abandon me?"[7] Davout agreed.
Napoleon won over many by lies; he won over those who knew him best with
the stark truth. Some truths, Napoleon found difficult to swallow, himself.
On March 25, he wrote to Marie-Louise, "I am the master of all France. All
the people, and the whole army are in the greatest enthusiasm. The self-styled
king has gone to England. I am waiting for you here in April, and for my son."[8]

The chronicle of the times, Le Moniteur, noted all this in its edition of
March 21, with its "laconic chilliness": "The king and the princes left in
the night. His Majesty the Emperor arrived at 8:00 P.M. in his palace of the
Tuileries." Pierre Serna paints the scene as a play, "without tail or head, where
the characters . . . enter and leave, by the courtyard, by the garden, without
ever meeting each other . . . Reading Le Moniteur from day to day, forces the
reader to ask himself if the country in question really is the same today as it

was the day before."[9] Joseph and Jérôme were on their way. Joseph was welcome to lodge in the Tuileries in the short term, but was told sharply to "set up your house in a modest tone."[10] Lucien returned, too, a shadow from the past. He had been a prisoner of the British for several years, captured trying to get to America when Napoleon seized Rome in 1810. Recently allowed back to Rome by Castlereagh, Joseph implored Lucien to return to the fold. Lucien's good relations with Pius VII were important to him, and this made him hesitate, but he also began to fear Murat after he refused to help him negotiate the passage of his army through papal territory. Lucien's dread of Murat's wrath, should he occupy Rome, more than loyalty, tipped him to his brother's side.[11] Joseph smoothed his way with Napoleon, and he arrived in Paris as very much "Joseph's man," to help him play a card he always kept up his sleeve for the French political classes: the liberalization of the regime. Lucien said later, "Our family never had its eldest for its head, prince Joseph, one of the most enlightened spirits of the age . . . one of the noblest characters whoever sat on a throne."[12] Napoleon made his three brothers princes, and gave the liberal opposition, so recently d'Orléans's men, a new standard to rally around in his brothers. Lucien took up residence in the Palais Royal, d'Orléans's residence. The absent faces on March 20, the characters offstage, spoke volumes, Marie-Louise first and foremost. Murat may have been in the field, but Caroline stayed in her capital, playing a game that had ceased to be a double one. Eugène did not budge from his in-laws' side, in Munich.

Even the army was not a monolith. As Napoleon made his way from Fontainebleau to Paris, whole units from the "camp of Melun" simply melted to his side. One of their captains left no doubt about it in his memoirs: "All the *chasseurs* and hussars flung themselves into the saddle in complete disorder . . . When the emperor's coach appeared . . . the soldiers, swords in hand, ran before it . . . and joined the column."[13] "My most beautiful campaign has not cost one drop of French blood," Napoleon crowed from Fontainebleau, the morning he marched on Paris.[14] In this, he did not lie. In the provinces, revolts broke out in most of the military divisions in support of Napoleon. Oudinot warned the government that his forces, in Metz, would defect at the first chance, never mind fight for Louis. Marshals who sought to bring their men to order were swept aside: Victor, who said he would go after Napoleon and deliver him for "the punishment he deserved," was hounded out by his own men at Châlons-en-Champagne, and fled.[15] The attitude of the marshals was far more nuanced, and reflected the ambivalence or outright hostility, of the masses of granite, the men of property Napoleon had made of them. Davout was the only marshal there to greet Napoleon on March 20. He never took the oath of loyalty, and had been harshly treated by the restored regime on his return from Hamburg in 1814. His hesitancy in surrendering until he had firm proof of the abdication saw him accused of refusing to acknowledge Napoleon's deposition and the restoration of the Bourbons, to which charge was added stealing from the Bank of Hamburg and committing "arbitrary acts which tended to render the French name odious."[16] He was completely exonerated, but Davout's was a rare case. Most of the marshalate were welcomed into the Bourbon army, if often with upturned nose. Their response to Napoleon's audacious return was a mosaic. While Ney and Soult bided their time, Masséna remained in Marseille and simply obeyed the orders that came to him, from whoever held Paris. He still professed his readiness to "die with the white flag in his hand" as late as March 29—it took some time for news to travel south—but by April 10, he reported the he had hoisted the tricolor over the city and issued a ringing proclamation to its people to rally to "the Great Napoleon," after Napoleon had chided him to "show a little energy."[17] Augereau had vociferously proclaimed his allegiance to the Bourbons in 1814, but on March 22, told his men at Caen that, "seduced by the noble illusion (of the happiness of the country), (Napoleon) had sacrificed his glory and his crown . . . He demands it back today; never have they been more sacred to us . . . We rally to the colors of the nation!" For Pierre Serna, this marshal from a humble background was now capable of speaking with "that wooden tongue" of his betters, so adapted to hypocrisy.[18] If so, it did not fool Napoleon. He knew the difference between a "weathercock" like Masséna—cynical but rational—and the likes of Augereau, who had gone too far in 1814, and now tried to bluster their way out of a corner. The former kept his post; the latter was stripped of his rank and allowed to slink off home. Oudinot was more honest. He told Davout he had to stay loyal to his oath to Louis, and would not play a double role: "I will serve no one."[19] Gouvion de St. Cyr, like Oudinot, had genuinely tried to make a stand against Napoleon, refusing to acknowledge the new regime until March 24, when he let his men put on the tricolor cockade, but Napoleon had already made up his mind, telling Davout on March 23: "St. Cyr is stripped of his command . . . if he comes to Paris, he will be declared a traitor to the country. Go find Madame St. Cyr and tell her what my intentions are for her husband, who has tried to lead his troops toward the Vendée; that he is a traitor to his country, and that his properties will be confiscated if he comes back (to Paris)."[20] Threatened so ferociously, St. Cyr still did not flee to Louis, but retired to his estates, and was left alone. Victor stood by his vehement words against Napoleon—that he would guarantee "the quick punishment of (Napoleon's) new crime"[21]—and followed Louis into exile. Once an ardent revolutionary, Victor, the son of a bailiff, became a loyal courtier. Napoleon still granted him a pension after he had been stripped of his rank.[22] Clearly, there were levels of disloyalty for Napoleon. For some, it turned on how they had behaved in the last days of his rule in 1814; for others, it was acceptable to make a personal decision not to serve, based on obligation, even after Napoleon recalled them all to the colors, but it was beyond the pale to incite French troops to against him.

Four of his marshals rode north with Louis on March 19: Berthier, "the emperor's wife," his closest companion in the field; Marmont, labeled openly as a traitor by Napoleon more than once for his defection in 1814; Macdonald, who had defended Louis steadfastly at Lyon and Paris; and Mortier, loyal to Napoleon to the end in 1814 but equally loyal to Louis a year later, in scotching d'Erlon's revolt. They were an ill-assorted crew, and their choices after getting Louis to safety, reveal how fraught was the world Napoleon had created for not just for himself, but for everyone else when he fled Elba. Marmont commanded the sad little "army" that led the king into exile, a role that only confirmed in many eyes the treacherous reputation he carried with him, "like the shadow of death." For Charles d'Agoult, a captain in the royal guards, he was "certainly the most slandered man of the century," and his troops were soon dubbed "the Judas company." Marmont had been at Napoleon's side since Egypt; he had been showered with honors. Now, fleeing in ignominy, "he found himself where he should not have been."[23] Napoleon saw him once almost as an adopted son, and now could not find words harsh enough for him.[24] Despite the rank and wealth he held under the Bourbons, no one ever trusted him again. When they fell forever in 1830, he again followed them into exile, dying in Venice in 1852. It was a pattern Napoleon had long discerned: the better he treated someone, be they a marshal or a sibling, the more likely they were to betray him. Generosity bred a comfortable life, the preservation of which weighed more heavily than honor or friendship. "Oh, what do you want? Who betrays me? Who speaks ill of me? Oh my God, Berthier and Marmont, who I loaded (with honors), how did they act?" he said to Gourgaud on Saint Helena.[25] "I was betrayed by Berthier, a silly goose I made into something of an eagle," he snarled to Las Cases.[26] Generosity and betrayal went in inverse proportion, an almost mathematical principle deeply embedded in his mind.

Macdonald gave Louis some hard advice on the road north, his judgment as severe, his eye as clear, as it had been a year before, when he saw Napoleon's end in sight: "Sire, he who quits the country, loses."[27] Napoleon thought that "vanity had lost Marmont,"[28] but he could not say the same of Macdonald. He rode with Louis as far as the border, then turned his horse around, went back to Paris, and enlisted as a simple grenadier in the National Guard, a corps devoted to the protection of public order and property. Napoleon believed Macdonald's treason stemmed simply from his noble birth; they were all like that—"I was wrong to employ nobles," obviously forgetting Davout as he spoke.[29] Mortier was, according to taste, either the epitome of Pierre Serna's "weathercock," or a man of scrupulous military dutifulness. When Louis decided to go into exile, he told his men, "Gentlemen, the king is leaving; I will stay loyal to him until he leaves France . . . I will not leave her, and I shall defend France from the foreigners." For Emmanuel de Waresquiel, Mortier had given himself an insurance policy in case Napoleon lost and the Bourbons returned.[30] Yet this was the kind of weathercocking Napoleon understood. He valued Mortier so highly, and was so worried by his hesitancy, that he told Fouché to "go find Madame Mortier and tell her how important the choice her husband makes is . . . that it is so important for him and for the state that she must go to him right away, or send someone trustworthy to persuade the marshal to . . . act as he should."[31] When Mortier at last answered Napoleon's call to the colors, he was entrusted with the critical role of organizing the defense of the Belgian frontier:

> He will . . . take all necessary measures that circumstances demand to complete the system of defense in this area . . . He is charged with doing all that is necessary to put our forts in the best possible position. He will pass in review the national guards: he will rally everyone to their duty; he will issue proclamations . . . and he will stimulate the zeal and patriotism of his fellow citizens.[32]

This was a powerful sign of trust in the draper's son who was so often given command of the guard artillery and cavalry. He was given command of the Young Guard at the outset of the Waterloo campaign, but fell ill with severe sciatica on the march, and was relieved before the battle.[33] It may have been a "convenient" illness,[34] but Napoleon did not see it thus. He told Gourgaud on Saint Helena, that although Mortier "did me ill by leaving the command of the Guard," it was his wife's fault, for Mortier was a brave man, if "easily led by his wife."[35] She was not always wrong. Mortier found favor under the July Monarchy, and was killed on July 28, 1835, in an assassination attempt on Louis-Philippe, during a military review his wife had urged him not to attend.[36]

Berthier felt "torn between remorse and sadness . . . obliged to drink the wine down to the dregs"[37] as he led Louis toward enemy territory as the captain of his personal guard. Berthier knew Napoleon better than anyone in the army, and had been instrumental in bringing many of the marshals over to Louis. When he said Napoleon had become a danger, he had to be believed.

Yet Louis never trusted him, convinced he was in touch with Napoleon on Elba. He had risen higher and been more lavishly rewarded than anyone under the empire—he was given his own principality of Neuchâtel, which he was forced to cede to the Swiss in 1814—and none felt the venomous backlash of the émigrés more. The Vicomte de Noailles greeted him with, "Well, Berthier, thanks to the Revolution, look! You're above me!" The Dowager Duchess d'Orléans took more tangible vengeance. She contested the validity of his ownership of forest of d'Etampes, once her family's fief: "(A)fter having been for so long the victim of laws of usurpers, (the Dowager Duchess) will avail herself of the laws of reparation of the legitimate government, knowing M. the Marshal will be delighted to contribute to them."[38] Yet, he led the way to Belgium, "biting his nails . . . full of troubles," Macdonald recalled.[39] His response was the most ambivalent of them all. At the frontier, he went neither with Louis, nor back to France, but rode to Bavaria, the home of his second wife, Maria-Elisabeth Franzisca of Bavaria-Birkenfeld, seeking refuge with his in-laws. When he asked to be relieved of his commission, Louis was glad to see the back of him.[40]

On March 26, Marmont, Augereau, Oudinot, Victor, and Gouvion St. Cyr were all stripped of their marshals' batons. None of them, not even Marmont, was condemned to death, but they were ordered to stay away from Paris.[41] These four men, along with Berthier, had observed closely the collapse of Napoleon's world in 1814, and all demanded he abdicate. They found no reason to change their minds a year later, even if some felt the pull of personal loyalty and had lost faith in the Bourbons in the meantime. They knew at first hand that France could not win another war, that Napoleon had left a country on its knees, and that "the flight of the eagle" was doomed to crash. Almost all the marshals who had fought in northern France in 1814—with Mortier and Ney the major (and still hesitant) exceptions—rejected Napoleon's call. Those who answered it—Davout, Soult, Suchet—had been elsewhere. They had seen neither the power of the coalition armies, nor the obstinacy of their emperor. Davout, besieged in Hamburg, remained steadfastly loyal: "He did not comprehend the vast changes . . . since 1812, nor did he understand the magnitude of the forces . . . drawn up against France in . . . 1815," in the judgment of his biographer.[42] The reasons for the decisions of individuals are many and complex, often unfathomable, but this correlation does not seem coincidental.

If Caulaincourt became foreign minister "as a gauge of Napoleon's loyal and pacific intentions,"[43] such hopes soon unraveled. The foreign ambassadors flooded out of Paris, a slap in the face to the man now officially branded an outlaw by the Congress of Vienna. Caulaincourt was then forced to ask French ambassadors to return to France. None did; they remained in Louis's service. France was completely isolated; the only foreign power to recognize Napoleon was the United States, which had made peace with Britain barely a month earlier.[44] This forced Caulaincourt to attempt to contact the other powers, Alexander in particular, through private, informal lines of communication. He got news from them, but none of it was good. The best France could hope for, according to Eugène, was that Alexander was still favorable to a regency,[45] although the duc d'Orléans was Alexander's openly preferred candidate to replace the Bourbons.[46] Louis's flight had only intensified the tsar's well-known loathing for them;[47] now he was "ready to send Louis XVIII and his family to the devil," his rage stoked further when he learned of the convention signed on January 3, by Austria, France, and Britain, which was largely aimed at him.[48] The question of who would sit on the French throne was still open for Alexander. None of this meant he would tolerate Napoleon on it. In the end, Fouché, not Caulaincourt, ran foreign relations, because only Fouché had the agents to make any contacts abroad. If his country was isolated diplomatically, Napoleon was isolated from reality, believing Talleyrand could convince Metternich to get Austria out of the coalition at the price of two million francs.[49] There was no sane reason for the allies to make peace, and they did not. They had nearly one million men under arms marching on France.[50] Napoleon's response to the threat from Spain was to ask Joseph to set up a parallel Bonapartist government in Paris, to organize a guerrilla war against the Bourbons—the term was his—and to publish a newspaper "to enlighten the Spanish, to make known to them our constitutional reforms, and to incite them to revolt and desertion."[51] Thierry Lentz found "no trace of any activity by the ex-king to execute (it)."[52]

Once in Paris, Napoleon's urgent concerns were not with the tidal wave swelling on his borders but with internal security, and that was possibly just as well in his state of mind. However deluded in diplomacy, Napoleon had few illusions about the country he now ruled again. His purges began at home, literally. "Replace the concierges of my palace who belonged to the king. I mean to keep none of them. They have contracted liaisons which are unsuitable," he told Bertrand.[53] "(M)y intention is that none of the former ministers or other prominent individuals who were employed under Louis XVIII should be allowed to stay in France or retain their properties . . . unless they recognize the Emperor Napoleon as the legitimate sovereign of France . . . (T)his declaration must be . . . simple, clear, without 'ifs' or 'buts.' Those who do not swear it will not stay in France and will have their properties sequestered."[54] So much for *ralliement*. The purges ran deep into the bureaucracy: "I know a great number of your employees hate my person and my government; bring me the list tomorrow of those who have to be chased out," Carnot was ordered on March 23.[55] His real fears boiled over to Cambacérès, when Napoleon detected a reticence to purge in his lawyer-in-chief: "You have men of marked malevolence in your offices . . . If you don't make changes, I will be obliged to make them myself, which is not how it should work."[56] The Bourbons had taken a great interest in the Imperial University, retaining its centralized, state-controlled structure, but bringing it under clerical influence and purging it, ideologically, placing the Catholic intellectual Louis de Bonald on its council. Napoleon acted swiftly: "Get me a project for a decree to reestablish it as it was organized last year . . . Get rid of those like M. Bonald, who have espoused obscurantist principles, which can mislead public opinion and corrupt youth. I want it by next Wednesday," Carnot was ordered.[57] The lycées had not escaped the attentions of either regime. Napoleon ordered the reinstitution of the drum roll between classes, in place of the clerical church bells, and a purge of the teachers, particularly in Paris where he wanted it all done "tomorrow" he told Carnot on May 8.[58] A new elite emerged from Napoleon's deep distrust of what he found. Within a week of his return, he told Savary, ". . . place within the Paris gendarmerie the whole company that came with me from Elba. They are faithful men and especially attached to my person for many years . . . use them for the most delicate missions."[59] The Paris gendarmerie was the elite of the elite, but had been crucial in securing the provisional government in 1814. Now, it was to be infiltrated. Even the guard cavalry was infected. Word reached Napoleon that one of its officers had cut off his moustache—the hallmark of a Guardsman—was dressing as a civilian, "and mouthing bad opinions."[60]

Beyond Paris, the provincial administration, once the bedrock of his system, was a treacherous shambles. The day after his return, Napoleon told Fouché, "Bring me a list tomorrow of all the prefects who have to be replaced. The same for the sub-prefects. I mean the ones who are so bad they cannot be left where they are for an instant."[61] Among the first to go were those of the provençal departments who had hounded him on his march north.[62] Sixty-one prefects were sacked immediately, and only twenty-two were retained or transferred, but replacements proved hard to find.[63] Sackings were followed by refusals to serve. It did not stop at the prefectures. "There are many . . . mayors who are very bad, you cannot get rid of them soon enough," he informed Carnot on March 27.[64] The municipal council of Paris was purged immediately; Napoleon soon had that of Lyon in his sights.[65] He delegated the work to Carnot and Fouché, the former wary of disrupting the machine, the latter only too happy to add to the mayhem.[66] The purge went on. By June, only eight of the prefects there in March were left.[67] By mid-May, Napoleon ordered Marseille put under a state of siege, its national guard purged and disarmed, and thirty known royalists imprisoned.[68] There was now chaos where once there had been order. In contrast, Napoleon's dire threats to the émigrés remained largely dead letters. With his many contacts in royalist circles, Fouché protected them, but did little to calm their fears. He found willing accomplices in many prefects, isolated men, little inclined to vex the local elite.[69] In the teeth of all this, Napoleon wrote to Marie-Louise, "I have sent you a man to tell you that all is going very well. I am adored here and the master of everything." "The man," Joseph de Stassart, was arrested in Munich; the letter never reached her.[70]

Napoleon had no illusions, whatever he told Marie-Louise. A political geography of France, "for and against," was clear in his mind. There were the "good provinces" of the east—Dauphiné, Franche-Comté, Alsace, and Lorraine—that had known the rigors of allied occupation, whose national guards could be relied on, where "good citizens" could be found to officer them.[71] Throughout these regions, local defense associations sprang up spontaneously, "federations," in response to the renewed reality of war.[72] Napoleon ordered "all which appears suspect" in the Vendée deported to the Champagne, Burgundy, and Dauphiné.[73] He had outrun his enemies, but now had to turn around to face them. "It seems the duc d'Angoulême is near Avignon, covering Provence . . . this gathering has to be dispersed," he told Davout.[74] D'Angoulême's stronghold was in Nîmes, near Marseille, which Napoleon still thought unreliable.[75] His redoubtable wife held Bordeaux. The émigrés led most of these rebellions—an old, ineffectual enemy—but Napoleon was not complacent: "Measures must be taken to repress them, because if they know nothing is being done to stop their uprisings, they will grow, and they are already growing, not diminishing."[76] The prominent royalist Guignard Saint-Priest family of Montpellier, "from where they led the whole province in insurrection," had to be arrested, he told Davout. They were not caught.[77] The army could be counted on, whatever the failings of the administration and police. Masséna soon turned on the weak royalist forces near him; Suchet easily dispersed them around Nîmes, with some brutality.[78] The duchesse d'Angoulême, with Lainé at her side, steadied herself for a siege, hoping for foreign help and that, by making a stand, she might rally Napoleon's troops to her, but neither the Spanish nor the Royal Navy came to her aid. Her hopes in tatters, she escaped by ship to London.[79] Old-fashioned, "princely rebellion" was brushed aside in 1815, as it had been in the past, but military control did not spell the end of royalist resentment. Military victory brought control, but little else. Lynch, the mayor who had turned Bordeaux over to the British the year before, promptly fled to England. "I see that we are at a loss to choose a mayor," Napoleon laconically remarked to Carnot. He proposed one of his courtiers, Pierre Portal, who declined.[80] Napoleon sensed this when Alexandre de Lameth, a leader of the revolution from the first hour, requested not to go to Toulouse as a commissioner: "He reminded me that it was he, in 1790, who moved the abolition of the *parlements* and he wishes, in consequence, not to be sent to a *parlementaire* city. That seems a good reason to me . . . Have the prefect of Toulouse replaced."[81] Napoleon had stirred very old hatreds.

Then there was the "wicked west." Napoleon had good reason to fear resistance there. The Chouan department of Maine-et-Loire was put under an old Corsican friend, Jean-Baptiste Galeazzini, a former mayor of Bastia who served Napoleon on Elba, "a clever man, and very capable of keeping up with the intrigues that could be hatching in the West."[82] Napoleon probably wished he had one such for every department. In truth, Napoleon's greatest weapon here was his enemies' weakness. Lacking arms and the support of cautious local elites—"the priests, landowners and the women are opposed to any rising," General Morand told Davout[83]—potential rebels hesitated, watching and waiting as the authorities did nothing. The west remained unmoved as Louis XVIII took flight, just as when his brother was guillotined in 1793. Napoleon soon put Morand, one of Davout's best commanders, in charge of the region. He swiftly secured the cities on the northern bank of the Loire, Angers and Nantes,[84] and sealed off the region from the south, once the duchesse d'Angoulême was driven from Bordeaux.[85] This was a "phoney war."

As in 1793, the specter of conscription roused the west to fury, not the fall of kings. The only universally popular thing Louis XVIII did was abolish conscription, making it impossible for Napoleon to restore it. The Council of State simply refused to support him for fear of public uproar, but he needed an army desperately. Deprived of his main method of recruitment, Napoleon had two sources of manpower left: reservists—men recently retired from the army—and the National Guard, men between twenty and forty who normally only served in their own departments. On March 28, Napoleon classified the *démi-soldes* and all soldiers on leave as reservists, who could simply be recalled to the colors as they had not technically left the army. This yielded

122,000 men on paper. By a sleight of hand, Napoleon also categorized the levy of 1815—120,000 men—as "on leave": They had been conscripted, but not actually called up, so they, too, were classed as reservists. Napoleon noted that thirty-seven thousand of them came forward voluntarily, "from the better disposed departments" of the East. He felt that many of the levy of 1815 rounded up in "the doubtful departments" in the West ought to be rejected, even though "we must find, right away, 80 to 90,000 men."[86] Two weeks later, he ordered 300,000 national guardsmen mobilized for service with the army. But with his administration a shambles, only 81,000 well-trained men were added to the army, along with 222,000 badly armed, half-trained men fit only for garrison duty.[87] Napoleon, himself, did not believe he would get as many as one hundred thousand from the veterans.[88] He admitted as much when he sent flying columns into the Var "to make the veterans rejoin, and traverse the communes (where) . . . this measure has failed."[89] Once rounded up, there were desertions. Napoleon complained to Savary that, especially around the capital, "the Gendarmerie does not pursue deserters energetically enough."[90] By mid-May, Napoleon envisaged another method of recruitment. Units of well-armed, nicely uniformed Young Guardsmen were to be sent to major provincial towns—Rouen and Amiens, first, then others—not to coerce or arrest, but "to use all means to recruit volunteers and attract retired soldiers . . . order them to beat the drum, parade the flag . . . do everything they can to get recruits."[91] Advertising, a new phenomenon, appeared. Carnot was confident he could mobilize ten times more national guardsmen by summer, and Napoleon thought he would have eighty thousand more men in the depots by July.[92] As soon as he left his capital for the front, he made it clear to Davout, from Laon, that he intended to reintroduce conscription, and raise 200,000 men.[93]

But time was against him, and this led him into desperate measures he had always avoided. The western departments had been spared heavy conscription even during the worst of the wars, but not now, a move Fouché thought regrettable in so inflammable a region.[94] Napoleon abandoned his own maxim, to avoid the mistake of the revolutionaries, and the price he paid was the same as in 1793—civil war. Mobilization proved easy, rebel leaders drawing on the deep-rooted paramilitary structures of Vendean society. Bolstered by promises of immediate help from the British, the revolt broke out in force on May 15. Gendarmerie brigades withdrew to safety; the rural bourgeoisie fled to Nantes.[95] In truth, the royalist mobilization was nothing like the scale of 1793, and many in its ranks considered it as dangerous a risk as "the flight of the eagle."[96] The local authorities exaggerated the numbers of rebels in arms—there were probably only fifty thousand in total by May[97]—but no one stopped them taking control in rural areas south of the Loire, the Vendean heartland. Here, the rebels were operating only inside their own "royalist sanctuary . . . akin to an empty scallop shell," as the revolt's historian, Aurélien Lignereux has aptly put it.[98] Increasingly, as in the past, they could not break out of their strongholds in the remote, thinly populated bocage. Napoleon took the terrified local republicans at their word, nonetheless. He poured artillery into the beleaguered cities of Nantes, Angers, and Saumur[99] and sent thirteen thousand good troops he could ill afford to spare, to the Vendée, units of the Young Guard among them, but they only sealed off the insurgent zone.[100] Napoleon wanted it over quickly, and organized eighteen hundred gendarmes and marines into three flying columns "to go crisscross the country and stifle these seditious movements." He ordered the arrest of the known royalist, Charles Autichamp, and his removal to Paris. Autichamp slipped away, formed a small army, and fought on.[101] In his frustration, Napoleon lashed out at the leaders. "Order General Delaborde to concentrate his forces and go to the house of La Rochejacquelein, and raze it to the ground. Sequester all his property. Through this act of severity, the Vendée will feel the renewal of all the evil it has worked these last ten years . . . This is the beginning of disasters for it."[102] Louis de la Rochejacquelein was the brother of a legendary rebel commander of the 1790s, and now a leader himself. He remained undeterred and died in combat a few weeks later.[103] Despite early defeats and internal wrangling among the rebel leadership,[104] the west continued to drain Napoleon's shallow pool of men.[105] North of the Loire, in the *chouan* country, a civil war between "whites" and "blues" sprang back into life at village level. The army was better organized by now, and the gendarmerie brigades held firm, but fear of reprisals in the countryside and of civil war within the walls of Angers and Nantes was still real enough among the "blues." The arrival in the towns of terrified refugees from the countryside stiffened the will to resist.[106] In Nantes, the events triggered by "the flight of the eagle" rekindled older loyalties, animosities and fears well predating Napoleon's rule. With its arsenal and access to the coast, Nantes was a target for the rebels, as in 1793. Memories of the assault of that year were very much alive, while Napoleon's first, Jacobin-tinged decrees sparked attacks on the nobility of the city by the laboring classes. A noble "fifth column" lurked within the walls, and some of its partisans were officers in the national guard. To counterbalance this unreliable element, an association was formed of three hundred *fédérés*, noted less for their loyalty to Napoleon than their republican pasts. Angers raised twelve hundred *fédérés*.[107] The movement spread to Rennes, now engulfed by Chouan raiders and in the grip of atavistic dread. About six hundred men enlisted in the Rennes *fédérés*, and they fought courageously not only in their own city, but all over the surrounding countryside to rescue isolated officials and known revolutionaries from the Chouans, just as their precursors had in the 1790s. They fought at Nantes, at the height of the siege, and were prepared to obey the order to become coast guards should the British appear. However, as the Canadian scholar R. S. Alexander has shown, most were bourgeois, moderate republicans of the 1790s, who balked at Napoleon's dictatorship in his last years and now distrusted his rediscovered Jacobinism, but Louis XVIII's behavior unnerved them more. They trembled at the sight of renewed counterrevolutionary violence, but refused to become another source of recruits for the next war, and stood on their undertaking to protect order and property, in the slender hopes of gaining a properly liberal constitution.[108] Their support was conditional and driven by fear. They had little love for Napoleon. For all that, they knew he would not murder them in their beds, unlike the Chouans.

The West was not alone. In the wake of the rout of d'Angoulême, the southeast lurched toward an ever bloodier civil war, fueled by sectarian divisions stretching back to the sixteenth century. Here, the Protestant peasantry of the rugged valleys of the Cevennes fell on the bedraggled remnants of d'Angoulême's forces like wolves, while their middle-class coreligionists proved loyal Bonapartists, seizing back their dominance of local administration when Napoleon purged the royalists. "One of the gravest errors contributing to the collapse of the Imperialist regime was to place in public office sworn enemies of our Revolution," declared the Protestant villagers of Générac.[109] Roles were reversed in the blazing heat of the meridional summer. As the royalists fell back on Montpellier, they were followed by *fédérés* of a very different kind from those of the West, who took the town and sacked it ruthlessly. The royalists went underground and plotted the revenge that would be theirs after Waterloo. D'Alphonse, a councillor of state sent by Napoleon to deal with the region, saw no good in any of this: "The same men who were prominent during one of our saddest epochs have emerged from the shadows," he told Fouché.[110] D'Alphonse was soon replaced by General Jacques Laurent Gilly, the Gard's deputy and a veteran who was wounded at Wagram.[111] Gilly was given draconian powers to "put towns under a state of siege, purge the military and the gendarmerie, form mobile columns" and do whatever had to be done to "maintain order."[112] The gendarmes were now suspect, but Gilly had the Protestant peasantry, the descendants of the Camisards who defied Louis XIV. Gilly thought them as an unruly mob,[113] but Napoleon needed all the friends he could get.

All of this was sparked by the recklessness of "the flight of the eagle." It was Napoleon's doing. Yet, buried in the heart of the civil war was the unease created by the restored monarchy among so many. The Bourbons played their part in paving the way for Napoleon. Louis proved himself a remarkably adept practitioner of *ralliement* and *amalgame* at the higher levels of government. His approach to who held the high and middling offices of state was infinitely less disruptive or vengeful than Napoleon's on his return. No transition was handled so softly, Pierre Serna has remarked. However, it was not so for the lower grades—"the little hands"—of the administration. Like the army, they saw many jobs disappear as the restored monarchy sought economies to cope with the financial ruin Napoleon left behind, and such men harbored loyalties to an empire that gave them work and status.[114] Apprehension stretched beyond their ranks. Less dramatic than the dread hanging over moderate men in Nantes or Montpellier, many landowners in the Var, in Provence, rallied to the *fédérés* because they feared the Bourbons might renege on their promises, and confiscate their *biens nationaux*.[115] They were typical. The Bourbons promised emphatically to respect the sale of *biens nationaux*, but when they proposed restoring all those properties still unsold to the Church in their efforts to bolster its presence in French society, suspicions of darker intentions were roused once this became law after fierce debate in the Chamber of Deputies.[116] The retraction of d'Artois's rash promise to abolish the hated *droits réunis* on alcohol raised hackles, but the perceived threat to property caused genuine terror, bringing people of many economic and social strata back to the values of the Revolution. It was no wonder Napoleon found a "good east" awaiting him, for Burgundy and the Champagne were places where peasants, as well as the moneyed classes, had done well out of *biens nationaux*.

There was a deeper problem, rooted in the birth of the restoration, which troubled many who were glad to see the back of Napoleon. Louis XVIII bridled at the constitution the Napoleonic Senate produced on April 6, 1814, with its emphasis on the sovereignty of the nation, and halted his journey back to Paris at St. Ouen, where he drafted one of his own—"the Charter"—before he reclaimed the capital. It granted the liberal opposition to Napoleon much of what it sought: a freer press, regular parliaments with the power to control taxation, an electorate composed of propertied men, given real responsibility for the practical governance of the country. The terms of Saint-Ouen were accepted by the Senate, but warily. As Munro Price has acutely observed, the spirit of the Charter lay in the words of its preamble, not its clauses. Like Napoleon, Louis accorded himself the sole right to initiate legislation. He granted his constitution to the French "by the free exercise of our royal authority." Might he then be able to withdraw it at will? Then there was Article Fourteen. The preamble made clear that the king was the source of all sovereignty, not the nation, and that he had the right to "frame all regulations and ordinances necessary for . . . the safety of the state." Could this mean he had the power to suspend the Charter whenever he saw fit? It was quickly interpreted just this way by d'Artois and the ultraroyalists around him, and by many on the left.[117] There was something more worrying still in the preamble for all who had supported the revolution in any of its many guises. Louis spoke of his wish to "reforge the chain of time," of reuniting the France of 1814 to its deeper past. For the Ultras, this meant the revival of the society of orders, bolstering not only the Church, but the nobility. Most, even d'Artois, realized this could not entail actually reviving the old estates as legal entities, but they openly vowed to strengthen the aristocracy at every turn.[118] Réné de Chateaubriand, who accepted the Charter wholeheartedly, wrote eloquently of the need for France to discard the Napoleonic professional bureaucracy, and replace it with its "natural leadership" at a local level, the nobility, the repositories of honor in society, just as the hereditary peers—whose very existence caused unease for many moderates[119]—were a necessary check on absolutism.[120] D'Artois and his followers lit upon such ideas with alacrity. For the liberals, the "chain of time" boded the return of feudal rights, just as the decision to close cafés on Sunday mornings and the growing independence of the clergy—some of whom preached hellfire on the owners of *biens nationaux* or refused to bury divorced people—betokened the rising power of the Church.[121] It did Louis XVIII no good once Napoleon returned. Benjamin Constant is an emphatic example of the "liberal dilemma." The sometime partner of Germaine de Staël—who was currently Talleyrand's mistress[122]—and an unrelenting critic of Napoleon, who described Louis's ministerial team as "reassuring" in May 1814, he wrote violent anti-Napoleonic pamphlets during the flight of the eagle, but changed sides when he felt Louis failed to crush the return of ancien régime practices.[123] There was no evidence to convict his government of pandering to the ultras, but a man can be convicted by the company he keeps, and so it was with Louis.

This left Napoleon with an incongruous coalition at his back. Alongside the true loyalists in the army, indifferent to constitutions or parliamentary government, were those Frédéric Bluche has termed "neo-Bonapartist Jacobins," who saw in Napoleon the Roman-style dictator needed to crush the

Bourbons, the savior who would restore the true Terrorist republic. Such men flocked to the *fédérés* in eastern France. Their resurgence marked the utter backfiring of Bourbon propaganda that luridly equated Napoleon with the Terror.[124] Nor did these dire predictions prevent moderate men from rallying to him, however tepidly. Events soon vindicated the judgment of Jean-Baptiste Say, a liberal intellectual who had gone to Egypt with Napoleon in 1798, that "The vast majority of those who marched with (Napoleon in 1815) did not do so from loyalty to his person or his principles, but out of hatred for the Bourbon government, through fear of d'Artois, d'Angoulême, of Berry and their lot."[125] Napoleon found his Jacobin supporters far less of a headache than the liberals. He played the old card that, whoever he was, he was not the Bourbons. His rhetoric pandered to those left. "(M)ake it well known," he told Carnot, "that the cause today is that of the people against the nobles, of the peasants against the landlords, of the French against the foreigner. You must appeal everywhere to the honor and patriotism of the people."[126] Much was made of the new, "republican" constitution being drawn up by a committee that contained Carnot and Philippe-Antoine Merlin de Douai—both members of the Committee of Public Safety—as well as Constant, while Lucien did the backroom work. Article 67 declared that the French people forbade forever the return of the Bourbons or any attempt to restore the old regime.[127] The language of the Terror came more easily to him than that of 1791. To appease the liberals, censorship was abolished as early as March 24, but in May, he cracked down on the royalist paper *Journal général de France*, and put Carnot in charge of it.[128] The same day, he told Fouché, "I think it best to confide the surveillance of different journals to people I designate," meaning Lucien, Maret, and Carnot.[129] Predictably, Constant often crossed swords with Napoleon as it became ever clearer that the emperor was determined to hold on to as much of his power as possible. Napoleon ceded over the composition of the new, broader electorate for the lower house, but the deputies—now "the representatives of the people"—were still chosen by electoral colleges in the final instance. However, the upper house—no longer the treasonous Senate—remained the Chamber of Peers, its Bourbon title, part of which was popularly elected, but there were also an unlimited number of hereditary peers, appointed by Napoleon. When Chateaubriand showed Louis the text, he remarked that it was merely "an improved Charter."[130] Ominously, Napoleon point-blank refused to rescind his decrees sequestering the properties of Marmont, Talleyrand, and the others, or his orders to bring them before the courts, should they return. Democracy, even liberal parliamentarianism of a conservative kind, never came naturally or willingly to Napoleon, but a certain Terrorist determination was rekindled, fanned by the deep-seated sense of betrayal he had nurtured since at least Wagram. This bitterness grew within him. On April 18, during the last days of work for the new constitution, Napoleon wrote to Cambacérès:

> A great number of people have refused (to take) the oath (of loyalty). What should be done as regards their persons and property? . . . A great many Frenchmen have followed the Count of Lille (Louis XVIII) . . . they have said they will only return at the head of 50,000 men. There are civil authorities in the same case . . . the former prefect of the Doubs issues orders in his department in the name of the king. What is to be done with their persons and property? . . . The agents employed abroad (the French ambassadors) who were recalled (to France) have declared they will continue to wear the white cockade and serve the Count of Lille: how should we act as regards their persons and property?[131]

He then sacked eleven generals, telling Mollien to strip them of their pensions or any other benefits they were drawing.[132] Most had served under Marmont. He set his face against many, but there was still room for mending old fences. The same day, he wrote to Masséna,

> Thank you for having held Toulon and Antibes, and Toulon above all (from the royalists). I trembled when I read the order that you may have received from the duc d'Angoulême to surrender that

precious depot to the English . . . I truly want to see you. If the
state of your health is such that you need to return to the Midi, I
shall get you back there from Paris.[133]

Masséna came, and was warmly received. Napoleon joked that he knew his
old friend would just as readily throw him into the sea as serve him. Masséna
pulled no punches: "Certainly, so long as I believed you were not recalled by
the majority of Frenchmen." Napoleon offered him a field command, but
his old comrade's health was broken, and he returned south. They parted on
good terms, never to meet again.[134] The prospect of Toulon in English hands
obviously stirred something deep in Napoleon, and he was grateful to the man
who had prevented his own first achievement turning to dust.

Whether his latest effort, his constitution, would prove Masséna right was
soon put to the test. Napoleon called his "improved Charter" the "Additional
Act to the Constitutions of the Empire." This meant that it did not actually replace the previous constitution for the moment, but only promised
to "rework" the earlier imperial texts at a later date.[135] The Bourbons had
been exiled from France for a generation and might be expected to be out of
step. Their problem was that too many of them refused to care if they were.
Napoleon now proved equally maladroit. He sniffed opposition like a spaniel
after game, and knew incongruous interests he had to reconcile, but he had
no more idea how to do so in April 1815, than on his bedraggled return from
Russia in December 1812. The whole project proved a dreadful miscalculation.
No one liked the way it had been done—drawn up behind closed doors by a
handpicked committee and then put to a plebiscite—when the demand was
for a constituent assembly, a real return to the roots of 1789, proving, perhaps,
that the tsar had not been the fantasist others made of him. Napoleon did
not like it, either, snarling on Saint Helena that "those liberal scum made me
lose a lot of time talking 'constitutions' to me."[136] Napoleon's priorities were
elsewhere, in every sense. It was all too provisional for anyone to feel secure.
The creation of a hereditary peerage drew the same appalled reaction from
Napoleon's Jacobin base as his reneging on universal suffrage. For Frédéric

Bluche, "The deception was all the more marked, because Napoleon had portrayed himself as a man of the Revolution." Constant had been away too long, as well. The liberals were not appeased by his handiwork, afraid that the lower chamber was still a prisoner of a powerful—and power-hungry—executive. As with the Charter, the right of dissolution, so recently and flagrantly abused by Napoleon, remained ill defined. These were the men who had changed sides many times before, and they were well capable of doing so again. They launched a bitter pamphlet war as soon as the "act" was made public on April 22. With so much in the balance, few liberal writers were openly hostile to Napoleon, but three quarters of them rejected the act.[137]

Napoleon pressed ahead, nonetheless, and the act was put to a plebiscite, in the tried and tested fashion of the regime since its inception. The plebiscite gave the right to vote to a larger electorate than that for the lower chambers of either Napoleon or the Bourbons: about 7,500,000 Frenchmen—roughly one in five—could vote, but only just over 1,600,000 did so.[138] This widespread indifference—or outright hostility in places like the West, where not even some mayors voted[139]—gives a far more accurate idea of the regime's levels of support than the crushing numerical victory of 1,554,112 "for" to a mere 5,743 "against," redolent of the "fixed" nature of plebiscites past.[140] The careful analysis of Frédéric Bluche confirms the hardening divisions within France, true to Napoleon's mental geography: Burgundy, the Champagne, Alsace, and Lorraine had the highest proportions of support for the act; in the West and Southwest, support was almost nonexistent.[141] Then came the elections for the new Chamber of Representatives in mid-May. They were organized in a pyramid of assemblies, each choosing electors, until the final tier elected the deputies. Napoleon left the good republican, Carnot, to organize the process, and allowed the liberal press free rein, but Fouché's hand was everywhere, with his extensive networks of influence, and newspapers in his pocket. He allegedly told Pasquier, "He'll have to go to the army before the month is out. Once gone, we will be masters of the game. I hope he wins one or two battles; he'll lose the third, and then our role will begin."[142] Fouché thrived in uncertainty, and the times were made for him. Abstention rates showed how unstable it all was: they were over 70 percent in the highest tier of electoral colleges, the departments. Only seventeen departments saw a turnout of over 50 percent. Most of the deputies elected were closely linked to the state—magistrates, civil servants, veterans. There were 620 in all.[143] About five hundred of them have often been classed as "liberals," although this is hard to quantify. Emphatically, however, the old Revolutionary Guard, Jacobin and moderate, was back in force, among them many friends of Fouché.[144] The new chamber was, without doubt, full of men who had no love for the Bourbons, but neither were they convinced that Napoleon was what they really wanted. This was a regime built on negatives: fear of the Bourbons, fear of invasion, fear of the politics of revenge. Nor had Napoleon any confidence in them. Only a few days after the elections, he dispatched "extraordinary commissioners" to the provinces as he had done the year before, a loud echo of the Terror, but hardly the act of a constitutional monarch. Napoleon had his reasons. The municipal elections were a triumph for the royalists in towns of less than five thousand people: 80 percent of those elected were Bourbon appointees.[145] *La France profonde* was simply out of his control.

Napoleon seemed set on outdoing Louis in poor judgment. He saved his worst for last. The doomed nature of the whole enterprise found pathetic visual expression in Napoleon's concoction of June 1, the *Champ de Mai*. It was held on the sacred revolutionary turf of the Champ de Mars, where Louis XVI had sworn loyalty to the new constitution in 1790, and where sans culottes paid with their lives protesting that same constitution in 1791. If the spatial message was muddled, the nomenclature was worse. *Champ de Mai* harked back to a Carolingian practice that supposedly brought together the free warriors of the kingdom to renew their allegiance to the crown. About ten thousand members of the electoral colleges came to Paris for it, not as many as were invited. They were mere spectators, there to fill up the Champ de Mars as Napoleon took his oath to the act. It began with a Mass, not what his supporters envisaged. Napoleon dropped his original idea to appear on horseback in the uniform of the national guard. Instead, he and his brothers arrived by coach and emerged looking like stuffed turkeys, playing at being peacocks.

They wore mock-Roman tunics, the brothers' of white velvet, Napoleon's of red, all with lace and cloaks on a hot day, slippers with tassels and ribbons on them, and plumed caps. He could have appeared in the battered tricorne hat and the uniform of his chasseurs, as the hero of Austerlitz. Instead, he looked like a bird trussed up for the oven, poured into a costume that showed how fat he had become, as the sweat poured off him.[146] His speech that day, punctuated by artillery salvos, was no more than a call to arms, with a mere nod to the act. Only toward the end of the ceremony did Napoleon break with protocol, leaving the stage spontaneously to distribute the eagles to the troops. "His men" thronged around him.[147] For a fleeting moment, the élan of 1804 and the brio of the flight of the eagle flickered. Napoleon pulled off this kind of jumble in 1804, on the tide of success—he had won wars and made peace—but in 1815 it seemed "a ridiculous parody" to one observer. The Marquis de Lafayette, a veteran of such things, called it a "juggling act," and he was right. Before the event, Fouché suggested Napoleon use the occasion to abdicate in favor of his son.[148] Behind the vanity and bluster were the politics of desperation that let Fouché get away with such a remark. Ahead lay a new coalition, more powerful than any before.

17

THE WAR OF THE SEVENTH COALITION: MARCH–JUNE 1815

❧ ──────────────────────────── ❧

Europe Rises

The flight of the eagle caught the victorious grandees at Vienna, quite literally, mid-waltz.[1] The news broke at a ball hosted by Metternich, and while he tried in vain to get the "band to play on," the dancers froze on the floor, staring at one another, stunned, as the very thought of Napoleon reverberated across the room "with the rapidity of an electric shock."[2] It left the Congress of Vienna stirred, but it remained unshaken. The old heads at its helm had lived through too much to be surprised by anything anymore. Some of them had protested long and loud that sending Napoleon only as far as Elba would lead to this, and now no one could contradict them. On March 7, Metternich was handed a note marked "secret" from the Austrian consul in Livorno with the news. He went, first, to Francis, asking him to work for a united front against Napoleon. By 8:30 A.M. the next morning, Alexander and Frederick-William agreed to form a Seventh Coalition against the man they now declared "the enemy and perturber of the peace of the world." Britain joined the renewed alliance a few days later, after a fierce debate in Parliament,[3] assuring the other allies continued huge subsidies[4] of seven million pounds sterling, almost 50 percent of all the income tax revenue raised in 1814.[5] The terms of the Treaty of Chaumont were reactivated, the major powers pledging to keep 150,000 men each in the field, for ten years if necessary.[6] The terms of the new alliance were concluded by March 25.

Their rivalries and tensions were far from forgotten, but decades of experience taught the allied leaders where their priorities lay. The previous months nearly saw the allies come to blows over the reorganization of Saxony and Poland, but these dangerous issues were already close to resolution.[7] Austria, and even Prussia, feared Alexander's expansionist ambitions in Poland. In one stormy meeting, the tsar challenged Metternich to a duel, and the Austrian diplomat wondered later if he "was leaving by the window, or the door." Poland was not repartitioned—the status quo antebellum was not restored—to the loss of Prussia and Austria. Yet, compromise was achieved: a virtually independent "Congress." Poland emerged, ruled by Alexander, but not as tsar.[8] Napoleon felt sure these disputes would make the Congress disintegrate, a view Caulaincourt thought mad.[9] Their tensions actually worked to his undoing, reinforcing the need for balance and negotiation. The Saxon-Polish crisis forced the three eastern powers to keep large numbers of troops on a war footing, while Metternich placed sizeable forces in Italy to watch Murat. Only Britain was relatively ill-prepared. The hardened veterans of the Peninsular army had been dispatched to America, with whom she was still at war.[10] Haggling soon began over the distribution of subsidies, and the small German states were generally suspicious of Prussia,[11] but for the leadership, the need for unity overrode all else. Alexander wrote to his mother, of the news from Elba, ". . . my conviction that this evil genius would end up one way or another brought down and destroyed, this conviction does not leave me, I base it on the words of our Holy Religion . . . A mass of 85,000 would be ready to combat and crush the evil genius if he tried to exercise his wicked empire even briefly."[12] He meant what he said.

Cool heads prevailed, but it was a wonder. Some of their personal lives were almost as turbulent as their diplomacy. Alexander spent much of his time philandering. His wife, the Empress Elizabeth, was on the verge of leaving him at Vienna when she fell in love for the second time with Adam Czartoryski, the leading advocate of Polish independence. He begged her to divorce the tsar and marry him on the same day the new coalition was formed. She said she had to remain loyal to him at such a time, and returned to Saint Petersburg, "to suffer in silence" and submit to the will of Providence.[13] To leave Alexander for him might have undone the fragile equilibrium Metternich, Alexander, and Castlereagh had only just achieved, and handed Napoleon the chaos he wanted. Then again, her resolution reflected that of many others. Castlereagh offered Wellington "the soft option" of remaining in Vienna as ambassador, or taking the field in Belgium, where Napoleon was most likely to strike first. Wellington did not hesitate, and hurried north from the fleshpots of Vienna.[14] Talleyrand and the state he represented were swept aside for the moment, "reduced to the rank of pretenders, like so many others," when Louis XVIII was excluded from the new alliance and the fate of France "after Napoleon" was left deliberately vague.[15] Yet in the midst of his humiliation, Talleyrand stood with the coalition. He had no compassion for the troops who rallied to Napoleon: "As many as can be must be killed, the rest should be sent to Siberia," he wrote to Sophie, Countess of Schönborn, his mistress in Vienna while his wife remained "safely" in France.[16] Behind all the glitter of the balls, the concerts and the banquets, was a steely resolve among the *bons viveurs* and practiced *roués* of old elite that Napoleon galvanized to his cost.

The squabbling among the allies worked against Napoleon in the most fatal way possible, in Belgium. Although the Congress had decided to hand Belgium to the kingdom of the Netherlands, this had yet to be ratified formally when Napoleon returned, nor had its borders been fixed precisely: The fate of Luxembourg, with its imposing fortress and strategic importance, was still in the balance. The loss of its share of Poland turned Prussia into a very expansionist state. It had first sought to annex all of Saxony, a loyal Napoleonic ally ripe, Berlin felt, for the diplomat's avenging knife, only to be thwarted by the common front of Austria, Britain, and France.[17] Prussia got roughly half of Saxony, but that did not stop her casting covetous eyes on Luxembourg, and even the Netherlands.[18] Hence, although Prussia was constrained to remove Kleist's forty-four thousand troops from Belgium, they still lurked nearby, in Aachen. Kleist's force was understrength and dispersed along the Rhine over 110 miles, but about 50,000 more troops were in Prussia's new Rhine province carved out of four former "French" departments.[19] Prussia kept its bargaining chips to hand, and they were not negligible. Blücher was able to muster 117,000 men when the call came.[20]

The British also had a presence in Belgium. Wellington had just over 110,000 men under his command but, like the Prussians, they were widely dispersed.[21] It was a polyglot force, composed mainly of troops from Hanover, Brunswick, and Nassau, and the King's German Legion, together with a few British Guard battalions and line regiments, whose main role was to shield the region while the fledgling army of the new Dutch kingdom took shape almost from scratch.[22] Until Napoleon's return, their purpose was to protect the Netherlands from Prussian ambitions, for where Prussia went, Russia went, too.[23] The Prussians regarded the British with suspicion. For their part, as long as there was the faintest hint that Prussia had territorial ambitions anywhere near the Channel coast, the British remained on their guard. This influenced organization on the ground. Wellington and Blücher maintained separate lines of communications, Blücher's running from southern Belgium into the Rhineland, and Wellington's from his headquarters in Brussels to the Channel at Ostend. Even when the Prussians were allowed back into Belgium as the crisis mounted, their respective headquarters—Brussels for Wellington, Namur for Blücher—were fifty miles apart.[24] For all their shortcomings, the Anglo-Prussians in Belgium were the only organized armies on Napoleon's borders.[25] The mutual unease among the allies gave them a stronger presence in and around the region, than might have been the case otherwise.

Wellington's arrival in Brussels presaged a wider strategy, and he went north with the promise that 700,000 men would soon assemble along the length of France's eastern borders.[26] The allied governments did their best. On May 13,

Alexander personally promised the British that 200,000 men under Barclay and 564 guns, then in Poland, would be on the Rhine by June 24.[27] This was only the vanguard. Berthier was among the first to see them coming. Ever since he left Paris with Louis, Berthier loathed the prospect of being branded an émigré. He soon found himself under round-the-clock police surveillance by the Bavarians, followed by agents even on his morning walks with his family. Isolated, the man known for his sobriety took to drinking several bottles of champagne in the morning, and it was in this state he saw the Russian cavalry moving up on June 1, and fell to his death from a tower window, his brains scattered on the courtyard below. Some said he was assassinated by French royalists intent on stopping him rejoining Napoleon, a wild theory generally rejected. The family, and one of his recent biographers,[28] insisted it was an accident. Suicide was the verdict of the Bavarian authorities, and was rapidly accepted by the rumor mill.[29] Emmanuel de Waresquiel has no doubt this was the cause.[30] This much is known: Consumed by doubts and despair in his refuge in Bamberg, he sought to return to France, to live quietly on his estates, but was denied a passport by the Bavarians; his doctor said he was in a state of "hypochondrial melancholy." His children's governess heard him mutter, as he watched the Russian cavalry pass, "This defile never ends . . . Poor France, what is going to befall you, and I am here!"[31] These were the last known words of the man Napoleon told Metternich "followed me around like a good boy."[32]

The Prussians began a general mobilization, despite their almost bankrupt finances. They had difficulty amassing even ten days' rations for the new levies, and rows soon flared over who was responsible for paying for the army in Belgium: the Dutch had promised to do so, but balked at the actual cost, and the Prussians felt Wellington had misled them over this. The British, in contrast, paid their own way in hard cash.[33] These problems continued during the spring, but British troops, weapons and supplies reached the Netherlands by mid-June, and Wellington's staff officers were now, after considerable nagging, mainly his Peninsular veterans.[34] He won other small, but important victories. The young Prince of Orange, the brave but raw heir to the Dutch throne, was dissuaded from retaining independent command of the Dutch forces, accepting a corps command under Wellington, who was made a Dutch Field Marshal and commander of all the Dutch forces, to square the circle.[35] Over two million pounds sterling of the entire war subsidy was poured into the Belgian sector.[36] British financial support was crucial at every turn, and Castlereagh defended it ferociously in Parliament, rebuffing Whig proposals to negotiate with Napoleon.[37]

Austrian mobilization, or lack of it, added to the fraught climate more than it helped. Schwarzenberg was appointed the allied supreme commander, and picked up where he left off in 1814: slowly. Charged with formulating the overarching allied strategy, it was seven weeks before "an inadequate concoction of generalities"[38] emerged that hinged on delaying until the allies amassed their full force. Only then would they drive on Paris "and the mass of the French army, wherever it might present itself."[39] The plan envisaged no overall control of the different armies: the British and Prussians in Belgium were to operate independently of the Austrians along the Rhine, and the Russian role was left vague. It lacked a sense of urgency: the Austrians could assemble 310,000 men but not quickly; the Russian advance was long and laborious. Schwarzenberg did not want to advance until June 16, but by then Napoleon's forces would be stronger and the field commanders knew it. Alexander flung Schwarzenberg's plan back in his face. Wellington proved an astute, more courteous critic. In private, Wellington was unnerved by his commander's vagueness and hesitancy. In fact, Schwarzenberg was overoptimistic. The Austrians were not ready by July 1, but they were the keystone of his redrawn plan. The allies assembled in five separate armies: Wellington and Blücher's 227,000 in Belgium; Schwarzenberg, now with 210,000 Austrians and southern Germans on the Upper Rhine; Barclay's 200,000 Russians, who would arrive late and form a strategic reserve in the middle Rhine; and 75,000 more Austrians, who were to drive along the Riviera.[40] This last force was a source of suspicion among the other allies, seen as a sign that Austria's real interest was territorial aggrandizement in Italy. Purely militarily, Wellington regarded it as a fatal "extension of the front."[41]

Austrian interest in the Riviera appeared even more sinister when the Coalition won its first victory. Murat sat in Ancona, in papal territory, with thirty-five thousand men, faced by fifty thousand Austrians. Having again declared himself "the liberator of Italy," there was now every reason to depose him. His call fell on deaf ears in Italy. At one point, vacillating as ever, Murat offered his services to the coalition, but then launched his troops north. He was not entirely misguided in this, because Napoleon had denounced his enterprise and warned him that his support was conditional on Murat returning to his status as a French vassal.[42] The Austrians fell back before him, but it was a ploy. Murat was drawn further north, occupying Bologna, and then Modena, at which point the Austrians counterattacked, forcing him back over the river Panaro, in bitter fighting. On April 16, he fled Bologna. The Austrians found a strong defensive position near Tolentino, on May 1, where they consolidated their forces, gave battle, and held firm. Murat came at them furiously the next day, his infantry driving the Austrians back from their positions, with pitiless bayonet work. He still inspired almost fanatical loyalty in his men and his staff, but true to form, he had not reconnoitered the ground properly. His cavalry, meant to support the advance, were trapped in narrow ravines, and slowed down as they tried to cross marshes Murat did not know were there. His flanks exposed, the Austrians drove him relentlessly back, and forced him to abandon the field. As Murat's biographer, Vincent Haegele remarks, it was a bitter irony that Murat, of all people, lost his last battle because he did not use his cavalry properly.[43] Most of his troops simply vanished, and he fell back on Naples with only nine thousand men. There, the local authorities negotiated a quiet surrender to the allies, while Murat tried vainly to raise the people against them. Meanwhile, Caroline had asked for and received five hundred British marines to keep law and order in the city, and was assured by the British she would be allowed to remain. One of them was none other than Neil Campbell.[44] Outfoxed and abandoned, Murat slipped out of Naples on May 20, in disguise, leaving Caroline behind as regent. He escaped to the island of Ischia, and then to the south of France, where he found refuge near Toulon. He offered his services to Napoleon, hoping to be given command of an "army of Italy" to retake Naples. Instead, Napoleon told him to keep his head down and his mouth shut. Murat flew into a predictable rage, wrote a stinging letter to Napoleon, and started off north, soon after Napoleon launched his offensive.[45] Caroline was told by the emissaries she sent to meet the Austrians that she was, purely and simply, deposed, and the Bourbons restored. As Naples turned out to welcome the Austrians, surrounded by a violent populace, Caroline took refuge on a British ship, forced to abandon her large train of luggage on the beach.[46] It took her to exile and imprisonment in Trieste, in violation of the terms of her agreement with the British. Perfidious Albion was more than a match for this most duplicitous of the Bonapartes. The political leadership of the Coalition was bitter, ruthless, and decisive in the demise of the Murats, and did not stop with them. On May 12, the sovereigns denounced the Treaty of Paris. All its terms were simply torn up.

The high command showed no such determination. Alexander was still exasperated by Schwarzenberg's imprecision and snail-like timetable of plans, particularly how little attention it gave to the role of the Russians, given the copious information he had provided. The protocol for the allied advance into France was not even signed until June 10. The advance for all the armies was set for June 24. Blücher's demands for an immediate attack, and Wellington's view that the Austrian presence would be enough if it was prompt, were set aside. Schwarzenberg won the argument: they were waiting for the Russians.[47] It mattered not. Napoleon was already on the march.

Napoleon's Sandcastle: France and Its Army, May–June 1815

As early as March 27, Napoleon made it clear to Davout that his main army would be in the north.[48] He knew the allies were not assembled anywhere except Belgium. Napoleon was not yet ready, himself, and said later he would rather have waited until autumn to fight,[49] but the allies were growing stronger by the week. If a decisive engagement was what he wanted—and he always did—there was no choice but to strike at Wellington and Blücher. Napoleon never committed his exact plans to paper and kept his troop buildup well hidden:[50] He quietly concentrated five corps—89,000 infantry, 22,000 cavalry, 11,000 gunners, 336 guns, and the guard—in a zone of only thirty kilometers.[51] This was a strike force. Yet, however scattered, the allies still outnumbered him considerably, however substandard some of the Dutch and German troops might be.[52] He did not feel strong enough to herd Wellington and Blücher together and destroy them with a single blow.[53] His plan hinged on defeating them individually, a confession of weakness, that revealed many others.

The Army of the North was composed almost entirely of veterans, good troops whose rank and file retained the same ferocious loyalty to Napoleon they displayed on his return to France. But this army was a façade. It contained almost of all the combat-ready troops Napoleon possessed. The Rhine and Alpine fronts, those in the path of the approaching Russian onslaught, were held by raw recruits and poorly armed, untrained national guards. In the event of an allied advance, the national guards were to abandon Alsace immediately and fall back into the Vosges.[54] The frontiers were not the only places Napoleon was prepared to yield. In late May, he felt that only one of Marseille's two forts could be defended against royalists in the city, and ordered the garrison's gunpowder and cartridges taken to Lyon. Nothing had been done by June, and Marseille was still not safe from "the popular movement."[55] "There are 4,000 well-armed national guards and many royalist companies . . . The national guard must be disarmed, and a new one formed composed of patriots and the people."[56] He ordered mass arrests; many nobles were to be expelled from the city; a "very severe police" was needed.[57] Five hundred gendarmes were sent from Corsica to garrison the forts.[58] Marshal Guillaume Marie-Anne Brune took command of the city. Once a protégé of Danton and a member of the radical Cordeliers Club during the Terror, he was a man of impeccable republican credentials, and in 1807, he fell foul of Napoleon for taking a surrender "in the name of the French army," not that of "His Imperial and Royal Majesty." He had not been employed since.[59] Now, he was just what Napoleon needed. The army retreated from the city, the second largest in France, into the forts. He wrote despairingly to Fouché that it was no better in Bordeaux or Montauban. Even Toulon was at risk. All their national guards had to be purged, and replaced by "friends of the Revolution." This alone would "change the face of the Midi." Nor did Lille, so close to the war zone, appear safe. Its national guard was "badly disposed" and had to be disarmed.[60] It was easier said than done. Carnot had summoned these units into being, armed them, and created a monster.

Napoleon's command was but a thin screen, a Japanese paper door, between France and conquest. He knew it. He ordered massive defenses built on the heights of northern Paris: The picturesque modern neighborhood of Montmartre bristled with earthworks and stakes; thirty artillery batteries—240 guns in all—were commanded for the city; 120,000 men were allocated to Davout to hold it, even if they were all second rate:[61]

> It would be shameful to strip too many troops from the capital, for its population, on which I must count, needs security. They cannot be forced (to serve) because this is a question of . . . public morale and, if they are unhappy, they don't want to do anything. I'm told that in Paris, (the authorities) are being too rigorous about that.[62]

Napoleon still feared and respected his volatile capital. He put Suchet in charge of Lyon, where the huge task of raising earthworks on its high ground "will result in putting Lyon in a safe position."[63] Napoleon knew the likelihood of defeat in the field, and mapped out his retreat well before the campaign. Neither great city was to be trusted. Despite his fiery Jacobin noises, the lack of muskets gave Napoleon a good reason not to distribute them "to the workers of Paris and Lyon, from whom they cannot be got back."[64]

The practical problems of 1814 had not changed. Horses, artillery, and muskets were all in desperately short supply. Hours of his frenetic, almost manic energies were poured into correcting this with pitifully little success. The war industries, which had struggled when at full tilt in 1814, had been largely dismantled under Louis.[65] "We need at least 100,000 muskets at Vincennes (the depot for Paris) and 100,000 on the Loire (for the reserve army) . . . I want the production at Tulle tripled. I also want it tripled at Versailles," to produce 235,000 weapons.[66] In truth, production never surpassed twenty thousand per month, plus the same number of repaired muskets. More than half of national guardsmen had no muskets; almost all ammunition went to the field army.[67] Often, national guards were armed with hunting rifles: "What is not good for the artillery will do well for the peasants," Napoleon told Davout.[68] The relentless search for horses yielded an increase of 70 percent between March and June: 27,864 cavalry mounts rose to 44,000; 7,765 artillery horses became 16,500 through a mixture of purchase and requisition.[69] Numbers can deceive; it was nowhere near enough. "The western departments furnish almost nothing . . . those of the Champagne . . . can furnish no more, because of the losses born in the last enemy invasion," which convinced Napoleon he could hope for only five thousand horses from this levy, not the eight thousand he originally demanded.[70] On June 1, Napoleon told Davout the artillery had to have priority over the cavalry—"Four batteries which arrive too late can cost me a battle."[71] On the eve of the campaign, five hundred Polish light horsemen, an elite unit, found themselves without mounts. Napoleon saw the mess he made too late: "I attach great importance to having the 500 Poles mounted as soon as possible," he told Davout, but confessed they had only 300 saddles.[72] As the army took the field, its supplies were shambolic. The depots on the route north had only four days' rations of bread—"our situation is shameful"[73]— and shortages continued on the march, creating the dispersal and delay that went with foraging. The army had not been paid, perhaps Napoleon's most pressing reason for a quick victory.[74]

Napoleon made all this worse. In Soult, Suchet, and more than anyone Davout, Napoleon still had his best field commanders, but he deployed them badly. The use made of Davout and Suchet was born of his deep pessimism about the campaign. A Midi swelling with resurgent royalism, a Vendée still in arms, a capricious capital, an obstreperous parliament that had found its voice, all this and more led him to keep Davout in Paris to "watch his back." The pathetic vulnerability of eastern France, menaced by the "never ending defiles" that so tortured Berthier, probably influenced putting Suchet, himself a Lyonnais, in charge there. Suchet's Army of the Alps numbered about thirty-eight thousand conscripts and national guards;[75] the eight thousand men of his Observation Corps in the Jura had no arms at all in June.[76] There he languished. Napoleon's plans needed men capable of independent command; there were none better than the victor of Auerstadt or the conqueror of Tarragona, but Napoleon's vulnerability at home denied him their genius. On Saint Helena, Napoleon wailed to Gourgaud, "If I had had Lannes or Bessières at the head of the Guard, this ill would not have befallen!"[77] He cried out for the dead, but there were those among the living he could easily have summoned, had he chosen to.

Soult was a different case. No one trusted Soult, yet none doubted his ability in the field. This was not what Napoleon chose to do with him. He made him his chief of staff. Ney had hated Soult with a passion since the Portuguese campaign of 1809, when the two drew swords on each other. They almost came to blows again as recently as February, while in Louis's service.[78] Ney was as much loved in the army as Soult was loathed, and with so many marshals dead, loyal to Louis, or seconded to other duties, he was also the senior field commander in the Army of the North. This did not make Soult an ideal choice as the chief liaison with the corps commanders. There were alternatives. Joseph pressed the case for Jourdan, who had fulfilled that role in Spain in Berthier's absence, whereas Soult's tenure of the same post had been a disaster.[79] Napoleon did not value Joseph's views on war. "He believed himself a great soldier . . . superior to Suchet, Masséna, or Lannes," he told Bertrand.[80] Jourdan was probably undone by his referee, rather than his record. Suchet was also discussed, but Napoleon wanted him where he was.[81] He had his eye on Soult for the role for some time. "He is a skillful man . . . with a good understanding of the details of warfare, and would make a perfect chief of staff," he remarked in 1811.[82] Napoleon could see what he wanted to see in someone, and so it was with Soult. Napoleon knew well Soult's shifty character, but Davout and he agreed that Soult was capable. Problems soon began, however. Soult assumed he had authority over the entire army, and was answerable only to Napoleon, but Napoleon had made him chief of staff only for the Army of the North. Conflict and confusion ensued when Davout, as minister of war, claimed that because the army was not yet in the field, he, not Soult, gave the orders. Napoleon tried to rectify it on May 16, declaring that Soult's authority was restricted to the Army of the North, and Davout controlled all other units. When Soult ignored this and continued issuing general orders, Davout threatened to resign. This was only sorted out when Napoleon joined the army in the field.[83] Napoleon had only three marshals with him on campaign: the deskbound Soult, Ney, and Grouchy, whose experience was almost entirely as a cavalry commander, and was a newly minted marshal, for his trivial victory over d'Angoulême a few weeks before. Murat's offer of his services was spurned. Napoleon still had experienced divisional commanders—Gérard, Vandamme, Reille, Lobau, and d'Erlon—but they had seldom led corps, so clear instructions from the chief of staff were more important than ever. In these circumstances, the absence of Soult, Davout, and Suchet from the battlefield is almost incalculable. None of this boded well. Napoleon learned of Berthier's end only days before he took the field. One observer remembered: "No one was better at hiding or simulating his emotions. But he seemed to have lost all power to dissimulate . . . [H]is face was contorted . . . and his gestures expressed more sadness as his smallest movements had something convulsive about them."[84] Carnot recalled that "He said that if Berthier returned, he would not have been able to stop himself taking him in his arms."[85] Monnier said he never heard Napoleon speak ill of him, and that he praised him as one of his best generals because he simply knew what to do. "I would really like to have seen Berthier in the uniform of a captain in Louis XVIII's guard," he told his minister with a sly grin,[86] but it was clear to all he dreaded going to war without him.

Few people worked more closely with Napoleon in these frenetic weeks that Carnot and Mollien, and they detected worrying signs in him. Mollien saw fundamental changes:

> His glance at work, once so confident and quick . . . became more
> circumspect: his plans appeared less sharp, his orders less absolute

and less energetic . . . In council . . . he prolonged discussions to make it look as if the decision was the work of everyone . . . His meditations had become laborious and irritating . . . A kind of weariness, that he had never known, would overcome him after several hours of work . . .[87]

Carnot pointed to Napoleon's equal determination to master detail, and his ability to work with the same minister for hours at a time. To do otherwise was not in Napoleon's character: "He believed that if he let go of the reins only a little, all power would slip from him," be it in minor administration or by accepting democracy.[88] The old knack for delegation was gone. Both men noted that Napoleon never appeared flustered. In this he remained master of himself, no matter how pressing the matter,[89] "habitually calm, thoughtful, and conserving without affectation a serious dignity."[90] Yet, these two men who were in intense, daily contact with Napoleon discerned deeper, disturbing currents. Mollien saw a fatalism in Napoleon, stemming from, he thought, his sheer exhaustion:

> . . . There were few traces of that audacity of the first years, of that self confidence that had never known an insurmountable obstacle: but in those other times, destiny had shown itself as submissive to him as men. In the Hundred Days, he was the first to say that destiny had changed for him, and that in it, he had lost an ally he could never replace.[91]

Carnot, if he is to be believed, stumbled upon a Napoleon with "qualities of the heart" he had never suspected when they worked together in the early days of the Consulate or when he gave him the Army of Italy nineteen years before. He found Napoleon weeping over the portrait of his son one day, and was so convulsed with sadness, Carnot had to lead him to his desk, something that deeply moved Carnot,[92] but was, in truth, worrying in a man under such pressure. From his return to Paris until his departure on campaign, Napoleon never let up on himself, working demonic hours even by his own standards, but Mollien saw this savage routine taking a new kind of toll on him. "He had no other distraction, no other source of rest, than private interviews; he sought them out, and what is even more odd, he preferred to summon people who, having served him previously, left him little surprised by the fantasies which his prodigious imagination had stunned others."[93] Even that benchmark for absolutist workaholics, Philip II of Spain, did not rise until 8:00 A.M., nor open his papers until 11:00 A.M., stopped at 9:00 P.M., and made time for two short walks. Above all, he had diversions.[94] Shorn of his wife and son, probably too ill to hunt, even had there been time, Napoleon had nothing to ease his growing impatience all around him saw. "He sensed he had played his last hand," Mollien reflected soon afterward.[95] As he led his army into the jaws of hell, there was then the question of its commander's state of mind and body. Such was the commander's condition when he quietly took his leave of Paris on June 12 to join the army.

Looking for a Fight: June 12–16

True to his controlling, increasingly secretive behavior, Napoleon revealed his plans to Carnot only hours before he left Paris, and the minister of the interior did not like what he heard. "You know we don't have a serviceable army," the blunt ex-Terrorist told him. Napoleon remained calm and amiable, equally true to form: "Calm down, Carnot . . . You know better than me how to organize a campaign, but I know better how to win a battle." Carnot argued they had time to turn France into "an armed camp" before the Russians arrived, and that Blücher and Wellington would not move without them, but Napoleon replied, "You're right in principle, but my politics need a stunning strike." Carnot remembered when he had said this before, on the eve of Marengo— "A victory will leave me as master, to do what I want." Carnot took from this that the search for a quick victory had more to do with shutting up the

Chambers than the allies.[96] Carnot had his own form of tunnel vision, but he knew political trouble when he saw it.

With his convulsed realm at his back, and his disheveled army beside him, Napoleon marched to the southern bank of the river Sambre, just below Charleroi. He made his headquarters at Beaumont, in the pouring rain, on the night of June 13–14, the anniversaries of Marengo and Friedland. He issued a bloodthirsty order of the day, recalling those victories, the odds they had all faced together and won against, the arrogance of the allies, concluding, "The rights, honors, and happiness of the nation will be reconquered by arms . . . the moment has come to conquer or perish!"[97] The Bourbons found a riposte. On the night of June 14, the commander of XIV Division of IV Corps, General Louis Bourmont, defected to the allies, along with his chief of staff and his whole headquarters, taking Napoleon's orders with him. They were questioned and sent on to Blücher, most of whose staff did not trust Bourmont, thinking it another of Napoleon's ploys. They knew by now where he was and what he meant to do, in any case.[98] It pulverized the French, however. Quick thinking by the senior officer who had not defected, General Étienne Hulot, got the news to Gérard, the corps commander. Rudderless, the division needed clear leadership. Gérard rallied them well, and got them going forward into action.[99] There were ripples of unease throughout the army. Napoleon had told Soult only a few days before to be emphatic in his circular to the troops, that the flight of the Bourbons and their appeal to foreign powers for support "destroys all the undertakings that might have been made to them," adding, "Without this phrase, I think this order of the day could do you harm in the eyes of shady men."[100] Bourmont's defection confirmed many such fears. Neither Soult nor Davout trusted Bourmont, and both opposed his appointment; Bourmont had fought with the Chouans before rallying to the Consulate, but went over to the Bourbons in 1814. As Napoleon approached Paris, in March, Bourmont—"confident from his experience in the Vendée"—even proposed leading a party of sharpshooters to ambush and kill Napoleon.[101] Napoleon had usually deployed him well away from France, but in 1815, he needed good commanders, and this was the price he paid.[102]

Carnot was stunned by his appointment, and by Napoleon's largesse when he found his sons' places and grants to attend an elite lycée: "Are you sure?" to which Napoleon replied, "That was then." Carnot pointed to Napoleon's ability to admit his mistakes—which he did over Bourmont—and his "natural generosity, when his own person was not in play."[103] Now was such a time, however. It was probably no coincidence that the following day, Napoleon wrote to Joseph, "The confiscation of the properties of the traitors . . . in Ghent is necessary."[104] The incident bore out the view of one observer that "the soldiers are more Napoleonists than their officers," who shared the fears of the masses of granite about the whole enterprise.[105]

The next day, June 15, was hot and dry. Napoleon got his troops into position to attack the scattered Prussian corps under Hans von Zieten, shielding Charleroi, in the early hours, entrusting the right wing to Grouchy and the left, to Ney. Napoleon and the guard held the center, supported by Vandamme and Lobau. The French were successful, and drove Zieten back by overwhelming force. Blücher and Wellington were caught off-guard, not by an attack per se, but by its swiftness. Zieten fell back in good order, but the fall of Charleroi drew Blücher out of Namur, as he rushed to support him, and so put himself in a dangerous forward position, exposed to a full French onslaught.[106] When Wellington did not react as quickly, Napoleon felt he had achieved the important objective of driving a wedge between the two armies. Accounts agree that Napoleon was at ease with the day's results,[107] but he was also reported as exhausted, worn out. He forced himself into the saddle at midnight, however, convinced there would be "a very important affair tomorrow."[108]

Chareloi revealed a myriad of flaws. Napoleon's orders were extremely complex: The central front was only five kilometers wide, so the timing of each division's advance across the bridges over the Sambre had to be precise to avoid congestion, but commanders took their own initiative, moving too early or too late. The attack began well before dawn, and units got lost in the dark. It proved too much for Soult. Orders arrived late or not at all; nor were they issued in duplicate, as Berthier had always done, knowing that one courier might not get through. Units ordered forward in the small hours did not reach the bridges until midafternoon. When they got there, the Prussians were waiting. They were taken too much by surprise to destroy the bridges, but reacted quickly to hold them. The light cavalry sent in first were easily driven back. Reille and d'Erlon then battled their way across the bridges after fierce hand-to-hand combat in the punishing summer heat.[109] The tide was turned by the arrival of Napoleon and the Young Guard, because Vandamme had not turned up, and he blamed Soult's confused orders for it.[110] It took the Marines and Sappers of the Guard to clear the main bridge. The early use of the guard was never a good sign.

Ney and Grouchy were well removed from Napoleon, and they did not do well. On the right, Grouchy overestimated the Prussian force before him, and did not attack until late in the afternoon, much reinforced and chided by Napoleon. By then, the Prussians had begun an orderly withdrawal. As for Ney on the left, he had barely arrived at the front, but was rushed into service. He was well behind the rest of the army, and reached Avesnes by coach only on June 14, to get the news that Napoleon needed him quickly. Unable to find a horse, he had to travel in a peasant's cart until he met the stricken Mortier, now relieved of command, from whom Ney bought a horse to get him the rest of the way.[111] Napoleon gave him verbal orders only, and sent him off to the front. Ney stayed out there, on his own, sticking to what he claimed were his orders, to push the Prussians up the road to Brussels. It all ended at dark, with the Prussian force intact, if in retreat. Reille and d'Erlon remained unsure whose orders they were under that day, Ney's or Napoleon's. Ney halted at Gosselies, just north of Charleroi, sent his report to Soult about 10:00 P.M., and went to bed.[112] It is not clear, even today, how far north Napoleon wanted Ney to push,[113] but the result was that allied troops were not dislodged from Quatre Bras, a cluster of farmhouses. It was also a crossroads, as the name suggests, where the north-south road from Charleroi to Brussels crosses the east-west road from Namur to Nivelles, and it was still in allied hands while Ney slept.

After Charleroi, the Prussians fell back to the northeast; alerted to Napoleon's advance, Wellington's army retreated northwest. Napoleon did not grasp that they were following a clear plan of their own. Wellington had been in—often acrimonious it must be said—talks with the Prussians since early April with Gneisnau, Blücher's chief of staff, who never overcame his distrust of Wellington.[114] He knew Blücher would soon arrive to take over command, and found it difficult to commit to any of Wellington's firmer ideas. However, one important point of agreement was reached, and it was no small achievement: Gneisnau saw, like Wellington, that if attacked, they had to make a stand to stop Napoleon taking Brussels, for diplomatic as much as military reasons. To do so, they had to coordinate intensely.[115] Blücher arrived on May 1, and met Wellington at Tirlemont two days later. Their meeting took place in the wake of a mutiny by two thousand Saxon troops in Liège under Prussian command, incensed at the prospect of part of their country being handed to Prussia, and themselves integrated into the Prussian army. Cries of "*Vive Napoléon*" rose from their ranks. They drove Blücher from the town, his then headquarters. It took several days and ten Prussian battalions to subdue them. A few Saxons fell back into the heavily wooded Meuse valley and held out for some days more. Blücher shot seven ringleaders and burned the Saxons' colors in front of the assembled prisoners. There were twelve thousand more Saxons in his army, and news of the spectacle disaffected them, to the point that they had to be shipped back to Germany. Until they were, Blücher had to detach considerable manpower to guard them. On the eve of talks with his ally, Blücher was deprived of 20 percent of his effectives. Napoleon's loss of Bourmont paled into insignificance. The initial promise to Wellington of eighty thousand men was now impossible,[116] but Wellington remained clear that it should not affect their ability to stop the French. Blücher agreed. Cooperation was promised, but it remained vague while they concentrated their scattered units. However, when Napoleon struck, they knew their respective zones of operation, and their priorities: Blücher would stand at Ligny; Wellington would hold the roads to Brussels.

It took some hours for definitive news that Napoleon had attacked at Charleroi to reach both men. Blücher was in Namur; Wellington at a ball in Brussels with his current mistress, Lady Frances Wedderburn Webster, which he did not leave. He wrote his first orders from the dinner table.[117]

Wellington knew nothing of the outcome at Charleroi, and stuck to his plan to concentrate his forces around Nivelles to hold the road.[118] He assumed Nivelles was at risk, and created a reserve behind it that could move toward any of the main routes, if threatened. His first orders shifted the bulk of the army toward the Prussians, but at the cost of weakening the western sector, and he advised Louis XVIII to be ready to flee Ghent at short notice.[119] It was only in the afternoon of the 15th that the advance units in Quatre Bras and Nivelles learned that Charleroi had fallen. The Dutch commanders in Ney's path, Constant and Hendrik George de Perponcher, were unsure whether to counter the advance at Nivelles as ordered, or at Quatre Bras, the fate of those first to know. Quatre Bras was lightly defended by only one thousand men and eight guns, but Constant took the initiative; he sent reinforcements and redeployed his other troops to support its commander, Prince Carl Bernhard of Saxe-Weimar-Eisenach. Their efforts put seventy-seven hundred men and sixteen guns at the ready.[120] As Wellington left Brussels early on the 16th, no one could tell him about the fate of the Prussians, but the Prince of Orange had gone up to Nivelles and Quatre Bras and soon gave Wellington his first clear news. He then started to move the bulk of his army to the danger zone between Quatre Bras and Nivelles, drawing them too close to Blücher for Napoleon to ignore.[121] The morning of June 16 was a scramble in the allied ranks, but it was not blind panic.

Ligny, June 16, 1815: "A Very Important Affair"

If Wellington was uncertain about where the blow might fall, Blücher was not. He came to the meeting at Tirlemont intent on fighting at Ligny, northeast of Charleroi.[122] The hour to do so had come. This was Napoleon's "very important affair."

Ligny is the largest of several small villages strung out along a brook of that name, with gradually rising ground behind them, a good artillery position. Blücher took advantage of it, installing most of his artillery on the heights.

The villages ran in an arch from Wagnlee in the east, through Le Hameau, Saint-Amand, and La Haye, to Ligny in the west. The bridges across the brook were fortified, as were the villages behind them, every house's walls potted with loopholes for snipers, each street, a gauntlet to be run by an attacker. Fortified villages were always among the grizzliest Napoleonic battlescapes, and so it proved at Ligny. Blücher kept this ground in his pocket for just such a day. His forces contained many raw recruits, *landwehr* militiamen, who were no match for French veterans in open combat, but well able fight at close quarters, where pure guts counted for more than drill.[123] Into this front line, about eleven kilometers wide, Blücher poured everything he had in the course of the morning, about 83,000 men in position, and 224 cannon.[124] He was chafing at the bit to give Napoleon the big battle they both wanted.

Having first assumed that Zieten's men in Saint-Amand were only a rear guard, Napoleon was delighted when he discerned Blücher's intentions. It meant altering his plan, which had been to strike at Wellington, but catching the whole Prussian army was too good to miss. Even so, he was outnumbered; when he detached Gérard's IV Corps from Ney and added them to Grouchy's forty thousand men, he could still only pit 63,000 men and 244 guns against Blücher. Ney was initially ordered to push on to Brussels, but Napoleon's plan now hinged on him making short work of token opposition at Quatre Bras, and then arriving to finish off Blücher. Ney had assured Napoleon there were only three thousand men holding Quatre Bras.[125] Napoleon also had to hope that his sudden change of plan was not too complex for Soult or his field commanders. For his part, Blücher knew his front was overextended, and to hold it safely, he, too, counted on help, certainly from Bülow's corps of thirty-one thousand men from Namur and, less hopefully, from Wellington. Wellington met Blücher briefly about midday under the windmill at Brye. At that point, neither was clear what Napoleon would do, but both knew that, as imposing as Blücher's host seemed, should Napoleon swing all his army against it, Wellington would be needed. Quatre Bras was the best position to reach Blücher from, but Wellington's reserve could not get there until late in the afternoon, at best. He also made it clear that holding the road to Brussels remained his priority, and departed saying he would help if not attacked, himself.[126] Both protagonists were engaged in a risky business.

The French assault began at 2:00 P.M., in blinding heat, when Vandamme's men attacked Hameau Saint-Amand. They were beaten back by a combination of massed artillery from the heights and infantry fire from the villages, followed by snipers moving through the fields, using the tall wheat for cover. The French rallied, and drove the Prussians out of the village with a ferocious bayonet charge that soon degenerated into hand-to-hand butchery. Sheer weight of numbers won them the village, only for Blücher to saturate it with cannon fire, setting the buildings alight. A Prussian counterattack followed, and drove the French back. Next, the French bombarded Ligny and the heights beyond, to soften it up for their attack and silence the Prussian guns. They wreaked havoc among the Prussians stationed below the heights in open ground, a formation Wellington told an indignant Gneisenau he found unwise. "The Prussians like to see their enemy," he snarled back.[127] The French advanced in columns, drums beating, to be met with murderously accurate fire from the village. All but one column was stopped in its tracks. Trapped in the village square, a hail of fire raining down on them, that column "was soon ejected with great loss of life."[128] Napoleon quickly launched another attack, but had learned his lesson and sent his men in, in skirmish order through the tall crops, making them less of a target. More guns were hurried up. The French fought their way into Ligny, some reaching the central square, but each step was met with a bayonet thrust, checked by sniper fire, thwarted by burning buildings. The fighting had lasted barely two hours, but the casualties were already frightening.[129] Let off the leash in the villages, fighting man-to-man, observers shuddered at the savagery shown by hardened veterans and raw conscripts alike.[130]

By about 3:30 P.M., Napoleon saw he had gained nothing at Saint-Amand, and his failure at Ligny confirmed that Blücher was much stronger than supposed. He had to change course, quickly. He had no reason to believe Ney was in difficulties with Wellington, and told Soult to order him to swing his whole force toward Ligny to envelop the Prussian right. "The fate of France is in your hands," Soult told Ney.[131] The guard was still some distance away, so Napoleon simply commandeered those of Ney's troops closest to Ligny, d'Erlon's corps, which had started its advance an hour late. Napoleon knew they would not be at Quatre Bras yet, but he did not tell Ney what he had done. Only minutes later, he learned that Ney was facing a strong British force; Napoleon had left him without a reserve, and unwarned of the fact. More urgently, he knew Ney was not coming soon, if at all.[132] Girard's division now attacked the Saint-Amand villages, and retook them. Blücher hit back, but the French were dug in, and gave the Prussians a taste of their own medicine. Seeing the Prussians in retreat, Girard charged in pursuit, and was cut down by a bullet through his lung. This only served to rouse his men. Blücher's response was to lead a counterattack in person, screaming, "My children, behave well! Don't allow the great nation (France) to rule over you again! Forward in God's name!"[133] With that, La Haye was recaptured, but not Le Hameau. Blücher had stabilized his line, but at horrendous cost. The fight for Ligny stagnated, too, by late afternoon, "the upper hand passed from one hand to the other . . . by the introduction of more meat to the grinder," in the gruesome, accurate words of the British scholar, Gareth Glover.[134]

Napoleon needed help. He ordered up Lobau's corps and told the guard to be ready to fight. When d'Erlon was spotted, about 5:30 P.M., things were so muddled he was taken for the enemy. Panic ensued, delaying Napoleon's assault. It did not help that d'Erlon arrived later than Napoleon supposed, or that he was moving north, not east as ordered. D'Erlon managed to come to the aid of neither Ney nor Napoleon. The confusion has been attributed by some to Napoleon's illegible handwritten order to him.[135]

It gave Blücher time to regroup. He needed it; his *landwehr* had fought bravely all day in blistering heat and the mounting stench of corpses. It was a dread baptism of fire for many, and they proved themselves, but the old warhorse knew exhaustion when he saw it. His only hope of victory was the arrival of Bülow and Wellington, but Napoleon's delay spurred him to another effort at about 6:30 P.M. The French, themselves on their knees, were driven from Le Hameau and La Haye. Many in Blücher's ranks were stragglers he rounded up, and he led them from the front. Not knowing whether d'Erlon was friend or foe, his left flank crumbling before Blücher, Napoleon unleashed the Young Guard, bands playing and flags flying. Its appearance roused Vandammne's tired men, and both villages were retaken. Ligny was on fire from one end to the other. In the course of this action, Napoleon learned that the mystery corps was d'Erlon's, but it was now heading away from him, toward Ney. Napoleon simply shrugged.[136] As gloom and heavy rain set in, Napoleon thrust six thousand Guardsmen at Ligny, supported by heavy cavalry and sixty guns, spearheaded by the *grognards* of the Old Guard. True to the dark spirit of the day, they bellowed "No quarter!"[137] One officer told his men that he would execute anyone who brought him a prisoner.[138] It proved just enough to break the Prussian lines, and drive them out, by about 7:30 P.M. Blücher could not contain himself. He called together thirty-two squadrons of cavalry, and led them in a furious charge on the guard. With their hallmark calm, the *grognards* redeployed from column and line, into the great squares, the *carrés*, as had first been taught to their predecessors in the Channel camps years before. Their iron discipline and bristling bayonets held off the Prussians, and the attack broke off about 9:00 P.M.[139] It cost them 170 presumed dead, and 400 wounded, 200 of whom tended to their own wounds, amid the piles of rotting Prussian corpses.[140] The battle of Ligny was all but over.

Blücher paid dearly for his daring. His horse, a beautiful white charger given him by the Prince of Wales, was shot from under him, and he lay pinned beneath it, semiconscious, for most of the action. He had only one aide-de-camp with him, and was lucky not to be captured by French patrols, who failed to notice him in the dark. He was then retrieved by a patrol of uhlans, Prussian lancers, and got to safety.[141] His headquarters was in chaos. Gneisenau and the staff had little control over Blücher, but Gneisenau had one clear objective, to stay close to Wellington because he did not trust him: If beaten by Ney, he might bolt for the coast. Gneisenau knew that if he did not get the remnants of the army toward Wellington, the Prussians were doomed. If caught isolated, Napoleon could pick them off. Tilly was mentioned as a possible headquarters, but the disorganized survivors were wandering north, of their own accord, toward Wavre, and so it was designated the rallying point. "The feet of the retreating men had already made the decision for the high command."[142]

About midnight, Napoleon retired to Fleurus, to the Château de la Paix. Ligny was his last victory. The horror of the day is in the casualty figures. Almost no prisoners were taken. Napoleon and Blücher whipped their men into a frenzy, and this was the result. As the French picked over the Prussian corpses, they saw that Blücher had thrown every unit he commanded at them. Only Bülow's corps was intact. Prussian losses are put between sixteen and twenty thousand—between 19 percent and a quarter of Blücher's forces. The discrepancy arises over how to count the eight thousand "missing," who deserted to inflict havoc and harm on the Flemish countryside.[143] The French did not keep detailed figures, but estimates place their losses at between eighty-three and ninety-one hundred. Three divisional commanders and five brigadiers were wounded. One brigadier was killed, as was Jean-Baptiste Girard, who died of his wounds a few days later.[144] Although his losses are proportionate to Blücher's, these were Napoleon's only good troops. At great cost, the Prussians were in flight. But there was another battle raging that day.

Quatre Bras: An Unforeseen Bloodbath, June 16, 1815

By the early hours of June 16, Saxe-Weimar knew Quatre Bras could not be held, but Wellington arrived about 10:00 A.M. and met with the Prince of Orange. Both felt the French were not present in enough strength to pose a threat. Napoleon presumed Wellington was falling back further north to defend Brussels. Soult told Ney he was to ascertain Wellington's route and stay in touch with Napoleon's right wing. Napoleon remained untroubled when he learned that Wellington had sent troops to Quatre Bras; it still appeared lightly garrisoned and Ney could sweep any resistance aside. Ney promptly sent in Reille's corps; d'Erlon was meant to support him, but as has been seen, d'Erlon was well behind Ney. Reille launched four battalions, in columns, at the Dutch lines, driving them back, first to Gemioncourt farm, and then to the crossroads, when French heavy cavalry stormed through fields full of ripe, tall wheat. It looked over by midafternoon, but the arrival of Dutch cavalry and the vanguard of Thomas Picton's 5th division, and then Wellington, himself, stayed Reille's advance.[145] Reille and Ney, both veterans of Spain, were wary of Wellington. As the French approached the woodland around the crossroads, and seeing so many fields high with wheat, they feared Wellington had concealed a stronger force than he showed them, as so often in Spain. The French pressed on, but cautiously. Wellington's reputation allowed the seventy-seven hundred defenders to hold off Ney's twenty-one thousand veterans and sixty guns.[146] A pattern emerged. Where the Dutch were well dug in, around Bossu Wood and the farms, the French found trouble, whereas in the wheat fields along the Namur-Nivelles road, the Napoleonic heavy cavalry reveled in charge after charge against brave but weak defenders, and got nearer the crossroads.

Around 3:00 P.M., Quatre Bras developed into a battle of escalation, as reinforcements poured in from both sides, and both front lines came under pressure. The French were checked at Pierrepont farm, and called up Jérôme's eight thousand-man division to take it. On the allied right, the Dutch holding the Nivelles road under Perponcher, who had borne the brunt of the first attacks with such courage, were wavering until Picton arrived in full force. British veterans relieved them. Wellington now had twenty-one thousand men at Quatre Bras; Ney had twenty-two thousand but needed d'Erlon desperately. Just when Brunswick appeared with more troops on the allied side, Napoleon—oblivious to Ney's real circumstances—purloined his reserve. The British First Guards Division then reached Nivelles. As they began to fall out, the Prince of Orange arrived and told them to get to Quatre Bras. They did so by a forced march in the scorching heat. Many fell by the wayside, but the bulk of the Guards reached the front "by sheer willpower and determination."[147] Ney, meanwhile, was pushing back the German troops holding Bossu Wood. Seeing Wellington's lines weakening, Ney committed his last reserves, still confident d'Erlon would appear. He was met by Picton's, who had been drilled in the tactics of Spain (few had fought there, and several brigades were Hanoverian):[148] as the French advanced in columns, the British line hit them at close range with a deadly volley, followed by a bayonet charge that sent them reeling backward. For Gareth Glover, "the French seemed to have learned nothing."[149] Skirmishers finally halted Picton.

At 3:15 P.M., the very moment Wellington turned from defense to attack, Ney learned that Napoleon had commandeered d'Erlon. He exploded at the poor staff officer Napoleon sent with a written order to take the crossroads, which Ney did not even read until the evening. "Tell the Emperor what you have seen. I am opposed by the whole of Wellington's army. I will hold where I am . . . I cannot promise any more," and made his point about d'Erlon.[150] Ney got orders to d'Erlon to turn around and head for Quatre Bras, saying nothing about Napoleon's orders to him. D'Erlon complied, as Napoleon saw for himself. Ney then went on the attack, throwing first his infantry and then the heavy cavalry at the Brunswick units, and swept them aside, almost reaching the road. The cavalry were rampant, but the 44th Foot stood firm, allowing the French horsemen so close, some said, they could almost touch them, before discharging a devastating series of volleys that all but annihilated them. The Black Watch were not so lucky. Taken unaware by French lancers, their square not fully formed; they were still able to see them off, but only after many isolated men were cut down. The French lancers were known in Spain for taking no prisoners, and many Scots were brutally butchered, even the wounded. Many were jabbed repeatedly. Many wounded allied troops had their throats cut on the field.[151] Reille had a particular predilection for cruelty in Spain, and the sight of red coats may have reignited it.

The French horse made chaotic headway, at one point crashing into a British field hospital and getting perilously close to Wellington. The duke fled, jumping a ditch full of his own men on his horse. The French were ousted from the house containing the hospital by the 92nd Highlanders, with much use of the bayonet. Between 4:00 and 5:00 P.M., some allied units were running out of ammunition, and Ney readied for a last, ferocious assault. He ordered Kellermann's cavalry into a suicidal charge to take the crossroads, at which Kellermann, always an aggressive commander since Marengo, balked, his force now so weakened. Ney, clearly cracking, bellowed at him, "What does it matter! Charge with what you have and ride the enemy into the ground. I'll bring the rest of the cavalry. Go! Go now!"[152] Kellermann did just that at 5:00 P.M. It almost worked. He caught the 69th Foot formed in a line, an easy target for cavalry, because the Prince of Orange countermanded their commander's order to form a square. They were cut to pieces, their colors lost, and probably presented to Ney.[153] Next, the 33rd Foot were swept aside and for a fleeting moment, the French held the crossroads. Ney had not kept his word. Isolated, Kellermann and his men were slaughtered by the artillery of the King's German Legion and the musket fire of two foot regiments. Kellermann's horse was shot from under him, but he got away.[154] It was 6:30 P.M. and even Ney knew it was over.

As Ney received Napoleon's order for the second time, ordering d'Erlon to Ligny, Wellington got his last, timely, infusion of new blood: Hackett's brigade of Charles Alten's 3 Division. He now had thirty-six thousand men and seventy guns in the field.[155] Wellington threw in his hard marching guards, regaining all the ground lost in the morning. By 9:00 P.M. the fighting stopped, the cries and moans of the dying wounded filling the night.[156] The French lost about four thousand men; the allies forty-eight hundred, half of them British.[157] David Chandler called it "a hard fought draw."[158] The French saw it as victory spurned. Napoleon knew nothing of Ney's predicament: "I am fighting the whole Prussian army—Ney's affair is only with Wellington's advance guard,"[159] a pathetic echo of Jena-Auerstadt. Ney blamed d'Erlon but, in the twin battle, Ney was not Davout, nor d'Erlon, Bernadotte; Soult was not Berthier; and Napoleon was not Napoleon without Berthier. He was still a Napoleon too ready to disparage his opponents. The Prussians were no longer the Prussians of Jena; Wellington had brought his winning ways with him to Flanders. Napoleon could not grasp this. He would pay for it.

June 17, 1815: A Pregnant Pause

Napoleon and Wellington awoke on the 17th not knowing what had happened beyond their own sectors. Blücher did not even know where he was. The battered old warhorse halted for the night at Mellery, where Gneisenau found him the next morning. Gradually, the Prussian retreat assumed coherence. Gneisenau was effectively in command of the retreat and did well. Communications between the three corps that fought at Ligny were restored only by midmorning, but news at last reached Bülow's IV Corps that Wavre was the concentration area. The Prussian supply column, adrift for some time, was at last located, and directed there. In the course of the day, the whole army was assembled at Wavre.[160] Napoleon's cavalry patrols left him badly misinformed about this. He was led to believe that the Prussians were in full flight, seemingly confirmed by the large quantities of stores and baggage they dumped as they retreated.[161] Post-battle intelligence had been a problem since at least 1809, and it was no better now. Yet Napoleon accepted the reports, and did not monitor their movements further. Grouchy was sent with thirty-five thousand men to shadow Blücher and keep him apart from Wellington, but the French worked on the false assumption that the Prussians were heading east for Liège and Namur, not north. Grouchy was only partially disabused of this by 10:00 P.M., thinking there were thirty thousand Prussians at Wavre, but the bulk of the army was heading to Namur. Thus, Napoleon was lulled into complacency about Blücher.

He remained in a worse haze about Wellington. When he stirred on the 17th, Napoleon was still convinced that Quatre Bras had been a small-scale encounter. He was inert throughout the morning, "a combination of false optimism and fatigue," for David Chandler.[162] Gareth Glover believes that Napoleon saw how shattered his men were after Ligny, and took a chance to rest them, because he deeply underestimated the Prussians' ability to rally.[163] The weather soon hampered pursuit, sudden torrential rain turning the roads into quagmires. Whatever, Napoleon left his commanders directionless on the night of June 16–17, issuing no orders. His behavior the next morning was simply odd. He toured the battlefield of Ligny, wallowed in the acclaim of his troops, and rambled to his staff about his opinionated new parliament.[164] Soult's poor staff work did not help, but Napoleon was foolish to leave him to his own devices at Fleurus all morning.[165]

The moment Napoleon heard that Wellington had held his ground, and deployed his whole army to do so, he swung into action. He now saw Wellington as his real problem, and saw a chance to catch him. He formed his cavalry into a vanguard, put himself at its head, and raced down the Nivelles-Namur road at breakneck speed toward Quatre Bras, with the infantry following by forced marches. He found Ney and his men barely bestirred.[166] Napoleon berated Ney for his inaction. Ney defended himself: Faced with Wellington's whole army, he could do no more. He had a point. His men were short of food, and he had to let them forage that morning. Ney was probably badly shaken by the desperation of the battle, and the déjà vu of a mauling by Wellington.[167] For his part, Wellington conducted a very orderly retreat, as he often had in Spain, and was organized enough to allow his men to have their breakfast before they pulled out.[168] Good planning ensured there was relatively little congestion on the road to Brussels. Because he did not delay, Wellington's retreat got underway before the rain began. "Napoleon was not so ill as to prevent him thinking straight,"[169] and he soon saw that Wellington had stolen a march on him, literally. He met a British cavalry rearguard, which offered very spirited opposition and inflicted casualties on him. Wellington would not be caught now.

Blücher was not the only one with a piece of ground in his pocket. Wellington fell back to the high ground on Mont-Saint-Jean, near the village of Waterloo. He seems to have spotted this position in August 1814, and probably visited it again, on June 14, just before the fighting began.[170] He had also received assurances from Blücher that two Prussian corps would support him there, if he made a stand. On the night of June 17, Wellington's men bivouacked as best they could, in the open air. Thunder and lightning burst over them, a good omen for the Peninsular veterans. Many of Wellington's victories came after such a night.[171] In the dark and under the downpour, Napoleon gave up the chase about 6:30 P.M. and bivouacked his own men around La Belle Alliance, making his headquarters in the farmhouse of Le Caillou. Initially worried that Wellington would slip away again, in the manner of Bennigsen, Napoleon was reassured when he saw the allied campfires on the slopes of Mont-Saint-Jean. At 4:00 A.M. on June 18, after scouting the forward posts, he at last got Grouchy's dispatch, sent at 10:00 P.M. Despite being six hours behind the Prussians, he assured Napoleon that, even should the main army change course for Wavre, he could prevent it reaching Wellington.[172] Napoleon simply accepted this, and left Grouchy without further orders all night.[173] He now knew the Prussians were within reach of Wellington and himself, but went to bed still "convinced that the Prussian army was a broken reed."[174]

The armies left the stench of death and the smoking ruins of destruction in their wake. Whole villages were reduced to rubble. Fields replete with ripe crops were trampled into pulp, beckoning starvation to come. Streams of refugees, clutching what they could of their lives, filled the roads north.[175] From beginning to end, the wars dealt out misery to all in their path. They began on Flanders' fields, in 1792. Here, they would end, but only after a final day of horror.

Waterloo, June 18, 1815

Napoleon awoke on June 18 on the ridge of La Belle Alliance, to see Wellington atop exactly the ground he chose. He could have done little to prevent Wellington occupying it, but his first mistake of the day was to be happy about it. All those who observed him at breakfast in Le Caillou that morning remarked on his brimming confidence. "If my orders are well executed, we will sleep in Brussels this evening," were words remembered by all.[176] Wellington was, indeed, a cautious general, but he was not the tentative worrywart Napoleon assumed him to be. Soult, in contrast, knew his opponent and was wary. Napoleon rounded on him: "Because you have been beaten by

Wellington you consider him a good general, but I tell you that Wellington is a bad general and the English are bad troops. The whole affair will not be more serious than swallowing one's breakfast."[177] His ingrained prejudices took over. The thought of Blücher routed, and the very sight of Wellington, banished the doubts he felt at his desk in Paris. Those endless defiles of Russians vanished into thin air: "The forthcoming battle will save France and will be celebrated in the world's annals."[178] "Yet once more he was painting pictures in his mind," John Hussey observed.[179] In the saddle, his mind concentrated on the task at hand, but as his vision focused, it narrowed, tipping him into delusion.

Ney saw so few troops on his morning reconnoiter, he assumed Wellington was pulling back. Napoleon knew better, but he underestimated the force arrayed on Mont-Saint-Jean and its environs: he judged only on what he saw. Blücher let Napoleon see his forces at Ligny; Wellington did the exact opposite. As so often in Spain, he hid his reserves on the reverse side of the ridge of Mont-Saint-Jean, not only to protect them from French artillery, but to fool Napoleon as to his real strength. It worked. The main Brussels-Charleroi road dissected the battlefield into two equal parts. To the east of the ridge were several small hamlets, La Haye, Smohain, and Frischermont, with many nooks and crannies around them. Below Mont-Saint-Jean lay two farm complexes on either side of the main road: Hougoumont, to the west, nestling in the valley between La Belle Alliance and Mont-Saint-Jean surrounded on three sides by woods, and La Haye Sainte to the east, closer to the ridge of Mont-Saint-Jean than Hougoumont, with a sand pit behind it. Wellington had occupied and fortified all these structures, although he had not given the same attention to La Haye Sainte as to other positions.[180] On the crest of Mont-Saint-Jean was Soignes Wood, directly behind Wellington's lines. Napoleon was certain he had made a grave error, putting himself so close to a dense woodland, believing Wellington had cut off his own retreat, but Wellington knew the terrain, and foresaw pulling back through its many paths in good order, well covered from French fire. Directly below the ridge was Mont-Saint-Jean farm and, below it, a partially sunken track running parallel to the ridge and covered by a thick hedgerow; it was full of allied troops, concealed from sight. The ridge's slope was gradual enough for cavalry charges and infantry assaults, but the track provided a natural break on any advance, a "speed bump" of sorts. It became the allied front line. When those attacks came, they were funneled upward, toward a curving ridge that was manned on three sides. The valley itself was covered in high standing wheat, used for concealment, was between La Belle Alliance and Mont-Saint-Jean and made for a very narrow battlefield, in marked contrast to Ligny. Wellington's force of 67,000 men and 157 guns[181] was not stretched. It was well-entrenched, but invisible. "This inoffensive gentle ridge almost devoid of visible troops was what the French army was about to attack."[182] Wellington had fashioned a series of deadly traps. John Hussey regards his deployments as "a fine piece of marquetry."[183] Gareth Glover rightly calls it "a battlefield of great subtlety."[184]

That was not how Napoleon saw it. He beheld a small zone of barely five thousand yards, its front lines only fifteen hundred yards apart,[185] near perfect for the blunt instrument for direct assault he proposed to unleash on Wellington with his 73,000 troops and 246 guns,[186] in a series of "unsophisticated frontal blows" in the English understatement of David Chandler.[187] Maximilien Foy, a divisional commander who recorded the staff meeting on the morning of the 18th, quoted Napoleon thus: "I shall play on them with my numerous artillery, I shall charge them with my cavalry to force the enemy to show themselves, and when I am certain of the point occupied by the English nationals, I shall march on them with my Old Guard." If this was not tainted by hindsight, then it shows Napoleon intended to attack in waves, as happened, and that he badly underestimated the allies' mettle.[188] It also reveals that he was not altogether sure where, exactly, Wellington had deployed his men, even on so small a battleground, but he attacked, just the same.

It had stopped raining, and Napoleon intended to strike at 9:00 A.M. The sodden nature of the ground dissuaded him, on advice from Drouot. Napoleon delayed until midday. It was a crucial error, buying Blücher precious time to reach Wellington. Napoleon discounted this danger, sure that the Prussians were still in disarray and too far off. Mounting his white Arab stallion, he reviewed his troops, commander and ranks bristling with confidence. At

11:00 A.M., he returned to Le Caillou, dictated his orders, and handed field command over to Ney. Napoleon has been much criticized for this. His absence from the field has been attributed to illness, which may well have been the case. There are many witnesses to his moments of fatigue and lethargy, bordering on apathy that day.[189] David Chandler dismisses this brusquely as overemphasized by apologists.[190] He was certainly in good form when he took his crucial decisions that morning, and batted away his subordinates' reservations. He chose to absent himself, and his failure to visit the sectors of the field was almost unprecedented. This compounded the problem of Ney. Napoleon knew his foibles all too well, but there was no one else left. It all points to his failure to take the engagement seriously enough at the outset. The British were bad troops, badly led. Ill or well, this prejudice did not leave him and so he mentally downgraded the coming battle in his mind. The real contest had been at Ligny, and he won it.

So, it began. June 18, 1815, was a Sunday. If Napoleon had the edge anywhere, it was in guns, and he unleashed them at 11:30 A.M. At about 1:00 P.M., the bombardment reached its crescendo. These were the twelve-pounders—the heaviest guns—of his "Grand Battery," among them the cherished artillery of the guard, "the Emperor's daughters."[191] Their job was to tear a gaping hole in Wellington's lines before the first attack, led by d'Erlon's division on the sunken track to the east of the road, between La Haye Sainte and Frischermont. They roared at Mont-Saint-Jean, and they were heard in Brussels. There were people in Kent who claimed to have heard them.[192] Grouchy heard them, too, but ignored them and stayed on the tail of the Prussians.

Meanwhile, as the first bombardment raged, something went badly wrong on another part of the field. West of the road, Reille's corps was ordered to envelop Hougoumont, as a diversion from d'Erlon's attack, but Hougoumont was a well-defended position, a potential thorn in his side, and Napoleon wanted it taken. He entrusted this personally to Jérôme and his 6th division of fifty-five hundred men, of Reille's corps. Jérôme led them in at 11:30 A.M., into what developed into a tenacious, costly daylong battle-within-a-battle. He had little idea what awaited him, nor did Napoleon. Wellington needed

Hougoumont to protect his right wing, and fortified it accordingly. The core of Hougoumont was a château, with its high stone walls, two courtyards and four entrances; it northern side was protected by a thick hedge and a sunken track. To the east was an orchard, surrounded by a high hedge; to the south, a large wood. Around the castle was a complex of buildings—kitchens, a barn, a chapel—all turned into redoubts. The Prince of Orange had reinforced the garrison that morning, with a mixture of troops from Brunswick, Hanover, and Nassau, and Wellington sent in thirteen companies of the Coldstream Guards, elite troops and masters of the bayonet, and units of the Scots Guards, about thirteen hundred men in all, placed in the orchard.[193] They were told to hold it at all costs.[194] Jérôme came to battle with a point to prove and a chip on his shoulder. Napoleon had not called upon him after what amounted to his desertion in Russia, and when Jérôme rallied to him in May, he did so "without pretension," saying he would lead a company if that was all his brother offered him. Napoleon gave him a division, but kept him on a tight leash. None of his Westphalien officers were allowed to follow him. "He will have only one German with him, a groom," he told Davout.[195] Jérôme fought well at Quatre Bras and was wounded. Lacking experience, but filled with resolve to fight, he was primed for bloodletting.

Jérôme first attacked the wood, sending in his skirmishers, followed by an infantry brigade, supported by artillery. They drove the German troops holding it across the orchard and back to the château, for the loss of their brigadier. They got close to the walls, but the Coldstreamers sallied forth, and drove the French from the wood. The British guns on the heights then pounded Jérôme's men, but they could not prevent the next, greater frontal assault on the château. The French were slaughtered, but diverted the British long enough for a flanking movement to storm the north gate and almost force it, driving them back inside the walls.[196] When the French reached the walls, crossing a death trap of open ground, some tried to climb into the garden, only to be bayoneted as they did so; others tried to seize the gun barrels that poked out of the loopholes in the wall. No one made it over the wall alive. Next, they tried to storm the gate. Jérôme's vanguard went at it with axes, firing at the defenders from point-blank range where gaps appeared. Led by the legendary Sub-lieutenant, Legros—known to his men as "the Enforcer"—he broke into the courtyard, axe in one hand, sword in the other. Bloodthirsty hand-to-hand combat followed, the French unaware they were unsupported. Isolated, the defenders cut them down from the safety of the buildings.[197] At this point, Jérôme's second-in-command, Guilleminot, advised calling off the assault, but support came from units of Foy's 9th division, and a renewed attack was made between 1:00 and 2:00 P.M. Foy's men got as far as the hedge protecting the orchard, where they suffered heavy losses from musket fire, but battled their way forward, drove the defenders back, and brought up a howitzer to blow open a gap in the defenses. They were stopped by defenders hiding on the edge of the orchard and the eastern wall. The French held the wood and the orchard, at great loss, but the château complex was still in allied hands. Neither Reille nor Napoleon gave any thought to calling off the fighting at Hougoumont,[198] but Reille's corps had been sucked into a secondary action when they were needed elsewhere if Napoleon's "sledgehammer" was to work. The fighting continued, the losses increasing at a frightening rate, but by now, the main action had shifted.

While "the Emperor's daughters" blasted the slopes of Mont-Saint-Jean and d'Erlon's corps got into place to attack the center of Wellington's lines, there was a rustling of the trees in the woods near Chapelle-Saint-Lambert, far on Napoleon's right. Hopes were raised, and swiftly dashed, that it was Grouchy. Instead, Napoleon learned it was the outliers of Bülow's corps.[199] Undaunted, he ordered d'Erlon to proceed, but he sent an urgent order to Grouchy to come up, badly miscalculating how long it would take him to receive it.[200] He remained confident he had time to sweep Wellington from his position, remarking to Ney that although the odds had shortened, they were still in his favor.[201] Nor was this the only problem. "The Emperor's daughters" had roared in vain. Wellington's men were well dug in; they were most certainly unnerved by the noise and the potential havoc—worse than any veteran ever heard, many recalled[202]—but the fearsome cannons had few clear targets; their shells "were often swallowed up into the soggy earth,"[203] and so did d'Erlon no real good. At 2:00 P.M. his men went forward, uphill, just the same. Had he known his plight, d'Erlon would have doubtless given far worse odds on the day's outcome than the 60–40 "for" that Napoleon offered Ney.

The going was heavy for d'Erlon, as his men drove on the farm complex below the ridge of Mont-Saint-Jean. There was about thirteen hundred yards between d'Erlon's four divisions—eighteen thousand men—and the allied front line. D'Erlon made things worse. The normal French formation for such attacks was the flexible mixture of line and column, which gave defenders a relatively narrow target in the head of a column, and allowed the infantry to redeploy easily if attacked by cavalry. Instead, d'Erlon, probably in agreement with Ney, arrayed his men in massive "battalion columns by division": each battalion was placed in line, with only a few paces between those in front and behind; the columns were wide, but shallow—one rank only—but it meant the whole division was packed together tightly, with as many as twenty-four ranks one after the other. There were gaps of about 200 meters between the four divisions, which meant it was difficult to coordinate them. The whole formation was inflexible, it could not adapt easily if attacked by cavalry.[204] The rationale for this deviation from the norm is difficult to know, but the results were soon horrendously clear. The corps set off with d'Erlon at their head, drums beating and in good voice, shouting *Vive l'empereur!*" and "Forward!"[205] Ahead lay no one, or so it seemed. As they climbed the ridge, the French guns had to cease firing, but Wellington's batteries opened up. The allies' guns were few in number, but they were very close and ripped into the tightly packed ranks. In front of them were their objectives, Wellington's forward positions of La Haye Sainte, the ridge, and the hamlet complexes of La Haye and Papelotte. Taking them would break Wellington's center and drive him off the heights, a trusted recipe for a rout.[206] Before them was the hedge, and the Dutch troops behind it now rose and fired, adding musketry to cannonballs. As Bourgeois's division, on the left, passed La Haye Sainte, it was caught in a crossfire from its defenders, the hedge and the sandpit, held by the 95th Foot. Bourgeois's officers were decimated, but his men showed bitter determination, driving the 95th from the sandpit and pushing on to the hedge, where Wellington had placed his weakest units. The Dutch had suffered heavy losses at Quatre Bras, and Bourgeois was now at their throats, his men sensing victory. The Dutch broke, some fleeing into the woods at the top of Mont-Saint-Jean. Behind the Dutch were Kemp and Pack's redcoats, advancing slowly but steadily in line. The French were too disorganized to check them, having scrambled through the hedge, when they received the British volleys. Nor could they regroup when the inevitable bayonet charge followed. Picton was killed by a musket ball immediately, but the attack went on. The front ranks fell to hand-to-hand combat, the French pressed closer to the British by the ranks to their rear, still advancing, with no idea what was happening.[207]

Then, the British cavalry under Edward Somerset charged into the French. On their way to the fray, they rode through the 92nd Highlanders, some of whom grabbed hold of the horsemens' stirrups to carry them to combat, thus endowing the battle with one of its most iconic moments. Kilted, bayonets fixed, they broke the French, and d'Erlon saw two thirds of his men fleeing back down the hill in mayhem.[208] Two eagles were lost, one seized by the Scots Greys, cavalry that Napoleon had so admired on their maneuvers the day before, if the words of a peasant are to be credited. Napoleon was still sure he would cut them to pieces.[209] He almost got his wish. The British cavalry, all units of the Union Brigade, charged on in a rush of blood, toward the French guns. They were out of control and even rode down some of their own infantry.[210] They were met by a French cavalry counterattack. The lancers came in first, spearing their targets, followed by the cuirassiers, the big men on the big horses, who set about the disheveled British with their dragoon swords. Napoleon timed this to perfection. Sir William Ponsonby was caught by lancers, surrounded, and killed, perhaps speared, perhaps shot.[211] His magnificent brigade collapsed around him. Drawn from all three kingdoms—hence its name—the Union Brigade now ceased to exist. The Scots Greys, Inniskilling Dragoons, 1st Royal Dragoons, and 2nd Royal North British Dragoons, rode twenty-five hundred strong against d'Erlon, and lost almost one thousand men in one action.[212] The survivors were saved when the Dutch troops who had been routed by d'Erlon rallied, and extricated what was left of them to safe positions on the ridge. The French, too, fell back.

A ferocious struggle developed around La Haye Sainte, the fortified farm complex on the crossroads, and the pivot of Wellington's line. It was held by four hundred men of the King's German Legion, mostly Peninsular veterans, under Major George Baring, a Hanoverian with a penchant for dueling and a veteran of the bitter fighting at Albuera.[213] D'Erlon saw its importance, and directed about two thousand men under Colonel Claude Charlet, to take it. Unlike Hougoumont, La Haye Sainte was not a discrete operation that got out of hand but, potentially, the key to Napoleon's plan. La Haye Sainte's buildings were solid, its courtyard was surrounded by a high stone wall, and its southern approach was shielded by an orchard, but Wellington had left it with weak points in his haste to shore up Hougoumont, diverting his engineers from it to Hougoumont, most crucially with one of its gateways unprotected after the men had torn down the gate for firewood on the night of June 17. There was only a makeshift barricade in place when battle began. Nor was any artillery positioned there. Exposed and easily cut off from support, no one thought about keeping the garrison supplied with ammunition. Napoleon knew its value to him and was unambiguous that d'Erlon had taken it, but gave no precise thought as to how, probably thinking that the sheer weight of d'Erlon's onslaught would sweep its defenders aside.[214] Astride the main road, on the edge of both sectors, Reille might normally have been expected to launch a parallel attack on it, but the escalation of fighting at Hougoumont extinguished any such hope.

The first French assault came after d'Erlon had driven the Dutch lines back toward the crest of Mont-Saint-Jean. He sent skirmishers, supported by cavalry, into the orchard, attacking from the east. Another column attacked the main gate and the buildings along the road, supported by cavalry. Baring positioned his men lying down in the orchard to present a smaller target, as he had learned in the Peninsula. It was a duel of the rapid fire of French muskets against the more accurate, but slower, British Baker rifles, and the French got the better of the first exchanges in the orchard but the defenders cut down the

French in droves when they attacked the buildings from the road. Baring led the fighting in the orchard and, although outnumbered, he held his ground, but taking heavy casualties, he withdrew to the farm buildings. The French on the road made for the main gate, led by Lieutenant Vieux, an engineer and alumnus of the prestigious Polytechnique, who set aside his scientific expertise for the moment, and went at the gate with an axe until he was wounded; another soldier took his place. Close to the walls, the French fell in droves, the dying and wounded writhing in agony as it proved impossible to recover them. The first attack had been beaten off.

At about 1:30 P.M., Wellington positioned himself above the crossroads under a tree known thereafter as "Wellington's Elm." He saw the danger immediately: As d'Erlon was driven back, several units attempted to relieve La Haye Sainte, but they were caught by French cavalry and badly mauled. A handful of men from the Lüneburg battalion made it into the shelter of La Haye Sainte, but more as disheveled refugees than reinforcements, their comrades scattered or cut down by the cuirassiers. The French swept into the kitchen garden on the north side of the buildings. To the south, the French now held the orchard, which brought them close to the broken, ill-defended barn door.[215] Only a makeshift blockade blocked the entrance, and it was fought over ferociously, as was the barn. The French who battled their way into the courtyard were slaughtered by fire from all sides. In macabre irony, the barn gate's barricade was now strengthened by the corpses of the French.[216] On the roadside, the French built barricades of their own, making it hard for the defenders to find their targets. Short of ammunition, their numbers dwindling, the end looked in sight for the Germans as d'Erlon at last brought up three batteries of twelve-pounders to simply level La Haye Sainte. The defenders were saved from certain massacre by the turning of the tide in the main sector. The great cavalry charge of the Union Brigade swept the guns away in its wake and bought Baring a brief respite. A company of 180 men of the King's German Legion arrived to bolster the defense, but they brought no ammunition, despite Baring's repeated requests.[217] Shrouded in a haze of gunpowder so thick at times "one couldn't see anything,"[218] saturated in the stench of sulfur and rotting corpses, the defenders of La Haye Sainte drew breath in the brief lull that fell over the whole main sector about 3:00 P.M.

No such lull descended on Hougoumont. About 2:00 P.M., French artillery on La Belle Alliance bombarded the site, setting fire to the roof of the barn, which housed the makeshift hospital. Desperate efforts were made to evacuate the wounded, but those who could not be saved perished in agony, their cries piercing the ears of the defenders, as the heat choked them and shells continued to rain down. Wellington gazed on all this and sent a note scribbled in pencil on a piece of goatskin to Macdonald, his commander there:

> I see the fire . . . You must however keep your men in those parts
> to which the fire does not reach. Take care that no men are lost
> by the falling in of the roof or floors. After they have fallen in
> occupy the ruined walls inside the garden: particularly if it should
> be possible for the enemy to pass through the embers in the inside
> of the house.[219]

He was obeyed. A junior officer stood in the barn door, his sword drawn, forbidding anyone to leave, and relented only as the floor gave way beneath him.[220] Regrouped, they fought on as more French troops were funneled into Hougoumont. They hacked their way into the barn and the south courtyard, where the Nassau troops took them on hand-to-hand, soon supported by Guardsmen fleeing a fire in the château. Those Frenchmen who did not fall back before the gate was shut were butchered. A renewed French assault swept the orchard, only to be thrown back by the Coldstreamers. Foy's men struck back, but were halted by fire from the Coldstreamers and the Nassauers holding the garden wall. Jérôme, seeing the complex in smoldering ruins, threw his men at them, only for them to be cut down in a ruthless crossfire. This was the last major assault, but no one could know that.[221] Quiet came to what remained of Hougoumont by about 4:00 P.M.

Both commanders had had their hearts in their mouths by then. Wellington saw how close d'Erlon came to breaking his lines, and watched in impotent rage as the flower of his cavalry destroyed itself. He had seen La Haye Sainte almost fall. Yet, he had met Napoleon's challenge and survived. Napoleon observed not only his main assault thrown back in ruins, but his strategy with it. D'Erlon's corps lay in bloody tatters, all its gains retaken. Only Pierre François Joseph Durutte's division, on the far right, achieved any degree of success, when it took Papelotte and held part of it against several attacks.[222] Significantly, Durutte had not drawn up his men like the other divisions, but in the more flexible column and line.[223] In the main sector, only Lobau's corps—now needed to shadow Bülow—and the Guard were relatively unscathed. His guns and gunners had been mauled badly in their brief encounter with British cavalry. Hougoumont continued to suck in Reille's corps, depriving Napoleon of between ten thousand and thirteen thousand men.[224] Casualties were difficult to calculate, so many corpses were charred by the fires beyond recognition, but the ditches were said to be full of British defenders, and the road piled high with the French. The allies lost as many as 850 men, perhaps double; the French as many as sixty-five hundred.[225] Had Jérôme prevailed, Wellington's front would have been dangerously extended, but he did not, while Reille's corps was badly damaged, and still in the same place.

What Wellington saw as he surveyed his lines was a weakened position that might well give way. He was still where he was, for all that. In stark contrast to Napoleon, Wellington moved about the combat zones. Ranging along the ridge, he saw both La Haye Sainte and Hougoumont for himself and responded accordingly. Napoleon did not budge from La Belle Alliance, thus unable to see Jérôme's repeated, flailing assaults or how long it took d'Erlon to think of using cannon against La Haye Sainte. It was, to put it mildly, very out of character. Unlike Wellington, by about 3:00 P.M., Napoleon needed an entirely new battle plan. The sledgehammer had failed, and been broken in the process. He was already running out of ammunition at Ligny, and went into Waterloo in dire straits. On the 17th, he told Davout to strip the northern fortresses of all he could find, but his orders were not dispatched until the afternoon of the 18th, in the midst of the battle. By then, his ranks were thinning; he ordered the 7th division—shattered at Ligny and bereft of Girard, their dying commander—up to the front. Then word came that Grouchy could not possibly reach him in time to fight that day, news that shook Soult to his core. Napoleon, "wasteful and extravagant," was running out of time, ammunition, and infantry.[226] He could break off the battle or try to end it quickly. Taking the latter course without hesitation, he turned to his heavy cavalry to smash Wellington's lines, and so ordered La Haye Sainte to be taken at all costs, but he left the details to Ney.

Ney rallied about three thousand men from d'Erlon's corps while artillery blasted away at the stout walls of La Haye Sainte, walls so thick no cell phone can work inside them today.[227] Ney threw his infantry at those walls at about 3:30 P.M., but they were hurled back with great losses, charging at the open gateway into the barnyard, clogged with the dead of the earlier attack. Ney galvanized the exhausted, wavering troops. The German defenders remembered their courage and ferocity, and they nearly prevailed. Some fought their way to the walls of the barn and forced the defenders back, using the loopholes against them to fire into the barn.[228] For all that, yet again no one thought to use light artillery on the gate. Ney's insistence on unsupported bayonet charges was "using a hammer to drive in a screw."[229] Courage and numbers took their toll. Running low on ammunition, the sheer weight of the French bearing down on the gate, the garrison was saved by, of all things, a massed French cavalry attack.

While the battle raged around La Haye Sainte, Ney assembled almost every regular cavalry unit on the field, including the light cavalry of the Guard—Napoleon's most spoiled children, the mounted chasseurs, among them—for a massed attack on the center of Wellington's line. At 4:00 P.M., forty-five hundred cuirassiers and five hundred light horse[230] charged up the steep slope, on sodden ground, bereft of infantry or artillery support. They galloped to the west of the main road, riding between Hougoumont and La Haye Sainte, under crossfire from both. Both garrisons breathed sighs of relief as the French host swept by, halting infantry attacks and shelling long enough for them to shore up their defenses.[231] Wellington saw what was coming. He pulled his men back from the ridgeline and formed them into squares, their front lines with fixed bayonets to keep cavalry at bay, their rear ranks with loaded muskets. He interspersed artillery between them, ordering the gunners to hold their fire as long as possible to wreak havoc on Ney, then either to scatter into the squares or hide under their guns until the attack ended. There were heavier guns behind them, on the highest ground.[232] It was a dangerous practice, requiring not just nerves of steel by the gunners, but in their having faith in their comrades in the squares not to give way. Without infantry support, and only one horse artillery battery, Ney was on a glorious suicide mission, and the cavalry commanders told him so, but when the guard light cavalry joined them—and only Napoleon could order this—they assumed Ney had Napoleon's agreement.[233] Desperate men do desperate things, and Napoleon was increasingly such a man. The battle had to end soon and this seemed not his best option, but his only hope.

It did not look hopeless to the troops awaiting the onslaught. As Ney's host cleared Hougoumont and La Haye Sainte, across those few yards before the ridge, the fighting died down and the French guns fell silent. All that could be heard was the steady trot of the horses, the clanking of the armor. Then, suddenly, they crested the ridge, their breastplates, plumed helmets, and sabers glinting. "Not a man present who survived could have forgotten in after life the awful grandeur of that charge . . . which, ever advancing, glittered like a stormy wave of the sea when it catches the sunlight . . . the very earth seemed to vibrate beneath their thundering tramp," wrote one British guardsman.[234] It did not last long. The guns between the squares let loose canister shot, round after round. The carnage was terrible, horses and men falling and writhing in agony, but still the French came on, only to receive musket fire from the squares. The charge as an exercise in shock and awe failed. The squares held firm, their ranks held their fire until they could almost feel the horses' breath on their faces. The gunners stood their ground, blasting Ney's men before scampering for the safety of the squares. A British private recalled, "the cavalry was the boldest we ever seed [sic], charged us many times, but we stood like a rock."[235] Many squares were badly battered, but there is no evidence even one was broken, still less destroyed.[236] The French fell back behind the ridge, reformed, and came again. Their horses tired, their ranks dispersed, a lacklustre charge by British light cavalry from behind the squares was enough to push them back over the ridge. It was far from over. Napoleon saw Ney's men repulsed, not once, but twice, yet he did not call off the attack. Instead, he ordered in Kellermann's cuirassiers and the heavy cavalry of the guard, his only mounted reserves.[237] Ney came at the allied lines again, and again, and again, for two hours. It is anyone's guess how many times.[238]

This was now a battle of wills. Ney led from the front, four horses shot from under him;[239] Wellington moved about the lines, cajoling, encouraging, simply being there as squares wavered and gunners' nerves frayed,[240] as once Napoleon had done. Allied nerves held; the gunners came and went with the charges, reloading and firing with murderous effect.[241] The French, worn out, increasingly just milled around the squares, tempting the ranks to fire at them unordered, hoping that they could prise them open, while the muskets were reloading, but to no avail.[242] The allied infantry learned fast: to fire at the horses offered a bigger target than the armored cuirassier, turning them into "upturned turtles."[243] It was Agincourt all over again. Discipline held, but if the squares presented an implacable face to Ney, "inside (them) we were nearly suffocated and smell from the burned cartridges . . . the loud groans of our wounded and dying were most appalling," one officer recorded.[244] The corpses of men and horses were piled up to buttress the squares as the death toll mounted. Slowly, what was left of Ney's force withdrew. Yet, even as their power waned, the cuirassiers could still strike terror by their very existence. When Wellington ordered a Hanoverian hussar regiment to charge them, in hopes of a complete rout, they outright refused, wheeled about, and rode all the way back to Brussels, where their appearance created panic.[245] There was no panic among the debris of the cavalry, just numbed exhaustion. The great gamble had failed. Napoleon watched on in horror, later claiming lamely that the attack had been premature. He lied.[246]

About 5:00 P.M., both commanders heard rumblings to the east. The Prussians were coming. For Wellington, it could not have come soon enough. He had held firm, but was unable to take the offensive. Napoleon's first reaction to Ney's failure was to order him to take La Haye Sainte. Just after 6:00 P.M., Ney went at it, and for the first time that day, he did so with a handful of cavalry and a few guns to support the infantry, "at last . . . the correct tactical formula."[247] It was as if it had taken all this time, and so much blood, to remind him of the lessons of the Channel camps. The guns blasted the buildings, driving what was left of the King's German Legionnaires into the courtyard. They saw Bülow's men coming in the distance, but ahead of them were two large columns of d'Erlon's corps, now free to climb over the walls and batter the gates almost unopposed, as the defenders, short of ammunition, had to slacken their fire. They still had their bayonets, and the first French troops into the yard were dispatched with cold steel; those first over the walls got the last rounds of ammunition. With so many officers dead or wounded, the order was given for the defenders to make for the allied lines individually. Only a handful fought their way out as units, one group fighting hand-to-hand with exhausted French troops, hacking their way through a narrow passage, giving and taking sword slashes to the face along the way. The French swarmed into their prize, hurriedly making it ready to repel a counterattack and to use it as a pivot for a new assault on the allied lines.[248] They took over what must have looked like an abattoir, not just from the corpses strewn about, but from those piled high as barricades. It would have smelled like an unsanitary pork butcher's, the charred flesh of the men incinerated in the buildings mingling with the sulfur.

Wellington now had a new nightmare. The Dutch troops sent to relieve La Haye Sainte were beaten back with heavy losses.[249] The Brunswickers who had held the center of the line so well for so long were beginning to crack, and Wellington—sharp enough to sense this—rushed in a brigade of the King's German Legion and a British brigade to replace them. Holding the crossroads was now imperative, and Lambert's brigade was placed there. The central position was held by the Inniskilling Foot—750 men in all—ordered in a square to withstand a charge. Instead, it was raked ruthlessly by Ney's guns, only 300 yards away.[250] Unable to fire a shot in defense, they lost 68 percent of their total: 71 percent of their officers and 63 percent of their ranks. An officer reported them "lying literally dead in a square."[251] They were told to hold at all costs, and did so. Wellington had now committed all his reserves simply to stop Ney. Like Napoleon, he had almost no heavy cavalry left. It was a matter of holding on until help came, and it did.

Napoleon had not even that ray of light by 6:00 P.M. Ney pleaded with him to commit the reserves and exploit the seizure of La Haye Sainte while Wellington was swaying. "Troops! Where do you want me to get them from? Do you want me to make you some?" came the sarcastic, exasperated response.[252] In fact, there were some. For some reason, all too typical of the chaos on La Belle Alliance, both men had forgotten the existence of many of Reille's units, left idle to the west of the main road throughout the day, who might have been used to great effect more than once. How or why this happened cannot be known, but it smacked of incompetence at every level. There was also the Imperial Guard. But now came the Prussians, that "broken reed."

The eastern sector was quiet for most of the day. Wellington anchored his left flank along an arch of hilly, woody, easily defended terrain between the villages of Papelotte, La Haye, and Frischermont in the north, to Plancenoit at its southern edge. It was held by thinly spread troops, mainly from Nassau, under Saxe-Weimar. Opposing them were light cavalry and skirmishers, backed by Lobau's division. The northern villages had been fought over, changing hands in the course of the day, but the sector was never allowed to escalate in the manner of Hougoumont. That changed dramatically, as Bülow's brigades filtered in to the area from 3:00 P.M. onward. By late afternoon, they amounted to about thirty thousand men, soon outnumbering the French two-to-one. Bülow struck at Plancenoit. This was one of the less spectacular, but most decisive points in the battle. Should the village be taken by Bülow, Napoleon's line of retreat would be cut. From 4:30 P.M. onward, Napoleon had all his commanders screaming in his ears. Ney's price of success was more men for the center, to finish off Wellington, or so he assumed; Lobau, in the east, raised the terrifying prospect of Prussians to his rear, a very real prospect, as his lines began to crack from 5:00 P.M. onward. They wanted more men, and they wanted them now. Ney's judgment had been dubious all day, but a captured

Prussian hussar made it clear the blue coats descending on Plancenoit were Bülow's, not Grouchy's, and they were attacking, pushed into it by Blücher, against Bülow's wishes, as much to relieve the pressure on Wellington as to cut off Napoleon's retreat.

It worked. Napoleon ordered forty-five hundred men of the Young Guard division under Duchesme to Plancenoit. By then, the village was in Prussian hands, but the Guard launched into street fighting, retaking the key position of the church, and clearing the houses of their defenders with the bayonet. Their triumph was brief. Nine thousand Prussian line infantry and Silesian *landwehr* counterattacked. Rocked by artillery and sustained fire from the Young Guard, they plowed on, captured the French guns, and drove the guard to the edge of the village.[253] Duchesme was shot in the head. He died in agony, two days later.[254] Two years before, the sight of Silesian *landwehr* routing the guard was laughable, even to Prussian officers. Now, it shook Napoleon to his core. What he could not know was that these troops were at the end of their tethers, having marched since dawn, or that Blücher's call for "forward" left them isolated. Zieten's corps had been following them, but seeing Wellington's dire straits, Karl von Müffling persuaded Zieten to go to Mont-Saint-Jean, not Plancenoit.[255] About 6:00 P.M., two and a half battalions of the Old Guard infantry, barely fifteen hundred men, were told to retake Plancenoit with the bayonet from ten times their number. They did so. The grenadier battalions of *grognards* advanced steadily by platoons, as the exhausted Prussians fell back before "the disciplined fury of the bayonet charge," taking no prisoners.[256] Within the hour, Plancenoit was secure.[257] The Young Guard, smarting from their humiliation, followed, occupying the burning village and cutting the throats of the Prussian wounded.[258] One unit of *grognards* pushed too far forward, and were driven back, but Plancenoit held out for another hour.[259] Each side lost about six thousand men. For Napoleon, among those losses were his very best, his "children." They were soon redeployed.

Napoleon's vision of hell took form: Blücher joined Wellington. His whole strategy collapsed before his eyes, as the blue Prussian coats streamed toward Mont-Saint-Jean. The Prussians had marched all day, jostled with each other through the narrow streets of Wavre—part of which was on fire at one point—slogged along muddy roads, and forded the swollen river Dyle, with their commanders arguing among themselves all the while. Now, they had come to deal Napoleon the death knell, the army he thought he had routed. When the French saw them, Napoleon did what was in his nature, he lied. He told Ney to tell the men that it was Grouchy's corps. He then played his last card. He had twelve battalions of the Old Guard left, and at 7:00 P.M., he sent ten of them against Wellington's central lines; the grognards at Plancenoit joined them. Napoleon's only reserve was now the battalion guarding Le Caillou and another near La Belle Alliance.[260] For the first time that day, Napoleon led his "children" into battle, across the valley toward Mont-Saint-Jean, to within 600 yards of the enemy lines, exposing himself to allied fire.[261] He turned command over to Ney only after his staff pleaded with him not to put himself in further danger. There is speculation he sought a heroic death.[262] That is impossible to know, but his presence galvanized his men. All eyes fell on the guard. The remnants of d'Erlon's and Reille's corps supported their attack; an artillery barrage prepared the way, and what cavalry could be found was deployed. Skirmishers preceded them. Napoleon organized it, and it was the first properly coordinated assault of the day, clear evidence of how sorely his presence around the field had cost him. Wellington was ready. The arrival of the Prussians enabled him to release troops to bolster his battered center. The arrival of the Hanoverian infantry was most welcome, while the First Foot Guards were now able to form a reserve at the crossroads. Wellington, too, now called up almost all his reserves.[263] The troops along the road laid down and took cover; the French guns pounded them with little impact.[264] The French skirmishers went forward, seemingly oblivious to the allied guns, only 600 yards away. Their efforts exhausted Wellington's batteries' ammunition and, as the guns fell silent, the guard took heart. The time had come.

Four battalions of the chasseurs of the guard, in columns, advanced across the ridgeline, following the route of the cavalry charges to the west of La Haye Sainte. They swept through some disorganized British guns, and marched unflinchingly toward what they saw, "a shaky line of British infantry."[265] But with Wellington, things were never as they seemed. At this point, the First Regiment of Foot stood up as one on Wellington's cry to their commander, "Now, Maitland, now's your time!" The *grognards* were only thirty paces away and took the full blast. Its commanders, at their head, fell almost as a man: both battalion commanders and General Michel were killed; General Friant was dragged away wounded; Ney lost his fifth horse of the day. Twenty percent of the ranks fell, at a stroke.[266] The First Foot were on their way to winning their new name, the Grenadier Guards, and the right to wear the same bearskins as the *grognards*. The French stalled, shaken at first, but calmly reformed into squares, and withdrew in good order.[267] The British followed with their usual bayonet charge, which began to break the square, but when support arrived from another chasseur battalion, Maitland pulled his men back.[268] It was the training of the Channel camps against the hard-learned lessons of Iberia.

A second wave came at the British when three guard battalions of grenadiers on the right of the chasseurs struck at the very weakest point of Wellington's line, the exhausted Hanoverian *landwehr*, now short of ammunition. They fell back under the battering of column and line, opening a dangerous gap in the line. The *grognards* seemed unstoppable. The Prince of Orange rallied the men and counterattacked, but was wounded and dragged from the field, the charge disintegrating around him. Wellington's presence on the field alone staved off the worst. He gathered the remains of the cavalry, put them in the path of the feeing Germans, and made them stand. The tide was turned by the Dutch, led by General David Chassé, known to his men as "the Bayonet." Initially placed in reserve, Chassé unleashed his batteries, and then, seeing the peril, threw his whole division at the Guard. Ney met his match. Some judged it a reckless attack; it was certainly bloody.[269] The *grognards* did not break, and a firefight ensued, but Chassé's bayonet charge—a "storm charge" with a ferocious roar from the Dutch—persuaded the Guard to retire, in good order, it is true, but repulsed, as were the Young Guard at Plancenoit, by long-despised opponents.[270]

Now, the remaining guards battalions moved up, hoping to exploit the weakened lines, where the First Foot were not yet reformed. Supported by infantry brought up from Hougoumont, they got further than any other attack that day, but were sent reeling by the initiative of a Peninsular veteran skilled in outpost fighting, who read Wellington's mind. Colonel Sir John Colborne wheeled his 1,000 men of the 52nd Foot around 45 degrees, with the words, "I'm going to make that column feel our fire." With that, he came up alongside the advancing guards—who were fully focused on the First Foot in front of them—and unleashed murderous, unceasing volleys of musket fire into their flank, as one rank leap-frogged the men in front, to let them reload. This startled even the *grognards*, and bought the First Foot crucial time to reform. Then came two simultaneous bayonet charges, by Colborne's men from the side, and the 1st Foot from the front. The guard simply crumpled and fell back.[271] They were seen by all, scrambling down the slope of Mont-Saint-Jean. "The Guard recoils!" went up all over the French lines, and Wellington ordered a full-scale bayonet charge to go after them. As dusk fell, around 8:00 P.M., the unthinkable had happened.

As the guard retreated, Napoleon's lie backfired on him. Those units closest to the oncoming Prussians saw soon enough they had been deceived. Dumbfounded consternation soon turned to blind panic among d'Erlon's battered men. Cries of "every man for himself" reverberated along the disintegrating lines.[272] Napoleon's army, his universe, were turning to dust around him as forty thousand Redcoats, at last, poured down the hill to engulf him, relieving Hougoumont as they went.

All Napoleon could do was rally the remnants of the guard, form them into three great squares, and try to cover the retreat of the debris of his "army of the North." The guard made a last, disciplined stand, Napoleon in their midst for some time. Just as crucially, the Young Guard held out at Plancenoit until about 9:00 P.M., keeping the road south open long enough for many to escape. The allies swept around the squares, and seized the heights of La Belle Alliance while the French scrambled down the southern slope for all they were worth. The British captured the guns there, and turned them on the guard in the valley below. Surrounded, the squares were defiant. When called upon to surrender, one officer, Cambronne, snapped back a term for human waste;

his name was used for a comfort break in polite French society henceforth. The squares soon collapsed. Cambronne, badly wounded and left for dead on the field, found his way into a comfortable English captivity before being repatriated to France.[273] Guardsmen scattered and made their way south in small groups or individually. One battalion made a last stand on La Belle Alliance, another at Hougoumont, before they were both overrun. At 9:00 P.M., Wellington and Blücher met in the inn at La Belle Alliance, but it was too dark and the allies were too exhausted to pursue the French much beyond the field. By 9:30 P.M., Napoleon left the field escorted by Polish lancers. He made, first, for Genappe, his designated rally point. When he found it in chaos, he pushed on through the deranged debris of the army, to Philippeville on horseback, leaving his coach and its contents to the mercy of the Prussians. He got there about 1:00 A.M. on the 19th. So began a flight that ended on Saint Helena.

Behind him was the last great carnage of a war begun in 1792. Hougoumont, Plancenoit, and La Haye Sainte had been pleasant, prosperous places that Sunday morning. Now, they were smoldering, stinking ruins. More than forty-three thousand men and over twelve thousand horses lay dead across the battlefield, in some places so deep they had to be trod over. Ripe crops lay crushed beneath them. The sight was surpassed in horror by the stench, and by the noises of the dying, the helpless, the maimed, running from agonized screams to muffled whimpers. Among them moved scavengers, stripping the dead and dying of anything of value. Had Wellington brought Goya with him as a war artist, the horror might have found true expression. It wasn't the eagle who flew from church spire to church spire. It was the angel of death. The great commanders and their hosts would not linger long here. Now, all roads led to Paris.

18

A LIFE UNRAVELS

Retreat, June 19–22, 1815

After Napoleon got some sleep at Philippeville in the early hours of June 19, he wrote to Joseph:

All is not lost. I suppose that when I unite my forces, there will be 150,000 men. The *fédérés* and the national guards who have spirit will give me 100,000 men; the battalions in the depots, 50,000. I will have 300,000 men to oppose the enemy immediately . . . I will raise 100,000 conscripts; I shall arm them with the rifles of the royalists and the bad national guards; I will hold *levées en masse* in Dauphiné, the Lyonnais, Burgundy, Lorraine, the Champagne; I will clobber the enemy, but someone has to help me . . . I will head for Lyon; I will surely find people there . . . I can have 50,000 men in three days, and with that I can buy Paris and France time to do their duty. The Austrians are marching slowly; the Prussians fear the peasants and dare not advance too far; it can all still be put right. Write to me about the effect this horrible scuffle will have had on the Chamber (of representatives). I believe that the deputies will be aroused to see that their duty . . . is to unite with me to save France.[1]

If Napoleon thought Blücher feared peasants, or advanced cautiously, he did not know his man, even after all these years. Later that day, Blücher wrote to his young wife, ". . . with my friend Wellington, I at once put an end to Napoleon's dancing. His army is completely routed . . . I had two horses killed under me yesterday. It will soon be over with Bonaparte."[2] The next day, he had two corps in Chareloi.[3] He kept it to himself that he meant to beat Wellington to Paris, their agreed goal. His supply lines stretched to breaking point, Blücher ordered his men to live off the land, and they obeyed with alacrity. The peasants fled in terror, as if mocking Napoleon's vision. Wellington moved more slowly, to preserve his supply chain as was his wont, but move he did. Napoleon's supplies were all but exhausted, while Wellington was able to provision not only himself but Blücher with munitions and a bridge train to ford the many rivers between Paris and himself.[4] Soult found it impossible to reform at Philippeville, and the rallying point was redesignated at Laon.

Napoleon always loved numbers. Now, his passion for them blotted out reality. His words to Joseph are an exercise in how to lie to yourself with statistics. His figures were not fantastical. Released from his desk, Soult did a good job of rallying and reorganizing the remains of the Army of the North in the following days, and did have about fifty-five thousand men in arms by late June. There were, indeed, 117,000 men to defend Paris, and 170,000 new recruits in the depots. After the carnage of Waterloo, Napoleon did still outnumber Wellington and Blücher, who had fifty-two thousand and sixty-six thousand men, respectively. But it was pure numerical advantage, and the tunnel vision that focused on but one sector of the war. Allied and French losses for the entire campaign were roughly equal—sixty thousand for Napoleon; fifty-five thousand for the allies[5]—but these men, killed, wounded, lost, deserted, were almost the only truly combat-worthy troops Napoleon possessed. The Young Guard was all but no more; 62 percent of its officers were lost. Only a handful of the Old Guard remained, but close to two thirds of its officers had fallen or been captured or wounded.[6] The heavy cavalry and their mounts were strewn across Mont-Saint-Jean. Some estimates put French losses at Waterloo, alone, at 40 percent.[7] All this was irreparable. As John Hussey reflects, "even if Wellington had lost the battle the French army would have been so desperately short of leaders that that its ability to continue a campaign against any half decent military force would have been in question."[8]

This is not to say the Army of the North had no fight left in it. Out of his brother's shadow stepped Jérôme. He withdrew from Hougoumont in good order, proved a great help to Soult, and rallied six thousand men to him at Laon by June 21. In the dying hours of the battle, amid the death throes of the "family project," Napoleon at last told him, "My brother, I regret that I only came to know you so late."[9] The supreme irony was that Grouchy's corps of about thirty-three thousand men[10] was now the bedrock of the army. Grouchy stuck to his orders on the 18th, spending most of it without news from Napoleon, battling around Wavre with Thielmann's corps of about seventeen thousand men. Their determined resistance allowed the main Prussian force to continue safely on its slow march to Placenoit and Mont-Saint-Jean. The fighting died away between Thielmann and Grouchy that night, with neither the wiser about the progress of the main battle. They had only rumors to go by, and Grouchy went on the offensive the following morning, driving the Prussians back. On the verge of breaking through, he was at last told of Napoleon's collapse.[11] He withdrew in very good order, but only after a row with Vandamme, one of his divisional commanders, that they push on and take Brussels by surprise.[12] Instead, Grouchy fell back on Namur, conducting a spirited rearguard action. The moment he learned of Napoleon's defeat, he suddenly reverted from a robotic subordinate to the resourceful independent commander he had been in the past, "a thinking general."[13] He stalled the Prussians, burning the bridges at Namur as he withdrew into France on June 22, and conserved his men, now the only hope left.[14] Napoleon added Grouchy to his list of people who lost him Waterloo almost as soon as he began reminiscing on Saint Helena. "He was going to win there. None of his actions presented him with less doubt in his eyes . . . Grouchy lost it . . . No one but himself," Las Cases said of a conversation in early December 1815, in a passage from his manuscript that he did not actually publish.[15] Grouchy duly entered the pantheon of Napoleonic villains[16]—one of the first to put the blame on him was Ney, in the Chamber of Representatives on June 22[17]—but Napoleon owed him a great debt. Grouchy headed first for Soissons, where Napoleon had ordered the Guard to rally, as the last step before Paris.[18] By then, events overtook them all.

Expulsion. June 21–25, 1815

"Someone has to help me," Napoleon blurted out to Joseph. That someone was the government, the elected chambers. Napoleon left Soult in charge, not knowing what had become of Grouchy—he assumed he had been defeated in the same letter—and went to Paris, riding through the night of June 20–21. He assumed that the men he still called "deputies," in a real Freudian slip, were afraid enough of the Bourbons to stand by him. The card he had played since Brumaire, that he was all that stood between them and a restoration, was no longer valid. The "representatives of the people" now made no such equation, and he was abruptly made aware of it.

Pierre Serna is right that Napoleon took a great risk by leaving 625 deputies behind him in Paris when he went on campaign, because this "could incarnate a form of sovereignty." They had already elected one of his most vociferous opponents, Jean-Denis Lanjuinais, as their president, a signatory of the act of his deposition only a year earlier.[19] Fiery debates raged during the campaign over demands to redraft the Additional Act and accusations that Caulaincourt had withheld evidence in a report he gave about the coalition. The legality of the offensive itself was brought into question, one representative asserting that only the legislature had the right to declare war. The atmosphere was like "an anarchic beehive" for one observer.[20] The whole tenor of the debates centered increasingly on asserting the primacy of the chambers over the executive. When the news of Waterloo broke, on June 20, Joseph summoned the council of ministers. He had too little concrete news from Napoleon to take action, but he shut down the press immediately. This could not stop Fouché, who probably knew of Waterloo before anyone, and probably leaked the news to his allies in the chambers.[21] This seems likely, because the demands for national unity made on the floor of the lower house that afternoon made scant mention of Napoleon.[22] The ground was well prepared. The news reached a volatile legislature, Fouché's natural habitat.

About 9:00 A.M. on June 21, an exhausted, disheveled Napoleon, still in his unwashed uniform, stumbled into this when he reached the Élysée, the modern residence of the French president, in a small open carriage lent him by the prefect of Laon.[23] Caulaincourt met him on the steps, and said he got the unbuffered account of the dread day, recorded in an official note: "It was the biggest loss. It was won. The army worked marvels; the enemy was beaten everywhere . . . The day over, the army was seized by a terror, a panic. It's inexplicable . . . Ney acted like a fool . . . They crushed my cavalry just at the moment I needed it . . . Grouchy didn't keep Bülow in check."[24] He slept briefly, then took a hot bath, during which he received his closest advisers, while most of the ministers assembled in the next room. He seems to have had little idea of what awaited him. His confidence may have been bolstered by the large crowd that gathered by the palace gates. The first of his counselors to see him were Davout and Cambacérès. Davout assumed he wanted to know the state of the army, but Napoleon asked, "what they are saying in Paris," to which Davout replied that they had not yet had time to know what had happened. He urged Napoleon to act quickly, to dismiss the chambers before they became a threat, and assume dictatorial powers. Privately, Davout felt Napoleon had already made a crucial error in returning to Paris. He should have remained with the army at Laon, and kept out of the clutches of the politicians. Above all, he needed to meet with his waiting ministers immediately.[25] Cambacérès gave him more concrete news, but rather different advice: "Sire, the Chamber of Representatives is hostile. They have no confidence (in you) and refuse to supply any more men or money, unless they control it . . . Either they must work with you and give you what you ask, or if they are against you, you either have to abdicate or overturn the Revolution . . . If they won't vote you men and money, you have to overstep the bounds."[26] Napoleon took his time to emerge; Davout had to go back in to the bathroom and ask him to hurry up. When Napoleon replied there was no need for haste, as Joseph was in control of things, Davout came close to losing his considerable temper, and Napoleon joined his council.[27] In the bath, he evolved from a man in shock to one in languor.

His brothers were in no such state when they met. Joseph agreed with Davout, that Napoleon should go back to the front and let him deal with Paris, because he could still manage the leaders of the liberals. Lucien agreed with Davout's other point: Napoleon should declare a dictatorship and send the chambers packing.[28] They were both in character in the crisis: Joseph, the diplomat, the consummate political broker of the Directory; Lucien, the hothead of the early years who had landed his family in exile and penury. Only Napoleon was not "himself": "I need great powers, a temporary dictatorship, to save the country. In the country's interest, I could seize this power; but it would be more useful, more 'national,' if it were given to me by the chambers."[29] His opacity displayed no concept of the politics of the last week or, indeed, the last months. It gave rise to a rare thing. An angry debate broke out. They all knew the mood of the chambers better than him, and—having quizzed his aides while he bathed—they knew more about Waterloo than he assumed.[30] Davout now stood alone in favor of a naked coup. Joseph and Fouché both kept silent. Regnauld de Saint-Jean-d'Angély, one of the original conspirators of Brumaire,[31] broached the heart of the matter, possibly primed by Fouché. He spoke of "the great sacrifices" that had to be made. When Napoleon pressed him to be precise, he blurted it out: the chambers wanted him to abdicate. No one supported him; Carnot swung to Davout's side, and Lucien returned to it. Napoleon obfuscated, outlining the military means he still thought he possessed, promising to defend Paris and Lyon, but concluding he would wait and see how the chambers responded.[32] His passivity at this, of all moments, is staggering. It echoed Louis XVI in 1789. Now, as then, they did not have long to wait before the chambers made their position clear.

Just after midday, while Napoleon met with his council, the chamber of representatives opened its session. The ferment of the last week boiled over. Fouché did not need to be there. He had found a "useful idiot," to invoke a famous phrase, to set the mayhem in motion. Lafayette, so often an inept if colorful revolutionary leader in 1789, took the floor. He got a motion passed that stirred memories of the Tennis Court Oath of June 17, 1789, declaring the chamber was in permanent session, indissoluble. Its wording left no doubt about where the representatives believed sovereign power lay: "Any attempt to dissolve (the chamber) is a crime of high treason: anyone found guilty of such an attempt will be a traitor to the nation, and will be judged as such." Four hundred national guardsmen were ordered up to defend the representatives.[33] Lafayette was Fouché's unwitting puppet, but he was the right man for the moment. Napoleon had stirred the embers of the Revolution since he landed in Provence. Now, from the mouth of its hero—ironically, the first general to be talked of as a Roman-style dictator[34]—the fire sparked into life. The motion also demanded that Carnot, Davout, Caulaincourt, and Savary present themselves before it, and account for what had happened. When the chamber of peers was informed of this, its members did not rally to Napoleon.

Napoleon was urged to go to the representatives in person when this news reached the Élysée. He declined, sending a deputation led by Lucien instead. He calmly told them to ask for the men and money he needed: "Are we a nation, or are we not a nation?" "Washington had the right to speak thus, but did Napoleon?" Cambacérès asked in his journal.[35] Lucien and the others were not well received. Antoine Jay, a protégé of Fouché, and now his mouthpiece, bellowed at Lucien:

> Go back to your brother and tell him that the assembly of the representatives of the people awaits a resolution from him which will bring him more honor than all his victories, that by abdicating power, he can save France, that his destiny presses him, that in a day, an hour, perhaps, there will be no more time. I ask that a commission (be formed) charged with inviting Napoleon

to abdicate, and to tell him that, should he refuse, the assembly will depose him.[36]

He was met with thunderous cheers. Lucien tried to argue back, but Lafayette picked up the baton of rebellion:

> You accuse us of neglecting our duties toward Napoleon. Have you forgotten the bones of our children, of our brothers . . . (on) the sands of Africa, on the banks of the Guadalquivir and the Tagus, or on those of the Vistula and the frozen deserts of Russia? For ten years, three million Frenchmen perished for one man, who still wants to fight on today, against Europe. If we have to reproach ourselves justly, it is for having shown too much perseverance. We have done enough for Napoleon; now, our duty is to save the country.[37]

The chamber rose against Napoleon, and the peers followed suit. As soon as Lucien ran back to the Élysée, Lanjuinais lost no time in naming the commission. It had the marks of a bloodless Thermidor, more than a reversal of Brumaire. Lafayette expressed years of pent-up rage. Jay's tone mattered as much as his words. The language was that of a fait accompli. There was no more mention of "the emperor," only of "your brother" or "Napoleon." The most dangerous among the deputies were not those who thundered, however, but those who grimaced in silence, as they had against Robespierre in the same room at Thermidor. "Fouché did not speak . . . in the Chamber on June 21, 1815, just as he had not in the Convention, on July 26 and 27, 1794," Emmanuel de Waresquiel notes astutely.[38]

Lucien made it plain to his brother: he could resort to force against the assemblies, or abdicate in favor of his son. There was now no other way to avoid being deposed. Napoleon roused himself briefly—"They would not dare!"—and lashed out at the ingratitude of Lafayette and Fouché. Davout had already abandoned his own advice, and told Napoleon it was useless to use force, "the time has passed to act"; the chambers may have acted illegally, but to repress them would mean civil war in Paris, with allied armies at the gates.[39] Fouché may have "worked" Davout; "Fouché breathed on him," one of his generals said, enigmatically.[40] but his assessment of the military position in Paris was indisputable.[41] "Force" lost its crucial advocate, and Napoleon admitted civil war had to be avoided.[42] Nothing decisive emanated from him, but the delegations were on their way to the Tuileries. Caulaincourt, a timid, silent figure until now, seeing Napoleon would not dissolve the chambers, counseled abdication.[43] Savary spoke forcefully, with a mixture of resignation and bluster: "Since they can't grasp that you are the only one who can save them, leave them to it . . . In eight days, the foreigners will come, shoot some of them and exile the others. You, go to America and enjoy the rest you've earned."[44] It was 6:00 P.M., and Napoleon remained irresolute. Hortense arrived, and they spent some time in the garden together, but what passed between them is uncertain. At literally the eleventh hour, Cambacérès, Joseph, Lucien, Fouché, and a few others went to the Tuileries to meet the two commissions from the chambers, headed by Lafayette. Cambacérès initially treated it simply as a briefing by the executive to the legislature, and he went on for two hours, until Lafayette exploded: No peace was possible while Napoleon was on the throne, and peace was what they wanted, not to find hopeless ways of delaying allied victory. Cambacérès refused to put abdication to the vote, but agreed that since the enemy would not deal with Napoleon, the chambers might send a delegation to Wellington. Fouché at last put his head over the parapet and supported this; Lucien and Joseph were aghast as were most of the ministers. The delegates rejected an attempt to allow Napoleon to appoint them, and this was the final blow: Napoleon was sidelined for all peace negotiations. Cambacérès showed he knew the game was up by his inaction; Fouché by breaking ranks openly for the first time. The real issue was still in the air, as dawn broke on the 22nd. Lafayette and Lucien crossed paths in the long corridors of the Tuileries at some point. The old hero of 1789 goaded the most volatile of the Bonapartes that if "his brother" did not abdicate, he would be sent for and deposed. He got the reply he should have expected:

"And me, I'll send La Bédoyère and a battalion of the Guard!"[45] Lucien would have been lucky to find one now.

The news was brought back to Napoleon in the Élysée, along with encouraging reports that Soult and Jérôme had rallied the army, and that Grouchy had turned up with his corps intact. Savary and Caulaincourt felt this was false hope. The real enemy was the commissioners, and they now arrived to confront Napoleon: It was abdication or deposition. After they left, Carnot and Lucien held out for a coup, even though Davout—who would have to carry it out—was opposed; Savary arrived with the news that the national guard had come out for the chambers. Joseph said he would support whatever Napoleon decided. At last, he agreed to abdicate in favor of his son. Cambacérès turned to the others, and looked straight at Lucien, saying coldly, "The allies will not accept now, what they refused last year." It had to be a pure and simple abdication. All present agreed that Napoleon did not react, that he knew his old collaborator was right, but he could do nothing else.[46] Napoleon then sat down, and dictated his last edict to Fouché, quill pen in hand, "allowing himself the luxury of paying homage to the one he had just brought down":[47]

Frenchmen,

At the beginning of the war to maintain national independence, I counted on the uniting of all the efforts, all the will, and on the agreement of all the national authorities: I had well founded hopes of success, and I have braved all the declarations of the foreign powers ranged against me.

Circumstances appear to have changed.

I offer myself as a sacrifice to the hatred of the enemies of France. That they may be sincere in their declarations that they want no more than my person! My political life is over, and I proclaim my son Emperor of the French, under the name of Napoleon II.

The present ministers will form a provisional council of government. In the interests I have for my son, I invite the chambers to

organize a regency in law, without delay. Unite for the public good,
and remain an independent nation.[48]

Napoleon knew his call for a regency was in vain. "You have nothing left
but the Bourbons," he told Maret and Lucien.[49] He had surrendered to the
chambers, to Fouché's machinations, in less than a day. T. S. Eliot said it: "this
is the way the world ends, not with a bang, but a whimper."

The next day, Carnot delivered the abdication, and was met with silence.
He did not mention Napoleon II, but Fouché proposed sending a five-man delegation to negotiate with the allied armies. It was a fool's errand, and Fouché
knew it, given his sources: they were to demand the accession of Napoleon II;
the personal safety to Napoleon; the integrity of French territory; and that
the Bourbons not be restored automatically," for France was to make up its
own mind.[50] Lafayette accepted the mission with alacrity. Arguments began
over the need to keep their word to Napoleon, but were scotched when news
came that the Peers supported electing a provisional executive. The chamber
moved quickly, and the results were significant: Carnot garnered the most
votes, with 324; Fouché came second with 293.[51] Clearly, the "war party"
consisted of more than Napoleonists. The chamber also sent Lanjuinais and
a delegation to "Napoleon Bonaparte," with "a vote of thanks for all he had
done." "Since this is your work," Napoleon told Lanjuinais, "you ought to
remind yourself that the title of emperor is not lost," and turned his back. In
his final humiliation, Napoleon rose in impotent rage, one observer remembered: "I abdicated in favor of my son. If the chambers do not proclaim him,
my abdication is null and void. I will take back my rights . . . You will see tears
of blood soon enough."[52] In fact, the army was dissolving. Desertions swelled
when news of the abdication broke, and the Army of the North now numbered
only twenty-nine thousand, with little artillery. Soult told Wellington of the
abdication, and asked for an armistice on June 24, as did Lafayette when he
arrived at Laon, reminding him that the allies had declared war on Napoleon,
not France.[53] Blücher ignored it all and pushed on. Soult resigned his commission two days later, and handed over to Grouchy, saving his skin, yet again.[54]

The day before, Fouché and the commission decided Napoleon had to be gotten out of Paris, for his own safety as much as for that of the capital. The chambers were too volatile to risk a vote on turning him over to the allies.[55] Davout was charged with telling him to clear off. He found a crowd of *démi-soldes* and deserters around the Élysée and, disciplinarian to the last, berated them and told them to get back to their units. Napoleon then berated him, in turn, with a chorus of "*Vive l'empereur*" wafting up from the windows behind him: "If I had wished to put myself at the head of these good and brave people . . . I would have put an end to those who had the courage to stand up against me only when they saw I was defenseless!" Davout reminded him of how it had come to this, perhaps the only person alive who could say so with authority. He reminded Napoleon of the price of civil war. If the deputies did not at least care for his personal safety, they would not ask this of him. Napoleon agreed, but the two men parted without even a handshake, never to meet again. It was a cold occasion, Davout recalled in notes he never made public in his lifetime.[56]

June 25, 1815, was Napoleon's last day in Paris. The chambers had already installed themselves in the Tuileries.[57] Napoleon, Joseph, and Lucien, joined by Jérôme, the mud of Picardy still on his boots, held their last family council. They agreed to try to reunite in America. Napoleon asked the new government to put two warships at his disposal to head for the United States, and cases began to be packed for the voyage.[58] Fouché agreed to the ships, but made it clear his departure depended on allied safe conduct. Le Havre, the major port of the Channel coast, was first mentioned for the departure, but Fouché insisted on the western port of Rochefort, tucked between La Rochelle and Bordeaux, a quiet, out-of-the-way place, hidden from the public eye. On June 26, Lafayette was told by Blücher's headquarters that safe conduct to America was a decision for the allied leaders. The negotiators, in turn, warned the government, "that we believe that his escape before negotiations are complete will be seen as bad faith on our part, and . . . could compromise the safety of France."[59] Lucien had a harebrained scheme to obtain safe conducts for all of them from the British government and went to Boulogne, in hopes of seeing Castlereagh's secretary in person. When it came to nothing, he ran for Italy. Joseph tried to persuade Jérôme to come to America with them,[60] but Fouché had gotten to him: "The commission of government thought it best that Your Highness takes himself away from Paris. I am charged with inviting you to do so."[61] Jérôme was probably worried he might lose his wife and child, and stayed in Paris only long enough to make contact with his in-laws. He returned to Württemberg, under their protection.[62] Joseph lurked at his estate with his family.

At about midday, Napoleon slipped out the Élysée under the escort of General Nicolas Becker, and went to Malmaison. Becker was a general of division who had fallen foul of Napoleon after Wagram, and was retired in 1811. Fouché chose him; Davout agreed: he would carry out orders, and protect Napoleon as far as Rochefort, but was not well disposed to him.[63] With his first jailer, Napoleon installed himself briefly in his old home with Josephine, his haven in what now must have seemed the halcyon days of the Consulate. For a few days, he enjoyed a deeply personal life. Hortense, Maria Waleska, and their son joined him there. He entrusted Joseph with his letters from Marie-Louise; Joseph also held on to the family's treasure chest.[64] All was not tranquil with Napoleon. He wrote to the government, offering his services to the country, as "General Bonaparte"—styling himself "the first soldier of the fatherland," and not without pedigree—for the duration of the war, casting himself as a selfless republican hero, promising to retire, like Cincinnatus, when victory was won: "By abdicating power, I have not in the least renounced the most noble duty of the citizen, the right to defend my country."[65] It was refused. He also drew up a proclamation to the armies, which he kept secret.[66]

He left Malmaison, and all those he held dear, on June 29, not a moment too soon. Fouché warned him the night before that the allies' attitude had hardened, and Napoleon barely avoided capture by Prussian hussars, sent to Malmaison expressly to seize him. They arrived on July 1, and were duly trounced by French cavalry in the vicinity of Versailles,[67] by which time Napoleon had reached Niort, on the edge of the Vendée. Joseph joined him there, having disguised himself as a traveling wine merchant.[68] Joseph had acquired several royal government passports from Fouché, who was only too glad to be rid of him, and one American passport in the name of "Surviglieri," the Italian for "watch him."[69] Three generals also joined Napoleon at Niort, Las Cases, Gourgaud, and Montholon, to each of whom he would dictate memoirs in his captivity. Together, they went on their way to Rochefort.

Captured, June 25–July 8, 1815

The environs of Niort were dangerous country, on the edge of the Vendean heartland, but Napoleon's troops won two engagements for him the day after Waterloo, at Thouars and Rocheservière. They secured his final line of retreat. Neither Waterloo nor the abdication influenced the government in Paris in its struggle with the Vendeans. Davout remained inflexible, insisting on the rebels' surrender, nor did the threats of retribution relent. This forced the Vendean leaders to peace talks, the "pacification of Cholet," on June 26. An uneasy calm fell on the bocage south of the Loire, but fighting went on in the Chouan country, north of the river. The great tides of history did not yet seep into the West. Civil war was just that, as both sides dug in, wary and well armed, to await events. The Chouan forces were on the brink of collapse when reinforcements arrived by sea, and the balance shifted in their favor. A brutal, atomized civil war broke out across Brittany over the summer. Nantes was besieged; Vannes was nearly taken. The empire was over, but the revolution raged on.[70]

As his party rode over the open, flat country between the bocage and the vineyards of Saint-Émilion to their south, toward the coast, Napoleon passed over the land like the rider of the Apocalypse on his pale horse. Behind him, the Vendée seethed in uneasy truce while, further north, the allies ground their way to Paris. To his south, across the Midi, a "white terror" ripped across the region, a revival of the chaos and brutality that followed Thermidor in 1794. Royalists reemerged to take revenge for the short-lived Jacobin spring of the 100 Days. On June 25, when the news of the abdication reached Marseille, the city erupted in violence between the garrison, loyal to Napoleon and barricaded in its forts, and the royalist Urban Guard, by now about 800 strong. Those suspected of "Bonapartism" were left defenseless and the most reliable figures speak of 250 dead and wounded, and 80 houses sacked. Caught up in this were the "Mameluke" community of about 250 to 300 people. They followed the French back from Egypt in 1801, and were still known as the "Egyptian refugees": interpreters, guides, collaborators of all sorts, who had to be saved from popular fury. In the intervening years, they became deeply identified with the regime, many serving in the Mameluke cavalry regiments, and in the 100 Days, they had shown themselves loyal to Napoleon. They were easily identified and were targeted along with other sympathizers. The cruelty with which the royalists dealt with them is well attested to—there were numerous lynchings—but how many perished is hard to establish. Their fate may have had a racist element, but their close identification with Napoleon sealed their fate.[71] Marseille's was as much an embattled Napoleonic garrison as any in Spain or Germany, and "collaborators" met the same fate. Napoleon's authority had collapsed here, and the royalist militias stepped into the vacuum.

It was the same across the Midi. If the "white terror" had a guiding hand it came from d'Angoulême, who slipped back from Spain whence he fled after he was driven out of Montpellier. He made Toulouse his capital, appointing officials—and sanctioning the purge of the incumbents—across Provence and Languedoc, justifying his quasi-autonomist actions by the extraordinary powers Louis had granted him during the 100 Days. Toulouse had been the seat of a sort of regional parliament, the Estates of Languedoc, before the revolution, and d'Angoulême played on local aspirations for a return to this, mixed with plain bloodlust for vengeance on the revolutionaries of the 1790s, Bonapartists and protestants. He began "at home," where General Jean-Pierre Ramel, the commander of what was left of the Toulouse national guard, was assassinated. In a matter of weeks, all protestants in the local administration across Languedoc were purged from office, replaced by Catholic ultras, their authority supported by local militia, the *battalions des miquelets.* The complete exclusion of protestants from all positions of influence, the cherished objective of royalists since 1789, was achieved within weeks of Waterloo. D'Angoulême proscribed Protestantism and made it illegal for a few months, classifying it as "revolutionary" and "bonapartist" by another name. By mid-July, most of the wealthy protestants of Nîmes had been attacked, their houses and businesses ransacked, in preplanned raids, causing many to flee. Arbitrary arrests proliferated, for the fortunate. Lynchings were more common. Marshal Brune, the commander of Marseille, was ambushed and killed as he tried to escape the city. The villages of the Cevennes lived through an orgy of violence in these weeks, as did Nîmes. The method was almost universal: Victims were dragged from their houses and shot in the head as soon as they were on the street. In the Cevennes, a report noted, "all the domains belonging to Protestants from Marguerittes to Vauvert . . . have been pillaged, devastated and set on fire." The protestants replied with economic warfare, shutting down vast sectors of the local economy. Fouché, once a ruthless "enforcer" of the revolutionary government in the provinces, sat powerless in Paris as d'Angoulême's men went about their work. The violence subsided by September, when Austrian troops entered the region, but political control was only recovered after the Bourbons fell, themselves, in 1830. Napoleon left his creations of *amalgame* and *ralliement* in cinders wherever he passed, whether marching to Paris, or fleeing from it, the furies of the armies of the East devouring his empire behind him. The hubris and nemesis of revolution and empire were telescoped into one human life, into one journey to the sea.

He reached Rochefort on July 3. On July 8, he and his companions crossed to the Île d'Aix, a small island in the harbor, the easier to embark. There were two French ships in its harbor, the *Saale* and the *Medusa*, as promised, but he also noted several British frigates and ships-of-the-line in view beyond the harbor. He did not find the promised safe conducts waiting for him. The commanders had been told Napoleon was bent on getting to America. They had orders not to let him escape and, if he tried, to seize him and remove him to a British port without delay.[72] Caught between the Royal Navy, rabid royalists, and, for all he knew, more uhlans on his tail, Napoleon was cornered at last. So was his country.

The day Napoleon reached Rocheport, Davout signed the capitulation of Paris. The fortnight between Napoleon's abdication and Davout's surrender were what might be called the life and death of the Second Republic, for that was what it was in the minds of many in the chambers, the self-styled government of France. As Napoleon negotiated with the Royal Navy, the provisional government gave up negotiating with the allies and accepted its fate, but not before much had transpired.

While the West and the South tore themselves apart in civil war, the North and East shuddered as the allied armies ground their way to Paris. The British became ill-disciplined at times, but the Prussians reveled in rapacious brutality. Blücher incarnated the wrath of his men: "If the Parisians don't kill the tyrant before we get there, we'll kill the Parisians," he wrote to Metternich, the day Napoleon abdicated.[73] He refused to speak French once on French soil, and boasted loudly of his thefts from grand châteaux, a beautiful painting of Pauline Bonaparte among them, lifted from Malmaison. He was "an incorrigible bear,"[74] and role model to his troops. Destruction and desolation fell upon Flanders and Picardy as the Prussians advanced, and it got worse, the closer they drew to Paris. No one of any class or political hue was spared. Château and cottage alike were ransacked. A prominent royalist, Ange-Étienne-Xavier Poisson de La Chabeaussière was found beaten and left for dead in his ruined country house. Whole villages were stripped not only of food, but of furniture, "not even a rope left for the wells," their women raped, their men battered.[75] The allied leaders and Wellington struggled to maintain the distinction between the war they decreed on Napoleon, and the French people. Frederick-William and his ministers adhered to this, but his commanders in the field simply brushed it aside. Blücher swept away what was left of the Army of the North in these days, too. An attempt was made to create a viable line of defense between Compiègne and Senlis, north of Paris, but morale had cracked, and Blücher took between 500 and 1,000 prisoners as he pushed on. The Army of the North fell back behind the defenses of northern Paris, soon joined by Grouchy's corps. By June 28, Blücher's headquarters was at Senlis, and his men were only ten miles from Notre-Dame, quartered around what is now Charles de Gaulle Airport.[76] His long-cherished objective—to take Paris and sack it—was within his grasp.

Behind the armies came the king and his court. Louis left Ghent on June 22, and crossed into France on June 24, halting first at Cateau, with d'Artois and his more reactionary ministers. Under their influence, Louis issued a vengeful declaration, full of menace, particularly because it named no names, and spoke only of "rewarding the good people." When they joined Wellington at Cambrai on June 26, the presence of more moderate counsels—the duke's among them, as well as Talleyrand—extracted a more moderate proclamation from Louis, who now "placed himself between the allied armies and the French people," as a protective shield. He had seen for himself the destruction Blücher had wrought. He announced a pardon for all save for "the instigators" of Bonaparte's "horrible plot." The Charter and much of the 1814 settlement were confirmed. It did not pass without bitterness. When the proclamation was read to the royal council, d'Artois reacted violently, and duc du Berry actually put his hand on his sword hilt, looking at Talleyrand.[77] If the proclamation of Cambrai was, indeed, "a declaration of war against all extremists,"[78] and a return to *ralliement* and *amalgame* in a new guise, it had yet to be felt within the heart of royal family.

Louis spoke of recalling his own parliament on his return to Paris, but even in his moderation, he lacked realism. The chambers sitting in Paris may have been of questionable legitimacy, but they were the only national government France possessed since the abdication, and they were speaking and legislating in the name of the "French people," not "Napoleon II." There was a mere handful of royalists in their midst; three of its five executive commissioners were regicides—Fouché, Carnot, and Nicolas Quinette (even though the first named was probing links to Louis)—and the representatives of the people refused to declare for Louis, or to support any candidate for king. Instead, they were discussing the reform of the Napoleonic Additional Act, clause by clause, even as the allies tightened the noose around their capital. Paris was still a place where royalists kept silent.

They were living in a bubble. Wellington and Blücher began to close the trap. Their main bone of contention was whether to wait for Wrede's Bavarian corps—the vanguard of the Austrian army—which had reached Châlons-en-Champagne by July 3, to seal off Paris completely, or risk an all-out assault. Wellington insisted on the former course, knowing Paris could be starved out, but Blücher pressed for an attack. The Army of the North, well dug in, was a different proposition to the disheveled force that struggled to retreat, however, and Wellington thought an assault on Paris could cost as many as ten thousand men.[79] Davout could muster about 78,000 men and 600 guns, enough to intimidate the Anglo-Prussians for a time.[80] It was a question of how and when the end would come. The city was short of supplies, tensions boiled over between the national guards and the fervently Bonapartist *fédérés*, who paraded busts of Napoleon about the streets and sought to stir a popular rising.[81] Beyond it all, the Austrians drew closer, the Russians, behind them. Davout and Fouché took charge of events, in their different ways, to break the deadlock before Paris was destroyed, and effect a second Bourbon restoration. Davout told Fouché on June 28 that there was no time to lose, but talks led by the new foreign minister, the bonapartist, Louis Bignon, failed because he insisted on terms the commanders were not free to accept, pressing Napoleon II's claim to the throne. Finally, on July 4, a purely military armistice was agreed among the commanders, whereby Blücher and Wellington agreed to leave the provisional government in place until further orders, and Davout agreed to evacuate the army from Paris to the Loire.[82] The troops proved amenable to this, largely because Fouché's friends, the bankers Laffitte and Perrégaux, authorized two million francs to pay them.[83] The army pulled out over July 4–5. Although Davout was convinced the Bourbons were the only viable source of authority, and felt firmly that Louis should enter Paris on his own before the allied troops, he and his commanders were not sufficiently reassured by the proclamation of Cambrai to submit the army to the king. Dejean and Kellermann called the armistice treason. Baron Eugène de Vitrolles, a deputy present, told Davout, "We don't speak the same French." "They discussed and caviled, while the wolves were at the door."[84] Fouché cultivated links to Wellington with limited success in hopes he would act as a broker between the government and Louis, but when it became clear the Bourbons would not recognize the provisional government, Fouché conceded every point, placing himself as the only figure in the executive on whom Louis could count. As his prevarications became widely known, the diehards in the chambers turned on him.[85] Fouché was on dangerous ground, but the timing was perfect. Entering a world he had lost control of, Louis immediately turned to him, as his minister of police. The Prussians entered Paris on July 6; the chambers recognized Louis, and he called his new team of ministers together at Neuilly, to swear allegiance to him. "Suddenly a door swung open," an observer recalled, "vice entered silently, supported by the arm of crime, M. de Talleyrand walking supported by Fouché; the infernal vision passed slowly before me, entered the king's cabinet, and disappeared."[86] The executive commission was dissolved the next day.

To the Ends of the Earth: July 8–October 17, 1815

While the allies settled into Paris, and Louis formed his new government, Napoleon remained stranded on l'Île d'Aix for a week. He knew his only hope was to throw himself on the mercy of the British, but he had to do his best to ensure they would be merciful. The commander of the British vessel *Bellerophon*, Captain Frederick Maitland, made it clear that as a state of war still existed, he would sink any French ship that left harbor. Plans were hatched to break out or slip away to sea, but Napoleon rejected them, and set about surrendering.[87] Joseph offered to give Napoleon his American papers and his place on *Le Commerce*, docked in Royan. Napoleon feigned his agreement and sent his brother off to make preparations. Joseph then received word Napoleon was not coming, and that he was to make for safety, which he duly did, eventually reaching New York.[88]

On July 13, Napoleon appealed directly to the Prince Regent: ". . . I have terminated my political career and I come, like Themistocles, to sit on the doorstep of the British people. I put myself under the protection of their laws," calling the Prince Regent "the most powerful, the most constant, and the most generous of my enemies."[89] When Napoleon invoked Themistocles, he drew a self-portrait for the Prince Regent of how he saw his past glory, his present plight, and, just possibly, his bright future. Themistocles led the Athenians in their struggle against Persia, masterminding their great victories on land and sea. The Spartans, Athens's rival in Greece, feared his prowess and insinuated rumors about him that forced him to flee the city, leading him to the Persians, whom he served well until his death. Napoleon's analogy with Themistocles at his height are obvious, but it is tempting to wonder if this was Napoleon offering his sword to the British, driven to it by the fickleness of his own people. Did Napoleon now see himself as the commander who could take revenge on America for Britain? Who would lead their armies against the nation he was set to embrace the day before? It is tempting to ask, in the climate of the times. Perhaps he had been influenced by the conduct of those around him—Soult and Marmont spring to mind—to transform the eagle into yet another weathercock. In truth, if Napoleon now resembled a classical hero on l'Île d'Aix, it was Hannibal, who had driven the enemies of his country to the very gates of Rome, only to let all initiative slip from him until he made his last stand before the walls of Carthage, his own capital, his former allies ranged against him. Livy told of the mood among the Carthaginians on the eve of the fall of the city: "At one moment, when they looked at Hannibal and the greatness of his achievements, they would regret having sued for peace. At the next they would reflect he had been . . . defeated on the battlefield . . . and that they had been driven from Spain and Italy."[90] As Scipio, the Roman commander who was his nemesis, told him: "It did not escape me, Hannibal, that it was the anticipation of your arrival that led the Carthaginians to scuttle the existing truce (to which you had given your word) as well as the hopes of peace." Hannibal was driven from Carthage after his defeat at Zama, leading an itinerant life, fomenting new wars against Rome among the Greek states of

Asia Minor and avoiding Roman assassins, finally committing suicide when his host betrayed him to the Romans.[91] They all knew their Livy. Blücher and the French ultras would have been only too pleased to reenact the classical past to the full. Napoleon boarded the *Bellerophon* on July 15, still hoping that he would be allowed to live as a guest of the British, although Maitland made it clear to Las Cases, Napoleon's negotiator, that his only remit was to take him to a British port, which he duly did. Gourgaud was sent to deliver Napoleon's letter to the Prince Regent in person, but was refused entry to Britain.[92] Napoleon avoided the assassin's dagger or the uhlan's lance, but little else. "Into the wide open jaws of the wolf," as Thierry Lentz puts it.[93]

On July 17, the *Bellerophon* anchored in the small Devon port of Torbay, and Napoleon was one of those rare human beings to get a view of his afterlife while still on earth. News of his presence soon spread, and before long the *Bellerophon* was surrounded by small craft from all along the Channel coast, while crowds swarmed into Torbay to catch a glimpse of him. Napoleon played to them shamelessly, appearing on deck regularly at 5:00 P.M. to take his bow. He was a modern celebrity. Fearful of security, Admiral George Keith Elphinstone moved the *Bellerophon* on to Plymouth. There, Napoleon got hold of British newspapers, and his illusions were punctured. The powers that be had no intention of allowing him to stay, or to go to America. The allied rulers left his fate to the British, and it was quickly decided. Wellington favored imprisonment in the Scottish highlands; there was talk of handing him over to Louis to be executed, but this was considered too dangerous, offering a martyr to the enemies of the Bourbons. They fell back on Saint Helena, a popular option in 1814.[94] Napoleon learned of this in Plymouth harbor on the last day of July. He exploded to Keith, "I am not a prisoner of war, but a guest in England . . . I am under the protection of the laws of your country. I prefer death to going to Saint Helena . . . I want to live freely in the heart of England, under the protection of your laws."[95] He continued to bombard Keith in similar vein during the long voyage to Saint Helena on the *Northumberland*, to which he was transferred. Others begged to differ with his view of matters. Napoleon seems to have forgotten his beloved Plutarch, when he ranged himself with

Themistocles. In his final judgment of Themistocles, Plutarch acknowledged his "gentility and greatness, his courage, but his ambition was also extreme, and drove him to so very many things for nothing more the vain glory and ridiculous presumption in deeds and words, that led him to the point where he wanted to have something singular, something more than all of the others or by the others."[96] The British establishment may have recalled this passage immediately to mind, as it escaped Napoleon's attention. Napoleon disembarked on Saint Helena on October 17. It was all over. If avoiding exile to this very place had been the real goal of the 100 Days, it ended in precise, not merely total, failure. By his own lights, Napoleon's end was ignominious.

He was not alone. Two days before Napoleon set foot on his prison island, Murat met his end before a firing squad in the Calabrian village of Pizzo, on October 13, 1815. After Waterloo, the Bourbons put a price of forty thousand francs on his head, and Murat escaped to Corsica. Offered safe conduct to join Caroline, he refused. He was determined to retake his kingdom, setting off with an "invasion force" of 250 men. They landed in Calabria on October 6. A storm wrecked most of his small fleet, and he washed up near Pizzo with only twenty-eight men, all in full dress uniform. They were met with resistance from the peasants and the local garrison while trying to unfurl their banners. He was tried by officers of the army he had created, under his own laws against "banditry," and condemned to death. Murat asked to be allowed to write to Caroline, but was refused. He died with great courage, refusing to sit down before the firing squad or wear a mask, and gave the command to fire himself. Some say his body was thrown into the sea, but it was more likely tossed into a communal grave, a ditch by the church, his bones mixed up with hundreds of others. His severed head was sent to the Bourbon court in Naples.[97]

The life of the world Napoleon had turned upside down went on as the *Northumberland* sought its destination. The allied victory emerged as all the more emphatic; the chaos in France did not abate. Murat was not alone of Napoleon's men in his fate. Louis took the step Napoleon rejected. Charles de la Bédoyère, who had "opened" Grenoble to Napoleon and been his aide-de-camp at Waterloo, was executed on August 19. Chateaubriand called it an act of "paternal severity."[98] Ney followed him on December 7, despite pleas for mercy from many sides.[99] A few weeks before, in contravention of the terms of Cambrai, Fouché drew up a proscription list for his new masters, of nineteen generals accused of treason, and thirty-eight others, to be placed under police surveillance. Among them were men who had not served Napoleon, but were simply known republicans. It all took place in a Paris of duels, punch-ups, and riots between newly emboldened royalists and Bonapartists, which erupted after the city fell to the Prussians.[100] Less dramatically, Sieyès, Cambacérès, and Roederer were expelled from the Académie Française. The ultra camp regarded all this as either only the beginning, or too lenient. Louis gave in over their demands for a purge of the administration. No less than sixty-four departments got new prefects,[101] but as with Napoleon's purges in the 100 Days, it stretched much further, leaving as many as 50,000 to 80,000 men sacked in its wake.[102]

This was nothing as compared to the army. The ultras in the chambers sought little short of its wholesale dissolution, prevented only by St. Cyr, now minister of war, and Macdonald, who took over command of the army on the Loire, and had Louis's trust. Grouchy fled to America, and Soult to the Prussian Rhineland. Both returned later, Soult to become minister of war, but the rank and file had no such political skill. All officers and men who had served Napoleon were ordered to return to their homes; all those over fifty were retired, thus "cleansing" the army of everyone who had fought for the revolution, as well as Napoleon. Their pensions were meager, if paid at all. The ultra chambers forced nearly twenty thousand officers out of the army over 1815–16. By a law of November 9, 1815, any officer who as much as "invoked the name of the usurper" could lose his pension. Confined to poor rural areas, forbidden to look for work in the large cities, an embittered, alienated body of articulate men was created at a stroke. The enlisted men were not as closely watched, and some became gendarmes or served in other branches of the local police. Officers and men alike existed on half pay if they were lucky, and lived in official ignominy, ostracized in places, even if they acquired status in their communities as living legends, creatures of an increasingly mythologized age.

Many never settled into a rural life they had long left behind.[103] Unwilling conscripts returned as displaced veterans. Napoleon's man management had worked too well. An army that was no more had become their family. One of Louis's first acts, on August 3, 1815, was to disband the Imperial Guard. Some among the remnants of the Young Guard were allowed to join the new royal army, a few in Louis's guards. The Old Guard became *démi-soldes*; most were put under police surveillance, whether with the colors or not. The last units to be dissolved were the cavalry—"These gentlemen belonged to a corps afflicted with troublesome prejudices," remarked the officer sent to disband them, whose own brother had fallen at Leipzig with the mounted chasseurs of the Guard. The last unit dissolved was a squadron of the Horse Grenadiers. They paraded into the market square of the small town of Preuilly, on the Loire, and handed over their eagle. The officers could not watch. They had been the last reserve at Waterloo, and now they were gone.[104] This is when, at heart, Napoleon's life really ended.

By November 20, a second Treaty of Paris was dictated to Louis: France was reduced to her prerevolutionary borders; an indemnity of 700 million francs was imposed on her, not repaid in full until the 1820s. The allied armies, under the overall command of Wellington, were to occupy all of northern and eastern France. By the end of July, there were 1,226,000 allied soldiers in France, costing the country 1,710,000 francs a day, by Castlereagh's calculations.[105] France was obliged to subsidize the refortification of her eastern frontiers by the Dutch, Prussians, Swiss, and Piedmontese, to hem her in. They had restored the Bourbons, but with no obligation to make life easy for them, or their subjects. Even royalists watched in horror as allied soldiers, on their government's orders, systematically looted the Louvre, in a long-meditated act of revenge for revolutionary and Napoleonic rapaciousness over the years.[106]

This roused Louis to action. On July 22, he addressed the tsar: "The conduct of the allied armies will soon reduce my people to arm themselves, as happened in Spain . . . I would rather live in a prison than remain here, a passive witness to the suffering of my children." He threatened to retire to Spain, which forced the allies to reduce and regularize the indemnities.[107]

Talleyrand resigned on September 22, to avoid association with the harshness of the occupation and the terms of the second Treaty of Paris. He was replaced by the duc de Richelieu, an émigré of moderate politics, who had governed Ukraine for Alexander as an enlightened reformer. Alexander was crucial in persuading him to accept, a sign of how influential the tsar, still in Paris, had become. Richelieu had originally refused to serve in a ministry containing Fouché.[108] This was solved when Fouché resigned under pressure from the ultras—the newly returned duchesse d'Angoulême chief among them—but it resulted in a victory for "the extreme center." He was replaced by Élie Decazes, a protégé of Louis Bonaparte who remained loyal to Louis XVIII in the 100 Days, and soon became a favorite.[109] These were the men who faced the restored regime's greatest test, when the elections to the new chambers under the Charter in late August, produced a majority for the ultras, and with it, the prospect of legalized civil war and bloodshed on a gargantuan scale. Louis's thirst for vengeance went only so far, however, and he and his ministers paid for it with unrelenting and increasingly violent verbal abuse from the ultra deputies, who were more concerned with pursuing the politics of revenge—of "white terror"—than supporting their king.[110] The law of July 24 declared that all the surviving regicides—those who had voted to execute Louis XVI in 1793—were given two months to leave France or face prosecution that could lead to death. The ultras soon cast their net far wider than the 391 deputies—many now dead—who had voted for Louis's execution. Their definition embraced any "political offense," which led to seventy thousand arrests and nine thousand condemnations.[111] That summer, Fouché, who had been exempted by Richelieu, drew up the first proscription lists, and ordered his old Terrorist comrade, Carnot, into exile. Carnot replied succinctly, "Where do you want me to go, traitor?" Fouché parried, "Wherever you like, imbecile." Carnot made first for Warsaw, and then Magdeburg, where he died in 1823.[112] The newly elected ultra majority deprived the king of the right to grant mercy, which made immediate execution possible, and demanded the execution of all surviving regicides, beginning with Fouché. Fouché was hastily named ambassador to Saxony, and fled to Prague. The former puppet master never saw France again.[113] He ended up in Trieste, a neighbor of the Bonaparte sisters, where he died prematurely aged and broken in 1820.[114]

The ultra majority increasingly alarmed both the government and the allies, Wellington chief among them.[115] Louis and his new ministry acted with authoritarian ruthlessness in the cause of moderation. Together, Richelieu and Lainé—now president of the Chamber of Deputies—agreed to Decazes's radical strategy to dissolve the chambers. Louis signed the decree on September 5, 1816. D'Artois and company found out about it from *Le Moniteur*. The same electorate, perhaps chastened by events, produced a more moderate majority that backed the king's ministers.[116] Gingerly, a fragile consensus of the center resumed the reins. It was left to Louis and Richelieu, émigrés par excellence, the "weathercock" Decazes, and the incarnation of moderation, Lainé, to pick up the pieces Napoleon had first assembled after Brumaire, and then rashly shattered in his final years. They did so in a country greatly reduced in the world.

About the time the *Northumberland* raised anchor in Plymouth, the advance guard of a huge Russian army marched into Paris, with over 200,000 more men close behind it. Among them were units of Alexander's Imperial Guard. They got the news of Waterloo when crossing from Russia into Poland; they kept on coming just the same. On September 10, while Napoleon was "all at sea" in every sense, his nemesis flaunted his power for all to see, friend and foe alike. On the open plains of the Champagne, near the pretty village of Vertus, below the hills now laden with ripe, green Chardonnay, the tsar reviewed 150,000 men and 540 cannons, a mere fraction of his forces.[117] There was now no doubt who was master.

EPILOGUE
BEYOND THE PALE

❧————————————————————————❧

Napoleon was born firmly within the pale, an insider of the Italian enclaves on Corsica, bastions of self-styled civilization surrounded by a barbaric periphery. He died as far outside a pale as could be, at the ends of the earth, on an island chosen exactly because it was far from anywhere. The hardliners at Vienna finally got their way. He was to be shackled to a barren rock, cast into a dark pit to live out his natural life.

Yet, there was nothing natural about Napoleon's life, and his ending was as abnormal, as devoid of precedent as his rise and demise. This was to do with the times, times so extraordinary to those who endured them, that they were deemed inexplicable to past or future generations.[1] Extraordinary times produced an extraordinary man, who was an extraordinary problem to be solved in an extraordinary way. The only precedent was the Satan of Revelation, as told by Milton. Even after the treacherous mayhem of the 100 Days, there was no serious question of killing the man many dubbed "the Ogre" or "the Beast," any more than that same "beast" sought the blood of those he felt had betrayed him in 1814. In an era of ceaseless bloodletting, on a continent strewn with rotting corpses, decimated landscapes, and ruined lives, it was held oddly barbaric to kill Napoleon. He would be left to rot in as safe a place as could be found. And so, for almost six years, it was. His daily life on Saint Helena was apt punishment for one who thrived on action. Where once he defeated armies, he now fought a daily, losing battle against the rats that devoured his chickens.[2] There was a rash of conspiracy theories that the British plotted Napoleon's assassination on Saint Helena, and they began to circulate as soon as the news of his death broke. His supporters were convinced of it; they needed an explanation for so premature a death.[3] There was no need to murder him or, rather, the governor of the island, Hudson Lowe, had his own method. The biggest single "event" of Napoleon's final years was when Lowe ordered him moved from the benign climate of Jamestown, on the coast, inland to Longwood House, in the most insalubrious part of the island's interior. Here, all Napoleon's accumulating ailments accelerated, as his cancer intensified. Yet, in a different age, it could have been worse. He might have met the fate of Murat or Ney. But, somehow, Napoleon was different. Those responsible would have been seen to have fallen victim, themselves, to the bloodlust of the Terror. They feared creating a martyr.

He did that for himself. The kerfuffle over his death mask, the legends spun around his death bed—that his last words were "Army . . . France . . . Josephine" among many—the demeaning caviling over what title to put on his headstone, that a comet had appeared in the skies over Saint Helena as he died, just as one had, in truth, on the day of his birth—all added to the image already set loose by the recollections he had dictated almost from the moment he set foot on his rock, to Bertrand, Las Cases, Gourgaud, and Montholon. His real energies were directed into their pens. The mawkish, callow would-be novelist of the garrison years[4] resurfaced in his final, boring posting, his storytelling skills well honed by a life of learning in propaganda, emotional blackmail, and political intrigue. Along the way, always a great reader, he had absorbed the romantic masterpieces of his beloved Goethe, of Scott, of Macpherson—a liar and fantasist, if a great one—and of his sworn enemy, Chateaubriand, whose weapons he now turned against him. More than the influence of others, Napoleon had a better story to tell than in his youth. It was without parallel, and it became a paradigm for the modern world, from which he was supposed to be cut off, narrated in the romantic language of the age from which he now heard nothing, all communication with the outside world blocked. He churned out a tissue of lies and fables, interspersed with enough hard truths and sharp recollections to evoke introspection and nostalgia in good measure from sympathetic ears of his own generation, and to elicit frustration and ambition from the bored youth of the next. He read the minds of his "children," the *démi-soldes*, his veterans, who still toasted his health in reunions, from Poland to Paris, and many places in between, and wherever they were asked by the young to recount their deeds under his eagles. There were thirty-five Napoleonic veterans' associations active in the Rhineland into the 1850s.[5] His was a tale of rags to riches, of the career open to the talent of genius, a genius who put his talent at the service of a whole generation and a whole continent, who did the impossible only to be betrayed by ingrates and inadequates. The "voice from the rock" roared one last call to arms.

His name and symbols outlawed, Napoleon was no longer the orchestrator of *amalgame* or the protector of the masses of granite. He took his place on the fringe of politics, alongside the revolutionary radicals. He was no longer the target of conspirators, he inspired them. His was the constituency of the marginalized, maladjusted veteran, and of restless, thwarted youth in the decades after Waterloo. The gamble taken in the 100 Days, to hitch his star to the Jacobin revolution, paid off in death. The "four gospels" dictated on Saint Helena served their purpose: chaos. *"Vive l'empereur"* was bellowed across the barricades in 1830, often more frequently than *Vive la République*. In one, tragic case, the consequences were fatal. So hated, feared, and reviled, even in death, was his father, that Napoleon-Francis lived the rest of his life a virtual captive in Vienna. When "Napoleon II" became a rallying cry during the revolutions of 1830, his time had come. He died after standing for hours in freezing rain, needlessly reviewing troops, on July 22, 1832, perhaps the last casualty of the Napoleonic Wars.

Yet, Louis-Philippe d'Orléans, King of the French since 1830, decided nonetheless to return the ashes of his family's bête noire to Paris, and reburied them in Les Invalides with ostentatious pomp and circumstance in December

1840—where they lie to this day—in the hopes that some Napoleonic stardust might sprinkle on his lacklustre regime, and by conjuring his ghost, Louis-Philippe might deflect some of the odium from himself for his Anglophile commercial treaties and flagging foreign policy. He went ahead with it in the face of a ludicrous "invasion" of Boulogne by Louis-Napoleon, son of the benighted Louis and Hortense, and fifty followers. It resulted in none of the surviving Bonaparte siblings, Louis, Joseph, or Jérôme, being allowed into France for the ceremony. "Behold the return to (Napoleon's) beloved France, where his family were still proscribed!" as Jacques-Olivier Boudon puts it.[6] Behind the farce lay a well-organized plot, which garnered some sympathy within the army. At his trial, Louis-Napoleon picked up the baton of the 100 Days, defiantly telling the court, "I represent before you a principle, a cause, and a defeat: the principle is the sovereignty of the people; the cause is that of the empire; the defeat, Waterloo." He did not stir a revolution, but even when a mob marched through Paris in September 1840, waving a tricolor and chanting "Long Live the Emperor Napoleon!" Louis-Philippe dared not halt his plans to return Napoleon's ashes.[7]

It was still hard to know where the farce of Boulogne ended and the lurking danger in the name and mystique of Napoleon began, even for the sharpest eyes. Writing about this time, Chateaubriand judged, "The famous delinquent in triumph is no more . . . Napoleon has need of no one to bestow merits upon him; he was born with enough of them."[8] The duality of that insight points to the many layers of Napoleon's legacy. In his own times, Chateaubriand saw clearly that Napoleon had been reduced to a specter on the margins. His name and memory rallied the dispossessed, the ingénues of younger generations, the subversives. Yet, Napoleon's merits laid foundations so deep and so widespread that even he, at his most cynical, shortsighted, and selfish, could not uproot them. The masses of granite turned on him to save his creation. Louis XVIII purged prefects; he did not abolish them, as Chateaubriand so hoped. Nor did he abolish the code, and when d'Artois, as Charles X, appeared to tamper with it, in an attempt to revive primogeniture, he did not last long. The code spread across Europe. Far and wide, it was either retained or restored as the decades passed. His construct of the public sphere, from the Gendarmerie to public, competitive examinations, endured. Napoleon was right: The code proved his most enduring legacy, as the deeds of the Grande Armée faded into the oral history of the cafés. The Spanish scholar Marta Lorente drives this home in the most unlikely context: "Napoleon triumphed on Spanish soil only after his death," when even that most recalcitrant of countries adopted both the code and the Council of State.[9] These victories, ubiquitous, enduring, and often mundane, took root at the behest of the same regimes that loathed and feared him, in the same years he was a "nonperson" for establishments everywhere. The real legacy of the romantic hero is found in the warp and woof of daily life.

There was a last sting in the tail of the bee. Louis-Philippe had indeed good reason to fear "the famous delinquent." In February 1848, his own regime came tumbling down like a house of cards, replaced by a republic, soon with a Bonaparte at its head, Louis-Napoleon, "Louis of Boulogne." It was quickly transformed by a cocktail of political guile and brute force into a Second Empire, which shot across of the European skies like a comet, only to crash in mayhem and horror like the first. Napoleon always set great store by Hortense. Her loyalty, intelligence, and resilience shone out as one of his siblings after the other imploded around him. The selfish incompetence of his brothers and, finally, in the cynical treason of his trusted Caroline, saw his ever slender hopes for the future of the dynasty come to rest on Hortense and her sons. She did not fail him. But that is another story.

ACKNOWLEDGMENTS

M any of the debts incurred in this project, which has taken over ten years to complete, have been acknowledged in the two previous volumes, but many of them merit repeating, and still more have been acquired in the life of this volume.

The present volume grew out of the project, "Napoleonic Civilization," which received a Major Leverhulme Fellowship, 2011–13. I am deeply grateful to the Leverhulme Trust for providing the springboard for this biography and much else. The wider project is still in progress with, hopefully, more to come in the years ahead. The Principal and Fellows of Lady Margaret Hall have accorded me sabbatical leave at crucial junctures during the writing, and their support is deeply appreciated. So has the comradeship and practical support of my fellow historians, Dr. Grant Tapsell and Dr. Josh Gibson, on whose competent shoulders so much as fallen over the last few years. They have been a great support. As my retirement looms, I wish their future careers every success. They have a right to it. The whole project would have been futile without the gargantuan labors of the Fondation Napoléon and its dynamic director, Thierry Lentz. The completion of their new edition of Napoleon's correspondence will revolutionize Napoleonic studies for generations, and I am grateful to be among the first of those working in the field to profit from it so much. Professor Tim Blanning, of Cambridge, guided me through seminal new material in German, and Professor Alexander Mikaberidze of Louisiana State (Shreveport) generously translated some important material in Russian for me. Their help has enriched this book, and I warmly thank them for their kindness.

There are some debts where the professional and the personal simply become inseparable. My agent, Robert Dudley, had been a constant support and without him, none of this would have come to pass. Robert is more than an agent. He is a friend of the best sort, and a fellow Worcester man to boot! Claiborne Hancock and Jessica Case at Pegasus Books kept faith in this project from start to finish, and I owe them very real thanks, and can only hope their faith will be rewarded. To Maria Fernandez and the production team at Pegasus, I thank them for their professional skills and their patience with me! Professor Michael "S" Siegel of Rutgers University drew the maps with the greatest skill. My friends and colleagues, Professor Alan Forrest and Dr. Ambrogio Caiani, read every word of this, for their sins, but their contribution reaches far beyond the intelligent and prescient reflections they passed on to me. Their friendship and support, often at times of ill health and fatigue, are impossible to calculate. To them, my deepest and abiding thanks. You are simply irreplaceable.

Without Professor Keith Channon and his teams at the cardiology units at the John Radcliffe and Manor hospitals of Oxford, I would not be here. At a time when medical services have been at breaking point across the world, the people I have had the good fortune to help me must be saluted for doing so much more than is to be expected of anyone. My wife, Sue, has been a constant and steadying support through a series of jolts—literally at one point!—and it is thanks to her, as well as Professor Channon, that this book, its author, and all their inherent faults, have made it over the line. There is, of course, our magic black cat, Woody, under whose watchful gaze all takes shape and nothing escapes, save the odd shrew!

Charlbury, Oxfordshire
St. Patrick's Day, 2022

ENDNOTES

Prelude: Into the Flames

1   Napoléon Bonaparte. *Correspondance Générale*, vol. x, *Un Grand Empire, mars 1810–mars 1811*, ed. Thierry Lentz, et al. (Paris, 2014), (afterward *CG*) to Fouché, Saint-Cloud, July 2, 1810, #23876, 314.

2   *CG*, x, to Savary, Saint-Cloud, July 1, 1810, Saint-Cloud, #23879, 315.

3   Ibid. to Decrès, Saint-Cloud, July 1, 1810, Saint-Cloud, #23874, 312. #23775, 313–14.

4   Nicola Todorov, *La Grande Armée à la Conquête de l'Angleterre. Le plan secret de Napoléon* (Paris, 2016).

5   The following account is based mainly on the excellent research of Christian Fileaux: "Drame à l'Ambassade d'Autriche," in *1810. Le tournant de l'Empire*, ed. Thierry Lentz (Paris, 2010), 51–60.

6   *Mémoires de Constant*, 4 vols. (Paris, 1830–31), iii, 245–46.

7   "Despite the celebrity, it is best not to use these memoirs," notes Jean Tulard tersely in his authoritative *Nouvelle Bibliographie Critique des Mémoires sur l'Époque napoleonienne*, Jean Tulard, ed. (Paris, 1991), 85.

8   *CG*, x, to Montaliver, Min of the Interior, Rambouillet, July 10, 1810, #23950, 343.

1: A New Order of Things

1   Cited in Thierry Lentz, *Nouvelle Histoire du Premier Empire*, vol. ii, *L'effondrement du système napoléonien, 1810-1814* (Paris, 2004), 27.

2   Peter Wilson, *The Holy Roman Empire. A Thousand Years of European history* (Milton Keynes, 2016), 37, 307.

3   *CG, x,* to Jérôme, Feb. 10, 1811, #25899, 1195.

4   Luigi Maschilli Migliorini, "Les fondements de l'Empire en 1810," in Thierry Lentz, ed., *Le Tournant de l'Empire en 1810* (Paris, 2010), 405–11, at 411.

5   Cited in Migliorini, "Les fondements," 410.

6   *CG, x,* to Davout, March 12, 1811, #26202, 1330.

7   For a detailed study: Nicolai-Peter Todorov, *L'administration du royaume de Westphalie de 1807 à 1813. Le dépaetement de l'Elbe* (Saarbrücken, 2011).

8   Claire de Rémusat, *Mémoires 1802–1808* (Paris, 1957 ed.), 367. For an excellent overview: Rebecca Rogers, "L'éducation des filles à l'époque napoléonienne," in *Napoléon et les Lycées* (Paris, 2004), Jacques-Oliviers Boudon, ed., 275–90.

9   Michael Broers, "*Les enfants du Siècle*': An Empire of Young Professionals and the Creation of a Bureaucratic, Imperial Ethos in Napoleonic Europe," in *Empires and Bureaucracy in World*

History. From Late Antiquity to the Twentieth Century, Peter Crooks, Timothy H. Parsons, eds. (Cambridge, 2016), 344–63 at 359.

10   On the colleges: Rebecca Rogers, *Les desmoiselles de la Légion d'honneur* (Paris, 1992).

11   Susan Jacques, *The Caesar of Paris* (New York, 2018), 382.

12   *CG*, x, to Josephine, Versailles, Aug. 10, 1810, #24309, 523.

13   Pierre Lascoumes, "Révolution ou réforme juridique? Les Codes Penaux Français de 1791 à 1810," in *Révolutions et Justice Penale en Europe. Modèles Français et Traditions Nationales 1780–1830/Revolutions and Criminal Justice. French Models and National Traditions 1780–1830*, Xavier Rousseau, Marie-Sylvie Dupont-Bouchart, Claude Vael eds., (Condé-sur-Noireau, 1999), 61–69, at 64.

14   Lascoumes, "Révolution ou réforme juridique?" 62.

15   Ibid., 64.

16   Cited in Alan Forrest, *Déserteurs et Insomis sous la Révolution et l'Empire* (Paris, 1988), 153.

17   The most influential formulation of this view is: Guy Jean-Baptiste Target, *Théorie de Code Penal* (Paris, 1893).

18   Lascoumes, "Révolution ou réforme juridique?" 65–66.

19   Michael Broers, *The Napoleonic Mediterranean. Enlightenment, Revolution and Empire* (London, 2017), 109–19.

20   Lentz, *Nouvelle Histoire*, iii, 293.

21   Ibid., 292.

22   Laurence Chatel de Brancion, *Cambacérès* (Paris, 2009), 505–17.

23   Cited in ibid., 517.

24   Ibid., 518.

25   Xavier Rousseau, "Une architecture pour la Justice. Organisation judiciaire et procedure penale (1789–1815)," in *Révolutions et Justice Penale en Europe*, op. cit., 37–58, at 47.

26   Cited in de Brancion, *Cambacérès*, 520.

27   Ibid., 519.

28   Dubois was a very distinguished doctor in his own field, who had been a member of the scientific Institute Napoleon founded in Egypt, and was promoted to the emperor's staff for his distinguished service at Eylau.

29   Cited in de Brançion, *Cambacérèces*, 524–25.

30   Cobblers were by general opinion among the lower rungs of the artisan class.

31   Cited in Jean Tulard, *Napoléon II* (Paris, 1992), 52.

32   Cited in Jean Thiry, *Le Roi de Rome, janvier 1811–juin, 1812* (Paris, 1968 ed.), 58.

33   Ibid., 61.

34   Tulard, *Napoléon II*, 53–54.

35   Ibid., 49.

36   Lentz, *Nouvelle Histoire,* ii, 126, note 1.

37   Thierry Lentz, *Joseph Bonaparte* (Paris, 2016), 382–83.

38   *Napoléon Bonaparte. Correspondance Générale*, xi, *Bruits et Bottes*, ed. Thierry Lentz, et al. (Paris, 2015), April 1811–Dec. 1811, to Caroline, April 20, 1811, #26774, 200.

39   Thiry, *Roi de Rome*, 234.

40   Ronald Ridely, *The Eagle and the Spade: Archaeology in Rome in the Napoleonic Era* (Cambridge, 1992).

41   Philip Mansel, *The Eagle in Splendour. Inside the Court of Napoleon* (London, 2015 ed.), 77.

42   Ibid., 73.

43   Ibid., 163.

44   Cited in Mansel, *Eagle in Splendour*, 79.

45   The two main sources, used rather uncritically by Jean Thiry in his *Le Roi de Rome* (Paris, 1968 ed.), are the memoirs of Napoleon's Chamberlain, Louis-François Joseph de Bausset, and

Claude-François de Menéval, who had worked first for Joseph, and succeeded Bourienne as Napoleon's private secretary after Bourienne's disgrace in 1802. Jean Tulard found that Bausset's memoirs were almost certainly written up by Balzac, and judges that "it is essential to suspect them"; Menéval was renowned for his discretion in life, but Tulard finds his objectivity suspect, and that it was unlikely that, even in his position, he knew as much as he claimed: Jean Tulard, *Nouvelle Bibliographie Critique des Mémoires sur l'époque Napoléonienne* (Paris, 1991), 35, 204–05.

46   Mansel, *Eagle in Splendour*, 76.

47   Cited in Henri Welschinger, *Le Roi de Rome, 1811–1822* (Paris, 1897), 29–30.

48   See Thiry, *Roi de Rome* (1968 ed.), 83–85 for unattributed examples of this kind, most probably drawn from Bausset.

49   Julie Hardwick, "Gender" in William Doyle (ed.) *The Oxford Handbook of the Ancien Régime* (Oxford, 2012) 187. Hardwick draws on an extensive scholarly literature.

50   Thiry, *Roi de Rome*, 115.

51   *CG*, xi, *Bruits et Bottes, Avril, 1813–Décembre, 1813*, to Madame de Montesquiou, Antwerp, Sept. 30, 1811, #28749, 1091.

52   Cited in Welschinger, *Roi de Rome*, 33.

53   Cited in ibid., 31.

54   Cited in ibid., 29.

55   Cited in Philip Dwyer, *Citizen Emperor. Napoleon in Power, 1800–1815* (London, 2013), 344–45.

56   Emmanuel Las Cases, *Le Mémorial de Sainte-Hélène*, eds. Thierry Lentz, Peter Hicks, François Houdecek, Chantal Prévot (Paris, 2017 ed.), 617. This is a new edition of the newly discovered original manuscript of Las Cases's book.

57   Cited in Mansel, *Eagle in Splendour*, 114.

58   Dwyer, *Citizen Emperor*, 385. Dwyer is wisely skeptical about theories concerning venereal disease that have circulated at times. He also raises the theory that Napoleon's sudden weight gain was caused by Fröhlich's Syndrome.

59   I am very indebted to my friend, Professor John Land, a noted surgeon, of University College London, for his learned opinions on the symptoms presented by Napoleon.

60   Las Cases, *Mémorial*, 616–17.

61   Ibid., 706.

62   Thiry, *Roi de Rome*, 115, 83.

63   Cited in Welschinger, *Roi de Rome*, 31–32.

64   Henry Lachouque and Anne S. K. Brown, *The Anatomy of Glory. Napoleon and His* Guard (Mechanicsburg, PA, 1998 ed.), 419–20.

65   *CG*, xi, to Madame Montesquiou-Fézensac, Rambouillet, May 17, 1811, #27094, 341.

66   The most detailed expression of this is in Thiry, *Roi de Rome*, 115.

67   Charles Thomas, *Le Maréchal Lannes* (Paris, 1891), 82.

68   Lannes had divorced his first wife a few months before, for committing adultery (she had an indisputably illegitimate child) while he was serving in Egypt, 1798–99.

69   Margaret Scott Chrisanon, *The Emperor's Friend: Marshal Jean Lannes* (Westport, CT, 2001), 93.

70   Thomas, *Lannes*, 89–93.

71   Ibid., 333.

72   Chrisanon, *The Emperor's Friend*, 248.

73   Ibid., 164–65, 176.

74   Henir Welschinger, *Le Pape et l'Empereur, 1804–1815* (Paris, 1905), 140–42.

75   Jacques-Olivier Boudon, *Napoléon et les Cultes* (Paris, 2002), 282.

76   Welschinger, *Le Pape et l'Empereur*, 144–46.

77   Cited in Lentz, *Nouvelle Histoire*, ii, 121.
78   Cited in Welschinger, *Le Pape et l'Empereur*, 147–48.
79   *CG*, x, to Savary, Jan. 4, 1811, #25634, 1087.
80   Cited in Welschinger, *Le Pape et l'Empereur*, 149.
81   Cited in ibid., 151.
82   *CG*, x, to Borghese, Governor-General, Turin, Jan. 2, 1811, #25608, 1077.
83   Lentz, *Nouvelle Histoire*, ii, 133.
84   *CG*, x, to Bigot, Jan. 5, 1811, #25636, 1087–88.
85   Cited in Welschinger, *Le Pape et l'Empereur*, 160.
86   Cited in Lentz, *Nouvelle Histoire*, ii, 123.
87   Boudon, *Napoléon et les Cultes*, 284–85. Lentz, *Nouvelle Histoire*, ii, 123.
88   Welschinger, *Le Pape et l'Empereur*, 164. Boudon, *Napoléon et les Cultes*, 286.
89   *CG*, xi. to Bigot, April 24, 1811, #26820, 220–22.
90   Boudon, *Napoléon et les Cultes*, 286.
91   Welschinger, *Le Pape et l'Empereur*, 164–66.
92   Michael Broers, *The Politics of Religion in Napoleonic Italy. The War against God, 1801–1814* (London, 2002), 161–66.
93   André Latreille, *L'église catholique et la Révolution française*, 2 vols. (Paris, 1970 ed.), ii, *1800–1815*, 225–26.
94   Welschinger, *Le Pape et l'Empereur*, 198–99.
95   Ibid., 201.
96   Ibid., 200–01.
97   Cited in ibid., 213–15.
98   *CG*, xi, to Bigot, Saint-Cloud, June 18, 1811, #27337, 468–70 (as an annexe).
99   Isser Woloch, *Napoleon and his Collaborators. The Making of a Dictatorship* (New York, 2001), 81–82.
100 Boudon, *Napoléon et les Cultes*, 278.
101 Victor Bindel, *Un Rêve de Napoléon. Le Vatican à Paris* (Paris, 1943).
102 Boudon, *Napoléon et les Cultes*, 287.
103 Ibid., 82, 132.
104 Ambrogio Caiani, "The Concile Nationale of 1811: Napoleon, Gallicanism and the Failure of Neo-Conciliarism," *Journal of Ecclesiastical History*, 70 (2019), 546–64.
105 Boudon, *Napoléon et les Cultes*, 287.
106 Welschinger, *Le Pape et l'Empereur*, 237–38.
107 Boudon, *Napoléon et les Cultes*, 288.
108 *CG*, xi, to Fesch, July 12, 1811, #27609, 607.
109 Boudon, *Napoléon et les Cultes*, 288.
110 Ibid., 288.
111 The most detailed, authoritative research on this is Caiani, "Concile," op. cit.
112 Welschinger, *Le Pape et l'Empereur*, 275–80.
113 Ibid., 252–53.
114 *CG*, xi, to Fesch, July 22, 1811, #27757, 665.
115 Cited in Welschinger, *Le Pape et l'Empereur*, 258.
116 Ibid., 245–49, 282.
117 Caiani, "Concile of 1811," 563.
118 *CG*, xi, to Bigot, Sept. 30, 1811, #28744, 1089–90.
119 Ibid., to Bigot, Oct. 6, 1811, #28778, 1103.
120 Cited in Lentz, *Nouvelle Histoire*, ii, 128.
121 Caiani, "Concile of 1811," 563.

122 Ibid., 563.

123 *CG*, xi (April 1811–Dec. 1811) to Bigot, Sept. 30, 1811, Antwerp, #28744, 1089–90.

124 Ibid., to Bigot, Oct. 26, Rotterdam, #28922, 1163.

125 Ibid., to Bigot, Sept. 30, 1811, Antwerp, #28744, 1089–90.

126 Ibid., to Savary, Nov.21, 1811, #29165, 1279.

127 Welschinger, *Le Pape et l'Empereur*, 322–23.

128 *CG*, xi, to Savary, Dec. 10, 1811, #29312, 1342.

129 Caiani, "Concile of 1811," passim.

130 Lentz, *Nouvelle Histoire*, ii, 131.

131 *CG*, xi to Bigot, Oct. 8, 1811, #28790, 1108.

132 Ibid., to Bigot, Oct. 22, 1811, Amsterdam, #28883, 1143–44. The dioceses were: Saint-Brieuc, Bordeaux, Ghent, Tournai, Troyes, and Alpes-Maritimes.

133 Ibid., to Bigot, Oct. 22, 1811, Amsterdam, #28884, 1144.

134 Ibid., to Bigot, Oct. 6, 1811, #28778, 1103.

135 Geoffrey Ellis, *Napoleon's Continental Blockade. The Case of Alsace* (Oxford, 1981), 163.

136 Nicholas François Mollien, *Mémoires d'un Ministre du Trésor Public 1780–1815* 3 vols. (Paris, 1898 ed.), iii, 20–24. It should be noted that these memoirs are among the most reliable and valuable of the period: In his *Nouvelle Bibliographie Critique* of the memoirs of the period, Jean Tulard notes only of Mollien, "indispensable": 211.

137 Gavin Daly, *Inside Napoleonic France. State and Society in Rouen, 1800–1815* (Aldershot, 2001), 178.

138 Mollien, *Mémoires*, iii, 27–28.

139 Ibid., iii, 25.

140 Ibid., iii, 28–32.

141 Daly, *Inside Napoleonic France*, 179.

142 *CG*, x, to Mollien, March 4, 1811, #26094, 1275.

143 Daly, *Inside Napoleonic France*, 179. Mollien, *Mémoires*, iii, 27.

144 Mollien, *Mémoires*, iii, 31–32.

145 Geoffrey Ellis, *The Napoleonic Empire* (Basingstoke, 2001 ed.), 117.

146 *CG*, xi, to Lacuée, Saint-Cloud, May 2, 1811, #26943, 279–80.

147 Ibid., to Gen. Clarke, Min of War, Saint-Cloud, May 7, 1811, #26998, 303–04.

148 Ibid., to Gen. Duroc, Saint-Cloud, May 7, 1811, #27002, 305.

149 Maurice Agulhon, *The Republican Experiment, 1848–1852* (Cambridge, 1983).

150 Cited in Alain Pillepich, *Milan, Capitale Napoléonienne 1800–1814* (Paris, 2001), 595.

151 Cited in Pillepich, *Milan*, 595–96.

152 Ibid., 596–97.

153 Ibid., *Milan*, 597.

154 Richard C. Cobb, *The Police and the People. French Popular Protest 1789–1820* (Oxford, 1972 ed.), 108.

155 Michael Rowe, *From Reich to State. The Rhineland in the Revolutionary Age, 1780–1820* (Cambridge, 2003), 205–06.

156 Cobb, *Police and the People*, 116.

157 Ibid., 108.

158 Cited in ibid., 106.

159 Ibid., 108–09.

160 Alan Forrest, "Experiencing the Continental System in the Cities of the French Atlantic," in Katherine B. Aasletad and Johan Joor, eds., *Revisiting Napoleon's Continental System. Local, Regional and European Experiences* (Basingstoke, 2015), 207–22, at 214.

161 Dwyer, *Citizen Emperor*, 341–43.

162   Cobb, *Police and the People*, 115.
163   *CG*, x, to Portalis, Compiègne, April 22, 1810, #23465, 120.
164   Ibid., to Savary, Fontainebleau, Oct. 25, 1810, #25063, 849.
165   Lentz, *Nouvelle Histoire du Premier Empire*, iii, *La France et l'Europe de Napoléon 1804–1814* (Paris, 2007), 641.
166   Mollien, *Mémoires*, iii, 37–38.
167   Cobb, *Police and the People*, 116–17.

2: The Great Empire, 1810–1812

1   Louis abdicated and fled his throne on July 3; Napoleon moved swiftly to annex the whole country to France. He stripped Jérôme of the coastal areas of the former kingdom of Hanover in August 1810, having given it to him in the wake of the war of 1806.
2   Jacques-Olivier Boudon, "Napoléon, les catholiques français et le Pape," in Lentz, *1810*, 131–48, at 137–38, 148.
3   Cited in Angela Valente, *Gioacchino Murat e l'Italia Meridionale* (Turin, 1965), 232–33.
4   John A. Davis, *Naples and Napoleon. Southern Italy and the European Revolutions 1780–1860* (Oxford, 2006), 131–32.
5   *CG*, xi, to Clarke, Min of War, Saint-Cloud, June 24, 1811, #27429, 523–24.
6   Cited in Lentz, *Nouvelle Histoire*, ii, 44.
7   Vincent Haegle, *Murat. La solitude du cavalier* (Paris, 2015), 626–27.
8   Jacques-Olivier Boudon, *Le Roi Jérôme. Frère prodigue de Napoléon* (Paris, 2008), 358.
9   Cited in Valente, *Murat*, 232.
10   Cited in ibid., 239–42.
11   *CG* xi, to Maret, For. Min. Saint-Cloud, June 20, 1811, #27365, 488.
12   Cited in Valente, *Murat*, 239–42.
13   Edward Gibbon, *The History of the Decline and Fall of the Roman Empire* (first published 1776, London, 1994 edition), ed. David Womersley, 36.
14   *CG*, x to Lebrun, Rambouillet, July 8, 1810, #23927, 333.
15   Ibid., to Lebrun, Rambouillet, July 9, 1810, #23931, 335–36.
16   Ibid., to Van de Poll, President of the Commission of Government, Rambouillet, July 9, 1810, #23932, 336.
17   Ibid., to Mme Boubers, Governess to the Dutch Princes, Rambouillet, July 10, 1810, #23936, 338.
18   Ibid., to Champagny, For. Min., Rambouillet, July 11, 1810, #23955, 345.
19   Ibid., to Gen Clarke, Min of War, Rambouillet, July 11, 1810, #23957, 346–47.
20   Ibid., to Gaudin, Min of Finances, Rambouillet, July 11, 1810, #23962, 348.
21   Don Alexander, *Rod of Iron: French Counter-insurgency Policy in Aragon during the Peninsular War* (Wilmington, VA, 1985), 352–61.
22   *CG*, x to Berthier, Compiègne, April 9, 1810, #23407, 96.
23   Michael Broers, *The Napoleonic Empire in Italy, 1796–1814. Cultural Imperialism in a European Context?* (Basingstoke, 2005), 135, 175.
24   *CG*, x to Reille, Saint-Cloud, July 3, 1810, #23892, 319.
25   John Lawrence Tone, *The Fatal Knot. The Guerrilla War in Navarre and the Defeat of Napoleon in Spain* (Charlotte, NC, 1994), 86–88, 102–03.
26   Tone, *Fatal Knot*, 104.
27   Ibid., 104–25.
28   Jean-Marc Lafon, *L'Andalousie et Napoléon. Contre-insurrection, Collaboration et Resistances dans le Midi de l'Espagne (1808–1812)* (Paris, 2007), 378–89.
29   André Fugier, *La Junte Supérieur des Asturias et l'Invasion française, 1810–1811* (Paris, 1930), 28–35.

30 *CG*, x to Clarke, Min of War, Saint-Cloud, July 10, 1810, #23907, 324.
31 Juan Mercader Riba, *Jose Bonaparte. Rey de España, vol. 1 1808–1813. Estrutura del Estado Español Bonapartista* (Madrid, 1983), 176–84.
32 Tone, *Fatal Knot*, 156–57.
33 Lafon, *L'Adalousie et Napoléon*, 57–404.
34 Ibid., 129.
35 Timothy Gribaudi, "Pacification, collaboration and resistance in Napoleonic Valencia, 1808–1814," (unpublished Oxford M.Phil. thesis, 2012), 55–60.
36 Fugier, *La Junte Supérieur*, 164–67.
37 Tone, *Fatal Knot*, 109–13.
38 *CG*, x to Berthier, Compiègne, April 17, 1810, #23439, 108–09.
39 Lentz, *Nouvelle Histoire*, ii, 176.
40 *CG*, x to Berthier, Saint-Cloud, July 31, 1810, #24175, 458–59.
41 *Mémoires de Masséna, rédigés d'après les documents qu'il a laissé*, ed. Gen. Koch (7 vols., Paris, 1850), vol. vii, 506.
42 *CG*, xi to Berthier, Saint-Cloud, April 21, 1811, #26787, 206. The sentence marked in italic was not published when the letter first appeared in Léon Lecestre, *Lettres inédits de Napoléon I* (Paris, 1892), vol. ii, 126.
43 Charles J. Esdaile, *Fighting Napoleon. Guerrillas, Bandits and Adventurers in Spain 1808–1814* (London, and New Haven, CT, 2004), 128.
44 *CG*, xi to Savary, Saint-Cloud, April 21, 1811, #26797, 209.
45 Ibid., to Berthier, Saint-Cloud, May 1, 1811, # 26921, 266.
46 Cited in Esdaile, *Peninsular War*, 323.
47 *CG*, xi to Berthier, April 4, 1811, # 26505, 51–2.
48 *CG*, xi to Gen. Clarke, April 1, 1811, #26449, 24.
49 Ibid., to Berthier, Le Havre, May 29, 1810, #23671, 229–30.
50 Esdaile, *Peninsular War*, 319.
51 Ibid., 324–25.
52 Ibid.
53 Ibid., 323–24. Esdaile's careful research has shown this was Masséna's rationale, rather than poor intelligence.
54 Cited in Rory Muir, *Wellington. The Path to Victory, 1769–1814* (New Haven, CT and London, 2013), 383.
55 Muir, *Wellington*, ii, 385.
56 For an excellent account of the battle: ibid., 324–26.
57 Ibid., 359–61.
58 Ibid., 366.
59 Ibid., 369.
60 Ibid., 367.
61 Ibid., 368–69.
62 Esdaile, *Peninsular War*, 333.
63 *Mémoires de Masséna*, vii, 509–11.
64 Ibid., 546–47.
65 Ibid., vii, 510–11.
66 Muir, *Wellington*, ii, 418.
67 *Mémoires de Masséna*, vii, 512–13.
68 Muir, *Wellington*, ii, 420–21.
69 Cited in ibid., 421.
70 Ibid., 425.

71 *Mémoires de Masséna*, vii, 551.

72 Ibid., 555.

73 Ibid., 367–68.

74 *CG*, xi, to Berthier, April 9, 1811, #26596, 96–97.

75 *Mémoires de Masséna*, vii, 604.

76 This is often cited, recently in David Buttery, *Wellington Against Masséna. The Third Invasion of Portugal, 1810–1811* (Barnsley, United Kingdom, 2007), 171.

77 *Mémoires de Masséna*, vii, 560.

78 Cited in ibid., vii, 515.

79 *CG*, xi, to Bessières, Boulogne, Sept. 20, 1811, #28706, 1073.

80 Ibid., to Mollien, Saint-Cloud, April 22, 1811, #26805, 212.

81 Ibid., to Berthier, April 9, 1811, #26596, 96–97.

82 Esdaile, *Peninsular War*, 356–57.

83 Cited in ibid., 357.

84 Gribaudi, *Napoleonic Valencia*, 31.

85 Charles J. Esdaile, *Outpost of Empire. The Napoleonic Occupation of Andalucía, 1810–1812* (Norman, 2012), 191. It should be noted that Esdaile's assessment that such behavior alienated the Andalucíans is somewhat contradicted by the careful research of Lafon, op. cit.

86 Cited in Lentz, *Joseph Bonaparte*, 382.

87 *Napoléon et Joseph. Correspondance intégrale, 1784–1818*, ed. Vincent Haegele (Paris, 2007), Joseph to Napoleon, Santa Maria de la Nieva, April 25, 1811, #1348, 709–10.

88 Lentz, *Joseph Bonaparte*, 383.

89 *Napoléon et Joseph*, Joseph to Napoleon, Burgos, May 1, 1811, #1349, 710–11.

90 Esdaile, *Peninsular War*, 323–33.

91 Agustín Guimera Ravina, "Bloquero imperfect, Guerra anfibia y liderazago: Cadiz, 1810," in Manuel-Reyes García Hurtado, ed., *La Armada española en el siglo xviii. Ciencia, hombres y barcas* (Madrid, 2010), 207–32.

92 Esdaile, *Peninsular War*, 339.

93 Cited in *CG*, xi, 1484.

94 Reinhard A. Stauber, "The Illyrian Provinces," in *The Napoleonic Empire and the New European Political Culture* (Basingstoke, 2012), eds. Michael Broers, Peter Hicks, and Agustín Guimerá, 241–53, at 242.

95 Peter Vodapivec, "Illyrian Provinces from a Slovene Perspective: Myth and Reality," in Ute Planert, ed., *Napoleon's Empire*, 252–63, at 252–53.

96 Stauber, "Illyrian Provinces," 243–43.

97 Paul W. Schroeder, *The Transformation of European Politics, 1763–1848* (Oxford, 1994), 407.

98 Marko Trogrilić and Josip Vrandečić, "French Rule in Dalmatia, 1806–1814: Globalizing a Local Geopolitics," in *Napoleon's Empire. European Politics in Global Perspective* (Basingstoke, 2016) Ute Planert, ed., 264–76, at 267.

99 Trogrilić and Vrandečić, "French Rule in Dalmatia," 271.

100 Ibid., 271.

101 Wolfram Siemann, *Metternich. Strategist and Visionary* (Eng. trans., Cambridge, Mass., 2019), 369–70.

102 These are studied in Michael Broers, "The Napoleonic Judicial System in the Illyrian Provinces, 1808–1813: An Exercise in Incongruity," in idem, *The Napoleonic Mediterranean. Enlightenment, Revolution and Empire* (London, 2017), 190–219.

103 Stauber, "Illyrian Provinces," 244–45.

104 Cited in Broers, "Napoleonic Judicial System," 216–17.

105 Todorov, *La Grande Armée*, 51.

106 Ibid., 60–61.

107 Ibid., 68.

108 Ibid., 75.

109 Ibid., 73.

110 Roger Knight, *Britain Against Napoleon. The Organisation of Victory 1793–1815* (London, 2013), 274.

111 Knight, *Britain Against Napoleon*, 282.

112 Cited in ibid., 283.

113 *CG*, x, to Josephine, Versailles, Aug. 10, 1810, #24309, 523.

114 Ibid., to Lebrun, Rambouillet, July 9, 1810, #23931, 335–36.

115 Ibid., to Lebrun, Rambouillet, July 10, 1810, #23948, 324–43.

116 Ibid., to Josephine, Rambouillet, July 8, 1810, #23926, 333.

117 Sylvie Humbert-Convain, *Le juge de paix et la repression des infractions dounanières en Flandre et en Hollande, 1794–1815: Contribution à l'histoire du système continental napoleonien* (Valenciennes, 1993), 197–209.

118 *CG*, x, to Deponthon, Cabinet Secretary, Rambouillet, July 15, 1810, #24004, 374–75.

119 Ibid., to Lebrun, Rambouillet, July 9, 1810, #23931, 335–36.

120 Johan Joor, "The Napoleonic period in Holland from a Dutch historical perspective," in *Napoleon's Empire*, 53–66, at 62.

121 *CG*, x, to Lebrun, March 19, 1810, #26321, 1385.

122 Johan Joor, "Resistance against Napoleon in the kingdom of Holland," in *Napoleonic Empire and the New European Political Culture*, 112–22, at 116.

123 Johan Joor, "'A very rebellious disposition': Dutch experience and popular protest under the Napoleonic regime (1806–1813)" in *Soldiers, Citizens and Civilians. Experiences and Perceptions of the Revolutionary and Napoleonic Wars, 1790–1820* (Basingstoke, 2009) eds. Alan Forrest, Karen Hagemann, and Jane Rendall, 181–204.

124 *CG*, xi, to Lebrun, Saint-Cloud, May 3, 1811, #26958, 286–87.

125 Ibid., to Davout, Fontainebleau, Oct. 4, 1810, #24781, 730.

126 Cited in Katherine B. Aalestad, "War Without Battles: Civilian experiences of economic warfare during the Napoleonic era in Hamburg," in *Soldiers, Citizens and Civilians*, 118–36, at 123.

127 *CG*, to Alexander, Feb. 28, 1811, #26020, 1244–46.

128 Boudon, *Jérôme*, 342–43.

129 Ibid., 344.

130 *CG*, x, to Jérôme, Feb. 10, 1811, #25899, 1195–96.

131 Cited in Boudon, *Jérôme*, 346–47.

132 Cited in ibid., 349.

133 Lentz, *Nouvelle Histoire*, ii, 35.

134 Boudon, *Jérôme*, 349.

135 Cited in ibid., 349.

136 Ibid., 352.

137 Nicola-Peter Todorov, *L'administration du royaume de Westphalie de 1807 à 1813. Le department de l'Elbe* (Saarbrücken, 2011), 556–57.

138 Aaslestad, "War Without Battles," 123–24.

139 Ibid., 125.

140 Cited in ibid., 124.

141 Ibid., 128–31.

142 *CG*, x, to Vice Admiral Decrès, March 1, 1811, #26033, 1251.

143 Schroeder, *Transformation*, 393.

144 Cited in François Crouzet, *L'Économie Britannique et le Blocus Continental* (Paris, 1987), 588.

145   Crouzet, *L'Économie Britannique*, 563.

146   *CG*, x, to Davout, Saint-Cloud, Aug. 19, 1810, #24360, 549.

147   *CG*, x to Davout, Saint-Cloud, Sept. 2, 1810, #24471, 592–93.

148   Ibid., to Davout, Fontainebleau, Sept. 28, 1810, #24702, 695–96.

149   Lentz, *Nouvelle Histoire*, ii, 104.

150   *CG*, x, to Collin de Sussy, Director-General of Customs, Nov. 28, 1810, #25373, 978.

151   Nicholas François Mollien, *Mémoires d'un Ministre du Trésor Public, 1780–1814* (Paris, 3 vols., 1898 ed.), iii, 101–2.

152   *CG*, x, to Mollien, March 9, 1811, #26164, 1311. The words "to me" are underlined in the original.

153   Cited in Crouzet, *L'Économie britannique*, 592.

154   Knight, *Britain Against Napoleon*, 412: In April 1813, merchants in the island were finally able to resume and smuggled an unprecendently large volume of goods into Germany.

155   Mollien, *Mémoires*, iii, 36.

156   Crouzet, *L'Économie Britannique*, 525–62.

157   *CG*, x, to Davout, March 13, 1811, #26217, 1336.

158   Ibid, to Davout, March 25, 1811, #26394, 1421.

159   Cited Boyd Hilton, *A Mad, Bad and Dangerous People? England 1783–1846* (Oxford, 2006), 212.

160   Hilton, *Mad Bad and Dangerous*, 224–25.

161   Crouzet, *L'Économie Britannique*, 581.

162   Ibid., 635, 640.

163   Ibid., 579–80.

164   Ibid., 615–28.

165   Cited in ibid., 625.

166   Ibid., 626–27.

167   Cited in ibid., 635, note 177.

168   David Andress, *The Savage Storm. Britain on the Brink in the Age of Napoleon* (London, 2012), 264.

169   Ibid., 270.

170   Ibid., 267–68.

171   Ibid., 264–65.

172   Ibid., 270, 273.

173   Hilton, *Mad, Bad and Dangerous*, 218.

174   Rasmus Glenthøj and Morten Nordhagen Ottosen, *Experiences of War and Nationality in Denmark and Norway, 1807–1814* (Basingstoke, 2014), 146.

175   Ibid., 148.

176   Thierry Lentz, *Nouvelle Histoire du Premier Empire*, i, *Napoleon et la Conquête de l'Europe, 1804–1810* (Paris, 2002), 542.

177   *CG*, x, to Champagny, Saint-Cloud, July 25, 1810, #24129, 441.

178   Lentz, *Nouvelle Histoire*, i, 543.

179   Glenthøj and Ottosen, *Experiences of War*, 149.

180   Lentz, *Nouvelle Histoire*, i, 543.

181   Glenthøj and Ottosen, *Experiences of War*, 149.

182   *CG*, x, to Charles XIII, King of Sweden, Saint-Cloud, Sept. 6, 1810, #24500, 605.

183   *Ibid,* to Champagny, Saint-Cloud, Sept. 7, 1810, 1:00 A.M., #24514, 609–10.

184   Dominic Lievin, *Russia and the Defeat of Napoleon. The Battle for Europe 1807 to 1812* (London, 2009), 95–96.

185   *CG*, xi, to Champagny, April 1, 1811, #26447, 23.

186 Both cited in Lentz, *Nouvelle Histoire*, i, 543.
187 *CG*, x, to Bernadotte, Saint-Cloud, Sept. 10, 1810, #24542, note 4, 621–22.
188 Cited in Lentz, *Nouvelle histoire*, ii, 73.
189 Crouzet, *L'Économie Britannique*, 598–601.
190 *CG*, x, to Davout, March 10, 1811, #26178, 1318.
191 Ibid, to Decrès, March 25, 1811, #26364, 1404–5.
192 Ibid, to Davout, March 25, 1811, #26396, 1422.
193 Crouzet, *L'Économie Britannique*, 615.
194 Knight, *Britain Against Napoleon*, 173–74.
195 Ibid., 447.
196 *CG*, viii (1808) to Champagny, Saint-Cloud, Sept. 2, 1808, #18807, 01920.
197 Ibid., to Soult, Saint-Cloud, Sept. 4, 1808, #18826, 1032.
198 Ibid., to Jérôme, Saint-Cloud, Sept. 6, 1808, #18834, 1035–36.
199 Ibid., to Soult, Saint-Cloud, Sept. 10, 1808, #18884, 1062.
200 Schroeder, *Transformation*, 409–10.
201 Christopher Clark, *The Iron Kingdom: The Rise and Downfall of Prussia, 1600–1947* (London, 2007 ed.), 339.
202 Ibid., 339–40. For the wider context of noble opposition: Ronald Berdahl, *The Politics of the Prussian Nobility: The Development of a Conservative Ideology, 1770–1848* (Princeton, NJ, 1988), 107–38.
203 Clark, *Iron Kingdom*, 322.
204 Ibid., 323.
205 Ibid., 326.
206 For the classic studies in English: William O. Shanahan, *Prussian Military Reforms (1789–1813)* (New York, 1945); Peter Paret, *Yorck and the Era of Prussian Reform (1807–1815)* (Princeton, NJ, 1966).
207 Cited in Clark, *Iron Kingdom*, 353.
208 Ibid., 351.
209 Lieven, *Russia*, 139.
210 David Chandler, *The Campaigns of Napoleon* (London, 1967 ed.), 872.
211 *CG*, xi, to Maret, Saint-Cloud, April, 27, 1811, #26869, 243–44.
212 Clark, *Iron Kingdom*, 351–52.
213 "L'Évangile selon Montholon," in *Napoléon à Sainte-Hélène*, ed. Jean Tulard (Paris, 1981), 595.
214 Cited in Clark, *Iron Kingdom*, 354.
215 Schroeder, *Transformation*, 411.
216 Cited in Marie-Pierre Rey, *Alexander I. The Tsar Who Defeated Napoleon* (DeKalb, 2012), 208.
217 Siemann, *Metternich*, 311. Paul Schroeder's belief that Metternich felt Prussia to be doomed, based on his memoirs, is lessened by Siemann's fresh research.
218 Clark, *Iron Kingdom*, 354–56.
219 Schroder, *Transformation*, 411.
220 Clark, *Iron Kingdom*, 352–53.
221 Ibid., 356.
222 Despite the care taken over this, Napoleon, and scores of historians ever since, refer to it incorrectly as "the Grand Duchy."
223 For a full account: Czubaty, *Duchy*, 63–77.
224 Ibid., 79.
225 Jarosław Czubaty, "Glory, Honour and Patriotism: Military Careers in the Duchy of Warsaw, 1806–1815," in *Soldiers, Citizens and Civilians*, 59–76, at 61–62.
226 Czubaty, *Duchy*, 81.

227 Jaroslav Czubaty, "What lies behind the glory? A balance sheet of the Napoleonic Era in Poland," in *Napoleon's Empire*, 173–86, at 176.

228 A small portion of southern Galicia remained under Vienna.

229 Alexander Grab, *Napoleon and the Transformation of Europe* (Basningstoke, 2003), 179–80.

230 For a comprehensive, masterly analysis of Napoleonic rule: Czubaty, *Duchy, passim.*

231 Ibid., 157.

232 W. H. Zawadzki, *A Man of Honour. Adam Czartoyski as a Statesman in Russia and Poland, 1795–1831* (Oxford, 1993), 147–49.

233 Cited in Rey, *Alexander,* 207–8.

234 Czubaty, *Duchy,* 153–54.

235 Cited in Rey, *Alexander,* 208–9.

236 Siemann, *Metternich,* 310.

237 Knight, *Britain Against Napoleon,* 181.

3: Lurching to War: Napoleon and Alexander: Posturing and Poise, 1810–1812

1 Schroeder, *Transformation,* 421.

2 Ibid, 422.

3 Lieven, *Russia,* 75.

4 Ibid., 91, 93, 183.

5 Olivier Varlan, *Caulaincourt. Diplomate de Napoléon* (Paris, 2018), 224–25.

6 Cited in Marie-Pierre Rey, *L'effroyable tragédie. Une nouvelle histoire de la champagne de Russie* (Paris, 2012), 33.

7 Lieven, *Russia,* 78–79.

8 *CG*, x, to Champagny, Feb. 10, 1811, #25892, 1192.

9 Lieven, *Russia,* 78–79.

10 Varlan, *Caulaincourt,* 222.

11 *CG*, x, to Alexander I, Feb. 28, 1811, #26020, 1244–46.

12 Serge Tatistcheff (ed.), *Alexandre I et Napoleon d'après leur correspondance inedite, 1801–1812* (Paris, 1891), 547–52.

13 Aleksandr A. Orlov, "Russia and Britain in International Relations in the Period 1807–1812," in *Russia and the Napoleonic Wars*, eds. Janet M. Hartley, Paul Keenan, and Dominic Lieven (Basingstoke, 2015), 84–96, at 88–89.

14 Lieven, *Russia,* 79.

15 Ibid., 22.

16 Knight, *Britain Against Napoleon,* 17–19.

17 Lieven, *Russia,* 63–64.

18 Rey, *Alexander I,* 122.

19 Lieven, *Russia,* 63–64.

20 *CG*, x, to Alexander I, Feb. 28, 1811, #26020, 1244–46.

21 Ibid, to Champagny, March 5, 1811, #26067, 1262.

22 Ibid, to Champagny, March 10, 1811, #26170.

23 *CG*, xi to Champagny, April 5, 1811, #26542, 67–68. The words were underlined by Napoleon.

24 *CG*, x to Alexander, Feb. 28, 1811, #26020, 1244–46.

25 Varlan, *Caulaincourt,* 229–30.

26 Ibid, 229.

27 Cited in ibid., 230.

28 Ibid., 230.

29 Ibid., 228.

30 Ibid., 21–26.
31 Ibid., 230–31.
32 Ibid., 231.
33 Rey, *Alexander*, 207–9.
34 Cited in ibid., 207–9.
35 *CG*, xi, to Champagny, April 5, 1811, #26542, 67–68. The words were underlined by Napoleon.
36 Lieven, *Russia*, 82–87.
37 Rey, *Alexander I*, 211.
38 Varlan, *Caulaincourt*, 232–37.
39 Cited in ibid., 234.
40 Rey, *Alexander I*, 227–29.
41 Lieven, *Russia*, 81.
42 Cited in Rey, *Alexander I*, 227.
43 Cited in ibid., 209.
44 Henri Troyat, *Alexander Ire, le sphinx du Nord* (Paris, 2008).
45 Cited in Lieven, *Russia*, 84–85.
46 *CG*, xi, to Champagny, April 17, 1811, #26705, 150.
47 Schroeder, *Transformation*, 426.
48 Migliorini, *Napoléon*, 363.
49 Ibid., 363. Maret was the son of a doctor.
50 Varlan, *Caulaincourt*, 238–39.
51 Cited in Rey, *Alexander*, 209.
52 *CG*, x, to Champagny, Feb. 17, 1811, #25952, 1217.
53 Ibid., to Champagny, Feb., 1811, #26002, 1234–35.
54 Ibid., to Champagny, April 8, 1811, #26572, 84–85.
55 Varlan, *Caulaincourt*, 241–42.
56 Cited in ibid., 254.
57 Cited in ibid., 250.
58 Cited in ibid., 248–49.
59 Cited in ibid., 251.
60 Cited in Welschinger, *Le Pape et l'Empereur*, 166, 169.
61 *CG*, x, to Alexander, Feb. 28, 1811, #26020, 1244–46.
62 Ibid., to Champagny, March 5, 1811, #26067, 1262.
63 Bessarabia.
64 Cited in Emmanuel de Waresquiel, *Talleyrand. Dernières Nouvelles du Diable* (Paris, 2011), 110–11.
65 For a brief account: Michael Broers, *Napoleon's Other War. Bandits, Rebels and their Pursuers in the Age of Revolutions* (Witney, 2010), 76–80.
66 Denis Sdvizkov, "*L'Empire d'Occident* faces the Russian Empire: inter-imperial exchanges and their reflection in historiography," in *Napoleon's Empire*, 159–72, at 164.
67 Schroeder, *Transformation*, 423.
68 Lentz, *Nouvelle Histoire*, ii, 209.
69 Cited in *Napoléon. De la Guerre*, ed. Bruno Colson (Paris, 2011), 434.
70 Cited in Rey, *Alexander*, 210.
71 John Bew, *Castlereagh. Enlightenment, War and Tyranny* (London, 2011), 312.
72 *CG*, xi, to Champagny, April 5, 1811, #26542, 67–68.
73 Rey, *Alexander*, 44.
74 Kerautret, "Napoléon et le mirage," 35–36.
75 *CG*, xi, to Cambacérèces, Düsseldorf, Nov. 3, 1811, #28990, 1195.

76   Lentz, *Nouvelle Histoire*, ii, 241.
77   Rey, *L'effroyable tragédie*, 49.

4: The Order of Battle: Autumn 1811–June 1812

1   *CG*, xi, to Clarke, Saint-Cloud, Nov. 12, 1811, #29023, 1211.
2   Ibid., to Clarke, Saint-Cloud, Nov. 12, 1811, #29030, 1214.
3   Ibid., to Clarke, Saint-Cloud, Nov. 12, 1811, #29032, 1215–16.
4   Ibid., to Clarke, Saint-Cloud, Nov. 12, 1811, #29034, 1217–18.
5   Ibid., to Clarke, Saint-Cloud, Nov. 12, 1811, #29036, 1219.
6   Ibid., to Clarke, Saint-Cloud, Nov. 12, 1811, #29031, 1215.
7   Cited in Rey, *Alexander*, 225.
8   Cited in de Brancion, *Cambacérécs*, 536.
9   Cited in ibid., 536.
10   Cited in ibid., 536.
11   *CG*, xii, *La Campagne de Russie, 1812*, to Berthier, January 16, 1812, #29762, 110–11.
12   Lentz, *Nouvelle* Histoire, ii, 256.
13   Thomas Munck, "Preface," in Pasi I Halainen, Michael Bregnsbo, Karin Sennefelt, and Patrik Winton, eds., *Scandinavia in the Age of Revolution. Nordic Political Cultures, 1740–1820* (Farnham, United Kingdom, 2011), xvii.
14   de Briancion, *Cambacérès*, 538.
15   Mollien, *Mémoires*, iii, 66–69.
16   Ibid, 111.
17   *CG*, xi, to Decrès, Dec. 6, 1811, #29285, 1330–31.
18   Ibid., to Berthier, Saint-Cloud, Nov. 30, 1811, #29217, 1298.
19   de Brancion, *Cambacérès*, 533–34.
20   *CG*, xii, to Cambacérès, Feb. 13, 1812, #29966, 231–32.
21   Ibid, to Joseph, Dec. 31, 1811, #29569, 1471.
22   Esdaile, *Peninsular War*, 370.
23   Lachouque and Brown, *Anatomy*, 198–200.
24   Esdaile, *Outpost of Empire*, 386.
25   Esdaile, *Peninsular War*, 370.
26   Ibid., 378.
27   Ibid., 502.
28   Muir, *Wellington*, ii, 446.
29   Esdaile, *Peninsular War*, 370–71. Tone, *Fatal Knot*, 130.
30   Tone, *Fatal Knot*, 128–29.
31   Ibid., 129–34.
32   Ibid., 132.
33   Ibid., 131–34.
34   Cited in ibid., 131.
35   Esdaile, *Peninsular War*, 371.
36   Muir, *Wellington*, ii, ii, 446.
37   Esdaile, *Peninsular War*, 378–79.
38   Cited in Muir, *Wellington*, ii, ii, 440.
39   Muir, *Wellington*, ii, ii, 439.
40   Ibid., 438.
41   Mollien, *Mémoires*, iii, 5–6.
42   Muir, *Wellington*, ii, ii, 439.
43   Ibid., 441–43.

44 Esdaile, *Peninsular War*, 380.
45 Cited in ibid., 380.
46 Esdaile, *Peninsular War*, 380–81.
47 Ibid., 382.
48 *CG*, xii to Berthier (annex of Berthier's letter to Marmont), February 18, 1812, #29995, 246–50.
49 Cited in Esdaile, *Peninsular War*, 382.
50 Ibid., 384.
51 Cited in ibid., 387.
52 Ibid., 387.
53 Ibid., 386.
54 Lentz, *Joseph Bonaparte*, 389.
55 Ibid., 389–90.
56 Muir, *Britain and the Defeat of Napoleon*, 198.
57 Bew, *Castlereagh*, 314.
58 Varlan, *Caulaincourt*, 260.
59 Mollien, *Mémoires*, iii, 79.
60 The summation of various remarks assembled in Jean Lucas-Dubretion, *Napoléon devant l'Espagne. Ce qu'a vu Goya* (Paris, 1946), 470.
61 Bew, *Castlereagh*, 308.
62 This process is traced in Charles J. Esdaile, *The Duke of Wellington and the Command of the Spanish Army* (London, 1990), *passim*.
63 Rey, *L'effroyable tragédie*, 53–54.
64 Ibid., 44.
65 Forrest, *Déserteurs*, 169.
66 Isser Woloch *The New Regime. Transformations of the French Civic Order, 1789–1820s* (New York, 1994), 418.
67 Forrest, *Déserteurs*, 67.
68 Ibid., 63.
69 Ibid., 68.
70 Ibid., 127.
71 Ibid., 241.
72 Ibid., 113.
73 Woloch, *New Regime*, 417.
74 Forrest, *Déserteurs*, 232.
75 Ibid., 234.
76 Woloch, *New Regime*, 418.
77 Ibid., 418–19.
78 Ibid., 419.
79 Ibid., 418.
80 Forrest, *Déserteurs*, 111.
81 Jacques Morvan, *Le soldat impérial*, 2 vols. (Paris, 1904), i, 333.
82 Chandler, *Campaigns*, 755.
83 Forrest, "Napoleon's Vision," 50.
84 Chandler, *Campaigns*, 753–54.
85 Lachouque and Brown, *Anatomy*, 190.
86 Brun, "La formation 'diplomatique.'" 49.
87 Lachouque and Brown, *Anatomy*, 232.
88 Ibid., 198–200.

89 Ibid., 220–21.

90 Alain Pigeard, 'Le rôle de Davout dans la champagne de 1812," in *1812, la campagne de Russie*, eds. Marie-Pierre Rey and Thierry Lentz, (Paris, 2012), 75–83, 77.

91 Morvan, *Soldat Impérial*, i, 333–35.

92 Chandler, *Campaigns*, 758.

93 Pigeard, "Le rôle de Davout," 76.

94 Cited in Chandler, *Campaigns*, 758.

95 Pigeard, "Le rôle de Davout," 77.

96 David Gates, *Napoleonic Wars, 1803–1815* (London, 1997), 208.

97 Morvan, *Soldat Impérial*, i, 334.

98 Gates, *Napoleonic Wars*, 208.

99 Houdecek, "La Grande Armée," 1347–48.

100 Chandler, *Campaigns*, 754.

101 Cited in Paul Britten Austin, "Oudinot," in *Napoleon's Marshals*, ed., David Chandler, (London, 1997), 382–400, 384.

102 Cited in ibid., 384.

103 Ibid., 400.

104 François-Guy Hourtoulle, "Ney," in *Dictionnaire Napoleon*, ed. Jean Tulard (Paris, 1989), 1236–38, 1236.

105 Brigadier Peter Young, "Ney," in Chandler, *Napoleon's Marshals*, 358–80, 360.

106 Morvan, *Soldat Impérial*, ii, 20.

107 Hourtoulle, "Ney," 1236.

108 Las Cases, *Le Mémorial de Sainte-Hélène* (2017 ed.) 223.

109 Ibid, 436, note 1.

110 Rory Muir, *Tactics and the Experience of Battle in the Age of Napoleon* (New Haven, CT, and London, 1998), 106.

111 M. Dugue McCarhy, "Cavalerie," in Jean Tulard, ed., *Dictionnaire Napoléon* (Paris, 1989), 386–94, 391.

112 Chandler, *Campaigns*, 758.

113 Lachouque and Brown, *Anatomy*, 219.

114 Dugue McCarhy, "Cavalerie," 391.

115 Paul Dawson, *Au gallop! Horses and Riders of Napoleon's Army* (Stockton-on-Tees, UK, 2013), 114–18.

116 Muir, *Tactics*, 107.

117 Andrzej Nieuazny, "Les Polonais de la Grande Armée," in Rey and Lentz, *1812*, 85–98, 86.

118 Jean-François Brun, "La formation 'diplomatique' de la Grande Armée," in Rey and Lentz, *1812*, 37–62, 39.

119 Brun, "La formation 'diplomatique'," 41.

120 Czubaty, *Duchy*, 171.

121 Brun, "La formation 'diplomatique'," 42.

122 Cited in Chandler, *Campaigns*, 754–55.

123 Brun, 'La formation "diplomatique",' 46–47.

124 Davis, *Napoleon and Naples*, 252.

125 Ibid., 220.

126 On Murat's officer corps: Walter Bruyère-Ostalls, "Les généraux français au service de Murat et la place de Naples dans le Grand Empire napoléonien (1808–1815)," in Pierre-Marie Delpu, Igor Moullier, and Mélanie Traversier, eds., *Le royaume de Naples à l'heure française. Revisiter l'histoire du "decennio francese" 1806–1815* (Villeneuve d'Ascq, 2018), 95–111.

127 Vincent Haegele, *Murat. La solitude du cavalier* (Paris, 2015), 632–34.

128 Brun, "La formation 'diplomatique'," 49.

129 Ibid., 44.

130 Houdecek, "La Grande Armée de 1812," 1355.

131 Brun, "La formation 'diplomatique'," 51.

132 Chandler, *Campaigns*, 755.

133 Brun, "La formation 'diplomatique'," 44, 46.

134 Chandler, *Campaigns*, 755.

135 Franco della Peruta, "War and society in Napoleonic Italy: the armies of the Kingdom of Italy at home and abroad," in John A. Davis and Paul Ginsborg, eds., *Society and Politics in the Age of Risorgimento* (Cambridge, 1991), 2648, 28.

136 Houdeck, "La Grande Armée de 1812," 1349–50.

137 Della Peruta, "War and society," 46–47.

138 Michael Broers, *Europe Under Napoleon, 1799–1815* (London, 1996), 170.

139 Esdaile, *Peninsular War*, 502.

140 Chandler, *Campaigns*, 754–55.

141 Rey's figures represent the most recent calculations, (*L'effroyable tragédie*, 53–54) but the actual number of the total Grande Armée of 1812 varies considerably. Geoffrey Ellis put it at not much more than 611,000, basing his figures on the work of Own Connelly: Ellis, *Napoleonic Empire*, 66; Owen Connelly, ed., *Historical Dictionary of Napoleonic France* (Chapel Hill, NC, 1985), 23. The French scholar François Houdecek sets it as high as 680,145 men: François Houdecek, "La Grande Armée de 1812," *Études*, 1333–35 in *CG*, xii, 1333. Houdeck's research is probably the most detailed.

142 Boudon, *Jérôme*, 364–65.

143 *CG*, xi to Jérôme, Düsseldorf, Nov. 3, 1811, #29003, 1200.

144 Ibid., to Jérôme, Dec. 10, 1811, #29309, 340–41.

145 Brun, "La formation "diplomatique'," 43–44.

146 Vincent Haegele, *Napoléon et les siens. Un système de famille* (Paris, 2018), 333.

147 Haegele, *Murat*, 626–27.

148 Ibid., 634, Davis, *Napoleon and Naples*, 142, 145–46.

149 Cited in Haegele, *Murat*, 634.

150 Haegele, *Napoléon et les siens*, 333.

151 *CG*, xii, to Claarke, Dresden, May 25, 1812, #39674, 605.

152 Forrest, "Napoleon's vision," 49.

153 Rey, *L'efforyable tragédie*, 79.

154 This is drawn from the succinct analysis by Gates, *Napoleonic Wars*, 206–7.

155 Chandler, *Campaigns*, 761.

156 Forrest, "Napoleon's vision," 49.

157 Cited in Chandler, *Campaigns*, 757.

158 Cited in ibid., 757.

159 Cited in ibid., 760.

160 Ibid., 758.

161 Houdecek, "La Grande Armée de 1812," 1359.

162 Chandler, *Campaigns*, 759–60.

163 Rey, *L'effroyable tragédie*, 73.

164 Ibid., 72.

165 Ibid.

166 Lachouque and Brown, *Anatomy*, 218.

167 Cited in Forrest, "Napoleon's vision," 47.

168 Cited in ibid., 49.

169   Cited in Haegele, *Murat*, 637–38.

170   Cited in Czubaty, *Duchy*, 171.

171   Ibid., 171.

172   Ibid., 170–71.

173   Nieuwazny, "Les Polonais de la Grande Armèe," 87.

174   Cited in Forrest, "Napoleon's vision," 49.

175   Chandler, *Campaigns*, 757–58.

176   Cited in Rey, *L'efforyable tragédie*, 43.

177   Lieven, *Russia*, 134.

178   Jean-Joël Brégeon, "Barclay de Tolly," in Rey and Lentz, *1812*, 197–212, 202–3.

179   Lieven, *Russia*, 134.

180   Brégeon, "Barclay de Tolly," 202–3.

181   Viktor M. Bezotonsnyi, "Factions and In-fighting among Russian Generals in the 1812 Era," in Lieven, et al., *Russia*, 106–18, 109.

182   Cited in Marie-Pierre Rey, "Le pouvoir, les élites et le people russe face à Napoléon et à la Grande Armée," in Rey and Lentz, *1812*, 185–95, 189.

183   Lieven, *Russia*, 103.

184   John P. LeDonne, "Ruling Families in the Russian Political Order, 1689–1825," *Cahiers des Études russes et soviétiques*, 28 (1987), 227–313, 304.

185   Rey, *Alexander*, 46.

186   LeDonne, "Ruling families," 305–6.

187   Brégeon, "Barclay de Tolly," 205.

188   Lieven, *Russia*, 37.

189   This is drawn from the excellent research presented by Dominic Lieven in *Russia*, 110–34.

190   Lieven, *Russia*, 134.

191   Ibid., 133.

192   Ibid., 175–76.

193   Rey, *L'effroyable tragédie*, 49.

194   Ibid., 49.

195   Siemann, *Metternich*, 386.

196   Knight, *Britain and the Defeat of Napoleon*, 177.

197   Ibid., 188.

198   Lieven, *Russia*, 52.

199   Schroeder, *Transformation*, 365.

200   Ibid., 358–59.

201   Cited in Muir, *Britain and the Defeat of Napoleon*, 185.

202   Lieven, *Russia*, 90.

203   Rey, *L'effroyable tragédie*, 72.

204   Muir, *Britain and the Defeat of Napoleon*, 228.

205   LeDonne, "Ruling Families," 304–5.

206   John Gooding, "The liberalism of Michael Speransky," *Slavonic and East European Review*, lxiv (1986), 401–24, 403.

207   Lieven, *Russia*, 89.

208   Ibid., 90.

209   Ibid.

210   Rey, *Alexander*, 231.

211   Ibid., 68.

212   Ibid., 105.

213   Cited in ibid., 231.

214 Liubov Melnikova, "Orthodox Russia against 'Godless' France: the Russian Orthodox Church and the 'Holy War' of 1812," in *Russia and the Napoleonic Wars*, 179–95, 184.

215 Cited in ibid., 187.

216 Cited in ibid., 185.

217 The controversial characterization of the Napoleonic Wars as "total" and comparable to twentieth century conflicts is the major theme of David A. Bell, *The First Total War: Napoleon's Europe and the Birth of Warfare as We Know It* (New York, 2007).

218 Cited in Lieven, *Russia*, 134–35.

219 Lieven, *Russia*, 218.

220 Cited in ibid., 217.

221 Rey, *Alexander*, 219–24.

222 Ibid., 298.

223 Cited in Victor Bezotosnyi, "L'organisation de l'Armée Russe," in *CG*, xii, 1377–88, 1381.

224 Ibid., 1381–82.

225 Ibid., 1381.

226 Lieven, *Russia*, 95.

227 Viktor Bezotosnyi, "Factions and in-fighting among Russian Generals in the 1812 era," in *Russia and the Napoleonic Wars*, 106–18, 116.

228 Chandler, *Campaigns*, 752.

229 Rey, *L'efforyable tragédie*, 65.

230 Chandler, *Campaigns*, 780.

231 Lieven, *Russia*, 138–39.

232 This estimate is based on Lieven's detailed research.

233 Bezotosnyi, "L'organisation de l'Armée Russe," 1383.

234 Ibid., 1379.

235 Cited in Lieven, *Russia*, 102.

236 Ibid., 103.

237 Cited in ibid., 103.

238 Chandler, *Campaigns*, 749–50.

239 Cited in Lieven, *Russia*, 104.

240 Ibid, 102–8.

241 Cited in Bezotosnyi, "L'organisation de l'Armée Russe," 1382.

242 Lieven, *Russia*, 108.

243 This section is based on in Bezotosnyi, "L'organisation de l'Armée Russe," 1383–84.

244 Lieven, *Russia*, 115–16.

245 Bezotosnyi, "L'organisation de l'Armée Russe," 1378–84.

246 Ibid, 1380.

247 Lieven, *Russia*, 147–48.

248 This is based on Chandler, *Campaigns*, 749–50 and Bezotosnyi, "L'organisation de l'Armée Russe," 1379–80.

249 Bezotosnyi, "Russian Generals in 1812," 108.

250 Chandler, *Campaigns*, 752.

251 Lieven, *Russia*, 44–45.

252 Ibid., 119.

253 Lentz, *Nouvelle Histoire*, ii, 324–25.

254 Cited in Kate Williams, *Josephine. Desire, Ambition, Napoleon* (London, 2013), 288.

255 *CG*, xii (1812) to Fredrick of Württemberg, Mainz, May 11, 1812, #30622, 578.

256 Dwyer, *Citizen Emperor*, 362–63.

257 Migliorini, *Napoléon*, 373.

258   Cited in Dwyer, *Citizen Emperor*, 363.
259   *CG*, xii (1812) to Prince Borghese, Dresden, May 21, 1812, #30651, 593–94.
260   Ibid., to Maret, Dresden, May 27, 1812, #30721, 628–29.
261   Cited in Rey, *L'efforyable tragédie*, 82.

5: Into the Abyss: The March on Moscow

1   Chandler, *Campaigns*, 770.
2   Ibid.
3   *Memoirs of General de Caulaincourt, Duke of Vicenza* (3 vols. London, 1950, trans. Hamish
     Miles) I, *The Russian Campaign*, 161.
4   Lieven, *Russia*, 145.
5   Herodotus, *The Histories* (London, 1972 ed., trans Aubrey de Sélincourt), 452–53.
6   Arrian, *The Campaigns of Alexander* (London, 1971 ed., trans Aubrey de Sélincourt), 112.
7   *Les vies des Hommes illustres de Plutarque*, vol. vii (Paris, 1818 ed., reprinted from that of 1769,
     trans. 1819 Aymot), vol. vii, 36.
8   Cited in Rey, *L'effroyable*, 84.
9   Chandler, *Campaigns*, 771.
10   Rey, *L'effroyable*, 88.
11   *CG*, xii (1812) to Berthier, Vilna, June 30, 1812, #31063, 785.
12   *Ibid*, to Berthier, Vilna, June 30, 1812, #31061, 783.
13   Chandler, *Campaigns*, 770.
14   *Memoirs of Caulaincourt*, i, 167.
15   Cited in Varlan, *Caulaincourt*, 261.
16   *Memoirs of Caulaincourt*, i, 173.
17   Ibid, i, 185.
18   *Correspondance du Maréchal Davout, Prince d'Eckmühl. Ses commandements, son Ministère,
     1801–1815* (4 vols. Paris, 1885), iii, no. 1062, to Berthier, Vidna, June 30, 1812, 362–63.
19   Cited in Rey, *L'effroyable*, 85.
20   Ibid., 85.
21   *Corresp Davout*, iii, no. 1057, to Berthier, Gora, June 24, 1812, 357–58.
22   Cited in Rey, *L'effroyable*, 86.
23   *Memoirs of Caulaincourt*, i, 166.
24   Ibid., i, 168.
25   Lachouque and Brown, *Anatomy*, 232.
26   Cited in Rey, *L'effroyable*, 87.
27   Ibid., 111.
28   *CG*, xii (1812) to Berthier, Vilna, July 2, 1812, #31081, 795.
29   Ibid., to Berthier, Vilna, July 2, 1812, #31080, 795.
30   Ibid., to Berthier, Kovno, June 27, 1812, #31055, 780.
31   Ibid., to William, Prince-Royal of Württemberg, Vilna, c. July 1812, #31067, 787.
32   Cited in Rey, *L'effroyable*, 112.
33   Cited in *CG*, xii (1812) to Alexander I, Vilna, July 1, 1812, #31068, 787–90, fn 1, 789–90.
34   Ibid., to Alexander I, Vilna, July 1, 1812, #31068, 787–90.
35   *Memoirs of Caulaincourt*, i, 171.
36   Jacques-Oliver Boudon in his preface to Varlan, *Caulaincourt*, 13.
37   *Memoirs of Caulaincourt*, i, 175–76.
38   *CG*, xii (1812), to Berthier, Vilna, June 29, 1812, #31056, 780–81.
39   John G. Gallaher, *The Iron Marshal. A Biography of Louis N. Davout* (Barnsley, United Kingdom,
     2000), 229–30.

40   Lieven, *Russia*, 153.
41   *Memoirs of Caulaincourt*, i, 159.
42   Chandler, Campaigns, 775, 755.
43   Ibid., 775.
44   Czubaty, *Duchy*, 176.
45   Nieuwazny, "Les polonaise," 89–92.
46   Boudon, *Jérôme*, 375.
47   *CG*, xii (1812), to Berthier, Vilna, July 5, 1812, #31115, 811–12.
48   Lieven, *Russia*, 153.
49   *CG*, xii (1812) to Berthier, Vilna, July 14, 1812, #31223, 868–69.
50   On Latour-Mauberg at Talavera: Muir, *Tactics*, 97. At Friedland: Chandler, *Campaigns*, 569.
51   Cited in Boudon, *Jérôme*, 378.
52   *CG*, xii (1812), to Jérôme, Vilna, July 8, 1812, #31167, 836–37. It is worth noting that this letter was not included in the original official correspondence complied by Napoleon III. It remained long buried in the Archives Nationales.
53   Gallaher, *Iron Marshal*, 232.
54   Ibid., 232.
55   Czubaty, *Duchy*, 176.
56   *Memoirs of Caulaincourt*, i, 187–88.
57   Gallaher, *Iron Marshal*, 230.
58   *Corresp Davout*, iii, no. 1075, to Berthier, Dobrowna, Aug. 7, 1812, 375–79. This is Davout's official report on the battle.
59   Lieven, *Russia*, 151–52.
60   This account of the battle is based on Gallaher, *Iron Marshal*, 234–35.
61   Rey, *L'effroyable*, 103.
62   This was essential to maintaining the line intact for armies of the time, and very hard to instill in training.
63   *Corresp Davout*, iii, no. 1075, to Berthier, Dobrowna, Aug. 7, 1812, 375–79.
64   Gallaher, *Iron Marshal*, 232–33.
65   *CG*, xii (1812) to Berthier, Biechenkovitchi, July 26, 1812, #31300, 924.
66   Gallaher, *Iron Marshal*, 237.
67   Zamoyski, *1812. Napoleon's Fatal March on Moscow* (London, 2013 edition), 191–92.
68   *Memoirs of Caulaincourt*, i, 177.
69   Lieven, *Russia*, 152.
70   *CG*, xii (1812) to Berthier, Vilna, July 6, 1812, #311321, 814–15.
71   Ibid, to Berthier, Vilna, July 10, 1812, #31184, 847–48.
72   Cited in Gallaher, *Iron Marshal*, 236.
73   *CG*, xii (1812) to Berthier, July 4, 1812, Vilna, #31100, 805.
74   Lieven, *Russia*, 150.
75   Chandler, *Campaigns*, 777.
76   Lieven, *Russia*, 154.
77   Cited in ibid., 151.
78   Chandler, *Campaigns*, 780.
79   Lieven, *Russia*, 151–52.
80   Ibid., 151.
81   *Memoirs of Caulaincourt*, i, 181–84.
82   Lieven, *Russia*, 154–56.
83   Cited in ibid., 157.
84   *Memoirs of Caulaincourt*, i, 184.

85   Chandler, *Campaigns*, 780.
86   Lachouque and Brown, *Anatomy*, 233.
87   *Memoirs of Caulaincourt*, i, 193–94.
88   Ibid., 194.
89   *CG*, xii (1812) to Berthier, Vitebsk, July 29, 1812, #31347, 329–30.
90   Ibid., to Berthier, July 29, 1812,Vitsek, #31344, 930–31.
91   Ibid., to Cambacérès, Aug. 15, 1812, Bivouac of Boyarinstevo, #31513, 1009.
92   *Memoirs of Caulaincourt*, i, 191.
93   Varlan, *Caulaincourt*, 262.
94   Chandler, *Campaigns*, 771.
95   Haegele, *Murat*, 640.
96   *Memoirs of Caulaincourt*, i, 187.
97   Ibid., 187.
98   *CG*, xii (1812) to Clarke, July 29, Vitebsk, #31352, 933.
99   The disintegration of the cavalry, the Young Guard, and the heavy casualties of all kinds taken
     by Davout's I Corps must surely seriously qualify the assertion by Adam Zamoyski that the
     losses on the march were actually beneficial to the Grande Armée: "The ranks had been cleared
     of the weakest who should never have been sent to war in the first place.": *1812*, 191.
100 *Memoirs of Caulaincourt*, i, 195.
101 Cited in Lieven, *Russia*, 158.
102 Cited in Zamoyski, *1812*, 204.
103 Ibid., 204–5.
104 Ibid., 206–7.
105 Ibid., 206.
106 Cited in Lieven, *Russia*, 159.
107 Ibid, 159.
108 Cited in Zamoyski, *1812*, 203.
109 Ibid., 198.
110 Lieven, *Russia*, 158.
111 Cited in ibid., 160–61.
112 Chandler, *Campaigns*, 781–82.
113 Cited in Zamoysky, *1812*, 210.
114 Lieven, *Russia*, 161–62.
115 Zamoysky, *1812*, 211.
116 Chandler, *Campaigns*, 782–83. Lieven, *Russia*, 159–62.
117 Lieven, *Russia*, 162.
118 Chandler, *Campaigns*, 783.
119 Lieven, *Russia*, 162.
120 Ibid., 164.
121 Chandler, *Campaigns*, 785.
122 Lieven, *Russia*, 164 and Chandler, *Campaigns*, 786–88 are both of this opinion.
123 *CG*, xii, to Cambacérès, August 12, 1812, #31507, 1006. *CG*, xii (1812) to Cambacérès, Aug. 15,
     1812, Bivouac of Boyarinstevo, #31513, 1009.
124 Chandler, *Campaigns*, 786.
125 Ibid., 783–84.
126 *Corresp Davout*, iii, no. 1085, to Berthier, Aug. 30, 1812, 389–91.
127 Gallaher, *Iron Marshal*, 238.
128 Chandler, *Campaigns*, 786.
129 *Corresp Davout*, iii, no. 1085, to Berthier, Aug. 30, 1812, 389–91.

130 Gallaher, *Iron Marshal*, 238.
131 Cited in Lieven, *Russia*, 165–66.
132 *Corresp Davout*, iii, no. 1085, to Berthier, Aug. 30, 1812, 389–91.
133 Ibid., no. 1085, to Berthier, Aug. 30, 1812, 389–91.
134 Ibid., no 1081, to Berthier, Aug. 21, 1812, 385–86.
135 Zamoyski, *1812*, 217.
136 Chandler, *Campaigns*, 788.
137 Zamoyski, *1812*, 213.
138 Czubaty, *Duchy*, 177.
139 *CG*, xii (1812) to Maret, Smolensk, Aug. 18, 1812, #31516, 1010.
140 Ibid., to Maret, Smolensk, Aug. 18, 1812, #31516, 1010, fn 4. This note was removed from Napoleon III's edition of the correspondence.
141 Chandler, *Campaigns*, 786. Lieven puts Russian losses at 11,000: Lieven, *Russia*, 165.
142 *Memoirs of Caulaincourt*, i, 210.
143 Zamoysky, *1812*, 219.
144 Ibid., 217.
145 Cited in ibid., 218.
146 Ibid., 220.
147 These words are struck out of the original text.
148 *CG*, xii (1812) to Berthier, Smolensk, Aug. 19, 1812, # 31526, 1014.
149 Cited in Lieven, *Russia*, 165.
150 Zamoysky, *1812*, 219.
151 Lieven, *Russia*, 165.
152 Ibid, 167.
153 Cited in Denis A. Sdvizhov, "The 'Maid of Orleans' of the Russian Army: Prince Eugen of Württemberg in the Napoleonic Wars," in *Russia and the Napoleonic Wars*, 119–35, 123.
154 Gallaher, *Iron Marshal*, 239.
155 Cited in ibid., 239.
156 *Corresp Davout*, iii, nos. 1077, 1079; 380, 381–83.
157 Most notably, Chandler, *Campaigns*, 789.
158 Haegele, *Murat*, 642.
159 *CG*, xii, to Davout, Smolensk, Aug. 22, 1812, #31556, 1024–25.
160 Gallaher, *Iron Marshal*, 240.
161 Ibid., 241–42.
162 Ibid., 242.
163 *Corresp Davout*, iii, no 1066, 366–67: ". . . seeing that nothing had yet been done to organize the provisional commission ordered by the Emperor, I thought it necessary to organize . . . a commission to administer the area and provide for the needs of the army."
164 *Memoirs of Caulaincourt*, i, 159 (on his family); 173 (on Tsar Alexander); 187–88 (on Jérôme); 192 (on the behavior of the Guard); 194–95 (on his field commanders).
165 Ibid., i, 195.
166 Chandler, *Campaigns*, 794.
167 *CG*, xii (1812) to Berthier, Vitebsk, July 30, 1812, #31357, 935–36.
168 Ibid., to Berthier, Vitebsk, Aug. 3, 1812, #31399, 954.
169 Ibid., to Berthier, Bienkovitchi, July 26, 1812, #31330, 924.
170 Ibid., to Davout, Vitebsk, Aug. 3, 1812, #31402, 955–56.
171 Lieven, *Russia*, 176.
172 *CG*, xii (1812) to Berthier, Vitebsk, Aug. 7, 1812, #31427, 967–68.
173 Glenthøj and Ottosen, *Experiences of War*, 179–80.

174 Lieven, *Russia*, 176–77.

175 *CG*, xii, to Berthier, Vitebsk, Aug. 7, 1812, #31427, 967–68.

176 Lieven, *Russia*, 176.

177 Ibid.

178 *CG*, xii (1812) to Berthier, Vitebsk, Aug. 10, 1812, #31456, 980–81.

179 Austin, "Oudinot," in *Napoleon's Marshals*, 393.

180 Lieven, *Russia*, 178–79.

181 *CG*, xii, to Berthier, Smolensk, Aug. 19, 1812, #31519, 1011–12.

182 Lieven, *Russia*, 179–81.

183 Ibid., 180.

184 Austin, "Oudinot," in *Napoleon's Marshals*, 391, 393.

185 Chandler, *Campaigns*, 780–81.

186 Cited in Zamoyski, *1812*, 203.

187 Lieven, *Russia*, 180–84.

188 *CG*, xii (1812) to Eugene, Vitebsk, Aug. 5, 1812, #31411, 959.

189 Ibid., to Maret, Velitchevo, Sept. 1, 1812, #31649, 1066.

190 *Memoirs of Caulaincourt*, i, 226.

191 Ibid, i, 229.

192 Napoleon's determination to finish the campaign quickly may have been influenced at this point by the news of Wellington's victory over Marmont at Salamanca on June 22. He received the first news on September 1, and his initial reaction was concern and annoyance that the reports gave him little clear information: *CG*, xii (1812) to Clarke, Gjatsk, Sept. 1, 1812, #31659, 1071–72.

193 Bessières and Mortier held this together, Bessières in charge of the cavalry; Mortier, the infantry. This had been the case since the Channel Camps.

194 Charles Esdaile, "The Misnamed Bayard: Bessières," in *Napoleon's Marshals*, 68.

195 *Memoirs of Caulaincourt*, i, 200.

196 *Memoirs of Caulaincourt*, i, 230–31.

197 Cited in Lieven, *Russia*, 186–87.

198 Ibid., 185–86.

199 Cited in ibid., 188.

200 Zamoyski, *1812*, 246–47.

201 Cited in Bezotosnyi, "Russian Generals," 112.

202 Lieven, *Russia*, 189–91.

203 Lieven, *Russia*, 195.

204 Cited in Zamoyski, *1812*, 256.

205 Chandler, *Campaigns*, 795–96. Lieven, *Russia*, 192.

206 Chandler, *Campaigns*, 796.

207 Cited in Zamoyski, *1812*, 258–59.

208 Lieven, *Russia*, 194.

209 Zamoyski, *1812*, 254.

210 Ibid., 257.

211 Gallaher, *Iron Marshal*, 248.

212 Ibid., 247.

213 Zamoyski, *1812*, 259. Lieven, *Russia*, 198 puts the French at about 125,000 but notes that the Russian total counted 30,000 men of the Moscow militia, who were not really frontline troops, thus evening the odds.

214 Chandler, *Campaigns*, 796.

215 Ibid., 796.

216 Lieven, *Russia*, 194.

217 Zamoyski, *1812*, 259–60.
218 Cited in Zamoyski, *1812*, 263–63.
219 Cited in Liubov Melnikova, "Orthodox Russia," 194–95, note 28.
220 *CG*, xii, to Marie-Louise, Moscow, Sept. 21, 1812, #31745, 1107.
221 Wilson-Smith, *Napoleon and His Artists* (London, 1996), 21, 264.
222 Cited in Welschinger, *Le Roi de Rome*, 35.
223 Lachouque and Brown, *Anatomy of Glory*, 238.
224 Cited in Zamoyski, *1812*, 263.
225 Cited in ibid., 260.
226 Lachouque and Brown, *Anatomy of Glory*, 238.
227 Cited in Chandler, *Campaigns*, 799.
228 Forrest, *Napoleon's Men. The Soldiers of the Revolution and Empire* (London, 2002), 72.
229 Zamoyski, *1812*, 266.
230 Cited in Lieven, *Russia*, 202.
231 Alexander Mikaberidze, *The Battle of Borodino. Napoleon against Kutuzov* (Huddersfield, 2010), 107.
232 Gallaher, *Iron Marshal*, 248–49.
233 Chandler, *Campaigns*, 800.
234 Zamoyski, *1812*, 270.
235 Gallaher, *Iron Marshal*, 25–51.
236 Zamoyski, *1812*, 270.
237 Ibid, 270–71.
238 Cited in ibid., 271.
239 Cited in ibid., 271.
240 Lieven, *Russia*, 203.
241 Cited in Gallaher, *Iron Marshal*, 249.
242 Zamoyski, *1812*, 273.
243 Lieven, *Russia*, 203.
244 Ibid., 203.
245 Mikaberidze, *Borodino*, 136.
246 Chandler, *Campaigns*, 801.
247 Cited in ibid., 801.
248 Zamoyski, *1812*, 274–75.
249 Chandler, *Campaigns*, 804.
250 Cited in Chandler, *Campaigns*, 805.
251 Zamoyski, *1812*, 279.
252 Cited in ibid., 278–79.
253 Cited in Zamoyski, *1812*, 280.
254 Lieven, *Russia*, 208; Zamoyski, *1812*, 280.
255 Lieven, *Russia*, 205.
256 Chandler, *Campaigns*, 806.
257 Lachouque and Brown, *Anatomy*, 238.
258 Ibid., 239.
259 Cited in Chandler, *Campaigns*, 806.
260 Cited in Mikaberidze, *Borodino*, 206.
261 Cited in Zamoyski, *1812*, 285.
262 Ibid., 274.
263 Lieven, *Russia*, 203–4. Mikaberidze, *Borodino*, 135–36, contests this, on the grounds that Kutaisov would have left in place clear orders for each battery that could be followed without his intervention.

264 Mikaberidze, *Borodino*, 105–06.

265 Zamoyski, *1812*, 287.

266 *CG*, xii, to Maret, Mojaïsk, Sept. 9, 1812, #31686, 1083.

267 Cited in Mkaberidze, *Borodino*, 206.

268 Cited in Zamoyski, *1812*, 280–81.

269 Lieven, *Russia*, 209.

270 See *Corresp Davout*, iv, 394–400.

271 Chandler, *Campaigns*, 807. Gallaher, *Iron Marshal*, 250.

272 *CG*, xii, to Berthier, Mojaïsk, Sept. 10, 1812, #31693, 1086.

273 Ibid, to Maret, Mojaïsk, Sept. 10, 1812, #31708, 1091.

274 Lieven, *Russia*, 229.

275 This was in his letter to Maret on September 9: *CG*, xii (1812) to Maret, Mojaïsk, Sept. 9, 1812, #31686, 1083.

276 *CG*, xii (1812) to Cambacérès, Borodino, Sept. 8, 1812, #31677, 1080.

277 Ibid., to Emperor Francis, Mojaïsk, Sept. 9, 1812, #31684, 108–83.

278 Ibid., to Maret, Mojaïsk, Sept. 9, 1812, #31686, 1083.

279 Mikaberidze, *Borodino*, 208. Mikaberidze provides a very thorough examination of the evidence from which casualty figures have been drawn, and their ideologically charged history: 207–19.

280 Ibid., 204–6.

281 *CG*, xii (1812) to Marie-Louise, Mojaïsk, Sept. 9, 1812, #31687, 1084.

282 Ibid., to Clark, Mojaïsk, Sept. 10, 1812, #31706, 1090. To the Bishops of the Empire, Mojaïsk, Sept. 10, 1812, #31707, 1091.

283 Ibid., to Cambacérès, Mojaïsk, Sept. 9, 1812, #31685, 1082.

284 Cited in Rey, *Alexander*, 252.

285 Gallaher, *Iron Marshal*, 250–51.

286 Cited in ibid., 251.

287 David Hopkin, "'The Tinderbox': Military Culture and Literary Culture from Romanticism to Realism," in *A History of the European Restorations* ii, *Culture, Society and Religion*, eds. Michael Broers, Ambrogio Caiani, and Stephen Bann (London, 2020), 130–40, 134.

6: Hell Is a Very Cold Place: Moscow

1   Cited in Zamoyski, *1812*, 286.

2   Ibid., 286–87.

3   Lieven, *Russia*, 209–10.

4   Alexander Mikaberidze, *The Burning of Moscow. Napoleon's Trial by Fire, 1812* (Barnsley, United Kingdom, 2014 ed.), 27.

5   Cited in Lieven, *Russia*, 210.

6   Cited in Zamoyski, *1812*, 289.

7   Cited in Zamoyski, *1812*, 290.

8   Mikaberidze, *Burning*, 67.

9   Lieven, *Russia*, 210–11.

10 Zamoyski, *1812*, 291.

11 Bezotosnyi, "Russian Generals in 1812," 112.

12 Zamoyski, *1812*, 291.

13 Cited in Zamoyski, *1812*, 291.

14 Cited in ibid., 289.

15 Cited in Lieven, *Russia*, 211.

16 Zamoyski, *1812*, 292–93.

17 Ibid., 292–93.

18   Cited in Zamoyski, *1812*, 289.

19   Cited in ibid., 53.

20   Ibid., 53–54.

21   Lieven, *Russia*, 212.

22   Cited in Zamoyski, *1812*, 294.

23   Mikaberidze, *Borodino*, 218. Junot's VIII Corps was given this task because it was so badly battered that Napoleon ordered it redesignated a division a few weeks later: *CG*, xii (1812) to Berthier, Moscow, Sept. 21, 1812, #31738, 1104.

24   Cited in Mikaberidze, *Burning*, 55.

25   *CG*, xii to Marie-Louise, Sept. 16, 1812, Moscow, #31727, 1099.

26   Mikaberidze, *Burning*, 16.

27   Cited in ibid., 18.

28   Cited in Mikaberidze, *Burning*, 55–56.

29   Both cited in Zamoyski, *1812*, 298.

30   Haegele, *Murat*, 645. Lieven, *Russia*, 212.

31   Mikaberidze, *Burning*, 70.

32   *CG*, xii, to Berthier, Sept. 14, 1812, Moscow, #31724, 1098; to Bessières, Moscow, Sept. 15, 1812, Moscow, #31726, 1098–99.

33   Zamoyski, *1812*, 293.

34   Cited in ibid., 297–98.

35   Mikaberidze, *Burning*, 75–77.

36   Ibid., 78–79, 86.

37   Cited in ibid., 74, 78.

38   Ibid., 79.

39   Most of the following account is based on the immaculate research of Alexander Mikaberidze's *Burning*, op. cit.

40   Moscow had been periodically ravaged by fires throughout the eighteenth century, the most recent of which was in January 1812. In response to this, the government had created an extensive system of water pumps manned by a full time professional fire brigade over 200 strong, and 100 fire engines (even if it was of questionable quality). Paris had acquired something equivalent only in 1810, after the fire at the Austrian ambassador's residence: Mikaberidze, *Burning*, 25–26.

41   Mikaberidze, *Burning*, 71.

42   Cited in ibid., 88.

43   Mikaberidze notes that all the witnesses agree on this: Caulaincourt, Meneval, and Gourgaud: Mikaberidze, *Burning*, 92.

44   *CG*, xii, to Marie-Louise, Moscow, Sept. 16, 1812, #31727, 1099.

45   Ibid., to Cambacérès, Moscow, Sept. 18, 1812, #31729, 1100.

46   Mikaberidze, *Burning*, 116.

47   Cited in Zamoyski, *1812*, 305.

48   Mikaberidze, *Burning*, 116–18.

49   Ibid., 119.

50   Cited in Gallaher, *Iron Marshal*, 251.

51   *Corresp du Davout*, iii, to Berthier, Sept. 21, 1812, #1090, 394–95.

52   Cited in Mikaberidze, *Burning*, 124.

53   Ibid., 126.

54   Lachouque and Brown, *Anatomy*, 243.

55   Ibid., 245.

56   Mikaberidze, *Burning*, 121–22.

57   *CG*, vol. xii (1812) to Berthier, Moscow, Sept. 21, 1812, #31738, 1104.

58   Ibid., to Berthier, Moscow, Sept. 21, 1812, #31739, 1104–5.

59   Ibid., to Maret, Moscow, Sept. 21, 1812, #31742, 1106–7.

60   Ibid., to Maret, Moscow, Sept. 30, 1812, #31784, 1123.

61   Ibid., to Maret, Moscow, Sept. 29, 1812, #31780, 1121–22.

62   Czubaty, *Duchy*, 178.

63   *CG*, vol. xii, to Maret, Moscow, Sept. 21, 1812, #31757, 1112–13.

64   *CG*, vol. xii to Maret, Moscow, Sept. 23, 1812, #31750, 1109–10.

65   Ibid., to Cambacérès, Moscow, Sept. 27, 1812, #31768, 1117.

66   Mikaberidze, *Burning*, 127.

67   *CG*, vol. xii, to Berthier, Moscow, Sept. 29, 1812, #31779, 1120–21.

68   Mikaberidze, *Burning*, 128–31.

69   Ibid., 131–33.

70   *CG*, xii, to Marie-Louise, Sept. 16, 1812, Moscow, #31727, 1099.

71   Lieven, *Russia*, 213–14.

72   Chandler, *Campaigns*, 815–16.

73   Ibid., 816–17.

74   *CG*, xii, to Tsar Alexander, Moscow, Sept. 20, 1812, #31736, 1103.

75   Zamoyski, *1812*, 313.

76   Mikaberidze, *Burning*, 150–51. Mikaberidze's thorough analysis concludes that Rostopchin
     did not actually order the fire, but his actions, particularly dismantling the fire brigade and the
     water pumps, must be seen as a deliberate policy of making a fire likely: 145–65.

77   Cited in Lieven, *Russia*, 241.

78   Zamoyski, *1812*, 307.

79   Rey, *Alexander*, 254.

80   Zamoyski, *1812*, 314–15.

81   Chandler, *Campaigns*, 817.

82   Lieven, *Russia*, 242–44.

83   Chandler, *Campaigns*, 819.

7: The Gauntlet: The Retreat from Moscow, October–December 1812

1   Lieven, *Russia*, 251.

2   Ibid., 251.

3   Ibid., 250.

4   Zamoyski, *1812*, 333–34.

5   Mikaberidze, *Burning*, 190–91.

6   Lieven, *Russia*, 251.

7   Lachouque and Brown, *Anatomy*, 247.

8   Lieven, *Russia*, 250–51.

9   Chandler, *Campaigns*, 819.

10   Ibid., 818.

11   *CG*, xii, to Maret, Moscow, Oct. 16, 1812, #31922, note 4, 1193.

12   *CG*, xii, to Maret, Moscow, Oct. 16, 1812, #31922, 1192.

13   Zamoyski, *1812*, 361.

14   Chandler, *Campaigns*, 818.

15   Lieven, *Russia*, 256.

16   Chandler, *Campaigns*, 820.

17   Cited in Lieven, *Russia*, 257.

18   Milaberidze, *Burning*, 198.

19   Cited in Chandler, *Campaigns*, 820.
20   Milaberidze, *Burning*, 197.
21   Cited in Lieven, *Russia*, 257.
22   Ibid., 256–57.
23   Milaberidze, *Burning*, 195.
24   Chandler, *Campaigns*, 819.
25   Zamoyski, *1812*, 362.
26   Milaberidze, *Burning*, 195.
27   Lieven, *Russia*, 252.
28   Ibid., 253.
29   *CG*, xii, to Berthier, Troïtskoïy, Oct. 20, 1812, #31951, 1208.
30   Cited in Zamoyski, *1812*, 370.
31   Eugene's wife, Amelie of Bavaria.
32   *CG*, xii, to Maret, Vereya, Oct. 27, 1812, #31974, 1220–21. To Marie-Louise, Borovsk, Oct. 26, 1812, #31972, 1219–20.
33   Lieven, *Russia*, 258.
34   *CG*, xii, to Maret, Berthier, Borovsk, Oct. 26, 1812, #31971, 1218–19.
35   Lieven, *Russia*, 258.
36   Ibid.
37   Chandler, *Campaigns*, 822. Lachouque and Brown, *Anatomy*, 250.
38   Chandler, *Campaigns*, 822.
39   Lieven, *Russia*, 259.
40   *CG*, xii, to Berthier, Borovsk, Oct. 26, 1812, #31971, 1218–19.
41   Ibid.
42   Ibid., to Cambacérès, Borovsk, Oct. 24, 1812, #31969, 1217–18.
43   Chandler, *Campaigns*, 823.
44   *Corresp Davout*, III, to Berthier, Oct. 28, 1812, #1134, 422–23.
45   *CG*, xii, to Berthier, Dorogobouj, Nov. 5, 1812, #32013, 1238.
46   Lieven, *Russia*, 261.
47   *CG*, xii, to Berthier, Dorogobouj, Nov. 5, 1812, #32019, 1239–40.
48   Cited in Forrest, *Napoleon's Men*, 152.
49   Caulaincourt, *With Napoleon in Russia* (New York, 1935), 274.
50   Lieven, *Russia*, 261.
51   Cited in Zamoyski, *1812*, 384.
52   Ibid., 383.
53   Dwyer, *Citizen Emperor*, 426.
54   Cited in Lieven, *Russia*, 261–62.
55   Cited in Chandler, *Campaigns*, 823.
56   Lieven, *Russia*, 263–64.
57   Chandler, *Campaigns*, 822.
58   Lieven, *Russia*, 264–65.
59   Chandler, *Campaigns*, 825.
60   Ibid., 825.
61   Zamoyski, *1812*, 391.
62   Lieven, *Russia*, 274–75.
63   *CG*, xii, to Berthier, Mikhailovka, Nov. 7, 1812, #32026, 1242–43.
64   Chandler, *Campaigns*, 824.
65   Lieven, *Russia*, 271–72.
66   Chandler, *Campaigns*, 827–28.

67   Zamoyski, *1812*, 408.

68   Chandler, *Campaigns*, 827.

69   Zamoyski, *1812*, 409.

70   Ibid., 410–11.

71   Ibid., 414–15.

72   Lachouque and Brown, *Anatomy*, 256.

73   Ibid., 257–58.

74   Zamoyski, *1812*, 421–24.

75   Lieven, *Russia*, 267–68. Zamoyski, *1812*, 424.

76   Cited in Zamoyski, *1812*, 427.

77   Ibid., 425–27.

78   Lieven, *Russia*, 268.

79   Cited in Chandler, *Campaigns*, 829.

80   Zamoyski, *1812*, 440.

81   Chandler, *Campaigns*, 829.

82   Ibid., 846.

83   *CG*, xii, to Berthier, Orcha, Nov. 18, 1812, #32061, 1260–61.

84   Chandler, *Campaigns*, 832–33.

85   Lieven, *Russia*, 274–76.

86   Zamoyski, *1812*, 458.

87   Bezotosnyi, "Russian Generals in 1812," 114.

88   Lieven, *Russia*, 276.

89   Varlan, *Caulaincourt*, 270.

90   Chandler, *Campaigns*, 835.

91   Zamoyski, *1812*, 463.

92   Lachouque and Brown, *Anatomy*, 262.

93   Zamoyski, *1812*, 463.

94   Zamoyski, *1812*, 465. The many accounts of this, compiled by Zamoyski, disprove the assertions made by many historians that Napoleon ordered the eagles burned after Krasnyi to avoid capture.

95   Chandler, *Campaigns*, 841–42.

96   Zamoyski, *1812*, 466–67.

97   Chandler, *Campaigns*, 842.

98   Cited in Zamoyski, *1812*, 464.

99   Chandler, *Campaigns*, 842.

100 Zamoyski, *1812*, 474–75.

101 Ibid., 478–79.

102 Chichagov calculated nine thousand dead on the eastern bank and seven thousand prisoners, probably the most reliable estimate: Zamoyski, *1812*, 479–80.

103 Zamoyski, *1812*, 473.

104 Chandler, *Campaigns*, 843–44.

105 Ibid., 845.

106 Lieven, *Russia*, 274.

107 Ibid., 277.

108 Zamoyski, *1812*, 471.

109 Cited in ibid., 473.

110 Chandler, *Campaigns*, 847.

111 Ibid., 846.

112 Ibid.

113   Lachouque and Brown, *Anatomy*, 264.

114   Chandler, *Campaigns*, 847.

115   Rey, *L'effroyable tragédie*, 282.

116   Ibid., 283.

117   Ibid., 284.

118   Chandler, *Campaigns*, 850.

119   Lieven, *Russia*, 282–83.

120   Lentz, *Nouvelle histoire*, ii, 335.

121   Cited in ibid., ii, 336–37.

122   de Brancion, *Cambacérès*, 547–50.

123   Ibid., 548.

124   *CG*, xii, to Clarke, Mikhailovka, Nov. 6, 1812, #32022, 1241.

125   Ibid., to Clarke, Mikhailovka, Nov. 6, 1812, #32023, 1241,

126   Ibid., to Clarke, Mikhailovka, Nov. 6, 1812, #32028, 1243.

127   Ibid., to Cambacérès, Smolensk, Nov. 11, 1812, #32038, 1247–48. None of Cambacérès's dispatches to Napoleon in Russia seems to have survived, so it is impossible to know with certainty whether he knew of Cambacérès's concerns about the loyalty of the Senate, but he had seen the proclamation and was alert to the plotters' intentions when he ordered this.

128   Ibid., to Cambacérès, Smolensk, Nov. 11, 1812, #32039, 1248–49. To Clarke, Smolensk, Nov. 11, 1812, #32040, 1249, to Savary, Smolensk, Nov. 11, 1812, #32047, 1252.

129   Lentz, *Nouvelle histoire*, ii, 339.

130   *CG*, xii, to Cambacérès, Smolensk, Nov. 14, 1812, #32052, 1254–55.

131   Chatel de Brancion, *Cambacérès*, 549.

132   *CG*, xii, to Savary, Smorgoni, Dec. 5, 1812, #32118, 1301.

133   Caulaincourt, *With Napoleon in Russia* (New York, 1935), 345.

134   Ibid., 386–87.

135   *CG*, xii, to Cambacérès, Smolensk, Nov. 14, 1812, #32052, 1254–55.

136   *CG*, xii, to Cambacérès, Benitsa, Dec. 5, 1812, #32106, 1297.

137   de Brancion, *Cambacérès*, 553.

138   Caulaincourt, *With Napoleon*, 389–90.

139   Lachouque and Brown, *Anatomy*, 265–66.

140   *CG*, xii, to Marie-Louise, Smorgoni, Dec. 5, 1812, #32115, 1300.

141   Caulaincourt, *With Napoleon*, 276–77.

142   Chandler, *Campaigns*, 850.

143   Rey, *L'effroyable tragédie*, 288–93.

144   Lieven, *Russia*, 283–84.

145   Ibid., 182–84.

146   Chandler, *Campaigns*, 850.

147   Ibid., 851.

148   Lieven, *Russia*, 291–92.

149   Clark, *Iron Kingdom*, 359–61.

8: From Delusion to Determination, December 1812–April 1813

1   Varlan, *Caulaincourt*, 275–76.

2   Caulaincourt, *With Napoleon in Russia*, 323.

3   Ibid., 345.

4   Ibid., 334.

5   Cited in Clark, *Iron Kingdom*, 336–37.

6   Caulaincourt, *With Napoleon in Russia*, 372.
7   Ibid., 277, 339.
8   Gates, *Napoleonic Wars*, 221.
9   Haegele, *Murat*, 652.
10   Lieven, *Russia*, 285.
11   Ibid., 118–19.
12   Caulaincourt, *With Napoleon in Russia*, 306, 287.
13   Ibid., 372.
14   Cited in Lieven, *Russia*, 287.
15   Ibid., 286.
16   Ibid., 286.
17   Caulaincourt, *With Napoleon in Russia*, 277.
18   Lieven, *Russia*, 297–99.
19   Chandler, *Campaigns*, 852.
20   Haegele, *Murat*, 651–53.
21   Siemann, *Metternich*, 321.
22   Cited in Varlan, *Caulaincourt*, 282.
23   Haegele, *Murat*, 653–54.
24   *CG*, xiii, *Le Commencement de la Fin, Janvier, 1813–Juin, 1813*, to Eugene, Jan. 22, 1813,
      #32388, 148.
25   Ibid., to Murat, Jan. 26, 1813, #32501, 206.
26   Ibid., to Caroline, Jan. 24, 1813, #32438, 173. This is the original text of the letter, found
      recently in the Russian State Archives. The text came into the hands of Castlereagh, who
      falsified it for political purposes; this was immediately known to be the case, but it was the only
      text available until now: fn 3, 173.
27   Haegele, *Murat*, 655–56.
28   Ibid., 652.
29   Siemann, *Metternich*, 318–19.
30   Lieven, *Russia*, 303.
31   Caulaincourt, *With Napoleon in Russia*, 350.
32   Ibid., 277–78.
33   Ibid., 350.
34   Ibid., 351.
35   *CG*, xiii, to Emperor Francis, Jan. 7, 1813, #32230, 57–60.
36   Siemann, *Metternich*, 308.
37   Ibid., 317–18.
38   Ibid., 363, which overturns the standard view set out in Schroeder, *Transformation*, 462.
39   Siemann, *Metternich*, 322.
40   *CG*, xii, to Emperor Francis, Dec. 12, 1812, Dresden, #32121, 1303.
41   Ibid, to Frederick-William III, Dec. 12, 1812, Dresden, #32127, 1305.
42   Clark, *Iron Kingdom*, 357.
43   Gates, *Napoleonic Wars*, 222–23.
44   Clark, Iron Kingdom, 360–62.
45   Ibid., 360.
46   Ibid, 357–58.
47   Siemann, *Metternich*, 322–24.
48   Clark, *Iron Kingdom*, 362.
49   Cited in Lieven, *Russia*, 294–95.
50   Cited in Clark, *Iron Kingdom*, 362.

51 Ibid., 362.

52 Ibid., 362–64. Dominic Lieven takes a much more positive view of the alliance: *Russia*, 299–301, based on a sense of mutual good faith between the two rulers.

53 Lieven, *Russia*, 303–04.

54 Clark, *Iron Kingdom*, 364.

55 Ibid., 364. Lieven, *Russia*, 304.

56 Napoleon's italics.

57 *CG*, xiii, to Eugene, March 5, 1813, #33017, 471–72.

58 Ibid., to Jérôme, March 5, 1813, #33091, 473.

59 *CG*, xii, to Jérôme, Dec. 23, 1812, #32132, 1307.

60 Ibid., to Clark, Moscow, Oct. 19, 1812, #31947, 1206.

61 Caulaincourt, *With Napoleon in Russia*, 302.

62 Broers, *Europe Under Napoleon*, 215.

63 Caulaincourt, *With Napoleon in Russia*, 302.

64 Muir, *Wellington*, ii, 464.

65 Caulaincourt, *With Napoleon in Russia*, 302.

66 Esdaile, *Outpost of Empire*, 369.

67 Muir, *Wellington*, ii, 463.

68 Esdaile, *Peninsular War*, 393.

69 Muir, *Wellington*, ii, 462–63.

70 Ibid., 466.

71 Ibid., 468.

72 Esdaile, *Peninsular War*, 394–95.

73 Muir, *Wellington*, ii, 471–474.

74 Esdaile, *Peninsular War*, 397.

75 Muir, *Wellington*, ii, 474.

76 Ibid., 474.

77 Ibid., 478–79.

78 Ibid., 474.

79 Ibid., 478.

80 James Marshal-Cornwall, *Marshal Massena* (Oxford, 1965), 251.

81 Cited in Lentz, *Joseph Bonaparte*, 390.

82 Esdaile, *Outpost of Empire*, 396.

83 Ibid., 396–97.

84 Lentz, *Joseph Bonaparte*, 391–92.

85 Gotteri, *Soult*, 380.

86 Cited in Lentz, *Joseph Bonaparte*, 392.

87 Esdaile, *Peninsular War*, 400.

88 Gotteri, *Soult*, 383.

89 Lentz, *Joseph Bonaparte*, 395–96.

90 Muir, *Wellington*, ii, 484.

91 Cited in ibid., 486.

92 Ibid., 488.

93 Gotteri, *Soult*, 381.

94 Muir, *Wellington*, ii, 488.

95 Cited in Gotteri, *Soult*, 384.

96 Ibid., 385.

97 Muir, *Wellington*, ii, 491. Charles J. Esdaile, *The Duke of Wellington and the Command of the Spanish Armies* (London, 1990), 85–107.

98   Cited in Muir, *Wellington*, ii, 519.
99   Ibid., 492.
100 *CG*, xiii, to Clarke, Jan. 3, 1813, #32182, 29–30.
101 Cited in Tone, *Fatal Knot*, 141.
102 Ibid., 141–43.
103 Muir, *Wellington*, ii, 520–21.
104 Cited in Knight, *Britain Against Napoleon*, 423–24.
105 Ibid., 429.
106 Cited in de Brancion, *Cambacérès*, 557.
107 Cited in Varlan, *Caulaincourt*, 282.
108 Caulaincourt, *With Napoleon in Russia*, 399.
109 Pierre Branda, "Introduction," *CG*, xiii (Jan. 1813–July 1813), 13–21, 15–16.
110 Lentz, *Nouvelle histoire*, ii, 399.
111 Forrest, *Deserteurs*, 52.
112 Woloch, *New Regime*, 420.
113 Cited in Forrest, *Deserteurs*, 60.
114 Ibid., 55, 61–62.
115 Jacques-Olivier Boudon, *Ordre et Désordre dans la France Napoléonienne* (Paris, 2008), 157.
116 Forrest, *Deserteurs*, 221.
117 Cited in ibid., 140.
118 Ibid., 87.
119 Ibid., 55.
120 Ibid., 236.
121 Caulaincourt, *With Napoleon in Russia*, 322.
122 Lentz, *Nouvelle histoire*, ii, 399.
123 Gates, *Napoleonic Wars*, 231.
124 Esdaile, *Peninsular War*, 429.
125 Branda, "Introduction," *CG*, xiii (Jan. 1813–July 1813), 15–16.
126 Esdaile, *Peninsular War*, 428–29.
127 Lachouque and Brown, *Anatomy*, 282.
128 Lentz, *Nouvelle Histoire*, ii, 360.
129 Lachouque and Brown, *Anatomy*, 281.
130 Cited in Gates, *Napoleonic Wars*, 232.
131 *CG*, xiii, to Clarke, Jan. 21, 1813, #32375, 141–42.
132 Ibid., to Clarke, Jan. 23, 1813, #32411, 159–60.
133 Ibid., to Clarke, Feb. 3, 1813, #32569, 246.
134 Gates, *Napoleonic Wars*, 232.
135 Cited in Gates, *Napoleonic Wars*, 232.
136 *CG*, xiii, to Lacuée, Jan. 23, 1813, #32433, 171.
137 Ibid., to Clarke, Jan. 23, 1813, #32417, 163.
138 Ibid., to Kellermann, Jan. 30, 1813, #32548, 233–34.
139 Branda, "Introduction," *CG*, xiii (Jan. 1813–July 1813), 16.
140 *CG*, xiii, to Clarke, Jan. 2, 1813, #32178, 28.
141 Ibid., to Defermon, Jan. 20, 1813, #32349, 130; to Lapécède, president of the Senate, Jan. 20, 1813, #32355, 132.
142 Ibid., to Lacuée, Jan. 23, 1813, #32431, 171.
143 Ibid., to Maret, Jan. 20, 1813, #32358, 133–34.
144 Ibid., to Lacuée, Jan. 31, 1813, #32556, 237–39.
145 Gates, *Napoleonic Wars*, 232.

146 Ibid., 235.

147 *CG*, xiii, to Jérôme, Jan. 18, 1813, #32332, 118–20.

148 Ibid., fn 8, 120–21.

149 Cited in: Gates, *Napoleonic Wars*, 231.

150 Georges Lefebvre, *Napoléon* (Paris, 1941), 523.

151 *CG*, xiii, to Le Marois, Jan. 30, 1813, #32549, 234.

152 Ibid., to Ferdinand-Joseph, March 2, 1813, #32942, 439.

153 Katherine B. Aaslesrad, "War without Battles: Civilian experiences and economic warfare during the Napoleonic era in Hamburg," in *Soldiers, Citizens and Civilians. Experiences and Perceptions of the Revolutionary and Napoleonic Wars, 1790–1820*, Alan Forrest, Karen Hagemann, and Jane Rendall, eds. (Basingstoke, 2009), 118–36, 130.

154 Migliorini, *Napoléon*, 399.

155 Caulaincourt, *With Napoleon in Russia*, 315, for this in "so many words."

156 Cited in Migliorini, *Napoléon*, 401.

157 The imagery is explored well by Philip Dwyer in *Citizen Emperor, passim.*

158 Cited in Lentz, *Nouvelle histoire*, ii, 348–49.

159 Ibid., 349.

160 de Brancion, *Cambacérès*, 559.

161 Caulaincourt, *With Napoleon in Russia*, 296.

162 de Brancion, *Cambacérès*, 561.

163 *CG*, xiii, to Louis, Jan. 16, 1813, #32315, 108.

164 Lentz, *Histoire nouvelle*, ii, 350.

165 de Brancion, *Cambacérès*, 559–60.

166 Cited in Woloch, *New Regime*, 419.

167 Ibid., 419.

168 Edward A. Whitcomb, "Napoleon's Prefects," *American Historical Review*, 79 (1974), 1089–118.

169 Caulaincourt, *With Napoleon in Russia*, 362–63.

170 de Brancion, *Cambacérès*, 361.

171 Cited in Lentz, *Nouvelle histoire*, ii, 360.

172 Caulaincourt, *With Napoleon in Russia*, 338, 341, 387, 369–70, 367–68.

173 Woloch, *New Regime*, 420–21.

174 Ibid., 423.

175 de Brancion, *Cambacérès*, 557.

176 Chateaubriand, *Mémoires d'Outre-Tombe,* i, 832.

177 de Brancion, *Cambacérès*, 561.

178 Caulaincourt, *With Napoleon in Russia*, 287.

179 Ibid., 277.

180 Emmanuel de Waresquiel, *Talleyrand. Le Prince Immobile* (Paris, 2003), 425–26.

181 Siemann, *Metternich*, 325–26.

182 de Waresquiel, *Talleyrand*, 424.

183 Philip Mansel, *Louis XVIII* (London, 1981), 162.

184 De Waresquiel, *Talleyrand*, 424.

185 Ambrogio A. Caiani, *To Kidnap a Pope. Napoleon and Pius VII* (New Haven, CT, and London, 2021), 225–29.

186 *CG*, xii, to Marie-Louise, Vilnius, July 8, 1812, #31169, 837.

187 Caiani, *To Kidnap a Pope*, 230.

188 *CG*, xii (1812) to Pius VII, Dec. 29, 1812, #32169, 1322–23.

189 Caiani, *To Kidnap a Pope*, 235.

190 Boudon, *Napoléon et les Cultes*, 317–18.

191 Cited in ibid., 318.
192 Cited in Caiani, *To Kidnap a Pope*, 238.
193 Caiani, *To Kidnap a Pope*, 241.
194 Cited in Lentz, *Nouvelle histoire*, ii, 353–54.
195 *CG*, xiii, to Bigot, Jan. 25, 1813, #32463, 185–86.
196 Boudon, *Napoléon et les Cultes*, 319.
197 *CG*, xiii, to Pius VII, Jan. 25, 1813, #32480, 196.
198 Cited in Caiani, *To Kidnap a Pope*, 243.
199 Ibid., 245.
200 Ibid., 242.
201 *CG*, xiii, to Bigot, March 9, 1813, #33111, 513.
202 *CG*, xiii, to Bigot, March 13, 1813, #33182, 552.
203 Boudon, *Napoléon et les Cultes*, 320–22.
204 Ibid., 321.
205 Caiani, *To Kidnap a Pope*, 243.
206 Ambrogio A. Caiani, *Louis XVI and the French Revolution* (Cambridge, 2012), 90–92.
207 *CG*, xiii, to Bigot, April 2, 1813, #33570, 717; to Savary, April 2, 1813, #33591, 731.
208 Caiani, *To Kidnap a Pope*, 244.
209 *CG*, xiii, to Bigot, Jan. 24, 1813, #32437, 172–73. In fact, these departments comprised one diocese: Le Mans.
210 Caulaincourt, *With Napoleon in Russia*, 315.

9: The Struggle for Germany, April 1813–August 1813

1 Munro Price, *Napoleon. The End of Glory* (Oxford, 2014), 38–39. Lieven, *Russia*, 290–91.
2 Siemann, *Metternich*, 331–33.
3 Ibid., 329.
4 Price, *End of Glory*, 62.
5 *CG*, xiii, to de Serra, Minister to the king of Saxony, Mainz, April 20, 1813, #33962, 882–83.
6 Lentz, *Nouvelle histoire*, ii, 404–5.
7 *CG*, xiii, to Germain, Minister to the Grand Duke of Würzburg.
8 Ibid., to Frederick I of Württemberg, Mainz, April 24, 1813, #34004, 901–2.
9 Lentz, *Nouvelle histoire*, ii, 404–5.
10 *CG*, xiii, to Frederick I of Württemberg, Mainz, April 18, 1813, #33906, 857.
11 Ibid., to Frederick I of Württemberg, Mainz, April 20, 1813, #33949, 877.
12 Boudon, *Jérôme*, 387–91.
13 *CG*, xiii (Jan. 1813–June, 1813), to Jérôme, April 20, 1813, Mainz, #33954, 879.
14 Ibid., to Reinhard, Ambassador to Westphalia, April 20, 1813, Mainz, #33960, 881–82.
15 Price, *End of Glory*, 58.
16 Cited in Lieven, *Russia*, 313.
17 Ibid., 313.
18 Gallaher, *Iron Marshal*, 274.
19 Bew, *Castlereagh*, 315–16.
20 Lieven, *Russia*, 313–14.
21 Ibid., 315.
22 *CG*, xiii, to Cambacérès, May 4, 1813, Pegau, #34115, 950.
23 Cited in Price, *End of Glory*, 61.
24 Cited in Lachouque and Brown, *Anatomy*, 293–94.
25 Lieven, *Russia*, 316.
26 Lachouque and Brown, *Anatomy*, 295.

27 *CG*, xiii, to Frederick of Württemberg, Nossen, May 7, 1813, #34163, 971.

28 Michael V. Leggiere, *Napoleon and the Struggle for Germany. The Franco-Prussian War of 1813*, ii, *The Defeat of Napoleon* (Cambridge, 2015), 4.

29 Cited in Lachouque and Brown, *Anatomy*, 291.

30 Cited in ibid., 292.

31 *CG*, xiii, to Berthier, Lützen, May 2, 1813, 8:00 A.M., #34088, 940.

32 Ibid., to Marie-Louise, May 2, 1813, #34098, 944.

33 Lentz, *Nouvelle histoire*, ii, 410.

34 *CG*, xiii, to La Maréchale Bessières, Colditz, May 6, 1813, #34139, 959.

35 Cited in Chandler, *Campaigns*, 881.

36 Lentz, *Nouvelle Histoire*, ii, 427.

37 Cited in Lentz, *Nouvelle Histoire*, ii, 428.

38 Ibid., 428–29.

39 *CG*, xiii, to Maret, Dresden, May 14, 1813, #34236, 1001.

40 *Napoléon à Sainte-Hélène*, Tulard, ed., 449.

41 *CG*, xiii, to Savary, Lützen, May 2, 8:00 P.M., #34102, 945.

42 Ibid., to Berthier, May 4, Pegau, May 4, 1813, 4:00 A.M. #34106, 946–47.

43 Cited in Price, *End of Glory*, 61.

44 *CG*, xiii (Jan. 1813–June 1813), to Emperor Francis, May 4, 1813, Pegau, #34116, 951.

45 Ibid., to Frederick of Württemberg, May 4, 1813, Pegau, #341117, 951.

46 Lieven, *Russia*, 317.

47 *CG*, xiii, to Serra, minister to Saxony, Dresden, May 8, 1813, #34172, 974.

48 Ibid., to Fouché, May 11, 1813, #34196, 985.

49 Leggiere, *Napoleon*, ii, 761.

50 Price, *End of Glory*, 56.

51 Siemanns, *Metternich*, 334.

52 Ibid., 326–27.

53 Chandler, *Campaigns*, 889.

54 Siemanns, *Metternich*, 334.

55 Cited in Price, *End of Glory*, 65–66.

56 *CG*, xiii, to Marie-Louise, Mainz, April 18, 1813, #33913, 860.

57 Charles-Éloi Vial, *Marie-Louise* (Paris, 2017), 122.

58 Price, *End of Glory*, 64.

59 Ibid., 69–70.

60 Chandler, *Campaigns*, 888.

61 The complete list is cited in Siemman, *Metternich*, 333–34.

62 Lieven, *Russia*, 319–20.

63 *CG*, xiii (Jan. 1813–June 1813), to General Bourgier, Dresden, May 13, 1813, #34225, 996–97.

64 *CG*, xiii, to Emperor Francis, Dresden, May 17, 1813, #34267, 1013–14.

65 Price, *End of Glory*, 71–72.

66 Lieven, *Russia*, 320.

67 *CG*, xiii, to Ney, Dresden, May 14, 1813, #34238 and 34239, 1002.

68 Chandler, *Campaigns*, 890.

69 *CG*, xiii, to Berthier, Dresden, May 18, #34274, 1017.

70 Ibid., to Mortier, Dresden, May 16, 1813, #34265, 1013.

71 Chandler, *Campaigns*, 894.

72 Ibid., 895.

73 Lieven, *Russia*, 322.

74 Chandler, *Campaigns*, 896.

75   Lieven, *Russia*, 322.

76   Cited in ibid., 322.

77   Chandler, *Campaigns*, 896.

78   Lachouque and Brown, *Anatomy of Glory*, 299.

79   *CG*, xiii, to Emperor Francis, Wurschen, May 22, 1813, #34294, 1025.

80   Lieven, *Russia*, 323.

81   Price, *End of Glory*, 74.

82   Las Cases, *Le memorial*, 296.

83   Price, *End of Glory*, 74.

84   *CG*, xiii, to Marie-Louise, Goerlitz, May 23, 1813, #34296, 1026.

85   Varlan, *Caulaincourt*, 284–85.

86   *CG*, xiv, *Leipzig, Juillet, 1813–Décembre, 1813,* to Marie-Louise, Dresden, July 2, 1813, #35158, 55.

87   Ibid., to Marie-Louise, Liegnitz, May 28, 1813, #34339, 1052.

88   Lieven, *Russia*, 322–23, gives the figures as twenty-five thousand French to almost eleven thousand allied losses. Chandler, Campaigns, 897, at twenty thousand each. Leggiere follows Lieven: *Napoleon*, ii, 5.

89   *CG*, xiii, to Berthier, Goerlitz, May 24, 1813, #34324, 1037–38.

90   Lieven, *Russia*, 324.

91   Price, *End of Glory*, 74.

92   Lieven, *Russia*, 325.

93   Ibid., 324–25.

94   Siemann, *Metternich*, 353–54.

95   Cited in ibid., 353.

96   Lieven, *Russia*, 326.

97   Cited in ibid., 327.

98   Price, *End of Glory*, 79.

99   *CG*, xiii, to Cambaérès, Dresden, June 18, 1813, #34818, 1254.

100   Cited in Siemann, *Metternich*, 351.

101   Varlan, *Caulaincourt*, 284.

102   Cited in Siemann, *Metternich*, 349, 351.

103   Ibid., 352.

104   Cited in Price, *End of Glory*, 75.

105   Leggiere, *Napoleon*, ii, 90.

106   Cited in ibid., 76.

107   Lieven, *Russia*, 333–38.

108   Muir, *Britain*, 253.

109   Price, *End of Glory*, 80.

110   Muir, *Britain*, 253.

111   Bew, *Castlereagh*, 317.

112   Caulaincourt, *With Napoleon*, 298–300.

113   Price, *End of Glory*, 85.

114   Cited in Lieven, *Russia*, 327–28.

10: The Last Summer: Dresden, the Final Victory, June–September 1813

1   Price, *End of Glory*, 89–94.

2   Siemann, *Metternich*, 353–55.

3   *CG*, xiv, to Marie-Louise, Dresden, July 1, 1813, #35135, 46.

4   *CG*, xiii, to Eugene, Neumarkt, June 1, 1813, #34398, 1089–90.

5   Varlan, *Caulaincourt*, 290–99.
6   Lieven, *Russia*, 334–37.
7   Ibid., 346–48.
8   Ibid., 349.
9   Ibid., 349–52.
10   Chandler, *Campaigns*, 900.
11   Lieven, *Russia*, 340.
12   Ibid., 348.
13   Ibid., 333–34.
14   Ibid., 338–39.
15   Chandler, *Campaigns*, 900.
16   Price, *End of Glory*, 56.
17   Chandler, *Campaigns*, 901.
18   Siemann, *Metternich*, 359–60.
19   *CG*, xiv, to Eugene, July 1, 1813, Dresden, #35129, 43–44.
20   Chandler, *Campaigns*, 901.
21   Lentz, *Nouvelle histoire*, ii, 439.
22   *CG*, xiii, to Frederick-Augustus, Goerlitz, May 25, 1813, #34528, 1039–40.
23   Ibid., to Maret, Bunzlau, May 25, 1813, #34329, 1040.
24   Ibid., to Le Marois, governor of Magdeburg, Dresden, July 3, 1813. #35175, 63.
25   Ibid., to Savary, Dresden, June 18, 1813, #34845, 1267–68.
26   Gallaher, *Iron Marshal*, 276–77.
27   Chandler, *Campaigns*, 902–03.
28   *CG*, xiv, to Eugene, Aug. 14, 1813, Dresden, #35902, 382.
29   Cited in Haegele, *Murat*, 664.
30   Esdaile, *Peninsular War*, 440–42.
31   Muir, *Wellington*, ii, 523.
32   Esdaile, *Peninsular War*, 452.
33   *CG*, xiv, to Clarke, Dresden, July 6, 1813, #35247, 92.
34   Esdaile, *Peninsular War*, 445.
35   Muir, *Wellington*, ii, 528.
36   Esdaile, *Peninsular War*, 446.
37   Muir, *Wellington*, ii, 528.
38   Esdaile, *Peninsular War*, 444.
39   Lentz, *Joseph Bonaparte*, 400.
40   Esdaile, *Peninsular War*, 450.
41   Muir, *Wellington*, ii, 532.
42   Esdaile, *Peninsular War*, 450.
43   Muir, *Wellington*, ii, 529.
44   Esdaile, *Peninsular War*, 452.
45   Gotteri, *Soult*, 436.
46   *CG*, xiv, to Cambacérès, July 1, 1813, Dresden, #35113, 36.
47   Ibid., to Joseph, July 1, 1813, Dresden, #35131, 44.
48   Ibid., to Clarke, July 1, 1813, Dresden, #35116, 38.
49   Ibid., to Cambacérès, July 1, 1813, Dresden, #35113, 36.
50   Ibid., to Soult, Dresden, July 1, 1813, #35140, 47–48.
51   Ibid., to Marie-Louise, Dresden, July 2, 1813, #35158, 55.
52   Esdaile, *Peninsular War*, 452.
53   Lentz, *Joseph Bonaparte*, 401.

54   Price, *End of Glory*, 97.

55   Siemann, *Metternich*, 354.

56   Ibid., 355.

57   Ibid., 356.

58   Jonathon Riley, *Napoleon as a General* (London, 2007), 180.

59   Siemann, *Metternich*, 358–59.

60   Ibid., 356–57.

61   Cited in Chandler, *Campaigns*, 902.

62   *CG*, xiv, to Berthier, Aug. 13, 1813, Dresden, #35873, 369–70.

63   Ibid., to General Bertrand, Aug. 13, 1813, #35876, 372.

64   Riley, *Napoleon as a General*, 182.

65   Cited in Chandler, *Campaigns*, 903.

66   *CG*, xiv, to Maret, Goerlitz, Aug. 24, 1813, #36070, 464–65.

67   Price, *End of Glory*, 118–19.

68   Leggiere, *Napoleon*, ii, 8–9.

69   Cited in Chandler, *Campaigns*, 904.

70   Lieven, *Russia*, 395.

71   Chandler, *Campaigns*, 906.

72   Lieven, *Russia*, 394–95.

73   Chandler, *Campaigns*, 906.

74   Lachouque and Brown, *Anatomy*, 308.

75   Cited in Lieven, *Russia*, 393–94.

76   Ibid., 395–96.

77   Ibid., 395.

78   Chandler, *Campaigns*, 908.

79   Ibid., 908.

80   Price, *End of Glory*, 122–23, neither agrees nor dismisses this, but notes that Clam was biased. Price stresses that it was too confused to be knowable.

81   Ibid., 124.

82   Ibid., 127.

83   Lachouque and Brown, *Anatomy*, 308.

84   Chandler, *Campaigns*, 908.

85   Lachouque and Brown, *Anatomy*, 308–09.

86   *CG*, xiv, to Berthier, Stolpen, Aug. 26, 1813, 1:00 A.M., #36094, 479.

87   Lachouque and Brown, *Anatomy*, 309.

88   Chandler, *Campaigns*, 908.

89   Lieven, *Russia*, 398–99.

90   Lachouque and Brown, *Anatomy*, 309.

91   Price, *End of Glory*, 126.

92   Chandler, *Campaigns*, 911.

93   Price, *End of Glory*, 126–27.

94   Siemann, *Metternich*, 361–62. Siemann gives the date of Moreau's wounding as September 1, but it happened earlier. He also says Moreau died on the spot; he lived on in agony for another week: Price, *End of Glory*, 127.

95   Chandler, *Campaigns*, 910–11.

96   Price, *End of Glory*, 127.

97   Chandler, *Campaigns*, 911.

98   Lachouque and Brown, *Anatomy*, 309.

99   *CG*, xiv, to Cambacérès, Dresden, Aug. 27, 1813, evening, #36105, 485.

100 Price, *End of Glory*, 129.

101 Chandler, *Campaigns*, 912.

102 *CG*, xiv, to Marie-Louise, Dresden, Aug. 27, 1813, evening, #36107, 485.

103 Ibid., to Berthier, Dresden, Aug. 28, 1813, #36108, 485–86.

104 Lachouque and Brown, *Anatomy*, 309.

105 *CG*, xiv, to Marie-Louise, Dresden, Aug. 29, 1813, #36117, 489.

106 Ibid., to Murat, Dresden, Aug. 29, 1813, #36127, 493–94.

107 Lieven, *Russia*, 400–3.

108 Price, *End of Glory*, 129–30.

109 Lieven, *Russia*, 408.

110 Price, *End of Glory*, 130.

111 Lieven, *Russia*, 404.

112 Ibid., 409.

113 Ibid., 410–11.

114 Price, *End of Glory*, 130.

115 Lieven, *Russia*, 411.

116 Ibid., 415.

117 Cited in ibid., 416.

118 Price, *End of Glory*, 133–34.

119 *CG*, xiv, to St. Cyr, Dresden, Sept. 1, 1813, #36167, 512–13.

120 Ibid., to Berthier, Dresden, Sept. 1, 1813, #36160, 508–9.

121 Siemann, *Metternich*, 364.

122 Ibid., 364.

123 *CG*, xiv, to Berthier, Dresden, Sept. 1, 1813, #36161, 509.

124 Ibid., to Berthier, Dresden, Sept. 1, 1813, #36157, 507.

11: Leipzig: The Battle Lost, September–October 1813

1 Leggiere, *Napoleon*, ii, 288.

2 *CG*, xiv, to Marmont, Dresden, Sept. 2, 1813, 3:00 A.M., #36183, 519.

3 Ibid., to Berthier, Dresden, Sept. 2, 1813, #36180, 518.

4 *CG*, xiv, to Marmont, Dresden, Sept. 2, 1813, 3:00 A.M., # 36183, 519.

5 Chandler, *Campaigns*, 914–15.

6 This is based on the best modern account of the action in Price, *End of Glory*, 135–36.

7 Lieven, *Russia*, 418–19.

8 Price, *End of Glory*, 137.

9 Cited in Leggiere, *Napoleon*, ii, 453.

10 Chandler, *Campaigns*, 915.

11 Leggiere, *Napoleon*, ii, 377.

12 Chandler, *Campaigns*, 315.

13 Gotteri, *Soult*, 447.

14 Ibid., 451.

15 Ibid., 447–48.

16 Muir, *Wellington*, ii, 538–39.

17 Cited in ibid., 540.

18 Cited in ibid., 540.

19 Ibid., 541.

20 Gotteri, *Soult*, 449.

21 Cited in Muir, *Wellington*, ii, 541–42.

22 Cited in ibid., 544.

23 Gotteri, *Soult*, 448.
24 Muir, *Wellington*, ii, 545.
25 Gotteri, *Soult*, 452–53.
26 Cited in Esdaile, *Peninsular War*, 470.
27 Cited in ibid., 468.
28 Ibid., 469–71.
29 Muir, *Wellington*, ii, 548.
30 Esdaile, *Peninsular War*, 471.
31 Cited in Muir, Wellington, ii, 555.
32 Leggiere, *Napoleon*, ii, 378.
33 Siemann, *Metternich*, 362.
34 Bew, *Castlereagh*, 318.
35 Like all treaties of the era, Teplitz was written in French.
36 Siemann, *Metternich*, 363.
37 Schroeder, *Transformation*, 480–81.
38 Lieven, *Russia*, 274–75.
39 Leggiere, *Napoleon*, ii, 587.
40 *CG*, xix, to Maret, Dresden, Oct. 3, 1813, #36631, 717.
41 Ibid., to Berthier, Dresden, Oct. 3, 1813, #36619, fn 2, 712.
42 Cited in de Brancion, *Cambacérès*, 571.
43 Muir, *Britain*, 290–92.
44 Lieven, *Russia*, 425.
45 Leggiere, *Napoleon*, ii, 100–1.
46 Lieven, *Russia*, 429–30.
47 Leggiere, *Napoleon*, ii, 488.
48 Ibid., 489.
49 Ibid., ii, 488.
50 Bruno Colson, *Leipzig. La Bataille des Nations, 16–19 octobre, 1813* (Paris, 2013), 22–24.
51 Leggiere, *Napoleon*, ii, 490–91.
52 Lieven, *Russia*, 436–37.
53 Colson, *Leipzig*, 21.
54 Lieven, *Russia*, 431–32.
55 Leggiere, *Napoleon*, ii, 491.
56 Cited in Colson, *Leipzig*, 28.
57 1774 Ibid., 30.
58 Cited in ibid., 31.
59 Ibid., 32.
60 Ibid., 32–33.
61 Leggiere, *Napoleon*, ii, 518–19.
62 Colson, *Leipzig*, 34–35.
63 Ibid., 36.
64 Cited in ibid., 36–37.
65 Cited in ibid., 37.
66 Cited in Price, *End of Glory*, 141.
67 Leggiere, *Napoleon*, ii, 624.
68 Price, *End of Glory*, 142.
69 Colson, *Leipzig*, 37.
70 Chandler, *Campaigns*, 919.
71 Colson, *Leipzig*, 39–40.

72   Lieven, Russia, 437.
73   Leggiere, *Napoleon*, ii, 491.
74   Cited in Colson, *Leipzig*, 40.
75   Lieven, *Russia*, 441.
76   Chandler, *Campaigns*, 922.
77   Colson, *Leipzig*, 41.
78   Chandler, *Campaigns*, 922–23.
79   Colson, *Leipzig*, 50.
80   *CG*, xiv, to Marmont, Reudnitz, Oct. 13, 1813, 10:00 P.M., #36825, 806.
81   Leggiere, *Napoleon*, ii, 601.
82   Cited in Colson, *Leipzig*, 77.
83   The description is by a Swiss officer, Jomini, also recently defected from Napoleon's service: Cited in Colson, *Leipzig*, 75.
84   Leggiere, *Napoleon*, ii, 624.
85   Ibid., 625.
86   Digby Smith, *Leipzig, Napoleon and the Battle of the Nations* (London, 2001), 69.
87   Lieven, *Russia*, 440–41. Colson, *Leipzig*, 76–77. Chandler, *Campaigns*, 923.
88   *CG*, xiv, to Gen. Arrighi, Duben, Oct. 14, 1813, 3:00 A.M., #36812, 799.
89   Cited in Colson, *Leipzig*, 70.
90   Ibid., 51.
91   *CG*, xiv, to Marshal Macdonald, Reudnitz, Oct. 15, 8:00 A.M., #36824, 805–6.
92   Colson, *Leipzig*, 52–68.
93   Ibid., 70.
94   Chandler, *Campaigns*, 922.
95   Cited in Colson, *Leipzig*, 79.
96   Ibid., 93.
97   Cited in ibid., 93.
98   Cited in ibid., 94.
99   Ibid., 95.
100 Ibid., 96.
101 Cited in ibid., 98.
102 Ibid., 99–102. Leggiere, *Napoleon*, ii, 627.
103 Chandler, *Campaigns*, 927.
104 Leggiere, *Napoleon*, ii, 627.
105 Chandler, *Campaigns*, 928.
106 Colson, *Leipzig*, 107–8.
107 Cited in ibid., 107.
108 Ibid., 109.
109 Ibid., 105.
110 Karen Hagemann, "'Unimaginable horror and misery': The Battle of Leipzig in October 1813 in civilian experience and perception," in *Soldiers, Citizens, Civilians*, 157–78, 165.
111 Chandler, *Campaigns*, 927–28.
112 Colson, *Leipzig*, 116–17.
113 Chandler, *Campaigns*, 930.
114 Colson, *Leipzig*, 118.
115 Chandler, *Campaigns*, 930.
116 Colson, *Leipzig*, 134–35.
117 Ibid., 138–43.
118 Chandler, *Campaigns*, 930.

119 Ibid., 930.
120 Colson, *Leipzig*, 172.
121 Ibid., 157.
122 Chandler, *Campaigns*, 926, 930.
123 Ibid., 925.
124 Cited in Leggiere, *Napoleon*, ii, 631.
125 Ibid, 627.
126 Colson, *Leipzig*, 174.
127 Ibid., 174–76.
128 Leggiere, *Napoleon*, ii, 630–31.
129 Colson, *Leipzig*, 174–75.
130 Chandler, *Campaigns*, 925.
131 Cited in Colson, *Leipzig*, 175–76.
132 Siemann, *Metternich*, 322–24.
133 Colson, *Leipzig*, 176–77.
134 Ibid,. 178.
135 Leggiere, *Napoleon*, ii, 630.
136 Chandler, *Campaigns*, 930.
137 Cited in Colson, *Leipzig*, 183.
138 Chandler, *Campaigns*, 930–31.
139 Cited in Leggiere, *Napoleon*, ii, 633.
140 Leggiere, *Napoleon*, ii, 634.
141 Colson, *Leipzig*, 185.
142 Leggiere, *Napoleon*, ii, 634.
143 Colson, *Leipzig*, 184.
144 Leggiere, *Napoleon*, ii, 636.
145 Colson, *Leipzig*, 186–87.
146 Ibid., 187–88.
147 Ibid., 190.
148 Ibid., 189.
149 Chandler, *Campaigns*, 931.
150 Colson, *Leipzig*, 194.
151 Cited in ibid., 192.
152 Ibid., 195.
153 Ibid., 203.
154 Ibid., 202.
155 Chandler, *Campaigns*, 932.
156 Colson, *Leipzig*, 204.
157 Cited in ibid., 207.
158 Chandler, *Campaigns*, 932.
159 Cited in Colson, *Leipzig*, 210.
160 Colson, *Leipzig*, 221–23.
161 Cited in Hagermann, "Unimaginable Horror," 162.
162 Colson, Leipzig, 240.
163 Ibid., 229–31.
164 Chandler, *Campaigns*, 933.
165 Siemann, *Metternich*, 367.
166 Cited in Colson, *Leipzig*, 233.
167 Ibid., 219–25.

168 Leggiere, *Napoleon*, ii, 686–87.
169 Colson, *Leipzig*, 220.
170 Ibid., 236.
171 Cited in ibid., 238.
172 Cited in ibid., 241.
173 Cited in Cited in ibid., 242.
174 Ibid., 247–48.
175 Cited in ibid., 253.
176 Cited in ibid., 255.
177 Ibid., 254.
178 Cited in ibid., 259.
179 Ibid., 260.
180 Cited in ibid., 260.
181 Ibid., 260.
182 Cited in ibid., 261.
183 Leggiere, *Napoleon*, ii, 721–22.
184 Colson, *Leipzig*, 276.
185 Leggiere, *Napoleon*, ii, 722–24.
186 Colson, *Leipzig*, 277.
187 Cited in ibid., 289.
188 Cited in ibid., 291.
189 Ibid., 293.
190 Ibid., 299.
191 Leggiere, *Napoleon*, ii, 725.
192 Ibid.
193 Colson, *Leipzig*, 298.
194 *CG*, xiv, to Bertrand, Leipzig, Oct. 19, 7:00 A.M., #36831, 809–10. This was sent on to Paris by telegraph on Oct. 22.
195 Leggiere, *Napoleon*, ii, 729–30.
196 Chandler, *Campaigns*, 935.
197 Leggiere, *Napoleon*, ii, 727.
198 Chandler, *Campaigns*, 936.
199 Cited in Leggiere, *Napoleon*, ii, 728.
200 Ibid., 729.
201 Ibid, 730–31.
202 Ibid., 734.
203 Cited in Colson, *Leipzig*, 319.
204 Cited in ibid., 322.
205 Lieven, *Russia*, 457.
206 Colson, *Leipzig*, 335.
207 Chandler, *Campaigns*, 935.
208 Colson, *Leipzig*, 338.
209 *CG*, xiv, to Clarke, Gotha, Oct. 25, 1813, #36854, 821.
210 Colson, *Leipzig*, 342–43.
211 Chandler, *Campaigns*, 936.
212 Leggiere, *Napoleon*, ii, 746.
213 Colson, *Leipzig*, 345.
214 Ibid., 381.
215 Ibid., 390.

216　Ibid., 346.
217　Cited in Rey, *Alexander*, 263.
218　Cited in Leggiere, *Napoleon*, ii, 759.
219　Siemann, *Metternich*, 367.
220　Ibid., 367.
221　Leggiere, *Napoleon*, ii, 747–48.
222　Lieven, *Russia*, 458.
223　Cited in Leggiere, *Napoleon*, ii, 759.
224　*CG*, xiv, to Cambacérès, Gotha, Oct. 25, 1813, #36850, 818–19.
225　Ibid., to Cambacérès, Gotha, Oct. 25, 1813, #36851, 819.
226　Ibid., to Cambacérès, Gotha, Oct. 25, 1813, #36853, 820.

12: The Frontiers Crumble: The End of Empire, October 1813–January 1814

1　　Colson, *Leipzig*, 389.
2　　Boudon, *Jérôme*, 394.
3　　*CG*, xiv, to Gen Lebrun, Frankfurt, Nov. 1, 1813, #36877, 832–33.
4　　*CG*, xiv, to Cambacérès, Mainz, Nov. 6, 1813, #36947, 860–61.
5　　Hagermann, "Unimaginable Horror," 164.
6　　Colson, *Leipzig*, 388.
7　　Ibid., 389–90.
8　　Leggiere, *Napoleon*, ii, 768–70.
9　　Ibid., 770.
10　Ibid., 775.
11　Ibid., 775–76.
12　Ibid., 797–98.
13　Ibid., 788.
14　Ibid., 794–95.
15　Ibid., 795–96.
16　Lieven, *Russia*, 473.
17　Ibid., 474.
18　*CG*, xiv, to Marshal Kellermann, Frankfurt, Nov. 1, 1813, #36874, 831.
19　Leggiere, *Napoleon*, ii, 790.
20　*CG*, xiv, to Marshal Kellermann, Frankfurt, Oct. 31, 1813, #36866, 827.
21　Chandler, *Campaigns*, 937–38.
22　Leggiere, *Napoleon*, ii, 769–70.
23　Ibid., 782.
24　Cited in ibid., 789.
25　*CG*, xiv, to Clarke, Mainz, Nov.3, 1813, #36917, 848.
26　Ibid., to Clarke, Gotha, Oct. 25, 1813, #36855, 822–23.
27　*CG*, xv, *Les Chutes 1814–1821*, to Berthier, Jan. 1, 1814, #37704, 22.
28　*CG*, xv, to Marshal Kellermann, Jan. 3, 1814, #37732, 36–37.
29　Ibid., to Berthier, Jan. 6, 1814, #37747, 43.
30　Ibid., to Clarke, Jan. 2, 1814, #37718, 28.
31　Ibid., to Montalivet, Min of Interior, Jan. 2, 1814, #37726, 34.
32　*CG*, xiii, to Montalivet, Min of Interior, Dec. 6, 1813, #37433, 1091.
33　Cited in Siemann, *Metternich*, 377–78.
34　Varlan, *Caulaincourt*, 333.
35　*CG*, xiv, to Clarke, Mainz, Nov. 3, 1813, #36912, 845–46.
36　Cited in Price, *End of Glory*, 154–55.

37   Siemann, *Metternich*, 376.

38   Lieven, *Russia*, 466.

39   Leggiere, *Napoleon*, ii, 790.

40   Cited in Price, *End of Glory*, 159.

41   Lieven, *Russia*, 467.

42   Ibid., 465–66.

43   Ibid., 472.

44   Siemann, *Metternich*, 375.

45   Leggiere, *Napoleon*, ii, 791.

46   Lieven, *Russia*, 470–71.

47   Siemann, *Metternich*, 375, 379.

48   Ibid., 374.

49   Lieven, *Russia*, 463.

50   Cited in Bew, *Castlereagh*, 328.

51   Cited in Siemann, *Metternich*, 376.

52   Varlan, *Caulaincourt*, 322–24.

53   Ibid., 321–22.

54   Siemann, *Metternich*, 377–78.

55   Cited in Leighton S. James, *Witnessing the Revolutionary and Napoleonic Wars in German Central Europe* (Basningstoke, 2013), 178–79.

56   Aaslestad, "War Without Battles," 131.

57   Lieven, *Russia*, 471.

58   Gallaher, *Iron Marshal*, 283–87.

59   Glenthøj and Ottosen, *Experiences of War*, 202–5.

60   Lieven, *Russia*, 473.

61   Cited in de Brancion, *Cambacérès*, 571.

62   Joor, "Resistance," 117–18.

63   *CG*, xiv, to Vice-Admiral Decrès, Saint-Cloud, Nov. 17, 1813, #37095, 926.

64   Ibid., to Gen. Lebrun, Saint-Cloud, Nov. 17, 1813, #37102, 928–31.

65   de Brancion, *Cambacérès*, 572–73.

66   *CG*, xiii, Mainz, to Marie-Louise, Nov. 6, 1813, #36956, 866.

67   Ibid., to Cambacérès, Mainz, Nov. 6, 1813, #36948, 861–62.

68   Ibid., to Letezia Bonaparte, Mainz, Nov. 6, 1813, #36954, 865.

69   Ibid., to Marie-Louise, Mainz, Nov. 6, 1813, #36956, 866.

70   *CG*, xv, *Les Chutes, 1814–1821* to Louis. Jan. 4–5, 1814, #37745, 42.

71   *CG*, xiv, to Cambacérès, Gotha, Oct. 25, 1813, #36852, 820.

72   Ibid., to Pauline, Gotha, Oct. 25, 1813, #36861, 825.

73   Ibid., to Mollien, Saint-Cloud, Nov. 17, 1813, 1:00 A.M., #37103, 931–32.

74   Esdaile, *Peninsular War*, 479.

75   Muir, *Wellington*, ii, 554.

76   Esdaile, *Peninsular War*, 476–77.

77   Cited in Muir, Wellington, ii, 553.

78   Cited in Esdaile, *Peninsular War*, 479.

79   Cited in Muir, *Wellington*, ii, 556.

80   Esdaile, *Peninsular War*, 477.

81   Muir, *Wellington*, ii, 556–57.

82   *CG*, xiv, to Clarke, Mainz, Nov. 6, 1813, #56952, 864.

83   Cited in Muir, *Wellington*, ii, 561.

84   Esdaile, *Peninsular War*, 478–79.

85   *CG*, xiv, to Eugene, Saint-Cloud, Nov. 12, 1813, #37005, 888.

86   Ibid., to Clarke, Saint-Cloud, Nov. 14, 1813, #37019, 893.

87   Ibid., to Collin de Sussy, Saint-Cloud, Nov. 20, 1813, #37192, 974.

88   *CG*, xiv, to Clarke, Saint-Cloud, Nov. 18, 1813, #37131, 945.

89   Ibid., to Clarke, Saint-Cloud, Nov. 25, 1813, #37288, 1020–22.

90   Ibid.

91   Esdaile, *Peninsular War*, 481.

92   *CG*, xiv, to Clarke, Paris, Dec. 15, 1813, #37564, 1145.

93   Ibid., to Clarke, Paris, Dec. 8, 1813, #37481, 1111.

94   Esdaile, *Peninsular War*, 481.

95   Ibid., 479–81.

96   Cited in Muir, *Wellington*, ii, 564.

97   Cited in ibid., 565.

98   Gotteri, *Soult*, 464.

99   *CG*, xiv, to Ferdinand VII, Saint-Cloud, Nov. 12, 1813, #37006, 888–89.

100   Caulaincourt, *With Napoleon in Russia*, 282.

101   *CG*, xiv, to Melzi, Dec. 25, 1813, #37676, 1201; to Elisa, Dec. 25, 1813, #37674, 1201.

102   Cited in Lentz, *Joseph Bonaparte*, 406.

103   Lentz, *Joseph Bonaparte*, 405–7.

104   *CG*, xv, to Joseph, Jan. 7, 1814, #37756, 47–48.

105   *Napoléon et Joseph*, Joseph to Napoleon, Jan. 7, 1814, #1345, 708.

106   *CG*, xiv, to Clarke, Nov. 26, 1813, Paris, #37306, 1028–29.

107   Cited in Vincent Haegele, "Joseph Bonaparte en 1814: l'impossible conciliation," in *1814. La campagne de France*, Patrice Gueniffey and Pierre Branda, eds. (Paris, 2016), 273–85, 276.

108   Cited in Lentz, *Nouvelle histoire*, ii, 488.

109   Haegele, *Murat*, 671.

110   *CG*, xiv, to Cambacérès, Gotha, Oct. 25, 1813, #36850, 818–19.

111   Haegele, *Murat*, 669–70.

112   Michel Lacour-Gayet, *Joachim et Caroline Murat* (Paris, 1996), 251.

113   *CG*, xiv, to Fouché, Saint-Cloud, Nov. 15, 1813, #37063, 909–10.

114   Lacour-Gayet, *Joachim et Caroline*, 238–39.

115   Cited in ibid., 229.

116   Ibid., 251.

117   Haegele, *Murat*, 673.

118   Davis, *Napoleon and Naples*, 261.

119   Ibid., 259–60.

120   Haegele, *Murat*, 672.

121   Ibid., 672–73.

122   Ibid., 673.

123   Lacour-Gayet, *Joachim et Caroline*, 266.

124   Cited in Haegele, *Murat*, 673.

125   Cited in Lentz, *Nouvelle histoire*, ii, 493.

126   Cited in ibid., 493–94.

127   Haegele, *Napoléon et les siens*, 352.

128   *CG*, xiv, to Eugene, Jan. 17, 1814, #37845, 86.

129   Haegele, *Murat*, 675.

130   Price, *End of Glory*, 127.

131   Siemann, *Metterich*, 382.

132   Cited in ibid., 382–83.

133 Price, *End of Glory*, 163–65.

134 Caulaincourt, *With Napoleon in Russia*, 291.

135 Price, *End of Glory*, 165.

136 Ibid., 168.

137 *CG*, xv, to Caulaincourt, Jan. 4, 1814, #37736, 38–39.

138 de Brancion, *Cambacérès*, 578.

139 Ibid.

140 de Brancion, *Cambacérès*, 578.

141 Price, *End of Glory*, 176.

142 de Brancion, *Cambacérès*, 578.

143 Price, *End of Glory*, 176–79.

144 de Brancion, *Cambacérès*, 579.

145 Lentz, *Nouvelle Histoire*, ii, 510.

146 Price, *End of Glory*, 178–79.

147 de Brancion, *Cambacérès*, 579.

148 Cited in Price, *End of Glory*, 179.

149 de Brancion, *Cambacérès*, 578–79.

150 Cited in Price, *End of Glory*, 180.

151 Cited in ibid., 180–81.

152 Ibid., 184.

153 Ibid., 181.

154 Ibid., 181–82.

155 Cited in de Brancion, *Cambacérès*, 579–80.

156 Cited in Price, *End of Glory*, 183.

157 June K. Burton, *Napoleon and Clio. Historical Writing, Teaching and Thinking during the First Empire* (Durham, NC, 1979).

13: The Fall of France: The End of Everything, January to May 1814

1 Michael Leggiere, *The Fall of Napoleon*, vol. I, *The Allied Invasion of France, 1813–1814* (Cambridge, 2007), 84.

2 Lieven, *Russia*, 475–76.

3 Ibid., 477–78.

4 Leggiere, *Fall of Napoleon*, 198–99.

5 Lieven, *Russia*, 472–73, 476.

6 Chandler, *Campaigns*, 950.

7 Lieven, *Russia*, 462.

8 Ibid., 472–73, 476.

9 Price, *End of Glory*, 159.

10 Leggiere, *Fall of Napoleon*, I, 94.

11 Chandler, *Campaigns*, 949.

12 Leggiere, *Fall of Napoleon*, I, 94–95.

13 Ibid., 93–94.

14 François Houdecek, "L'autre visage de la campagne de France: Napoléon face aux désordres de l'armée," in Gueniffey et Branda, *1814*, 73–87, at 79–80.

15 Lentz, *Nouvelle histoire*, iii, 502–04.

16 Houdecek, "L'autre visage," 74–75.

17 Leggiere, *Fall of Napoleon*, I, 68.

18 Chandler, *Campaigns*, 949.

19 Lachouque and Brown, *Anatomy*, 337.

20   Chandler, *Campaigns*, 951.

21   Lieven, *Russia*, 478.

22   Leggiere, *Fall of Napoleon*, I, 65.

23   Lieven, *Russia*, 474.

24   Lachouque and Brown, *Anatomy*, 337.

25   Ibid., 337.

26   *CG*, xv, to Clarke, Jan. 11, 1814, #37799, 63–64.

27   Ibid., to Gen. Bertrand, Jan. 13, 1814, #37816, 71.

28   Ibid., to Clarke, Jan. 2, 1814, #37718, 28.

29   Leggiere, *Fall of Napoleon*, I, 270–71.

30   *CG*, xv, to Montalivet, Min of Interior, Jan. 2, 1814, #37726, 34.

31   On January 2, Napoleon ordered all troops east of Langres-Vesoul to be paid as frontline troops, establishing this as the war zone: *CG*, xv, to Daru, #37720, 29–30.

32   *CG*, xv, to Clarke, Jan. 4, 1814, #37738, 39–40.

33   Ibid., to Clarke, Jan. 11, 1814, #37802, 64–65.

34   Leggiere, *Fall of Napoleon*, I, 507.

35   Muir, *Wellington*, ii, 567.

36   Leggiere, *Fall of Napoleon*, I, 507.

37   Ibid., 383.

38   Jean-François Brun, "La prudence autrichienne à l'origine de la défaite de Napoléon?" in *1814. La campagne de France*, eds. Patrice Gueniffey & Pierre Branda (Paris, 2016), 119–62, 127–28.

39   *CG*, xv, to Clarke, Jan. 6, 1814, #37749, 44.

40   Leggiere, *Fall of Napoleon*, I, 73.

41   Chandler, *Campaigns*, 946–47.

42   Cited in Lieven, *Russia*, 477.

43   Chandler, *Campaigns*, 874.

44   Leggiere, *Fall of Napoleon*, I, 269.

45   Ibid., 272.

46   Chandler, *Campaigns*, 951.

47   *CG*, xv, to Montalivet, Min Interior, Jan. 2, 1814, #37718, 28.

48   Leggiere, *Fall of Napoleon*, I, 382.

49   Lieven, *Russia*, 477–78.

50   *CG*, xv, to Berthier, Jan. 18, 1814, #37853, 89.

51   Ibid., to Berthier, Jan. 17, 1814, #37835, 80.

52   Ibid., to Clarke, Jan. 17, 1814, #37840, 82.

53   Leggiere, *Fall of Napoleon*, I, 166.

54   Ibid., 185.

55   Chandler, *Campaigns*, 949.

56   Leggiere, *Fall of Napoleon*, I, 169.

57   Ibid., 177–78.

58   Ibid., 182–83.

59   Ibid., 437.

60   Ibid., 420–21.

61   *CG*, xv, to Clarke, Jan. 18, 1814, #37857, 90–91.

62   Ibid, to Clarke, Jan. 18, 1814, #37858, 91.

63   Leggiere, *Fall of Napoleon*, I, 175.

64   Ibid., 182.

65   Ibid., 162–63.

66   Cited in ibid., 165.

67 *CG*, xiv, to Elisa, Dec. 25, 1813, #37674, 1201.

68 *CG*, xv, to Borghese, Jan. 17, 1814, #37837, 81.

69 Ibid., to Eugene, Jan. 17, 1814, #37845, 86.

70 Leggiere, *Fall of Napoleon*, I, 68.

71 Drawn from Annie Crépin, "*La conscription des années sombre et le devenir de l'instituion*," in *1814. La campagne de France*, Partrice Gueniffey and Pierre Branda, eds. (Paris, 2016), 41–54.

72 Chandler, *Campaigns*, 946.

73 Leggiere, *Fall of Napoleon*, I, 69.

74 *CG*, xv, to Berthier, Jan. 1, 1814, #37704, 22.

75 Alan Forrest, "*Les partisans de la campagne de France: mythe or réalité?*" in Gueniffey and Branda, *1814*, 17–27.

76 Crépin, "La conscription," 47.

77 *CG*, xv, to Clarke, Jan. 18, 1814, #37860, 92, note 3.

78 Ibid., to Clarke, Jan. 18, 1814, #37860, 92.

79 Ibid., to Molé minister of justice, Jan. 18, 1814, #37864, 93.

80 Crépin, "La conscription," in Gueniffey and Branda, *1814*, 46–49.

81 *CG*, xv, to Clarke, Jan. 18, 1814, #37859, 91.

82 Ibid., to Clarke, Jan. 18, 1814, #37861, 92.

83 Cited in Lentz, *Joseph Bonaparte*, 410.

84 Haegele, "Joseph Bonaparte en 1814," 281.

85 Cited in ibid., 280–81.

86 *CG*, xv, to Joseph, Jan. 24, 1814, #37914, 118–21. In fact, Joseph reported that the Guard numbered only twenty-two battalions: *Napoléon et Joseph*, Joseph to Napoléon, Jan. 27, 1814, #1403, 755.

87 *CG*, xv, to Joseph, Jan. 24, 1814, #37914, 118–21.

88 *Napoléon et Joseph*, Joseph to Napoleon, Jan. 27, 1814, #1403, 755.

89 *CG*, xv (1814-1821) to Joseph, Jan. 24, 1814, #37914, 118–21.

90 Cited in Lentz, *Joseph Bonaparte*, 409.

91 Lentz, *Nouvelle histoire*, ii, 518.

92 *CG*, xv, to Savary, Jan. 21, 1814, #37883, 103.

93 Ibid., to Savary, Jan. 21, 1814, #37883, 103.

94 Caiani, *To Kidnap a Pope*, 256–58.

95 Broers, *Politics of Religion*, 94, 99.

96 Caiani, *To Kidnap a Pope*, 260–61.

97 Varlan, *Caulaincourt*, 336.

98 Caiani, *To Kidnap a Pope*, 253.

99 Ibid., 255–57.

100 *CG*, xv, to Marshal Kellerman, Jan. 24, 1814, #37915, 122.

101 Leggiere, *Fall of Napoleon*, I, 488–90.

102 *CG*, xv, to Victor, Vitry, Jan. 26, 1814, #37221, 124.

103 Leggiere, *Fall of Napoleon*, I, 486–88.

104 Chandler, *Campaigns*, 958.

105 Lieven, *Russia*, 479–81.

106 Cited in ibid., 481.

107 Ibid., 482.

108 Cited in ibid., 482.

109 Chandler, *Campaigns*, 964.

110 David Rouanet, "Troyes dans la tourmente de 1814," in Gueniffey and Branda, *1814*, 229–54, 235.

111 *CG*, xv, to Caulaincourt, Piney, Feb. 2, 1814, #37971, 148.

112 Ibid., to Joseph, Piney, Feb. 2, 1814, #37973, 149.

113 Cited in Siemann, *Metternich*, 382.

114 Ibid., 382.

115 Lieven, *Russia*, 485.

116 Siemann, *Metternich*, 383.

117 Varlan, *Caulaincourt*, 348.

118 Chandler, *Campaigns*, 955.

119 *CG*, xv, to Joseph, Troyes, Feb. 5, 1814, #38008, 165–66.

120 Ibid., to Joseph, Troyes, Feb. 5, 1814, #38008, 165–66. In fact, Joseph had proposed only leaving "a prince at the head of a provisional administration" between the departure of the empress and any allied entry of the city: Haegele, ed., *Napoléon et Joseph*, Joseph to Napoleon, Feb. 5, 1814, #1412, 760.

121 Ibid., to Joseph, Troyes, Feb. 5, 1814, #38009, 166.

122 Haegele (ed.), *Napoléon et Joseph*, Napoleon to Joseph, Nogent, Feb. 8, 1814, #1428, 770–71.

123 *CG*, xv, to Savary, Troyes, Feb. 6, 1814, #38015, 168.

124 Catholic devotions asking for mercy and intercession, often at time of great fear.

125 *CG*, xv, to Cambacérès, Nogent-sur-Seine, Feb. 7, 1814, #38020, 170–71.

126 Haegele (ed)., *Napoléon et Joseph*, Joseph to Napoleon, Feb. 8, 1814. #1434, 774.

127 Ibid., Joseph to Napoleon, Feb. 3, 1814, #1409, 758; Joseph to Napoleon, Feb. 5, 1814, #1411, 759.

128 Ibid., Napoleon to Joseph, Nogent, Feb. 8, 1814, #1428, 770–71.

129 Lieven, *Russia*, 487.

130 Lachouque and Brown, *Anatomy*, 353–55.

131 Lieven, *Russia*, 488.

132 Chandler, *Campaigns*, 969.

133 For a succinct summary: Bruno Colson, "Napoléon et la campagne de France dans la pensée militaire," in Gueniffey and Branda, *1814*, 55–72.

134 Cited in Varlan, *Caulaincourt*, 356.

135 Ibid., 351–52.

136 Cited in Siemann, *Metternich*, 378.

137 Varlan, *Caulaincourt*, 355–57.

138 Siemann, *Metternich*, 383–84.

139 Cited in ibid., 386.

140 Underlined in the text.

141 *CG*, xv, to Francis I, Nogent-sur-Seine, Feb. 21, 1814, #38280, 295–96.

142 Lentz, *Joseph Bonaparte*, 411–13.

143 *Napoléon et Joseph*, Joseph to Napoleon, Feb. 17, 1814, #1493, 805.

144 Ibid., Joseph to Napoleon, Feb. 18, 1814, #1497, 807.

145 Ibid., Joseph to Napoleon, Feb. 20, 1814, #1509, 813.

146 Cited in Brancion, *Cambacérès*, 586.

147 Varlan, *Caulaincourt*, 357–58.

148 Lieven, *Russia*, 492–93.

149 Cited in Siemann, *Metternich*, 386.

150 Cited in Chandler, *Campaigns*, 977.

151 Ibid., 978.

152 Lieven, *Russia*, 489.

153 Cited in Chandler, *Campaigns*, 979.

154 *CG*, xv, to Joseph, Montereau, Feb. 20, 1814, #38246, 280.

155 Ibid., to Augereau, Nogent-sur-Seine, Feb. 21, 1814, #38250, 281–82.
156 Jean-Philippe Rey, *Derniers combats pour l'Empire, Lyonnais, Dauphiné, Savoie* (Lyon, 2014).
157 Lieven, *Russia*, 491–92.
158 Cited in Bew, *Castlereagh*, 343.
159 Siemann, *Metternich*, 387–89.
160 Cited in Bew, *Castlereagh*, 343.
161 Siemann, *Metternich*, 387.
162 Lieven, *Russia*, 497–98.
163 Cited in Bew, *Castlereagh*, 344.
164 Cited in ibid., 346.
165 Cited in Vial, *Marie-Louise*, 145.
166 Cited in ibid., 145–46.
167 Siemann, *Metternich*, 390–91.
168 Rouanet, "Troyes," 244–46.
169 Ibid., 247–49.
170 Chandler, *Campaigns*, 984.
171 *CG*, xv, to Joseph, Fismes, March 4, 1814, #38427, 367–68.
172 Lieven, *Russia*, 498–99.
173 *CG*, xv, to Joseph, La Ferté, March 2, 1814, #38407, 358.
174 Lieven, *Russia*, 498–99.
175 Lachouque and Brown, *Anatomy*, 372.
176 Cited in ibid., 372–73.
177 Chandler, *Campaigns*, 988.
178 Lieven, *Russia*, 499–502.
179 Lachouque and Brown, *Anatomy*, 373.
180 Chandler, *Campaigns*, 989.
181 Lachouque and Brown, *Anatomy*, 373.
182 Chandler, *Campaigns*, 989.
183 Lieven, Russia, 502.
184 Chandler, *Campaigns*, 990.
185 Lieven, *Russia*, 502.
186 Ibid., 502–3.
187 Chandler, *Campaigns*, p. 991.
188 Haegele, ed., *Napoleon et Joseph*, Napoleon to Joseph, Chavignon, March 10, 1814, #1575, 843.
189 Lachouque and Brown, *Anatomy*, 375.
190 Lieven, *Russia*, 503–4.
191 Cited in Lentz, *Joseph Bonaparte*, 414.
192 Cited in ibid., 415.
193 Brancion, *Cambacérès*, 586.
194 Cited in Lentz, *Joseph Bonaparte*, 415.
195 *CG*, xv, to Cambacérès, March 14, Reims, #38518, 407–8.
196 Cited in Vial, *Marie-Louise*, 146–47.
197 *CG*, xv, to Cambacérès, March 14, Reims, #38519, 408–9.
198 Vial, *Marie-Louise*, 148–49.
199 *CG*, xv, to Cambacérès, March 14, Reims, #38518, 407–8.
200 Vial, *Marie-Louise*, 148.
201 De Waresquiel, *Talleyrand*, 433.
202 Cited in ibid., 436.
203 Ibid., 435–36.

204 Cited in ibid., 435.

205 Ibid., 62.

206 Cited in ibid., 433.

207 *CG*, xv, to Cambacérès, La Ferté, March 3, 1814, #38417, 362–63.

208 Cited in De Waresquiel, *Talleyrand*, 433.

209 *CG*, xv, to Cambacérès, Reims, March 14, 1814, #38519, 408–9.

210 Varlan, *Caulaincourt*, 361.

211 Lieven, *Russia*, 505.

212 Brun, "La prudence autrichien," 143, fn 25.

213 Lieven, *Russia*, 509.

214 Price, *End of Glory*, 214.

215 Chandler, *Campaigns*, 997.

216 Lachouque and Brown, *Anatomy*, 383.

217 Chandler, *Campaigns*, 996–997.

218 Ibid., 998.

219 Lachouque and Brown, *Anatomy*, 384–85.

220 Chandler, *Campaigns*, 999.

221 Ibid., 997.

222 Lieven, *Russia*, 509.

223 Ibid., 510.

224 Ibid., 509.

225 *CG*, xv, to Berthier, Saint-Dizier, #38625, 457.

226 *CG*, xv, to Marie-Louise, Bar-sur-Aube, March 28, 1814, 458.

227 Jean-Philippe Rey, "Lyon et sa région dans la défaite," in Guenifey et Branda, *1814*, 255–70, 258–59.

228 Chandler, *Campaigns*, 999–1000.

229 Ibid., 1001.

230 Bew, *Castlereagh*, 148.

231 Cited in de Waresquiel, *Talleyrand*, 436.

232 *CG*, xv, to Méneval, Soissons, March 12, 1814, #38510, 404.

233 Ibid., to Marie-Louise, Soissons, March 14, 1814, #38530, 414.

234 Ibid., to Savary, Reims, March 14, 1814, #38535, 415–16.

235 Ibid., to Cambacérès, Reims, March 17, #38576, 433.

236 Muir, *Wellington*, ii, 572.

237 Ibid., 570–73.

238 Cited in ibid., 572.

239 Price, *End of Glory*, 208.

240 Forrest, *French Atlantic*, 211.

241 Price, *End of Glory*, 208–11.

242 Ibid., 210.

243 Muir, *Wellington*, ii, 575.

244 Lentz, *Joseph Bonaparte*, 416–17.

245 Price, *End of Glory*, 218.

246 Lentz, *Joseph Bonaparte*, 418–19.

247 Price, *End of Glory*, 218.

248 de Brancion, *Cambacérès*, 588.

249 Cited in Lentz, *Joseph Bonaparte*, 419.

250 Cited in Vial, *Marie-Louise*, 151.

251 Lentz, *Joseph Bonaparte*, 419. Vial, *Marie-Louise*, 151.

252 Lentz, *Joseph Bonaparte*, 415.

253 Lieven, *Russia*, 514.

254 Lentz, *Joseph Bonaparte*, 421–22; De Waresquiel, *Talleyrand*, 440.

255 Cited in Lentz, *Nouvelle Histoire*, ii, 560.

256 Ibid., 561.

257 Lieven, *Russia*, 515.

258 Lentz, *Nouvelle Histoire*, ii, 561; Lieven, *Russia*, 515.

259 Lieven, *Russia*, 514.

260 Lentz, *Nouvelle Histoire*, ii, 561.

261 *CG*, xv, to Marie-Louise, Fontainebleau, March 31, 1814, #38632, 461; to Berthier, Fontainebleau, March 31, 1814, #38629 and 38629, 458–59.

262 *CG*, xv, to Caulaincourt, Fromenteau, March 31, 1814, #38630, 459–60.

263 Lentz, *Nouvelle Histoire*, ii, 562.

264 Lieven, *Russia*, 516.

265 Siemann, *Metternich*, 392.

266 Pierre Serna, *La République des Girouettes. 1789–1815 et au-delà une anomalie politique. La France de l'extrême centre* (Seyssel, 2005), *passim*.

267 De Waresquiel, *Talleyrand*, 440.

268 Price, *End of Glory*, 117.

269 Ibid., 220.

270 Caiani, *Louis XVI*, *passim*.

271 Cited in Siemann, *Metternich*, 394.

272 De Waresquiel, *Talleyrand*, 442.

273 Price, *End of Glory*, 224.

274 Ibid., 228.

275 Ibid.

276 Chandler, *Campaigns*, 1001.

277 Price, *End of Glory*, 229.

278 De Waresquiel, *Talleyrand*, 441.

279 Ibid., 444.

280 Price, *End of Glory*, 228.

281 De Waresquiel, *Talleyrand*, 444.

282 Serna, *Girouettes*, 150–51.

283 The entire text can be found in Lentz, *Nouvelle histoire*, ii, 566–67.

284 Lentz, *Nouvelle histoire*, ii, 567.

285 Las Cases, *Mémorial*, Lentz et al., eds., 277.

286 Serna, *Girouettes*, 155.

287 Ibid., 151–55.

288 Ibid., 153.

289 Munro Price, *The Perilous Crown. France between Revolutions, 1814–1848* (Basingstoke & Oxford, 2007), 53.

290 Varlan, *Caulaincourt*, 372.

291 Cited in ibid., 394.

292 Price, *End of Glory*, 232–33.

293 Cited in ibid., 233.

294 Ibid., 233.

295 Las Cases, *Mémoriale*, Lentz, et al., eds., 279.

296 Serna, *Girouettes*, 153–55.

297 Cited in Price, *End of Glory*, 238.

298   Cited in Varlan, *Caulaincourt*, 391.

299   Cited in ibid., 391–92.

300   Cited in ibid., 392.

301   *CG*, xv, to Caulaincourt, Fontainebleau, April 11, 1814, #38651, 470–71.

302   Cited in Varlan, *Caulaincourt*, 395.

303   Price, *End of Glory*, 241.

304   *Nouvelle Bibliographie Critique*, ed. Tulard, 32–33: "We have here a model, sadly rare, of what editions of memoirs ought to be."

305   Pierre Hillemand, "Napoléon a-t-il tenté de se suicide à Fontainebleau?" *Revue de l'Institut Napoléon*, 119 (1971): 71–78.

306   *CG*, xv, to Maria Walewska, Fontainebleau, April 14, 1814, #38666, 478.

307   *CG*, xv, to Marie-Louise, Fontainebleau, April 8, 1814, #38649, 469–70.

308   Ibid., to Josephine, Fontainebleau, April 16, 1814, #38665, 477.

309   Vial, *Marie-Louise*, 155.

310   *CG*, xv, to Marie-Louise, Fontainebleau, April 3, 1814, #38641, 465–66.

311   Vial, *Marie-Louise*, 155.

312   On the myth: Vial, *Marie-Louise*, 154. Most of this began with Chateaubriand, who was not present.

313   Vial, *Marie-Louise*, 157–58.

314   Ibid., 158–59.

315   Lentz, *Joseph Bonaparte*, 427–28.

316   Vial, *Marie-Louise*, 169.

317   Lentz, *Joseph Bonaparte*, 426.

318   Lentz, *Nouvelle histoire*, ii, 586.

319   de Brancion, *Cambacérès*, 591–92.

320   Vial, *Marie-Louise*, 169–71.

321   Ibid., 163.

322   Lentz, *Joseph Bonaparte*, 429–30.

323   Lachouque and Brown, *Anatomy*, 420–21.

324   Cited in Price, *End of Glory*, 243.

325   Lachouque and Brown, *Anatomy*, 420–21.

14: Elba: A Nervous Exile, April 1814–February 1815

1   Lachouque and Brown, *Anatomy*, 421.

2   Cited in Dwyer, *Citizen Emperor*, 495–98.

3   Price, *End of Glory*, 245–50.

4   Boudon, *Jérôme*, 414–23.

5   Lentz, *Joseph Bonaparte*, 428–29.

6   Varlan, *Caulaincourt*, 397–98.

7   Ibid., 398.

8   Ibid., 397.

9   Cited in Lieven, *Russia*, 518–19.

10   Varlan, *Caulaincourt*, 396–97.

11   Cited in ibid., 398.

12   Rey, *Alexander*, 273.

13   Cited in Siemann, *Metternich*, 395.

14   Bew, *Castlereagh*, 355–56.

15   Ibid., 357.

16   *CG*, xv, to Marie-Louise, Fontainebleau, April 19, 1814, #38671, 479–80.

17   Lentz, *Nouvelle histoire*, III, 172–75.
18   Ibid., 177–78.
19   Migliorini, *Napoléon*, 428.
20   Dwyer, *Citizen Emperor*, 500.
21   Ibid., 502.
22   Lentz, *Nouvelle histoire*, III, 204.
23   Ibid., 197.
24   Ibid., 195, note 4.
25   *CG*, xv, to Taillade, Comdt of the Fleet, Longone, Sept. 16, 1814, #38878, 589.
26   Ibid., to Bertrand, Portoferraio, Feb. 9, 1815, #38999, 646.
27   Ibid., to Bertrand, Portoferraio, Oct. 21, 1814, #38916, 606.
28   Ibid., to Bertrand, Portoferraio, Jan. 18, 1815, #38983.
29   Ibid., to Bertrand, Portoferraio, Oct. 30, 1814, #38930, 615.
30   Ibid., to Bertrand, Portoferraio, Dec. 24, 1814, #38962, 630.
31   Dwyer, *Citizen Emperor*, 507–8.
32   Vial, *Marie-Louise*, 188–90.
33   Lentz, *Nouvelle histoire*, iv, 270–78.
34   Ibid., 280.
35   Cited in Davis, *Naples and Napoleon*, 262–63.
36   Mansel, *Louis XVIII*, 197–98.
37   Mark Braude, *The Invisible Emperor: Napoleon on Elba* (London, 2018), 172.
38   Lentz, *Nouvelle histoire*, iv, 280–81.
39   Bew, *Castlereagh*, 405–6.
40   Lentz, *Nouvelle histoire*, iv, 281.
41   Mansel, *Louis XVIII*, 197.
42   Dwyer, *Citizen Emperor*, 512.
43   Ibid., 514.
44   Lentz, *Nouvelle histoire*, iv, 276.
45   Ibid., 285.
46   Ibid., 260, 262.
47   Cited in Dwyer, *Citizen Emperor*, 512.
48   Ibid., 513.
49   Cited in Lentz, *Nouvelle histoire*, iv, 273.
50   Cited in Braude, *Invisible Emperor*, 221.
51   Braude, *Invisible Emperor*, 240.
52   Ibid., 221
53   Cited in Lentz, *Nouvelle histoire*, iv, 273.
54   Cited in ibid., 271.
55   Braude, *Invisible Emperor*, 203.
56   *CG*, xv, to Murat, Portoferraio, Feb. 17, 1815, 39010, 650.
57   Ibid., to Murat, Portoferraio, Feb. 17, 1815, 39011, 650.

15: The Flight of the Eagle

1   Cited in Bernal Díaz, *The Conquest of New Spain* (Eng. trans J. M. Cohen, London, 1963 ed.), 84.
2   Marshall-Cornwall, *Massena*, 255.
3   Cited in Lentz, *Nouvelle histoire*, iv, 291.
4   Cited in Marshall-Cornwall, *Massena*, 255.
5   Emmanuel de Waresquiel, *Cent Jours, la tentation de l'impossible, mars–julliet 1815* (Paris, 2008), 117.

6   Lentz, *Nouvelle histoire*, iv, 292.

7   De Waresquiel, *Cent Jours*, 109.

8   Ibid., 109–11.

9   Price, *Perilous Crown*, 73–75.

10   Both cited in Lentz, *Nouvelle histoire*, iv, 294–95.

11   Ibid., iv, 294.

12   Cited in ibid., 296.

13   From the official government journal, *Le Moniteur* of March 23, 1815, cited in ibid., 301.

14   Cited in de Waresquiel, *Cent Jours*, 175.

15   Cited in ibid., 176.

16   Cited in Price, *Perilous Crown*, 71–72.

17   Lentz, *Nouvelle histoire*, iv, 300.

18   Cited in de Waresquiel, *Cent Jours*, 178.

19   Ibid., 177.

20   Ibid., 176.

21   Ibid., 178–80.

22   Cited in Lentz, *Nouvelle histoire*, iv, 303.

23   *CG*, xv, to Marie-Louise, March 11, 1815, Lyon, 39025, 662–63.

24   Ibid., to Joseph, March 12, Lyon, 39029, 664–65.

25   Vial, *Marie-Louise*, 226–28.

26   Cited in Haegele, *Murat*, 689.

27   Cited in Lentz, *Nouvelle Histoire*, iv, 363.

28   Davis, *Naples and Napoleon*, 263.

29   Lentz, *Joseph Bonaparte*, 441.

30   Cited in Haegele, *Murat*, 691.

31   Davis, *Naples and Napoleon*, 264.

32   Haegele, *Murat*, 691.

33   Cited in Davis, *Napoleon and Naples*, 263.

34   Haegele, *Murat*, 696.

35   Cited in Lentz, *Nouvelle histoire*, iv, 364.

36   Ibid., 116, note 2.

37   *CG*, xv, to Ney, Auxerre, March 17, 1815, 39033, 665–66.

38   Ibid., to Ney, Lyon, March 13, 1815, 39030, 665.

39   de Waresquiel, *Cent Jours*, 240–41.

40   Cited in ibid., 242.

41   Lentz, *Nouvelle histoire*, iv, 306.

42   Cited in de Waresquiel, *Cent Jours*, 244.

43   *CG*, xv, to Ney, Auxerre, March 17, 1815, 39033, 665–66.

44   Cited in Lentz, *Nouvelle histoire*, iv, 295–96.

45   Ibid., 307.

46   Cited in ibid., 307.

47   Mansel, *Louis XVIII*, 222.

48   Gotteri, *Soult*, 472.

49   Both cited in cited in De Waresquiel, *Cent Jours*, 215.

50   Lentz, *Nouvelle histoire*, iv, 310.

51   Cited in de Waresquiel, *Cent Jours*, 203.

52   Cited in Lentz, *Nouvelle histoire*, iv, 309.

53   Cited in de Waresquiel, *Cent Jours*, 244.

54   Gotteri, *Soult*, 470–71.

55   Mansel, *Louis XVIII*, 191, 200.
56   De Waresquiel, *Cent Jours*, 169.
57   Gotteri, *Soult*, 472–73.
58   De Waresquiel, *Cent Jours*, 195.
59   Ibid., 194–95.
60   Gotteri, *Soult*, 471.
61   Ibid., 474–75.
62   Ibid., *Soult*, 475.
63   De Waresquiel, *Cent Jours*, 194–95.
64   Cited in Gotteri, *Soult*, 475.
65   Ibid., 475.
66   Price, *Perilous Crown*, 74.
67   Mansel, *Louis XVIII*, 223.
68   Lentz, *Nouvelle histoire*, iv, 310–11.
69   Ibid., 311; Mansel, *Louis XVIII*, 223.
70   de Waresquiel, *Cent Jours*, 199.
71   Cited in ibid., 199.
72   Cited in ibid., 212.
73   Cited in ibid., 200.
74   Ibid., 233.
75   Ibid., 248–51.
76   Cited in Price, *Perilous Crown*, 77.
77   de Waresquiel, *Cent Jours*, 256.
78   Lentz, *Nouvelle histoire*, iv, 312–13.
79   Cited in Mansel, *Louis XVIII*, 226–27.
80   de Waresquiel, *Cent Jours*, 41.
81   Ibid., 227.
82   Cited in ibid., 47–48.
83   This account draws mainly on that in de Waresquiel, *Cent Jours*, 44–51.

16: The Politics of Desperation: March–June 1815

1   Cited in Lentz, *Nouvelle histoire*, iv, 317.
2   Ibid., 316.
3   de Brancion, *Cambacérès*, 599.
4   Mollien, *Mémoires*, iii, 419.
5   Varlan, *Caulaincourt*, 409–11.
6   de Brancion, *Cambacérès*, 597–98.
7   Cited in Gallaher, *Iron Marshal*, 300.
8   *CG*, xv, to Marie-Louise, March 25, 1815, 39083, 685.
9   Serna, *Girouettes*, 164–65.
10   *CG*, xv, to Joseph, March 25, 1815, 39081, 684.
11   Haegele, *Napoléon et les siens*, 362–63.
12   Lentz, *Joseph Bonaparte*, 445.
13   Cited in ibid., 316.
14   *CG*, xv, to Madame Fortunée Hamelin, Fontainebleau, March 20, 1815, 39037, 668.
15   Lentz, *Histoire nouvelle*, iv, 338–39.
16   Cited in Gallaher, *Iron Marshal*, 297.
17   Cited in Marshall-Cornwall, *Massena*, 259.
18   Cited in Serna, *Girouettes*, 229–30.

19   Cited in Lentz, *Nouvelle histoire*, iv, 338.
20   *CG*, xv, to Davout, March 23, 1815, 39051, 673.
21   Cited in Lentz, *Nouvelle histoire*, iv, 338.
22   Arnold, 'Victor,' in Chandler, ed., *Napoleon's Marshals*, 517.
23   De Waresquiel, *Cent Jours*, 298.
24   Serna, *Girouettes*, 525.
25   *Napoléon à Sainte-Hélène*, Tulard, ed., 455.
26   Las Cases, *Mémoriale*, 373.
27   Cited in de Waresquiel, *Cent Jours*, 310.
28   Las Cases, *Mémorial*, 191.
29   Ibid., 373.
30   De Waresquiel, *Cent Jours*, 310.
31   *CG*, xv, to Fouché, March 23, 1815, 39059, 676.
32   Ibid., to Davout, April 29, 1815, 39446, 837–38.
33   Randal Gray, "The Big Mortar. Mortier," in *Napoleon's Marshals*, 324.
34   The opinion of Emmanuel de Waresquiel: *Cent Jours*, 311.
35   "Évangile selon Gourgaud," in Jean Tulard, ed., *Napoléon à Sainte-Hélène* (Paris, 1981), 463–64.
36   Gray, "The Big Mortar. Mortier," 325.
37   De Waresquiel, *Cent Jours*, 310.
38   Cited in Franck Favier, *Berthier. L'ombre de Napoléon* (Paris, 2015), 266–67.
39   Cited in Favier, *Berthier*, 271.
40   Ibid., 274.
41   *CG*, xv, to Davout, March 26, 1815, 39091, 688.
42   Gallaher, *Iron Marshal*, 308.
43   Cited in Varlan, *Caulaincourt*, 412.
44   Peace had been concluded between them at Ghent in December 1814, but Congress ratified the treaty, only in February 1815, and hostilities continued into the spring.
45   Varlan, *Caulaincourt*, 414.
46   De Waresquiel, *Talleyrand*, 494.
47   Rey, *Alexander*, 277.
48   De Waresquiel, *Talleyrand*, 492.
49   Varlan, *Caulaincourt*, 411–21.
50   Chandler, *Campaigns*, 1016–17.
51   *CG*, xv, to Joseph, May 2, 1815, #39509, 862.
52   Lentz, *Joseph Bonaparte*, 445.
53   *CG*, xv (1814–1821) to Bertrand, March 25, 1815, 39072, 680.
54   Ibid., to Carnot, 1 Paris, 1815, 39178, 723.
55   Ibid., to Carnot, March 23/24, 1815, 39063, 678.
56   Cited in Lentz, *Nouvelle histoire*, iv, 406.
57   *CG*, xv, to Carnot, March 26, 1815, 39090, 687.
58   Ibid., to Carnot, May 8, 1815, #39555, 80.
59   Ibid., to Savary, March 26, 1815, 39097, 690.
60   Ibid., to Gen. Corbineau, May 5, 1815, #39531, 870.
61   *CG*, xv, to Fouché, March 21, 1815, 39040, 669–70.
62   Lentz, *Nouvelle histoire*, iv, 407.
63   Ibid.
64   *CG*, xv, to Carnot, March 27, 1815, 39102, 692.
65   Ibid., to Carnot, April 2, 1815, 39185, 726.

66   Lentz, *Nouvelle histoire*, iv, 409.

67   Ibid., 408.

68   *CG*, xv, to Davout, May 18, 1815, #39682, 938.

69   Aurélien Lignereux, *Chouans et Vendéens contre l'Empire. 1815, L'autre guerre des Cent-Jours* (Paris, 2015), 79.

70   *CG*, xv, to Marie-Louise, April 4, 1815, 39211, 741.

71   Ibid., to Carnot, March 27, 1815, 39101, 691.

72   Lentz, *Nouvelle histoire*, iv, 427.

73   *CG*, xv, to Davout, May 20, 1815, #39694, 942.

74   Ibid., to Davout, March 27, 1815, 39118, 697.

75   Lentz, *Nouvelle histoire*, iv, 419.

76   *CG*, xv, to Cambacérès, April 14, 1815, 39306, 780.

77   Ibid., to Davout, April 30, 1815, #39460, 843.

78   Gwynne Lewis, *The Second Vendée. The continuity of counter-revolution in the Department of the Gard 1789–1815* (Oxford, 1978), 175.

79   Lentz, *Nouvelle histoire*, iv, 419.

80   *CG*, xv, to Carnot, April 13, 1815, #39298, 777.

81   Ibid., to Carnot, April 16, 1815, #39341, 793–94.

82   Ibid., to Carnot, March 25, 1815, 39072, 680–81.

83   Cited in Lignereux, *Chouans*, 67.

84   *CG*, xv, to Davout, March 29, 1815, #39147, 709.

85   Ibid., to Davout, March 30, 1815, #39158, 716–17.

86   *CG*, xv, to Davout, May 29, 1815, #39864, 1014.

87   John Hussey, *Waterloo. The Campaign of 1815*, 2 vols. (Padstow, 2019), I, 318.

88   *CG*, xv, to Davout, May 5, 1815, #39532, 871.

89   Ibid., to Davout, May 13, 1815, #39614, 908.

90   Ibid., to Savary, May 5, 1815, #39542, 874.

91   Ibid., to Gen. Drouot, May 17, 1815, #39678, 936–37.

92   Hussey, *Waterloo*, I, 216, 318.

93   *CG*, xv, to Davout, Laon, June 12, 1815, #40038, 1081.

94   Cited in Lignereux, *Chouans*, 69.

95   Ibid., 71–78.

96   Ibid., 93.

97   Ibid., 71.

98   Ibid., 101.

99   *CG*, xv, to Davout, May 20, 1815, #39709, 948.

100   Lignereux, *Chouans*, 101.

101   *CG*, xv, to Davout, May 13, 1815, #39615, 908.

102   Ibid., to Davout, May 20, 1815, #39694, 942.

103   Lignereux, *Chouans*, 169.

104   Ibid., 146.

105   Hussey, *Waterloo*, I, 218.

106   Lignereux, *Chouans*, 101–18.

107   Ibid., 108–12.

108   R. S. Alexander, *Bonapartism and Revolutionary Tradition in France. The Fédérés of 1815* (Cambridge, 1991), 107–26.

109   Cited in Lewis, *Second Vendée,* 177.

110   Cited in ibid., 177.

111   *CG*, xv, to Carnot, May 2, 1815, #39478, 852.

112 Ibid., to Davout, May 2, 1815, #39497, 859.
113 Lewis, *Second Vendée*, 179–81.
114 Serna, *Girouettes*, 160–61.
115 Lentz, *Nouvelle histoire*, iv, 428.
116 Price, *Perilous Crown*, 55, 70.
117 Cited in ibid., 59.
118 Ibid., 58–59.
119 Bluche, *Bonapartisme*, 105.
120 Réné de Chateaubriand, "Réflexions politiques sur quelques écrits du jour et sur les interest de tous les français," Nov. 27, 1814. in Chateaubriand. *Grands ecrtis politiques*, 2 vols., ed. Jean-Paul Clement (Paris, 1993) I, 137–300.
121 Lentz, *Nouvelle histoire*, iv, 243–45.
122 Brian E. Vick, *The Congress of Vienna. Power and Politics after Napoleon* (Cambridge, MA, 2014), 118.
123 Bluche, *Bonapartisme*, 104, note 16.
124 Ibid., 102.
125 Cited in ibid., 102.
126 *CG*, xv, to Carnot, May 10, 1815, #39583, 891–92.
127 Bluche, *Bonapartisme*, 104–05.
128 *CG*, xv, to Carnot, May 19, 1815, #39684, 939.
129 Ibid., to Fouché, May 19, 1815, #39686, 939–40.
130 Cited in Lentz, *Nouvelle histoire*, iv, 377.
131 *CG*, xv, to Cambacérès, April 18, 1815, #39360, 801–2.
132 Ibid., to Mollien, April 18,1815, #39372, 807–8.
133 Ibid., to Masséna, April 18, 1815, #39371, 807.
134 Marshall-Cornwall, *Masséna*, 261.
135 Lentz, *Nouvelle histoire*, iv, 377.
136 Cited in ibid., 387.
137 Bluche, *Bonapartisme*, 105–6.
138 Ibid., 107–9.
139 Ibid., 114.
140 Ibid., 107–8.
141 Ibid., 107–18.
142 Cited in Lentz, *Nouvelle histoire*, iv, 389.
143 Ibid., 389–90.
144 Ibid., 391.
145 Ibid., 392.
146 Lentz, *Nouvelle histoire*, iv, 400–2.
147 Dwyer, *Citizen Emperor*, 543–44.
148 Lentz, *Nouvelle histoire*, iv, 400.

17: The War of the Seventh Coalition: March–June 1815.
1 Rhys Johns, "Turning the Clock Back? The Politics of Time in Restoration Europe, 1815–1830," in *European Restorations*, ii, 17–27, at 17.
2 Cited in Jones, "Turning the Clock Back?," 17.
3 Bew, *Castlereagh*, 391–94.
4 Ibid., 390.
5 Hussey, *Waterloo*, I, 63.
6 Ibid., 61.

7   Vick, *Congress of Vienna*, 17–18.

8   Siemann, *Metternich*, 426–28.

9   Varlan, *Caulaincourt*, 517–18.

10   Hussey, *Waterloo*, I, 57.

11   Ibid., 63–65.

12   Cited in Rey, *Alexander*, 286.

13   Ibid., 280–81.

14   Bew, *Castlereagh*, 390–91.

15   De Waresquiel, *Talleyrand*, 492.

16   Ibid., 496.

17   Siemann, *Metternich*, 429.

18   Schroeder, *Transformation*, 560–63.

19   Hussey, *Waterloo*, I, 98–99.

20   Chandler, *Campaigns*, 1015.

21   Ibid., 1017.

22   Hussey, *Waterloo*, I, 88–89.

23   Schroeder, *Transformation*, 562.

24   Chandler, *Campaigns*, 1016–17.

25   Hussey, *Waterloo*, I, 104.

26   Ibid., 102–03.

27   Ibid., 253.

28   Frédéric Hulot, *Le Maréhal Berthier* (Paris, 2007), 287.

29   Favier, *Berthier*, 278–79.

30   De Waresquiel, *Cent Jours*, 342.

31   Favier, *Berthier*, 277–78.

32   Cited in De Waresquiel, *Cent Jours*, 342.

33   Gareth Glover, *Waterloo. Myth and Reality* (Huddersfield, 2020), 19.

34   Hussey, *Waterloo*, I, 144–48; Glover, *Waterloo*, 21.

35   Ibid., 152.

36   Ibid, 156.

37   Bew, *Castlereagh*, 395.

38   Hussey, *Waterloo*, I, 249.

39   Cited in ibid., 248.

40   Chandler, *Campaigns*, 1015.

41   Cited in Hussey, Waterloo, I, 251.

42   Lentz, *Nouvelle histoire*, iv, 463.

43   Haegele, *Murat*, 694.

44   Lentz, *Nouvelle histoire*, iv, 464.

45   Haegele, *Murat*, 692–98.

46   Haegele, *Napoléon et les siens*, 365.

47   Glover, *Waterloo*, 19–20.

48   Hussey, *Waterloo*, I, 85.

49   Cited in Lentz, *Nouvelle histoire*, iv, 467.

50   Glover, *Waterloo*, 36.

51   Chandler, *Campaigns*, 1020.

52   Hussey, *Waterloo*, I, 218. Lentz, *Nouvelle histoire*, iv, 468–69.

53   Chandler, *Campaigns*, 1016–17.

54   *CG*, xv, to Gen. Rapp, May 14, 1815, #39631, 914.

55   *CG*, xv, to Davout, June 6, 1815, #39961, 1055.

56 Ibid., to Davout, May 22, 1815, #39742, 963.

57 Ibid., to Davout, May 22, 1815, #39750, 965–66.

58 Ibid., to Savary, June 6, 1815, #39975, 1059.

59 Lt. Col. Alan Shepperd, "The Patagonian. Brune," in Chandler, *Napoleon's Marshals*, 80–91.

60 *CG*, xv, to Fouché, June 1, 1815, #39893, 1026–27.

61 Ibid., to Davout, April 30, 1815, #39456, 841.

62 Ibid., to Davout, May 25, 1815, #39797, 986.

63 Ibid., to Davout, May 2, 1815, #39485.

64 Ibid., to Davout, May 29, 1815, #39862, 1012–13.

65 Hussey, *Waterloo*, I, 223.

66 *CG*, xv, to Davout, March 23, 1815, #39053, 674.

67 Hussey, *Waterloo*, I, 319.

68 *CG*, xv, to Davout, May 27, 1815, #39833, 1001.

69 Hussey, *Waterloo*, I, 318.

70 *CG*, xv, to Davout, May 22, 1815, #39765, 969–70.

71 Cited in Hussey, *Waterloo*, I, 319.

72 *CG*, xv, to Davout, Laon, June 11, #40033, 1079.

73 Ibid., to Davout, Laon, May 16, 1815, #39667, 932.

74 Hussey, *Waterloo*, I, 318–19.

75 Lentz, *Nouvelle histoire*, iv, 458.

76 *CG*, xv, to Davout, June 3, 1815, #39920, 1036.

77 *Napoléon à Sainte-Hélène*, Tulard, ed., 463.

78 Gotteri, *Soult*, 477.

79 Hussey, *Waterloo*, I, 321.

80 *Napoléon à Sainte-Hélène*, Tulard, ed., 617.

81 Glover, *Waterloo*, 36.

82 Cited in Hussey, *Waterloo*, I, 323.

83 Gallaher, *Iron Marshal*, 305–6.

84 Cited in Favier, *Berthier*, 281.

85 *Mémoires sur Carnot*, 2 vols., Hippolyte Carnot, ed., (Paris, 1907), ii, 457.

86 Mollien, *Mémoires*, iii, 431.

87 Ibid., 428–31.

88 Carnot, *Mémoires*, ii, 455–56.

89 Ibid., 455.

90 Mollien, *Mémoires*, iii, 430.

91 Ibid., iii, 430.

92 Carnot, *Mémoires*, ii, 458–59.

93 Mollien, *Mémoires*, iii, 430–31.

94 Geoffrey Parker, *Imprudent King. A new life of Philip II* (New Haven, CT, and London, 2014), 113–17.

95 Mollien, *Mémoires*, iii, 424.

96 Carnot, *Mémoires*, 506–7.

97 Cited in Hussey, *Waterloo*, I, 334.

98 Glover, *Waterloo*, 38.

99 Hussey, *Waterloo*, I, 355–56.

100 *CG*, xv, to Soult, June 3, 1815, #39933, 1046.

101 De Waresquiel, *Cent Jours*, 222.

102 Hussey, *Waterloo*, I, 322–23; 366–68.

103 Carnot, *Mémoires*, ii, 457–58.

104 *CG*, xv, to Joseph, Charleroi, June 16, 1815, #40051, 1090.

105 Lentz, *Nouvelle histoire*, iv, 456–57.

106 Chandler, *Campaigns*, 1026–27.

107 Glover, *Waterloo*, 40–42.

108 Cited in Hussey, *Waterloo*, I, 364.

109 Chandler, *Campaigns*, 1026–27.

110 Hussey, *Waterloo*, I, 348–49.

111 Glover, *Waterloo*, 39.

112 Hussey, *Waterloo*, I, 359.

113 For a succinct appraisal that concludes Napoleon did not think about taking Quatre Bras: Glover, *Waterloo*, 41.

114 Hussey, *Waterloo*, I, 102.

115 Ibid., 120.

116 Hussey, *Waterloo*, I, 173–77.

117 Ibid., 421.

118 Glover, *Waterloo*, 47–48.

119 Hussey, *Waterloo*, I, 425–27.

120 Ibid., 447.

121 Ibid., 452–53.

122 Ibid., 172. Hussey points out that this negates assumptions that the stand made there was a result of the talks.

123 Glover, *Waterloo*, 59.

124 Ibid., 60.

125 Hussey, *Waterloo*, I, 572.

126 Ibid., 494.

127 Hussey, *Waterloo*, I, 499.

128 Glover, *Waterloo*, 61.

129 Ibid., 61–62.

130 Hussey, *Waterloo*, I, 521.

131 Cited in ibid., 572.

132 Hussey, *Waterloo*, I, 575–76.

133 Cited in Glover, *Waterloo*, 62–64.

134 Ibid., 64.

135 Chandler, *Campaigns*, 1043.

136 Ibid., 1045.

137 Glover, *Waterloo*, 65.

138 Lachouque and Brown, *Anatomy*, 480.

139 Chandler, *Campaigns*, 1044.

140 Lachouque and Brown, *Anatomy*, 480.

141 Hussey, *Waterloo*, I, 535.

142 Cited in ibid., 538.

143 Glover, *Waterloo*, 66–67, opts for the lower figure. in Hussey, *Waterloo*, I, 535, for the higher.

144 Hussey, *Waterloo*, I, 539.

145 Glover, *Waterloo*, 69–71.

146 Chandler, *Campaigns*, 1048–49.

147 Glover, *Waterloo*, 74–75.

148 Hussey, *Waterloo*, I, 424.

149 Glover, *Waterloo*, 75.

150 Cited in Chandler, *Campaigns*, 1051.

151   Glover, *Waterloo*, 78–79.
152   Cited in Hussey, *Waterloo*, I, 553.
153   The 69th lost both its regimental colors and the king's colors. On their fate: Glover, *Waterloo*, 82.
154   Chandler, *Campaigns*, 1053.
155   Ibid., 1053.
156   Glover, *Waterloo*, 86.
157   Chandler, *Campaigns*, 1055.
158   Ibid., 1056.
159   Cited in ibid., 1053.
160   Glover, *Waterloo*, 89.
161   Ibid., 91.
162   Chandler, *Campaigns*, 1058.
163   Glover, *Waterloo*, 91.
164   Hussey, *Waterloo*, ii, 23.
165   Ibid., 21–22.
166   Glover, *Waterloo*, 91–93.
167   Hussey, *Waterloo*, ii, 26–27.
168   Glover, *Waterloo*, 90.
169   Ibid., 91.
170   Ibid., 96, for a learned account of how the site was chosen.
171   Ibid., 95.
172   Ibid., 91, 95.
173   Chandler, *Campaigns*, 1063.
174   Ibid., 1063.
175   Glover, *Waterloo*, 90.
176   Cited in Hussey, Waterloo, ii, 80.
177   Chandler, *Campaigns*, 1007.
178   Cited in Hussey, Waterloo, ii, 80.
179   Ibid., 80.
180   Ibid., II, 70.
181   Glover, *Waterloo*, 108.
182   Hussey, *Waterloo*, ii, 70.
183   Ibid., 63.
184   Glover, *Waterloo*, 102.
185   Chandler, *Campaigns*, 1064.
186   Glover, *Waterloo*, 102.
187   Chandler, *Campaigns*, 1067.
188   Cited in Hussey, *Waterloo*, ii, 81.
189   Ibid., 373, for a summary.
190   Chandler, *Campaigns*, 1092.
191   Hussey, *Waterloo*, ii, 91–92. Estimates vary considerably, but the generally accepted figure is that 24 twelve pounders comprised the Grand Battery: ibid., 112–13.
192   Glover, *Waterloo*, 111.
193   Chandler, *Campaigns*, 1072–73.
194   Hussey, *Waterloo*, ii, 105–6.
195   Cited in Boudon, *Jérôme*, 438.
196   Hussey, *Waterloo*, ii, 107–8.
197   Glover, *Waterloo*, 115–18.
198   Hussey, *Waterloo*, ii, 107–9.

199 Ibid., 132, on the debate about when Napoleon knew Bülow's whole corps was close to him.
200 Chandler, *Campaigns*, 1076–77.
201 Cited in Hussey, *Waterloo*, ii, 114–15.
202 Glover, *Waterloo*, 124.
203 Chandler, *Campaigns*, 1073.
204 Glover, *Waterloo*, 126.
205 Ibid., 127.
206 Hussey, *Waterloo*, ii, 116–17.
207 Glover, *Waterloo*, 127.
208 Chandler, *Campaigns*, 1078–79.
209 Cited in ibid., 1066.
210 Glover, *Waterloo*, 138–40.
211 On the shaky evidence: Glover, *Waterloo*, 139. It is known the lancers caught him.
212 Chandler, *Campaigns*, 1079.
213 Brendan Simms, *The Longest Afternoon. The 400 Men Who Decided the Battle of Waterloo* (London, 2015), 8, 11–12.
214 Simms, *Longest Afternoon*, 17–21.
215 Ibid., 27–32.
216 Glover, *Waterloo*, 159.
217 Ibid., 160.
218 Cited in Simms, *Longest Afternoon*, 30.
219 Cited in Hussey, *Waterloo*, ii, 139.
220 Glover, *Waterloo*, 119.
221 Ibid., 119–20.
222 Ibid., 165–67.
223 Chandler, *Campaigns*, 1077.
224 Hussey, *Waterloo*, ii, 109 for the lower estimate; Glover, *Waterloo*, 120 for the higher.
225 Hussey, *Waterloo*, ii, 140.
226 Ibid., 130.
227 Simms, *Longest Afternoon*, 37.
228 Ibid., 37–39.
229 Hussey, Waterloo, ii, 141.
230 Glover, *Waterloo*, 146. Chandler, *Campaigns*, 1080.
231 Simms, *Longest Afternoon*, 39.
232 Glover, *Waterloo*, 146.
233 Hussey, Waterloo, ii, 143–44.
234 Cited in Chandler, *Campaigns*, 1081.
235 Cited in Glover, *Waterloo*, 147.
236 Ibid., 151.
237 Hussey, *Waterloo*, ii, 147–48.
238 Glover, *Waterloo*, 148.
239 Chandler, *Campaigns*, 1085.
240 Ibid., 1080.
241 The French have often been criticized for not trying to spike the cannons when they held them after a charge (Chandler, *Campaigns*, 1081), but cavalry did not usually carry spikes with them: Glover, *Waterloo*, 148.
242 Glover, *Waterloo*, 149–50.
243 Cited in ibid., 151.
244 Cited in Chandler, *Campaigns*, 1084.

245 Glover, *Waterloo*, 153.
246 Chandler, *Campaigns*, 1080.
247 Ibid., 1085.
248 Simms, *Longest Afternoon*, 49–53.
249 Glover, *Waterloo*, 163–64.
250 Chandler, *Campaigns*, 1085.
251 Hussey, *Waterloo*, ii, 183–84.
252 Chandler, *Campaigns*, 1085.
253 Lachouque and Brown, *Anatomy*, 485.
254 Chandler, Campaigns, 1084.
255 Hussey, *Waterloo*, ii, 200–3.
256 Glover, *Waterloo*, 174.
257 Chandler, *Campaigns*, 1086.
258 Lachouque and Brown, *Anatomy*, 486.
259 Chandler, *Campaigns*, 1086.
260 Glover, *Waterloo*, 176.
261 Chandler, *Campaigns*, 1087.
262 Glover, *Waterloo*, 177.
263 Ibid., 177.
264 Chandler, *Campaigns*, 1088.
265 Glover, *Waterloo*, 178.
266 Hussey, *Waterloo*, ii, 217–18.
267 Ibid., 218.
268 Ibid.
269 Ibid., 217, gives a good survey of the Dutch and British sources, and himself doubts the impact
     of the attack.
270 Glover, *Waterloo*, 181–82.
271 Hussey, *Waterloo*, ii, 218–220.
272 Chandler, *Campaigns*, 1087.
273 Lachouque and Brown, *Anatomy*, 490.

18: A Life Unravels

1   *CG*, xv, to Joseph, Philippeville, June 19, 1815, #40057, 1094.
2   Cited in Hussey, *Waterloo*, ii, 254–55.
3   Ibid, 260–61.
4   Glover, *Waterloo*, 217–18.
5   Chandler, *Campaigns*, 1093–94.
6   Hussey, *Waterloo*, ii, 251.
7   Lentz, *Nouvelle histoire*, iv, 496.
8   Hussey, *Waterloo*, ii, 251.
9   Cited in Boudon, *Jérôme*, 442.
10 Glover, *Waterloo*, 212.
11 Ibid., 212–16.
12 Hussey, *Waterloo*, ii, 259.
13 Ibid., 259.
14 Glover, *Waterloo*, 218–20.
15 Las Cases, *Mémorial*, 222.
16 Chandler, *Campaigns*, 1087.
17 La Bédoyère blamed Ney in the same session: Lentz, *Nouvelle histoire*, iv, 519–22.

18   Chandler, *Campaigns*, 1095.
19   Serna, *Girouettes*, 181, 183.
20   Cited in Lentz, *Nouvelle histoire*, iv, 510–11.
21   Lentz, *Joseph Bonaparte*, 452.
22   Lentz, *Nouvelle histoire*, iv, 511.
23   Ibid., 506.
24   Cited in Varlan, *Caulaincourt*, 427.
25   Cited in Gallaher, *Iron Marshal*, 311–5.
26   Cited in de Brancion, *Cambacérès*, 602–3.
27   Gallaher, *Iron Marshal*, 312.
28   Lentz, *Joseph Bonaparte*, 452.
29   Cited in Lentz, *Joseph Bonaparte*, 452.
30   Lentz, *Nouvelle histoire*, iv, 508–9.
31   Woloch, *New Regime*, 91.
32   Lentz, *Nouvelle histoire*, iv, 509.
33   Cited in ibid., 512.
34   David A. Bell, *Men on Horseback. The Power of Charisma in the Age of Revolution* (New York, 2020), 100–2.
35   de Brancion, *Cambacérès*, 603.
36   Cited in Lentz, *Nouvelle histoire*, iv, 514.
37   Ibid., 514.
38   De Waresquiel, *Cent Jours*, 483.
39   Cited in Gallaher, *Iron Marshal*, 312.
40   Cited in de Waresquiel, *Cent Jours*, 484.
41   Gallaher, *Iron Marshal*, 313.
42   Lentz, *Nouvelle histoire*, iv, 515.
43   Varlan, *Caulaincourt*, 429.
44   Cited in Lentz, *Nouvelle histoire*, iv, 515–16.
45   Cited in ibid., 517.
46   Cited in de Brancion, *Cambacérès*, 603.
47   De Waresquiel, *Cent Jours*, 483.
48   Cited in Lentz, *Nouvelle histoire*, iv, 518.
49   Lentz, *Nouvelle histoire*, iv, 518.
50   Hussey, *Waterloo*, ii, 281.
51   Lentz, *Nouvelle histoire*, iv, 521.
52   Cited in ibid., 521.
53   Ibid., 521.
54   Glover, *Waterloo*, 221.
55   Lentz, *Joseph Bonaparte*, 455.
56   Cited in Gallaher, *Iron Marshal*, 317–18.
57   Lentz, *Nouvelle histoire*, iv, 523.
58   Ibid., 527.
59   Cited in Hussey, *Waterloo*, ii, 283.
60   Lentz, *Joseph Bonaparte*, 454.
61   Cited in Boudon, *Jérôme*, 445.
62   Boudon, *Jerome*, 445–46.
63   Gallaher, *Iron Marshal*, 318.
64   Lentz, *Joseph Bonaparte*, 454.
65   *CG*, xv, To the Provisional Government, Malmaison, June 27, 1815, #40064, 1108.

66   Lentz, Nouvelle histoire, iv, 526–27.

67   Hussey, *Waterloo*, ii, 310–12.

68   Boudon, *Jérôme*, 445.

69   Lentz, *Joseph Bonaparte*, 456.

70   Lignereux, *Chouans*, 220–50.

71   Vincent Denis and Mathieu Grenet, "Armée et (désordre) urbain pendant les Cent Jours à Marseille: le 'massacre des Mamelouks' en juin 1815," *Revue historique des armées*, 283 (2016), 25–37.

72   Hussey, *Waterloo*, ii, 325–26.

73   Cited in de Waresquiel, *Cent Jours*, 457.

74   Cited in ibid., 458.

75   Ibid., 455.

76   Hussey, *Waterloo*, ii, 300–1.

77   De Waresquiel, *Cent Jours*, 461–63.

78   Ibid., 463.

79   Hussey, *Waterloo*, ii, 313.

80   Ibid., 306–7.

81   De Waresquiel, *Cent Jours*, 475.

82   Hussey, *Waterloo*, ii, 317–19.

83   De Waresquiel, *Cent Jours*, 476.

84   Ibid., 476–77.

85   Ibid., 486–87.

86   Cited in Serna, *Girouettes*, 186.

87   Hussey, *Waterloo*, ii, 329.

88   Lentz, *Joseph Bonaparte*, 459.

89   *CG*, xv, to the Prince Regent, July 13, 1815, Rochefort, #40066, 1103.

90   Livy *Hannibal's War* (Oxford, 2006, trans. J. C. Yardley), Book xxx, chapter 28, 595.

91   Livy, *Rome's Mediterranean Empire* (Oxford, 2007, trans. Jane D. Chaplin), Periochae, book 39, 253.

92   Philip Dwyer, *Napoleon. Passion, Death and Resurrection, 1815–1840* (London, 2018), 11.

93   Lentz, *Joseph Bonaparte*, 455.

94   Dwyer, *Napoleon*, 13–15.

95   *CG*, xv, to Admiral Keith, July 31, 1815, on board the *Bellerophon*, #40067, 1104.

96   *Les vies des homes illustres de Plutarque*, op. cit. 152.

97   Haegele, *Murat*, 702–06.

98   Cited in Serna, *Girouettes*, 189.

99   Mansel, *Louis XVIII*, 325.

100 Serna, *Girouettes*, 188–89.

101 Ibid., 189.

102 Mansel, *Louis XVIII*, 327.

103 Alan Forrest, *The Legacy of the French Revolutionary Wars. The Nation-in-arms in French Republican Memory* (Cambridge, 2009), 64–69.

104 Lachouque and Brown, *Anatomy*, 495–99.

105 De Waresquiel, *Cent Jours*, 501.

106 Mansel, *Louis XVIII*, 267.

107 De Waresquiel, *Cent Jours*, 502.

108 Ibid., 506.

109 Mansel, *Louis XVIII*, 264–66.

110 Ibid., 327–28.

111 Serna, *Girouettes*, 191.

112   Price, *Perilous Crown*, 83–84.

113   Serna, *Girouettes*, 190.

114   De Waresquiel, *Talleyrand*, 516.

115   Price, *Perilous Crown*, 82.

116   André Jardin and André-Jean Tudesq, *Restoration and Reaction, 1815–1848* (Eng. trans., Cambridge, 1983), 30–33.

117   Modest Bogdanovich, *Istoriya tsarstvovaniya imperatora Aleskandra I i Rossii v ego vreamya* (Saint Petersburg, 1871), v, 51–78. This information was given to the author and rendered into English by his colleague and friend Professor Alexander Mikaberidze, of Louisiana State University (Shreveport), to whom I wish to convey my deepest thanks.

Epilogue: Beyond the Pale

1   This is explored lucidly in Peter Fritzsche, *Stranded in the Present. Modern Time and the Melancholy of History* (Cambridge, MA, 2004).

2   Dwyer, *Napoleon*, 39–40.

3   Ibid., 140–41.

4   Andy Martin, *Napoleon. The Novelist* (Cambridge, 2000), *passim*.

5   Ute Planert, "Napoleon as an Icon of Political Liberalism in Restoration Germany," *European Restorations*, ii, 157–67.

6   Boudon, *Jérôme*, 507.

7   Sudir Hazareesingh, *The Legend of Napoleon* (London, 2004), 203–8.

8   Réné de Chateaubriand, *Mémoires d'Outre-Tombe* (Mesnil-l'Estrée, 1948 ed.), ii, 653–54.

9   Marta Lorente, 'The New Spanish Councils,' in *Napoleonic Empire and the New European Political Culture*, 293.

INDEX